SPARTA
BEYOND THE MIRAGE

Editors

Anton Powell

and

Stephen Hodkinson

Contributors

Nikos Birgalias, Jacqueline Christien, Michael Clarke, Andrey Eremin, Thomas J. Figueira, Michael Flower, Noreen Humble, Michael Lipka, Marcello Lupi, Nino Luraghi, Norbert Mertens, Ellen Millender, Daniel Ogden, Stefan Rebenich

The Classical Press of Wales

First published in 2002 by
Gerald Duckworth & Co. Ltd
and the Classical Press of Wales

This paperback edition 2023
The Classical Press of Wales
15 Rosehill Terrace, Swansea SA1 6JN
classicalpressofwales@gmail.com
www.classicalpressofwales.co.uk

Distributor in North America, e-book distributor world-wide
ISD,
70 Enterprise Drive, Suite 2,
Bristol, CT 06010, USA
Tel: +1 (860) 584-6546
Fax: +1 (860) 516-4873
www.isdistribution.com

ISBN paperback 978-1-914535-30-7; hardback 0-715631837;
e-book 978-1-914535-20-8

A catalogue record for this book is available from the British Library.

Typeset by Ernest Buckley, Clunton, Shropshire, and by Louise Jones; printed and bound in the UK by Gomer Press, Llandysul, Ceredigion, Wales.

The Classical Press of Wales, an independent venture, was founded in 1993, initially to support the work of classicists and ancient historians in Wales and their collaborators from further afield. It now publishes work initiated by scholars internationally, and welcomes contributions from all parts of the world.

The symbol of the Press is the Red Kite. This bird, once widespread in Britain, was reduced by 1905 to some five individuals confined to a small area known as 'The Desert of Wales' – the upper Tywi valley. Geneticists report that the stock was saved from terminal inbreeding by the arrival of one stray female bird from Germany. After much careful protection, the Red Kite now thrives – in Wales and beyond

SPARTA: BEYOND THE MIRAGE

Contents

Page

Introduction *Stephen Hodkinson* (University of Manchester) vii

I. Representations of Sparta

1. Herodotus and Spartan despotism 1
Ellen Millender (Reed College)

2. Spartan *atē* at Thermopylai: semantics and ideology at Herodotus, *Histories* 7.234 63
Michael Clarke (National University of Ireland, Maynooth)

3. Was *sōphrosynē* ever a Spartan virtue? 85
Noreen Humble (University College Cork)

4. Three evocations of the dead with Pausanias 111
Daniel Ogden (University of Wales, Swansea)

II. Invention and Tradition

5. Iron money and the ideology of consumption in Laconia 137
Thomas J. Figueira (Rutgers University)

6. Iron money in Sparta: myth and history 171
Jacqueline Christien (University of Paris x, Nanterre)

7. The invention of tradition in classical and hellenistic Sparta 191
Michael Flower (Franklin and Marshall College)

8. Notes on the influence of the Spartan Great Rhetra on Tyrtaeus, Herodotus and Xenophon 219
Michael Lipka (University of Patras)

III. Subject Populations

9. Helotic slavery reconsidered 227
Nino Luraghi (Harvard University)

10. Helotage and Spartan social organization 249
Nikos Birgalias (Open University of Greece)

11. Settlements of Spartan *perioikoi*: *poleis* or *kōmai*? 267
Andrey Eremin (Samara State University)

12. οὐκ ὁμοῖοι, ἀγαθοὶ δέ: the *perioikoi* in the classical Lakedaimonian *polis* 285
Norbert Mertens (Berlin)

IV. HISTORIOGRAPHICAL RECEPTION

13. Sparta compared: ethnographic perspectives in Spartan studies 305
Marcello Lupi (University of Naples)

14. From Thermopylae to Stalingrad: the myth of Leonidas in German historiography 323
Stefan Rebenich (University of Mannheim)

Index 351

INTRODUCTION

Stephen Hodkinson

The papers in this volume were originally given at the meeting of the international seminar on Spartan history held in September within the first Celtic Conference in Classics at the National University of Ireland, Maynooth. The seminar constituted the third such meeting in a series whose first two seminars are represented by volumes on *The Shadow of Sparta* (Powell and Hodkinson 1994) and *Sparta: New perspectives* (Hodkinson and Powell 1999). The decision to hold the 2000 meeting within the broader context of a conference in Classics signals the increasing interaction between researchers on Sparta and on other aspects of antiquity. Indeed, several authors in this volume are noted for their work on a range of classical subjects and here bring their expertise from other fields to bear on the interpretation of Spartan history and society.

The Introduction to *Sparta: New perspectives* referred to 'the notable resurgence of Spartan studies which has taken place around the world during the last generation' (Hodkinson 1999, ix). This resurgence has gathered pace in the last few years with the publication of over twenty volumes since 1998.[1] The vitality of current Spartan scholarship has had a notable impact within Greece itself, following the recent appearance of two entire issues devoted to Sparta in the weekly historical magazine of the national daily newspaper *Eleutherotypia*.[2] One sign of this vitality is that eleven of the fourteen scholars represented in the present volume are new contributors to the Sparta seminar series. As in our previous volume, participation is international in character: our contributors hail originally from no fewer than nine different countries: Canada, France, Germany, Greece, Ireland, Italy, Russia, the UK and the USA.

We have entitled this volume *Sparta: Beyond the Mirage*. In organizing the seminar, we did not attempt to impose a common theme upon our speakers, but gave them the freedom to select the subjects and themes they themselves judged most pressing within the present setting of Spartan research. Despite the diversity of academic backgrounds and of subject matter, however, most of the papers at the seminar revolved around issues connected with the varying images of Sparta from antiquity to the present day – a shared focus which accurately reflects the central preoccupation of much current historical research.[3] The concept of a Spartan 'mirage' was originated in 1933 by the French historian François Ollier, whose two-volume work, *Le Mirage spartiate*, highlighted the ongoing tradition of idealized distortions and inventions regarding the character of Spartan society in the works of non-Spartan writers in both Greek and Roman antiquity. Ollier's initiative was extended a generation later by E.N. Tigerstedt's massive (and often underrated) three-volume study of *The Legend of Sparta in Classical Antiquity* (1965–78). Whereas Ollier's study focused primarily upon idealizations of Sparta's society, Tigerstedt also gave emphasis to negative portrayals of her customs and institutions. At around the same time Elizabeth Rawson's groundbreaking study, *The Spartan Tradition in European Thought* (1969), examined the continuing mirage of Sparta within medieval and modern thought, whose positive or negative representations typically reflected contemporary social or political concerns. More recently, partly in consequence of the borrowing from modern history of the concept of 'the invention of tradition' (Hobsbawm and Ranger 1983), attention has focused upon the Spartans' own role in originating, or collaborating in the development of, many of the idealized images of her past and contemporary society.[4]

Despite this steady accumulation of insights into the diverse forms of the Spartan mirage and the different ways in which surviving accounts of her history and society are affected by distortion and invention, twentieth-century historical scholarship was somewhat slow to adopt the perspectives initiated by Ollier. As Michael Whitby (2002, 11) has recently commented, 'After Ollier it should have been difficult to study Sparta without constantly being aware of the need to assess the distorting effects of the varying ancient perceptions'. Only within the last 15–20 years, however, has that truly been the case. Even into the 1980s, despite certain earlier notable exceptions, many historical discussions continued to treat the ancient evidence on its own terms and to combine the testimony of sources from diverse periods without serious consideration of their temporal context or the social and political influences upon their writings.[5] Even today, there is dispute about what conclusions may legitimately be drawn from such consideration.[6] For example, when an allegedly classical practice or institution is first mentioned in a late source, how (and by what criteria) does one judge whether it is late invention or an authentically classical phenomenon missing from the contemporary historical record due to the paucity of evidence? Similarly, when assessing the effect that the agenda of an ancient writer has had on his presentation of Sparta, how does one distinguish (to phrase the alternatives in their grossest form) between genuine information, distortion and pure invention? In navigating this contested terrain, the papers in this volume make, as our sub-title indicates, some notable contributions to advancing our understanding of Spartan society beyond the various manifestations of the Spartan mirage outlined above.

Part I deals with representations of Sparta in a variety of historical and literary sources. The opening two papers discuss Herodotus, the 'Father of History', whose portrayal of Sparta as the 'Greek Other', 'the only Greek state that Herodotus treats in [an] ethnographic manner', has been the subject of considerable recent interest.[7] Continuing a series of articles investigating the impact of fifth-century Athenian self-representations upon contemporary characterizations of their Spartan enemies,[8] Ellen Millender examines how Herodotus' depiction of Sparta's hereditary kingships conforms to the image of the barbarian autocrat which runs throughout his work. Although sensitive to Athens' anti-Spartan ideology and emphasizing the Spartans' role as champions of Greek freedom, Herodotus' account of the Persian wars reflects a fundamentally Athenocentric perspective in which the Spartans' resistance to Persia, even in their 'finest hour' at the battle of Thermopylai, is ascribed to the despotism of their *nomos* (law or custom), symbolic of the autocratic nature of the Spartan *polis*. This interpretation finds echoes in Michael Clarke's paper – part of a larger project aimed at understanding the world-picture of archaic Greece through study of its language (cf. Clarke 1999) – which brings the methods of cultural and cognitive linguistics to bear on Herodotus' characterization of the three hundred Spartans who gave their lives alongside King Leonidas. The pejorative connotations of the words used to describe the Spartan warriors imply a senseless self-sacrifice dictated by obedience to the *nomos* that they must remain in the company of their king, an insight which raises interesting questions about the relationship of Spartan military ethics to those elsewhere in Greece.

Noreen Humble continues her examination of the standard assumption that *sōphrosynē* (moderation) was regarded by classical writers as a characteristically Spartan virtue. Having previously demonstrated that this association is not present in Xenophon, our main source for classical Sparta (Humble 1999), she undertakes here a broad survey of other writers from the fifth century BC to Plutarch. The association is largely limited to idealizing contexts: in the classical period to laconizing oligarchs, subsequently to pro-Spartan accounts of the third-century revolution, and from there to Plutarch's *Lykourgos*, whose influence upon modern ideas is mainly responsible for modern assumptions.

Daniel Ogden's paper, deriving from his general study of Greek and Roman necromancy (Ogden 2002), focuses upon three interrelated episodes involving evocations of the dead concerning another hero of the

Persian wars, the regent Pausanias. Although Thucydides is our earliest extant source for the incidents which culminated in Pausanias' death, there is reason to believe that he has purposely rationalized pre-existing accounts, omitting one episode entirely and purging the other two of their necromantic elements, which can be reconstructed with the aid of later, supposedly less reliable, sources. Quite apart from the implications for Thucydides' historical methods, Ogden's study constitutes a valuable reminder of the religious elements which frequently surrounded Spartan politics.[9]

The papers in Part II explore the complex interaction between invented and genuine Spartan traditions. The article by MICHAEL FLOWER represents the published version of an oral paper, first given in 1994, which has played an influential role in disseminating the modern historical concept of 'invented tradition' within the discourse of historians of classical Sparta.[10] Yet, as he observes, although several recent studies have applied the concept to good effect, others continue to proceed without acknowledgement of this significant phenomenon. Flower himself argues for a very strong version of its impact on Spartan history and historiography. Examining the creation and subsequent representation of a range of institutions, he concludes that throughout their history the Spartans ascribed new practices to the Lykourgan past so frequently and systematically that no synthetic account of Spartan institutions is possible. Evidence in later sources can therefore be used as testimony to earlier practice only if corroborated by earlier sources.

Some scholars will no doubt prefer less radical judgements, as can be seen in this section from the articles by THOMAS FIGUEIRA and JACQUELINE CHRISTIEN, both of which encompass the controversial subject of Sparta's iron money. In the absence of earlier literary or archaeological evidence for its existence, Flower suggests that the supposedly ancestral iron money was invented by conservative Spartans during the political controversy of 404 BC as an alternative currency to the foreign coinage introduced by Lysander. Figueira too exposes the ahistorical character of certain common ancient traditions about the iron currency and he agrees that the anti-Lysandrian arguments in 404 were tapping the authority of an imagined past. He argues, however, that this currency was not simply a construct, but a historical entity introduced by the Spartan authorities (perhaps in the late sixth or early fifth century) in reaction to the regional predominance of silver coinage. He interprets the iron money, with its exclusive legitimacy and purposely reduced fiduciary value, as an anti-money largely confined to official contexts which was designed to exclude wealth in precious metals from civic transactions. Christien also accepts some reality to ancient accounts of the iron currency. In contrast to Figueira, however, who views the currency as flat iron ingots (associated with the Lakonian dialect term *pelanor*), she connects it with iron spits dedicated at Spartan sanctuaries and also suggests a somewhat wider role within private exchange, linking it with genuine issues of iron coinage in other *poleis*. As part of her long-term survey of the history of the use of coinage at Sparta, she argues that behind the confused traditions regarding the debates in 404 lay a controversial proposal by Lysander that Sparta should start minting her own coinage.

In recent years scholars have generally abandoned older images of Sparta as a conservative, unchanging society for a more nuanced picture which, while recognizing some degree of continuity, also emphasizes that Spartan society was subject to ongoing processes of adaptation and change.[11] As already indicated, one difficulty for historians, especially given the paucity of surviving evidence, is accurately to distinguish genuine elements of continuity and tradition from the products of later invention. Michael Lipka's paper provides a careful demonstration of continuity linking a body of texts on Spartan politics which were written over a period of approximately three hundred years. Close similarities of content and/or syntactical construction indicate that depictions of the compact between the Spartan *polis* and its kings by Herodotus (6.56–8) in the fifth century and by Xenophon (*Lak. Pol.* 13 and 15) in the fourth derive from the seventh-century legal text commonly known as the 'Great Rhetra'. These similarities also suggest that the fragment of the Rhetra quoted in Plutarch's *Lykourgos* was originally part of a more extensive compact defining important aspects of the Spartan political order. Interestingly, when viewed within the framework of these other texts, Herodotus' description of the prerogatives of the kings takes on a constitutionalist character which differs markedly from the image of despotism produced by his overall treatment of Sparta within the *Histories*.

Over the last dozen or so years the non-Spartiate populations of Lakonia and Messenia have been the subject of increasing study,[12] a focus reflected in this volume by the set of papers on the helots and *perioikoi* in Part III. Advances in our understanding of the character of helotage during the 1990s have been based above all upon a deepened awareness of the distorting effects of certain ancient representations of helotage, including the 'globalizing' approaches of those writers who lumped helotage together with other collective servile populations, such as the Penestai of Thessaly, in order to produce a general definition of such helotic-type statuses.[13] Nino Luraghi's paper, which forms part of a current series of revisionist articles on the helots,[14] criticizes similar globalizing approaches by those scholars who have sought to categorize helotage in terms of modern legal or sociological definitions of serfdom.[15] Such misleading definitions, he suggests, have underpinned modern perceptions of the Lakonian and Messenian helots as pre-existing homogeneous ethnic groups subjugated within their own territories. Deploying comparative evidence, he argues that the helots' condition was not significantly different from that of agrarian chattel-slaves elsewhere in Greece. Rather than outsiders conquered in an early act of mass enslavement, the helots were more probably impoverished members of the community (comparable to poor Athenians at the time of Solon) taken into servitude at a somewhat later date, in concert with the other major changes that established the classical Spartan order. Nikos Birgalias too is concerned with the interaction between helotage and Sparta's social organization. He concurs with Luraghi in casting doubt upon the existence of a pre-existing Messenian political identity and in viewing the context for the development of helotage as analogous to that of seventh-century Attica. Birgalias questions the severity of the problem posed for the *homoioi* by the helots. He suggest that ideas of class-war between them were partly a product of fifth-century Athenian-inspired ideology and of the independent Messenia of the fourth century onwards. For Birgalias the system of helotage, at its inception, was progressive and represented a pioneering form of security for poorer sections of the population.

The *perioikoi* have, with certain notable exceptions,[16] often been treated as the poor relations of Spartan research, seriously understudied in comparison with the dominant Spartiate elite and the servile helot population. The recent revival of perioikic studies has been stimulated above all by three main influences: first, the systematic project of the Copenhagen Polis Centre (CPC), which has approached the position of perioikic communities as a significant case-study in its attempt to frame general propositions regarding the dependent status of most ancient Greek *poleis* (Shipley 1997; Hall 2000); secondly, the increasing application within different regions of the Greek world of the technique of intensive archaeological survey, exemplified in the case of Spartan territory by the *Laconia Survey* (Shipley 1992; Cavanagh *et al.* 1996, 2002) and the *Pylos Regional Archaeological Project* (Alcock *et al.* in preparation); thirdly, the notable interest in the position of the *perioikoi* shown by Russian ancient historians (e.g. Zaikov 1988, 1994). All three influences are evident in the papers in this volume by Andrey Eremin and Norbert Mertens, both of which address the twin questions which lie at the heart of recent historical research. In what sense, if any, did the *perioikoi* possess citizenship within the political framework of Spartan rule? And can perioikic settlements or communities be regarded as *poleis*, as they are often described by ancient writers? The two contributions show some interesting similarities and differences.

Mertens' paper, which develops his recent Berlin MA dissertation (1999), concentrates upon the period between the Persian wars (480–79 BC) and the battle of Leuktra (371 BC). He tackles the above questions through analysis of the historical sources, focusing upon a critique of the principles and propositions put forward by scholars working under the aegis of the CPC. He concurs that the *perioikoi* were members of the citizen-body of the Lakedaimonian *polis*, which embraced both the Spartiates and the *perioikoi*, although only the former possessed full political rights. On the basis of the CPC's own criteria, however, he dissents from their proposition that the perioikic communities can be regarded as *poleis* in their own right, arguing instead that they were integrated components of the Lakedaimonian *polis*. Furthermore, he questions the general categorizations of communities employed by the project, especially that of the 'dependent *polis*', calling for appreciation of a more varied spectrum of levels of integration which would permit a more nuanced depiction of the position of perioikic communities. In contrast, Eremin's paper, which performs a valuable role in outlining the insights of recent Russian research (cf. Eremin 1993), addresses these questions through a long-term historical perspective. Arguing that the *polis* was not just a simple grouping of citizens, but a structured organization of those citizens involving specific social relations between quasi-kinship groups such as *phylai*, his study focuses upon developments in the internal organization of perioikic communities, which are examined through a combination of archaeological and literary evidence for the process of synoikism. He concludes that the relatively late dating of these synoikisms indicates that the communities in question had previously been *kōmai* not *poleis*. Furthermore, he dismisses the notion of a Lakedaimonian *polis* (and hence any idea of perioikic citizenship), given the absence of any structured organization involving constituent *phylai*. Although disagreeing on this last point, the two papers, despite their diverse methods, produce similar conclusions in other respects. Each disagrees with the conclusions of recent research that perioikic communities can be regarded as *poleis*; and they concur in disputing the proposition of the CPC that the prime test of a community's *polis* status should be the labels applied by the Greeks themselves, preferring instead to form their judgements on the basis of more objective criteria. This engagement with the ideas emerging from the Copenhagen project is a good example of the ongoing interaction between current research on Sparta and on Greek history in general.

Part IV of the volume comprises two articles dealing with the growing field of the historiographical reception of Sparta, including what might be called 'the mirage of Sparta within modern history-writing'. As Rawson was aware, the Spartan tradition in European thought has exercised an impact not only upon social and political theorists but also upon other members of the intelligentsia, including both the early forerunners and the later professional exponents of academic scholarship.[17] Building upon his recent monograph on Spartan age classes and marriage practices (2000), MARCELLO LUPI sketches what he terms 'another chapter of the Spartan mirage': the history of how modern historiography has attempted to interpret Spartan customs on the basis of ethnographic parallels. Following in the footsteps of early modern missionaries and travellers, who likened Spartan customs to those found among peoples of the New World, scholars in the early years of the twentieth century treated Spartan society as a fossil, 'an authentic museum of ancient customs' (Schurtz 1902), which could be compared to those in modern 'primitive' societies. From the 1920s onwards, however, comparative study fell out of favour within both classics and anthropology; and, subsequently, even scholars like Finley and Cartledge who have wished to re-open a dialogue, have argued that ethnographic parallels cannot illuminate classical Sparta but only her lost early history. Reacting against such restrictions, Lupi advocates a return to comparative study through a new method in tune with current anthropological approaches, which proceed via critical scrutiny of the categories employed in comparison. He illustrates this method through a case study in which problematizing the category of marriage permits the reconciliation of two sources (Hagnon and Plutarch) who have interpreted the same practice in the disparate terms, respectively, of pre- and post-marital sexual relations.

STEFAN REBENICH's contribution – which forms part of a series of articles on the role of classical scholarship within the National Socialist era (e.g. Rebenich 2001a, 2001b) – returns us full-circle to the starting-place of this volume: a Spartan king and the battle of Thermopylai. His paper on the myth of Leonidas in German historiography constitutes a timely addition to recent studies both of the modern legend of Thermopylai (e.g. Macgregor Morris 2000a, 2000b) and of the role of Sparta within German politics and culture (Rawson 1969, 306–43; Christ 1986). From the mid-nineteenth century to World War I, German historical scholarship, despite some criticism, celebrated Leonidas and Thermopylai as paradigms of patriotism and heroism. Thus were the foundations laid for a more intensive development of these images under Nazi rule. Owing to the allegedly close racial connection between Spartans and Germans, and also to their supposedly common Nordic background, Sparta came to play the role of an exemplar within National Socialist education. Within this context, Leonidas was often portrayed in both academic and popular historiography as the ideal historical representative of a Führerstaat, an example which Adolf Hitler himself invoked when resolving in 1945 to remain in Berlin to meet his end.

Acknowledgements

The editors thank the trustees of the A.G. Leventis Foundation for their support of the 2000 Sparta seminar and of the Celtic Conference in Classics of which it formed part. They also convey their gratitude to Professor David Scourfield, Head of the Department of Ancient Classics at the National University of Ireland, Maynooth, for generously providing the venue for the Conference.

Notes

[1] Baltrusch 1998; Cavanagh and Walker 1998; Meier 1998; Richer 1998; Birgalias 1999; Hodkinson and Powell 1999; Koutoulas 1999; Hodkinson 2000; Hupfloher 2000; Kourinou 2000; Link 2000; Lupi 2000; Cartledge 2001a, 2001b; Cartledge and Spawforth 2001; Dreher 2001; Förtsch 2001; Koliopoulos 2001; Sommer 2001; Cavanagh *et al.* 2002; Lipka 2002; Pomeroy 2002; Whitby 2002.

[2] *Eleutherotypia*, *E Istorika*, 61, 14 December 2000; 87, 14 June 2001.

[3] Cf. Whitby 2002, 11, and the title of Paul Cartledge's recent collection of essays (2001a), *Spartan Reflections*.

[4] e.g. Kennell 1995; Cartledge and Spawforth 2001, ch. 14.

[5] For criticism of these tendencies within modern scholarship on Spartan landownership, Hodkinson 1986; 2000, 65–75. The most notable earlier exception is Chester Starr's important article on 'The credibility of early Spartan history' (Starr 1965), on which see Hodkinson 1997a, 83 and Whitby 2002, 21.

[6] Cf. the claim of Glen Bowersock that, 'A recent tendency to confine the traditions recorded by ancient witnesses to the epoch in which they wrote has produced an unbalanced, fragmented, and ultimately unpersuasive account of classical Sparta' ('Premessa' [Preface] to Lupi 2000, 5).

[7] Cartledge 1993, 80–2 (quotation at p. 80). His perspective derives inspiration from the work of Hartog 1988 (cf. esp. 152–6, 329–30, 335–9 for his brief discussions of Herodotus and Sparta). For one subject on which Herodotus does *not* treat Spartan practice as alien to that of other Greeks, Hodkinson 2000, 19–20.

[8] Millender 1999, 2000.

[9] Cf. Hodkinson 1983, 273–6.

[10] For an example of the influence of Flower's paper upon my own work, see Hodkinson 1997a, 84–7.

[11] Among older approaches, cf. Chrimes (1949, v), whose work aimed 'to trace constitutional and social survivals back to their roots in the past'. Among more recent depictions, cf. Kennell 1995; Thommen 1996.

[12] e.g. On the helots, Talbert 1989; Ducat 1990; Cartledge 1991; Hodkinson 1992; 1997b; 2000, 113–49; Singor 1993; Whitby 1994; Paradiso 1997; Figueira 1999; Lombardo 1999; Alcock 2002; Alcock and Luraghi forthcoming. On the *perioikoi*, Shipley 1992, 1997; Lotze 1993/94; Zaikov 1988, 1994; Kennell 1999; Hall 2000.

[13] Ducat 1990; 1994, 16. Cf. also Hodkinson 1992; Whitby 1994.

[14] Luraghi 2001; 2002; forthcoming.

[15] e.g. the definition of helots as 'state serfs' by de Ste Croix 1981, 147, 149; Cartledge 1987, 172; 1988, 39. de Ste Croix's definition (1981, 135–6) is based upon the 1956 UN Supplementary Convention on the Abolition of Slavery, the Slave Trade and Practices similar to Slavery. For criticism of the definition of helots as serfs, Finley 1985, 65, 184–5, 221 n. 5. For a general critique of such globalizing approaches, Hodkinson forthcoming.

[16] e.g. Cartledge 2001b, originally published in 1979.

[17] Cf. also, recently, Hodkinson 2000, 9–17; and Humble, this volume.

Bibliography

Alcock, S.E.

2002 'A simple case of exploitation? The helots of Messenia', in P. Cartledge, E.E. Cohen and L. Foxhall (eds.) *Money, Labour and Land in Ancient Greece: Approaches to the economies of ancient Greece*, London and New York, 185–99.

Alcock, S.E. et al.

in prep. 'The Pylos Regional Archaeological Project. Part IV: Historic Messenia, Geometric to late Roman', *Hesperia.*

Alcock, S.E. and Luraghi, N. (eds.)

forthcoming *Helots and their Masters in Laconia and Messenia: Histories, ideologies, structures.*

Baltrusch, E.

1998 *Sparta: Geschichte, Gesellschaft, Kultur*, Munich.

Birgalias, N.

1999 *L'odyssée de l'éducation spartiate*, Athens.

Cartledge, P.

1987 *Agesilaos and the Crisis of Sparta*, London.

1988 'Serfdom in classical Greece', in L. Archer (ed.) *Slavery and Other Forms of Unfree Labour*, London, 33–41.

1991 'Richard Talbert's revision of the Spartan-helot struggle: a reply', *Historia* 40, 379–81.

1993 *The Greeks: A portrait of Self and Others*, Oxford and New York.

2001a *Spartan Reflections*, London.

2001b *Sparta and Lakonia: A regional history, 1300–362 BC*, 2nd edn, London and New York.

Cartledge, P. and Spawforth, A.

2001 *Hellenistic and Roman Sparta: A tale of two cities*, 2nd edn, London and New York.

Cavanagh, W.G., Crouwel, J., Catling, R.W.V. and Shipley, G.

1996 *Continuity and Change in a Greek Rural Landscape: The Laconia Survey, II, Archaeological data, BSA* Suppl. Vol. 27, London.

2002 *Continuity and Change in a Greek Rural Landscape: The Laconia Survey, I, Results and interpretation, BSA* Suppl. Vol. 26, London.

Cavanagh, W.G. and Walker, S.E.C. (eds.)
1998 *Sparta in Laconia: The archaeology of a city and its countryside*, London.

Chrimes, K.M.T.
1949 *Ancient Sparta: A re-examination of the evidence*, Manchester. Reprinted 1999.

Christ, K.
1986 'Spartaforschung und Spartabild', in K. Christ (ed.) *Sparta*, Darmstadt, 1–72. Repr. in his *Griechische Geschichte und Wissenschaftsgeschichte*, Historia Einzelschriften 106, Stuttgart 1996, 9–57.

Clarke, M.
1999 *Flesh and Spirit in the Songs of Homer*, Oxford.

de Ste. Croix, G.E.M.
1981 *The Class Struggle in the Ancient Greek World*, London. Corrected paperback imprint, 1983.

Dreher, M.
2001 *Athen und Sparta*, Munich.

Ducat, J.
1990 *Les Hilotes*, *BCH* Supplément XX, Paris.
1994 *Les Pénestes de Thessalie*, Paris.

Eremin, A.
1993 'The problems of ancient Spartan history in post-war British and American historiography', Synopsis of candidate thesis [in Russian], Kazan State University.

Figueira, T.J.
1999 'The evolution of the Messenian identity', in Hodkinson and Powell (eds.) *Sparta: New perspectives*, 211–44.

Finley, M.I.
1985 *The Ancient Economy*, 2nd edn, London.

Förtsch, R.
2001 *Kunstverwendung und Kunstlegitimation im archaischen und frühklassischen Sparta*, Mainz am Rhein.

Hall, J.M.
2000 'Sparta, Lakedaimon and the nature of perioikic dependency', in P. Flensted-Jensen (ed.) *Further Studies in the Ancient Greek Polis*, Stuttgart, 73–89.

Hartog, F.
1988 *The Mirror of Herodotus: The representation of the Other in the writing of history*, Berkeley. English trans. of French original, Paris 1980; rev. and augmented edn 1992.

Hobsbawm, E. and Ranger, T. (eds.)
1983 *The Invention of Tradition*, Cambridge.

Hodkinson, S.
1983 'Social order and the conflict of values in classical Sparta', *Chiron* 13, 239–81.
1986 'Land tenure and inheritance in classical Sparta', *CQ* n.s. 36, 378–406.
1992 'Sharecropping and Sparta's economic exploitation of the helots', in Sanders *Philolakôn*, 123–34.

1997a 'The development of Spartan society and institutions in the archaic period', in L.G. Mitchell and P.J. Rhodes (eds.) *The Development of the Polis in Archaic Greece*, London and New York, 83–102.

1997b 'Servile and free dependants of the Spartan *oikos*', in Moggi and Cordiano (eds.) *Schiavi e Dipendenti*, 45–71.

1999 'Introduction', in Hodkinson and Powell (eds.) *Sparta: New perspectives*, ix–xxvi.

2000 *Property and Wealth in Classical Sparta*, London.

forthcoming 'Spartiates, helots and the direction of the agrarian economy: towards an understanding of helotage in comparative perspective', in Alcock and Luraghi (eds.) *Helots and their Masters*.

Hodkinson, S. and Powell, A. (eds.)

1999 *Sparta: New perspectives*, London.

Humble, N.

1999 '*Sōphrosynē* and the Spartans', in Hodkinson and Powell (eds.) *Sparta: New perspectives*, 339–53.

Hupfloher, A.

2000 *Kulte im kaiserzeitlichen Sparta: eine Rekonstruktion anhand der Priesterämter*, Berlin.

Kennell, N.M.

1995 *The Gymnasium of Virtue: Education and culture in ancient Sparta*, Chapel Hill and London.

1999 'From *perioikoi* to *poleis*: the Laconian cities in the late hellenistic period', in Hodkinson and Powell (eds.) *Sparta: New Perspectives*, 189–210.

Koliopoulos, K.

2001 *E Ypsēlē Stratēgikē tēs Archaias Spartēs (750–192 p.Ch.)*, Athens.

Kourinou, E.

2000 *Spartē: Symbolē stē mnēmeiakē topographia tēs*, Athens.

Koutoulas, D.

1999 *Archaia Spartē*. Thessalonike.

Link, S.

2000 *Das frühe Sparta: Untersuchungen zur spartanischen Staatsbildung im 7. und 6. Jahrhundert v.Chr.*, St Katharinen.

Lipka, M.

2002 *Xenophon's* Spartan Constitution*: Introduction, text, commentary*, Berlin and New York.

Lombardo, M.

1999 'Le donne degli Iloti', in F. Reduzzi Merola and A. Storchi Marino (eds.) *Femmes-esclaves: Modèles d'interprétation anthropologique, économique, juridique*, Naples, 129–43.

Lotze, D.

1993/94 'Bürger zweiter Klasse: Spartas Periöken. Ihre Stellung und Funktion im Staat der Lakedaimonier', *Sitzungsberichte der Akademie der Wissenschaften zu Erfurt. Geisteswissenschaftliche Klasse* 2, 37–51.

Lupi, M.

2000 *L'Ordine Delle Generazioni: Classi di età e costumi matrimoniali nell'antica Sparta*, Bari.

Luraghi, N.

2001 'Der Erdbebenaufstand und die Entstehung der messenischen Identität', in D. Papenfuss and V.-M. Strocka (eds.) *Gab es das griechische Wunder? Griechenland zwischen dem Ende des 6. und der Mitte des 5. Jahrhunderts v. Chr.*, Mainz, 279–301.

2002 'Becoming Messenian', *JHS* 122.

forthcoming 'The imaginary conquest of the helots', in Alcock and Luraghi (eds.) *Helots and their Masters.*

Macgregor Morris, I.

2000a '*To make a new Thermopylae*: hellenism, Greek liberation, and the battle of Thermopylae', *Greece and Rome* 47, 211–30.

2000b 'The Age of Leonidas: the legend of Thermopylae in British political culture, 1737–1821', PhD diss., University of Manchester.

Meier, M.

1998 *Aristokraten und Damoden. Untersuchungen zur inneren Entwicklung Spartas im 7. Jahrhundert v. Chr. und zur politischen Funktion der Dichtung des Tyrtaios*, Stuttgart.

Mertens, N.

1999 'Die periöken Spartas', MA diss., Freie Universität Berlin.

Millender, E.G.

1999 'Athenian ideology and the empowered Spartan woman', in Hodkinson and Powell (eds.) *Sparta: New perspectives*, 355–91.

2000 'Spartan literacy revisited', *Classical Antiquity* 20, 121–64.

Moggi, M. and Cordiano, G. (eds.)

1997 *Schiavi e Dipendenti nell'Ambito dell'Oikos e della Familia*, XXII Colloquio GIREA, Pisa,

Ogden, D.

2002 *Greek and Roman Necromancy*, Princeton.

Ollier, F.

1933–43 *Le Mirage Spartiate: Étude sur l'idéalisation de Sparte dans l'antiquité grecque*, 2 vols., Lyon and Paris.

Paradiso, A.

1997 'Gli iloti e l'*oikos*', in Moggi and Cordiano (eds.) *Schiavi e Dipendenti*, 73–90.

Pomeroy, S.B.

2002 *Spartan Women*, New York.

Powell, A. and Hodkinson, S. (eds.)

1994 *The Shadow of Sparta*, London and New York.

Rawson, E.

1969 *The Spartan Tradition in European Thought*, Oxford.

Rebenich, S.

2001a 'Alte Geschichte in Demokratie und Diktatur: Der Fall Helmut Berve', *Chiron* 31, 457–96.

2001b 'Zwischen Anpassung und Widerstand? Die Berliner Akademie der Wissenschaften von 1933 bis 1945', in B. Näf and T. Kammasch (eds.) *Antike und Altertumswissenschaft in der Zeit von Faschismus und Nationalsozialismus*, Mandelbachtal and Cambridge, 203–44.

Richer, N.
1998 *Les Éphores: Études sur l'histoire et sur l'image de Sparte (VIIIe–IIIe siècles avant Jésus-Christ)*, Paris.

Sanders, J.M. (ed.)
1992 *Philolakôn: Lakonian Studies in honour of Hector Catling*, London.

Schurtz, H.
1902 *Alterklassen und Männerbünde*, Berlin.

Shipley, G.
1992 '*Perioikos*: the discovery of classical Lakonia', in Sanders (ed.), *Philolakôn*, 211–26.
1997 '"The other Lakedaimonians": the dependent perioikic *poleis* of Laconia and Messenia', in M.H. Hansen (ed.) *The Polis as an Urban Centre and as a Political Community*, Acts of the Copenhagen Polis Centre, vol. 4, Copenhagen, 189–281.

Singor, H.W.
1993 'Spartan land lots and helot rents', in H. Sancisi-Weerdenburg *et al.* (eds.) *De Agricultura: In memoriam Pieter Willem de Neeve*, Amsterdam, 31–60.

Sommer, S.
2001 *Das Ephorat. Garant des spartanischen Kosmos*, St Katharinen.

Starr, C.G.
1965 'The credibility of early Spartan history', *Historia* 14, 257–72. Reprinted in his *Essays in Ancient History*, eds. A. Ferrill and T. Kelly, Leiden 1979, 145–59; and in Whitby 2002, 26–42.

Talbert, R.J.A.
1989 'The role of the helots in the class struggle at Sparta', *Historia* 38, 22–40.

Thommen, L.
1996 *Lakedaimonion Politeia: Die Entstehung der spartanischen Verfassung*, Historia Einzelschriften 103, Stuttgart.

Tigerstedt, E.N.
1965–78 *The Legend of Sparta in Classical Antiquity*, 3 vols., Stockholm, Göteborg and Uppsala.

Whitby, M.
1994 'Two shadows: images of Spartans and helots', in Powell and Hodkinson, *The Shadow of Sparta*, 87–126.

Whitby, M. (ed.)
2002 *Sparta*, Edinburgh.

Zaikov, A.V.
1988 'Perioikoi in the structure of the Spartan polis' [in Russian], *Antichnaya Drevnost' I Sredniye Veka*, Sverdlovsk, 19–29.
1994 'Poleis of the Spartan perioikoi' [in Russian], in *Antichnyj I Srednevekovyj Gorod*, Ekaterinburg and Sevastopol, 63–6.

1

HERODOTUS AND SPARTAN DESPOTISM

Ellen Millender

Scholars have long recognized that autocratic government plays a central role in Herodotus' organization of his *Histories*, in which the polarization of Greek and barbarian operates around the factor of political difference.[1] Tales of hybristic Eastern monarchs figure at both the beginning and the end of this work, which recounts the affairs of numerous autocrats throughout its entirety and concentrates on the triumph of Greek freedom over barbarian despotism in Books 7–9. Although Herodotus occasionally recounts positive aspects of various autocratic regimes, as in the case of Peisistratus (1.59),[2] he more often than not presents autocratic rule as inferior to Greek self-government in general and democratic constitutionality in particular.[3] Herodotus repeatedly contrasts absolute rule with the blessings of freedom or self-government, and his account includes two vehement attacks on one-man rule.[4] The first occurs in the Persian Otanes' speech in the constitutional debate (3.80.2–5), and the Corinthian Socles offers the second example in his vivid description of the Cypselid tyranny (5.92).[5] Together with the *Histories'* numerous damning portraits of kings and tyrants, these speeches reveal Herodotus' belief that the power of any individual over a community is arbitrary, prone to become tyrannical, and inimical to freedom.[6]

When one considers how central the opposition between constitutional government and autocracy is to Herodotus' account of the Persian Wars, the role of the Spartan kings in the *Histories* poses an interesting problem: where do the Spartan dyarchs belong in Herodotus' political framework? The Spartan dyarchy occupies a special position in the *Histories* as a rare example of the survival of kingship in the Greek world. Herodotus' work also includes accounts of the hereditary kingships of Macedon and Cyrene, but these societies possess a marginal position in relation to the rest of Greece and play far less important roles in the *Histories* than Sparta.[7] The Spartan kingship, consequently, offers a unique opportunity to evaluate the effect of Herodotus' anti-autocratic bias on his depiction of a Greek kingship, one, moreover, that was constitutionally limited by other organs of government.

This paper argues that Herodotus' portrait of Sparta's hereditary dyarchy in many respects conforms to the pattern of the tyrant that runs through the *Histories.* I suggest that the explanation lies not in Herodotus' ignorance of Sparta's constitutional structure but rather in the strong influence that Athenian democratic practice and ideology exerted on his account of the victory of Greek constitutional government over barbarian tyranny. Against the standard of a Hellas politically defined by fifth-century Athenian democracy, the Spartan kingship in Herodotus' hands not only becomes the antithesis of Athenian constitutional government but also operates as an indicator of Spartan political otherness. In his characterization of the Spartan dyarchy, Herodotus repeatedly uses the same ideologically charged nexus of terms, themes, and symbols with which both he and several contemporary Athenian-based authors conceptualized barbarian autocracy. In the first two sections of this paper, I examine this construction of Spartan despotism in Herodotus' account of the dyarchs' prerogatives and burial rites (6.56–60) and his individual portraits of Spartan personal rule. The third section analyzes the ideological framework underpinning Herodotus' representation of all forms of autocracy, especially the Lacedaemonians' hereditary kingship.

I. Herodotus and the Spartan royal funeral

Most of the disparate information on Sparta included in the *Histories* clusters around the figures of the Spartan kings and renders Herodotus' portrait of Sparta essentially a series of royal biographical sketches. For example, he constructs the bulk of his narrative of Spartan internal history around the stories of the birth and rivalry of Cleomenes I and his half-brother Dorieus (5.39–48), the conflict between Cleomenes and Demaratus (6.50–1, 61–70), and Cleomenes' madness and demise (6.74–84). He similarly situates several accounts of Sparta's external affairs in the context of his extended treatment of Cleomenes, including the tyrant Aristagoras' visit to Sparta (5.38, 49–51), Sparta's conflict with the young Athenian democracy (5.70, 72–6), and Sparta's early-fifth-century war with Argos (6.76–81).

In contrast with his detailed treatment of the Spartan kings, Herodotus' presentation of the other governmental bodies that constituted Sparta's 'mixed' constitution – the gerousia, the ephorate, and the ecclesia – appears rather sparse. The disparity in Herodotus' treatment of the other organs of government, however, implies neither a lack of interest in, nor ignorance of, Sparta's constitutional structure. Herodotus does not provide a detailed analysis of the various components of the Spartan system, but comments scattered throughout the text reveal his basic understanding of the organs of Spartan government, along with their respective prerogatives and duties.[8] In addition to his reference to the political structures reputedly established by Lycurgus (1.65.5), Herodotus occasionally alludes to the powers that the ephors exercised,[9] including their reception and expulsion of foreign visitors (3.148.2; 9.7.1–10.1),[10] their guardianship of the hereditary succession of the two Spartan royal dynasties (5.39.2, 40.1, 41.2), their judicial role in the trial of Cleomenes I after the battle of Sepeia *c.* 494 (6.82.1), their authority to order out a levy and appoint its commander (9.10.1), and their possible accompaniment of kings (or, in this case, a regent) on campaign (9.76.3).[11] Although Herodotus gives far less attention to the gerousia, he reveals his knowledge of their joint deliberations with the dyarchs (6.57.5) and their role in the protection of the hereditary succession (5.40.1).[12] His information concerning the Spartan assembly is similarly minimal, but he twice refers specifically to the assembly's meetings (6.58.3; 7.134.2). Herodotus also describes various activities of 'the Spartans' or 'the Lacedaemonians', from which one can infer the numerous constitutional responsibilities and duties of the ecclesia.[13]

Herodotus' focus on the Spartan kings to the detriment of the other elements of Spartan government and society may be a consequence of his biographical approach to history, which probably reflects both the oral nature of his sources and the interests of his audience.[14] The structure of the Spartan constitution also probably contributed to this imbalance, especially when one compares the relatively long reigns of the kings and the annual tenure of the ephorate. The more conspicuous duties and activities of the kings may likewise have provided more material for a historian than the less sensational and, perhaps, less accessible functions of the other officers of state.

However, Herodotus' description of the prerogatives and burial rites of Sparta's hereditary kings, the Agiads and the Eurypontids (6.56–60), suggests that his interest in the Spartan dyarchy has more complex roots. While scholars have tended to attribute Herodotus' treatment of these Spartan *nomoi* to his general interest in anthropological topics and fascination with Spartan customs in particular,[15] this explanation fails to account for the unique position that Herodotus' digression on Lacedaemonian royal customs occupies in the *Histories.* Sparta is the only Greek *polis* given an ethnography by Herodotus, an anomaly that is even more striking when one considers the important function that ethnography performs in the *Histories.*[16] Ethnography provided Herodotus with a useful methodological tool with which to encounter and make sense of his world. It enabled him to come to terms with foreignness present in the cultures he was investigating by providing a discourse through which he could decipher and, in turn, interpret differences he detected between non-Greek societies and Hellas.[17] More importantly, as François Hartog has shown, Herodotus used ethnographic material as a mirror to present to his Greek audience a reverse image of itself. Comparative cultural research, in other words, helped Herodotus to define, against a background of Greek knowledge, what was alien and what it meant to be Greek.[18] Ethnography, moreover, allowed Herodotus 'to give historical significance to the Greek-barbarian antithesis' by making the polarity between barbarian tyranny and Greek freedom the basis of his account of Greece's victory over the East.[19] By supplying an ethnography of the Spartan kingship, Herodotus, therefore, implicitly places Lacedaemon on the non-Greek end of the Greek-barbarian antithesis that structures his ethnographic discourse and treats Spartan kingship as a key signifier of Spartan political difference.

Herodotus sets the stage for his elaboration of Spartan otherness in his discussion of the Spartan dyarchy's origins (6.52–5). After relating the Spartan account (6.52), he suggests his preference for the 'Greek' version, which traces the Spartan kings back to Perseus, son of Danaë (6.53.1). Herodotus then explains that while the Dorian kings can rightly be considered Greek in nationality as far back as Perseus, their relation to his mother Danaë effectively makes them Egyptian in origin (6.53.2; cf. 2.91.5–6). By next inserting the Persians' alternative genealogy of Perseus into this analysis of Spartan royal lineage, Herodotus obliquely emphasizes another possible connection between the dyarchs and Eastern barbarians, in this case the Assyrians (6.54). The Spartan kings' relation to Perseus also links them with Perses, the eponymous founder of the Persians (cf. 7.61.3, 150.2). At the end of this section, Herodotus even more emphatically refers to the dyarchs' Egyptian extraction, when he ponders how Egyptians came to the Peloponnesus and what they did to make themselves kings in that part of Greece (6.55).[20] While Herodotus notes connections between other Greek peoples and non-Greeks (cf. 1.56.2, 57; 2.49.3; 5.57–61, 65.3), both the critical positioning of this passage just before his account of Spartan *nomoi* and his insistence on the 'Greek' account of the dyarchs' origins make it worthy of careful consideration.[21]

Through his discussion of the Spartan kings' Egyptian extraction, Herodotus provides an unusual variant of the more traditional account of the Spartiate dyarchy's lineage, which traces the two royal families to Heracles (cf. 6.52.1; 7.204, 220.4; 8.131.2).[22] He further distances Spartan ethnicity when he claims that both the name and parents of Heracles, the traditional forefather of the Spartan kings, are Egyptian in origin as well (2.43.2). Herodotus' choice of Egypt as the Spartan dyarchy's source assumes even greater significance when one considers the position that Egypt occupies in the *Histories.* Before commencing his treatment of Egyptian customs, Herodotus sets up a polarity between the Egyptians and the rest of mankind, or, more particularly, the Greeks (2.35.2).[23] By linking the Spartan kings with the Egyptians, Herodotus thus effects a significant distinction between the Spartans and the other Greeks.

Herodotus' affirmation of the Spartan kings' foreign origins appropriately introduces his extended treatment of Spartan *nomoi* at 6.56–60, which opens with a description of the prerogatives (γέρεα) that the Spartans accorded their kings during their lifetime (6.56–7). He then examines the kings' funeral honors in a striking passage that stresses Spartan otherness, given that elsewhere it is only the burial and mourning customs of non-Greek peoples that arouse his interest (6.58):[24]

> The kings have received these prerogatives from the Spartan commonwealth during their lifetime, and when they die they receive the following honors. Horsemen carry news of the death throughout Laconia, and women go about the city beating cauldrons. When this has been accomplished, two free people from each house, one man and one woman, are compelled to put on mourning or incur heavy penalties if they fail to do so. The Lacedaemonians observe the same custom at the deaths of their kings as the barbarians of Asia, for most of the barbarians observe the same custom upon their kings' deaths. For, whenever a king of the Lacedaemonians dies, not only the Spartiates, but also a certain number of the perioeci from all over Lacedaemon, are obligated to attend the funeral. When the perioeci, the helots, and the Spartiates themselves have been assembled in the same place to the number of many thousands, mingled with the women, they zealously strike their foreheads and make endless lamentation, declaring that the most recently deceased king was the best king they had ever had.[25]

Herodotus, the traveler and ethnographer, was bound to take an interest in foreign funerary rites. Varying from society to society, such practices provided him with an index of civilization as well as a basis for the comparison of the different groups included in his study. His recognition of funerary practice as a cultural discriminator appears most clearly in his account of Darius' examination of Greek and Indian attitudes toward the proper disposal of the dead (3.38.2–4). More importantly, funeral customs, similar to the other practices and rituals that Herodotus describes in the *Histories*, function in his work as an important indicator of difference between the Greek and non-Greek worlds.[26]

Herodotus' unusual treatment of Spartan funerary *nomoi* builds upon the image of Spartan alterity, implied earlier in his discussion of the dyarchy's foreign origins, by means of an explicit analogy between the funeral honors of the Spartan kings and the mourning procedures for non-Greek monarchs (6.58.2). In the passages immediately following his description of Lacedaemonian royal obsequies, Herodotus further situates Spartan funerary rites on the fringes of the civilized world by means of two additional analogies between Spartan customs and what he views as their homologues in the non-Greek world (6.59–60).[27] The first analogy continues the association Herodotus had earlier indirectly established between Sparta and Persia through yet another royal custom: just as the new Spartan king cancels all outstanding debts to himself or the commonwealth, the Persian king at the beginning of his reign forgives all cities their arrears of tribute (6.59). The second analogy links the Spartans with the Egyptians through a discussion of the inherited professions of herald, flautist, and cook that exist in both societies (6.60).[28] This analogy strengthens the connections that Herodotus had made earlier between the Spartans and the Egyptians in terms of their deference to the elder members of their respective societies (2.80.1), their practice of war as a hereditary calling (2.164–68),[29] and their especial disdain for trade and handicrafts (2.166–67).[30] Herodotus' association of Spartan and Egyptian professions, moreover, implicitly returns the reader to his account of the Spartan kings' Egyptian origins that introduces the Spartan ethnography at 6.53–5.

Herodotus' explanation of Spartan royal obsequies by means of such analogies with the non-Greek world further underlines Spartan difference by subverting the usual function that comparison performs in his ethnographic discourse. In the *Histories* comparison effects the domestication and translation of the exotic.[31] Herodotus, like all ethnographers, needs to help his Greek audience make sense of the foreign cultures he treats in the *Histories.* Through comparison, and especially the related form of analogy, he makes the foreign familiar by establishing correspondences between features of the society or culture being recounted and elements of the world to which he recounts them.[32] For example, when Herodotus attempts to describe the portion of Egypt lying between the ranges of mountains above Memphis, he remarks that this area must have once been a gulf of the sea, similar to (ὥσπερ) the countryside around Ilium, Teuthrania, Ephesus, and the plain of the Maeander (2.10.1). Herodotus again refers to the Maeander in order to describe the winding course of the Nile beyond Elephantine (2.29.3).

Herodotus' 'translation' of Spartan royal obsequies by means of analogies with the non-Greek world works in the opposite direction. Instead of making the foreign familiar, Herodotus' use of analogy in his description of Spartan royal funeral rites renders them foreign. Herodotus can only explain these customs by establishing correspondences with barbarian rituals (6.58.2):

> νόμος δὲ τοῖσι Λακεδαιμονίοισι κατὰ τῶν βασιλέων τοὺς θανάτους ἐστὶ ὡυτὸς καὶ τοῖσι βαρβάροισι τοῖσι ἐν τῇ Ἀσίῃ· τῶν γὰρ ὦν βαρβάρων οἱ πλεῦνες τὠυτῷ νόμῳ χρέωνται κατὰ τοὺς θανάτους τῶν βασιλέων.

Through this process of defamiliarization, Herodotus highlights the otherness of these particular Spartan *nomoi* and classes them with foreign phenomena for which he fails to provide Greek analogies. Occasionally, Herodotus recounts features of the non-Greek world lacking homologues in Greece that would facilitate their presentation to his audience. Faced with this difficulty, Herodotus adduces foreign parallels to explain such foreign phenomena. This operation occurs, for example, in his description of the Nile's course through Libya, which he effects by means of an analogy with the Ister's course (2.34.2; cf. 2.33.2–4).[33] Likewise, Herodotus recounts the Libyan Nasamones' penchant for polygamy and promiscuous sexual relations by means of an analogy with Massagetan *nomoi* (4.172.2).[34] Herodotus' treatment of both the Nile's course and the Nasamones' sexual *mores* implies that the body of knowledge he shares with his audience is not sufficient for making sense of such phenomena. Similarly, Herodotus' treatment of Spartan royal funeral customs suggests that they, too, are not part of the matrix of common knowledge and shared cultural vocabulary that forms the basis of communication between him and his audience. Spartan royal obsequies, in other words, remain both unintelligible and untranslatable in the face of the hellenic cultural vocabulary that Herodotus has at his disposal.

In addition to Herodotus' explicit association of Spartan and barbarian funerary practices and his consequent defamiliarization of these particular Lacedaemonian *nomoi*, several other elements in his digression on the dyarchs' funeral honors enhance its portrait of Spartan alterity, especially in political terms. As Hartog has pointed out in his examination of the *Histories*' account of Scythian royal burial rites, Herodotus' very interest in the nature of royal burial in Sparta cannot help but refer the reader back to his account of Scythian obsequies (4.71–2).[35] A few noteworthy aspects of the Spartan ceremony further help to link Sparta not only with Scythia but also with the barbarian world in general and simultaneously separate Sparta from the rest of the classical Greek world, particularly democratic Athens.

The Spartan mourners, for example, make endless lamentation: οἰμωγῇ διαχρέωνται ἀπλέτῳ (6.58.3), a practice that several fifth-century Athenian-based authors treat as a feature of the barbarian world.[36] Aeschylus' *Persae*, produced in 472, furnishes the earliest extant evidence of this characterization through its presentation of Persian emotional abandonment following the defeat of Xerxes at Salamis. Aeschylus effects this characterization by means of a continued emphasis on Persian lamentation throughout the tragedy, which culminates in an unusually lengthy and impassioned dirge (909–1076).[37] In a number of fifth-century tragedies, such behavior also became a frequent characteristic of mythical non-Greek societies, which tragedy had gradually Orientalized.[38] This treatment is explicit in Euripides' *Hecuba* of *c.* 424, where the chorus of captive Trojan women perform a long lament (59–215) until the Greek Odysseus' entry temporarily halts the Trojan *thrēnos* and asserts the primacy of the Greek, male, spoken voice of rationality over the female lament sung by the barbarians.[39]

Herodotus also locates the practice of highly emotional forms of lamentation in various parts of the non-Greek world, including Egypt, Babylonia and Persia.[40] Among the many examples he cites, three offer close parallels to the Spartans' mourning: (1) the Persians' loud and lengthy lament in response to Cambyses' impending death (3.66.1), (2) the Persians' unappeasable grief upon learning of their defeat at Salamis (8.99.2), and (3) the Persian army's endless lamentation (οἰμωγῇ τε χρεόμενοι ἀπλέτῳ) while mourning the death of Masistius, the commander of the Persian cavalry (9.24). Herodotus' specific use of the tragic term οἰμωγή to denote both Persian and Spartan lamentation once again links Sparta with Persia and situates the Spartan ritual in a non-Greek context.[41] More importantly, as Hartog has noted, 'these statutory lamentations naturally stand in opposition to the legislation of other cities and in particular to the laws of Athens which, ever since Solon, had prohibited the funeral lament (*thrēnos*) or had laid down a code for its use, limiting it to women'.[42] Thucydides reveals that the public funeral of the fifth-century democracy continued to keep lamentation to a minimum, subordinating private mourning to the public ceremony that served to celebrate and praise the dead (2.34.4, 44.1, 46.2).[43]

As I have argued elsewhere, the Spartans' largely speechless demonstration of mourning further associates them with the barbarian world, where non-verbal communication commonly occurs through signs or tokens.[44] Through their avoidance of articulated speech and preference for brief, formulaic expressions of praise for their dead king, the Spartan mourners, more importantly, exhibit an attitude toward speech that is generally characteristic of autocratic regimes in the *Histories*.[45] Under the rule of the despot, subjects, like slaves, lack free speech and fear its consequences.[46] Such expressions of grief also distance the Lacedaemonians from democratic Athens and its burial ceremony for soldiers fallen in battle. While the Athenian civic ceremony reduced the visual spectacle to a minimum and gave precedence to speech celebrating the *polis*, the Spartan ritual described by Herodotus reduces speech to a mere formula that celebrates the dead dyarch and, through him, the institution of the hereditary dyarchy.[47]

The dyarchs' funeral ceremony underlines Spartan political alterity not only through the mourners' mode of lamentation but also through the Lacedaemonians' practice of zealously beating their foreheads while lamenting their dead king: κόπτονταί τε τὰ μέτωπα προθύμως (6.58.3). This custom even further separates Sparta from Athens, where Solon had banned such violent treatment of the body, especially on the part of women,[48] and refers the reader to the non-Greek world, where Herodotus repeatedly locates acts of disfigurement,[49] including funerary self-mutilation.[50] By striking their foreheads, the Lacedaemonians call to mind Herodotus' Scythians, who mutilate their heads in response to the news of their king's death (4.71.2), and the Carians, who beat their breasts and cut their foreheads in lamentation following the sacrifice at the festival of Isis at Busiris (2.61.2).[51] The Spartans' beatings, however, particularly associate Lacedaemonian royal funeral rites with Herodotus' portrayal of autocracy, in which mutilation and disfigurement often function as an exercise of power.[52] Throughout the *Histories* despots assert their authority, threaten, humiliate, and punish by means of physical disfigurement. Cambyses, for example, affirms his mastery over Egypt by mutilating Amasis' exhumed corpse (3.16), while Xerxes punishes the Lydian Pythius' insolent plea to exempt his eldest son from war by turning the young man's severed halves into a makeshift gateway for the Persian army (7.39.3). The role that mutilation plays in the establishment of despotic authority appears most clearly in Herodotus' account of the Persian Zopyrus' self-mutilation (3.154–60). Zopyrus shaves his head, hacks off his own nose and ears, and scourges himself, in order to make the Babylonians believe that he is a fellow victim of Darius (3.154.2). When Darius demands to know who could have perpetrated such an outrage, Zopyrus claims that only his monarch, Darius, would have the power to inflict such bodily abuse (3.155.1).[53]

Although the mutilation that attends the Spartan royal funeral is less extreme than that practiced by these Herodotean despots and functions as a part of the ritual of lamentation,[54] it parallels the various marks of slavery that both physically and symbolically demarcate ruler and ruled in the barbarian world.[55] This delineation of power relations reveals itself throughout the Spartan ceremony, most explicitly in (1) the requirement that two free people from each household, a man and a woman, don mourning on pain of harsh penalties (6.58.1), and (2) the obligation of all Spartiates and a specified number of their subject neighbors to attend the funeral (6.58.2).[56] Together with their unarticulated expression of lamentation and the other constraints that circumscribe the mourning process, the Spartans' ritual defilement demonstrates their subservient position in relation to the king.[57]

Herodotus' description of the funeral ceremony as one of the privileges (γέρεα) that the Spartan kings could claim from the *polis* also lends a despotic flavor to the Lacedaemonians' royal funeral ceremony (6.56, 57.5; cf. 7.104.2). Instead of being a right to which all citizens are equally entitled, the funeral becomes one of the prerogatives of Sparta's hereditary kings that set them apart from the rest of the *polis.* Functioning as a γέρας, the funeral associates Sparta with several autocratically-governed societies in Herodotus' account,[58] in which both the giving and receiving of special privileges play a fundamental role.[59] In addition to the perquisites that the Spartan kings receive from their subjects, Herodotus uses the term γέρας to refer to the Persian kingship itself (3.85.1; 7.3.3) and the prerogatives of the hereditary kings of Cyrene (4.162.2, 165.1). By describing the Spartan dyarch's funeral by means of this term, Herodotus again stresses Spartan political alterity.[60]

Despite the 'despotic' tenor of Herodotus' portrait of Lacedaemonian royal obsequies, scholars – with the exception of Hartog – have failed to note the unusual nature of this passage.[61] Even Hartog's treatment of these rites remains incomplete, because he neither elucidates the historical principles that control Herodotus' depiction of Spartan royal funerary practices nor questions why Herodotus, who is so selective in his inclusion of Spartan material, discusses Spartan royal obsequies in such detail. The question of Herodotus' selectivity is an important one, since he chooses to describe a funeral ceremony that was an exceptional example of Spartan burial habits and fails to provide an account of the burial ritual of the average Spartiate to parallel his earlier description of the average Scythian's obsequies (4.73).[62]

By focusing on the exceptional ritual of the Spartan royal funeral, Herodotus portrays Sparta as a society whose political structures forge a link with the non-Greek world, where autocratic government was the norm.[63] In political terms, the Spartan ceremony functions as an institution that reifies and supports an autocratic political structure. By honoring the city's hereditary dyarchs, Spartan royal obsequies simultaneously celebrate the very institution of kingship. Through their speechless display, self-mutilation, obligatory attendance, and compulsory externalization of their lamentation, the Lacedaemonian mourners abase themselves and establish the absolute superiority of the dead king. The symbolic death that the city undergoes through the suspension of all commercial and political activity during a prescribed ten-day period of mourning following the funeral (6.58.3), in turn, signifies the dyarch's embodiment of the Spartan commonwealth.[64] The fact that the compulsory, despotic elements of the royal funeral emanate not from autocratic kingship but from the Spartan *polis*, which observes these rites as one of several prerogatives it bestows upon its dyarchs, adds yet another layer to this complex portrait of Spartan autocracy. By forcing themselves and their subject neighbors to recognize and honor the dyarchs' extraordinary status, the Spartiates – and their *polis* by extension – become veritable despots in their own right and further identify Sparta as a society organized on despotic principles. It is by operating as a symbol of hierarchy and despotism that the royal funeral propels the constitutional dyarchy of the Spartans across the political divide separating Greeks from non-Greeks in the *Histories* and situates it in a polarity with Greek constitutionality.

II. Herodotus' despotic dyarchs

Although Herodotus' ethnography of Spartan royal obsequies emphasizes the autocratic nature of the Spartan kingship, his scattered depictions of the dyarchs do not wholly conform to the pattern of tyranny that, in large part, structures the *Histories*. For example, Herodotus provides extensive evidence that illuminates the unique constitutional position of the Lacedaemonian dyarchs, as rulers circumscribed by both their own collegiality and Sparta's other political organs. Herodotus' account of the extended conflict between the Agiad Cleomenes I and the Eurypontid Demaratus well illustrates the restrictions that collegiality could put in the way of either king's exercise of authority (6.50–70; cf. 5.74–6). His description of Cleomenes' engineering of Demaratus' deposition (6.61–67.1), along with three other accounts of Spartan dyarchs brought into court on criminal charges (6.72, 82, 85), also demonstrates that the kings could be tried before the high court composed of the ephors and gerousia and, if found guilty, deposed. Other examples of the ephors' and elders' ability to modify kingly behavior run through the *Histories*, including their intervention in Anaxandridas' domestic affairs to secure the Agiad succession (5.39–40).

Herodotus demonstrates his awareness of the constitutional limits of the Spartan dyarchy,[65] but he does not present the Spartan kings as either ineffectual or controlled by the other officers of state. His depiction of the dyarchy (and especially Cleomenes I), on the contrary, reveals that the Spartan kings could exercise considerable influence on Spartan politics, particularly in the realm of foreign affairs.[66] In his accounts of Cleomenes' reception of Maeandrius *c.* 516 (3.148) and Aristagoras in 499 (5.38.2, 49–51), Herodotus makes the Agiad king the principal, if not the only, representative of Spartan diplomacy and fully responsible for the negotiations that took place during these visits.[67] Herodotus' description of Sparta's conflict with Athens following the deposition of the Peisistratids, in addition, presents Cleomenes as the author of Spartan foreign policy and in control of certain expeditions from their inception (5.70, 72, 74).[68] His account of Cleomenes' conduct of the war against Argos *c.* 494 likewise demonstrates this dyarch's full control over the expedition.[69] Herodotus suggests that Cleomenes alone was responsible for the choice of route, the conduct of the campaign, and the final decision to spare the city of Argos (6.76–82). Although Demaratus obstructed Cleomenes' attempt to punish the leading medizers in Aegina (6.50–1, 61.1), Cleomenes' activities on this island reveal a similar independence and assertion of royal authority (6.49–50, 61.1, 64, 73).[70]

As Herodotus recognized, numerous factors made it possible for the Spartan dyarchs to become dynamic political leaders, especially their hereditary role as Sparta's military leaders.[71] In addition to his important military role in Spartan society, the king possessed an exceptional status in relation to his fellow citizens both in life and in death, which rightly led Max Weber to describe the Spartan dyarchy as an example of 'family-charismatic' kingship.[72] Herodotus reminds his audience several times of the dyarchy's lineal descent from the semi-divine Heracles (6.52.1; 7.204, 220.4; 8.131.2), which set the kings above their fellow Spartiates and mortal men in general. His mention of the close connection between the dyarchs and the twin Dioscuri, who accompanied them on their expeditions (5.75.2), also suggests that the kings functioned as guarantors of the divine protection of Sparta and further emphasizes the semi-divine nature of the Spartan kingship.[73] Similarly, the dyarchs' hereditary priesthoods of Zeus Lacedaemonius and Zeus Uranius, together with their responsibility for conducting necessary sacrifices before setting out on expeditions (6.56.1), indicate their symbolic role as guardians of the state's continued well-being.[74]

Herodotus' account of the special prerogatives of the dyarchs (6.56–8) further underlines their extraordinary position in Spartan society. Their numerous privileges at both public sacrifices and regular meals, especially their double rations (6.57.1–4), allowed them to exercise their patronage by inviting guests to dine with them on both occasions. The kings' right to appoint *proxenoi* and the Pythian messengers (6.57.2), along with their various judicial prerogatives (6.57.4), also served as important sources of patronage and potential political influence. Both kings, in addition, would have been able to exercise influence through their participation in the gerousia (6.57.5).[75] Finally, the elaborate funeral ceremony of the Spartan dyarchs (6.58), to quote Paul Cartledge, 'symbolized, indeed created the honorand's posthumous status as a hero of more than merely mortal nature and thus naturally complemented and continued the charismatic status he had enjoyed in his lifetime'.[76]

Herodotus' account thus presents a complex portrait of the Spartan kings, as subject to constitutional limits and yet empowered by both the charismatic nature of their position in Sparta and their many opportunities to exert personal leadership in this highly militaristic society. His depiction of the Spartan dyarchy, however, possesses yet another dimension that both counters and diminishes his treatment of the kings as constitutional rulers and leaves a far more lasting impression upon the mind of his reader. Throughout the *Histories* Herodotus provides numerous accounts of the Lacedaemonian dyarchs that build upon the vivid image of Spartan despotism created in his ethnography of the Spartan royal funeral, by constructing Sparta as a society organized around the principles of absolute kingship.[77]

In his extended treatment of Cleomenes' reign, for example, Herodotus recounts several intra- and inter-dynastic struggles over the Spartan kingship's hereditary succession, which, as Moses Finley has argued, 'belong to the courts of tyrants and barbarian monarchs, not to a Greek *polis*'.[78] The first of these occurs in his account of the circumstances surrounding Cleomenes' birth and accession (5.39–48). In his description of King Anaxandridas' attempts to produce an heir, Herodotus depicts the hereditary principle of succession as both capricious and disruptive. The need to ensure the succession forces King Anaxandridas to violate Spartan custom by taking a second wife (5.40.2) and produces strife first between his two wives and later between their offspring – Cleomenes and Dorieus (5.42). The Agiads' practice of hereditary succession, more importantly, secures the throne for Cleomenes, a madman who becomes king on account of his birth rather than any manly virtue (ἀνδραγαθίη) he might possess (5.39.1).

Herodotus' account of the struggle between Cleomenes and Demaratus reveals similar inherent defects in the royal succession of the Eurypontid house (6.50–70). Irregular marriage again plays a central role in the story of Demaratus' path to kingship, as Herodotus recounts King Ariston's acquisition of his third wife by cruelly tricking his best friend into giving up his own wife (6.61–2). This improper marriage endangers the royal succession, since Ariston's new wife appears to give birth to the future King Demaratus before the customary 'ten' months have passed (6.63.1–2, 69.1–4) and later admits her own doubts concerning her son's paternity (6.69.4–5). Hostility between the two houses, in the form of Cleomenes' ongoing conflict with Demaratus, also puts the succession in jeopardy when Cleomenes employs the stock allegation of illegitimacy to oust Demaratus and replace him with Leotychidas, a member of a collateral branch of the Eurypontid house (6.61–67.1).

Through the theme of the royal succession, Herodotus associates the Spartan dyarchy with several despotic regimes in which the succession appears equally arbitrary and subject to disturbances, especially the Persian monarchy. Herodotus' description of the circumstances surrounding Cyrus' (1.107–28) and Darius' (1.209–10; 3.61–87) acquisition of the γέρας of the Persian kingship demonstrates both the vicissitudes and intrigue that could similarly accompany the Persian royal succession. The parallels between the Spartans' and Persians' custom of hereditary succession become particularly clear in Herodotus' account of the exiled king Demaratus' role in securing the Persian kingdom for Xerxes (7.2–3). Darius' choice of an heir from among his seven sons produces discord between his first and second wives and their children reminiscent of that attending the succession of the Agiad Cleomenes. Like Cleomenes, Xerxes ostensibly gains the throne on the basis of his birth rather than any other consideration. His accession, however, becomes even more arbitrary through the chance involvement of the Spartan king, Demaratus. According to Herodotus, this exiled dyarch advised Xerxes to base his claim to succession on the argument that Darius was already on the Persian throne when Xerxes was born.[79]

Herodotus' claim that Atossa's great power would have guaranteed Xerxes' accession to the throne with or without Demaratus' help (7.3.4) forges yet another link between Persia and Lacedaemon, where women similarly play an important political role as the wives and mothers of kings. As Herodotus' detailed treatment of the mechanics of both Persian and Spartan succession shows, women wield significant power in the context of autocracy through their ability to support or endanger the succession and thereby affect the very political structure of the state. Demaratus' mother, for example, disrupts the hereditary succession of the Eurypontids through her reputed beauty, her foreshortened pregnancy, and the rumors impugning her sexual fidelity (6.61–9). Demaratus' mother, of course, remains an essentially passive political player and does not politically intervene in the succession as directly as the Persian Atossa. However, Herodotus' portrayal of another royal mother, Argeia, suggests that Spartan queens were as capable as Atossa of actively influencing the succession. According to Herodotus, the clever mother of the twin founders of the Agiad and Eurypontid houses desired that both of her sons be made kings and was thus ultimately responsible for the foundation of the dyarchy (6.52.2–7).[80]

The heavy layer of folklore surrounding Herodotus' discussion of the Spartan royal succession further locates the Lacedaemonian kingship in a particularly Eastern context. In his account of Cleomenes' irregular succession (5.39–42.2), Herodotus employs the theme of the struggle between two wives to bear heirs and continue the blood-line of the family, which generally runs as follows: the husband takes a second wife to bear an heir when the first wife proves barren; strife occurs between the two wives in which the second wife and/or her coterie taunt and harass the first beloved wife; and the first wife soon bears children of her own, who become the favorites of their father.[81] The motif of strife between the barren first wife and the fecund second wife occurs throughout Near Eastern folklore, including the biblical accounts of the conflict between Sarah and Hagar (Gen. 16, 1–6), Rachel and Leah (Gen. 30, 1–24), and Hannah and Peninah (Sam. I 1, 1–19).

Herodotus' treatment of Demaratus' birth is similarly overlaid with folklore, both in the description of Demaratus' mother's metamorphosis from an ugly child into the fairest of all Spartan women (6.61.2–5) and her account of Demaratus' possibly heroic paternity (6.69.1–4). Herodotus' use of folkloric elements and focus on the circumstances surrounding the births of these Spartan kings link them with several of the more notable autocrats in the *Histories* – Pisistratus (1.59.1–3), Cyrus (1.107–13), and Cypselus (5.92β1–δ2) – whose birth phenomena provide veritable forecasts of their later regimes. The bad omens presaging Pisistratus' birth serve as a warning against his later introduction of tyranny into Athens, just as Astyages' dreams of the water and vine issuing from his daughter and covering all of Asia predict Cyrus' later sovereignty over that region (1.130.3). Similarly, the prophecies that forecast the birth of a rolling rock and lion to Eetion and Labda appropriately describe the later Cypselus, who murders, exiles, and despoils many of his fellow Corinthians (5.92ε2).[82] The peculiar circumstances attending Cleomenes' and Demaratus' births likewise provide clues concerning their later reigns, particularly Cleomenes' supposed madness and lack of manly merit (5.39.1, 42.1) and Demaratus' association with rape and illegitimacy (6.62–3).

The central position of these and other folkloric motifs in Herodotus' depictions of the Lacedaemonian dyarchs reveals the extent to which Herodotus' portrait of the Spartan kingship conforms to a model of absolute rule that was developing throughout much of the fifth century. The influence of conventional notions of tyranny on Herodotus' treatment of the Spartan dyarchs becomes clear in the many parallels that the *Histories* establish between the Lacedaemonian kings and the Persian Otanes' portrait of autocracy in his speech in favor of popular government in the constitutional debate (3.80.2–5).[83] After recalling the most recent examples of untrammeled rule under the Achaemenid Cambyses and the Magus (3.80.2), Otanes launches into a generalized diatribe against one-man rule.[84] The organizing principle of his portrait of autocracy is *hybris*, which manifests itself in the ruler's penchant for wickedness, impiety, violence, envy, and transgression (3.80.3–5):[85]

> How can monarchy be a well-adjusted thing, when it provides the possibility for a man to do what he wishes without being subject to any account? Monarchy would place even the best of all men holding this position of power outside of his wonted thoughts. For *hybris* arises in him as a result of the presence of good things, and envy is engendered in man from the beginning. Possessing these two tendencies, he possesses all wickedness; sated [with power] he commits many reckless deeds, some from *hybris*, some from jealousy. It is true that the tyrannical man should be free from envy, since he possesses all good things, but the opposite occurs in his dealings with his citizens. He envies the best of them merely for continuing to live, takes pleasure in the worst of the citizens, and is most disposed to listen to slander. Of all men he is the most inconsistent; if you admire him with moderation, he is vexed because he is not paid extreme attention, and if someone pays him extreme attention, he is angry at him for being a flatterer. But the worst things of all I am now going to mention: he disturbs ancestral usages, does violence to women, and kills men without trial.[86]

Among the variety of hybristic modes of behavior that tyrants characteristically exhibit, Otanes emphasizes violence against women (3.80.5).[87] His portrait of the despot receives support from numerous accounts in the *Histories* in which potentates transgress the customary bonds between the sexes by violating women, engaging in abnormal sexual relations, and displaying immoderate and often destructive forms of sexual desire.[88] Significantly, this very theme of excessive and unnatural desire (ἔρως) brackets Herodotus' narrative of the rise and fall of various Eastern empires. The *Histories* opens with the tragic story of the Lydian Candaules, whose ἔρως for his wife is so overpowering that he violates Lydian custom concerning modesty and eventually brings about his own death and Gyges' usurpation of his throne (1.8–12). Near the conclusion of his work, Herodotus recounts the Persian Xerxes' similarly destructive ἔρως for his sister- and daughter-in-law (9.108–13).[89] In between these two tales, Herodotus provides examples of equally abnormal and violent sexual relations, including Cambyses' illegitimate relations with his sisters (3.31–2) and the tyrant Periander's uxoricide and necrophilia (3.50.1; 5.92η3).[90]

At several points in the *Histories*, Herodotus also locates irregular marriages, aberrant sexual relations, and excessive forms of ἔρως in the Spartan royal houses.[91] King Anaxandridas' strong attachment to his wife, who has failed to produce an heir, not only jeopardizes the hereditary succession of the Agiad dynasty but also ultimately forces him to violate Spartan custom by taking a second wife (5.40.2).[92] Mad Cleomenes, the issue of this irregular union, is rumored to have indulged in an adulterous liaison with the wife of his Athenian *xeinos*, Isagoras, thereby violating the bonds of both *xenia* and matrimony (5.70.1).[93] Both Ariston and Demaratus reveal a similar disrespect for the legitimate bonds of marriage by stealing their wives from other men, the former through deceit and the latter through force.[94] King Ariston's passion (ἔρως) for the wife of Agetus is so strong that he schemes against his friend to obtain her. After proposing an exchange of gifts, he persuades the unsuspecting Agetus to swear to give him whichever of his possessions he should demand and then asks for Agetus' wife (6.61–2).[95] Demaratus, by means of another underhanded plot, deprives Leotychidas of his intended bride, Percalus, by carrying her off and marrying her himself (6.65.2).[96] By seriously disrupting the Eurypontid succession,[97] the unnatural passion of both father and son links them with the Lydian Candaules, whose excessive ἔρως brings about his own deposition (1.12), and the Persian Xerxes, whose similarly unhealthy love eventually results in a rebellion that endangers his position and causes serious disruption in both the royal court and the kingdom as a whole (9.113). According to Herodotus, the Spartan regent Pausanias reputedly fell prey to a similarly transgressive ἔρως to become tyrant of Greece, which inspired his illegitimate betrothal to the Achaemenid Megabates' daughter (5.32).[98] While Pausanias' passion arises from political ambition rather than sexual *hybris*, Herodotus' stretching of the meaning of ἔρως as a metaphor for the Spartan regent's 'lust' for power reveals his interest in effecting yet another parallel between the Spartan dyarchs and their barbarian counterparts.

Along with sexual violence, Otanes treats the violation of traditions as characteristic of the unaccountable ruler (3.80.5). Herodotus provides copious instances of such hybristic behavior on the part of various Greek and non-Greek autocrats, especially *hybris* in the form of sacrilege. Cambyses' trangressions against both Persian and Egyptian religious *nomoi* upon his invasion of Egypt furnish the most infamous example of despotic violation of religious propriety in the *Histories.* The ostensibly mad king orders the exhumation, mutilation and burning of Amasis' corpse (3.16.1–4), mortally wounds the sacred bull Apis (3.29), orders that the priests in charge of Apis be scourged (3.29.2), exhumes and opens ancient coffins at Memphis (3.37.1), derides the image in the temple of Hephaestus (3.37.2), and transgresses the sacred boundaries of the temple of the Cabeiri, where he mocks and burns the images (3.37.3). The Persian satrap Artaÿctes provides another instance of despotic sacrilege when he desecrates the tomb of Protesilaus in the Chersonesus by stealing its treasure, planting and farming the precinct, and having intercourse with women in the shrine (9.116). Other examples of impiety on the part of autocrats range from belief in both their invincibility (2.169.2) and their superiority to other mortals (1.30.2, 34.1, 204.2; cf. 4.91.2) to highly sacrilegious attacks on natural forces, such as the pharaoh Pheros' spearing of the Nile (2.111.1–2) and Xerxes' lashing of the Hellespont (7.35.2).[99]

The Spartans in the *Histories* demonstrate an attention to religious matters that at first seems to run counter to the impiety frequently exhibited by barbarian despots.[100] They not only appear to have an unusually close relationship with the oracle at Delphi[101] but also observe their religious festivals so strictly that they repeatedly place sacral obligations before their duty to aid their allies against the Persians.[102] Although instances of Spartan religiosity run through Herodotus' text, they are almost completely overshadowed by his detailed treatment of Cleomenes I, the powerful monarch who dominates the accounts of Sparta in the fifth and sixth books of the *Histories.*[103] Herodotus offers a complex portrait of this king that vacillates between stock tales of tyrannical *hybris* and occasional glimpses of a dynamic and largely successful reign.[104] Cleomenes' attitude toward the divine similarly oscillates, in his case between the typical Spartan respect for the gods and an often brutal disregard for religious proprieties.[105] In his dual role as military and religious leader, Cleomenes performs the customary crossing-sacrifices before leaving the boundaries of Lacedaemon and shows respect for both geographical and divinely-ordained boundaries in his attack on the Argives.[106] When he fails to receive favorable omens for his crossing of the Erasinus, he does not follow the tyrannical pattern of punishing the offending body of water (cf. Hdt. 1.75.4–6, 189.2; 2.111.1–2; 7.35.2) but rather sends his men to the region of Tiryns by sea (6.76). Later, when he realizes that his burning of the sacred grove of Argos has led him to take the wrong 'Argos', he abides by Apollo's prophecy and returns to Sparta without having conquered the city of Argos (6.80, 82).[107]

While Herodotus at times portrays Cleomenes as a pious, constitutionally limited monarch and provides information on the less sensationalistic aspects of his reign, his lengthy account of the dyarch focuses a great deal of attention on Cleomenes' various acts of impiety and wickedness.[108] Cleomenes' reputation for sacrilege begins during his second invasion of Attica, when he shows wanton disregard for the warning of the priestess of Athena on the Acropolis, barring Dorians from entering the sanctuary (5.72.3–4). Although Cleomenes' Achaean roots justify his entry, his violation of sacred space parallels the behavior of numerous despots in the *Histories*, particularly Cambyses (3.37.3), Miltiades II (6.134–6), and Xerxes, whose invasion of Greece constitutes the most extreme transgression of boundaries.[109] The same disregard for religious proprieties makes possible Cleomenes' subornation of the Pythia at Delphi to ensure the success of his attempt to depose Demaratus (6.66.2–3, 74.1, 75.3, 84.3).[110]

Most significantly, Herodotus makes Cleomenes' impiety the basis of his discussion of the factors that contributed to the king's eventual madness and grotesque demise (6.75.3). According to Herodotus, the Greeks in general attributed Cleomenes' end to his bribery of the Pythia, the Athenians blamed it on his desecration of the precinct of Demeter at Eleusis, and the Argives attributed it to his burning of the sacred grove of Argos after butchering those who had taken refuge there. In his ensuing elaboration of the Argive version of Cleomenes' end, Herodotus provides a detailed account of the battle of Sepeia *c.* 494, which emphasizes the Spartan dyarch's repeated offences against religious and moral order. After defeating the Argives in battle, Cleomenes surrounds those who have escaped to the sacred grove of Argos, lures out and murders fifty of them by means of a ruse, and then burns the remaining fugitives to death (6.80).[111] On the heels of this impious holocaust, Cleomenes sacrilegiously offers sacrifice at the temple of Hera and has his helots manhandle the priest who attempts to stop him (6.81), acts that closely parallel Cambyses' violation of religious custom in Egypt (3.29.2).[112]

When he asserts his authority by having the priest at the Argive Heraeum dragged from the altar and flogged, Cleomenes furnishes the only instance of Greek use of the whip in the *Histories* and further conforms to the pattern of the tyrant established throughout the text.[113] Among the various acts by which Herodotean despots demonstrate their power over both the living and the dead, whipping plays an important role, especially as a designator of Persian monarchy.[114] While Cyrus' scourging of a disobedient playmate during a game in which he plays 'king' reveals his true royal lineage (1.114.3), Zopyrus implies that such punishment is characteristic of the Persian kingship (3.155.2; cf. 3.154.2, 157.1), and Xerxes boastfully describes his control over his army as compulsion under the lash (7.103.4; cf. 7.22.1, 56.1, 223.3).

Similar to his autocratic Persian counterparts, Cleomenes uses physical disfigurement to affirm his power not only over strangers but also, more importantly, over his fellow countrymen. Under the influence of madness, Cleomenes turns his penchant for physical abuse on the Spartiates, smashing his staff into the face of anyone he happens to encounter (6.75.1). Cleomenes' maltreatment of the Spartiates performs in reverse the role that the Lacedaemonian mourners' self-mutilation plays in the royal funeral ceremony. Both acts serve to draw a distinction between the ruler and his subjects and, accordingly, emphasize the absolute nature of the Spartan dyarchy.

Even though Cleomenes' attacks on his fellow Spartiates eventually land him in the stocks and briefly remind the reader of the constitutional aspect of the Spartan kingship, the ensuing account of his death immediately reasserts Herodotus' presentation of this dyarch as a despot. After Cleomenes' relatives finally place the mad king in the stocks, he forces his helot guard to give him a dagger by threatening him, most probably, with some sort of physical punishment.[115] The deranged dyarch then uses the dagger to tear gashes into his legs and eventually cuts himself into strips (6.75.2–3). Herodotus' description of Cleomenes' self-mutilation accords with the transgression that characterizes his reign in the *Histories* and appropriately concludes an account of his life that begins with an allusion to his madness (5.42.1).

The Spartan dyarch's tragic end also links him with several Herodotean despots who similarly experience violent deaths that parallel the violent behavior they had exhibited when alive. The Achaemenid Cyrus' bloodthirsty desire to conquer the Massagetae, for example, results in the Massagetan queen Tomyris' appropriately bloody mutilation of his corpse (1.205–14). Pheretime of Cyrene, who avenges her son's death by brutally murdering and mutilating a number of the citizens of Barce (4.202), suffers a similarly 'illustrative' death, when her body undergoes a form of self-mutilation by festering and breeding worms (4.205).[116] Cleomenes' horrifying demise especially recalls the untimely death of Cambyses, who accidentally pierces himself in the leg with his sword while mounting his horse and dies from the same type of gangrenous wound that he had earlier inflicted on the Apis bull's thigh (3.64.3, 66.2; cf. 3.29).[117] Both rulers, in a sense, live and die 'by the sword'; they inflict upon themselves the same physical defilement that figures so largely in the despot's relations with his subjects.

Herodotus' statement concerning the brevity of Cleomenes' reign and his lack of a male heir (5.48; cf. 7.205.1) even further emphasizes the despotic nature of Cleomenes' rule. In order to draw a moral lesson from history concerning the nature of absolute rule, Herodotus has distorted both the chronology and reality of Cleomenes' reign. By ruling 'for no long time', Cleomenes conforms to the fifth-century conception of the tyrant, whose impiety and violation of *nomoi* characteristically lead to punishment through untimely death.[118] His failure to produce a male child and the consequent extirpation of his line upon his death also closely associate Cleomenes with those Herodotean autocrats who suffer this punishment for similarly transgressive behavior, particularly Astyages (1.109.3) and Cambyses (3.66.2).[119]

From the illegitimate circumstances of his birth to the gruesome spectacle of his death, Herodotus' Cleomenes functions as the very embodiment of tyrannical *hybris*. His reign is characterized by madness,[120] violence, and transgression: he burns, mutilates, and strikes his enemies, exhibits an excessive taste for revenge, indulges in sexual relations contrary to *nomos*, treats religious sanctuaries and figures with the utmost impiety, and meets with an appropriately violent and supposedly untimely death. As Alan Griffiths has noted, most of these aspects of Cleomenes' reign find direct parallels in Herodotus' account of the Persian despot Cambyses.[121] Most likely drawing on a repertoire of classical tyrant-tales, Herodotus presents these kings as 'two almost contemporary, deranged, dipsomaniac, priest-flogging, skin-stripping, sacrilegious, sadistic warrior kings who are misled by place-name oracles and expire in circumstances symbolically retributive of their capricious cruelties'.[122] One has to wonder why Herodotus would depict Cleomenes as Cambyses' Doppelgänger and have him conform so closely to Otanes' generalized portrait of autocracy, given his understanding of Sparta's complex constitutional structure and the often limited position that the dyarchy occupied within it. One must also question why Herodotus focuses so much attention on this mad king and why he provides accounts of other Spartan kings – Ariston, Demaratus, and Anaxandridas – that emphasize transgressive traits associating them with a number of the barbarian autocrats featured in the *Histories*.[123] Alternatively, it is curious that Herodotus provides so little information concerning Leonidas and furnishes the dyarch who epitomizes Spartan bravery and steadfastness with a relatively one-dimensional portrait in his account of the battle of Thermopylae (7.204–33). One might speculate that Leonidas' iconic status made it impossible for Herodotus to attribute to him those stock tyrannical traits exhibited by the other Spartan dyarchs in the *Histories*.[124]

By offering a disproportionately detailed treatment of the hybristic Cleomenes and furnishing several other kings with stock tyrannical traits, Herodotus suggests that tyrannical *hybris* is as standard a feature of Spartan kingship as it is of the other forms of autocracy he describes in the *Histories* (cf. 3.80.3–5). As I argue in the final section of this paper, Herodotus' skewed treatment of the Spartan dyarchy – and particularly his depiction of Cleomenes as an exemplar of despotism – must be understood in the context of Sparta's extended hegemonic rivalry with democratic Athens, the city-state that significantly influenced Herodotus' assessment of political institutions and constitutions and shaped his attitude toward absolute rule.[125]

III. The ideological roots of Herodotus' despotic dyarchs

Herodotus' anti-autocratic bias undoubtedly had several sources, including his own experience of tyranny in Halicarnassus[126] and his refuge in Samos, where he came into contact with popular traditions concerning the tyrant Polycrates' rule.[127] Herodotus' experience of despotic government, however, was largely conditioned within the context of Athenian imperialism and democratization. While Herodotus grew up amid the continued struggle between Persian and Athenian influence in the Aegean, both his life in Halicarnassus and his stay in Samos brought him into close contact with the political reality of the Athenian empire.[128] Even more influential was Herodotus' direct experience of democratic Athens, where he probably spent time between 450 and 444/3 and possibly during the Peloponnesian War.[129] At Athens Herodotus would have encountered a generalized hostility to all forms of one-man rule, which particularly manifested itself in Athenian tragedy throughout much of the fifth century.[130] His sojourn at Athens, more importantly, would also have acquainted him with an increasingly pervasive democratic ideology, which eulogized the Athenian democracy's role in the repulse of the Persians and helped to bolster Athenian hegemony in the Aegean against Persian, and later Spartan, claims. On the tragic stage, the Ur-democracy repeatedly defended hellenic *nomos* and demonstrated its unique worthiness of Greek hegemony in such tragedies as Euripides' *Heracleidae* of *c.* 430 and *Supplices* of *c.* 422. Up on the Acropolis, the Periclean building program initiated a spate of public sculpture that celebrated the triumph of democratic freedom over barbarian tyranny. In the Ceramicus, private mourning rites yielded to celebrations of the democratic city and those soldiers who had given their lives in its defense. Herodotus, visiting Athens during the height of its power, would thus have been virtually bombarded by Athenian democratic ideology and rhetoric, in which the opposition between tyranny and democracy occupied a central position.[131]

The power of Athenian democratic discourse becomes an important factor when we consider the probability that Herodotus delivered recitations before an Athenian audience.[132] As Martin Ostwald has pointed out, Herodotus repeatedly explains foreign phenomena by means of analogies that would 'make sense only to an audience as intimately familiar with Athens and Attica as only the Athenians are likely to have been'.[133] For example, he recounts the outermost circuit wall of Ecbatana by means of a comparison with the wall surrounding Athens (1.98.5). In his discussion of Babylon's wealth, Herodotus inserts a parenthesis to explain the Persian cubic measure ἀρτάβη by providing its equivalent in Attic measures (1.192.3). When he later wishes to describe the distance between Heliopolis and the sea, Herodotus uses the distance from the altar of the twelve gods in Athens to the temple of Olympian Zeus in Pisa as a guide (2.7). He similarly describes the Scythian coast and the peninsula inhabited by the

Tauri by means of an analogy with Attica and the promontory on which Sunium is located (4.99.4–5). Finally, Herodotus uses the Attic term δῆμος when he mentions the Spartan township of Pitana, although the Laconian term would be κώμα (3.55.2).

Herodotus' use of analogies between other areas of the Greek world and the foreign world he recounts, demonstrates that his audience was not simply Athenian, but rather panhellenic.[134] Nevertheless, the relative frequency with which Herodotus explains foreign phenomena against the background of knowledge shared with an Athenian audience is noteworthy, since the relationship between speaker and audience has a significant impact on the construction of narrative. The nexus of shared values, cultural vocabulary, and experience that exists between them circumscribes the development of the text and makes the process of communication possible.[135] Herodotus' relationship with Athens as an audience, therefore, would have necessitated a familiarity not only with Athenian topography and history but even more so with the currents of thought that were circulating in Athens at the time, and especially the democratic ideology that permeated fifth-century Athenian society. The interactive nature of Herodotean history-making would have played a large part in the shaping of his account, as the historian and his audience jointly participated in both the creation and confirmation of traditions that conformed to the audience's view of its past as well as its present.[136]

The very fact that Athens is the only major city on the Greek mainland that Herodotus employs to make sense of non-Greek phenomena suggests, more importantly, that Athens became a frame of reference in his construction of both the Greek and non-Greek worlds. His portrayal of the political polarization of hellene and barbarian shows how far the Athenian democracy, rather than Hellas as a whole, operates as a cultural and political standard in his text. Although many Greek city-states participated in the struggle to preserve Greek freedom, Athens' democracy functions as the exemplar of Greek constitutionality in the *Histories.* Herodotus, for example, makes democracy, rather than oligarchy, the foe of despotism in the constitutional debate (3.80–2), which largely focuses on the pros and cons of democratic (3.80.6, 81.1–3, 82.4) and monarchical (3.80.2–5, 82.1–2, 5) constitutions.[137] The arguments that all three Persian conspirators put forward concerning the rule of the people, in addition, demonstrate that they have the Athenian democracy in mind rather than a generalized notion of popular government.[138] Under government conducted by τὸ πλῆθος, all offices are assigned by lot, magistrates are held responsible for their conduct in office, and all issues are decided by public debate (3.80.6): πάλῳ μὲν ἀρχὰς ἄρχει, ὑπεύθυνον δὲ ἀρχὴν ἔχει, βουλεύματα δὲ πάντα ἐς τὸ κοινὸν ἀναφέρει. All three of these aspects of government by the commons found parallels in later fifth-century Athenian democratic practice, and Otanes' use of the term ὑπεύθυνον and his earlier description of the monarch as unaccountable (ἀνεύθυνος) clearly reflect Athenian democratic practice and theory. The *euthyna* was a long-standing feature of Athenian political life at least from the time of Solon and later became a central component of the democracy after Ephialtes' reforms.[139]

Megabyzus' view of the *dēmos* as an ignorant, violent, and irresponsible mob (3.81.1–2), moreover, echoes examples of anti-democratic sentiment that occur throughout Athenian literature in the second half of the fifth century, especially the criticism of popular government offered by both the Old Oligarch (Ps.-Xen. 1.1–8) and Euripides' Theban herald in his *Supplices* of *c.* 422 (417–25).[140] Megabyzus' description of the commonalty as 'rushing thoughtlessly into affairs like a river in flood' (3.81.2) also parallels images of the *dēmos* as an uncontrollable and impetuous force that occur in Athenian tragedy in this period. Euripides, for example, has Hecuba describe the '*dēmos*' of the Achaean army as the kind of mob that can get out of hand and run wilder than a raging fire (*Hec.* 606–8). Euripides' Menelaus similarly compares the excessive emotionality and impetuosity of the *dēmos* to a fire that rages out of control (*Or.* 696–701).[141]

While the constitutional debate presents democracy as the antithesis and enemy of despotism, other passages in the *Histories* demonstrate Herodotus' conviction that this form of government played a significant role in the repulse of the barbarian. Probably echoing current Athenian democratic rhetoric, Herodotus repeatedly attributes Athenian growth and military success in the late sixth century to the simultaneous overthrow of the Peisistratid tyranny and the establishment of the Cleisthenic democracy (5.66.1, 78, 91.1),[142] a connection that had important ramifications for the later struggle between Hellas and Persia.[143] Herodotus further suggests that this combination of ἰσηγορίη and military strength effected the young democracy's defeat of the Persians at Marathon (6.109–10).[144] Most striking, however, is Herodotus' explicit praise of Athens' role in the hellenes' ultimate victory over the Persians, in which he implies that the Athenians' intertwined military might, freedom, and self-determination enabled them alone to make the fateful decision to save the Greeks from barbarian tyranny and slavery (7.139.5).[145]

Herodotus' reliance on the Athenian democracy as a political reference point obviously shaped the politically-based antithesis that he erects between the Greeks and barbarians. This reliance, more importantly, colored his treatment of the political structure, and especially the hereditary dyarchy, of Athens' later Lacedaemonian rivals. The strong influence that Athenian democratic ideology exerted on his account of the Greeks' victory over barbarian tyranny facilitated his construction of another politically organized polarity between democratic Athens and an autocratic Sparta. This ideology, which viewed Athens' nascent democracy as the force underpinning both Athens' rise to power and central role in the defeat of the Persians, most clearly lies behind Herodotus' account of the Spartans' repeated attempts to re-establish tyranny in Athens after their key participation in the deposition of the Peisistratidae.

This is not surprising, when one considers the Spartans' significant role in Athenian history as the first foes of Athens' developing democracy in the late sixth century. According to Herodotus, Cleomenes twice attempted to install Isagoras, his cuckolded *xeinos*, as tyrant but failed in both attempts when he encountered resistance, first from the Athenian *demos* (5.70–2) and later from his Corinthian allies and Demaratus (5.74–6). While Herodotus attributes these first two attempts to restore tyranny in Athens to Cleomenes' initiative, he makes the Lacedaemonians responsible for the later expedition to restore Hippias and quash the development of democracy at Athens (5.90–1, 93.2). Herodotus claims that the Spartans made this final attempt for two reasons: (1) their discovery of the Alcmaeonids' corruption of the Pythia and prophecies of future disasters at the hands of the Athenians (5.90) and (2) their belief that an Athens oppressed by despotism would be weak, while an Athens free of tyranny could become a match for Sparta itself (5.91). Their allies, however, rejected the proposed expedition against Athens (5.93.2), apparently persuaded by the Corinthian Socles' impassioned speech on the horrors of tyranny, which begins by underlining the immoral and perverse nature of the Spartans' desire to restore tyranny in Greece (5.92α1–2).

Herodotus' interest in and relatively lengthy treatment of these Spartan attempts to destroy Athens' budding democracy – given their failure and relative inconsequence[146] – reflect the important position that these events occupied in fifth-century Athenian civic memory. Several elements of his account, however, reveal that the memory of Spartan intervention in late-sixth-century Athenian politics became distorted over time. Herodotus' explanation of the roots of the Spartans' hostility toward the young Athenian democracy, for example, closely associates them with both Greek tyrants and foreign despots in the *Histories* and thereby places the Lacedaemonians into the same political camp as Hellas' barbarian enemies. Herodotus repeatedly mentions the existence of strong ties of ritualized friendship between the Spartans and the Peisistratids (5.63.2, 90.1, 91.2) and makes the bonds of *xenia* the primary reason behind Cleomenes' interference in Athenian affairs on behalf of Isagoras (5.70.1). Both the

Spartans' desire to reduce the Athenians to obedience (πειθαρχέεσθαι) and their fear of Athens as a growing rival (5.91.1–2) are also modes of behavior characteristic of Eastern despots in the *Histories*.[147] Especially noteworthy is Herodotus' use of the verb κατέχειν in his account of the Spartans' interest in restoring tyranny at Athens (5.91.1). As Sara Forsdyke has pointed out, 'in addition to its basic connotations of compulsion and force, the verb κατέχειν is used repeatedly by Herodotus to characterize Peisistratus' tyranny and seems to be part of the ideologically charged set of terms and concepts that were used to evoke the contrast between tyranny and democracy'.[148]

Herodotus' description of Cleomenes' initial attempt to support Isagoras further stresses Spartan political alterity. When Cleomenes seizes the Acropolis to counter the Athenian *dēmos'* resistance, he patterns himself after both the would-be tyrant Cylon (5.71.1) and the Peisistratids (5.64.2–65) and provides a parallel to the later Persian attack on Athens (8.51–3) in his attempted violation of Athena's sanctuary (5.72.3–4). Through their association with such despots, the Spartans in this account – particularly Cleomenes – cease to be simply the enemies of Athenian democracy and become the foes of Greek freedom and equality in general.

Of course, one may counter that the Corinthian Socles twice demonstrates shock at the Spartans' support of tyranny (5.92α1, 92η5) and explicitly mentions the Spartans' inexperience of this type of government (5.92α2). Herodotus' focus on the Lacedaemonians' ongoing hostility to the very establishment of democracy at Athens, however, overshadows Sparta's reputation for putting down tyranny in Greece (cf. Thuc. 1.81.1). Herodotus, in addition, provides an implicitly negative treatment of the Lacedaemonians' central role in the deposition of the Peisistratids, which – not coincidentally – gradually became effaced by the Tyrannicides in Athenian public memory (cf. Thuc. 6.53.3–59). He makes the Spartans' involvement in the overthrow of the Peisistratids a function of their own gullibility and Alcmaeonid bribery (cf. 5.63.1–2, 90.1, 91.2) and fails to allow for Spartan initiative. For example, Herodotus never considers the possibility that the Spartans' ousting of the medizing Peisistratids formed part of a larger anti-Persian policy along with Cleomenes' later intervention in Aegina at Athens' request (6.49–50, 61.1, 64, 73).[149] It is also true that the Spartans ultimately abandoned their planned reinstallation of tyranny in Athens in the face of opposition from their allies in 506 (5.75) and in 504 (5.93.2), but this change in policy reflects Sparta's growing dependence on its allies in the developing Peloponnesian League rather than any self-imposed restraint or recognition of the perversity of Lacedaemonian interference in Athenian politics.

As Herodotus' treatment of the Spartans' repeated attempts to reinstall a tyrant in Athens reveals, these events colored later memories and versions of Sparta's complicated involvement in late-sixth-century Athenian politics. His account of Spartan interference in Athens shows that these episodes also gradually assumed greater significance as Athenian political self-consciousness developed in the context of the Persian Wars, the consolidation of Athens' hegemony in the Aegean after the Greeks' victory, and Athens' increasing discord with Lacedaemon. At some point after the Persian Wars, Athenian democratic ideology, which crystallized in tandem with Athens' changing hegemonic goals, forged a link between the Athenians' successful opposition against the re-establishment of internal Peisistratid tyranny and their defense of Hellas against Persian despotism.

Because of his central role in Sparta's attempts to restore tyranny in Athens, Cleomenes naturally loomed large in fifth-century Athenian political thinking as an enemy of democracy. It was Athens' growing rivalry with Sparta, however, that ultimately turned Cleomenes into an ideal despot and thereby conceptually strengthened the Athenians' bid for power. As Thucydides shows in his *History*, the Athenians utilized their role at Marathon and their contribution to the defense of Hellas against Xerxes to defend their hegemony against Spartan claims (1.73.4–5, 74, 75.1, 144.4; 6.83.2). Herodotus reflects the Athenians' distortion of the Persian Wars for the sake of ideological interests by repeatedly suggesting that Athens contributed more than any other Greek city to Xerxes' defeat (7.139.5, 144.2–3; 8.57–63, 75–80, 136.2–3) and by stressing the Athenians' unusual level of commitment to the cause of hellenic freedom (7.139.5; 8.3.1, 109.1, 142.3, 143–144.3; 9.5, 7α2, β1). Those same Athenian ideological interests underlie Herodotus' similarly distorted presentation of Cleomenes – and the Lacedaemonians by extension – as inimical to the freedom and equality so cherished by the Greeks and as more politically akin to the non-Greek enemies of Hellas than the Greek city-states alongside whom the Spartans helped to preserve Hellas from barbarian despotism.

While Herodotus is very aware of Athens' anti-Spartan ideology and takes pains to demonstrate how, and with what justification, it arose, his treatment of both Athens and Sparta in the *Histories* demonstrates that he is not simply the tool of Athenian ideology and never fully commits himself to an anti-Spartan stance. As many scholars have argued, Herodotus focuses upon Spartan commitment to Greek freedom in a number of passages and places Sparta and Athens on the same side politically – against barbarian despotism.[150] Herodotus frequently reveals admiration for Spartan bravery and fortitude, especially in his account of Sperthias' and Bulis' sacrificial voyage to Persia to atone for the Spartans' earlier murder of Darius' heralds (7.134–7). In response to the satrap Hydarnes' attempt to persuade them to medize, the Lacedaemonians offer a resounding eulogy of the freedom that the Greeks so highly value (7.135.3).[151] Numerous scholars, in addition, see in the speeches of the exiled Spartan king Demaratus on the eve of the battle of Thermopylae Herodotus' belief that Spartan constitutionality and courage played the decisive role in the eventual defeat of the Persians (7.102, 104; cf. 7.209).[152] Finally, both Herodotus' presentation of Spartan fortitude and unswerving patriotism at Thermopylae (7.219–28) and his description of Spartan bravery at Plataea (9.71; cf. 64.1) emphasize Sparta's commitment to Greek freedom.[153]

One cannot dismiss these positive treatments of Sparta's role in the Persian Wars. However, they co-exist with Herodotus' systematic association of Sparta with the many barbarian autocracies featured in his work and never fully undermine it. The *Histories* does not present a monolithic portrait of Lacedaemon, and several factors contribute to Herodotus' complex treatment of this society. First, Sparta's position as the most powerful of the Greek states at the end of the sixth century and the beginning of the fifth, together with its decisive role in the Persian defeat, both earned Herodotus' admiration and ensured Sparta a prominent position as one of the principal defenders of Hellas in the *Histories.* Herodotus makes Sparta's status as the leading state in Greece during this period perfectly clear in his accounts of Croesus' alliance with the Spartans (1.6.2, 56.1–2, 69–70.1), the visits to Sparta of the Ionian embassy (1.141.4, 152), Maeandrius (3.148), and Aristagoras (5.49–51), and the hellenic coalition's choice of Sparta as its leader in the struggle against Xerxes (7.149.2, 159, 161.2; cf. 8.3.2). Both his treatment of the Spartans' courageous sacrifice at Thermopylae and his warm praise of their victory at Plataea (9.64.1, 71), more importantly, reveal his esteem for the Lacedaemonians and awareness of their important contribution to the final victory over the Persians.[154] No historian, not even an obvious ideologue, could totally ignore or distort Sparta's participation in the preservation of Hellas' freedom.

Herodotus, in addition, rarely treats any city-state or individual in his work with consistency, as his portrayal of both Sparta and Athens demonstrates. Herodotus reveals respect for Athens' resolution and fortitude in the Persian Wars (cf. 7.139; 8.3.1)[155] as well as for the successful young Athenian democracy (5.66.1, 78, 91.1), but his work demonstrates that his admiration was tempered by his awareness of less palatable aspects of Athens and its democracy.[156] He draws attention, for example, to Athens' early imperial ambition (8.3.2; cf. 5.32; 6.133; 8.111; 9.106.3) as well as the impetuosity and lack of common sense demonstrated by the Athenian *dēmos* (3.81; 5.97.2; cf. 1.60.3–5). In his account of Aristagoras' lack of rhetorical success with the the Spartan Cleomenes, Herodotus even favorably compares Sparta with Athens, where that Milesian tyrant used words to achieve his ends soon after being expelled from Sparta (5.97; cf. 5.55). According to Herodotus, the arguments that had failed to convince Cleomenes, together with a host of empty promises, prevailed in Athens, since it was apparently easier to impose upon thirty thousand Athenians than upon a Spartan king (5.97.2).

Finally, Herodotus holds a number of oppositions in balance simultaneously, often without fully working out their logic and any ensuing inconsistencies among them.[157] While Herodotus makes the polarity between Greek freedom and barbarian tyranny the guiding principle of the text, a lesser, yet crucial, opposition also exists between the main Greek protagonists, Athens and Sparta.[158] This dual schema of polarity often becomes quite complicated, as Herodotus in effect creates a triangular arrangement among Athens, Sparta, and the barbarians. He manages, however, to maintain both binary oppositions by making Sparta at once Athens' foil and one of the main representatives of Hellas against its barbarian enemies.[159] When Herodotus provides information on both Athens and Sparta in parallel *logoi* in the first and fifth books (1.56.2–68; 5.39–48, 55–96) and on the Spartan kingship and events in the reigns of Cleomenes I, Demaratus, and Leotychidas II in the mainly Greek narrative of the sixth book (6.50–86), the Spartans often tend to exhibit behavior antithetical to standard Greek *mores* and more akin to barbarian conduct.[160] Alternatively, when he recounts Leonidas' and the Spartans' struggle against the Persians at Thermopylae, Sperthias' and Bulis' encounters with individual Persians, and the Spartans' victory at Plataea, he tends to focus on the main opposition between Greek and non-Greek and portrays the Spartans as representatives of Hellas.[161]

Sparta functions as the champion of Greek freedom most explicitly in Herodotus' account of the dialogue between the Persian king Xerxes and the exiled Spartan dyarch Demaratus after the Persians' crossing of the Hellespont (7.101–5; cf. 7.209.2). In reply to Xerxes' question concerning his Greek opponents and their willingness to stand up to the Persians' huge force, Demaratus delivers a eulogy of the Spartans' commitment to hellenic freedom (7.102.2) and then explains that *nomos* commands their steadfastness in battle (7.104.4–5):

> So it is with the Lacedaemonians: fighting singly, they are no worse than any other men, but fighting together, they are the best soldiers among all men. For although free they are not free in every respect. *Nomos* is master over them, and they fear it far more than your subjects fear you. Whatever this master

> commands, they do; and its command is always the same: never to retreat in battle, however great the odds, but always to remain at their posts and either conquer or die.[162]

However, as I have argued elsewhere, even this panegyric of Spartan courage and lawfulness underlines the autocratic nature of the Spartan *polis*.[163] Demaratus' description of Spartan *nomos* as δεσπότης is striking, since Herodotus uses the term δεσπότης to refer to the ruling party in the relationship between owner and possession, master and slave, king and subjects, tyrant and subjects, and god and man.[164] By means of this terminology, the exiled dyarch suggests that *nomos* exercises a type of arbitrary authority at Sparta that parallels these relationships and that the Spartans, consequently, construct their society's power relations according to the despotic model. This model of power strengthens the link that Herodotus elsewhere forges between the Lacedaemonians and the barbarians, who repeatedly reveal an inability to live under more constitutional forms of rule (cf.1.97.2; 2.147.2; 3.83.1–2) and even conceptualize their relations with the gods in despotic terms (cf. 1.212.3; 4.127.4).

Demaratus' description of the Lacedaemonians' despotic *nomos*, when combined with Herodotus' depiction of the Spartan royal funeral ceremony and his individual portraits of Spartan personal rule, creates a powerful representation of Sparta as a society in which despotism not only operates on multiple levels but even becomes the guiding principle behind Spartan bravery in warfare. As the epitaph honoring the Spartans killed at Thermopylae suggests, the compulsion exercised by the dyarchs, by the Spartan *polis* itself, and by the *nomos* commanding steadfastness in battle likewise underpinned the Lacedaemonians' courageous stand at Thermopylae (7.228.2): 'Go, stranger, tell the Spartans that here, obeying their orders, we lie dead.'[165]

Through the implication both here and elsewhere in the *Histories* that compulsion motivated Spartan participation in the Persian Wars,[166] Herodotus once again reflects his Athenian contemporaries' distortion of the Persian Wars as a result of their extended hegemonic rivalry with the Lacedaemonians. As both Herodotus (7.139.5; 8.143–144.3; 9.7α2, β1) and Thucydides (1.74) demonstrate, the Athenians attributed their intrepid opposition to the Persians to a conscious choice to preserve hellenic freedom rather than to the kind of compulsion exercised by the 'invisible whip' of Spartan *nomos* or Xerxes' more tangible μάστιξ (cf. 7.22.1, 56.1, 103.4, 223.3).[167] Combining their distorted portrait of Spartan kingship with this implied polarity between Sparta's compelled bravery and the Athenians' more spontaneous brand of courage, Herodotus' Athenian contemporaries attempted not only to enhance their idealized role in the Persian Wars as the true champion of panhellenism and hellenic freedom but also, more importantly, to tarnish the Spartans' envied position as the 'liberators of the hellenes' on the eve of the Peloponnesian War.[168]

Notes

[1] On the central role that various forms of personal rule play in the *Histories*, see Hartog 1988, 323–39; Munson 1993, 39–41. See also Asheri 1988, 1.lv–lvi. On the theme of tyranny and its important function in the organization of the *Histories*, see also Hirst 1938, 97–110; Lang 1944, 65–82, 166–275; Lateiner 1984, 258, and 1989, 170–86; Gammie 1986, 171–95. See also Raaflaub 1987, 221–48, who recognizes Herodotus' interest in tyranny but believes that Herodotus is mainly interested in elucidating the development of Athens as a *polis tyrannos*. *Contra* Waters 1971; 1972, 138–47; and 1985, 131–3; and Cragg 1976, 68, who argue that Herodotus is not especially interested in tyranny or autocracy *per se* but includes numerous accounts of despots because they are historically necessary to his work. Waters also argues that Herodotus' biographical approach to history would have drawn him to tyrants, impressive figures around whom striking tales would have collected. On Herodotus' focus on the political polarization of Greek and barbarian, see Redfield 1985, 116–17; Lateiner 1985b, 79–103, and 1989, 16, 154–5, 165–6, 170; Hartog 1988, 340, 368; Cartledge 1990, 37–8.

[2] Herodotus' portrait of Peisistratus, however, tends to be more negative than positive. After his brief praise of Peisistratus' rule (1.59.6), Herodotus recounts Peisistratus' stratagem with Phye (1.60), his improper treatment of his Alcmaeonid wife (1.61.1), his use of foreign forces to gain the tyranny (1.61.2–4), and his strengthening of his basis of power by means of mercenaries and the taking of hostages from prominent Athenian families (1.64.1). Herodotus' account of Deioces' rise to power similarly vacillates, this time between the portrait of the clever and wise dispenser of justice and the power-hungry man obsessed with the trappings of sovereignty (1.96–100).

[3] On Herodotus' anti-tyrannical bias, see, esp., Hirst 1938, 97–110; Ferrill 1978, 391–8; Lateiner 1984, 263–7, and 1989, 153–5, 166, 170–1, 182–3. *Contra* Waters 1971; 1972, 139–47; and 1985, 131–3; and Cragg 1976, 68, who argue that Herodotus does not demonstrate any particular attitude toward tyrants as a group. See also Flory 1987, 120–44; Gray 1996. Ferrill 1978 not only disproves the old assumption that Herodotus uses the word τύραννος in the neutral sense of 'ruler' but also offers a balanced view of Herodotus' treatment of tyranny (397): 'It is true that he does not always paint the tyrants as totally wicked and perverse men. Neither did Aristotle, although the philosopher leaves no doubt about his view of tyranny.' Cf. Munson 1993, 40.

[4] For the freedom-despotism opposition, see, e.g., 1.62.1, 95.2; 2.147.2; 3.83.3, 142, 143.2; 4.137; 5.55, 65.5–66, 78, 91; 6.5, 22, 109; 7.135.3; 8.142. This opposition becomes pointed in Herodotus' accounts of peoples among whom

one-man rule is popular and who he believes must prefer slavery to freedom (cf. 1.62.1; 3.143.2). For other, more generally negative, treatments of one-man rule, see, e.g., 1.95–101; 5.37.2; 6.104; 7.164.1.

[5] On Herodotus' probable sympathy with Otanes' political viewpoint, see Tigerstedt 1965–78, 1.86; Berve 1967, 1.197; Lateiner 1984, 261–2, 272, and 1989, 168, 185. See also Nakategawa 1988, 260. *Contra* Waters 1971, 11–12; 1972, 141; and 1985, 132. Strasburger 1955, 7, 12 ff. regards Socles' speech as particularly personal to Herodotus and consequently as a 'key-position' for understanding Herodotus' attitude to Athens. *Contra* Waters 1971, 13–14.

[6] On Herodotus' equation of tyranny and kingship, see Hartog 1988, 325–40; Munson 1993, 40–1. For the opposing viewpoint that Herodotus did not have a negative viewpoint toward all forms of one-man-rule, see Ferrill 1978, 392, 395, 397; Davie 1979, 161–3; Lateiner 1984, 265, and 1989, 171. Ferrill 1978, 385–99 questions the traditional thesis that Herodotus failed to distinguish among the terms βασιλεύς, τύραννος, and μούναρχος. See also, more recently, Lévy 1993. For this traditional reading of Herodotus, see, e.g., Andrewes 1956, 27; Waters 1971, 6–7, and 1985, 117 n. 31; Flory 1987, 119–20. While Ferrill's argument is compelling, the very fact that the term βασιλεύς can be used to describe Greek tyrants (3.42.2, 44.1, 52.4, 136.2; 5.35.1, 92ε2; 6.23.1; 7.161.1), that the term τύραννος is often used of legitimate, Oriental monarchs (1.6.1, 7.2, 86.4; 3.80.4, 81.2) as well as the Macedonian Alexander (8.142.5), and that the term μούναρχος can apply equally to Oriental kings (1.55.1; 3.80.2–3 and 6, 82.1 and 3–5), Greek kings (5.61), and Greek tyrants (5.46.2; 6.23.4, 24.1; 7.154.1, 165) implies a very close relationship among these three types of leadership and their occupation of the same conceptual framework. Ferrill 1978, 391–3 himself points out the ease with which a μούναρχος could become a τύραννος. See also Andrewes 1956, 26; Fisher 1992, 347–8. Oost (1972, 10–30; 1974, 119–20; and 1976, 224–36) discusses various tyrants' use of the title of 'king' but then goes too far in his attempt to make such usage proof of various tyrants' actual status as legitimate kings.

[7] Kings of Macedon: 5.17.2–22; 7.173.3; 8.34, 121.2, 136–44; 9.1.1, 44–46.1. Kings of Cyrene: 4.159–67, 200–5. Herodotus also mentions a single king of Argos at 7.149.2 but makes no further comments on the Argive kingship and actually refers to Pheidon, who was most probably a hereditary king of Argos, as a τύραννος (6.127.3). On the hereditary kingship of the Temenids in Argos, see Drews 1983, 58–71, who carefully examines all of the extant evidence and arrives at the judicious conclusion that the Argive kings were hereditary military commanders during the archaic period and the first half of the fifth century. Herodotus also uses the terms βασιλεύς and μούναρχος to describe the following Greek rulers: Polycrates of Samos (3.42.2), Periander of Corinth (3.52.4), Aristophilides of Tarentum (3.136.2), Aristagoras of Miletus (5.35.1), Telys of Sybaris (5.44.1), the Bacchiads of Corinth (5.92β2), Scythas of Zancle (6.23.1 and 4, 24.1), and Gelon of Syracuse (7.161.1). Although the Pythia refers to the Bacchiads of Corinth as μούναρχοι (5.92β2), Herodotus himself makes it clear that they constituted an oligarchy. For the other references, see Ferrill 1978, 389–91, who reasonably argues that almost all of these figures are tyrants rather than

hereditary kings and that references to them as kings have far more to do with the nature of Herodotus' sources on these rulers than with their actual status and the legitimacy of their rule. Three of these cases (3.42.2, 52; 7.161), for example, use the term βασιλεύς in direct discourse and suggest that the term βασιλεύς would have been more flattering to the rulers in question than τύραννος. Similarly, it would make sense that Aristagoras, despite his reputation as an unpopular tyrant (5.37.2), viewed himself as a veritable βασιλεύς. In two other cases these terms occur in accounts favorable to these rulers: the Sybarites refer to their ruler Telys as a βασιλεύς, while their enemies refer to him as a τύραννος (5.44); and the account of Scythas provides a very positive treatment of this ruler's reputation for virtue (6.24). The only figure who may actually represent another example of Greek kingship is Aristophilides of Tarentum (3.136.2), especially when one considers Tarentum's status as a Spartan colony. On the possibility of a legitimate, constitutional monarchy at Tarentum, see Dunbabin 1948, 385; Ferrill 1978, 390; Drews 1983, 36–8. For a different viewpoint on the presence of kingship in Greece, see Oost 1972, 10–30; 1974, 119–20; and 1976, 224–36. For a general discussion of Greek kingship, see Carlier 1984.

[8] *Contra* Waters 1985, 131, who claims, with little foundation, that Herodotus was not given access to the 'arcana' of Spartan government and that the earliest description of its institutions and procedures occurs in Xenophon. On Herodotus' treatment and understanding of the Spartan constitutional structure, see Carlier 1977, 67 and Cragg 1976, 82–99, who argues that while Herodotus is interested in the nature of Spartan government, he lacks interest in constitutional formalities and terminology. As Cragg rightly points out (id. 86, 160), Herodotus prefers to demonstrate the function of an office in action, when it becomes important to the narrative, rather than abstractly. Herodotus' presentation of the Spartan constitutional structure, of course, has its weaknesses, including his use of vague, imprecise language. For example, he uses the general term ἄρχοντες (cf. 3.46.1; 6.106.1) for magistrates who, judging from their reception of foreigners, were most likely the ephors. On this and other problems with Herodotus' elaboration of Spartan constitutional matters, see Wüst 1935; Cragg 1976, 91, 93, 95–6. On the general and ambiguous terms ancient authors employed to designate the ephors, see also Richer 1998, 265–70.

[9] For an exhaustive treatment of the ephors' functions, see Richer 1998, esp. 323–505.

[10] See also Hdt. 3.46.1 and 6.106.1 and, above, n. 8.

[11] Although Herodotus does not comment upon the role of the ephors at Plataea, Xenophon makes it clear that in his time two ephors customarily accompanied the king on campaign (*Lac. Pol.* 13; *Hell.* 2.4.36). Many scholars, therefore, assume that the ephorate also performed this function in the early fifth century. See, e.g., Lewis 1977, 44; Cartledge 1987, 17, 106, 128. See also Thommen 1996, 132; Richer 1998, 413.

[12] On Herodotus' treatment of the council of elders, see Cragg 1976, 95–6. On the gerousia, see Andrewes 1954 and 1966, 2–5, 18; de Ste Croix 1972, 131–7; Cartledge 1987, 121–5.

[13] These unspecified groups, for example, receive and send envoys and messengers (1.66.3, 67.5, 69.2, 82.1, 152; 4.145.3–4; 6.52.4–5, 66.1; 7.136.2, 157.1, 239.1; 8.114.1, 132.1, 141.1–2, 142.1; 9.6), establish alliances (1.69.3, 70.1, 77.2; 6.108.2, 4), pass laws (1.82.7), vote on various expeditions (1.152.2–3; 5.50.3, 91; cf. 6.50), send expeditions (1.152.2; 5.63–4; 7.206.1), declare war and peace (3.44.1; 5.63.2, 64.1, 91; 7.149.2), grant citizenship (4.145.5; 9.33, 35.1), and oversee the royal succession (5.42.2). On the Spartan ecclesia in general, see Andrewes 1966, 1–20; de Ste Croix 1972, 126–30; Cartledge 1987, 129–31.

[14] Oral tradition, as a rule, tends to gravitate toward outstanding personalities, to whom stories of both a factual and fanciful nature tend to attach themselves. See Lang 1944, iv–v, 271, 278; Cragg 1976, 165. On the impact of oral tradition on Herodotus' composition of the *Histories*, see Thomas 1989, esp. 15–94, 238–86. See also Murray 1987; Evans 1991, 89–146.

[15] Consider, for example, Herodotus' discussion of the rarity with which the Lacedaemonians granted citizenship to outsiders (9.35.1) and their practice of combing their long hair before battle (7.208.3, 209.3). On Herodotus' interest in Spartan customs, see Finley 1968, 156; Rawson 1969, 20; Cragg 1976, 88, 205–6, 210, 219. See also Waters 1985, 40, who argues that Herodotus' narrative may have necessitated such an analysis, since a firmer grasp of the status and powers of the Spartan kings would lead to a better understanding of Sparta's conduct of warfare and foreign policy in general.

[16] Immerwahr 1966, 118–19, 121, 318, 319 notes the ethnographic nature of Herodotus' digression on the prerogatives of the Spartan kings but does not attempt to analyze this treatment. See also Cragg 1976, 210; Lévy 1999, 131. Cartledge 1979, 233 also recognizes the significance of this treatment but attributes it to Herodotus' interest in what he calls 'the anachronistic ossification of Spartan society'. See also Flory 1987, 106; Munson 1993, 43; Thommen 1996, 86; and Cartledge 1987, 105, 332–3, who again calls attention to the unusual nature of Herodotus' account of the Spartan kings. Cartledge rightly points out that Herodotus' purpose is to make the oddity of the Spartan kingship stand out in high relief, but he does not pursue this point to its logical conclusion. Fitzhardinge 1980, 142 similarly notes that 'only the dual monarchy seemed to Herodotus so unusual as to warrant special explanation' but does not elaborate on this point. Rawson 1969, 20 believes that Herodotus' treatment of Sparta as something 'sui generis' was the product of his time and was 'nourished by the ethnographic literary tradition upon which early historiography built'. For this type of analysis, see also Finley 1968, 156.

[17] On ethnography as a means of translation, see Crapanzo 1986, 51; Hartog 1988.

[18] Hartog 1988. See also Laurot 1981, 39–48; Lateiner 1987, 90, and 1989, 145–7.

[19] Lateiner 1985b, 79–103, at 89, and 1989, 16. See also Cartledge 1990, 31–8. Although Herodotus' treatment of non-Greeks is generally impartial and non-racist, the Greek-barbarian polarity in both political and cultural terms is fundamental to his history of the Persian Wars. See Lateiner 1985b, 94.

[20] Hdt. 6.55: καὶ ταῦτα μέν νυν περὶ τούτων εἰρήσθω· ὅ τι δέ, ἐόντες Αἰγύπτιοι, καὶ ὅ τι ἀποδεξάμενοι ἔλαβον τὰς Δωριέων βασιληίας, ἄλλοισι γὰρ περὶ αὐτῶν εἴρηται, ἐάσομεν αὐτά· τὰ δὲ ἄλλοι οὐ κατελάβοντο, τούτων μνήμην ποιήσομαι.

[21] The only scholar who appears to deal with these passages is Benardete 1969, 171–2. While Benardete notices the repeated links between the Spartans and various non-Greek peoples, he appears to see nothing odd about Herodotus' treatment of Sparta and accordingly does not question the role that these particular passages play in the work as a whole.

[22] Although Pausanias later claims that both Tyndareus (3.1.4) and the Heracleidae (2.18.7) were the descendants of Perseus, he makes no mention of any Egyptian connection.

[23] Although Herodotus admits similarities and borrowings between Egypt and Greece (2.48.2, 49–53, 79.2, 81, 91.4, 109.3, 123.2–3, 171, 177.2), Egypt mainly functions in his work as the antithesis of Hellas. On Herodotus' treatment of such similarities and borrowings, see Lloyd 1990, 229–30. On the central role that Egypt plays in Herodotus' ethnographic discourse, see Lateiner 1985b, 83, and 1989, 147–9; Lloyd 1990, 219–21, 229. See also Hartog 1988, 213–15, who describes Herodotus' treatment of Egypt as a classic example of the figure of inversion, whereby difference becomes exaggerated and takes on the form of anti-sameness. For other examples of this process, see Hdt. 1.133.3–4, 140.2–3; 3.104.2–3; 4.181.3–4.

[24] Besides the lone Greek example of Sparta, Herodotus examines the burial and mourning customs of several non-Greek peoples, including the Babylonians (1.198), the Egyptians (2.85–90), the Scythians (4.71–3), and the Thracians (5.4–5, 8). See also Hdt. 1.140.1–2 (Persians), 1.216.3 (Massagetae); 3.16.2–4 (Persians and Egyptians), 3.24 (Ethiopians), 3.99–100 (Indians).

[25] Hdt. 6.58: ταῦτα μὲν ζῶσι τοῖσι βασιλεῦσι δέδοται ἐκ τοῦ κοινοῦ τῶν Σπαρτιητέων, ἀποθανοῦσι δὲ τάδε· ἱππέες περιαγγέλλουσι τὸ γεγονὸς κατὰ πᾶσαν τὴν Λακωνικήν, κατὰ δὲ τὴν πόλιν γυναῖκες περιιοῦσαι λέβητας κροτέουσι. ἐπεὰν ὦν τοῦτο γένηται τοιοῦτον, ἀνάγκη ἐξ οἰκίης ἑκάστης ἐλευθέρους δύο καταμιαίνεσθαι, ἄνδρα τε καὶ γυναῖκα· μὴ ποιήσασι δὲ τοῦτο ζημίαι μεγάλαι ἐπικέαται. νόμος δὲ τοῖσι Λακεδαιμονίοισι κατὰ τῶν βασιλέων τοὺς θανάτους ἐστὶ ὡυτὸς καὶ τοῖσι βαρβάροισι τοῖσι ἐν τῇ Ἀσίῃ· τῶν γὰρ ὦν βαρβάρων οἱ πλεῦνες τὠυτῷ νόμῳ χρέονται κατὰ τοὺς θανάτους τῶν βασιλέων. ἐπεὰν γὰρ ἀποθάνῃ βασιλεὺς Λακεδαιμονίων, ἐκ πάσης δεῖ Λακεδαίμονος, χωρὶς Σπαρτιητέων, ἀριθμῷ τῶν περιοίκων ἀναγκαστοὺς ἐς τὸ κῆδος ἰέναι· τούτων ὦν καὶ τῶν εἱλωτέων καὶ αὐτῶν Σπαρτιητέων ἐπεὰν συλλεχθέωσι ἐς τὠυτὸ πολλαὶ χιλιάδες, σύμμιγα τῇσι γυναιξὶ κόπτονταί τε τὰ μέτωπα προθύμως καὶ οἰμωγῇ διαχρέονται ἀπλέτῳ, φάμενοι τὸν ὕστατον αἰεὶ ἀπογενόμενον τῶν βασιλέων, τοῦτον δὴ γενέσθαι ἄριστον.

[26] Hartog 1982, 143 rightly points out that 'la mort est signe d'altérité et elle intervient, dans le grand partage, toujours recommencé, entre le même et l'autre'. See also Hartog 1988, 133–4; Asheri 1990, 146–50.

[27] Cf. Hartog 1988, 152 on the context of 'otherness' that these comparisons create and in which Herodotus situates his discussion of Spartan funeral

ceremonies. See also Lévy 1999, 132.

[28] On the role that hereditary occupational differentiation played in the Greeks' conceptualization of 'primitive' societies as coherent entities, see Humphreys 1983, 52. Isocrates' *Busiris* later claimed that the Spartans adopted many of their customs from the Egyptians (17–19).

[29] As Lloyd 1990, 229 points out, Herodotus is treating the μάχιμοι as the Egyptian equivalent of the Spartan ὁμοῖοι at 2.164–8.

[30] By means of this passage, Herodotus links Sparta not only with Egypt but also with the rest of the barbarian world. Cf. 5.6.2. While Herodotus notes that all Greeks share this disdain for trade and handicrafts, his emphasis on the Spartans' hostility towards trade and manufacturing strengthens the link between the Spartans and the Egyptians that he makes at several points in the *Histories.* On the Spartans' probable participation in various banausic enterprises, see Ridley 1974, 281–92; Cartledge 1976a, 90; 1976b, 115–19; and 1979, 183–4; Fitzhardinge 1980, 41–2. They argue against Cook's (1962, 156) theory that only the perioeci handled artistic production in Laconia.

[31] Hartog 1988, 225; cf. 225–30. On the Greeks' use of analogy to make sense of unfamiliar phenomena, see Lloyd 1966, 172–420, esp. 187–90, 209, 305, 345, 417.

[32] As Hartog 1988, 133–47 shows in his examination of Herodotus' ethnographic analysis of the Scythians, this process of cultural translation involves the processes of rendering the foreign familiar to the Greeks and presenting its foreignness simultaneously. Because of this dual process, one frequently finds Herodotus' text vacillating between the familiar and the alien. See also Hartog 1988, 225–30. See Said 1978, 58–9, 71–2; Clifford 1986, 101; and Crapanzo 1986, 52, who demonstrate that such vacillation is a normal element in ethnographic representation.

[33] On the analogy between the Ister and the Nile, see Hartog 1988, 229–30.

[34] For other examples of this process, see Hdt. 3.24.2, 37.2, 97.2, 101, 106.2; 4.168.1, 186.1, 198.2.

[35] Hartog 1982, 150, and 1988, 152.

[36] Hall 1989, 149; cf. id. 84. Hall (1989, 44, 83–4, 103–5, 131–2) argues that when Athens' democratic ideology first developed to legitimize Athenian leadership in the Aegean against the barbarian, contemporary tragedy increasingly treated unrestrained emotionalism in general, and endless lamentation in particular, as features of the barbarian world. See also Loraux 1986, 46; Hartog 1988, 143.

[37] On the final section of this lament and its production of an effect of 'near-hysteria', see Scott 1984, 156–8. On Aeschylus' presentation of Persian lamentation, see Else 1977, 78; Hall 1989, 83–4, 131–2.

[38] Hall 1989, 101–59 discusses the invention of the 'mythical barbarian'.

[39] Hall 1989, 132.

[40] For examples of funerary lamentation in Herodotus, see 1.198 (Babylon and Egypt); 2.79.3 (Egypt), 2.85.1 (Egypt); 5.8 (Thracians); 9.24 (Mardonius and Persian army). For examples of more generalized lamentation, see 1.109.1

(Harpagus), 1.111.2 (house of Harpagus); 2.40.4 (Egyptians), 2.61 (Egyptians), 2.121γ1 (Egyptians); 3.14.3–10 (Egyptians), 3.64.2 (Cambyses), 3.65.7 (Cambyses), 3.66.1 (Cambyses and Persian nobles), 3.119.3 (Intaphrenes' wife); 5.4.2 (Thracians); 8.99.2 (Persians).

[41] Hartog 1988, 154. See also Cartledge 1987, 334.

[42] Hartog 1988, 154. On Solon's funerary legislation, see [Dem.] 43.62; Plut. *Sol.* 21.6; cf. 12.8; Cic. *Leg.* 2.59 ff. For modern discussions of this legislation, see Alexiou 1974, 14–15, 18–22; Garland 1981, 54, 87–8, and 1985, 26–30, 33–4; Humphreys 1983, 86.

[43] Thucydides alludes to private ritual lamentation in his description of the Athenian public burial (2.34.4) and has Pericles refer to it at the conclusion of the *epitaphios* (2.46.2). Both Thucydides' general description of the ceremony (2.34) and the tone of the *epitaphios* itself, however, suggest that emotional displays of mourning were viewed as subsidiary to the public funeral. As Loraux 1986, 44 points out, the *epitaphios* prohibits the bewailing of the dead (2.44.1) by means of a formula that reappears in other *epitaphioi* (cf. Lys. 2.77, 80; Pl. *Menex.* 248c5). Although ritual lamentation continued to have a place in the Athenian funeral, it nevertheless played a far less central role there than in the Spartan ceremony described by Herodotus. See Loraux 1986, 45–6.

[44] Millender 2001, 154–5. On barbarian non-verbal communication see, e.g., Hdt. 3.21.2–3; 4.127.4, 131–2 and Lateiner 1987, 87–107.

[45] On the Spartans' reputation for brevity of speech in both Herodotus and other fifth-century authors, see Millender 2001, 150, 154–5.

[46] See Millender 2001, 155 and n. 163. One should also note the initial unwillingness of Sparta's allies to voice their disapproval of Sparta's proposal to restore tyranny at Athens (5.92–3). See Gray 1996, 383.

[47] See Hartog 1982, 148, 151, and 1988, 154–6. See also Loraux 1986, 45–7 for an interesting comparison of Athenian and Spartan funeral ceremonies in which she contrasts the heroic *thrēnos* and the funeral oration and examines the nature of praise in each ceremony.

[48] See Plut. *Sol.* 21.5; Cic. *Leg.* 2.59 ff. and Hartog 1988, 155. Note in particular the language of Plut. *Sol.* 21.6: ἀμυχὰς δὲ κοπτομένων καὶ τὸ θρηνεῖν πεποιημένα καὶ τὸ κωκύειν ἄλλον ἐν ταφαῖς ἑτέρων αφεῖλεν.

[49] Herodotus' view of mutilation as a typical 'barbaric' custom comes through most clearly in the speech delivered by the Spartan regent Pausanias following the Greek victory at Plataea. In response to the Aeginetan Lampon's request that the Greeks impale Mardonius' head in revenge for Xerxes' decapitation of Leonidas (cf. 7.238), Pausanias points out that such an act is far more appropriate for foreigners than for Greeks (9.79.1). Although it may appear contradictory to the above argument that Herodotus has a Spartan make this statement, the narrative necessitates that a Spartan adopt this role. Since Lampon discusses vengeance against Xerxes for his decapitation of Leonidas, it would make sense that his request be addressed to the man who was both victor at Plataea and Leonidas' 'successor'. Herodotus, it should be noted, also occasionally attributes this type of behavior to Greek despots and other Greeks whom he wishes to put in a class

with non-Greek peoples, such as Pheretime of Cyrene (4.202.1) and Cleomenes of Sparta (6.75.3, 81). On mutilation as a barbarian practice, see Laurot 1981, 44; Hartog 1982, 147–9, 151, and 1988, 142–3, 155; Lateiner 1987, 92–3; Hall 1989, 26–8, 44, 105, 131, 205.

[50] Hartog 1988, 155. In addition to those examples discussed below, see Hdt. 2.85, on Egyptian mourning customs and 1.140.1, where Herodotus claims that Persian corpses are not buried until they have been mangled by a bird or dog.

[51] By beating themselves upon the head, the Spartan mourners also recall the clever Egyptian thief who eventually became Rhampsinitus' son-in-law. Herodotus reports that this thief, attempting to steal his brother's corpse from Rhampsinitus' guards by making them drunk, staged an accident in which he loosened several skins carrying wine. Feigning frustration at this turn of events, the thief cried aloud and beat his head (2.121δ2). On the nature and symbolic role of Scythian mutilation during royal funerals, see Hartog 1982, 147–9, 151, and 1988, 142–7, 155, 333.

[52] On mutilation as the exercise of power in barbarian communities, see Hartog 1982, 147–9, and 1988, 142, 332–4; Hall 1989, 158–9; Munson 1993, 40. Lateiner (1984, 266; 1987, 92–3; and 1989, 29, 138–9, 153, 180) views the practice of mutilation in a similar way, arguing that it is a practice that can only flourish under despotism. See also Asheri 1990, 142 on branding as a mark of slavery.

[53] See Hartog 1988, 333. Mutilation as a royal prerogative receives support from Herodotus' account of Intaphrenes' violent treatment of Darius' guards and consequent punishment (3.118–19). For other examples of mutilation practiced by barbarians, see Hdt. 1.74.6, 114.3, 214.4; 2.2.5, 36.3, 37.2, 86–8, 104.2–4, 121β2 and ε4, 131.2, 162.5; 3.8.1, 69.5, 79.1, 118, 130.2, 132.2, 154.2–155.2, 159.1; 4.26.1, 43.2, 62.4, 64–5, 68.3, 70, 80.5, 103.3, 202.1; 5.114.1; 6.32; 7.35.3, 233.2, 238.1; 8.90.3, 118.4; 9.112. Cf. Herodotus' account of Xerxes' 'physical' punishment of the Hellespont by means of scourging and branding (7.35.1). See also Lateiner 1987, 114.

[54] Hartog 1988, 155 claims that Sparta represents an intermediate state somewhere between the Scythians and the Athenians, practicing neither systematic embalming nor true mutilation. His implicit assumption that the Spartans' beatings upon their heads do not involve the cutting of the skin, however, is questionable on several grounds. Herodotus uses the middle form of the verb κόπτειν to describe the Spartans' beatings, a verb that can mean, among other things, both to strike and to cut. The verb often seems to embody both of these meanings simultaneously, as the *Histories* demonstrates. At several points in his work, Herodotus uses κόπτειν and the related form κατακόπτειν to describe an act of cutting that results from striking, smashing or crushing. See, e.g., Hdt. 1.48.2, 73.5, 207.6; 2.42.6, 94.2, 172.3; 3.96.2, 98.4; 4.71.1. These two meanings of the verb more explicitly shade into one another in Herodotus' description of the Carians' mutilation of their foreheads with knives at the festival of Isis at Busiris (2.61.2): τὰ μέτωπα κόπτονται μαχαίρῃσι. Evidence from other sources further indicates that such beatings upon the head constituted a form, albeit mild, of

mutilation. Euripides provides a striking image of this manifestation of mourning in a speech uttered by Helen in the tragedy that bears her name. Bewailing the vanity of the Trojan War, Helen claims that Hellas has beaten her hands against her head and has moistened the soft skin of her cheek with bloody blows (*Hel.* 370–4): βοὰν βοὰν δ᾽ Ἑλλὰς | κέλαδησε κἀνοτότυξεν, | ἐπὶ δὲ κρατὶ χέρας ἔθηκεν, | ὄνυχι δ᾽ ἁπαλόχροα γένυν | δεῦσε φονίαισι πλαγαῖς. Cf. Aesch. *Cho.* 423–8. The fact that such beatings were specifically banned by Solon (see, above, n. 48) also undercuts Hartog's view that such beatings situate the Spartans in an intermediate state between Athens and the barbarian world. The violence implicit in such beatings and their correspondence to barbarian practices in the *Histories* closely associates the Lacedaemonians with the non-Greek world in Herodotus' account.

[55] Cf. Athenaeus' description of the funeral of the tyrants of Erythrae (259e). On the ceremony at Erythrae, see Reiner 1938, 49–50. See also Hartog (1982, 147, 149, and 1988, 142, 146, 155, 333) on the similar role that royal funerary mutilation plays in Scythian society.

[56] On the despotic aspect of the Spartan royal funeral, see Hartog 1982, 151–2, and 1988, 153–5; Loraux 1986, 46; Munson 1993, 44. On ἀνάγκη as a term describing 'the compulsion of monarchical rule', see Munson 1988, 95 n. 18, and 1993, 44. The language in 6.58.1–2, quoted in n. 25 above, underlines the compulsion that underpins the entire ceremony.

[57] This mode of mourning again links the Spartans with the Scythians, who similarly externalize their lamentation and celebrate their dead king through both the marks they make upon their bodies and an elaborate visual display around the king's tomb (4.71.2–72).

[58] With only one exception, Herodotus uses the term γέρας in connection with both Greek and non-Greek societies organized around the principles of autocracy: 1.114.2 (Persia); 2.168.1 (Egypt); 3.85.1 (Persia), 104.2 (Sparta), 142.4 (Maeandrius of Samos); 4.143.1 (Persia), 162.2, 165.1 (Cyrene); 6.56, 57.5 (Sparta); 7.3.3 (Persia), 29.2 (Persians), 134.1 (Sparta), 154.1 (Gela); 8.125.1 (Sparta); 9.26.5 (Sparta). The one exception occurs at 9.27.5, where the Athenians claim that their feat of arms at Marathon entitled them to the honor of holding the left wing of the Greek army at Plataea. Herodotus' use of this term to refer to the unique privileges of the Egyptian warrior class (2.168) is also noteworthy. Through its focus on a hereditary warrior caste and its detailed list of the daily rations given to members of the Egyptian king's annual bodyguard, this passage offers a striking parallel to Herodotus' description of the Spartan kings' peacetime privileges (6.57.1–3) and once again links Sparta with Egypt. See, above, n. 29.

[59] Although Herodotus occasionally uses the term γέρας to refer to an honor (4.143.1; 8.125.1; 9.27.5) and to certain types of offices (1.114.2; 7.134.1, 154.1), in his text the term most often signifies special privileges accorded to specific members or groups (2.168.1; 3.142.4; 4.162.2, 165.1; 6.56, 57.5; 7.29.2, 104.2; 9.26.5). Even when Herodotus uses the term γέρας to refer to offices, such as that of the heralds at Sparta (7.134.1) and the priesthood of the chthonian goddesses at Gela (7.153–154.1), he demonstrates that these offices are held as

privileges rather than through more democratic processes. See also the tyrant Maeandrius' attempt to garner the priesthood of Zeus the Liberator for his family in return for giving up his tyranny (3.142.4).

[60] *Contra* Munson 1993, 43, who argues that the various royal privileges conferred upon the Spartan kings make the Spartan kingship conform to a hellenic model. Munson offers kingship in Cyrene (Hdt. 4.162.2, 165.1) and Homeric Greece (*Il.* 12.310–21) as other examples. See also Thuc. 1.13. On γέρας as a term signifying Homeric kingship, see also Carlier 1977, 74 n. 37, who argues that Herodotus' use of this term with all of its Homeric resonances rather paints a picture of a limited monarchy. Cf. Carlier 1984, 255, 273. While it is true that barbarian monarchs do not receive γέρεα from their subjects, such privileges are a common feature of both Greek and barbarian societies that are ruled by autocrats. The Spartan kings' privileges, therefore, not only underline the monarchical structure of their society but also link the Spartans with groups such as the Persians and the Egyptians. See Tigerstedt 1965–78, 1.104.

[61] Hartog 1982, 150–2, and 1988, 152–6. Cf. Finley 1968, 151.

[62] On the striking difference in treatment between that accorded to the kings and that accorded to the average Spartiate, see Cartledge 1987, 335; Hodkinson 2000, 262–3. For detailed descriptions of Spartiate burial practices, see Nafissi 1991, 277–341; Richer 1994; Hodkinson 2000, 237–70.

[63] Cf. Lateiner 1989, 148 on Herodotus' preoccupation with exceptions in his treatment of Egypt: 'The fact that he fastens on the exceptions and struck by the contrasts to Greece, forgets to notice that they are only occasional in Egypt, only strengthens our point, namely that Herodotus sought the surprising in order to demonstrate a thesis, Egyptian polarity to the rest of mankind, especially to the Greeks (2.35.1–2).' See also Asheri 1990, 141.

[64] Cf. Munson 1993, 44. See also Loraux 1986, 46: 'Thus the Spartan community came together to proclaim in a threnos the absolute superiority of the dead king, and for ten days the city, its political life suspended, gave itself over entirely to lamentation, as if to ward off a death that endangered the very principle of its continuity.'

[65] In his account of the dyarch's privileges at 6.57.4, Herodotus also reveals his knowledge of the kings' comparatively limited judicial powers.

[66] Cleomenes' role in the *Histories* supports a theory concerning the Spartan kingship that Cloché 1949, 113–38, 343–81 first put forward. Through a detailed examination of the careers of the Spartan kings from Cleomenes I (*c.* 520–488) to Cleomenes III (237–291), Cloché concludes that while the Spartan monarchy was constitutionally-based, nevertheless 'sans violer la loi, des princes habiles et résolus pouvaient très bien renforcer l'efficacité de leurs fonctions'. See also Tigerstedt 1965–78, 1.68; de Ste Croix 1972, 125, 138–48; Thomas 1974, 257–70, esp. 258–60; Carlier 1977, 65–84; Cartledge 1987, esp. 4, 18, 106, 205–6. On the limits of royal power, see Carlier 1984, 240–324; Thommen 1996, 85–90. On Cleomenes' direction of Spartan foreign policy, see, esp., Cloché 1949, 120–3; de Ste Croix 1972, 140–1; Carlier 1977, 70–84; Thommen 1996, 87–90, 92–6.

[67] In the former episode, Herodotus mentions the ephors, but their only

responsibility consists of their expulsion of Maeandrius at the request of Cleomenes. See also Hdt. 6.84, where Herodotus suggests a similarly dominant role for Cleomenes in the Spartans' dealings with the Scythians. See Thommen 1996, 87–8.

[68] On the nature of royal initiative in Sparta's campaigns in Athens during the late sixth century, see de Ste Croix 1972, 141, 150–1 n. 158; Thomas 1974, 262; Thommen 1996, 88–9.

[69] See de Ste Croix 1972, 141; Thomas 1974, 262.

[70] See de Ste Croix 1972, 141; Thomas 1974, 262; Carlier 1977, 78–9. Herodotus' accounts of Leonidas' command at Thermopylae (7.220–2) and Pausanias' conduct of the battle at Plataea (9.46–7, 53–7, 60–4, 76, 78–81) further demonstrate the kings' (or regent's) prerogatives in war. In his digression on the kings' prerogatives, Herodotus also claims that the dyarchs had the right to wage war on whatever land they pleased and that any Spartan who attempted to prevent them from exercising this prerogative would be 'liable to the curse' (6.56). Scholars have offered a variety of interpretations of this passage, most reading it as anachronistic and hopelessly in conflict with other passages in the *Histories.* See, e.g., de Ste Croix 1972, 149–51; Cartledge 1987, 105–6. See also Carlier 1977, 70–75 and 1984, 259–65; Thommen 1996, 86–7. Herodotus, however, says nothing in this passage about the declaration of war and the voting of the expedition and, therefore, does not counter the other evidence he provides on the assembly's (and sometimes the ephorate's) control of these processes. Cf. Andrewes *HCT* 4.74, who rightly insists that the statement 'cannot mean that the king had a right to "declare" war on any land he chose, for Herodotus is speaking of his own time, when such decisions were conspicuously taken by the assembly'. Herodotus' formulation of this privilege does not contradict fifth-century Spartan practice, and we may read the passage as a statement of the kings' control over the direction of the operations once the city declared war and appointed the commander, and the ephorate called up the army.

[71] As Cartledge 1987, 205–6 aptly puts it, 'a prescriptive right to the supreme command of citizen and allied armies in a militarized state like Sparta was potentially a passport to undying fame abroad and enormous political influence at home'. See also Tigerstedt 1965–78, 1.68; de Ste Croix 1972, 139; Thomas 1974, 258–60, 262–3, 270; Carlier 1977, 77 ff., esp. 82–3. All of these studies conclude that the kings' military leadership was the key to their power as well as the fact that personal leadership remained a considerable factor in determining state policy. When the kings successfully met Sparta's special military requirements, their personal leadership and 'auctoritas' made it possible for them to be motive forces in Spartan history.

[72] Weber 1978, 1285. On the charismatic nature of the Spartan dyarchy, see Finley 1968, 152; de Ste Croix 1972, 139; Cartledge 1987, 24, 95, 104–10, 128, 336–40.

[73] See Carlier 1977, 76 n. 42. See also Cartledge 1987, 338. Herodotus offers another indication of the Spartan dyarchs' supra-mortal stature in his account of the Aeginetans' attempt to punish Leotychidas (6.85.2–3). The Spartan Theasides,

in his warning to the Aeginetans not to carry off Leotychidas, suggests the 'sacrosanctity' of the kingship. Cf. Plut. *Agis* 19.9. See de Ste Croix 1972, 139.

[74] See Cartledge 1987, 105; cf. 337.

[75] On the Spartan kings and patronage, see Cartledge 1987, 108–9. For a more general discussion of Spartan patron-client relationships, see Hodkinson 2000, 335–68.

[76] Cartledge 1987, 340. Cf. Xen. *Lac. Pol.* 15.9, *Hell.* 3.3.1.

[77] On Herodotus' treatment of the Spartan kings as 'true royalty', see Immerwahr 1966, 198; Finley 1968, 151–2; Hartog 1988, 338.

[78] Finley 1968, 152. See also Immerwahr 1966, 197–8; Cartledge 1987, 104.

[79] One should note Demaratus' claim that this was the custom of succession in Sparta. Herodotus' account of Demaratus' advice to Xerxes thus effects an important linkage between Sparta and Persia through cultural – in this case, political – borrowing. Cf. Immerwahr 1966, 198.

[80] On the important role that mothers and marriage play in the Spartan succession, see Immerwahr 1966, 197; Cragg 1976, 203–4. See also Millender 1999, 356–7.

[81] See Lang 1944, 103–11 for a discussion of the motif of the favorite younger son. In Herodotus' account, Dorieus and his brothers assume this role (5.41–2).

[82] On the role of birth phenomena in Herodotus, see Lang 1944, 111–20.

[83] One should also note the other parallels that exist between the Spartan dyarchs and the various autocrats who inhabit Herodotus' *Histories*. The exiled Demaratus' writing of a secret message to the Lacedaemonians (7.239.3–4), for example, links him with the many Herodotean tyrants and monarchs who employ the written word in a myriad of ways. On the written word as a symbol which fifth-century Athenian-based sources use in their representations of autocratic rule, see Steiner 1994, 7, 127–85; Millender 2001, 142, 152. See also Hartog 1988, 277–8, 288. The powerful Spartan women Herodotus describes in detail, especially Gorgo (5.51.2–3, 7.239.4) and Argeia (6.52.2–7), also link the Lacedaemonians with many of the autocratic courts that figure so largely in the *Histories*. See Millender 1999, 355–91, esp. 356–7.

[84] On Otanes' speech as a paradigm for the various autocratic régimes featured in the *Histories*, see Wüst 1935, 59–60; Lang 1944, 71; Pearson 1954, 141–2; Lateiner 1984, 260, 272, and 1989, 165, 171; Gammie 1986, 171–95. *Contra* Flory 1987, 131.

[85] See Fisher 1992, 128, 344, 346–9 on the central role that *hybris* plays in the Herodotean portrait of the autocrat.

[86] Hdt. 3.80.3–5: κῶς δ᾽ ἂν εἴη χρῆμα κατηρτημένον μουναρχίη, τῇ ἔξεστι ἀνευθύνῳ ποιέειν τὰ βούλεται; καὶ γὰρ ἂν τὸν ἄριστον ἀνδρῶν πάντων στάντα ἐς ταύτην τὴν ἀρχὴν ἐκτὸς τῶν ἐωθότων νοημάτων στήσειε. ἐγγίνεται μὲν γάρ οἱ ὕβρις ὑπὸ τῶν παρεόντων ἀγαθῶν, φθόνος δὲ ἀρχῆθεν ἐμφύεται ἀνθρώπῳ. δύο δ᾽ ἔχων ταῦτα ἔχει πᾶσαν κακότητα· τὰ μὲν γὰρ ὕβρι κεκορημένος ἔρδει πολλὰ καὶ ἀτάσθαλα, τὰ δὲ φθόνῳ. καίτοι ἄνδρα γε τύραννον ἄφθονον ἔδει εἶναι, ἔχοντά γε πάντα τὰ ἀγαθά· τὸ δὲ ὑπεναντίον τούτου ἐς τοὺς πολιήτας πέφυκε· φθονέει γὰρ τοῖσι ἀρίστοισι περιεοῦσί τε καὶ ζώουσι, χαίρει δὲ τοῖσι κακίστοισι τῶν

ἀστῶν, διαβολὰς δὲ ἄριστος ἐνδέκεσθαι. ἀναρμοστότατον δὲ πάντων· ἤν τε γὰρ αὐτὸν μετρίως θωμάζῃς, ἄχθεται ὅτι οὐ κάρτα θεραπεύεται, ἤν τε θεραπεύῃ τις κάρτα, ἄχθεται ἅτε θωπί. τὰ δὲ δὴ μέγιστα ἔρχομαι ἐρέων· νόμαιά τε κινέει πάτρια καὶ βιᾶται γυναῖκας κτείνει τε ἀκρίτους.

[87] On the connection between *hybris* and sexual offenses committed against 'respectable' women, see Fisher 1992, 41, 78–9, 104–9, 127–9, 236–40.

[88] As Lateiner 1984, 265–6 demonstrates, Herodotus' emphasis on abnormal sexual activities and the confusion of sex and power illustrates the *hybris* of autocrats throughout the work. See also Benardete 1969, 137–8; Hartog 1988, 331–2. For useful discussions of Herodotus' general presentation of and attitude toward different sexual *mores*, see Pembroke 1967; Rosellini and Saïd 1978; Lateiner 1989, 137–8.

[89] Cf. Lateiner 1985a, 97. Lateiner 1989, 141–2 also notes the similarity of the opening and closing scenes of the *Histories* in their depiction of the violation of *nomoi* and its consequences. See also Wolff 1964, 51–8; Gammie 1986, 185–7. On the theme of transgressive or excessive ἔρως, see Benardete 1969, 137–8. See also Konstan 1983, 12, 19; Hartog 1988, 330; and Hall 1989, 208 on the despotic nature of excessive ἔρως.

[90] See also Herodotus' story of Mycerinus' illicit passion for his own daughter (2.131.1). In addition to these examples, one should also consider Herodotus' hints at sexual impropriety in his description of Peisistratus' relations with his Alcmaeonid wife (1.61.1).

[91] Cf. Immerwahr 1966, 198.

[92] By clinging to his wife at the risk of imperiling the succession, Anaxandridas calls to mind the Lydian Candaules' excessive and similarly dangerous ἔρως for his wife (Hdt. 1.8–12). One should note that the proposal to take a second wife came from the ephors and elders and that Anaxandridas only yielded to their advice when presented with the threat that his disobedience would force the Spartans to take unpleasant measures against him (5.40). His practice of bigamy, nevertheless, links him with other barbarian autocrats, such as Cyrus (3.3). The Spartan *polis'* sanctioning of such an arrangement, in addition, further associates it with such barbarian autocracies.

[93] While Herodotus does not fully commit himself to accepting this charge against Cleomenes, his inclusion of this rumor is noteworthy, since his account includes several other examples of transgressive ἔρως on the part of Spartan dyarchs.

[94] See Boedeker 1987, 188–9, who places both stories under the rubric of the 'Helen pattern'. See also Immerwahr 1966, 197, who believes that the motif of 'irregular marriage' is local to Sparta and 'has a connection, in Spartan mythology, with the rape of women'. On the Spartan myth of 'Raubehe', see Merkelbach 1957, 22.

[95] As Gray 1995, 192, 206 points out, both Ariston's lust for another man's wife and despotic compulsion of his subject and friend, Agetus, link him with several barbarian autocrats in the Histories. See also Flory 1987, 44. By using an underhanded scheme to secure Agetus' wife, Ariston parallels several other Herodotean

autocrats who similarly concoct plans to secure the sexual favors of otherwise unavailable women, especially Cambyses (3.31) and Xerxes (9.108). One should also note the similarities between Ariston's surprising request of Agetus and the unexpected demands by which both Artaÿnte and Amestris gain control over Xerxes (9.109–10). On the motif of the unexpected request, see Gray 1995, 198.

[96] Demaratus' seizure of Percalus is not wholly illegitimate, since he obtained his bride by means of the marriage-capture ritual before she had consummated her relationship to Leotychidas. Nevertheless, Herodotus' account presents this marriage as a veritable rape achieved through deception and violence and focuses on the role that Demaratus' seizure of his bride played in this dyarch's eventual deposition at the hands of Leotychidas and Cleomenes (6.65). On the aberrant nature of Demaratus' 'marriage by capture', see Millender 1999, 364. By sanctioning both this marriage practice and Ariston's theft of his wife, the Spartan *polis* is again on a par with the barbarian autocracies in the *Histories* that legitimate similar practices. Particularly noteworthy in this regard is the Persian law that Cambyses exploited in his desire to marry his sister (3.31).

[97] Ariston's hasty marriage eventually produces doubts concerning Demaratus' legitimacy (6.63.1–2, 68–9), and Demaratus' rape of Percalus later makes Leotychidas an active participant in his kinsman's deposition (6.65.2–3).

[98] See Benardete 1969, 137–8, who demonstrates that Herodotus uses the term ἔρως to signify unhealthy desire for sex (1.8.1 *bis*; 2.131.1; 3.31.2; 6.62.1; 9.108.1 and 2, 113.2) and for tyranny (1.96.2; 3.53.4; 5.32). As Benardete points out, Pausanias seems to combine the two aspects of the term.

[99] See also Cyrus' threatening of the river Gyndes (1.189.2) and Croesus' physical violence against the Halys river (1.75.4–6). For other examples of impious behavior on the part of tyrants and kings, see Hdt. 6.134–5; 7.238; 8.77, 109.3. On the despot's transgression of social, religious and sexual *nomoi* in general, see Hartog 1988, 331–2.

[100] On Spartan religion and religiosity, see Holladay and Goodman 1986, 151–60; Parker 1989, 142–72.

[101] See Hdt. 1.65.2–4, 66–7; 5.63.1–2, 5.90.2–91.1; 6.52.4–5, 66, 76, 80, 82; 7.220.3–4; 8.114. Consider also the Pythioi, the permanent officials appointed by the kings who were responsible for consulting Delphi on public business, mentioned by Hdt. 6.57.2–4 and Xen. *Lac. Pol.* 15.5. The Spartans' strong reliance on divination appears in Herodotus' account of their grant of citizenship to the Iamid seer Tisamenus and his brother (9.33–5). On the Spartans' keen interest in divination, see Parker 1985, 306–9, 318–19 and 1989, 154–61. Robinson 1992, 131–2 and 1994, 363–9 discusses the Spartans' religiosity and their role as the victims of hoaxes involving bribed oracles.

[102] Consider, for example, their probable celebration of the Carneia and consequent failure to aid the Athenians at Marathon in 490 (6.106) and their celebration of the Hyacinthia and delay in sending a force to Boeotia in 479 (9.7). Although the Spartans did send out a small force under Leonidas during the Carneia (7.206), Herodotus makes it clear that the threatened loss of central Greece to the Persians made such an expedition necessary and also points out that

the bulk of the Spartans remained behind in order to observe the festival. On the Spartans' observance of festivals and its effect on their role in the Persian Wars, see Cragg 1976, 196, who discusses earlier viewpoints on this issue. See also Cartledge 1979, 204–5, 207; cf. 286; Holladay and Goodman 1986, 157–60.

[103] In contrast to the scattered depictions of Spartan religiosity, Herodotus provides a sustained portrait of impiety in his lengthy accounts of Cleomenes, as I argue below.

[104] Scholars have long commented on Herodotus' inconsistent treatment of Cleomenes and have tended to argue that the tradition concerning Cleomenes had not yet solidified when Herodotus wrote his account. See, e.g., Lang 1944, 207–8; Tigerstedt 1965–78, 1.89–91; Cragg 1976, 39, 176–7; Evans 1991, 186. For detailed discussions of Cleomenes' reign, see Klein 1973; Cawkwell 1993; Devereaux 1995.

[105] See Forrest 1980, 86; Murray 1980, 252; Griffiths 1989, 76 n.37. See also Bradford 1994, 62–3 on Cleomenes' dealings with the divine.

[106] For other examples of the Spartan practice of these crossing-sacrifices, see Thuc. 5.54.1, 55.3, 116.1. Xenophon (*Lac. Pol.* 13.2–5) offers a detailed description of these preliminary sacrifices. See Parker 1989, 156–7.

[107] Cleomenes' misunderstanding of the oracle is noteworthy, since it parallels Cambyses' murder of the 'wrong' Smerdis and death at the 'wrong' Ecbatana (3.64) as well as Arcesilaus III's failure to understand the meaning of the oracle that warned him against burning his enemies to death and traveling to Barca (4.164.4). On the motif of the mistaken oracle, see Lang 1944, 206–7; Fontenrose 1978, Q93 and 68–9; Griffiths 1989, 58.

[108] On Cleomenes' impiety as the central motif of the Cleomenes *logos*, see Immerwahr 1966, 192–3, who argues that Herodotus accentuates this aspect of Cleomenes' kingship because of the Spartans' general reputation for piety.

[109] Lateiner 1985a, 87–100, and 1989, 126–35 discusses the theme of transgression and the importance of the crossing of boundaries in Herodotus. See also Hartog 1988, 330–1; Fisher 1992, 367–81, esp. 376–8.

[110] Cleomenes also demonstrates 'divine megalomania' during his brief sojourn in Arcadia, where he attempts to make the local leaders swear an oath of loyalty by the Styx (6.74.1). See Griffiths 1989, 60.

[111] Through his burning of the sacred grove, Cleomenes parallels two other Herodotean despots who dispose of their enemies through a similar process of entrapment and incineration: Sesostris' brother (2.107.1) and Arcesilaus (4.164.2). The parallels among the three passages in the *Histories* are striking. As Griffiths 1989, 57 points out, the detail of the brushwood piled up around the grove is significant and points to Herodotus' use of a generic motif. For other examples of despots using fire, see Hdt. 2.111.3; 3.37.3, 45.4; 5.92η3. For holocaust stories in general, see Hdt. 1.176.1; 2.100.4; 7.107.2 and Griffiths 1989, 57, who points out the Near Eastern background to these stories (cf. Judges 9, 46 ff.). On this stock trait of the despot, see Lateiner 1984, 264, and 1989, 170.

[112] Griffiths 1989, 58 also points out the similarities between Cleomenes' driving out of the priest and insistence on sacrificing in person, and Herodotus' account

of the Argive ruler Pheidon, who supposedly kicked out the Elean judges and took over the management of the Olympic games himself at some point in the archaic period (6.127.3).

[113] Cf. Hartog 1988, 332.

[114] See Hdt. 1.114.3; 3.16.1 and 6, 29.2, 130.2, 154.2, 157.1; 7.22.1, 35.1, 54.3, 56.1, 103.4, 223.3; 8.109.2. On whipping as characteristic of despotism, especially among the Persians, see Gigante 1956, 116; Momigliano 1979, 146; Laurot 1981, 45; Lateiner 1984, 266; 1987, 92; and 1989, 29, 153, 180; Hartog 1988, 332. Compare Herodotus' discussion of the Scythians' return home after spending almost three decades in Media (4.1–4). According to Herodotus, they managed to defeat their slaves in battle by brandishing horse-whips, which reminded the slaves of their inferior status (4.3.4).

[115] Cleomenes' despotic compulsion of his subject (= the helot) links him not only with Ariston (see, above, n. 95) but also with Herodotean despots in general. On the importance of the master/subject antithesis in the *Histories*, see Gray 1995, 201–10.

[116] The death of Miltiades II, tyrant of the Chersonesus, from a gangrenous thigh is equally appropriate when one recalls that he received his wound while sacrilegiously entering and tampering with the precinct of Demeter on Paros (6.134.2, 136.2–3). On the notion of 'illustrative' death, see Lefkowitz 1981, 3, 10 n. 27.

[117] Compare Histiaeus' thigh wound (6.5.2) and Miltiades II's death from a festering leg wound (6.134.2, 136.2–3). On the similarities among these deaths, see Immerwahr 1966, 192; Gammie 1986, 191; Hartog 1988, 337–8; Griffiths 1989, 61.

[118] See Macan 1895, 2.83; Immerwahr 1966, 193 n. 13; Cragg 1976, 64. Vansina 1973, 106 and 1985, 105–6 discusses the 'exemplary function' of history and the process by which traditions become distorted into providing examples of ideal types. He cites as an example the Kuba king, who, fifty years after his death, became the type of tyrant who kills and tortures out of sheer sadism. Similar to the Herodotean account of the Spartan Cleomenes, Bushongo tradition made this king die an untimely death despite the fact that he reigned for a longer time than most other kings. For a different interpretation of Herodotus' statement at 5.48, see Cawkwell 1993, 507. See also Griffiths 1989, 53–4, who substitutes εἰ for οὐ and uses apodotic ἀλλά to arrive at a very different translation of Hdt. 5.48: 'For while it is true that Kleomenes had a pretty long reign, still he died without an heir . . .' Griffiths, however, does not offer sufficient defense for his emendation and admits (72 n. 4) that this use of apodotic ἀλλά normally occurs in direct or reported speech.

[119] Compare the elder Miltiades and his nephew Stesagoras (6.38.1–2). See Lateiner 1985a, 98, and 1989, 142.

[120] As Otanes points out, the absolute ruler's position in and of itself can drive even the best man's thoughts from their wonted course (3.80.3). Herodotus uses the term ὑπομαργότερος to describe both Cambyses' and Cleomenes' madness (3.39.1; 6.75.1), as well as that of the equally disturbed and despotically-inclined Charilaus of Samos (3.145.1). Madness in Herodotus is almost always

a characteristic of autocrats, especially those in barbarian lands. See Hdt. 1.109.2, 212.2; 3.25.2, 30.1, 33, 34.1 and 3, 35.1–2 and 4, 37.1, 38.1–2, 61.1; 5.42.1; 6.84.1. By opening his account of Cleomenes with a reference to his madness (5.42.1), Herodotus stresses an attribute that closely associates Cleomenes with such autocrats and simultaneously calls attention to this linkage. On Herodotus' use of descriptions designating 'madness', see Munson 1991, 50–1 and nn. 10–11. See also Brown 1982, 397–9, 402–3.

[121] Griffiths 1989, 51–78, esp. 67, 70–1.

[122] Griffiths 1989, 70. Despite his awareness that Herodotus consciously crafted the image of an absolute and almost despotic Cleomenes, Griffiths does not see that Cleomenes and several other Spartan kings exhibit stock tyrannical traits that not only link them with Cambyses but also conform to Otanes' general portrait of one-man rule. On the parallels between Cambyses and Cleomenes, see also Bichler 1985, 125–47, at 137 n. 44; Hartog 1988, 337–8; Munson 1991, 50–1. Lang 1944, 80–1, 210 discusses the similarities between Cleomenes and Cambyses in terms of their *phthonos* and madness.

[123] Even Leotychidas does not fully escape this treatment, for Herodotus' account of this dyarch focuses upon his lawlessness in the form of perjury and greed (6.65.3, 72). See Millender 2002, 36, 38–9. For a fuller discussion of the links Herodotus forges between Demaratus and barbarian autocrats, see Millender 2002, 33–6.

[124] Cf. Harvey 1979, 260, who notes that 'Leonidas was the great hero of Thermopylae. Already by the time of Herodotus the events of that battle had been distorted so as to emphasize the heroic self-sacrifice of Leonidas. The same tendency might explain the suppression of facts about his earlier life which would have been discreditable to him.' Leonidas' heroic stature may likewise explain Herodotus' noteworthy claim that since Leonidas had two elder brothers, Cleomenes and Dorieus, he had put the possibility of becoming king right out of his mind (7.205): ἀπελήλατο τῆς φροντίδος περὶ τῆς βασιληίης. This description distances Leonidas not only from other Spartan kings but also from the general run of autocrats described by Otanes, who inevitably go out of their minds as a result of their position (3.80.3). See, above, n. 120.

[125] One, of course, must admit the probability that at least some of the negative information concerning Cleomenes in the *Histories* originated from this king's enemies in Sparta. See, e.g., Cartledge 1979, 143; and Cawkwell 1993, 507–9, who goes too far, however, in his claim that Herodotus simply swallowed Spartan misinformation concerning Cleomenes without question. While Herodotus undoubtedly used Spartan, Athenian, and likely other sources of information in his depiction of Cleomenes, both the similarities between Cleomenes and Cambyses and Cleomenes' conformation to the pattern of the tyrant in the *Histories* suggest that Herodotus' Athenian sources played a fundamental role in Herodotus' construction of Cleomenes' reign.

[126] See Millender 1996, 140.

[127] On Herodotus' relationship with Samos, see Cole 1912; Mitchell 1975, 79–91; Tölle-Kastenbein 1976. Lang 1944, 155–8, 262–9 discusses the various

folklore-motifs that organize Herodotus' portrayal of Polycrates. On the role that popular legend played in the Herodotean portrait of Polycrates, see Lateiner 1984, 264, and 1989, 170–1; Gammie 1986, 190. For a general discussion of Herodotus' treatment of Polycrates, see Tölle-Kastenbein 1976, 13–29.

[128] For evidence of Halicarnassus' membership in the Delian League and tributary record, see *ATL* 1.224–25; 3.20, 53, 209, 213, 242, 270. See also Hornblower 1982, 5, 25, 28–9, who points out that Halicarnassus demonstrated an unusual degree of loyalty to Athens in comparison with the other Carian cities. One should also note that the late 450s was a period that witnessed the continued struggle between Athenian and Persian imperial ambitions and the deposition of dynasties in several cities in Ionia and Caria. Especially significant are the changes in the listing of the Carian cities Idyma (*ATL* 1.288) and Syangela (*ATL* 1.414), which are mentioned in conjunction with dynasts before 449 and alone thereafter. Idyma: *ATL* 1.171, 288–9, 446, 492, 531, 554; 3.9, 23, 53, 212, 240. Syangela: *ATL* 1.414–15, 446, 448, 551–2, 554; 2.82; 3.6, 27, 54, 213–14, 273. The changes in the designation of these tributaries would suggest the collapse or overthrow of their ruling dynasties, perhaps with the aid of the Athenians. See Eddy 1973, 243; Graf 1985, 98.

[129] On the nature of the evidence for Herodotus' visit, see Jacoby 1913, 226–42, 274 ff.; Myres 1953, 11–15; von Fritz 1967, 1.123–35; Podlecki 1977, 246–65; Asheri 1988, 1.xii–xiii; Ostwald 1991, 138–48. The only explicit evidence comes from Eus. *Chron.* Ol. 83.4, which states that the Athenian *boule* honored Herodotus for having read his books to them, and Diyllus (*FGrH* 73 F 3 = Plut. *Mor.* 862b), who reports that Herodotus received from Athens a gift of ten talents on the motion of a certain Anytus. The evidence at first appears slender, but much of Herodotus' work suggests a familiarity with Athens that argues for a visit of some duration. Consider, for example, his description of physical features of the city and Attica (cf. 1.98.5; 2.7; 4.99.4–5; 5.63.4, 77.3–4, 89.3; 6.103.3; 8.53.1) and his obvious use of Athenian sources, family traditions, and civic traditions. See Thomas 1989, esp. 165–72, 238–51, 261–82. Most scholars believe that Herodotus visited Athens and made it his settled abode for an unspecified period of time in the middle of the fifth century. See, esp., Ostwald 1991, 137–48. See also Asheri 1988, 1.xii–xiii. *Contra* Podlecki 1977, 246–65, who fails both to explain away the vast amount of evidence that supports Herodotus' visit to Athens and to recognize Herodotus' need to visit one of the main participants in the Persian Wars. On the latter point, see Waters 1985, 75, who correctly points out that 'when one considers that Herodotus' life spanned the greatest years of Athens' power and brilliance, it is inconceivable that an intelligent man of his wide interests, composing an account of great wars in which the city played one of the chief parts, had not spent some time in the commercial, maritime, intellectual and artistic capital of the world'. See, however, Thomas 2000, 4–27, who discusses Herodotus' intellectual and cultural milieu and (11) argues that 'Athens was only one of several stops' made by traveling intellectuals and stresses the important influence that east Greece had on Herodotus' composition of the *Histories*. On the possibility of Herodotus' presence in Athens again during the Archidamian War or

even later, see Meyer 1899, 196 ff.; Fornara 1971a, 25, and 1971b, 43 n. 13. See also Asheri 1988, 1.xiv. How and Wells 1928, 1.9 argue that the later passages in Herodotus (i.e. 6.91; 7.137, 233; 9.73) 'would hardly have been known to him had he not returned to Athens'.

[130] For negative depictions of the despot, see, e.g., Aeschylus' depiction of Xerxes in the *Persae* and his portrayal of Zeus in the *Prometheus Vinctus*, Soph. *OT* 874 ff., the figure of Creon in Sophocles' *Oedipus at Colonus* and *Antigone*, and Eur. *Supp.* 404–405, 428–55. See also Aesch. *Ag.* 918–30, 1354–5, 1364–5; *Cho.* 973–4. Hall 1989 discusses the almost wholly negative presentation of Oriental despotism in fifth-century Greek tragedy.

[131] On the strong influence that Athenian democratic ideology exerted on Herodotus' treatment of Spartan society and institutions as well as his construction of Spartan power relations, see Millender 1996, 94–184 and 2002. For a more general discussion of the effect of this ideology on Herodotus' *Histories*, see Forsdyke 1999 and 2001. On the opposition between despotism and democracy in Athenian democratic ideology, see also Lanza 1977; Bleiken 1979, 157; Raaflaub 1983, 522–3; Giorgini 1993, 16–38, 142–86; Millender 1996 and 2002; Forsdyke 2001.

[132] On Herodotus' delivery of lectures, see Evans 1991, 89–90; Thomas 2000, 20, 257–69. Johnson 1994 questions the evidence for Herodotus' public lectures. On historians and their audiences, see Momigliano 1978.

[133] Ostwald 1991, 138–9.

[134] On analogies between the non-Greek world and other areas of the Greek world, see Hartog 1988, 225. Herodotus explains foreign phenomena by means of comparisons with analogous features in Lesbos (1.202.1), Anatolia (2.10.1, 29.3), Cyrene (2.96.1), the Aegean islands (2.97.1), Ephesus (2.148.2), Samos (2.148.2, 168.1), Delos (2.170.2), and southern Italy and Sicily (4.99.5). He also refers to customs common to all Greeks (2.171.2). On Herodotus' references to his audience, see Jacoby 1913, 278. For the view that Herodotus' work was aimed at a wider spectrum of Greeks, see, e.g., Jacoby 1913, 354; Fornara 1971b, 74; Cragg 1976, 15.

[135] See, e.g., Said 1979; Asad 1986, 141–64; Hartog 1988, 7–8. Lévi-Strauss 1966, 257–8 underlines the importance of the social group or public for whom texts are written. See also White 1978, 104.

[136] See Evans 1991, 128 on the important role of the *logioi* and their public recitations in the shaping of tradition. As Thomas 1989, 238–82 argues, Herodotus' *Histories* reflect a wide variety of traditions, including popular or *polis* traditions. On such *polis* traditions, see Thomas 1989, 197–206. See also Forsdyke 2001, who considers the influence exerted on Herodotus' composition by *polis* traditions reflecting fifth-century Athenian political beliefs and values.

[137] The term δημοκρατίη nowhere appears in the debate, and the debaters use a number of expressions to describe government by the masses: ἐς μέσον... καταθεῖναι τὰ πρήγματα (3.80.2), πλῆθος...ἄρχον (3.80.6), ἐς τὸ πλῆθος...φέρειν τὸ κράτος (3.81.1; cf. 3.80.6, 82.1), δήμῳ...χράσθων (3.81.3), δήμου ἄρχοντος (3.82.4) and especially ἰσονομίη (3.80.6, 83.1). Following numerous scholars,

I believe that Herodotus intends his reader to see these terms as equivalent to δημοκρατίη. This is particularly clear with the last term, since Herodotus claims at 3.83.1 that Otanes was Πέρσῃσι ἰσονομίην σπεύδων ποιῆσαι and later states the case in the following terms: Ὀτάνεα γνώμην ἀποδέξασθαι ὡς χρεὸν εἴη δημοκρατέεσθαι Πέρσας (6.43.3). See Larsen 1948, 6; Ehrenberg 1950, 526–8, 530; Vlastos 1953, 337–66 and 1964, 1–6 (but see 7 ff.); Evans 1981, 81 and 1982, 58; Nakategawa 1988, 260; Lateiner 1989, 168, 273 n. 16. Ostwald 1969, 120 claims that Herodotus is undoubtedly thinking only of *demokratia* when he speaks of *isonomia* but argues (97, 101–20) against any equation between the two terms. According to Ostwald (97), *isonomia* 'is not a name for a form of government but for the principle of political equality, which, though it is of course more closely associated with a democratic constitution than with any other, is not necessarily confined to it'. Ehrenberg 1950, 535–6 also recognizes that unlike *demokratia, isonomia* is not a constitution but argues that Herodotus, through his ignorance of constitutional issues, did not realize the difference between the two terms. See also Sealey 1974, 253–95; Asheri and Medaglia 1990, 298–9.

[138] See Ehrenberg 1950, 528; Tigerstedt 1965–78, 1.86; Evans 1982, 58; Lateiner 1984, 268, and 1987, 182, 273 n. 16.

[139] See Lateiner 1989, 167. Compare Aesch. *Pers.* 213, where the unaccountability of the king is clearly contrasted with Athenian democratic accountability. For a detailed history of the procedure of the *euthyna* at Athens, see Ostwald 1986, esp. 7, 12–14, 27–8, 40–2, 47–83, 208–9, 211–12, 436–41, 518.

[140] For other examples of negative comments on the 'rabble', see Eur. *Hec.* 865–68; *IA* 450, 517, 1357; *Supp.* 727; Thuc. 3.37.1.

[141] It may be noteworthy that it is the Spartan Menelaus who offers this criticism of the *dēmos.*

[142] See Immerwahr 1966, 119–20; Lateiner 1984, 268; Nakategawa 1988, 271. *Contra* Fornara 1971b, 48–9, at 48, who argues that Herodotus rather praises freedom over despotism. The close connection between ἰσηγορίη and democracy, however, would seem to argue against his conclusion. Although ἰσηγορίη is a component of δημοκρατίη rather than another word for this type of government, most scholars believe that Herodotus' use of the term at 5.78 again demonstrates that he was thinking of Athens' democratic constitution. On the difference and connection between the two terms, see Griffith 1966, 115–38; Woodhead 1967, 129–40; Ostwald 1969, 109; Nakategawa 1988, 257–75. See also Ostwald 1991, 141.

[143] On the significance of this connection, see Nakategawa 1988, 271. See Lateiner 1984, 272, and 1989, 170 on Herodotus' unusual stress on the advantages that Athens reaped from its overthrow of tyranny and development of self-government. See also Lateiner 1989, 185 on the connection between freedom, constitutional government, and Athenian success in Herodotus. Ostwald 1969, 108–9 discusses the connection between ἰσηγορίη and the victories of the young democracy in 506.

[144] Millender 2001, 151, and 2002, 47. As Loraux 1986, 205 points out, the open debate described by Herodotus, which allowed the Greeks to make the best

decisions possible and defeat the barbarians, was more specifically a feature of Athenian democracy as opposed to the supposed Spartan aversion to such debate (cf. 9.6–10). See also Nakategawa 1988, 270–1. On the important role that open expression and debate plays among the Greeks in general in the *Histories*, see Lateiner 1987, 182–3.

[145] See Millender 2002, 46–7.

[146] Cf. Forsdyke 2001, 335 n. 15.

[147] On the fear of a growing rival as 'a motive reminiscent of Eastern monarchs', see Immerwahr 1966, 203. For other examples, see 1.46.1 (Croesus and Persia), 1.163.3 (Arganthonius and Persia), 1.190.2 (Babylonians and Persia), and 3.1.2 (Amasis and Persia).

[148] See Forsdyke 2001, 332–3, who (336–7) notes the close parallels in language and imagery between the Spartans' statement at 5.91.1–2 and Atossa's description of her dream in Aeschylus' *Persae* (ll. 194–6). It is also striking that Herodotus uses the verb κατέχειν in his description of the Spartan Leonidas' detention of the Thebans at the battle of Thermopylae (7.222) and Cleomenes' occupation of the Athenian Acropolis in 508 (5.72.3). See Forsdyke 2001, 333, nn. 10–11. Gray 1996, 381 notes that the term that Herodotus uses to describe the Lacedaemonians' control of the Peloponnesus, κατεστραμμένη (1.68.6), is regularly used of Eastern domination over subject peoples (1.27.1, 28.1, 171.1, 177) and that Herodotus expresses the Spartans' rise (1.66.1) in the same terms as Cypselus' (5.92δ1). Compare Arieti 1995, 83, who discusses similarities between the Spartans and Croesus: 'Croesus perhaps identifies with Sparta's situation: he too had misunderstood a prophecy, in his case the dream about Atys; like Sparta, by the extravagance of his gifts he has propitiated the god and can expect an outcome as satisfactory as Sparta's. Moreover, the Spartans have no reluctance about waging aggressive wars of expansion; their motive in attacking the Arcadians and Tegeans had been discomfort with peace.'

[149] See Jeffery 1976, 126; Cartledge 1979, 146; Cawkwell 1993, 513 ff.

[150] See, e.g., Andrewes 1956, 14; Tigerstedt 1965–78, 1.86, 92–100, 103; Finley 1968, 157; Ostwald 1972, 283–7; Cragg 1976, 65, 66, 68; de Ste Croix 1977, 138; Lateiner 1984, 268, and 1989, 170, 182–5.

[151] See Tigerstedt 1965–78, 1.92, who rightly argues that 'Sparta here becomes the incarnation of Greek love of liberty and manliness, the representative of Greece against the barbarians'.

[152] See, e.g., Tigerstedt 1965–78, 1.93–6; Fornara 1971b, 50–1 n. 25; Cragg 1976, 103; Ostwald 1991, 142.

[153] Herodotus' detailed account of the events leading up to the battle of Plataea, however, seriously undercuts his praise of the Lacedaemonians' achievements in that battle (8.140–9.58). See Millender 2002, 42–4.

[154] Some scholars even argue that Herodotus was positively biased in favor of Sparta. Cragg 1976, 61–2 discusses earlier scholarship on this point. See also Fornara 1971b, 49–50; Forrest 1984, 6–8; Evans 1991, 86, 88.

[155] See also Hdt. 8.136.2, 143–4; 9.7, 27.5–6.

[156] On Herodotus' criticism of Athens, see, esp., Strasburger 1955, 1–25; Waters

1972, 136–7, 148–9, and 1985, 122–3; Podlecki 1977, 255–6; Evans 1991, 85–8; Ostwald 1991, 141–2.

157 Humphreys 1987, 216. At several points in his work, Herodotus even subverts the polarization of hellene and barbarian that largely structures the *Histories*. For example, he notes cultural similarities and borrowings between Greeks and barbarians, especially the Egyptians. See, above, n. 23. Herodotus also occasionally compares Greeks unfavorably to non-Greeks, as in his account of Xerxes' reception of the Spartan ambassadors Sperthias and Bulis (7.136.2; cf. 133–4).

158 On Herodotus' interest in the contrast between Athens and Sparta, see Immerwahr 1966, 199–230, 259, 265, 299, 303–5.

159 See Hartog 1988, 218–24, esp. at 218, 224 on Herodotus' treatment of the conceptual relationships existing among the Scythians, Amazons, and Greeks (4.110–17). As Hartog argues, this account reveals Herodotus' insistence on maintaining the binary opposition between Greeks and non-Greeks, despite the fact that this particular section of his work deals with two non-Greek peoples, the Amazons and Scythians, with the Greeks providing an absent framework of cultural norms. In order to convey the otherness of the Amazons to his Greek audience, Herodotus applies his customary schema of inversion to the relationship between the Scythians and Amazons and transforms his Scythians into quasi-Greeks.

160 By 'Greek narrative', I refer to the preponderance of purely Greek material in Book 6, which largely builds a picture of the relations among the Greeks before Xerxes' invasion. On Herodotus' inclusion and placement of the Greek material in the *Histories*, see Immerwahr 1966, 34–40.

161 This complex balancing of polarities may help to explain the Spartan regent Pausanias' claim that mutilation is an act far more proper for barbarians than for Grccks (9.79.1). Although Pausanias' statement may appear ironic given the Spartans' violent treatment of their heads in the context of the royal funeral (6.58.3), Herodotus' narrative necessitates Pausanias' role as the Greek representative of moderation in the series of events following the battle of Plataea. See, above, n. 49.

162 Hdt. 7.104.4–5: ὣς δὲ καὶ Λακεδαιμόνιοι κατὰ μὲν ἕνα μαχόμενοι οὐδαμῶν εἰσι κακίονες ἀνδρῶν, ἀλέες δὲ ἄριστοι ἀνδρῶν ἀπάντων. ἐλεύθεροι γὰρ ἐόντες οὐ πάντα ἐλεύθεροί εἰσι· ἔπεστι γάρ σφι δεσπότης νόμος, τὸν ὑποδειμαίνουσι πολλῷ ἔτι μᾶλλον ἢ οἱ σοὶ σέ. ποιεῦσι γῶν τὰ ἂν ἐκεῖνος ἀνώγῃ· ἀνώγει δὲ τὠυτὸ αἰεί, οὐκ ἐῶν φεύγειν οὐδὲν πλῆθος ἀνθρώπων ἐκ μάχης, ἀλλὰ μένοντας ἐν τῇ τάξι ἐπικρατέειν ἢ ἀπόλλυσθαι.

163 Millender 2002, esp. 33–47. Scholars have generally viewed Demaratus' response to Xerxes as a wholly positive eulogy of Spartan valor and lawfulness. See, e.g., Gigante 1956, 114 ff.; Ostwald 1969, 31; Waters 1971, 97; Cragg 1976, 103, 201; de Ste Croix 1977, 138; Hartog 1988, 334; Lateiner 1989, 155; Cartledge 1990, 38; Munson 1993, 42. See also Lévy 1999, 130–1.

164 Owner and possession: 3.134.2; 5.29.1; 7.88.2; master and slaves: 1.129.4; 4.43.7; 6.83.2; king and subjects: 1.8.3, 11.4, 90.2, 91.1, 111.2, 112.3, 115.2;

2.2.4; 3.1.4, 14.9, 34.2, 35.4, 62.3, 85.2, 89.3; 4.126, 136.4; 5.105.2; 7.5.2, 9.1, 35.2, 38.1–2, 147.3; 8.68α1, β1, 88.2, 100.2, 102.2, 118.3; 9.111.1 and 5, 116.3; cf. 5.18.3; tyrant and subjects: 5.78; god and man: l.212.3; 4.127.4.

[165] Hdt. 7.228.2: ὦ ξεῖν', ἀγγέλλειν Λακεδαιμονίοις ὅτι τῇδε | κείμεθα τοῖς κείνων ῥήμασι πειθόμενοι. See Millender 2002, 42.

[166] On the role that both compulsion and fear play in Sparta's conduct of war in the *Histories*, see Millender 2002, 40–5.

[167] Millender 2002, 45–7. For the description of Spartan *nomos* as an 'invisible whip', see Benardete 1969, 191. See also Millender 2002, 40 n. 19.

[168] As I have argued elsewhere (Millender 1996, 363–73), Herodotus continued to write and publish his composition during the first phase of the Peloponnesian War and perhaps even later, if we follow the arguments offered by Fornara (1971a, 28–32). For the view that the *Histories*, as we have them, are a product of the early years of the Peloponnesian War, see also Fornara 1971b, 43, 44, 74, 86; Evans 1991, 90. It is not surprising, therefore, that Herodotus would reflect what we may justly deem 'propaganda' that was circulating around the time of the outbreak of the Peloponnesian War. Thucydides' account of the debate at Sparta in 432, for example, reveals that the Athenians made effective use of their role in the Persian Wars as a propaganda weapon (1.73.2–75). In this speech the Athenians justify their empire, in part, on the grounds that their role as 'the saviors of Hellas' during the Persian Wars had earned them their later hegemony. As Evans (1979, 113–14) has pointed out, Herodotus' encomium of Athens' participation in the hellenes' victory over the Persians (7.139) bears a striking resemblance to the Athenians' defense of their empire at the debate at Sparta. Both defenses of Athenian courage emphasize the central role that Athenian sea-power played in the Persian defeat and underline the primacy of Salamis over the Greek victories on land (cf. Hdt. 7.139.2–4; Thuc. 1.73.4, 74.1–2 and 4). Both Herodotus (7.139.3) and Thucydides' Athenians (1.73.4), moreover, assume that the strategical weakness of the Peloponnesians in the face of Persia's superior navy eventually would have left the Spartans isolated by the gradual reduction or surrender of their allies. See Millender 1996, 371–3.

Bibliography

Alexiou, M.

1974 *The Ritual Lament in Greek Tradition*, Cambridge.

Andrewes, A.

1954 *Probouleusis: Sparta's contribution to the technique of government*, Oxford.

1956 *The Greek Tyrants*, London.

1966 'The government of classical Sparta', in E. Badian (ed.) *Ancient Society and Institutions: Studies presented to V. Ehrenberg on his 75th birthday*, Oxford, 1–20.

Arieti, J.A.

1995 *Discourses on the First Book of Herodotus*, Lanham, London, and New York.

Asad, T.
1986 'The concept of cultural translation in British social anthropology', in J. Clifford and G.E. Marcus (eds.) *Writing Culture: The poetics and politics of ethnography*, Berkeley, 141–64.
Asheri, D.
1990 'Herodotus on Thracian society and history', in O. Reverdin (ed.) *Hérodote et les peuples non grecs: neuf exposés suivis des discussions par Walter Burkert et al.*, Fondation Hardt, 35 (Geneva), 131–63.
Asheri, D. (ed.)
1988 *Erodoto, Le Storie, Libro I*, testo e commento, Milan.
Asheri, D. and Medaglia, S. M. (eds.)
1990 *Erodoto, Le Storie, Libro III*, testo e commento, Milan.
Benardete, S.
1969 *Herodotean Inquiries*, The Hague.
Berve, H.
1967 *Die Tyrannis bei den Griechen*, 2 vols., Munich.
Bichler, R.
1985 'Die "Reichsträume" bei Herodot: Eine Studie zu Herodots schöpferischer Leistung und ihre quellenkritische Konsequenz', *Chiron* 15, 125–47.
Bleicken, J.
1979 'Zur Entstehung der Verfassungstypologie im 5. Jahrhundert v. Chr. (Monarchie, Aristocratie, Demokratie)', *Historia* 28, 148–72.
Boedeker, D.
1987 'The two faces of Demaratus', in D. Boedeker (ed.) *Herodotus and the Invention of History, Arethusa* 20, 185–207.
Bradford, A.S.
1994 'The duplicitous Spartan', in A. Powell and S. Hodkinson (eds.) *The Shadow of Sparta*, London and New York, 59–85.
Brown, T.
1982 'Herodotus' portrait of Cambyses', *Historia* 31, 387–403.
Carlier, P.
1977 'La vie politique à Sparte sous le règne de Cléomene 1er: essai d'interprétation', *Ktema* 2, 65–84.
1984 *La Royauté en Grèce avant Alexandre*, Strasbourg.
Cartledge, P.
1976a 'A new fifth-century Spartan treaty', *LCM* 1, 87–92.
1976b 'Did Spartan citizens ever practise a manual *tekhne*?', *LCM* 1, 115–19.
1979 *Sparta and Lakonia: A regional history 1300–362 BC*, London.
1987 *Agesilaos and the Crisis of Sparta*, London.
1990 'Herodotus and "the other": a meditation on empire', *EMC/CV* 34, n. s. 9, 27–40.
Cawkwell, G.
1993 'Cleomenes', *Mnemosyne* 46, 506–27.
Clifford, J.
1986 'On ethnographic allegory', in J. Clifford and G.E. Marcus (eds.) *Writing*

Culture: The poetics and politics of ethnography, Berkeley, 98–121.
Cloché, P.
1949 'Sur le rôle des rois de Sparte', *LEC* 17, 113–38, 343–81.
Cole, E.E.
1912 'The Samos of Herodotus', Diss., Yale University.
Cook, R. M.
1962 'Spartan history and archaeology', *CQ* n.s. 12, 156–8.
Cragg, K.M.
1976 'Herodotus' presentation of Sparta', Diss., University of Michigan.
Crapanzo, V.
1986 'Hermes' dilemma: the masking of subversion in ethnographic description', in J. Clifford and G.E. Marcus (eds.) *Writing Culture: The poetics and politics of ethnography*, Berkeley, 51–76.
Davie, J.N.
1979 'Herodotus on monarchy', *G&R* 26, 160–8.
de Ste Croix, G.E.M.
1972 *The Origins of the Peloponnesian War*, London.
Den Boer, W.
1954 *Laconian Studies*, Amsterdam.
Devereaux, G.
1995 *Cléomène le roi fou*, Aubier.
Drews, R.
1983 *Basileus: The evidence for kingship in Geometric Greece*, New Haven and London.
Dunbabin, T.J.
1948 *The Western Greeks: The history of Sicily and south Italy from the foundation of the Greek colonies to 480 BC*, Oxford.
Eddy, S.K.
1973 'The cold war between Athens and Persia, 448–412 BC', *CP* 68, 241–58.
Ehrenberg, V.
1950 'The origins of democracy', *Historia* 1, 515–48.
Else, G.F.
1977 'Ritual and drama in Aischyleian tragedy', *ICS* 2, 70–87.
Evans, J.A.S.
1979 'Herodotus and Athens: the evidence of the encomium', *AC* 48, 112–18.
1981 'Notes on the debate of the Persian grandees in Herodotus 3.80–82', *QUCC* 7, 9–84.
1982 *Herodotus*, Boston.
1991 *Herodotus, Explorer of the Past*, Princeton.
Ferrill, A.
1978 'Herodotus on tyranny', *Historia* 27, 385–98.
Finley, M.I.
1968 'Sparta', in J.-P. Vernant (ed.) *Problèmes de la guerre en Grèce ancienne*, Paris, 143–60. Reprinted in B.D. Shaw and R.P. Saller (eds.) *Economy*

and Society in Ancient Greece, London, 1981, 24–40; and *The Use and Abuse of History*, 2nd edn, London, 1986, 161–78.

Fisher, N.R.E.
1992 *Hybris: A study in the values of honour and shame in ancient Greece*, Warminster.

Fitzhardinge, L.F.
1980 *The Spartans*, London.

Flory, S.
1987 *The Archaic Smile of Herodotus*, Detroit.

Fontenrose, J.
1978 *The Delphic Oracle: Its responses and operations with a catalogue of responses*, Berkeley.

Fornara, C.
1971a 'Evidence for the date of Herodotus' publication', *JHS* 91, 25–34.
1971b *Herodotus: An interpretative essay*, Oxford.

Forrest, W.G.
1980 *A History of Sparta 950–192 BC*, 2nd edn, London.
1984 'Herodotus and Athens', *Phoenix* 38, 1–11.

Forsdyke, S.
1999 'From aristocratic to democratic ideology and back again: the Thrasybulus anecdote in Herodotus' *Histories* and Aristotle's *Politics*', *CP* 94, 361–72.
2001 'Athenian democratic ideology and Herodotus' *Histories*', *AJP* 122, 329–58.

Gammie, J.
1986 'Herodotus on kings and tyrants: objective historiography or conventional portraiture?', *JNES* 45, 171–95.

Garland, R.
1981 'Greek attitudes and observances in regard to death', Diss., Univ. of London.
1985 *The Greek Way of Death*, Ithaca.

Gigante, M.
1956 *Nomos Basileus*, Naples.

Giorgini, G.
1993 *La città e il tiranno: il concetto di tirannide nella Grecia del VII–IV secolo a. c.*, Milan.

Gomme, A.W., Andrewes, A. and Dover, K.J.
1945–81 *A Historical Commentary on Thucydides*, 5 vols., Oxford.

Graf, D.F.
1985 'Greek tyrants and Achaemenid politics', in J.W. Eadie and J. Ober (eds.) *The Craft of the Ancient Historian: Essays in honor of Chester G. Starr*, Lanham, London, and New York, 79–123.

Gray, V.
1995 'Herodotus and the rhetoric of otherness', *AJP* 116, 185–211.
1996 'Herodotus and images of tyranny: the tyrants of Corinth', *AJP* 117, 361–89.

Griffith, G.T.
1966 'Isegoria in the assembly at Athens', in E. Badian (ed.) *Ancient Society and Institutions: Studies presented to Victor Ehrenberg on his 75th birthday*, Oxford, 115–38.

Griffiths, A.
1989 'Was Kleomenes mad?', in A. Powell (ed.) *Classical Sparta: Techniques behind her success*, London, 51–78.

Hall, E.
1989 *Inventing the Barbarian: Greek self-definition through tragedy*, Oxford.

Hartog, F.
1982 'La mort de l'autre: les funérailles des rois scythes', in G. Gnoli and J.-P. Vernant (eds.) *La mort, les morts dans les sociétés anciennes*, Cambridge, 143–54.
1988 *The Mirror of Herodotus: The representation of the other in the writing of history*, trans. J. Lloyd, Berkeley.

Harvey, F.D.
1979 'Leonidas the regicide? Speculations on the death of Kleomenes I', in G.W. Bowersock, W. Burkert, and M.C.J. Putnam (eds.) *Arktouros: Hellenic studies presented to Bernard M. W. Knox on the occasion of his 65th birthday*, Berlin, 253–60.

Hirst, G.M.
1938 'Herodotus on tyranny versus Athens and democracy (a study of book III of Herodotus' History)', in *Collected Papers*, Oxford, 97–110.

Hodkinson, S.
2000 *Property and Wealth in Classical Sparta*, London.

Holladay, A.J. and Goodman, M.D.
1986 'Religious scruples in ancient warfare', *CQ* n.s. 36, 151–71.

Hornblower, S.
1982 *Mausolus*, Oxford and New York.

How, W.W. and Wells, J.
1928 *A Commentary on Herodotus*, 2 vols., Oxford.

Humphreys, S.
1983 *The Family, Women, and Death*, London.
1987 'Law, custom and culture in Herodotus', in D. Boedeker (ed.) *Herodotus and the Invention of History*, *Arethusa* 20, 211–20.

Immerwahr, H.R.
1966 *Form and Thought in Herodotus*, Cleveland.

Jacoby, F.
1913 'Herodot', *RE* suppl. 2, 205–520.

Jeffery, L.H.
1976 *Archaic Greece: The city-states c. 700–500 BC*, London.

Johnson, W.A.
1994 'Oral performance and the composition of Herodotus' Histories', *GRBS* 35, 229–54.

Klein, S.C.
1973 'Cleomenes: A study in early Spartan imperialism', Diss., Univ. of Kansas.

Konstan, D.
1983 'The stories in Herodotus' Histories: Book I', *Helios* 10, 1–22.
Lang, M.L.
1944 'Biographical patterns of folklore and morality in Herodotus' *History*', Diss., Bryn Mawr.
Lanza, D.
1977 *Il tiranno e il suo pubblico*, Turin.
Larsen, J.A.O.
1948 'Cleisthenes and the development of the theory of democracy at Athens', in M.R. Konvitz and A.E. Murphy (eds.) *Essays in Political Theory Presented to George H. Sabine*, Ithaca, 1–16.
Lateiner, D.
1984 'Herodotus' historical patterning: "The constitutional debate"', *QS* 20, 257–84.
1985a 'Limit, propriety, and transgression in the Histories of Herodotus', in M.H. Jameson (ed.) *The Greek Historians: Literature and history, papers presented to A. E. Raubitschek*, Saratoga, 87–100.
1985b 'Polarità: il principio della differenza complementare', *QS* 22, 79–103.
1987 'Nonverbal communication in the *Histories* of Herodotus', in D. Boedeker (ed.) *Herodotus and the Invention of History, Arethusa* 20, 83–119.
1989 *The Historical Method of Herodotus, Phoenix*, suppl. 23, Toronto, Buffalo, and London.
Laurot, B.
1981 'Idéaux grecs et barbarie chez Hérodote', *Ktema* 6, 39–48.
Lefkowitz, M.
1981 *The Lives of the Greek Poets*, London and Baltimore.
Lévi-Strauss, C.
1966 *The Savage Mind*, London.
Lévy, E.
1993 '*Basileus* et *turannos* chez Hérodote', *Ktema* 18, 7–18.
1999 'La Sparte d' Hérodote', *Ktema* 24, 123–34.
Lewis, D.M.
1977 *Sparta and Persia*, Leiden.
Lloyd, A.B.
1990 'Herodotus on Egyptians and Lydians', in O. Reverdin (ed.) *Hérodote et les peuples non grecs: neuf exposés suivis des discussions par Walter Burkert et al.*, Fondation Hardt, 35 (Geneva), 215–44.
Lloyd, G.R.E.
1966 *Polarity and Analogy: Two types of argumentation in early Greek thought*, Cambridge.
Loraux, N.
1986 *The Invention of Athens: The funeral oration in the classical city*, trans. A. Sheridan, Cambridge, Mass., and London.
Macan, R.W.
1895 *Herodotus: The fourth, fifth and sixth books*, 2 vols., London.

Merkelbach, R.
1957 'Sappho und ihr Kreis', *Philologus* 101, 1–29.
Meyer, E.
1899 *Forschungen zur alten Geschichte*, vol. 2, Halle.
Millender, E.G.
1996 '"The teacher of Hellas": Athenian democratic ideology and the "barbarization" of Sparta in fifth-century Greek thought', Diss., University of Pennsylvania.
1999 'Athenian ideology and the empowered Spartan woman', in S. Hodkinson and A. Powell (eds.) *Sparta: New perspectives*, London, 355–91.
2001 'Spartan literacy revisited', *ClAnt* 20, 121–64.
2002 'Νόμος Δεσπότης: Spartan obedience and Athenian lawfulness in fifth-century Greek thought', in E. Robinson and V. Gorman (eds.) *Oikistes: Studies in constitutions, colonies, and military power in the ancient world offered in honor of A.J. Graham*, Leiden, 33–59.
Mitchell, B.M.
1975 'Herodotus and Samos', *JHS* 95, 75–91.
Momigliano, A.
1978 'The historians of the classical world and their audiences: some suggestions', *ASNP* Series 3, 8.59–75.
1979 'Persian empire and Greek freedom', in A. Ryan (ed.) *The Idea of Freedom: Essays in honour of Isaiah Berlin*, Oxford, 139–51.
Munson, R.
1988 'Artemisia in Herodotus', *ClAnt* 7, 91–106.
1991 'The madness of Cambyses (Herodotus 3.16–38)', *Arethusa* 24, 43–65.
1993 'Three aspects of Spartan kingship in Herodotus', in R.M. Rosen and J. Farrell (eds.) *Nomodeiktes: Greek studies in honor of Martin Ostwald*, Ann Arbor, 39–54.
Murray, O.
1980 *Early Greece*, London.
1987 'Herodotus and oral history', in H. Sancisi-Weerdenberg and A. Kuhrt (eds.) *Achaemenid History, vol. 2, The Greek Sources*, Leiden, 93–115.
Myers, J.L.
1953 *Herodotus, Father of History*, Oxford.
Nafissi, M.
1991 *La Nascita del Kosmos: Studi sulla storia e la società di Sparta*, Naples.
Nakategawa, Y.
1988 'Isegoria in Herodotus', *Historia* 37, 257–75.
Oost, S.I.
1972 'Cypselus the Bacchiad', *CP* 67, 10–30.
1974 'Two notes on the Orthagorids of Sicyon', *CP* 69, 118–20.
1976 'The tyrant kings of Syracuse', *CP* 72, 224–36.
Ostwald, M.
1969 *Nomos and the Beginnings of the Athenian Democracy*, Oxford.
1972 'Isokratia as a political concept (Herodotus 5.92α1)', in S.M. Stern,

A. Hourani, and V. Brown (eds.) *Islamic Philosophy and the Classical Tradition: Essays presented by his friends and pupils to Richard Walzer on his seventieth birthday*, Oxford, 277–91.
1986 *From Popular Sovereignty to the Sovereignty of Law: Law, society and politics in fifth-century Athens*, Berkeley.
1991 'Herodotus and Athens', *ICS* 16, 137–48.

Parker, R.
1989 'Spartan religion', in A. Powell (ed.) *Classical Sparta: Techniques behind her success*, London, 142–72.

Pembroke, S.
1967 'Women in charge: the function of alternatives in early Greek tradition and the ancient idea of matriarchy', *JWI* 30, 1–35.

Podlecki, A.J.
1977 'Herodotus in Athens?' in K.H. Kinzl (ed.) *Greece and the Early Mediterranean in Ancient History and Prehistory: Studies presented to Fritz Schachermeyer on the occasion of his 80th birthday*, Berlin, 246–65.

Raaflaub, K.A.
1983 'Democracy, oligarchy, and the concept of the "free citizen" in late fifth-century Athens', *Political Theory* 11, 517–44.
1987 'Herodotus, political thought, and the meaning of history', in D. Boedeker (ed.) *Herodotus and the Invention of History*, *Arethusa* 20, 221–48.

Rawson, E.
1969 *The Spartan Tradition in European Thought*, Oxford.

Redfield, J.
1985 'Herodotus the tourist', *CP* 80, 97–118.

Reiner, E.
1938 *Die rituelle Totenklage der Griechen*, Stuttgart and Berlin.

Richer, N.
1994 'Aspects des funérailles à Sparte', *Cahiers du Centre Gustave-Glotz* 5, 51–96.
1998 *Les Éphores: Études sur l'histoire et sur l'image de Sparte (VIIIe–IIIe siècles avant Jésus-Christ)*, Paris.

Ridley, R.T.
1974 'The economic activities of the perioikoi', *Mnemosyne* 27, 281–92.

Robinson, E.W.
1992 'Oracles and Spartan religious scruples', *LCM* 17.9, 131–2.
1994 'Reexamining the Alcmaeonid role in the liberation of Athens', *Historia* 43, 363–9.

Rosellini, M. and Saïd, S.
1978 'Usages des femmes et autres nomoi chez les "sauvages" d'Hérodote: essai de lecture structurale', *ASNP* Series 3, 8.949–1005.

Said, E.
1978 *Orientalism*, London.

Scott, W.C.
1984 *Musical Design in Aeschylean Theater*, Hanover, New Hampshire.

Sealey, R.
1974 'The origins of demokratia', *ClAnt* 6, 253–95.
Steiner, D.
1994 *The Tyrant's Writ: Myths and images of writing in ancient Greece*, Princeton.
Strasburger, H.
1955 'Herodot und das perikleische Athen', *Historia* 4, 1–25.
Thomas, C.G.
1974 'On the role of the Spartan kings', *Historia* 23, 257–70.
Thomas, R.
1989 *Oral Tradition and Written Record in Classical Athens*, Cambridge.
2000 *Herodotus in Context: Ethnography, science and the art of persuasion*, Cambridge.
Thommen, L.
1996 *Lakedaimonion Politeia. Die Entstehung der spartanischen Verfassung*, Stuttgart.
Tigerstedt, E.N.
1965–78 *The Legend of Sparta in Classical Antiquity*, 3 vols., Stockholm.
Tölle-Kastenbein, R.
1976 *Herodot und Samos*, Bochum.
Vansina, J.
1973 *Oral Tradition: A study in historical methodology*, Harmondsworth.
1985 *Oral Tradition as History*, London and Nairobi.
Vlastos, G.
1953 '*Isonomia*', *AJP* 74, 337–66.
1964 'Isonomia politike', in J. Mau and E.G. Schmidt (eds.) *Isonomia: Studien zur Gleichheitsvorstellung im griechischen Denken*, Berlin, 1–35.
von Fritz, K.
1967 *Die griechische Geschichtsschreibung*, vol. 1, Berlin.
Waters, K.H.
1971 *Herodotus on Tyrants and Despots: A study in objectivity*, *Historia Einzelschrift* 15, Wiesbaden.
1972 'Herodotus and politics', *G&R* 19, 136–50.
1985 *Herodotus the Historian: His problems, methods and originality*, Norman, Okla.
Weber, M.
1978 *Economy and Society: An outline of interpretive sociology*, 2 vols., G. Roth and C. Wittich (eds.) Berkeley, Los Angeles, and London.
White, H.
1978 *Tropics of Discourse: Essays in cultural criticism*, Baltimore.
Wolff, E.
1964 'Das Weib des Masistes', *Hermes* 92, 51–8.
Woodhead, A.G.
1967 'Ισηγορία and the council of 500', *Historia* 16, 129–40.
Wüst, K.
1935 'Politisches Denken bei Herodot', Diss., Munich.

2

SPARTAN *ATĒ* AT THERMOPYLAE? SEMANTICS AND IDEOLOGY AT HERODOTUS, *HISTORIES* 7.223.4

Michael Clarke

As I write this article the Afghan phase of America's 'War on Terror' seems to be nearing an end. For the second time – arguably the third, if the Gulf War is included – the world's major power has achieved victory by following a strategy designed to avoid the death in combat of a single member of its own armed forces. The strangeness of this policy is heightened by contrast with the deliberate acceptance of self-destruction by the men whose actions on September 11th sparked off the war. Since that day a fundamental question has been posed about the ethics of human conflict, a question that would have seemed merely theoretical a year ago: is it the act of a brave man or a fool to throw away one's own life for a cause, be it vengeance or sheer defiance of an enemy? For the few in the Western media who tried to explain the terrorists' willingness to die, it was possible to talk only in terms of brainwashing: the Darwinist Richard Dawkins, for example, compared "the afterlife-obsessed suicidal brain" to a pigeon tricked by repeated food rewards into guiding a missile to its target by pecking at its image on a screen.[1] That such things were written is a measure not only of people's horror and anger at the deaths of innocents, but also of the strength of the contemporary consensus that deliberate self-sacrifice is unnatural and grotesque, the result of madness rather than heroism.

It is strange to consider the gulf that divides this norm from the founding ideals of many of the states in which we live. In my own country, Ireland, it is only in the last few years that a new political mood has allowed us to leave behind the iconography of suicidal rebellions, hunger-strikes, and martyrdoms on the scaffold. In Ireland and throughout Europe the imagery and ideology of militant nationalism was articulated in its clearest form in the nineteenth century, and among its most powerful sources of validation was the paradigm of the ancient Greeks' defiance of Persia. I quote from the best-known of Ireland's nationalistic anthems, which was taught to schoolchildren up to my own generation:

> When boyhood's fire was in my blood
>   I read of ancient freemen,
> For Greece and Rome who bravely stood
>   THREE HUNDRED MEN and THREE MEN:
> And then I prayed I yet might see
>   Our fetters rent in twain,
> And Ireland, long a province, be
>   A NATION ONCE AGAIN!

Today these words may sound quaint or even absurd, but they reflect a deeply serious ideological programme: the song's author, Thomas Davis (1814–45), was one of the foremost intellects behind the doctrine of military and cultural resistance that led eventually to the achievement of independence from Britain. Few of those who learnt the song would have recognized the 'THREE MEN' as Horatius and his companions on the bridge, although Macaulay's *Lay of Horatius* endured long as a set text for twelve-year-olds; but very many, I guess, would have understood that the 'THREE HUNDRED MEN' were the Spartans who died with Leonidas in the straits of Thermopylae. For Davis and his successors, Thermopylae not only provided high cultural authority for militant nationalism but also mirrored the exploits of the heroes of native Irish tradition, who took their stand 'in the gap of danger'[2] to lay down their lives rather than submit to an imperialist aggressor. *A Nation Once Again* stands among countless tokens of the power that the 'heroic and extraordinary deeds'[3] of the Three Hundred have held in the international mythology of European patriotism, as an enactment for the principle that a man should choose death rather than accept the loss of freedom.[4]

To use Thermopylae in this way, as proof of the doctrine that 'from the graves of patriot men and women spring living nations',[5] was in part to re-invent the Greek conception that those who die for their country in battle achieve the same status as is accorded to the heroes of myth. Simonides depicted the fame of the dead of Thermopylae in such terms in a choral song, which was probably composed soon after the event and sung thereafter by the men of Sparta:[6]

> τῶν ἐν Θερμοπύλαις θανόντων
> εὐκλεὴς μὲν ἁ τύχα, καλὸς δ' ὁ πότμος,
> βωμὸς δ' ὁ τάφος, πρὸ γόων δὲ μνᾶστις, ὁ δ' οἶκτος ἔπαινος·
> ἐντάφιον δὲ τοιοῦτον οὔτ' εὐρὼς
> οὔθ' ὁ πανδαμάτωρ ἀμαυρώσει χρόνος. (fr. 531 *PMG*)

Those who died at Thermopylae met with a glorious chance and a beautiful death; their tomb is an altar; in place of wailing they have remembrance, and their lamentation is praise. Neither decay nor all-subduing time can obscure such a burial-song [funeral-gift? shroud?].

The glory of the fallen is evoked in terms that closely recall the ideology of Homer's heroes, for whom courage is bound up with an aspiration to the surrogate immortality that results from eternal fame (see e.g. *Il.* 12.310–21). This principle was enshrined in the poetry of Tyrtaeus (see esp. fr. 12.31–2 West)[7] and recurs, for example, in the recasting of Homeric imagery in the surviving fragments of Simonides' elegiac celebration of the victories at Artemisium and Plataea (see esp. fr. 11W).[8] The cults established for the dead of Plataea and Marathon,[9] and the rhetorical set-pieces that portrayed the dead of the Persian Wars as immortalized heroes (e.g. Isocrates, *Panegyricus* 84 ff.), testify to the prevalence of this theme in panhellenic culture: 'a beautiful death is the greatest reward of virtue'.[10] On the face of it, Thermopylae seems to present an unproblematic, if extreme, example of the practical acting-out of that ideal; but I hope to be able to show that the reality is more complex, and that the potential for a rejectionist response to the deeds of the Three Hundred was already present in Greek and even in Spartan thought in the fifth century BC. Despite the phrase 'their tomb is an altar' in the Simonides fragment quoted above, it is remarkable that the evidence suggests that the Three Hundred were never heroized as a group, as were those who fell at Plataea and Marathon.[11] Starting from this clue, my aim is to explore the implications of two hard words in Herodotus in order to suggest that doubt or ambivalence about the 'glorious chance' is already a reality for the author of our earliest surviving account of the battle, and that this ambivalence hinges on the difference between the causal logic of Leonidas' own self-sacrifice and that of his followers – a factor which, so far as I know, has been obscured in modern patriotic images of Thermopylae as well as in scholarly literature on the subject.

It is almost a truism among scholars that fifth-century warfare was characterized by an intense awareness of Homeric models, both in the real-life battlefield and in the thinking of intellectuals like Herodotus. On the one hand, Homer's educational authority seems to have provided soldiers and generals with their practical ideals, so that 'as the spiritual descendants of Homeric chieftains, *strategoi* felt the burdens of the heroic ethos';[12] on the other, it is familiar that Herodotus' narrative of Thermopylae is infused with elements of the 'Homeric spirit', including close verbal and thematic echoes,[13] so that his account of the Spartans' last stand begs to be seen as an enactment of the inherited ideal. As Immerwahr puts it,

The heroism of Leonidas and the Spartans stands out as an example of courage such as exists only in death, and Herodotus adds a few Homeric touches to his narrative, since the Homeric hero is the prime representative of absolute standards of value, exceeding the standards of the *polis* with its requirements of valour.[14]

But is the relationship between Herodotus and Homer really so simple and straightforward? Here is Herodotus describing how the Three Hundred, betrayed and encircled by the Persians' flanking movement, fought to the death against their foes:

> The Greeks around Leonidas, as if making their final journey to death, went much further than before towards the narrowest part of the pass... Being aware of the death that was coming to them from those who were going around the mountain, they showed forth the greatest strength they had against the barbarians, *parachreōmenoi* and *ateontes*. The spears of most of them were broken by now, but they fought on with their swords against the Persians... (7.223.4).

I have left the participles *parachreōmenoi* and *ateontes* in Greek, because they are difficult and repay careful consideration in turn.[15] The verb *parachraomai*, like many compounds in *para-*,[16] often has a sinister or negative connotation, meaning to 'misuse' or 'abuse' something.[17] Herodotus applies it to the action of one who disregards a command or a prophetic utterance (1.108.4; 8.20.1) or one who treats his own followers with foolish contempt that leads to disaster (2.141.1; cf. 5.92a2). In the Thermopylae passage it appears without a direct object, and it is particularly instructive to compare the one other instance where Herodotus uses it in this way (4.159.6). There it refers to soldiers throwing their lives away in folly: the Egyptians allowed themselves to be slaughtered by the Cyrenaeans 'because they attacked them like men who were ignorant about how to fight Greeks, *parachreōmenoi*': 'heedless', 'regardless', abandoning prudence and circumspection. The close verbal parallel suggests that in the Thermopylae passage something negative is being said about the Spartiates' behaviour, that they were ignorant or foolish in allowing themselves to be killed.

So far, this is merely a hint: but in the second participle the tone of condemnation becomes unmistakable. The verb *ateō* is extremely rare: it occurs nowhere else in prose and only once in earlier literature, in the twentieth book of the *Iliad*.[18] Whether or not Herodotus is deliberately echoing this passage, it offers the only reliable model for interpreting his use of the word. Apollo in disguise has cajoled Aineias into pitting himself against Achilles (20.79–85), and Aineias is foolish enough (*nēpios*, 264, 296) to believe that he has a chance of success. Poseidon descends to the battlefield to rescue him, and after whisking him away to safety he admonishes him against trying to face one so far beyond his strength:

> Αἰνεία, τίς σ' ὧδε θεῶν ἀτέοντα κελεύει
> ἀντία Πηλεΐωνος ὑπερθύμοιο μάχεσθαι,
> ὃς σεῦ ἅμα κρείσσων καὶ φίλτερος ἀθανάτοισιν;
> (*Il.* 20.332–4)

Aineias, which of the gods commanded you, *ateōn* as you were [*or* who commanded you, so *ateōn* against the gods][19] to stand and fight against overspirited Achilles, who is at once stronger than you and dearer to the immortals?

From the context alone, our word seems to refer to recklessness or folly; and this makes it irresistible to take *ateō* as a derivative of the noun *atē*, an interpretation that goes back to ancient scholarship.[20] Here we must be careful. As a matter of principle, when a verb is built on the stem of a noun its meaning will be determined by the most fundamental or prototypical sense of the noun, rather than by its connotations or its potential for poetic elaboration. However, understanding of *atē* as a word and as a concept has often been distorted by the fact that it looms large in the conflict between Achilles and Agamemnon in the *Iliad*, with two key speeches revolving around highly-wrought rhetorical depictions of Atē personified as a daughter and agent of Zeus on the cosmic level (Phoenix, 9.502–14; Agamemnon, 19.86–139).[21] Her role in these speeches is to bring ruin and destruction on her victims, either as an actor in the cycle of Zeus' punishment of wrong-doers or as a wayward meddler in the thoughts of both gods and mortals. Because of the literary prominence of these speeches, translators and commentators have tended to treat *atē* as a rather mystical concept, rendering it as divinely-inspired 'ruin', 'delusion', 'blinding'.[22] None of these translations adequately mirrors the range of ways in which Homer uses the word outside the two rhetorical passages, and it is plainly unsatisfactory to collapse two such creative (and probably anti-traditional) discourses into the word's basic definition. This can only be established if we set aside the creative articulations and focus instead on more straightforward instances of the word's application.

Briefly: *atē* is the appropriate word when Homer or a character refers with disapproval to such things as the behaviour of Achilles and Agamemnon in their quarrel (19.270–5), or Paris' action in bringing Helen to Troy (6.356), or Patroclus' when he physically and emotionally collapses after trying to assail Troy on his own (16.805). Similarly it names the act or experience of a man who kills a kinsman and is exiled from his people (24.480); Agamemnon regards himself as subject to *atē* when he says that the other Achaeans have failed to fulfil their promise to fight bravely for him (8.237), or that Zeus has failed in his promise to give him victory at Troy (2.111=9.18); Dolon believes that Hector misled him by or into many *atai* when he tricked him into going on a ruinously dangerous night expedition into enemy territory (10.391). From this range of uses a simple but precise definition emerges: *atē* is behaviour or thought that involves harm to oneself, whether originating in manipulation by someone else or in one's own wrong thinking. The latter especially is liable to seem an extraordinary phenomenon, the sort of thing that later seems like folly or madness; and it is typical of such a force, mysterious and destructive in its power, that it can be explained by skilled speakers (like Phoenix and Agamemnon) as a divine being originating with Zeus. Now the psychological basis of such behaviour is commonly seen in negative terms, as a taking away of mental substance: thus one of the ways Agamemnon describes his *atē* is by saying that Zeus 'took away his *phrenes*', deprived him of his wits or the stuff of his consciousness (19.137). In this context we can be further guided by the curious fact that *atē* also appears in archaic legal language with the meaning of a monetary fine, to be paid over as compensation to the wronged party in disputes over such matters as inheritance or the management of real estate. The word is found in this sense in several areas of Greece, most famously in the Law Code of Gortyn[23] but also in Laconia and Pamphylia.[24] It is certain that the two senses of the word go back to a single original meaning in Bronze Age Greek;[25] there should, then, be some common factor between the two, representing the original focus of meaning from which both are derived. It is easy to see that the common factor is the idea of *taking something away*:[26] the one who is subjected to the fine must give up a sum of money, and in Homer the person whose breast is emptied of the 'breath of thought' becomes witless, foolish and incapable of rational behaviour.[27] This, then, is the fundamental meaning of *atē* and the semantic core of the derived verb *ateō*. We can at last return to Poseidon's words to Aineias: when the god wants to dissuade him from a reckless combat against impossible odds, he tells him that he has been behaving as one who is deprived of mental substance and is, in effect, self-destructively insane. Unless we fall into special pleading, we must conclude that Herodotus is describing the Spartiates' impulse towards death in terms of the same psychological phenomenon.

So stated, this runs counter to our usual expectations about the ancient reputation of Sparta and about Herodotus' response to it. The route to a solution, I suggest, begins with the fact that Thermopylae was strategically of little help to the defence of Greece. Since the action delayed the Persians for a few days and no more, and attempts to explain the action in terms of practical military advantage have yielded no convincing results,[28] the commonsense modern solution is to explain the Spartans' act in terms of its propaganda value, as a demonstration of the reality of their discipline under their devotion to the Law, which they feared more than the Persians, driven into battle under the cracking whips of overseers (Hdt. 7.223.3, etc.), could ever fear their king. In J.T. Hooker's words, 'No matter that the occasion was a resounding defeat: the system [sc. of Spartan military discipline] was fully vindicated by a Spartan army, and a Spartan king, at Thermopylae.'[29] But if one reads Herodotus straight, within the narrative context the motivating factor is entirely different. Explaining why Leonidas sent away most of the allies but could not retreat himself, Herodotus says that by remaining Leonidas won great fame (*kleos*) and 'the prosperity (or 'blessedness', *eudaimoniē*) of Sparta was not wiped away (*exēleipheto*)' (7.220.2). He explains this strange statement by citing the prophecy that the Delphic Oracle gave to Sparta before the war:

> ὑμῖν δ', ὦ Σπάρτης οἰκήτορες εὐρυχόροιο,
> ἢ μέγα ἄστυ ἐρικυδὲς ὑπ' ἀνδράσι Περσεΐδῃσι
> πέρθεται, ἢ τὸ μὲν οὐχί, ἀφ' Ἡρακλέου δὲ γενέθλης
> πενθήσει βασιλῆ φθίμενον Λακεδαίμονος οὖρος.
> οὐ γὰρ τὸν ταύρων σχήσει μένος οὐδὲ λεόντων
> ἀντιβίην· Ζηνὸς γὰρ ἔχει μένος· οὐδέ ἕ φημι
> σχήσεσθαι, πρὶν τῶνδ' ἕτερον διὰ πάντα δάσηται.
> (7.220.4)

As for you, O people of Sparta of the broad dancing-floors, either your great and glorious city will be sacked by men of Perseus' race, or else this will not happen, but the land of Lakedaimon will mourn the death of a king of Heracles' race; for the strength neither of bulls nor lions will restrain him, force pitted against force; for he has the force of Zeus; and I say that he will not be restrained, before he takes one of these two choices/destroys one of the two.

I will not speculate about whether this prophecy was forged after the event,[30] nor about what its precise original meaning may have been if it is genuine.[31] It is enough that Herodotus, with his general trust in oracular prophecy and Delphi in particular,[32] believes it and cites it to explain why Leonidas had to act as he did: the death of a Heraclid king[33] in battle was demanded as a substitute for the destruction of his country. The prophecy reflects an ancient mythical pattern, whereby the land is threatened with disaster – usually invasion – and can be saved only by the ritualized death of a member of the royal family.[34] Like much of the sacral lore of Greek kingship, such myths are comparatively poorly attested in the documents that have come down to us: our principal source is their enactment or recreation on the tragic stage by Euripides, who was evidently exploring one of the stranger byways of traditional lore through myths associated with human sacrifice.[35] The clearest examples are the killing of the king's daughter in the *Erechtheus* and the self-sacrifice of Menoikeus in the *Phoenissae*.[36] Erechtheus is driven to sacrifice his daughter when the Delphic oracle reveals that this is the only way to ensure victory against the invaders (see esp. frr. 360, 362 Nauck). In the *Phoenissae*, Teiresias announces a prophecy that only Menoikeus' death will save the city from destruction by the Seven; the boy tricks his horrified father into thinking that he is about to escape into hiding, and then hurls himself from the topmost pinnacle (834–1018). It is idle to ask whether these particular examples are inventions by Euripides or old stories that had been half-forgotten by the Athenian public before he revived them;[37] what matters is that this mythical pattern was still meaningful in the fifth century, even in a city where kingship was all but abolished.

The plot thickens when we look beyond tragedy to the half-submerged myths recorded by the early historians. From Hellanicus there survives the outline of an intriguing story of one of the legendary kings of Athens:

> The Dorians made war on the Athenians, and the god prophesied to the Dorians that they would capture Athens, unless they killed Kodros the king. Kodros learnt this, so he dressed himself in cheap clothes like a woodcutter and took a sickle, and he went to the palisade of the enemy camp. Two of the enemy met him: he hit one of them and smote him down, but the other, not knowing who he was, struck him down and killed him.[38]

When we map this strange story onto that of Leonidas and the Delphic prophecy, the two emerge as precisely parallel: there is no reason to believe that the one was modelled artificially on the other, and the two are best seen as variants or allomorphs of a single traditional paradigm.[39] Against this background in mythopoeic story-patterns, it emerges that in the Herodotean version the reasoning behind Thermopylae cuts across any question of military advantage, whether strategy or propaganda: the kernel of the whole is that the king offers himself up to death as a substitute for the destruction of his country, with the result that in due course the barbarians fail to cross the Isthmus and Lakonia is saved when Attica, for example, is ravaged. From Herodotus' point of view, the significance of this chain of cause and effect is only deepened if one points out that the real 'meaning' of Thermopylae was that it inspired the allies to similar heroism in the later engagements of the war. If the lasting result of Leonidas' death was to bring about such change of mood and so influence the future cohesion of the alliance, or merely to ensure that fewer Greek states would Medize during Xerxes' advance,[40] then the details of what happened in men's minds and acts become another example of the mysterious and unforeseen ways in which prophecies are liable to be fulfilled.

The prophecy, of course, makes no mention of the deaths of other warriors. Why did Leonidas not go out alone like Kodros? The immediate answer to this question must have lain in Spartan custom, which demanded that when the king went into battle he was to be accompanied by an elite bodyguard of precisely three hundred Spartiates.[41] The Spartiate does not retreat, he comes back with his shield or on it, and his death in battle earns him quasi-heroic funeral honours.[42] Such is the *nomos* of the Spartans, the law on which Herodotus has us meditate before Thermopylae in the dialogues between Demaratus and Xerxes (7.209), the law that was seen as so fixed and certain that the public was amazed a generation later when Spartans surrendered at Pylos in order to save themselves from certain death (Thuc. 4.40.1); and the worst disgrace of all would be earned by the warrior who abandoned the king when he had fallen in combat.[43] Here, then, lies the deepest tragedy of Thermopylae as Herodotus presents it: the demands of the oracle and the demands of Spartan law combine to place these men in a position where they must throw away their lives or suffer the disgrace and humiliation that came with the label of *tresantes*.[44] It would, of course, be a mistake to reduce Herodotus' analysis of Thermopylae to a single value-judgment. Here as elsewhere his voice refuses to be reduced to a simple, univocal message,[45] just as in his finely nuanced approach to the question whether the Athenians or the Spartans deserve the name of the saviours of Greece: even if all others had deserted them the Spartans might have stood firm and died nobly (*gennaiōs*) at the Isthmus (7.139.3), but by doing so they would have achieved little or nothing in the long run. Nonetheless, Herodotus' choice of words in our passage shows decisively that he sees the Spartiates' decision to accept death as something more problematic than an example of pure military excellence. The implementation of the patriotic ideal entails the profitless waste of the warriors' own lives, and in this sense the Spartiates are driven by their own heroic discipline into an act of reckless folly.

Although it is impossible to distinguish sharply between Herodotus' own interpretation and the thinking behind the form into which the story had already been cast by his informants, we can go some way towards tracing the ultimate provenance of this vision of what happened at Thermopylae. A narrative in which Leonidas' purpose was the mystical salvation of the land through his own death will probably have seemed exotic in fifth-century Athens, where presumably such things belonged squarely in the past; but there is every reason to think that at Sparta the deaths of kings in battle retained more of their sacral and mythical associations. Herodotus himself describes the custom of bringing the king back in effigy if he died in battle abroad, so that the effigy (*eidōlon*) could be given a funeral in the absence of his corpse (6.58.3);[46] and there is evidence that the bones of Leonidas were brought back to Sparta forty years after his death (Paus. 3.14.1),[47] perhaps because they were seen as having heroic power in a similar way to that held by the bones of Orestes, whose possession ensured the safety of Sparta in its wars (Hdt. 1.67–8).[48] All this suggests that, whether or not Herodotus' story of Leonidas' motivation is historically true, the story probably goes back to a Spartan source. Interestingly, that source or something very like it seems also to have been an influence on other early versions of the Thermopylae narrative. Although Diodorus' summary of Ephorus' lost narrative omits any mention of the Delphic prophecy, it is very likely that it figured in the original account,[49] and a version even closer than Herodotus' to the story of Kodros may well have been the original setting for Diodorus' story of Leonidas making a surprise attack on Xerxes' tent by night, as if seeking to achieve his own death as quickly as possible (11.8.5–10.3).[50] Diodorus preserves other stories that make best sense if we see the Three Hundred as caught in a trap. According to Diodorus, the Spartan ephors (like modern historians) pointed out that the force of three hundred was too small to hold the pass against the barbarians: to which he gave the secret answer 'that they were indeed few for preventing the barbarians getting through the passes, but that they were very many for the deed that they were setting out to do' (11.4.3).[51] He refused to take any except grown men with living sons, and he even tried to send away the youngest soldiers before the battle to run bogus errands, as if unwilling to throw their lives away needlessly alongside his own: the deaths of all who would stay there were assured, and on the final day 'he ordered them to prepare their breakfast quickly, saying that they were going to dine in Hades' (11.9.4). If there is heroism in these images, there is also a sense of futility and horror, with men caught in the unfolding of a sequence of events that leads inescapably to their deaths.

The significance of this articulation of the tragedy of Thermopylae will perhaps be clarified if we set it against the overall patterning of Homeric and fifth-century attitudes to military virtue. It is vital first to realize that Homer never espouses the principle that self-destruction in battle is intrinsically good or admirable.[52] This point is well illustrated by the differing responses of Homeric heroes to the extreme danger they face when isolated from their comrades in battle: the brave or foolhardy man may try to force himself to face even a challenge beyond his strength, but one can still assert that it is wisdom to withdraw when the odds are known to be impossible (see Menelaus at *Il.* 17.98–9, comparing 11.409–10, 21.568–70, 22.126–30). The extent to which Achilles welcomes his coming death exactly matches the extent to which he is gripped by beast-like savagery;[53] and even in the language of speeches there is only one passage where a character comes close to depicting death in battle as a good thing. Hector urges his men to face down the Achaeans in the battle by the ships:

> ὅς δέ κεν ὑμέων
> βλήμενος ἠὲ τυπεὶς θάνατον καὶ πότμον ἐπίσπηι,
> τεθνάτω· οὔ οἱ ἀεικὲς ἀμυνομένωι περὶ πάτρης
> τεθνάμεν· ἀλλ' ἄλοχός τε σόη καὶ παῖδες ὀπίσσω,
> καὶ οἶκος καὶ κλῆρος ἀκήρατος… (*Il.* 15.494–8)

And if any of you is struck by spear or sword and finds death, let him die: it is no shame for him to die in defence of his fatherland, for his wife and children will be safe thereafter, his household and his farm unharmed…

Here the exception proves the rule: his justification of the acceptance of death is the fact that it saves homeland and family. Even without pushing the point that Hector at this moment is deluded and dangerous as he trusts in false signs from Zeus and hastens his own death,[54] the train of thought shows that if death in battle is good it is good because of the practical benefits it achieves for those one loves. When warriors rally their comrades to stand firm against the enemy, they never say that death is to be sought, not even that death is better than disgrace – glory is a consolation for the fact that life is short, not a reason to make it even shorter than it has to be (see e.g. *Il.* 12.322–8), and Aias himself represents the fear of disgrace as a force that will lead to survival in battle as part of the quest for glory:

> ὦ φίλοι, ἀνέρες ἔστε, καὶ αἰδῶ θέσθ' ἐνὶ θυμῶι,
> ἀλλήλους τ' αἰδεῖσθε ἀνὰ κρατερὰς ὑσμίνας·
> αἰδομένων δ' ἀνδρῶν πλέονες σόοι ἠὲ πέφανται…
> (*Il.* 15.563–4)

Friends, be men, put fear-of-disgrace in your thoughts, and be abashed before each other along the forceful ranks; when men fear disgrace, more survive than are killed…

Irresistibly, this moderate and practical sense of heroic ideology leads one to think of the speaker's later failure to preserve the very doctrine he here expresses, when an inability to accept the diminution of his reputation will lead him to infatuation and suicide.

Against this background a gulf seems to yawn between Spartan ideology and the overall shaping of Greek military ethics. On this point Nicole Loraux has deftly pointed out a contrast between Spartan and other evocations of patriotic fighting:[55] where Athenian rhetoric, for example, locates heroism in the unflinching refusal to fear death,[56] at Sparta the warrior's 'beautiful death' is presented as something desirable as an end in itself. The only surviving articulation of this principle is in the poetry of Tyrtaeus, where death is battle is presented as something to be actively pursued:

> μηδ' ἀνδρῶν πληθὺν δειμαίνετε, μηδὲ φοβεῖσθε,
> ἰθὺς δ' ἐς προμάχους ἀσπίδ' ἀνὴρ ἐχέτω,
> ἐχθρὴν μὲν ψυχὴν θέμενος, θανάτου δὲ μελαίνας
> κῆρας <ὁμῶς> αὐγαῖς ἠελίοιο φίλας. (fr. 11.3–6 West)

Do not fear the press of men, do not retreat, let each man hold his shield straight against the foremost fighters, holding his own life an enemy and the black spirits of death as dear to him as the rays of the sun.

In this poetry death is presented as inherently beautiful, almost erotic (fr.10.27–30 West). We are told that Tyrtaeus' elegies were officially sanctioned for instilling idealism into Spartan soldiers,[57] and at first sight it seems as if the doctrine is simple and univocal, with Tyrtaeus' 'official' authority underlined by his careful re-evocation of Homeric themes and images. However, it is important to see that images like this are likely to have been presented as idealized hyperbole rather than as recommendations to be followed in practice. The Homeric passages reworked or alluded to by Tyrtaeus are not in the voice of the primary narrator but in the voices of his characters, producing heightened and even exaggerated ideas and images in highly wrought rhetoric. The passage cited above, for example, most closely echoes Priam's speech of self-pity at the thought of his own death (*Il.* 22.37–76) and Idomeneus' defensive answer to Meriones' suggestion that he may be a coward (*Il.* 13.275–94). Even within the surviving fragments of Tyrtaeus, the exhortation to seek death in battle is balanced by more pragmatic evocations of the warrior ideal: for example, he urges that the bravest warriors who excel in close combat will themselves 'die in fewer numbers' as well as protecting those they defend (fr. 11.11–13 W), closely recalling Aias' words cited above from the *Iliad*.[58] As with all systems of military training based on presenting young men with exaggerated models of excellence, it is possible that the inculcation of the Spartan military ideal involved a real danger of excessive literalism. According to a story about the first Messenian war preserved by Diodorus (8.27.2),[59] after listening to Tyrtaeus on the eve of battle the Spartans were filled with such enthusiasm for death that they labelled themselves with identity badges, for the convenience of those who would gather their corpses afterwards: the story chimes exactly with Herodotus' story of the Spartans combing their hair before Thermopylae in anticipation of death (7.208), and the behaviour of the Spartans in both battles can be seen as indications not of simple courage but of a warrior ethos that has been pushed beyond the limits of sanity.

The evidence collected so far is cast into sharp relief by a later episode from Herodotus' account of the war, where we gain an unusual inkling of the problematic relationship between Tyrtaean heroism and contemporary standards of excellence. Herodotus is recounting the troubles undergone by the two from among the Three Hundred who survived because they had been separated from the force before the battle took place. One of these men, Pantites, had been sent away from his comrades with a message, an echo or forerunner of the story which Diodorus represents as Leonidas' ruse to spare his men's lives. Herodotus tells us that Pantites 'was so much dishonoured (*ētimōto*) that he hanged himself' (7.232): his suicide is identical in spirit to that of Aias but perhaps involves a further twist of self-humiliation, because hanging is traditionally the way of suicide used by women, so that Pantites was symbolically acting out the loss of his claim to manhood. The other survivor, Aristodemos, who was sent home before the battle because of an eye infection, tried to cope with his shame in a way that is still more revealing. He fought again at Plataea, where in Herodotus' opinion he 'showed the greatest heroism of all' (*aristos egeneto makrōi*, 9.71.2), but when honours were awarded by the allies he was passed over:

> When a meeting was held to adjudge who had shown the greatest valour, the Spartiates present considered that although Aristodemos had performed great deeds he had done so out of a desire to be seen being killed, because of the blame that was on him, raging (*lussōnta*) and abandoning the battle-line. Poseidonios, on the other hand, had acted as a valorous man without desiring to be killed, and was thus the better of the two. But maybe they said this out of envy. All the men I have mentioned who had died in the battle were treated with honour except Aristodemos: because of his desire to be killed, Aristodemos was not honoured (9.71.3–4).

It is striking that Aristodemos' behaviour is characterized with the verb *lussaō*, derived from the sinister word *lussa*.[60] *Lussa* is one of the key Homeric words for the wild ferocity of the warrior at his most reckless, dangerous and beast-like.[61] It derives from the root meaning 'wolf',[62] and when a warrior is full of *lussa* he is fey or berserk, destructive to himself as well as others. Euripides introduces the personified Lussa to represent the madness that drove Heracles to murder his children (*Heracles* 822 ff.), and the same goddess lies behind the destruction of Pentheus in the *Bacchae* (977 ff.). Herodotus' wording seems deliberately to recall Homer, as *lussa* and its cognates are not used in classical prose except as a technical term for the disease rabies.[63] Linguistically, then, this closely resembles the earlier use of epic *ateō* for the behaviour of the Three Hundred when they throw away their lives: on a literary level, at least, Herodotus invites us to consider both instances of battle-fury in terms of the problematic aspects of Homeric heroism.

The historian distances himself from the condemnation of Aristodemos, in effect espousing the opposite of the attitude to heroic self-destruction that we saw implied in the Thermopylae passage: here as elsewhere he refuses to be pinned down to a single dogmatic voice. As often, however, the most precious information in the passage is his record of the opinion which he rejects: it was the Spartiates themselves who judged that Aristodemos' heroism was flawed because he was deliberately seeking death. Whether sincerely or not, they are able to voice a rejection of the extremist version of the Tyrtaean ideal in favour of the same sense of heroic calculus that we saw informing Aias' rallying-call in the battle by the ships in the *Iliad*: bravery need not and should not involve the reckless waste of one's own life, which is seen as an act of culpable folly. In the tension between the two passages we have a possible clue to the original context of the disapproving attitude represented by *parachreōmenoi te kai ateontes*. If the condemnation of Aristodemos' behaviour reflects an official Spartan line on needless self-destruction in battle, then it may be that Herodotus' suggestion of *atē* among the Three Hundred likewise goes back to a version of the Thermopylae story that was framed with the needs of the Spartan military machine in view. Leonidas' followers may have been glorious defenders of Greece, but their extremism was also a dangerous model for future soldiers if the object of wars was to be victory.

Lack of evidence makes it difficult to go further in trying to reconstruct the complexities of Spartan military ideology in the context of Thermopylae. Here as elsewhere we are at the mercy of our Athenocentric sources, which tend to present Spartan values and practices as monolithic and unchallenged from within,[64] and only a few stray hints like the story of Aristodemos allow us an inkling of the internal dynamics of the Spartan military system. Our view of the relationship between Homeric and Spartan ideals might be clarified if we had more of Simonides' elegies on the battles of the Persian wars, which would enable us to see at first hand how the poetry and ideology of Homeric heroism were recreated in the fifth century.[65] By way of conclusion, however, it is intriguing to speculate in this context about the most famous of all Greek memorials of Thermopylae, Simonides' epitaph for the Three Hundred themselves:

> Ὦ ξεῖν', ἀγγέλλειν Λακεδαιμονίοις ὅτι τῇδε
> κείμεθα, τοῖς κείνων ῥήμασι πειθόμενοι.
> (Epigram no. XXII Page)

I suppose we are all led to think that this is heroic understatement, perhaps deliberately modelled on the famous Spartan brevity: 'Stranger, go tell the Lakedaimonioi that we lie here, obeying their commands.' But can it also be read in another way, a way that allows one to hear a note of reproach? 'Stranger, go tell the Lakedaimonioi that this is why we died – because we obeyed their precepts.' Death is all the Three Hundred achieved by pursuing the Spartan ideal to its ultimate end, and their grave is neither marked by their names nor commemorated by such honours as were given to those who laid down their lives in pursuit of victory rather than in fear of shame.[66]

Acknowledgements
I am grateful to Mark Humphries for helpful comments during the preparation of this article, and to the editors of this volume for their searching and thoughtful responses to the first draft.

Notes

[1] 'Religion's guided missiles', *Guardian*, 15th September 2001.

[2] This formula *i mbearna bhaoil*, proverbial in modern Irish and included in the evocation of a rebel ambush in the National Anthem, occurs already in one of the poetic passages of the saga *Táin Bó Cúailnge* (Recension I, l. 3049), where it refers to the defiant stand of the hero Cú Chulainn at a ford on the border of Ulster, warding off the enemy host single-handed while his countrymen lie stricken and powerless behind him. The structural resemblance to Thermopylae is obvious: and Davis refers explicitly to 'the gap of danger' in another of his songs, *Lament for the Milesians* (Davis 1945, 197), which expresses the same message as *A Nation Once Again* through paradigms from Irish rather than classical examples of heroic defiance.

[3] Diodorus Siculus 11.9.2.

[4] See in general Rawson 1969, esp. 268–343 *passim*; Morris 2000.

[5] Patrick Pearse, speech at the graveside of the patriot O'Donovan Rossa (1915). See Lyons 1979, 90–92.

[6] Nothing is known for certain about the context of these lines. Bowra (1961, 346–9) speculated that the song was composed for a cult honouring the Three Hundred as a group. He identified the *sēkos* of the fragment as the precinct of the shrine (cf. LSJ s.v. *sēkos* II), and the *entaphion* as their funeral-gift, which would continue to be given forever as part of the cult. Against this, Podlecki (1968, 258–62) shows that the wording cannot be mapped onto the vocabulary and practices of a cult: he also asks how, if Bowra were right, direct evidence for such a cult would have disappeared when those for the dead at Marathon and Plataea are so well attested. Podlecki argues that the song may have been composed to be sung in the Spartan messes; but this remains speculative. Given the allusive complexity and verbal indeterminacy that characterize choral lyric, it is just possible that the song was associated with the original versions of the cults of Maron and Alpheios or of Leonidas himself. See below, n. 11, and cf. Flower

1998. West 1975, 309, even speculates that the reference to Thermopylae in the first line originated as a gloss.

[7] See Fuqua 1981, with Stehle 2001, 115–17.

[8] See esp. Boedeker 2001; Rutherford 2001, with n. 65 below.

[9] See Boedeker 1995, 1998.

[10] Simonides, Epigram VII.2 Page, on the dead of Thermopylae.

[11] In Pausanias' time there were shrines at Sparta for Leonidas (3.14.1) and for Maron and Alpheus (3.12.9), whom Herodotus also singles out for particular praise on account of their outstanding performance at Thermopylae. On the silence of the sources concerning any collective shrine, see esp. Podlecki 1968, n. 6 above.

[12] Wheeler 1991, 151.

[13] See e.g. Nagy 1987; Romm 1998, ch. 2 passim, esp. 19–20.

[14] Immerwahr 1966, 263. Cf. Romm 1998, 191–2.

[15] The only modern discussion of these words known to me is that by Loraux (1995, 72): 'The hoplite vocabulary lacks a term for martial frenzy… As the Spartans' deaths reached back beyond hoplite tradition to enact the mad exploits of mythical warriors, Herodotus selects his vocabulary for the black death from the Homeric register.'

[16] See for example Goldhill 1990.

[17] See LSJ s.v. παραχράομαι. I know of no modern analysis of the word.

[18] The only later attestation is worthless for our purposes, being an isolated fragment of Callimachus with no contextual information and almost certainly modelled directly on the *Iliad* example (see next note).

[19] I take *theōn* as partitive genitive with *tis*, not as objective genitive with *ateonta*. The possibility of the latter has been suggested by the genitive in the only other attestation of the verb, Callimachus' *Mousaōn kenos anēr ateei* (fr. 633 Pheiffer = schol. on *Il.* 20.332), but there it is easier to take *Mousaōn kenos* as a unit: 'the man empty of the Muses (i.e. the man without poetic inspiration) *ateei*'. With this passage discounted there is no authority for an objective genitive with any word of the *atē* family (thus Pfeiffer ad loc., followed by Y. Gerhard in *LfgrE* s.v. *ateōn*).

[20] The scholiast glosses it 'being in *atē*, that is damaged and having no care for oneself', and Hesychius has *ateonta: atōmenon*. The transmitted form must be scanned ᾱ̓τέ̄οντᾰ, with synizesis: this is difficult, but probably represents a development from an original form *ᾰ̓Ϝᾰτῶ̄ντᾰ, here masked by contraction after loss of digamma and subjected to diectasis with the alternation between *–e-* stems and *–a-* stems which is a feature of post-Homeric transmission. For this explanation see Chantraine 1948–53, i.361; Risch 1974, §112f; Y. Gerhard in *LfgrE* s.v. *ateōn*. In his *Dictionnaire* (s.v.) Chantraine is more tentative.

[21] If we allow the speeches of Phoenix and Agamemnon to mould our definition, I cannot improve on Mark Edwards' summary: "Ate in Homer may be summed up as the heroes' personification of the impulse which led to a foolish and disastrous act, an act which with hindsight appears inexplicable and hence is attributed to an outside, i.e. superhuman, agency" (1991, 247). However, it can still be argued that this collapses at least two complex and creative discourses into an assessment

of what the word means in the first place. On this point see esp. Neuberg 1993, with Dawe 1967.

22 See for example LSJ s.v. ἄτη; Dodds 1951, 5; Doyle 1984, 7 and ch. 1 *passim*; Stallmach 1968, esp. 53–9. Seiler's analysis (1951) of the semantic relationship between *atē* and the cognate verb *aaomai* remains problematic, because if (as he argues) the central reference is to error and delusion, it is difficult to see how there could have been a single starting-point for this and the legal meaning of a fine (as opposed, for example, to a foolish or criminal act punished by a fine).

23 For survey and discussion see Bile 1990 and Bile 1988, 326, with Willetts' translation (1967).

24 See Schwyzer 1923, 511.4 (Gythion in Laconia); 686.6 (Pamphylia); and cf. 424.5 (Elea).

25 See Ruijgh 1957, 106–10; Bile 1990. Intriguingly, in mainstream thought and poetry of the classical period there was still a tendency to associate *atē* with the forced payment of money: witness the Delphic aphorism ἐγγύα, πάρα δ' ἄτα (Plato, *Charmides* 165A; Cratinus Iunior, fr. 12 Kassell-Austin), roughly 'When a pledge (= surety) is given, *atē* is nearby', and Epicharmus' description of Atē as the daughter of Pledge (fr. 268 Kaibel), expressing the same idea in terms that recall the personified Atē of the *Iliad*.

26 In his incisive discussion Neuberg (1989) arrives at the definition 'afflictions one regards as somehow the outgrowth of one's own deeds', which also chimes well with the legal sense of the word at Gortyn.

27 Clarke 1999, 101–6.

28 See for example Burn 1984, 407; Lazenby 1979, 134; Hope Simpson 1972; Evans 1964; Grant 1961. The problem, and the solution offered by Leonidas' response to the oracle, are presented in masterly fashion by Hammond (1996).

29 Hooker 1989, 134. Cf. Cartledge 1979, 201–6, on Leonidas as a 'kamikaze'.

30 For example Parke and Wormell (1956, vol. 2, p. 44; see also id., *CQ* 43 [1949] 139) dismiss it without explanation as 'evidently a forgery' produced to boost Spartan morale after Leonidas' death. Hammond (1996, 3–7) shows it is much more likely that the oracle is genuine: he considers it unbelievable that the Spartans would not have consulted the oracle before the war, or that the genuine response could have been replaced by a forgery and lost from the historical record.

31 Hart suggests (1993, 65) that it may have originally been an instruction to recall the exiled Demaratus.

32 On Herodotus and oracles see most recently Harrison 2000, 122–57.

33 Notice how his Heraclid ancestry is stressed at the outset of the battle-narrative (7.208.1).

34 On such myths see esp. Kearns 1990, 328 ff.; Kearns 1989, 44–63; Hughes 1991, 73–9; and note Plutarch, *Pelop*. 21, including Leonidas in a list of human sacrifices that brought success in war.

35 On the mythical background cf. Burkert 1983, 58–72.

36 Witness the willing self-sacrifice of Iphigeneia in the *Iphigeneia at Aulis*, of Makaria in the *Heraclidae*, and of Polyxena in the *Hecuba*, and see Wilkins 1993, xxiii–xxiv, with further refs.

[37] Mastronarde (1994, 28–9, 391–3) is the latest of many to suggest that the self-sacrifice of Menoikeus was introduced into the myth by Euripides, but even if this is true there is no reason to doubt that the underlying pattern is more ancient. In the *Phoenissae*, intriguingly, before Teiresias reveals the prophecy he mentions that he has just returned from Athens, alluding obliquely to Erechtheus' sacrifice of his daughter (852–7); this need not imply that one myth has been modelled on the other, only that Euripides and his audience will have associated them with each other in a thematically significant way.

[38] Hellanicus, fr. 125 Fowler = *FgrH* no. 323a F 24; see also Pherecydes, fr. 154 Fowler = *FgrH* no. 154. See also Lycurgus, *In Leocratem* 86; Plato, *Symposium* 208D; Pausanias 1.19.5.

[39] I do not understand why Kearns (1990, 328; more cautiously, 1989, 56–7) suggests the story of Kodros may be modelled on that of Leonidas: there is no evidence either way, and it is better in principle to see both as equally traditional representations of a single story-pattern. See also Hughes 1991, 74–5.

[40] Cf. Hdt. 7.206, with Hammond 1996, 12.

[41] Hammond 1996, 5, citing Hdt. 7.124.3, Thuc. 5.72.4, Xen. *Lac. Pol.* 4.3; Lazenby 1985, 53.

[42] See esp. Aelian, *V.H.* VI.6, with Richer 1994, 55. The validity of Aelian's evidence has, however, been severly doubted: see Hodkinson 2000, 245, 247–8.

[43] e.g. Pausanias 9.13.10.

[44] V. Ehrenberg in *RE* VI A 2 (1936), s.v. τρέσαντες.

[45] Cf. Hammond 1996, 9, 14; more generally Gould 1989, 119–20.

[46] Richer 1994, 70 ff.

[47] Connor 1979; Richer 1994, 73–97.

[48] Boedeker 1993.

[49] By careful comparison between the different elements taken from Ephorus' account in those of Diodorus and Justin, Hammond shows (1996, 3–7) that the oracle must have played an important part in the putative early account on which Ephorus' version was based.

[50] Cf. Flower 1998, suggesting that this story may derive from a choral song, perhaps by Simonides himself.

[51] Hammond 1996, 16. See also Plutarch in *Sayings of Spartans*, *Moralia* 225D no. 3.

[52] Cf. the measured discussion in Renehan 1987.

[53] Clarke 1995.

[54] Cf. Redfield 1975, 145–53.

[55] Loraux 1995, 63–74.

[56] See for example Plato, *Apology* 28b2 ff. and Lycurgus, *In Leocratem* 97 ff., which express this principle even when the paradigms they cite are from Tyrtaeus and the self-destructive Achilles of the later books of the *Iliad*.

[57] See esp. Lycurgus, *In Leocratem* 107; Plutarch, *Cleomenes* 2.3, Athenaeus, 14.630 f.

[58] Stephen Hodkinson points out to me that this passage is recalled in Xenophon's discussion of Spartan bravery, *Lac. Pol.* 9.2. See also Loraux 1995, 66–70.

[59] Richer 1994, p. 56 n. 25, with further sources.

[60] Cf. Loraux, loc. cit. (above, n. 55) for the link between Aristodemos' *lussa* and the *atē* of the men of Thermopylae.

[61] See *Il.* 8.229; 9.239, 305; 13.53; 21.542; 22.70.

[62] See Lincoln 1975; Padel 1992, 163–4.

[63] See LSJ s.v. *lussa* II.

[64] On this issue in various contexts, see for example Millender 1999, on Spartan women; Hodkinson 1999, esp. 149–60, on athletics; Hodkinson 2000, ch. 8 on burial practices.

[65] In particular, in fr. 11 West Simonides narrates (or alludes at length to) the death of Achilles before embarking on his main narrative, probably that of Plataea; but what survives is not enough to clarify the nature of the link in terms of ideology or vocabulary (see esp. Rutherford 2001, 38).

[66] Cf. Den Boer 1954, 295 n. 10, suggesting that the summary epitaph indicates reduced honour for the Three Hundred. By contrast, the names of those who died at Plataea were inscribed on the spot and tended with honour (Plutarch, *Aristides* 21.5; see Richer 1994, 62–3).

Bibliography

Bile, M.

1988 *Le Dialecte crétois ancien*, Paris.

1990 'Les homérismes des lois de Gortyne', *Cretan Studies* 2, 79–95.

Boedeker, D.

1993 'Hero cult and politics in Herodotus: the bones of Orestes', in C. Dougherty and L. Kurke (eds.) *Cultural Poetics in Archaic Greece*, Cambridge, 164–77.

1995 'Simonides on Plataea: narrative elegy, mythodic history', *ZPE* 107, 217–29.

1998 'The new Simonides and heroization at Plataea', in N. Fisher and H. van Wees (eds.) *Archaic Greece: New approaches and new evidence*, London and Swansea, 231–49.

2001 'Paths to heroization at Plataea', in Boedeker and Sider (eds.) *The New Simonides*, 148–63.

Boedeker, D. and Sider, D. (eds.)

2001 *The New Simonides*, Oxford.

Bowra, C.M.

1961 *Greek Lyric Poetry*, 2nd edn, Oxford.

Burkert, W.

1983 *Homo Necans*, English edn, Berkeley.

Burn, A.R.

1984 *Persia and the Greeks*, 2nd edn, London.

Cartledge, P.

1979 *Sparta and Lakonia*, London.

Chantraine, P.
1948–53 *Grammaire Homérique*, Paris.

Clarke, M.
1995 'Between lions and men: images of the hero in the *Iliad*', *GRBS* 36, 137–59.
1999 *Flesh and Spirit in the Songs of Homer*, Oxford.

Connor, W.R.
1979 'Pausanias 3.141.1: a sidelight on Spartan history', *TAPA* 109, 21–8.

Davis, T.
1945 *Essays and Poems*, Dublin.

Dawe, R.D.
1967 'Some reflections on *atē* and *hamartia*', *HSCP* 72, 89–123.

Den Boer, N.
1954 *Laconian Studies*, Amsterdam.

Dodds, E.R.
1951 *The Greeks and the Irrational*, Berkeley.

Doyle, R.E.
1984 Atē, *its Use and Meaning*, New York.

Edwards, M.W.
1991 *The* Iliad*: A Commentary*, vol. 5, Cambridge.

Evans, J.A.S.
1964 'The "final problem" at Thermopylae', *GRBS* 4, 231–7.

Fisher, N.R.E.
1989 'Drink, *hybris* and the promotion of harmony in Sparta', in A. Powell (ed.) *Classical Sparta: Techniques behind her success*, London, 26–50.

Flower, M.A.
1998 'Simonides, Ephorus and Diodorus on the battle of Thermopylae', *CQ* 48, 365–79.

Fuqua, C.
1981 'Tyrtaeus and the cult of heroes', *GRBS* 22, 215–26.

Goldhill, S.
1990 'Supplication and authorial comment in the *Iliad*: *Iliad* Z 61–2', *Hermes* 118, 373–6.

Gould, J.
1989 *Herodotus*, London.

Grant, J.R.
1961 'Leonidas' last stand', *Phoenix* 15, 14–27.

Hammond, N.
1996 'Sparta at Thermopylae', *Historia* 45, 1–20.

Harrison, T.
2000 *Divinity and History: The Religion of Herodotus*, Oxford.

Hart, J.
1993 *Herodotus and Greek History*, London.

Hodkinson, S.
1999 'An agonistic culture? Athletic competition in archaic and classical

Spartan society', in Hodkinson and Powell (eds.) *Sparta: New Perspectives*, 147–88.
2000 *Property and Wealth in Classical Sparta*, London.

Hodkinson, S. and Powell, A. (eds.)
1999 *Sparta: New Perspectives*, London and Swansea.

Hooker, J.T.
1989 'Spartan propaganda', in A. Powell (ed.) *Classical Sparta: Techniques behind her success*, London, 122–41.

Hope Simpson, R.
1972 'Leonidas' decision', *Phoenix* 26, 1–11.

Hughes, D.D.
1991 *Human Sacrifice in Ancient Greece*, London.

Immerwahr, H.
1966 *Form and Thought in Herodotus*, Cleveland.

Kearns, E.
1990 'Saving the city', in O. Murray (ed.) *The Greek City*, Oxford, 323–34.
1989 *The Heroes of Attica*, *BICS* Suppl. no. 57, London.

Lazenby, J.F.
1985 *The Spartan Army*, Warminster.
1979 *The Defence of Greece*, Warminster.

Lincoln, B.
1975 'Homeric *lussa*', *IF* 80, 98–105.

Loraux, N.
1995 *The Experiences of Tiresias*, English edn, Princeton.

Lyons, F.S.L.
1979 *Culture and Anarchy in Ireland 1890–1939*, Oxford.

Mastronarde, D.
1994 *Euripides* Phoenissae, Cambridge.

Millender, E.
1999 'Athenian ideology and the empowered Spartan woman', in Hodkinson and Powell (eds.) *Classical Sparta: Techniques behind her success*, 355–92.

Morris, I. Macgregor.
2000 '*To make a new Thermopylae*: hellenism, Greek liberation, and the battle of Thermopylae', *Greece and Rome* 47, 211–30.

Nagy, G.
1987 'Herodotus the *logios*', *Arethusa* 20, 175–84.

Neuberg, M.
1993 '*Ate* reconsidered', in *Nomodeiktes: Greek Studies in Honor of M. Ostwald*, Ann Arbor, 491–504.

Padel, R.
1992 *In and Out of the Mind*, Princeton.

Parke, H.W. and Wormell, D.E.W.
1956 *The Delphic Oracle*, London.

Podlecki, A.J.
1968 'Simonides: 480', *Historia* 17, 257–75.

Rawson, E.
1969 *The Spartan Tradition in European Thought*, Oxford.
Redfield, J.
1975 *Nature and Culture in the* Iliad, Chicago.
Renehan, R.
1987 'The *Heldentod* in Homer: one heroic ideal', *CPh* 82, 99–116.
Richer, N.
1994 'Aspects des funérailles à Sparte', in *Cahiers du Centre Glotz V*, Paris, 51–96.
Risch, E.
1974 *Wortbildung der homerischen Sprache*, 2nd edn, Berlin.
Romm, J.
1998 *Herodotus*, New Haven.
Ruijgh, C.J.
1957 *L' Élément achéen dans la langue épique*, Assen.
Rutherford, I.
2001 'The new Simonides: toward a commentary', in Boedeker and Sider (eds.) *The New Simonides*, 33–54.
Schwyzer, E.
1923 *Dialectorum Graecorum Exempla Epigraphica Potiora*, Leipzig.
Seiler, H.
1954 'Homerisch *aaomai* und *atē*', in *Sprachgeschichte und Wortbedeutung*, Festschrift Debrunner, Bern, 409–17.
Stallmach, J.
1968 *Ate: Frage des Selbst- und Welverständnisses des frühgriechischen Menschen*, *Beiträge zur klassischen Philologie* 18, Meissenheim.
Stehle, E.
2001 'A bard of the Iron Age and his auxiliary Muse', in Boedeker and Sider (eds.) *The New Simonides*, 106–19.
West, M.L.
1975 'Some lyric fragments reconsidered', *CQ* 25, 307–9.
Wheeler, E.L.
1991 'The general as hoplite', in V. Davis (ed.) *Hoplites*, London, 121–70.
Wilkins, J.
1993 *Euripides* Heraclidae, Oxford.
Willetts, R.F.
1967 *The Law Code of Gortyn*, Berlin.

3

SŌPHROSYNĒ REVISITED: WAS IT EVER A SPARTAN VIRTUE?

Noreen Humble

In the proceedings of the last Sparta conference I argued that Xenophon, contrary to the opinion of modern scholarship, did not attribute the virtue *sōphrosynē* to the Spartans; in fact, he was carefully avoiding making *sōphrosynē* a Spartan virtue.[1] But because Xenophon's views on this issue had been misrepresented and because the attribution of *sōphrosynē* to the Spartans does instinctively seem to be perfectly reasonable, it may be instructive to look more closely at the ancient evidence with several questions in mind. What actually is the evidence for Spartan *sōphrosynē*? Have the views of other authors been misrepresented in modern scholarship? Why does the attribution seem so reasonable?

I. The evidence from the fifth century BC

Herodotus appears to be the first ancient writer who provides some potentially relevant evidence.[2] Cognates of *sōphrosynē* are twice used with reference to Spartans.[3] First, the Scythian Anacharsis reports back to his king that among the Greeks only the Spartans listen and converse *sōphronōs* (4.77). Secondly, Damaratos later says, in conversation with Xerxes, that no *sōphrōn* man would reject kindness of the sort Xerxes has shown to Damaratos (7.104.9). This second example is indefinite, referring to any sensible man, and so nothing more than a commonplace. The first example, however, is certainly an attribution of *sōphrosynē* to the Spartans, though admittedly in a limited way: listening and conversing *sōphronōs* is a different matter from acting *sōphronōs* or possessing *sōphrosynē*. Herodotus goes on to remark that the story was only a silly invention of the Greeks[4] and makes nothing of *sōphrosynē* as a characteristic of Spartans in his lengthier discussion about the state. *Eunomia* is the concept upon which he dwells in connection with Sparta (1.66 ff.). It would hardly be fair to say, therefore, that Herodotus singles out *sōphrosynē* as the characteristic virtue of the Spartans; but it could be that his one statement might reflect some sort of tradition or even be the starting point of such a tradition.

Sōphrosynē is connected with Sparta in Thucydides in a much more notable way.[5] Thucydides says that the Spartan king Archidamos was reputed to be *sōphrōn* (1.79.2).[6] To no other character in the work is this virtue directly attributed.[7] At 1.68.1 Thucydides has the Corinthians comment on Spartan *sōphrosynē*. They point out that the Spartan spirit of trust towards one another is mirrored by distrust of others, resulting in *sōphrosynē* at home but also ignorance (*amathia*) and passivity concerning affairs abroad (1.68–69).[8] The Corinthians go on to paint a negative portrait of Sparta as a slow and hesitant power in contrast to the swift daring of the Athenians. Four times in the course of his speech to the Spartans, countering this view put forth by the Corinthians, Archidamos refers to the concept of *sōphrosynē*. The first time, at 1.80.2, is simply the rather general phrase 'if you consider prudently (*sōphronōs*)'— a variation on a formula which is used widely in many non-Spartan contexts.[9] The next three instances are more striking. At 1.84.2 he counters the accusation that Spartans are slow and cautious (1.84.1) by saying that they can equally well be described as behaving with sensible prudence (*sōphrosynē euphrōn*), substituting the negative connotations suggested by slowness (*to bradu*) with the positive connotations suggested by *sōphrosynē*;[10] and at 1.84.3 he remarks that 'a sense of shame is founded above all on *sōphrosynē* and valour upon fear of reproach; and we are well-advised because we are trained with too much lack of understanding (*amathesteron*) to scorn the laws and too sensibly (*sōphronesteron*) and severely to allow us to disobey them.'[11] Finally at 8.24.4 is the authorial comment that 'the Chians alone after the Lakedaimonians of all those I have perceived, were both prosperous (*ēudaimonēsan*) and prudent (*esōphronēsan*)'.[12] Thus Thucydides draws attention to Spartan *sōphrosynē* early on and then again near the end of his work, and the first and last references are in his own voice.[13]

Thucydides also associates *sōphrosynē* more widely with oligarchy in general (as 8.24.4 shows),[14] and more specifically with the oligarchic element in Athens, and this connection is important for the discussion at hand. Two portions of Thucydides' discussion of *stasis* are relevant. First at 3.82.4 he writes:

> And people exchanged the conventional value of words in relation to the facts, according to their own perception of what was justified. For reckless daring was considered loyal bravery; far-sighted hesitation was considered specious timidity, moderation (*to sōphron*) was considered a screen for cowardice (*tou anandrou*).[15]

And then at 3.82.8 is the remark:

> For faction leaders in the various cities used specious names on each side, the one by honouring popular equality before the law, the other prudent

> aristocracy (*aristokratias sōphronos*); and while in speech they made caring for the common good their prize, they contested in every way to overcome each other, daring the most terrible things.

After first warning of the tendency for words to be misapplied in times of *stasis*,[16] Thucydides gives examples of both *sōphrosynē* and aristocracy being misused. Oligarchs are shown to appropriate *sōphrosynē* as a slogan for themselves,[17] in contrast to the intemperate democratic mob.[18] Confirmation of this ideological appropriation of a virtue that was commonly aspired to and valued by everyone[19] is the fact that the concept, in Thucydides, tends to be avoided by the opposing political faction.[20]

There is another piece of late fifth-century evidence which shows these two associations – the association of *sōphrosynē* with Sparta and with oligarchs – coming together.[21] Kritias, a member of the oligarchic faction and a prominent laconizer,[22] in a fragment from his poetic *Politeia Lakedaimoniōn* praises the restrained drinking habits of the Spartans which are 'well suited to the deeds of Aphrodite and to sleep, the harbour of troubles, and to the most delightful of goddesses to mortals, Health, and the neighbour of Piety, *Sōphrosynē*' (D-K 88b6 19–22).

We have, therefore, evidence from two elite writers of a connection between *sōphrosynē*, Sparta and the oligarchs in Athens, many of whom were laconophiles, including, most prominently, Kritias. The use of the term in these works is certainly at times ideologically driven.[23] If we look at *sōphrosynē* in non-elite texts, i.e. material destined for a mass audience, examples of Athens being *sōphrōn* can be found,[24] examples of oligarchic appropriation of the concept can be found,[25] but, unsurprisingly, examples of a link with Sparta are virtually non-existent.[26] The Kritian and Thucydidean evidence, therefore, allows the following conclusion to be drawn: the association of *sōphrosynē* with Sparta appears to belong to the conservative oligarchic element in Athens.[27] This group is either (a) applying to Spartans a term it had appropriated for itself, or (b) picking up a term used by Spartans of themselves,[28] in the same way that it picked up superficial physical affectations.

II. The evidence from the fourth century BC

In the fourth century, along with some material to support the conclusions from the fifth-century evidence, two other trends appear in the extant material, one in oratory the other in philosophy. In oratory there are a number of cases in which Spartans are said to have possessed *sōphrosynē*. Isokrates, for example, in the *Areopagiticus* (*c.* 358/7 or 355), notes that the Spartans had made themselves masters of the Peloponnese because of living *sōphronōs* and their military skill, but had lost supremacy when they tried to extend their rule (7). In *On the Peace* (*c.* 355) the Spartans are said to have governed themselves *sōphronestata* until they grasped at empire (104). And in the *Panathenaicus* (*c.* 339) Menelaus is presented as a model of *sōphrosynē* and *dikaiosynē* in contrast to present day Spartans (72). There is a clear example also in Aeschines' *Against Timarchus* (346/5). In an anecdote prefaced by the remark that it is good to imitate the virtue of foreigners, Aeschines tells of a member of the Gerousia exhorting his countrymen to beware of listening to advice from someone who has led a shameful life (180–1).[29] The Gerousia is described as having been composed of men who have been *sōphrōn* from boyhood to old age. This 'fact' is reported again at the end of the anecdote.

There are several important points to be made about this oratorical evidence. First, Spartans of the past, not contemporary Spartans, are said to be *sōphrōn*. Secondly, in both orators *sōphrosynē* is more frequently connected with early Athens.[30] The passage from Aeschines is followed first by the comment 'in order that I may not seem to flatter the Lakedaimonians, I will also recall our ancestors', and then by an example recalling ancestral measures to protect the *sōphrosynē* of children (182). Indeed, early on in the speech Solon, Draco and other lawgivers were said to have been greatly concerned with *sōphrosynē* (6–7). In the same speech, then, both ancestral Athens and ancestral Sparta are said to have placed great weight on *sōphrosynē*. In Isokrates, in the above-cited passage from *On the Peace* (104), the Athenians as well as the Spartans are said in the past to have governed themselves *sōphronestata*.[31] And the whole of the *Areopagiticus* pleads for a return to the golden days of embryonic democracy under Solon and Kleisthenes: success, Isokrates says, comes to those who govern their city *arista* and *sōphronestata* (13); the ancestral constitution made people better and *sōphronesterous* (20); the Areopagus, it is repeatedly noted, exemplified *sōphrosynē* (37 twice; 38); their forefathers measured happiness by their *sōphrōn* government (*ek tou sōphronōs oikein*, 53). Many examples of this line of thinking are also found in the *Panathenaicus*.[32]

Thirdly, the appeal to past Sparta on moral grounds does not happen until well after Sparta's collapse as a dominant power. Isokrates, for example, does not comment on Spartan *sōphrosynē* in his writing until around 358 BC and Aeschines, still later, remarks in *Against Timarchos* on the inherent danger of appealing to things Spartan (182). Even at this late date when Sparta and Athens are no longer at loggerheads, there is an acknowledgement that a mass audience may still not accept praise of Sparta.[33] Fourthly, the appeals to earlier times, now safely past, are to encourage moral behaviour and adherence to particular political views in the present and are subordinate to the particular point of the speech.[34] Thus Isokrates' panhellenic leanings coupled with political reality meant that he did, at times, promote Spartan partnership with Athens, which meant praising Sparta.[35] Aeschines, on the other hand, is trying to prove that Timarchos is unfit for public office because of immoral behaviour (3: *autōi aischrōs bebiōkoti*). So not only does he set the whole case up as a defence of *sōphrosynē* (6), he also includes an anecdote showing a *sōphrōn* Spartan warning against following the political advice of someone who had led a shameful life (180: *bebiōkotos men aischrōs*). The Spartan anecdote is created to replicate what Aeschines is saying about Timarchos, and, as Fisher points out, 'the Gerousia probably functions in the anecdote as a parallel institution to the Areopagos, that was praised earlier: both are given the specific role of defending the moral standards of political life'.[36]

Apart from this attribution of *sōphrosynē* to past Spartans, Isokrates also gives us evidence that laconizers, who were still plentiful during the fourth century,[37] continued, in the manner of Kritias, to associate *sōphrosynē* with Sparta. In the *Panathenaicus* Isokrates notes that blind laconophiles praise Sparta by comparing her *sōphrosynē* and *peitharchia* (obedience to rule) with Athenian carelessness (111). The comment is used in an argument against a Spartan sympathiser,[38] and later, in the same argument, Isokrates uses *sōphrosynē* and *peitharchia* to characterize a land power (115). It is likely that the echo is deliberate[39] and that Isokrates is here using the laconizers' own language in his counter-attack.

More startling still, however, are two other Isokratean references.[40] One comes from the *Archidamos*, an oration put in the mouth of Archidamos III and set in an assembly meeting during which the Spartans are addressed by the Corinthians on the subject of alliance with Thebes in 366.[41] Archidamos is made to express confidence in Sparta's good government and moderate living (*sōphronōs zēn*), willingness to fight to the death and fear of reproach (59). This is the only example, thus far, outside Thucydides of a Spartan being made to extol *sōphrosynē* as a Spartan virtue. Admittedly the purpose of the speech is debated,[42] but even so, Isokrates' aim would surely have been to make it sound as authentically Spartan as possible and the sentiments could easily have come from laconizers, if they did not come directly from the Spartans themselves. The other reference leads to the same conclusion. In the *Letter to Archidamos*, Isokrates asks 'who would be at a loss, if he wished to relate the courage of your whole state, its *sōphrosynē* and the constitution ordained by your ancestors?' (4).

Philosophy provides us with an entirely different picture, despite its clearly elitist nature and attraction to Sparta. Xenophon is no Kritias, though he is often considered a laconizing oligarch in modern scholarship, nor does he follow the same line as Thucydides.[43] Instead, his avoidance of attributing *sōphrosynē* to Spartans is much more in line with Plato and Aristotle who believe that the Spartans did not cultivate *sōphrosynē*. For example, in Plato's *Republic*, though the timocratic regime (545c–8d) and man (548d–50c), which are thin disguises of the Spartan regime and a Spartiate, are only one step removed from Plato's ideal form of government, *sōphrosynē* does not figure at all in the discussion of them. Characteristic of this regime is a secret craving for and hoarding of wealth, and, later, in the discussion of the transition from oligarchy to democracy, it is noted that it is impossible to honour wealth and possess *sōphrosynē* at the same time (555c).[44] And in the *Laws*, a dialogue in which there is a Spartan interlocutor and in which *sōphrosynē* figures heavily as the prerequisite for all virtue,[45] the Athenian speaker is critical of the Spartan and Cretan systems because their whole way of life is devoted to success in war; they have no institutions to teach them how to live in peace – i.e. they possess *andreia* but not *sōphrosynē* (625c–32c). The only unambiguously positive reference is at *Laws* 692a where the Athenian admires the fact that the Spartan lawgiver tempered the rashness of the kings with the prudent power of old age (*tēn kata gēras sōphrona dunamin*); yet even here the link is between *sōphrosynē* and old age rather than *sōphrosynē* and Sparta.[46] Aristotle's view about Sparta's lack of *sōphrosynē* is similar. In the *Politics* he points out that most military states perish if not at war because their lawgiver did not consider how to educate the citizens about leisure (1334a6–10). The virtues necessary to lead a life of leisure are justice, wisdom and *sōphrosynē* (1334a11–40). Sparta, however, only cultivates one virtue – *andreia* – with a view to war (1324b8–9, 1334a40, 1338b11–39).

Yet Plato was intimately connected with late-fifth-century laconizing oligarchs – Kritias was his mother's cousin – and he does provide further evidence that these men appropriated the virtue of *sōphrosynē* for themselves and that Sparta is connected with this appropriation. In the one dialogue that Plato devoted to a discussion of *sōphrosynē*, the *Charmides*,[47] Kritias plays a key role. Sparta figures only indirectly in the dialogue through the behaviour and attitudes of Socrates' interlocutors, Kritias and his young cousin Charmides, both of whom were counted among the 30 tyrants.[48] Since Charmides is said by Kritias to possess *sōphrosynē*, Socrates asks him first what he considers the virtue to be. Charmides initially suggests quietness (*hēsuchiotēs*), which Socrates then playfully and ironically associates with slowness (*bradutēs*). It is difficult to say with certainty that Plato is asking his audience here to recall Thucydides, but the connection is striking both in light of the speech of Archidamos and his equation of *bradutēs* with *sōphrosynē* (Th. 1.84.1–2; see above), and in light of the political affiliations of Kritias and Charmides.[49] When the definition of *sōphrosynē* as *bradutēs* is found wanting, *aidōs* (modesty) is suggested, and commentators note that both definitions reflect Charmides' conservative upbringing and ideals elsewhere connected with Sparta.[50] As expected, neither definition satisfies Socrates and the dialogue shifts to the more mature Kritias, with whom the definition gradually progresses to knowledge of good and evil. The whole discussion in the end is about the Socratic paradox that all virtue is knowledge and, as customary, Socrates' interlocutors are shown not to understand what it is they claim to know about – *sōphrosynē*. The irony in the choice of two interlocutors whose later lives were paradigms of lack of *sōphrosynē*[51] extends also to the fact that in their later lives they continued to profess *sōphrosynē* even while acting otherwise.

The favouring of the virtue by the members of the oligarchic faction and their association of it with Sparta may also be behind a passage from *Alkibiades I* in which Socrates says to Alkibiades (122c):[52]

> If again you reflect on the Spartans' *sōphrosynē*, discipline, friendliness, affability, magnanimity, discipline, courage, stamina, endurance, competitive spirit and ambition, you would regard yourself as a child in all these respects.

This is part of a larger argument in which Socrates points out to Alkibiades that he falls far short of the Persian and Spartan kings in many respects, particularly regarding lineage and wealth. Debate over the authenticity and dating of this dialogue[53] has led to varying views of this passage. Whoever the author, Denyer's common sense interpretation of the context of this passage is surely correct: '[Socrates] exploits Alcibiades' vulnerability to rhetoric, stirs up his competitiveness, and appeals to his respect for breeding...[in order to] turn these things against themselves, so that Alcibiades will come to be a philosopher.'[54] To this might be added that in this passage Socrates is also exploiting the very rhetoric which men like Alkibiades would themselves use of Spartans.

One final fourth-century source requires comment. Athenaeus preserves the following comment from the *Hellenica* of Theopompus (F20 = Athen. 12.543b–c) about Lysander: 'he was a lover of toil and able to look after private men as well as kings, being *sōphrōn* and master of all pleasures'. Athenaeus cites the passage as evidence that not everyone believed that Lysander was notorious for luxury. While there is no evidence that Theopompus was anything other than an admirer of Lysander,[55] there is also not enough left of his writings for us to examine his use of *sōphrosynē* in general.[56] But since the *Hellenica* was composed sometime in the 350s or 340s[57] it is not improbable that Theopompus, like the fourth-century orators, is appealing to the Spartan past to reinforce a moral point.

The fourth-century evidence for Spartan *sōphrosynē*, therefore, gives us confirmation of the fifth-century evidence, and reveals two new approaches. Plato's *Charmides* and the possibly Platonic *Alkibiades I* confirm that laconizing oligarchs in the fifth century appropriated *sōphrosynē* for themselves and that it was associated by them with Sparta. Isokrates, in the *Panathenaicus*, provides evidence that this line of thinking was still around in the fourth century. Like Thucydides, he also puts praise of Spartan *sōphrosynē* into the mouth of a Spartan. At the same time, in mass-oriented texts there are now, where there were not in the fifth century, references to Spartan *sōphrosynē*, though they are always to past Sparta and only occur well after Sparta had lost her power. And in philosophy not even past Sparta is allowed the virtue; philosophers argue that Sparta never cultivated *sōphrosynē* in the first place.

III. The evidence from the third century BC to Plutarch

Far fewer ancient authors make reference to Spartan *sōphrosynē* after the fourth century BC.[58] Apart from an interesting reference in Polybius (6.48.3–7; on which see below),[59] the next writer in whom there is a noticeable emphasis on Spartan *sōphrosynē* is Plutarch.[60] Not surprisingly, given the temporal distance of Plutarch from his subject matter, another shift in the presentation of Spartan *sōphrosynē* is found. The subtle differences in Plutarch's approach are important to highlight for two reasons. First, he has influenced our image of Sparta more than any other ancient author[61] and it is all too easy to retroject his evidence onto earlier sources. Secondly, he is still inevitably used as a 'historical' source in the absence of, and even in the presence of, earlier ancient material.[62]

The Plutarchan references can be divided into two groups, those in the *Apophthegmata Lakōnika*, and those in the *Parallel Lives*. Scholarly opinion is generally agreed that the former is a collection of sayings and anecdotes which Plutarch seems to have taken from previous hellenistic collections and used as working notes for his Spartan *Lives*.[63] All but the sayings ascribed to Lykourgos (*Mor.* 225f–9a) appear to refer to the period before the revolutions of Agis and Kleomenes; the Lykourgan sayings, on the other hand, do show evidence of the rhetoric of the third-century revolution, so they post-date the revolution.[64] There are four relevant passages. At 213c, Agesilaos, speaking to some people in Asia about the title of the Persian king, says 'with respect to what is that man greater than I, unless he is more just and more moderate (*sōphronesteros*)'.[65] At 225f Lykourgos is depicted as wanting to lead Spartans from their present lifestyle into a more moderate (*sōphronesteran*) way of life. At 228b are comments on the *sōphrosynē* of women in the time of Lykourgos. And finally at 242b a poor Spartan girl, when asked what her dowry will be, says the family *sōphrosynē*.

Five Spartans figure as subjects in the *Parallel Lives* (composed between *c.* 96 and 120 AD). In the *Agis and Kleomenes* can be found the following references. Agis (7.2) says that 'he could not equal other kings in terms of property…but if, by *sōphrosynē*, simplicity and greatness of soul, he should surpass their luxury and establish equality and partnership among his citizens, he would truly obtain the name and reputation of a great king'. Kleomenes notes the danger of speaking about *sōphrosynē* of the young after Agis' death (23[2].1); his own life is said to be a paradigm of *sōphrosynē* (34[13].1); he is also described as a man bringing back the ancestral constitution to that *sōphrona* and Dorian way of life and law of Lykourgos (37[16].4); his wife is described as *sōphronestatēs* (43[22].2); and, finally, when given a pension by Ptolemy, Kleomenes uses it to keep himself and his friends living simply and moderately (*sōphronōs*, 53[32].3). In the *synkrisis* (the closing comparison found at the end of most of the pairs of Greek and Roman *Lives*) Agis and Kleomenes are described as making themselves 'leaders in simplicity and *sōphrosynē*' despite being brought up in a corrupted Sparta (1.2), and their reforms were based on the finest example, the ancestral rhetras concerning *sōphrosynē* and equality (2.3).

References abound also in the *Lykourgos*: at 5.6 Lykourgos' institution of the Gerousia is said 'to provide safety and *sōphrosynē* concerning the greatest matters'; at 11.4 is the story of the young man who poked out Lykourgos' eye and who, by living with Lykourgos, became most orderly and most moderate (*sōphronikōtatos*); at 12.4 boys are said to frequent the *syssitia* as though being brought to schools of *sōphrosynē*; at 14.1 Plutarch disagrees with Aristotle and says Lykourgos did indeed try to make moderate (*sōphronizein*) the women; at 15.5 the limitation of intercourse between young couples is said to provide training in *enkrateia* and *sōphrosynē*; at 15.7 it is noted that a women's *sōphrōn* behaviour was thought admirable; at 17.2 boys choose as their leader the most prudent (*sōphronestaton*) and warlike of the *Eirens*; at 26.1 it is reported that it is not the swiftest or the strongest who are elected to the Gerousia but the best and most prudent (*sōphronestaton*) of the good and prudent (*sōphrosin*); and finally at 31.1 is the comment that Lykourgos organized things so that men would become free, self-sufficient and moderate (*sōphronountes*). Also, in the *synkrisis*, both Numa and Lykourgos are said to have *sōphrosynē* (1.1) and both are said to have led their people to *sōphrosynē* (2.1).

The concept is less noticeable, though not totally absent, in the *Agesilaos* and *Lysander*. In the former it is found only once: '[in Asia] a marvellous opinion prevailed of his *sōphrosynē*, his simplicity of life and his moderation (*metriotētos*)' (*Ages.* 14.1).[66] In the *Lysander*, though there is a more ambiguous moral lesson than that found in most of the *Lives*,[67] Plutarch attributes *sōphrosynē* to Lysander twice in the *synkrisis*: at 3.1 he comments: 'Lysander showed everywhere a lifestyle so *sōphrona* and Spartan and restrained', and in the closing lines Plutarch assigns first place in *enkrateia* and *sōphrosynē* to Lysander, compared with generalship and bravery for Sulla (5.5). Also in the *synkrisis* is the comment that Lysander was sent out as a leader from a particularly well governed and moderate (*sōphronousēs*) Sparta (1.3).

Obviously some sense of Plutarch's use of *sōphrosynē* in general is necessary before closer analysis of the references above. An examination of his *oeuvre* reveals, as it did for the other sources discussed thus far, a complex picture, which, unsurprisingly, shows that Spartans are not the sole possessors of the virtue.[68] For example, if we look at the pair of leaders compared with Agis and Kleomenes, the Gracchi, we find no less than five relevant references.[69] Pompey is more in possession of this virtue than Agesilaos.[70] Sulla is said not to have had this virtue (*Sulla* 35.5) but to have tried to instil it into the Romans anyway (*Lys./Sulla* 3.2, 3.5). And in the *Numa*, there are two references, similar to the two in the *synkrisis*.[71] On the whole, in fact, *sōphrosynē* and its cognates appear reasonably widespread and important in the *Lives*.[72] And we do not have to look far to determine why *sōphrosynē* would be so generally important to Plutarch. North has quite rightly noted that

> the two major influences on the prose literature of the hellenistic and Graeco-Roman periods were philosophy and rhetoric, and there is at least one point at which the two streams converge: the cardinal virtues.[73]

Still there is a higher incidence of the term and its cognates in the *Agis/Kleomenes* and the *Lykourgos* than in any other of the *Lives* and this needs to be accounted for.

Clearly general laconophilia is not the answer because there is not a striking incidence of *sōphrosynē* in the *Agesilaos* and *Lysander*. Indeed, when transferring *Apoph. Lak.* 213c to the *Agesilaos*, Plutarch leaves out the reference to *sōphrosynē* (*Ages.* 23.5); and Lysander is hardly an overwhelmingly positive role model.[74] It is also not enough to say simply that Plutarch uses *sōphrosynē* so heavily in the *Lykourgos* and *Agis/Kleomenes* for the same reason that it crops up in fourth-century oratory, i.e. with reference to the idealized past.[75] If this were the sole reason we might expect to see similar heavy usage of the concept in the *Solon* and it is not there. Yet because the *topos* is perfectly reasonable in the context of both *Lives*, if Plutarch himself is not deliberately inserting it, the answer must be that he is picking it up from his sources. The most likely place is in his main source for the *Agis/Kleomenes*,[76] Phylarchos, who, on the evidence of Polybius and Plutarch, was biased heavily in favour of Kleomenes.[77] It is entirely plausible that Phylarchos preserved the rhetoric of the third-century revolution,[78] which was so concerned with restoring 'Lykourgan' Sparta and which could conceivably have employed the *topos* of referring to the *sōphrosynē* of past/Lykourgan Sparta and pressed for a return to the same.[79] In particular the references at *Ag./Kleom.* 37(16).4 and *Ag./Kleom.-Gracchi* 1.2, 2.3 encourage this train of thought. Further, it would follow naturally that the men leading the revolution, Agis and Kleomenes, would be portrayed as exemplifying a virtue they were trying to promote (*Ag./Kleom.* 7.2, 34[13].1, 53[32].3 and *Ag./Kleom.-Gracchi* 1.2). Without the full text of Phylarchos this remains simply inference, but an examination of the other instances of Spartan *sōphrosynē* which are traceable in the sources does allow interesting conclusions to be drawn about the instances which can not be traced directly.

In the *Agesilaos* and *Lysander*, *sōphrosynē* is not a dominant virtue, nor – perhaps coincidentally – is it dominant in the extant source material. Agesilaos has the virtue in Xenophon's encomium (*Ag.* 5.4.7 and 11.10), but the only other ascription to him is in the *Apophthegmata Lakōnika* (213c). If Agesilaos had become a model of *sōphrosynē* in the hellenistic period, it certainly is not reflected widely in Plutarch's working notes. The same holds true for Lysander whose *sōphrosynē* is noted, as far as we can tell, only by Theopompus.[80] In examining the instances of *sōphrosynē* in the *Lykourgos*, however, we are clearly hampered by the loss of so many works on the Spartan constitution which were available to Plutarch and which might have presented a tradition of Spartan *sōphrosynē*.[81] All that can be said with certainty is that *sōphrosynē* does not play a role in the two extant works of this type, that by Xenophon and Plutarch's *Instituta Laconica*. This latter work is a collection of information about the Spartan way of life and customs and is, like the *Apophthegmata*, considered to be part of Plutarch's working notes compiled from an earlier work or works. The dating of the earlier material is disputed but it is at least generally agreed to post-date the third-century revolution.[82] And while the *Instituta Laconica* has been shown to underlie much of what Plutarch records in the *Lykourgos*,[83] it is not the source for comments about *sōphrosynē*. Still, likely sources can be suggested. For example, *Lyk.* 5.6 and 26.1, concerning the *sōphrosynē* of the Gerousia, have a precedent in Plato (*Lg.* 691e–2a).[84] Also, the two references to female *sōphrosynē* (14.1 and 15.7) have a clear link to Aristotle's direct criticism of Lykourgos for not restraining the women (*Pol.* 1260b12–70a16),[85] the Lykourgan saying at *Mor.* 228b, and the saying of the anonymous Spartan woman (242b). The other Lykourgan saying (225f) about Lykourgos wanting to make the Spartans more *sōphrōn* could be behind *Lyk.* 31.1, the more specific example of Alcander (11.4), and the two references in the *synkrisis* (1.1, 2.1).

What is striking is that all references to Lykourgos either possessing *sōphrosynē* or inculcating it in the Spartans can be traced back only as far as a work which post-dates the revolutions of Agis and Kleomenes, the *Lykourgan Apophthegmata*. Plato's comment about the Spartan lawgiver using the *sōphrōn* power of old age to balance the constitution (*Lg.* 691e–2a) is the closest prior reference; but in it Plato does not actually attribute *sōphrosynē* to Lykourgos or suggest that instilling *sōphrosynē* in Spartans was Lykourgos' aim, and he quite clearly shows elsewhere his belief that *sōphrosynē* was lacking at Sparta. All other pre-revolutionary references are either to contemporary Sparta (as in Thucydides and Kritias) or Sparta before her collapse (as in Isokrates and Aeschines) without mention of Lykourgos. It looks, therefore, very much as though the specific linking of Lykourgos with *sōphrosynē* may have been part of the revolutionary rhetoric in the same way that the introduction of the concept of equality of property was, as Hodkinson has recently demonstrated.[86]

Indeed, within Plutarch's own works the pattern of Spartan *sōphrosynē*, and particularly Lykourgan-inspired *sōphrosynē*, is nearly identical with Hodkinson's findings concerning equality of property. First, the association of Lykourgos and *sōphrosynē* in the *Apophthegmata* is found only in the post-revolutionary *Lykourgan Apophthegmata* (225f and 228b). The two examples in the pre-revolutionary *Apophthegmata* (213c and 242b) have nothing to do with Lykourgos. Secondly, though the *Instituta Laconica* is post-revolutionary, it neither shows signs of revolutionary rhetoric concerning equality, nor does *sōphrosynē* make an appearance in it. Thirdly, there are, in the *Agis/Kleomenes*, a considerable number of references to both *sōphrosynē* and equality and indeed there are two instances where the two concepts are directly linked (*Ag./Kleom.* 23[2].1 and *Ag./Kleom.-Gracchi* 2.3). Finally, in the *Lykourgos*, just as Plutarch's references to Spartan equality echo the revolutionary rhetoric found in the *Agis/Kleomenes*, so too do his references to *sōphrosynē*.[87] The parallel extends wider still. Just as there are examples of the concept of equality connected with Sparta before the third-century revolution, though none concerns equality of property,[88] so too there are pre-revolutionary precedents for Spartan *sōphrosynē*, though none of them connects the virtue with Lykourgos.

There may be a danger of pressing this analogy too far, since *sōphrosynē* is not a concept to be pinned down in the same way as equality of property. But there is corroborating evidence in Polybius for this idea that the association of *sōphrosynē* with Lykourgos is linked to the third-century revolution. Polybius, while being much closer in time than Plutarch to the revolution, is manifestly hostile both to Plutarch's main source, Phylarchos, and to the Kings' revolutionary plans and so might be expected to present an entirely different picture.[89] In a digression on the nature of political constitutions and on why Rome's is superior to successful constitutions in the past, including that of Sparta, Polybius points out that the Lykourgan equality of land division and the simple and common diet were instituted for the purpose of making the lives of the citizens *sōphronas* (6.48.3). He goes on to state that where *andreia* and *sōphrosynē* are found in a soul or a city, neither will be easily overcome and that the problem with Sparta is that Lykourgos did this for individual Spartans but did not make the city *sōphrōn* (6.48.4–7). As Hodkinson points out, though Polybius was hostile to the Spartan revolution, the influence of its propaganda is clear in the reference to Lykourgan equality of land ownership.[90] It also appears to have influenced his comments on Lykourgos' concern with *sōphrosynē*. The notion of the importance of uniting both *andreia* and *sōphrosynē* may reflect, as North points out, the influence of Platonic doctrine;[91] but Plato never said that Lykourgos instilled *sōphrosynē* in individual Spartans or set up the land division or diet with a view to encouraging *sōphrōn* behaviour.

Even, therefore, with the loss of Phylarchos, it seems plausible to argue that Plutarch's particular emphasis on *sōphrosynē* in the *Agis/Kleomenes* and the *Lykourgos* is linked closely with the source material he used.[92] Even though his source base for the *Lykourgos* was much greater than that for the *Agis/Kleomenes*, as Hodkinson has shown – and as this study confirms – the content of the *Lykourgos* is influenced significantly by the rhetoric surrounding the third-century revolution. The specific linking of Lykourgos himself with *sōphrosynē* appears to be, like the call for a return to Lykourgan equality of property, a construct of the revolution.[93]

IV. Conclusion

The evidence, then, for a connection of Spartans with the virtue *sōphrosynē* is widespread, occurring in different types of source material over a long period of time. The focus and resonance of the attribution change from author to author as well as over time. In the fifth and fourth centuries BC, authors across a range of literary genres provide substantial evidence that *sōphrosynē* was used in a politically charged way by laconizing oligarchs, with reference to themselves and to the Spartans with whom they aligned themselves. Further, twice, during this same period, words are put into the mouths of Spartans to the effect that *sōphrosynē* was important in Sparta. Whether this reflects what Spartans themselves would have actually said is unclear. In the fourth century opposing strands of thought are found in orators and philosophers. In oratory *sōphrosynē* is attributed to past Sparta. Praise of Spartan *sōphrosynē* in these cases is not of the same sort as that given by the laconizing oligarchs. It is included specifically to back up an argument and not infrequently it is accompanied by a reference to Athenian *sōphrosynē*. Philosophers, on the other hand, while approving of certain aspects of Sparta's way of life, are agreed on the fact that *sōphrosynē* was not cultivated in Sparta at any time, past or present.

The other major body of evidence on Spartan *sōphrosynē* is found among Plutarch's works and, in general, a different tone is found to that in the earlier evidence.[94] In his *Lykourgos* and *Agis/Kleomenes*, in which there is a high incidence of the term and cognates, the rhetoric of the third-century Spartan revolution has been shown to have had a significant influence. So pervasive was this rhetoric that even Polybius, who was hostile to the revolution, preserved it in his work. The most significant point is that during the revolution *sōphrosynē* became attached to Lykourgos in a way that previously it had not been; like the notion of equality of property, it became an 'invented tradition'.[95] That this rhetoric does not infiltrate the *Agesilaos* and *Lysander* also provides us with further insight into Plutarch's selective and creative use of his source material.

In the extant sources, then, examples of Spartan *sōphrosynē* can be narrowed down to three groups: laconizing oligarchs, orators (if it can be used to heighten their point, and used only after Sparta has lost its power), and the third-century Spartan revolutionaries (as reflected in Plutarch). So the answer to the main question 'was *sōphrosynē* ever a Spartan virtue?' is 'for some people in some contexts'. However, because our idea of Sparta is so extraordinarily conditioned by what Plutarch says, particularly in his *Lykourgos*, we are perhaps more prone than we should be to accept the very reasonableness of the attribution of *sōphrosynē* to Spartans. The fact that Plutarch has been an enormously popular and central source for the ancient world since the fifteenth century[96] means that, although we can deal with our conscious understanding of the growth of the Spartan mirage, it is more problematic to overcome the Plutarchan Sparta of the collective unconscious. We moderns still come to study Sparta with Plutarch's picture already in place in our minds, as Hodkinson's account of images of Spartan egalitarianism from the sixteenth to twentieth centuries has amply demonstrated.[97] It is, therefore, all too easy to retroject Plutarch's account onto the earlier evidence, particularly onto a work like Xenophon's *Lakedaimoniōn Politeia*, the only other surviving complete treatise on the Spartans outside Plutarch's *oeuvre*.

Acknowledgements

Earlier versions of this paper were given in Manchester (1998) and Maynooth (2000). I am grateful to the audiences on both occasions for valuable comments and suggestions. A Government of Ireland Post-Doctoral Award has provided me with congenial circumstances in which to write up the paper. Thanks too are due to Nick Fisher and Keith Sidwell who commented on various drafts, to Michael Flower for allowing me to peruse in advance his paper for this volume, as well as to the editors of this volume. Where I have taken their sage advice, the paper has been much improved. Responsibility for the views presented and for any errors or omissions rests fully with myself.

Notes

[1] Humble 1999.

[2] As noted by Rawson 1969, 20.

[3] Herodotus does not actually use the noun *sōphrosynē* (on this see North 1966, 28–9).

[4] This is an interesting enough statement in its own right, and possibly an early example of the formation of an image (as Rawson 1969, 20 suggests), though it may seem so only because we have the later image in mind.

[5] As has frequently been pointed out. See, for example, Chrimes 1949, 125; Tuckey 1951, 7; Tigerstedt 1965–78, 1.128–40; North 1966, 70 n.91, 102–4, 111; Rawson 1969, 21–2; Edmunds 1975, 75; Wilson 1990, 51, 56–7; Hornblower 1991–96 on 1.79.2; Rhodes 1994, 206.

[6] There is considerable debate surrounding the meaning of the term here, as to whether it is being used in an encratic (i.e. simply to mean physical self-control, equivalent to *enkrateia*) or an intellectual (i.e. prudence) sense (see Humble 1999, 340 for the distinction); but Westlake's suggestion (1968, 123) that the two adjectives are meant to be understood in terms of what the words meant in Sparta itself and that this was somehow different from what they meant in Athens, seems unnecessarily complex.

[7] See Hussey 1985, 123–5 on how Thucydides presents Archidamos as a rather exceptional Spartan.

[8] Again there is some dispute about what *sōphrosynē* means here, but I incline towards the view that the term here means prudence (Hornblower 1991–6 on 1.68.1) rather than the view that it stands for general orderliness and law-abidingness in Sparta (*HCT ad loc.*).

[9] e.g. 1.40.2, 3.44.1, 4.18.4 (Spartans to Athenians), 4.60.1, 4.61.1, 4.64.4, 5.101, 6.11.7; and see North 1966, 56 and Humble 1999, 344. *HCT* on 1.86.2 suggests that Sthenelaïdas' use of the phrase *ēn sōphronōmen* in the speech answering Archidamos may be deliberately picking up Archidamos' use of the concept. This may be so but it is perhaps not wise to make too strong an argument on the back of a widely used generic phrase; see also n. 13 below.

[10] Cf. also Pelling 1991, 123 and Price 2001, 151. *Sōphrosynē* is, of itself, a positive virtue, on which see Irwin 1977, 288 n. 15. Dover 1974, 67–8 characterizes it as

'negative' because it restrains someone from doing wrong, but, as Irwin points out, it would be hard to find anyone saying '*Sōphrosynē* is bad'. Tigerstedt 1965–78, 1.139 and Greenstein-Millender 1996, 312 n. 105 both consider *sōphrosynē* in this instance to be, if not a negative quality, at least a passive one. If this were so, there would not be much point in Archidamos' rhetorical shift. *To bradu* is not a synonym of *sōphrosynē*.

[11] This first part of the translation is from Dover 1974, 119. The meaning of the passage is disputed. For a useful discussion see Hornblower 1991–6 on 1.84.3. *Amathia* and *sōphrosynē* are also linked at 3.37.3 (Kleon speaking in the Athenian assembly). The similarity with Archidamos' sentiments is noted by *HCT* on 3.37.4, but discussion of Kleon's speech tends to centre on the Periklean echoes. It is likely that Kleon simply has conservative oligarchic sentiments in mind.

[12] See North 1966, 113 on Thucydides' 'expressed admiration for Spartan stability'; see also Hornblower 1987, 162 and Wilson 1990, 56–7. Thucydides had previously commented on Sparta's *eunomia* at 1.18.1 and in this he follows Herodotus (cf. 1.65–6) and is followed by Plato (*Krito* 52e), neither of whom (see above and below) make any notable point about Spartan *sōphrosynē*.

[13] There are other instances of *sōphrosynē* and its cognates which some modern scholars have interpreted as having Spartan overtones. For example, North 1966, 108 (and *HCT* on 3.59.1) argues that this is why the Plataeans make use of *sōphrōn* twice (*sōphrona charin*, 3.58.1; *sōphroni oiktōi*, 3.59.1) in their appeal to Sparta. Yet, she also notes that *sōphrosynē* is used elsewhere 'with the implication "merciful"' without Spartan connotations. The same interpretative problem surrounds 1.120.3 where in their appeal to the Spartans the Corinthians make use of the generic phrase *andrōn sōphronōn estin* (e.g., Wassermann 1953, 200 n. 17 makes a connection). Rhodes 1994 on 3.62.2 and 3.65.3 (the speech of the Thebans countering a Plataean speech before Spartans) also argues for a Spartan connection, though by contrast North 1966, 112–13 argues the *sōphronistēs* in 3.65.3 has a straightforward political sense (i.e. non-oligarchic and non-Spartan). Not every use of *sōphrosynē* and cognates is linked to specific ideologies and none of the above examples is as clear cut as those I have cited in the body of the paper. See also n. 9 above.

[14] Which includes Sparta. See Wilson 1990, *passim* and *HCT* on 8.64.5.

[15] See Price 2001, 39 ff. for a valuable discussion about the meaning of this passage. My translation follows his closely.

[16] In which positive behaviour (*to sōphron*) is called cowardice. This is the same type of rhetoric that the Corinthians used against the Spartans and which Archidamos tried to counter in his speech (see above).

[17] *HCT* on 8.64.5 following North 1966, 44 and 102 and also Hornblower 1987, 162 and 1991–6 on 3.82.8. Also see n. 27 below.

[18] This ideological appropriation of *sōphrosynē* as an oligarchic virtue can be compared to the use of the term *dēmos* as a sociological construct (*hoi polloi*) by elite writers in the late fifth century, both terms retaining their wider, less charged meaning outside the ideological battle-ground: *sōphrosynē* as a virtue aspired to by all and *dēmos* meaning *hoi politai*; on which see Ober 1999, 117–19.

[19] For example, see North 1966, 116 on contemporary, non-ideological usage of *sōphrosynē* in Andocides.

[20] See North 1966, 102 ff., followed by *HCT* on 8.24.4 and Wilson 1990, 51–2. In the speeches of Pericles the term is avoided while the concept is preached (Wilson 1990, 52). Diodotos, on the other hand, does use the term (3.42.5, 3.43.5 are less generic than 3.44.1) possibly echoing Kleon's speech (as suggested in MacLeod 1978, 73; and see n. 11 above). Also the term *tois sōphrosi* at 4.28.5, used of the opponents of Kleon, seems not to be ideologically loaded (see North 1966, 111, *HCT* on 4.28.5 and Hornblower 1991–96 on 4.28.5).

[21] As noted by Tigerstedt 1965–78, 1.157; North 1966, 95; Rawson 1969, 30; and Hodkinson 1994, 189. See also North 1966, 96 on Kritias as external evidence for the views found in Thucydides.

[22] Xenophon (*HG* 2.3.34) has him state that the Spartan *politeia* was the best.

[23] See Ober 1989, 43–9 on elite and mass ideologies in general.

[24] See North 1966, 45–50 and 72.

[25] On *sōphrosynē* as an oligarchic political slogan in Aristophanes see North 1966, 66 and 97–9; Edmunds 1975, 78 n. 18; and Dunbar 1995, 706.

[26] The only possibly pertinent passage is in Sophocles *Ajax* in which Odysseus is the model of *sōphrosynē* (North 1966, 55 and 58–61) and Menelaus the antithesis. If what is said about Menelaus is meant to be interpreted as a commentary on contemporary Spartans, are we to read Menelaus' comments on *sōphrosynē* (1073 ff.: 'nor would a camp be governed *sōphronōs* any longer if it does not have the defence of fear or shame') as indirect evidence of Spartan self-attribution, and the fact that he clearly does not practise what he preaches as a critical Athenian commentary on this? Certainly often Euripides' mythical Spartan figures are far from possessors of *sōphrosynē* (e.g. *Andromache* 445–63, and Helen in the *Troades*). And in comedy, Aristophanes' jokes about Spartans are generally concerned with superficial aspects such as unkempt long hair, funny dialect, emaciation, and tattered clothing (see Greenstein-Millender 1996, 196 for discussion and references).

[27] Tigerstedt 1965–78, 1.158: 'love of Sparta...was merely the reverse side of the intense hatred for the Athenian democracy which denied them [conservative upper classes] power and enjoyment'.

[28] Ollier 1933–43, 112, for example, thinks that the sentiments are indeed Spartan.

[29] Fisher 2001, 329–30 has reasonably argued that the comment by the Spartan *gerōn* that 'they would not for a long time inhabit an unravaged Sparta' places the anecdote in the past.

[30] The point may be obvious but it is not unimportant since scholars seem to mention Aeschines with regard to Spartan *sōphrosynē* more than Isokrates (e.g., Rawson 1969, 45; Hodkinson 1994, 195; Fisher 1994, 373–5, 382). Yet the Aeschines passage under question is of the same nature as many similar comments in Isokrates.

[31] There is a tendency for the practices of ancestral Athenians and past Spartans to resemble each other in the fourth-century orators. The most striking example is the fourth-century tradition of Tyrtaeus as an Athenian (Plato *Lg.* 629a; Lykourgos

Against Leokrates 106). On this and the appeal of Solon see North 1966, 15; Rawson 1969, 40; Fisher 1994; and Thomas 1994.

[32] *Panath.* 138, 140, 151, 197.

[33] On the passage from Aeschines see Fisher 2001, 327–9. On mass and elite audiences see Ober 1989, 43–9.

[34] See Ober and Strauss 1990, 250–5 and, more specifically on Isokrates' appropriation of democratic slogans to present his oligarchic point of view, Ober 1999, 158.

[35] See Usher 1990 on the *Panegyricus* and Gray 1994 on the *Panathenaicus*. Both note that even when Sparta is praised, the praise is never unqualified. Tigerstedt 1965–78, 1.180–1 and 196–200 also discusses the political expediency of Isokrates' comments on Sparta but he believes that Isokrates 'shared the Laconism of the Athenian upper class' (202).

[36] Fisher 1994, 374.

[37] See Fisher 1994 for further evidence regarding these laconizers.

[38] See Gray 1994, 250–3 on Isokrates' implicit acknowledgment of the 'existence of the tribe of Spartan sympathizers'.

[39] Certainly elsewhere in Isokrates, even in this particular speech, *sōphrosynē* does not consistently appear in lists of Spartan virtues (cf. *Panath.* 216–7, 258; *On the Peace* 102).

[40] North 1966 does not refer to them. Tigerstedt 1965–78, 1.198 refers to the first but glosses over it by translating *sōphronōs zēn* as 'to live simply'. Rawson 1969, 41–2 also notes the first passage without comment.

[41] For a brief account of the event see Xenophon *HG* 7.4.6–11 where there is no mention of Archidamos.

[42] It is generally held to be a rhetorical exercise but whether or not it had a political purpose is uncertain. See Fisher 1994, 391 n. 56 for some suggestions and prior views.

[43] See Humble 1999.

[44] Cf. *Alk. 1* 122d–3b in which Socrates reminds Alkibiades about the great wealth of the Spartans, particularly on their hoarding of wealth. Surely, this, *contra* Tigerstedt (n. 54 below), further undermines the seriousness of the praise.

[45] Most often in its encratic sense of self-control over pleasures. On which see Stalley 1983, 4–5.

[46] See North 1966, 191–2.

[47] It is primarily the intellectual sense of *sōphrosynē* which is at the heart of this dialogue. See North 1966, 154 and Irwin 1977, particularly 19–21 and 87–8.

[48] Both men are spoken of by Xenophon, who notes that while Kritias associated with Socrates he behaved with *sōphrosynē* (*Mem.* 1.2.12; see also n. 22 above). Charmides is also mentioned in the *Memorabilia* where he is presented as a modest and retiring young man (3.7), though he is not said by Xenophon to possess *sōphrosynē*.

[49] Tuckey 1951, 7 also connects Charmides' first definition of *sōphrosynē* with Archidamos' speech but with regard to *eukosmos* not *bradutēs*.

[50] See Guthrie 1975, 164–5 (with broad examples), Saunders 1987, 166 n. 7

(with no examples), and Schofield 2000, 191 (with reference to Thucydides). None notes that *aidōs* is strongly associated with the Spartan way of life by Xenophon in the *Lak. Pol.*

[51] North 1966, 154 and Kahn 1996, 186.

[52] The translation is essentially Tigerstedt's (1965–78, 1.278).

[53] Regarding authenticity in particular, compare the scepticism of Gribble 1999, 260–2 with the defence of Denyer 2000, 14–26.

[54] Denyer 2000, 8 (and 184 where he comments on the unlaconic length of the passage). Tigerstedt 1965–78, 1.278 denies authenticity on the grounds that the flattering description of Sparta cannot be explained away as irony but he gives no reason for denying an ironic slant.

[55] See Flower 1994, 71–83 (on Sparta), 73–5 (on Lysander); and Rawson 1969, 54–5.

[56] The only other two instances are again connected with an opposition to luxury but not connected with Spartans: (a) F 62 = Athen. 526d–f where the Calchedonians who had once been a most *sōphrōn* and most *metrios* people are said to have been corrupted utterly by luxury under the influence of the Byzantians; and (b) F 224 = Athen. 166f–7c where there is the comment that not one of Philip's companions knew how to live *sōphronōs*.

[57] Flower 1994, 29.

[58] Chrimes 1949, 125 notes that the virtue appears in Spartan inscriptions. But these primarily honour women (in line with the long tradition of *sōphrosynē* as a female virtue) and are late second century AD. Tigerstedt 1965–78, 2.202–5 cites Dio of Prusa and makes rather a lot of his connection of *sōphrosynē* with Sparta. The two main references are 34.49–51 (after the Persian wars the Spartans confined themselves to Sparta and to becoming self-controlled (*hauton esōphronize*) and achieved greatest *eudaimonia* during this time but then lost all this, as the Athenians did, when they grasped at empire), and 50.1 (about the Gerousia surpassing all others in *sōphrosynē*). A further indirect and more limited reference can be found at 2.59–60 concerning *sōphronas* dances. On the other hand, Athenians in the time of Peisistratos are also referred to as *sōphrōn* (7.108.3) and in the course of flattering the Prusians and attributing a great number of virtues to them, including *sōphrosynē*, he compares them generally to Spartans and Athenians in the past (44.10–11). These few references among the great number of uses and applications of *sōphrosynē* in his works are not as significant as Tigerstedt implies (see n. 92 below).

[59] Tigerstedt 1965–78, 2.121 and North 1966, 247 draw attention to the passage.

[60] This has not been discussed by modern scholars. Ollier 1933–43, 195–214 makes no comment. North's (1966, 248) examination of Plutarch, regrettably brief, includes only the remark that he considers *sōphrōn* Lykourgos along with Numa, Aristides, Cato, Coriolanus and, above all, Alexander. Rawson 1969, 111–12 also is brief with no reference to *sōphrosynē*. By contrast, Tigerstedt 1965–78, 2.53–64 and 226 ff. is expansive, but even so he does not comment on Spartan *sōphrosynē* in Plutarch.

[61] See Tigerstedt 1965–78, 2.226; Rawson 1969, 130; and Hodkinson 2000, 14–15, 52–60.

[62] A glance at most of the scholarship on the third-century Spartan revolution reveals that even where there is acknowledgement of Plutarch's manipulation of his material, the same material is used without hesitation to provide an account of the period. Erskine 1990, 123–31 sounds a good note of caution about the *Agis*.

[63] Hodkinson 2000, 38–41 following Tigerstedt 1965–78, 2.25–7.

[64] Hodkinson 2000, 40–1, 45 and Tigerstedt 1965–78, 2.82–5.

[65] This anecdote is also included in the *Sayings of Kings and Commanders* (*Mor.* 190f).

[66] Shipley 1997, 196 links this list with the aims of the *syssitia* in the *Lykourgos*.

[67] For a recent treatment see Duff 1999, 161–204.

[68] North 1966, 248: 'in both the *Moralia* and the *Lives*, Plutarch makes sophrosyne profoundly important for education and morality'.

[69] Concerning their mother (*Gracchi* 1.4); both possessed *andreia* and *sōphrosynē* (2.1); Tiberius surpassed Gaius in *sōphrosynē* (2.3); a general statement to the effect that being educated *sōphronōs* fixes and orders the mind (10.4); Gaius excelled his elders in *sōphrosynē*, simplicity and love of labour (23[2].1). This last reference is very similar to the only reference in the *Agis*.

[70] Pompey is loved because he lived his life with *sōphrosynē* (*Pomp.* 1.3); he is *sōphrōn* by nature (18.2); *sōphrosynē* is used of him in the sense of chastity (53.2).

[71] Numa is called *sōphrōn* (*Numa* 4.3) and he tried to make *sōphrōn* (*sōphronizein*) the people (16.4).

[72] Duff 1999, 264 comments on the importance of the theme in the *synkriseis* too. Some of his examples refer simply to general instances of moderate/self-controlled behaviour without the use of the catch-word. Frazier 1996, 193–5 discusses references to *sōphrosynē* (but misses some and does not discuss the use of cognates) and random passages which show examples of self-control.

[73] North 1966, 245. See also Frazier 1996, 177–95 on the philosophic background to Plutarch's use of the cardinal virtues.

[74] See Stadter 1992, 54 n. 38 on Plutarch's general tone towards Sparta.

[75] *Lys.-Sulla* 1.3 is perhaps the only clear-cut example of this *topos* in use in the Spartan *Lives*; see also n. 94 below.

[76] On the sources for the *Agis/Kleomenes* see Marasco 1981, 1.24–42.

[77] See Polybius 2.56–63 on Phylarchos. Plutarch shows doubt about Phylarchos' version of events at *Ag./Kleom.* 26(5).3 and 49(28).1. See also Hodkinson 2000, 43.

[78] See Powell 1999, 401 ff.

[79] Marasco 1981, 2.358–9 on 23(2).1 suggests that 'l'inserimento della *sōphrosynē* fra le caratteristiche dell'educazione spartana sembra rispondere ad un desiderio di adeguare l'*agōgē* al pensiero di Platone' ('the insertion of *sōphrosynē* among the characteristics of Spartan education seems to respond to a desire to adapt the *agōgē* to the thought of Plato'); also see 2.460 on 34(13).1 with reference to Plato *Rep.* 390a.

[80] As noted by Bertinelli et al. 1997, 420. Certainly Athenaeus is reporting Theopompus as the exception concerning Lysander's *sōphrosynē* (Athen. 12.543b: 'nearly all report that Pausanias and Lysander were famous for their luxury'). It might be argued that because Plutarch often highlights Lysander's unspartan qualities (on which see Pelling 1988, 268–74) the absence of *sōphrosynē* if a Spartan quality, is perfectly explicable. However, he is termed *sōphrōn* in the *synkrisis* and this argument would not account for the absence of the term in the *Agesilaos*.

[81] Such as those by Kritias, Aristotle (from whom quite a lot is assumed to have derived), Dicaearchus, Persaeus of Citium, Sphairos, Dioskorides (on which see Boring 1979, 64–73) and possibly also Pausanias, Lysander and Thibron (Boring 1979, 50–4). On Plutarch's sources for the *Lykourgos*, see Manfredini and Piccirilli 1998, xl–xlii.

[82] See Kennell 1995, 20–3 and Hodkinson 2000, 38–40 and 48 ff., who also notes that much of the material can be traced back to Xenophon and Aristotle. Among the numerous problems surrounding the dating of the work is a reference to the defeat of Greece by Rome in 146 BC (240b). Kennell has argued that the first seventeen chapters at least date back to the third-century Spartan revolution, to the work of the Stoic philosopher Sphairos, who was close to King Kleomenes and wrote two works on Sparta, *On the Laconian constitution* and *On Lycurgus and Socrates* (Kennell 1995, 102–7). On the possible role of Sphairos in making certain that the Lykourgos of the revolution did not clash with the traditional Lykourgos, see the plausible suggestions of Erskine 1990, 135–8.

[83] See Hodkinson 2000, 48–50.

[84] Plutarch refers directly to Plato though he does substantially change the passage from the *Laws*, keeping the medical metaphor but bringing *sōphrosynē* to the fore. Cf. also Aeschines *Against Timarchus* 180; and Dio of Prusa 50.1.

[85] At *Lyk.* 14.1 Plutarch is directly referring to Aristotle *Pol.* 1270a7–8, but where Aristotle uses the phrase *agein hupo tous nomous* Plutarch uses the verb *sōphronizein*.

[86] See Hodkinson 2000, 37 ff. and Flower (this volume).

[87] Compare particularly *Ag./Kleom.* 37(16).4 and *Ag./Kleom.-Gracchi* 2.3 with *Lyk.* 31.4 and *Lyk.-Numa* 2.1. And see on this Tigerstedt 1965–78, 2.81.

[88] There are, for example, several early references to some sort of equality in daily life at Sparta. Thucydides uses the word *isodiaitoi* ('an equal style of living'); Xenophon states at *Lak.* 7.3 'what seriousness could wealth hold there [i.e. in Sparta] where Lykourgos ordered that they bring equal things (*isa*) to the provisions and that they lead similar lives (*homoiōs diaitasthai*)'. The same combination of equality and similarity is found in a highly tendentious passage in Isokrates (*Areopagiticus* 61): Isokrates says that Sparta is the most democratic state 'because concerning the choosing of their magistrates, their daily life and their practices we might see among them equality (*tas isotētas*) and similarity (*tas homoiotētas*) stronger than among others'.

[89] Hodkinson 2000, 50–2.

[90] See Hodkinson 2000, 51 on this as the earliest extant reference to the concept.

[91] North 1966, 247.

[92] Plutarch's contemporary, Dio, for example, who can hardly have had cause to refer to Phylarchos, in his few references to Spartan *sōphrosynē* resembles the practices of the fourth-century BC orators rather than Plutarch (see n. 58 above).

[93] The idea that Spartan women possessed *sōphrosynē* may (despite *Mor.* 242b which is presumed to be of a pre-revolutionary date) also be a similar construct of the revolution (see the post-revolutionary references in the *Lykourgan Apophthegmata* 228b, *Ag./Kleom.* 43[22].2 and *Lyk.* 14.1, 15.5, 15.7). Cf., by contrast, e.g., Euripides *Andr.* 601 (*ei mē gunaikas sōphronas paideuete;* on which see Cartledge 2001, 114); Xenophon (*Lak.* 3.4) where he comments on Spartan youths being more *sōphron* than Spartan women (with Cartledge 2001, 219 n. 121); and Aristotle for whom they live licentiously (*Pol.* 1269b22–3: *zōsi akolastōs*; for the opposition of *sōphrosunē* and *akolasia*, see Arist. *EN* 1117b23–33 and Plato *Grg.* 507c). Plato (*Lg.* 637c) and Aristotle (*Pol.* 1270a1) also comment on the 'freedom' (*anesis*) of Spartan women.

[94] The only instance in Plutarch of a laconizing oligarch praising Spartan *sōphrosynē*, in the manner of Kritias or of Isokrates' mock opponents in the *Panathenaicus*, is found in the *Cimon*. There Plutarch has Cimon say at his trial in 463 that if he was working for anyone it would be the Spartans whose simplicity and *sōphrosynē* he was happy to imitate (14.4). There is nothing in the *Alkibiades* to compare with the pseudo-Platonic *Alkibiades I.* Though Phokion is said to have sent his son to the Spartan *agōgē* (*Phok.* 20.2), his own *sōphrōn* education was Athenian (4.1). He is also called a guardian of *sōphrosynē* (38.1) but Plutarch connects him, in this regard, to Socrates not to any Spartan model (38.2). Aristides is said to have emulated and admired Lykourgos (*Arist.* 2.1) but *sōphrosynē* is only once attributed to him directly and the context has nothing to do with Sparta (*Arist./Cato Maj.* 6.1); his reputation is, rather, for justice (e.g. *Arist.* 2.2, 23.3, 24.2; cf. Hdt. 8.79 where Herodotus calls him most just). And there is a similar dearth of examples of the type of rhetoric about past Sparta that was found in the oratory of Isokrates and Aeschines. *Lys./Sulla* 1.3 definitely falls in this category and see also *Aristides* 23.7 (the Spartans, once they are shown that their leaders had been corrupted, retired and were said to prefer that their citizens be *sōphrōn* and abide by their customs than that they rule all Greece). See also n. 58 above for the use of the rhetorical *topos* by Dio of Prusa.

[95] To use the words of Flower (this volume).

[96] See Rawson 1969, 130 (and *passim*) and Duff 1999, 3–5.

[97] Hodkinson 2000, 9–17.

Bibliography

Bertinelli, M.G.A., Manfredini, M., Piccirilli, L. and Pisani, G.
1997 *Plutarco. Le Vite di Lisandro e di Silla*, Milan.

Boring, T.A.
1979 *Literacy in Ancient Sparta*, Leiden.

Cartledge, P.
2001 *Spartan Reflections*, London.
Chrimes, K.M.T.
1949 *Ancient Sparta: A re-examination of the evidence*, Manchester.
Denyer, N. (ed.)
2001 *Plato: Alcibiades*, Cambridge.
Dover, K.J.
1974 *Greek Popular Morality: In the time of Plato and Aristotle*, Indianapolis/Cambridge.
Duff, T.
1999 *Plutarch's Lives: Exploring virtue and vice*, Oxford.
Dunbar, N.
1995 *Aristophanes. Birds*, Oxford.
Edmunds, L.
1975 'Thucydides' ethics as reflected in the description of stasis (3.82–3)', *HSCP* 79, 73–92.
Erskine, A.
1990 *The Hellenistic Stoa: Political thought and action*, London.
Fisher, N.
1994 'Sparta re(de)valued: some Athenian public attitudes to Sparta between Leuctra and the Lamian War', in A. Powell and S. Hodkinson (eds.) *The Shadow of Sparta*, London, 347–400.
2001 *Aeschines. Against Timarchos*, Oxford.
Flower, M.A.
1994 *Theopompus of Chios: History and rhetoric in the fourth century BC*, Oxford.
Frazier, F.
1996 *Histoire et morale dans les Vies Parallèles de Plutarque*, Paris.
Gomme, A.W., Andrewes, A. and Dover, K.J.
1945–81 *A Historical Commentary on Thucydides*, 5 vols., Oxford.
Gray, V.
1994 'Images of Sparta: writer and audience in Isocrates' *Panathenaicus*', in A. Powell and S. Hodkinson (eds.) *The Shadow of Sparta*, London, 223–71.
Greenstein-Millender, E.
1996 '"The Teacher of Hellas": Athenian democratic ideology and the "barbarization" of Sparta in fifth-century Greek thought', Diss. Pennsylvania.
Gribble, D.
1999 *Alkibiades and Athens*, Oxford.
Guthrie, W.K.C.
1975 *A History of Greek Philosophy*, vol. 4, Cambridge.
Hodkinson, S.
1994 '"Blind Ploutos"? Contemporary images of the role of wealth in classical Sparta', in A. Powell and S. Hodkinson (eds.) *The Shadow of Sparta*, London, 183–222.
2000 *Property and Wealth in Classical Sparta*, London.

Hornblower, S.

1987 *Thucydides*, London.

1991–6 *A Commentary on Thucydides*, 2 vols., Oxford.

Humble, N.

1999 '*Sōphrosynē* and the Spartans', in S. Hodkinson and A. Powell (eds.) *Sparta: New Perspectives*, London, 339–53.

Hussey, E.L.

1985 'Thucydidean history and Democritean theory', in P. Cartledge and F.D. Harvey (eds.) *CRUX: Essays presented to G.E.M. de Ste Croix on his 75th Birthday*, London, 118–38.

Irwin, T.

1977 *Plato's Moral Theory: The early and middle dialogues*, Oxford.

Kahn, C.H.

1995 *Plato and the Socratic Dialogue: The philosophical use of a literary form*, Cambridge.

Kennell, N.M.

1992 *The Gymnasium of Virtue*, Chapel Hill.

MacLeod, C.W.

1978 'Reason and necessity: Thucydides iii 9–14, 37–48', *JHS* 98, 64–78.

Manfredini, M. and Piccirilli, L. (eds.)

1998 *Plutarco. Le Vite di Licurgo e di Numa*, 4th edn, Milan.

Marasco, G.

1981 *Commento alle biographie plutarchee di Agide e Cleomene*, 2 vols., Rome.

North, H.

1966 *Sophrosyne*, Ithaca.

Ober, J.

1989 *Mass and Elite in Democratic Athens*, Princeton.

1999 *The Athenian Revolution*, Princeton.

Ober, J. and Strauss, B.

1990 'Drama, political rhetoric, and the discourse of Athenian democracy', in J.J. Winkler and F.I. Zeitlin (eds.) *Nothing to do with Dionysos? Athenian drama in its social context*, Princeton 1990, 237–70.

Ollier, F.

1933–43 *Le mirage spartiate: étude sur l'idéalisation de Sparte dans l'antiquité grecque*, 2 vols., Paris.

Pelling, C.

1988 'Aspects of Plutarch's characterization', *ICS* 13, 257–74.

1991 'Thucydides' Archidamus and Herodotus' Artabanus' in M.A. Flower and M. Toher (eds.) *Georgica: Greek Studies in Honour of George Cawkwell*, London, 120–42.

Powell, A.

1999 'Spartan women assertive in politics? Plutarch's Lives of Agis and Kleomenes', in S. Hodkinson and A. Powell (eds.) *Sparta: New perspectives*, London, 393–419.

Price, J.J.

2001 *Thucydides and Internal War*, Cambridge.

Rawson, E.
1969 *The Spartan Tradition in European Thought*, Oxford.

Rhodes, P.J. (ed.)
1994 *Thucydides. History III*, Warminster.

Saunders, T.J. (ed.)
1987 *Plato. Early Socratic Dialogues*, Harmondsworth.

Schofield, M.
2000 'Approaching the *Republic*: Introduction', in C. Rowe and M. Schofield (eds.) *The Cambridge History of Greek and Roman Political Thought*, Cambridge, 190–2.

Shipley, D.R.
1997 *Plutarch's Life of Agesilaos: Response to sources in the presentation of character*, Oxford.

Stadter, P.A.
1992 'Paradoxical paradigms: Lysander and Sulla', in P.A. Stadter (ed.) *Plutarch and the Historical Tradition*, London and New York, 41–55.

Stalley, R.F.
1983 *An Introduction to Plato's Laws*, Oxford.

Thomas, R.
1994 'Law and the lawgiver in the Athenian democracy', in R. Osborne and S. Hornblower (eds.) *Ritual, Finance, Politics*, Oxford, 119–33.

Tigerstedt, E.N.
1965–78 *The Legend of Sparta in Classical Antiquity*, 3 vols., Stockholm, Göteborg and Uppsala.

Tuckey, T.G.
1951 *Plato's Charmides*. Cambridge.

Tuplin,C.
1994 'Xenophon, Sparta and the *Cyropaedia*', in A. Powell and S. Hodkinson (eds.) *The Shadow of Sparta*, London, 127–81.

Usher, S.
1990 *Greek Orators III. Isocrates*, Warminster.

Wassermann, F.M.
1953 'The speeches of King Archidamus in Thucydides', *CJ* 48, 193–9.

Westlake, H.D.
1968 *Individuals in Thucydides*, Cambridge.

Wilson, J.R.
1990 'Sophrosyne in Thucydides', *AHB* 4.3, 51–7.

4

THREE EVOCATIONS OF THE DEAD WITH PAUSANIAS

Daniel Ogden

Three traditions associate Pausanias, son of Cleombrotus, regent of Sparta and vanquisher of the Persians, with necromancy. These traditions can be shown both to be ancient and to be deeply coherent with each other. Of particular interest is the necromantic tale that lurks beneath Thucydides' story of the man of Argilos.[1]

1. The evocation of Pausanias

We are told that (around 470)[2] the ephors, having finally decided to arrest Pausanias for Persian treachery, chased him into a chamber in the precinct of Athene Chalkioikos, probably the temple cella,[3] wherein he became a suppliant. He was then starved to death in it, as we learn from a puzzling series of narratives that speak of him being bricked up either into the chamber itself or into the precinct as a whole, with the ephors then (roofing and) de-roofing the chamber (or precinct as a whole), ostensibly for purposes of surveillance or exposure. This is Thucydides' version of the aftermath:

> When, in the chamber as he was, Pausanias was on the point of giving up the ghost (*apopsuchein*), they realized this and brought him out of the shrine still just about breathing, but as soon as he was brought out he died. They were going to throw him into the Caeadas, where they threw criminals, but then they decided to put him in the ground (*katoruxai*) somewhere nearby. Later on (*husteron*), the god in Delphi responded to the Spartans that they should transfer his burial (*taphon*) to the place at which he died (and now he lies in the forecourt of the precinct, as pillars testify in writing), and that, since what they had done constituted a pollution (*agos*), they should repay to Chalkioikos two bodies in exchange for one. And so they made two bronze statues and dedicated them as in place of Pausanias. Thucydides 1.134

Other sources, such as Plutarch and Pausanias-periegetes, add interesting details:

> In like manner [i.e. in a manner akin to Callondes' placation of the ghost of Archilochus at the Tainaron *nekuomanteion*, for which see below], the

> Spartans received an oracle that they should propitiate the soul (*psuchēn*) of Pausanias, and so evocators (*psuchagōgoi*) were summoned from Italy. They made a sacrifice and drew the ghost (*eidōlon*) away from the temple.
> Plutarch *Moralia* 560ef (*Slow vengeance*)

> Beside the altar of Chalkioikos stand two effigies of Pausanias, who commanded at the battle of Plataea... [The tale of Pausanias and Cleonice, for which also see below, follows.] The Spartans, in fulfilment of the command of Delphi, made the bronze effigies and honour the demon Epidotes, saying that he averted the anger of Hikesios [*or*: of the attacking ghost (*hikesios*)][4] over Pausanias.
> Pausanias 3.17

> When Pausanias had been destroyed by starvation they took the roof off, dragged him out of the temple still breathing and cast him out. Because of this a pestilence seized them. The god prophesied that the pestilence would cease (*pausasthai*) whenever they propitiated the demons (*daimones*) of Pausanias, so they set up a statue to him, and the pestilence ceased (*epausato*).
> Aristodemus *FGH* 104 F 8 (fourth-century AD)

Further accounts of the tale are to be found elsewhere in Plutarch (in his *Parallel stories*, where Chrysermus of Corinth is cited, and in his fragmentary *Homerikai Meletai*), and also in Diodorus (from Ephorus?), Nepos, Ps.-Themistocles, and the *Suda*.[5]

The use of the replacement statues rings true enough in an early Spartan context. Herodotus tells that the Spartans buried effigies (*eidōla*) of their kings who died far away.[6] What relationship, if any, did these have to the pair of effigies of the Dioscuri that traditionally accompanied the Spartan kings into battle?[7]

It is initially tempting to disentangle two latent parallel tales within this complex tradition, which might be entitled 'the anger of Athene' and 'the anger of Pausanias'. The 'anger of Athene' runs as follows:

> Pausanias dies in the forecourt and is duly buried. But Athene is still angered by the violation of the supplication. She sends pestilence. Delphi tells the Spartans to 'give her back her suppliant'. Due reburial of Pausanias in the forecourt and the erection of statues for Athene's sake follow. Athene is placated.

The 'anger of Pausanias' runs as follows:

> Pausanias' ghost is angry at his deprivation of due burial. It terrorizes visitors to the precinct. Delphi tells the Spartans to bring in the evocators, who perform a sacrifice and charm the ghost away from the temple, accomplish the first due burial for Pausanias in the forecourt and erect statues for Pausanias' sake. The ghost of Pausanias is placated.

Such a differentiation helps us to make sense of the interwoven strands of logic that underpin the narrative. But there remains a bond at deep level between on the one hand the theme of the killing of suppliants of Athene and the ensuing intervention of Delphi, and on the other hand the theme of the placation of both the goddess and the ghosts of the dead with double statues. This can be seen from a comparison with Justin's apparently equally traditional tale of the youths of Siris:[8]

> When [the people of Croton and Metapontum] first took the city of Siris, in storming it they slaughtered fifty youths embracing the statue of Athene, together with the priest of the goddess in his robes of office amidst the altars. When they were afflicted by pestilence and civil disturbances on account of this, the Crotoniates first approached the Delphic oracle. They received the reply that there would be an end to their troubles if they placated the violated godhead of Athene and the ghosts of those who had been killed. And so, when the Crotoniates had begun to manufacture life-size statues for the young men and in particular for Athene, the Metapontines too, on learning of the god's oracle, thought they should seize for themselves the peace of the ghosts and the goddess first, and set up miniature stone effigies for the young men and placated the goddess with offering-cakes. And so the pestilence was laid to rest on both sides, since the one city had strenuously excelled in magnificence, the other in expedition.
> Justin 20.2[9]

So, if we do detect traces of two different tales in the Pausanias tradition, it is more likely that we are witnessing an originally unitary tale in the process of diverging than two originally distinct tales in the process of converging. Perhaps the goddess originally sent pestilence in part *because* deprived of cult when the ghost frightened her worshippers away.

There are a number of reasons for thinking that the ghost-story element of the tradition of Pausanias' death existed before Thucydides, that he was aware of it, and that he suppressed it.

(a) The most compelling indication that the ghost story existed before Thucydides is found in his reference to the dedication of the double figures (in bronze, and apparently representing Pausanias).[10] Double 'replacement' figures (*kolossoi*) are specifically associated with the placation of ghosts in archaic and even Mycenean Greek culture. This is clear from Justin's tale of the youths of Siris, in which Athene is placated by a single statue and offering-cakes, whereas the ghosts of the dead youths are each placated by double statues. Each pair of replacement effigies at Siris consisted of a large and a small, of which the smaller at any rate was made of stone (were the larger ones stone too, or bronze, by implicit contrast?). In this way they strongly resemble the pair of stone 'menhirs', flat oblong stones with head-like protruberances at the top, one around four feet tall, the other two feet tall, found in a Mycenean cenotaph chamber-tomb at Midea, the function of which was evidently to replace the (single) missing body.[11]

A seventh-century BC grave from Thera (Schiff's grave) similarly contained no bones but two rough-carved stone statuettes, this pair, however, of the same height, *c.* eight inches.[12] Perhaps these effigy-pairs were rationalized as standing for body and soul. Such a hypothesis seems particularly attractive in the cases of the large-and-small pairs at any rate, when we bear in mind archaic vase illustrations of Sarpedon's ghost quitting his body in the form of a parallel but miniature version of the body itself, as this body is carried from the field by personifications of Sleep and Death.[13] Indeed Richer has proposed precisely such an interpretation for the Pausanias statue-pair.[14]

In the fourth-century BC redaction of ancient purification rules supposedly given to Cyrene by Delphi, one is to lay an attacking ghost (*hikesios*) by proclaiming its name for three days, if one knows it. If one does not, one is to lay it by addressing it as 'O person, whether a man or a woman', making male and female dolls from earth or wood, entertaining them to a meal, and depositing them in unworked woodland.[15] Here it may be that the doll-pair was rationalized rather as representing each of the two sexes. These provisions in turn have much in common with those of a recently discovered sacred law from Selinus, which instruct a killer pursued by an angry ghost (*elasteros*; cf. *alastōr*) to rid himself of it by inviting the ghost to an outdoor meal and addressing it there.[16]

The Cyrenean law sheds crucial light on Pausanias-periegetes' narrative of regent Pausanias' death. It is normally assumed that the Hikesios placated in this narrative is Zeus Hikesios, Zeus of Suppliants, and therefore that he acts as a functional alternative to Athene Chalkioikos.[17] This is impossible. It is difficult enough that Zeus should step in to avenge a wrong done to Athene, but decisive is the fact that the averter of Hikesios' anger, Epidotes, is himself Zeus (or an aspect thereof): Hesychius tells that he was given this name in Sparta.[18] Now, Zeus cannot avert the anger of Zeus. Rather, it is clear that just as in the Cyrenean law two effigies placate an attacking ghost defined as a *hikesios*, so too in Pausanias-periegetes' narrative the Hikesios placated by the two effigies is the attacking ghost of Pausanias. Almost certainly the term is a common noun, not a proper one, and is therefore wrongly printed capitalized in all texts.[19] However, Greek's use of the term *hikesios* to mean both 'attacking ghost' and 'suppliant' was not an arbitrary equivocation.[20] The tale of Pausanias' death associates the two meanings closely, for the regent is shown as both suppliant and attacking ghost. We shall have more to say on this term's semantic field below.

A further parallel for the use of effigies in the placation of ghosts relates to their brazen nature rather than their duality. Pausanias-periegetes tells that the ghost of Actaeon devastated the country around Orchomenos by throwing rocks. Delphi commanded the Orchomenians to cover such remains of Actaeon as they could find with earth, make a bronze image of the ghost, and then rivet it with iron to rock.[21]

(b) As Burkert notes, Thucydides' introduction of the Delphic solution is undermotivated. In context it almost appears to be a solution without a prior problem. The *agos*, to which the Spartans are told they are subject, has not apparently manifested any effect so far. A logical motivation for the Spartans' consultation of Delphi seems to have dropped out to be replaced by weak temporal connective, 'later on' (*husteron*). Burkert's plausible solution is that in the gap belonged the terrorizing ghost, and that Thucydides has suppressed it.[22]

(c) The ghost story perhaps casts two linguistic shadows over Thucydides' narrative. First, Fontenrose sees in Thucydides' use of the word *agos* a reflection of the ghost and the haunting.[23] This does seem particularly likely in view of the fact that Pausanias-periegetes tells that Pausanias himself had tried and failed to wipe out the *agos* of the murder of Cleonice by supplication at the temple of Chalkioikos.[24] Secondly, the word that Thucydides applies to the death of Pausanias, *apopsuchein*, may be read as connoting 'give up the ghost': is this a sly tribute to the missing ghost?[25]

(d) Thucydides' detail (repeated by Nepos) that the Spartans first contemplated throwing Pausanias' body down the Caeadas, but then decided to bury him, is curious: this inconsequential dead-end seems out of place in the context of his fast-paced narrative. But when viewed in the context of other sources that assert that the Spartans did actually throw his body down the Caeadas (namely Plutarch/Chrysermus, Aristodemus and the *Suda*), the significance of Thucydides' detail becomes clear: its primary function is not narrative but agonistic, in his usual way.[26] Thucydides is thus acknowledging but denying an already well-established tradition that Pausanias' body was indeed thrown down the Caeadas.[27] Why? Perhaps because he felt the motif of the denial of due burial to be too intimately bound up with the motif of the angry ghost.

This leads to a further linguistic point. The motif of due burial denied may yet be cautiously reflected in the word that Thucydides applies to the initial disposal of the body: *katoruxai* perhaps connotes mechanical rather than due burial, which is denoted in turn by the subsequent *taphon*.[28] That the mere insertion of a corpse into the ground was not tantamount to due burial is best illustrated by ancient haunted-house stories. In Plautus' *Mostellaria* the spoof story that the slave spins, to keep the master from returning to his own house, has it haunted by the ghost of Diapontius, whom the former owner murdered and buried, without due burial, inside the house.[29] Pliny the Younger and Lucian tell variants of a tale in which a philosopher braves out the night alone in a haunted house with a ghost, which, after failing to terrify him to death or drag him down to hell, leads him through the house and points at a spot on the ground. The next day the spot is dug to reveal the remains of a maltreated corpse, unduly buried.[30] It is noteworthy that in these haunted-house tales the ghost haunts the spot where its body lies without due burial. If this notion were to be read back into the tale of Pausanias (which it need not be), then it would imply that Pausanias' body did after all lie near the temple, since the ghost was able to frighten those that approached it. However, ghosts did have the ability to haunt at once both the place in which their bodies lay and the place of their death. Thus, during the period of his provisional and inadequate burial in the Lamian gardens, Caligula contrived to haunt both the gardens and the building in which he had been cut down.[31]

(e) There is possibly another case of 'rationalization' in Thucydides' Pausanias material. The single most hackneyed and recycled element of the tradition relating to the death of Pausanias was the motif of his 'Spartan mother' leading the way in bricking him up into the chamber.[32] While we cannot prove that Thucydides knew it, a ready context exists for his 'rationalizing' suppression of it: his established distaste for the mention of women and of female causes in particular.[33]

We may conclude that the 'anger of Pausanias' element in the tradition was an old one, that Thucydides knew it, and that he (almost) eliminated it in favour of the 'anger of Athene' element. Indeed, it may well have been Thucydides' (or someone else's) isolation of this strand of the tradition that contributed more than anything to the apparent differentiation of the two latent stories within it.

2. The evocation of Cleonice

A related tradition tells of Pausanias' killing of Cleonice and of his own ensuing necromancy of her ghost, supposedly in or soon after 479.[34] This is presented as a direct cause of his own miserable death at Sparta. In paralleling the themes of that episode (wrongful killing, attempted necromantic placation) the Cleonice tale forms a 'diptych' with it:

> It is told that Pausanias sent for a virgin of Byzantium, Cleonice by name, of distinguished parents, in order to subject her to sexual disgrace. Her parents sent the girl out to him, under compulsion and through fear. She asked the men before the bedroom to remove the light, and approached the bed in silence through the darkness. Pausanias was already asleep. But she stumbled into the lamp-stand and accidentally overturned it. He was disturbed by the noise and drew the dagger at his side, thinking that an enemy was coming against him. He struck the girl and dropped her to the ground. She died from the blow, but would not permit Pausanias to be at peace. During the night she

> would visit him as a ghost in his sleep, and declare this hexameter in anger,
>
> Go to justice; hubris is a very bad thing for men.
>
> The allies took this outrage particularly badly, and, with Cimon, forced him out of the city. Chased out of Byzantium, and hounded to distraction by the ghost, as it is said, he fled to the oracle of the dead (*nekuomanteion*) at Heraclea.[35] He called up the soul of Cleonice and tried to beg off her anger. She came before his vision and said that he would quickly be delivered from his troubles when he was in Sparta, making a riddle, as it seems, about the death that was awaiting him. Anyway, many tell this tale. Plutarch *Cimon* 6

The following passage sits within Pausanias-periegetes' treatment of the two bronze statues of Pausanias, quoted above:

> I heard from a man of Byzantium that Pausanias was detected in his plotting, and was the only one of the suppliants (*hiketeusantōn*) of Chalkioikos to be deprived of immunity, for no other reason than that he was unable to wash away the pollution (*agos*) of murder. For when he was based at the Hellespont with the Spartan ships and those of the other Greeks, he conceived a desire for a Byzantine girl. And so right at the beginning of the night those detailed to do so brought Cleonice (for that was the girl's name) to him. At this point Pausanias was asleep, and the noise of her arrival woke him up. For as she approached his side she accidentally knocked over a burning lamp. Since Pausanias was guilt-ridden about his betrayal of Greece and for that reason in the continual grip of restless confusion and fear, he leaped up and there and then struck the girl with his sword. It turned out that Pausanias could not escape this pollution (*agos*), despite being in receipt of all sorts of purifications from and undertaking supplications (*hikesias*) before Zeus *Phuxios* ('the Deliverer'), and despite the fact that he even went to Phigalia in Arcadia to the evocators (*psuchagōgoi*). And he paid the penalty it was reasonable for him to pay to Cleonice and to the god. And the Spartans, in fulfilment of the command of Delphi [etc., as quoted above]. Pausanias 3.17

This tale too is told elsewhere in a second version by Plutarch, in his *Slow vengeance*, and also by Aristodemus.[36] It is evidently considerably older than Plutarch, who first attests it for us, as is indicated by the fact that he already says that it was told by many. Some think that Plutarch's source was Nymphis of Heraclea (early third century BC) because of Plutarch's location of the consultation at Heraclea (in contrast to Pausanias-periegetes' location of it at Phigalia), on the grounds that Nymphis is known to have spoken of the hubris of Pausanias,[37] and that Plutarch read him and cites him elsewhere.[38] It may well have come to Aristodemus, directly or indirectly, from the mid-fourth-century historian Ephorus.[39]

Comparison with two traditions attaching to Periander shows that the story-type itself is attested already in the fifth and possibly even in the sixth century (i.e. actually before the historical setting of the Cleonice tale). The

Cleonice tradition sits midway between the two Periander traditions, which initially appear unrelated to each other, and thus reveals the fundamental relationship between all three traditions.

The first Periander tradition is his famous evocation of his wife Melissa at the Acheron *nekuomanteion* in Thesprotia, for which Herodotus is the principal source,

> On one day he stripped all the women of Corinth on account of his wife Melissa. For he sent messengers to her, to Thesprotia, to the river Acheron, to the *nekuomanteion*, on the question of the deposit of a guest-friend. Melissa appeared and said that she would neither indicate nor declare where the deposit lay, for she was cold and naked. The clothes that had been buried with her were no use to her because they had not been burned. As witness to the truth of these assertions stood the fact that Periander had thrown his loaves into a cold oven. When these utterances were reported back to Periander (for the token was proof: Periander had had sex with Melissa's corpse), he immediately afterwards issued an edict that all the women of Corinth should go out to the Heraion. So they came out as to a festival in their finest adornments, but he posted his bodyguards in ambush and stripped them all alike, free and slave, piled their clothing up into a trench and burned it with a prayer to Melissa. After doing this he sent to Melissa a second time and she told him where she had put the guest-friend's deposit. Herodotus 5.92

Just as Pausanias found himself attracted to Cleonice, so too Periander experienced an intense erotic attachment towards Melissa, as is best demonstrated by his subsequent necrophilia with her corpse; Nicolaus of Damascus' account explicitly ascribes this to erotic desire.[40] As Pausanias had accidentally killed Cleonice, so too Periander had himself unintentially killed Melissa in an unthinking fit of rage (Diogenes Laertius uses the word *akousion*). She had been slandered by his concubines – presumably with the allegation of sexual infidelity – and he had kicked her or thrown a footstool at her, whilst she was pregnant.[41] Periander's necrophilia is also indicative of strong repentance thereafter. As Pausanias called up the ghost of Cleonice at a *nekuomanteion* to placate it, so too Periander called up Melissa's ghost at a *nekuomanteion* and placated it. Herodotus does not present placation as Periander's initial goal in his evocation, although the act of placation that he proceeds to undertake does constitute the focal episode of his tale.[42] The Melissa tale seemingly antedates Herodotus.[43] It exhibits structural similarities with a tale that Strabo tells elliptically with a tentative ascription to Stesichorus, whose *floruit* was probably the first half of the sixth century.[44] An unnamed tyrant of Corinth was betrothed to Rhadine, but she was loved by her cousin; the tyrant killed them both and dispatched their bodies from Corinth in a chariot; he then repented and had their bodies brought back for due burial. The obvious candidate for the 'bad' tyrant of Corinth is of course Periander himself.[45] It looks as though sexual jealousy was the reason for this killing too, so we can reconstruct an erotic attachment and a concomitantly passionate killing; repentance is explicit, and the bestowal of burial upon the corpse would constitute placation; admittedly there is no indication of an actual ghost in Strabo's allusive summary.

The second Periander tradition to bear upon the Cleonice tradition is that of Periander and his mother, Crateia, 'Power'. Parthenius tells that Crateia fell in love with Periander, and deceived him into having regular sex with her as a secret lover in a darkened room. Eventually, keen to discover the identity of his lover, he concealed a lamp in the chamber, which he suddenly revealed when his lover arrived. In horror at the discovery, he leaped at his mother to kill her, but was restrained from doing so by a demonic apparition (*daimonion phasma*). Periander went mad and starting killing citizens, while his mother committed suicide.[46] The links with the Cleonice tradition this time are different, but nonetheless clear: the darkened room; the woman approaching the bed for illicit sex; the pivotal significance of the lamp; the unreflecting, passionate attempt to kill; the ensuing distractedness of the man; the (eventual) death of the woman. And the ghost motif appears in the demonic apparition that prevents Periander from killing his mother.[47]

The Corinthian traditions exhibit comparable structures to the tale of Pausanias and Cleonice. In doing so they indicate that the story-type is an old one and that it may even have existed before the time of Pausanias himself.

3. The evocation of the man of Argilos

A number of sources tell the tale of Pausanias and the man of Argilos. Other accounts, such as that of Nepos, offer some interesting variants, but the story is first found in Thucydides. The ephors await proof of Pausanias' treachery with the Persian satrap:

> A man of Argilos [*anēr Argilios*], who was to take Pausanias' last letter to Artabazus, and who had formerly been his boy-lover and was intensely loyal to him, became an informer. For he had taken fear when he had considered that none of the messengers before him had ever come back. He made a copy of the seal, in case he should be wrong or in case Pausanias should ask to alter the text, and opened the letter. In it, in accordance with the sort of thing he suspected, he found it written that he should be killed.
>
> 133. When he had shown them the letter the ephors were more persuaded, but they still wanted to hear Pausanias himself admit something. They contrived a plot. The man went to Tainaron as a suppliant [*hiketou*] and

built a hut [*or*: tent] divided in two by a partition [*skēnōsamenou diplēn diaphragmati kalybēn*]. He concealed some of the ephors inside. Pausanias came to him and asked him the reason for his supplication [*hiketeias*], and they heard everything clearly. The man accused Pausanias of writing his death-warrant, and went through everything else in sequence. He said that although he had never betrayed Pausanias in the services he had performed him by going to the king, he had been given the same reward as the majority of his servants – death. Pausanias admitted these things and tried to persuade him not to be angry [*ouk eōntos orgizesthai*] about the current situation. He gave him a pledge of security should he get up from the altar and urged him to go on his way as quickly as possible and not hinder his project.

134. The ephors heard this in accurate detail and went off. Now that they knew for sure, they planned his arrest in the city... [the chase into Chalkioikos ensues.] Thucydides 1.132–4

And Nepos:

In the meantime, a certain Argilios, a young man, whom Pausanias had loved sexually when he was a boy, was given by him a letter for Artabazus, and he came to suspect that there might be something written in the letter about himself, since none of the people that had been sent on such a mission to the same place had come back. So he undid the letter and broke the seal, and realized that he would die if he took the message to its destination. There was also in the letter information about the agreement between Pausanias and the king of Persia. He handed the letter over to the ephors. The stolid caution of the Spartans should not be missed at this point. For they were not induced to arrest Pausanias even on the evidence of this man, and they thought it wrong to employ any force against him unless he compromised himself. So they gave instructions to the informer about what they wanted done. There is a temple of Poseidon on Tainaron, the violation of which the Greeks hold to be a crime. The informer fled there and sat down on the altar. Near this altar they made a place under the ground, from which it could be heard if anyone said anything to Argilios. Some of the ephors descended into this. When Pausanias heard that Argilios had fled to the altar, he came there in an agitated state. When he saw him sat on the altar as a suppliant of the god he asked him what the cause was of such a hasty plan. Argilios revealed to him what he had learned from the letter. Immediately, Pausanias, more upset still, began to beg him not to broadcast it or to betray him, when he had deserved so well of him. If he pardoned him for this and saved him from the charges he was facing, he would be richly rewarded. When the ephors had learned these things, they thought he would be better arrested in the city. When they had set out for the city and Pausanias was returning there after having, as he thought, placated Argilios, and was just about to be arrested, he realized that he was walking into a trap from the facial expression of one of the ephors. He managed to flee into the temple of Athene, who is called Chalkioikos, a few paces in advance of his pursuers. Nepos (*Pausanias*) 4.4–5

This tale is also told by Diodorus and Aristodemus.[48] There are several oddities about Thucydides' version, if viewed as a supposedly straight piece of historical narrative, and scholars, notably Cawkwell and Westlake, have remarked upon them.[49] Why should Thucydides specify that the messenger comes from Argilos (near Amphipolis in Thrace) and what is the significance of this?[50] Why did the man of Argilos live to take the last letter to the king when he had already taken others? Are his ruminations on the disappearance of preceding messengers credible? Why did he not just go home to Argilos after opening the letter? Why, accordingly, was Pausanias fooled by the gesture of supplication, which made the man more rather than less vulnerable? Why the need for the elaborate hut? How did the ephors know when Pausanias was coming and so to hide? Is it not curious that after all this Pausanias should be asking the man of Argilos to continue with his mission? Why did the ephors decline to arrest Pausanias before he had returned all the way to the city? Why is Thucydides unaware of or glossing over the great distance between Sparta and Tainaron?[51] These oddities can be largely explained by a detailed comparison with the Cleonice tradition, with which, on the surface, the Argilos tale appears to have little in common.

In the first place, the man-of-Argilos episode plays exactly the same functional role as the Cleonice episode, in that, in all the sources for it except for Aristodemus, it directly causes the death of Pausanias, just as the death of Cleonice directly causes the death of Pausanias in all of its four versions. And Aristodemus is very much the exception that proves the rule, because he is the only one of the sources to tell both the story of Cleonice and that of the man of Argilos. He has then, obviously, to tell them in sequence, and cannot make them both the direct cause of the death of Pausanias, so his solution is to tell the Cleonice story first and then resolve it by hypothesizing some satisfactory act of placation (distinct from the death of Pausanias), so that he can clear the ground for the story of the man of Argilos, which can lead directly to the death of Pausanias, as usual.

More specifically, both the man-of-Argilos episode and the Cleonice episode are shown to cause Pausanias' death by forcing him to reveal his treachery with Persia. This is central to the man-of-Argilos tale, and it is stated to be the result of the Cleonice *agos* by Pausanias-periegetes, although he does not begin to explain how so. The obvious assumption is that he was driven to reveal himself by the hounding of the ghost of Cleonice.

In addition to the functional equivalences of the two tales, there is also a basic equivalence between their central vignettes: in both cases Pausanias undertakes a special journey to a special enclosed chamber; in both cases this is to hold an interview with a person with whom he has an erotic connection; in both cases Pausanias' purpose is to beg off the anger of the person from him, for his very preservation.

These basic correspondences make it clear that there is some deep link between the two tales, but what is the nature of the link? Two models are available. The first, more 'conservative' model runs as follows: Thucydides is by far the earliest source, writing less than a hundred years after the events described, and with an impeccable reputation for historicity, truth and accuracy; Cleonice is not directly attested until six hundred years after the events described, and then first in a woolly and poorly 'historical' source, Plutarch. Therefore the myth of Cleonice has evolved over five hundred years out of the 'true' history of the man of Argilos.

The second model is more daring, and may have significant implications for the way we understand Thucydides' handling of his material, or that of his sources. It runs as follows. The tale of Cleonice and the tale of the man of Argilos both derive from a single or closely related group of necromantic-consultation narratives that explained the death of Pausanias and formed a narrative diptych with it. The Cleonice tale, although only first attested so much later, preserves the necromancy theme, whereas Thucydides (or his source) has rationalized the necromantic elements out of the man-of-Argilos tale. In other words, the man of Argilos was originally, like Cleonice, a ghost that Pausanias sought to placate in necromancy.

The second model is to be preferred for a number of reasons. First, the demonstrated close similarity between the Cleonice tale and the Melissa tale, the latter of which is present in essentials in Herodotus, indicates that necromantic tales of this general nature were already about before Thucydides wrote, and may, for that matter, indicate that they were about even before the death of Pausanias. Secondly, the demonstrated existence of a ghost story behind Thucydides' own tale of the death of Pausanias renders it plausible that a ghost story should lurk behind his related tale of the man of Argilos. Thirdly, and following on from this, Thucydides' demonstrated rationalizing exclusion of the ghost story from his tale of the death of Pausanias makes it plausible that he should have similarly excluded the ghost story from the tale of the man of Argilos. Fourthly, as we shall see, key details in Thucydides' story can be easily and sharply contextualized in necromantic terms, which constitutes a more than credible coincidence if the first model is applied.

The most compelling necromantic context is the actual setting of the story. Whilst Tainaron did indeed shelter suppliants,[52] it was also the home of a *nekuomanteion*. The association between the succouring of living suppliants and the evocation of the dead may at first sight appear an arbitrary one, but the curious term *hikesios*, which, as we have seen, seemingly equivocates between '(living) suppliant' and 'attacking ghost', offers a hint that it may be more significant. An attacking ghost may not much resemble a humble suppliant, but it does in its own way make petition through its attacks – for peace for itself. This is particularly clear in the tales of the deaths of Pausanias himself and of Cleonice. And as we have seen, the Heraclea oracle of the dead offered Cleonice the means of stipulating what she required for peace. In yoking the shelter of suppliants with an oracle of the dead, then, Tainaron perhaps sought to offer peace to all *hikesioi* alike, dead or alive.

The ancient sources make it clear that the *nekuomanteion* was a cave adjacent to the temple of Poseidon, at which Thucydides locates his story of the man of Argilos.[53] The remains of the modest temple of Poseidon, latterly a chapel, close to the tip of Cape Matapan, are prominent enough, and the remains of a small cave, 15 metres deep and 10–12 metres wide, its roof now collapsed, stand just below it. In antiquity a two-metre-thick ashlar wall fitted with a doorway was built across its entrance. Before the entrance stood a rectangular precinct.[54]

This *nekuomanteion* was the site of a mythical event of extraordinary similarity to Pausanias' interview with the man of Argilos and indeed to his interview with Cleonice. It concerns the supposed aftermath of the killing of the seventh-century poet Archilochus in battle:

> The man who killed Archilochus in battle was called Callondes, as it seems, but he had Corax ['Crow'] as a nickname. At first he was thrown out by the Pythia as having killed a man who was sacred to the Muses, but he then had recourse to prayers and supplications, and attempted to justify himself with arguments, and he was bidden to go to the house of Tettix ['Cicada'] to propitiate the soul of Archilochus. This was Tainaron. For they say that Tettix the Cretan came there with a fleet and founded a city and settled the area around the oracle of the dead (*psuchopompeion*). In the same way an oracle was given to the Spartans that they should propitiate the soul of Pausanias. So the evocators were sent for from Italy. They made a sacrifice and drew his ghost (*eidōlon*) away from the temple. Plutarch *Moralia* 560ef
> = Archilochus T141 Tarditi

Plutarch alludes to the tale elsewhere, and it is also told by Aelian.[55] In this Archilochus story too we have again the central vignette of a man journeying to a *nekuomanteion*, represented as a special chamber, to beg off the anger of the ghost of a person he has killed. If Pausanias too journeyed to Tainaron, to a special chamber, to beg off a person's anger, is there not a strong case for asking whether or not he went to the *nekuomanteion* and whether that person too was dead?

Was the 'man of Argilos' really a man of Argilos? The usages of the term *Argilios/Argilius* by Nepos and Aristodemus in fact clearly make the term a proper name, not an ethnic, as Jacoby realized,[56] although translators of and commentators upon these texts have doubtless been deterred from acknowledging this owing to an inappropriately reverential attitude towards Thucydides' text, or rather towards an unsophisticated reading of the same. It should be noted too that although Thucydides himself almost certainly does use *Argilios* as an ethnic, according to the text as we have it, his scholiast reported a debate among ancient scholars as to whether he was using the term as an ethnic or proper name. If Argilios was a proper name, we may expect it to be a speaking one, like Cleonice, and the meaning it must in this case bear is clear and appropriate. The noun *argilos* means earth or clay, whilst an *argilla* is a hole in the ground, and is used by one source to describe the underground holes inhabited by the 'Cimmerians' that once supposedly managed the *nekuomanteion* at Cumae.[57] The boy-lover is therefore 'Chthonic', 'Of the earth', an entirely appropriate name for a ghost. It becomes apparent that Thucydides or his source has recast the proper name *Argilios* as the ethnic of Argilos in an act of rationalization.

The peculiar and seemingly arbitrary partitioned hut may well then be a refraction of the *nekuomanteion*. The coincidence that the temple of Poseidon was a humble building divided by a partition wall is probably just that, although it is worth noting that a weak case has been put forward for identifying the temple itself with the *nekuomanteion*.[58] More significant is the fact that Nepos knew a version of the man-of-Argilos tale in which the chamber in which the ephors hid to overhear Pausanias' admission of treachery was configured rather differently from in the other accounts. As we have seen, he tells that Argilios went to sit on Poseidon's altar, but that the ephors made an underground hole (*locum…sub terra*) adjacently to the altar. Some of the ephors descended into this hole (*descenderunt*) to listen.[59] It is difficult not to see this hole as a refraction of the *nekuomanteion* cave itself, which nestles just below the temple, and it has indeed been suggested that we should think that the ephors hid in this.[60] It must be admitted that one could not hear a conversation at the temple altar from inside the cave, however.

Let us tie up some loose ends, although this inevitably involves further speculation. If Argilios was a ghost, angry at Pausanias, how did he come to die and have cause for such anger? The answer lies readily to hand: when employed as a messenger by Pausanias he did not, after all, open the letter and therefore betray Pausanias, but he took it, loyally and unquestioningly, like a dutiful boy-lover, to the Persian satrap and was duly killed for his efforts. That such favours and such loyalty should be rewarded by Pausanias with death would constitute just cause for the ghost's anger and bitterness. The ghost will then have discussed with Pausanias not the details of his attempted killing but the details of his actual killing, and this is, understandably, a favourite topic of ghosts, in and out of the context of evocation.[61] I offer a tentative, hypothetical reconstruction of a pre-rationalized version of the Argilos tale:

1. Pausanias entrusts the letter for his satrap to his boy-lover, who duly and dutifully takes it, and who is then killed in accordance with the letter's coda.
2. His betrayed, angry, restless ghost terrorizes Pausanias, and drives him to the Tainaron *nekuomanteion*, supposedly to ask about its placation, just as the ghost of Cleonice drives him to the Heraclea *nekuomanteion*, to ask about its placation.
3. The ghost – not the living man, of course – in the meantime also manifests itself to the ephors and tells them its story in its quest for peace through vengeance upon Pausanias.[62]
4. The ephors remain unsure whether to trust the ghost's allegations, as well they might. This was perhaps less to do with mistrust of the written word (the letter's role in the original tale was in any case perhaps spent by now), than with mistrust of allegations emanating from a ghost.[63] The ghost consequently challenges the ephors to come to the *nekuomanteion*.
5. Pausanias duly arrives at the *nekuomanteion*. In the course of begging off the ghost's anger he inevitably admits his responsibility for the murder and thereby his Persian treachery.

It has been convenient to set up our investigation into the man of Argilos as a battle between a resolutely necromantic 'original' tradition and a resolutely and innovatively rationalizing Thucydides. This may be an oversimplification. We have exploited Nepos' account of the man of Argilos to help prick Thucydides' rationalizing bubble: it is Nepos that gives us *Argilius* as a proper name and Nepos that gives us the ephors descending into a hole in the ground (and note also that Nepos applies the word *placare* to what Pausanias attempts to do to Argilios, so appropriate to the appeasement of a ghost). But despite all this Nepos' account is in itself every bit as rationalizing as Thucydides', albeit in some respects clearly independent of him. It is possible that his narrative derives ultimately from a Thucydidean rationalizing tradition into which some different aspects of the original necromantic tale have been reintegrated, or possibly Thucydides himself was merely one rationalizer among many.[64] Nonetheless, the general impression is that Thucydides is here treating his source material in a cavalierly procrustean fashion to make it fit his preconceptions about how the world works. It is unclear to what extent we should suspect him of taking a similar attitude to his source materials of various kinds in the rest of his work. Perhaps the difficulty can be contained: the excursuses on Pausanias and Themistocles are after all recognized to be anomalous within Thucydides' text, and distinctive above all for their 'Herodotean' feel.[65]

Postscript (1)

What was the ultimate source of the Pausanias stories discussed here? It has been argued that they belong, broadly, to a traditional story-type that may even have antedated Pausanias' own life. But it is impossible to tell when and where these story-patterns were first applied to the historical figure of Pausanias. With the ghost-of-Pausanias tale and the man-of-Argilos tale the trail goes cold with Thucydides himself, not least because of this author's deliberate and high-handed erasure of his own tracks.[66] With the Cleonice tale the trail goes cold, at best, with Ephorus or Nymphis, as we have seen. If a society constructs such tales around a historical figure, then it is because that figure is supremely interesting to it. Now, if we had reason to think that Pausanias was merely a figure of local interest in Sparta, we could be confident that it was in Sparta itself that such traditions were woven around him. But Pausanias was of course a figure of limitless interest to all the Greeks who believed that he had delivered them from the Persians in 480–79: everyone had reason to go weaving. How much significance should be attributed to local colour in these tales? The ghost-of-Pausanias tale's focus on the temple of Athene Chalkioikos together with its pair of Pausanias statues, and the man-of-Argilos tale's focus on the configuration of Tainaron, may – just – argue for a local Spartan origin. But then Athene Chalkioikos was perhaps, for all its humbleness, the most famous building in Sparta, its Eiffel Tower or Empire State, and the Tainaron oracle was open to all. Nor does the *cui bono* exercise work here. If the tales appear, in part, to portray Pausanias in a derogatory light, we should not for that reason alone presume that they were developed by his enemies within or without the Spartan state. As I have argued before, seemingly derogatory traditions can, paradoxically, be seen as a way of thinking about greatness for the Greeks.[67]

Do these tales tell us anything of Spartan religion and government? Not much, unfortunately. Since these tales are not in themselves historical, they cannot be taken as direct evidence for the ephors' preparedness – or lack of it – to act or make policy on the basis of ghostly utterances. However, that the Spartan state somehow or other presided over the oracle of the dead at Tainaron remains a fact, and this fact alone makes it plausible enough that it should indeed have been prepared to act on the basis of ghostly utterances.

The only other necromantic episode associated with Sparta, of which I am aware, is the marvellous tale of Cleomenes and the head of Archonides. The reputedly mad Cleomenes had sworn to his friend Archonides that he would include him in all his affairs, should he come to the throne. Upon accession he decapitated him and kept his head preserved in a jar of honey. He kept true to his word by holding a discussion with the head whenever he was about to embark upon an enterprise.[68] This tale seemingly carries overtones of skull-necromancy and accordingly provides further evidence for those who wish to find ghosts influencing the formation of policy in the city. But it is of course as much a myth as any of the tales we have been looking at in this piece.

The fact that Sparta had its own oracle of the dead should not be taken to indicate that Sparta was especially more interested in what the dead had to say than any other Greek state. We know of other oracles of the dead at the Acheron, at Avernus and at Heraclea Pontica, and there were perhaps many more besides.

Postscript (2): the afterlife of Cleonice

Admirers of Cleonice, frustrated by the brevity of her notices in the ancient sources, may find some solace in Sir Edward Bulwer-Lytton's unfinished novel, *Pausanias the Spartan*, written in 1859. Here her role is worked up into that of a full-blown romantic heroine, one of a beauty self-consciously contrasted with that of the Victorian age's 'women of the north'. Her speeches display a cultivation derived from a Milesian mother, and she advocates a variety of Pythagoreanism strikingly anticipatory of the Christian faith. Her beliefs license a scornful reference to the Necromancer of Heraclea, which the completion of the novel would doubtless have rendered ironic.[69]

Abbreviations

FGH Jacoby 1923–58
LIMC *Lexicon Iconographicum Mythologiae Classicae* (1981–)
SEG *Supplementum Epigraphicum Graecum* (1923–)

Notes

[1] This essay unites and remoulds material from diverse parts of Ogden 2001b. Readers are referred to that work for further discussion on all matters relating to the practice of necromancy, and in particular for reconstructions of the oracles of the dead; cf. also Ogden 2001a.

[2] If the chronology of the episode is difficult, this is no doubt due in part to the heavily mythologized nature of the tradition. For debates see, e.g., Gomme 1945, 397; White 1964; Rhodes 1970, 396–9; Cawkwell 1971, 47 and 51; Oliva 1971, 151; and Hornblower 1991, 213.

[3] *Pace* Classen 1919 on Thucydides 1.134.

[4] The variant translations reflect the uncertainty over whether the term *hikesios* here is to be read as a proper noun or a common one, as is discussed below.

[5] Plutarch *Moralia* 308b (*Parallel stories*) = Chrysermus of Corinth *FGH* 287 F 4; Plutarch *Homerikai Meletai* F1 Bernardakis (also at Sandbach's Loeb Plutarch vol. xv, p. 241 F126) = Scholiast Euripides *Alcestis* 1128; Diodorus 11.45 (cf. Tigerstedt 1965–78, i, 218–19 for the possible derivation from Ephorus); Nepos 4.5; Ps.-Themistocles 4.15 Hercher/Doenges (*c.* 100 AD, and somewhat contemporary with Plutarch, therefore: cf. Doenges 1981, 49–63); *Suda* s.v. *Pausanias.*

[6] Herodotus 6.58. Cf. Schäfer 1957 and Faraone 1992, 184.

[7] Herodotus 5.75; cf. Richer 1994, 85–8.

[8] I can see no definitive way of dating the origins of Justin's tale. However, at the risk of *petitio principi*, the apparent fact that it is cognate with the Pausanias tradition implies the existence of a common ancestor, one necessarily earlier than the first attestation of either story. The theoretical alternative, that Justin's tale is descended directly from the Pausanias tradition, is implausible. I note also that Justin's tale has a similar feel to the archaic traditions reviewed in Ogden 1997.

[9] Cf. Faraone 1991, 185.

[10] Thucydides does not affirm (or deny) that the figures directly represented Pausanias, but the later sources are satisfied that they did, including Pausanias-periegetes, who saw them (albeit not the original Pausanias for comparison!). The claims of Aristodemus and the *Suda* that there was only one effigy should not detain us in the face of Pausanias' autopsy. Doubtless they filtered the second statue out of the account for failure to appreciate its function. The excavation of Chalki-oikos found no trace either of the bronze statues or of the pillars (nor did it shed any light on the bricking-up episode – rather, the tradition of this episode is itself the principal key to the intepretation of the site: Dickins 1906–7). A tentative case has been made for the identification of the stone 'Leonidas' statue, now the glory of the Sparta museum, but already buried when Pausanias-periegetes visited the site, as a third effigy of Pausanias (Woodward 1923–5, 263–6).

[11] An early legend about Alcmene, who came from Midea, has Zeus send Hermes (the *psuchopompos*) to replace her dead body with a stone, which the Heraclids then set up in a wood (cf. below on the Cyrenean sacred law) and made the place a heroon for Alcmene (Pherecydes *FHG* 3 F 84 = Antoninus Liberalis 33; cf. Plutarch *Romulus* 28). See Persson 1931, 108–17 and plate xxix; Picard 1933; and Faraone 1991, 183–4. The Midean menhir-pair makes potentially interesting the claim of the Scholiast on Thucydides 1.134 that two pillars were set up for Pausanias, although the information may derive merely from a combination of Thucydides' own reference to (plural) pillars and to the two statues.

[12] Hiller von Gaertringen 1903, especially 304–6 and figs. 492–3; Kurtz and Boardman 1971, 179 and 258, fig. 34; and Faraone 1991, 184. A further effigy-

cenotaph is known from fifth-century BC Western Locri, a pot-burial with the remains replaced with a female bust; cf. Kurtz and Boardman 1971, 259 fig. 56, and Faraone 1991, 184.

13 The iconography of Sleep and Death carrying Sarpedon off is catalogued and discussed in detail by Mainoldi 1987; see especially Paris, Louvre F388 (*LIMC* Sarpedon no. 7; cf. no. 6); and Metropolitan Museum of Art, 1972, 11.10 (*LIMC* Sarpedon no. 4). See also Shapiro 1993, 132–65, and Sourvinou-Inwood 1995, 326–7. The poetic source is Homer *Iliad* 16.454; cf. 14.231.

14 Richer 1994.

15 *SEG* 9.72.111–21. See Faraone 1991, 180–7, with further bibliography on the law at 181 n. 55, and, for a briefer summary of the same material, 1992, 82–3; cf. also Faraone 1993 on Meiggs and Lewis no. 5 for more on *kolossoi* at Cyrene.

16 Published by Jameson et al. 1993; cf. pp. 54–6, 76, and, for the term *elasteros*, 116–20. The text introduced us to ἐλάστερος as a common noun for the first time, although the term was already known from other inscriptions as an epithet of Zeus (LSJ *Supplement* s.v.).

17 Thus Hitzig 1899 and Levi 1971 ad loc. But Wide 1893, 14–17 and 272 rightly detached Hikesios from Zeus. Some editors are less committal in identifying Hikesios as Zeus, but still make him a god: Meyer 1954; Papachatzis 1963–74; Rocha-Pereira 1973; and Musti et al. 1991. Our sources preserve no other mention of a Hikesios in Sparta.

18 Hesychius s.v. *Epidōtas*. Epidotes is therefore the Spartan equivalent of the Zeus *Phuxios* from whom Pausanias had himself sought purification over the death of Cleonice (Pausanias 3.17).

19 *SEG* 9.72.110–19: Ἱκέσιος ἐπακτός· αἴ κα ἐπιπεμφθῇ ἐπὶ τὰν οἰκίαν... κολοσὸς ποιήσαντα ἔρσενα καὶ θήλειαν ἢ καλίνος ἢ γαΐνος ὑποδεξάμενον παρατιθέμεν τὸ μέρος πάντων· Pausanias 3.17: Λακεδαιμόνιοι δὲ ἐκτελοῦντες πρόσταγμα ἐκ Δελφῶν τάς τε εἰκόνας ἐποιήσαντο τὰς χαλκᾶς καὶ δαίμονα τιμῶσιν Ἐπιδώτην τὸ ἐπὶ Παυσανίᾳ τοῦ ἱκεσίου μήνιμα ἀποτρέπειν τὸν Ἐπιδώτην λέγοντες τοῦτον.

20 Cf. Faraone 1992, 181 nn. 60–1.

21 Pausanias 9.38; cf. Fontenrose 1978, 130–1, and Faraone 1991, 187–8. The riveting to rock was evidently to stop the ghost wandering around.

22 Burkert 1962, 49; cf. Faraone 1991, 186–7 n. 79. Burkert is surely right, but it is worth noting that Diodorus, whose account is strongly similar to Thucydides', brings the Spartans to Delphi to ask about a matter other than the one upon which the response is given, and that this is an ancient and hallowed technique for bringing people to oracles in traditional narratives, as is demonstrated by its use by Herodotus in connection with Battus (4.150) and Cypselus (5.92).

23 Fontenrose 1978, 129.

24 Pausanias 3.17.

25 A different explanation at Westlake 1977, 106 with n. 62.

26 For Thucydides' agonistic atttitude in the writing of history, cf. 1.20 (against Herodotus and others) and 1.97 (against Hellanicus).

27 Rhodes 1970, 389 shares the view that Thucydides is being combative and

attempting to establish one view in the face of another in this narrative. Cawkwell 1971, 50, however, seems to take this detail to derive from the inscriptions in the precinct forecourt that Thucydides implies he read. This would be an oddly garrulous detail for any inscription of this period, let alone a Laconic one.

[28] A similar phenomenon may be noted in the parallel accounts of Diodorus and Nepos (references above). Diodorus uses *katachōsai* and Nepos uses *infoderunt*, the latter contrasting with a subsequent *sepultus*.

[29] Plautus *Mostellaria* 449–531.

[30] Pliny *Letters* 7.27 and Lucian *Philopseudes* 29–31.

[31] Suetonius *Caligula* 59; cf. Cumont 1949, 84–5 and 319, and Felton 1999, 10.

[32] The story is preserved by Diodorus, Nepos, Plutarch/Chrysermus, Aristodemus, and the *Suda*, as cited above. Polyaenus 8.51 calls her 'Theano'. Plutarch/Chrysermus gives the bricking-up to Pausanias' father, but attributes the denial of burial to the mother.

[33] Wiedemann 1983 and Harvey 1985; cf. also Gomme 1945 on Thucydides 1.134.

[34] Again, inasmuch as the tale is heavily mythologized, it is difficult to site chronologically. While Pausanias-periegetes locates the killing of Cleonice during the original period of Pausanias' command at Byzantium, Plutarch locates it after his dismissal from it. See Blamire 1989 on Plutarch *Cimon* 6. If we want a 'historical' hook onto which to hang this tradition, then we may look to the claim that when Pausanias was at Byzantium he sued for the hand of the daughter of Megabates (Herodotus 5.32) or even of Xerxes himself (Thucydides 1.128, Diodorus 11.44, Justin 2.15.14 and *Suda* s.v. *Pausanias*).

[35] For the *nekuomanteion* at Heraclea Pontica, see Hoepfner 1966 and 1972.

[36] Plutarch *Moralia* 555c (*Slow vengeance*); Aristodemus *FGH* 104 F 8.

[37] Nymphis of Heraclea *FGH* 432 F 9.

[38] Plutarch *Moralia* 248d = Nymphis of Heraclea *FGH* 432 F 7; cf. Blamire 1989 and Carena et al. 1990 on Plutarch *Cimon* 6.

[39] See Jacoby 1923–58 on *FGH* 104 F 4–10.

[40] Nicolaus of Damascus *FGH* 90 F 58.

[41] Herodotus 3.50 and Diogenes Laertius 1.100.

[42] Macan 1895 ad loc. makes a convincing case for the placation of Melissa having been the original prime goal of the necromancy.

[43] That there was at any rate one older, hexameter, version of the tale is perhaps indicated by the presence of the heavily dactylic phrase in Herodotus' narrative, ἐς ὄρυγμα Μελίσσῃ ἐπευχόμενος κατέκαιε ('...into a trench, and burned it with a prayer to Melissa'); cf. Stern 1989, 15–16. The word *nekuomanteion*, beginning with three short syllables, could not have appeared in a hexameter.

[44] Stesichorus F278 Campbell = Strabo C347.

[45] Cf. Herodotus 5.92 etc.

[46] Parthenius *Erotica pathemata* 17. The tale is alluded to by Plutarch *Moralia* 146 and Diogenes Laertius 1.96, who cites Aristippus' first book *On ancient luxury*. That tyrants should have sex with their mothers was a productive theme.

Oedipus Tyrannus (etc.) aside, the Athenian tyrant Hippias dreamed of sex with his mother (Herodotus 6.107). Another Corinthian, Diocles, was so disgusted by his mother's incestuous passion for him that he abandoned the city (Aristotle *Politics* 1274a).

[47] Who is the ghost? We might be tempted to suggest that it is Melissa again. Possibly, but insofar as the tale is situated within Periander's traditional biography it takes place prior to the death of Melissa. Parthenius says that Periander was still a young man at the time – hence the beauty that attracted his mother to him – while Plutarch makes it clear that Melissa was alive and well long after the debacle with his mother (*Moralia* 146d).

[48] Diodorus 11.45 and Aristodemus *FGH* 104 F 8.2–3.

[49] Cawkwell 1971, 50–2 and 57–8 n. 27, and Westlake 1977, 95 with n. 4 (citing many incredulous scholars); cf. also Podlecki 1976, 298, and Powell 1989,185–6. Cawkwell also observes that the Spartans cared much more about helot revolts than Persian treachery, and that it would have been Pausanias' treatment with the helots that would have been the real cause of his downfall (qualified by Hornblower 1991, 219).

[50] Cawkwell 1971, 50 and 57–8 n. 27 (cf. Podlecki 1976, 296) is rightly baffled by the Argilian-ness; he suggests an emendation to *Aigilios*, to be read as an ethnic for the Spartan locality of *Aigila* (found at Pausanias 4.17.1). For Gomme 1945 on Thucydides 1.132 the man from Argilos was a slave, and this is why Pausanias could imply that he had the power to punish him. But Pausanias was in any case hubristic and regent. And why specify the ethnic origin of a slave?

[51] This problem concerns Hornblower 1991, 219 on Thucydides 1.133.

[52] Thucydides himself tells of suppliant helots who fled there, and whom the Spartans raised up and then put to death (1.128 and 135); this became a grievance for the Athenians. Polybius 9.34 refers to it as an asylum sanctuary in around 240 BC, and Plutarch similarly in the first century BC. Perhaps it was this sanctuary of Poseidon at which Cleombrotus II sought refuge in 241 BC (Plutarch *Agis* 16 and *Cleomenes* 22). See Schumacher 1993, 72.

[53] Strabo C363; Pausanias 3.25 (a little confused); Pomponius Mela 2.51 (cf. 1.103); Scholiast Aristophanes *Acharnians* 509. More fantastic literary descriptions are found at Seneca *Hercules Furens* 662–96 and Statius *Thebaid* 2.32–57. There are countless further geographically unspecific references to Tainaron as an underworld entrance in ancient poetry.

[54] The site is clearly described and illustrated by Cummer 1978; plans, photographs and discussions also at Moschou 1976; Papachatzis 1976; Günther 1988; Musti et al. 1982– on Pausanias 3.25; and Schumacher 1993, 72–4. The identification is all but certain.

[55] Plutarch *Numa* 4; *Suda* s.v. *Archilochos* = Aelian F83 Domingo-Forasté (Teubner) = Archilochus T170 Tarditi; cf. also Galen *Protreptici* 9.1 and Hesychius s.v. *Tettigos hedranon*.

[56] Jacoby 1923–58 on Aristodemus *FGH* 104 F 8.

[57] Strabo C244; cf. Maximus of Tyre 8.2.

[58] Schumacher 1993, 73–4, without real argument. Perhaps he takes his lead

from Pausanias-periegetes' confusing reference to a 'temple made like a cave' (3.25). But the temple does not in any case appear to have resembled a cave; it is better to assume Pausanias is inaccurately speaking of the cave made like a temple.

[59] Nepos 4.4; not exactly a 'trap-door in the temple', as Podlecki 1976 sees it.

[60] By Günther 1988, 60, who also contemplates the possibility that the hole in which they hid was a well adjacent to the temple.

[61] Cf., e.g., Elpenor at Homer *Odyssey* 11.61–5; Diapontius at Plautus *Mostellaria* 497–504; Deiphobus at Virgil *Aeneid* 6.511–29; and Thelyphron at Apuleius *Metamorphoses* 2.29.

[62] For the manifestation of ghosts before third parties, to whom they appeal for revenge upon their killers, cf., e.g., Cicero *On Divination* 1.57.

[63] For mistrust of ghosts' claims to identify their killers, cf. Apuleius *Metamorphoses* 2.29.

[64] There has been speculation as to the nature of Thucydides' source for the man-of-Argilos story. Westlake 1977, 97–107 argues for a written source, and chooses first Charon of Lampsacus (*FGH* 262), and second Stesimbrotus of Thasos (*FGH* 107, who is identified as the source of the paired excursus on Themistocles by Carawan 1989); Hornblower 1991, 211 refuses to speculate.

[65] See Gomme 1945, 26–8 and 446; Rhodes 1970, 387; Podlecki 1976, 297; Westlake 1977, 95; Carawan 1989, 144; Powell 1989, 185–7; and Hornblower 1991, 211–12. It is noteworthy too that another rationalized myth, that of Telephus, is found in the Admetus tale in the Themistocles excursus (Thucydides 1.136–7): cf. Wilamowitz-Moellendorf 1902, 1.ii 31; Gomme 1945 ad loc. and Hornblower 1987, 15.

[66] Thucydides 1.21.

[67] Ogden 1997.

[68] Aelian *Varia historia* 12.8.

[69] See Lytton 1999 especially 430–1 and 463. It was evidently Pausanias-periegetes' account of the episode that had come to Byron's attention: 'The buried Prophet answered to the Hag / Of Endor; and the Spartan Monarch drew / From the Byzantine maid's unsleeping spirit / An answer and his destiny – he slew / That which he loved, unknowing what he slew, / And died unpardoned – though he called in aid / The Phyxian Jove, and in Phigalia roused / The Arcadian Evocators to compel / The indignant shadow to depose her wrath, / Or fix her term of vengeance – she replied / In words of dubious import, but fulfilled.' (*Manfred* II.iii.181–91; the play was first performed in 1834.)

Bibliography

Blamire, A.

1989 *Plutarch. Life of Cimon*, with translation and commentary, London.

Burkert, W.

1962 '*Goēs*: Zum griechischen "Schamanismus"', *RhM* 105, 36–55.

Carawan, E.

1989 'Stesimbrotus and Thucydides on the exile of Themistocles', *Historia* 38, 144–61.

Carena, C., et al.
1990 *Plutarco. Le vite di Cimone e di Lucullo,* Mondadori Commentaries, Verona.
Cawkwell, G.L.
1971 'The fall of Themistocles', in *Auckland Classical Studies Presented to E.M. Blaiklock*, London, 39–58.
Classen, J.
1919 *Thucydides I* , 5th edn, Berlin.
Cummer, W.
1978 'The sanctuary of Poseidon at Tainaron, Lakonia', *AM* 93, 35–43 and pls. 17–18.
Cumont, F.
1949 *Lux Perpetua*, Paris.
Dickins, G.
1906–7 'Laconia, I. Excavations at Sparta, 1907. 7. The hieron of Athena Chalkioikos', *BSA* 13, 137–54.
Doenges, N.A.
1981 *The Letters of Themistocles*, edited with introduction, translation and commentary, New York.
Faraone, C.A.
1991 'Binding and burying the forces of evil: the defensive use of "voodoo" dolls in ancient Greece', *CA* 10, 165–205.
1992 *Talismans and Trojan horses: Guardian statues in Greek myth and ritual*, Oxford.
1993 'Molten wax, spilt wine, and mutilated animals: near eastern and early Greek oath ceremonies', *JHS* 113, 60–80.
Felton, D.
1999 *Haunted Greece and Rome. Ghost stories from classical antiquity*, Austin.
Fontenrose, J.
1978 *The Delphic Oracle*, California.
Gomme, A.W.
1945 *A Historical Commentary on Thucydides,* vol. 1, Oxford.
Günther, K.
1988 'Der Poseidontempel auf Tainaron', *Antike Welt* 19.2, 58–60.
Harvey, F.D.
1985 'Women in Thucydides', *Arethusa* 18, 67–90.
Hiller von Gaertringen, F.
1903 'Das von A. Schiff entdeckte Grab', in *Theräische Gräber*, Berlin, 291–307.
Hitzig, H.
1899 *Pausaniae Graeciae Descriptio*, vol. 1.2, Leipzig.
Hoepfner, W.
1966 *Forschungen an der Nordküste Kleinasiens ii.1: Herakleia Pontike – Eregli: eine baugeschichtliche Untersuchung*, Ergänzungsbände zu den Tituli Asiae Minoris nr. 1, Vienna.
1972 'Topographische Forschungen', in D. Asheri, W. Hoepfner and

A. Erichsen, *Forschungen an der Nordküste Kleinasiens i*. Ergänzungsbände zu den Tituli Asiae Minoris nr. 5, Vienna, 37–46. with plans 4–5 and plates 1–3.

Hornblower, N.S.R.
1987 *Thucydides*, London.
1991 *A Commentary on Thucydides*, 2+ vols., Oxford.

Jacoby, F.
1923–58 *Die Fragmente der griechische Historiker*, 15 vols., Berlin.

Jameson, M.H., Jordan, D.R. and Kotansky, R.D.
1993 *A Lex Sacra from Selinus*, *GRBS* Supplement, Durham, N.C.

Kurtz, D.C. and Boardman, J.
1971 *Greek Burial Customs*, London.

Levi, P.
1971 *Pausanias: The Guide to Greece*, translation with notes, 2 vols, London.

Macan, R.W.
1895 *Herodotus. The fourth, fifth and sixth books*, London.

Mainoldi, C.
1984 *L'image du loup et du chien dans la Grèce ancienne d'Homère à Platon*, Paris.

Meiggs, R., and Lewis, D.M.
1969 *A Selection of Greek Historical Inscriptions*, Oxford.

Meyer, E.
1954 *Pausanias. Beschreibung Griechenlands*, Zurich.

Moschou, L.
1975 'Τοπογραφικὰ Μάνης', *AAA* 8, 160–77.

Musti, D. et al.
1982– *Pausania. Guida della Grecia*, Mondadori Commentaries, Verona.

Ogden, D.
1997 *The Crooked Kings of Ancient Greece*, London.
2001a 'Totenorakel in der griechischen Antike', in K. Brodersen (ed.) *Prognosis. Studien zur Funktion von Zukunftsvorhersagen in Literatur und Geschichte seit der Antike*, Münster, 39–60.
2001b *Greek and Roman Necromancy*, Princeton.

Oliva, P.
1971 *Sparta and her Social Problems*, Prague.

Papachatzis, N.D.
1963–74 Παυσανίου Ἑλλάδος περιήγησις, 5 vols., Athens.
1976 'Ποσειδῶν Ταινάριος', *Arch.Eph.* 102–25.

Persson, A.W.
1931 *The Royal Tombs at Dendra near Midea*, Lund.

Picard, C.
1933 'Le cénotaph de Midéa et les 'colosses' de Ménélas (ad Aesch. *Agamemn.* v. 414 sqq.)', *RPh* 7, 341–54.

Podlecki, A.J.
1976 'Themistocles and Pausanias', *Rivista di filologia e d'istruzione classica* 104, 293–311.

Powell, A.
1989 'Mendacity and Sparta's use of the visual', in A. Powell (ed.) *Classical Sparta: The techniques behind her success*, London, 173–92.
Rhodes, P.J.
1970 'Thucydides on Pausanias and Themistocles', *Historia* 19, 387–400.
Richer, N.
1994 'Aspects des funérailles à Sparte', *Cahiers du Centre G. Glotz* 5, 51–96.
Rocha-Pereira, M.H.
1973 *Pausaniae Graeciae descriptio* vol. i Libri i–iv [Teubner], Leipzig.
Schäfer, H.
1949 'Pausanias (25)', *RE* 36, 2563–78.
Schäfer, J.
1957 'Das Eidolon des Leonidas', in K. Schauenberg (ed.) *Charites: Festschrift E. Langlotz*, Bonn, 223–33.
Schumacher, R.W.M.
1993 'Three related sanctuaries of Poseidon: Geraistos, Kalaureia and Tainaron', in N. Marinatos and R. Hägg (eds.) *Greek Sanctuaries: New Approaches*, London, 62–87.
Servais, J.
1960 'Les suppliants dans la loi de Cyrène', *BCH* 84, 112–47.
Shapiro, H.A.
1993 *Personifications in Greek Art*, Kichberg and Zürich.
Sourvinou-Inwood, C.
1995 *'Reading' Greek Death*, Oxford.
Stern, J.
1989 'Demythologisation in Herodotus', *Eranos* 87, 13–20.
Tigerstedt, E.N.
1965–78 *The Legend of Sparta in Classical Antiquity*, 3 vols., Stockholm.
Westlake, H.D.
1977 'Thucydides on Pausanias and Themistocles: a written source?', *CQ* 27, 95–110.
White, M.E.
1964 'Some Agiad dates: Pausanias and his sons', *JHS* 84, 140–52.
Wide, S.
1893 *Lakonische Kulte*, Leipzig.
Wiedemann, T.E.J.
1983 '*Elachiston en tois arsesi kleos*. Thucydides, women and the limits of rational analysis', *G&R* 30, 163–70.
Wilamowitz-Moellendorf, U., von.
1902 *Griechisches Lesebuch*, 2 vols., 4 parts, Berlin.
Woodward, A.M.
1923–5 'Excavations at Sparta, 1924–5. 4. The acropolis', *BSA* 26, 240–76.

5

IRON MONEY AND THE IDEOLOGY OF CONSUMPTION IN LACONIA

Thomas J. Figueira

In this paper, I intend to contextualize Spartan iron money as a socio-economic phenomenon, and, specifically, to locate it within a classification of monetary media in archaic and classical Greece.[1] These include not only coins in various metals but also other signifiers of value. We shall test the hypothesis that Sparta's iron money represents the vestige of a common, early stage in monetary development (cf. Müller 1839; Köhler 1882) against the alternative paradigm of Spartan re-institutionalization, i.e., an ideologically conditioned process of incremental, conservative social evolution (Finley 1982, 24–40).

To start, let us clarify terminology. The phrase 'iron money' unfortunately evokes the image of coins in base metals, analogous to the bronze fractions that became common, starting from western Greece, in the third quarter of the fifth century (Price 1968; Figueira 1998, 497–8). Spartan iron money could indeed be juxtaposed with Byzantine iron coins (Pollux *Onomasticon* 7.105). Yet, as another passage in Pollux specifies, unlike Byzantine coins, units of Spartan money had great mass.[2] That feature attracted considerable comment, starting with our first witness, Xenophon.[3] The *Apophthegmata Laconica* puts unit weight at an Aiginetic *mna*.

A gloss in Hesychius calls a piece of Spartan money a *pelanor* (s.v. πέλανορ, π 1286 Latte).[4] That is Laconian dialect for *pelanos*, of which the most helpful connotation involves cakes, often flat and round, offered in ritual settings.[5] Therefore, the units of Spartan money were flat iron ingots, rather like grotesquely magnified coin blanks, weighing 614–30 g. or 1 pound, 5–6 ounces. Identifications of various artifacts as *pelanors* have been received skeptically.[6] The evidence outside Laconia for monetary *pelanors/pelanoi* is weak.[7] The *pelanor* was equivalent to a *tetrakhalkon*, which another Hesychian gloss calls a ἱππόπορ (s.v., ι 848; cf. 849). This may be a corruption of a Spartan word ἵππορ, Laconian for ἵππος (horse), so that the *pelanors* were possibly stamped with a horse or horse head. A craft industry, exploiting plentiful, high-grade ore at the Laconian town of Boai, provides a precondition for choosing this monetary medium, but not its rationale (Steph. Byz. s.v. Λακεδαίμων; Daimachos *FGH* 65 F 4; cf. Xen. *HG* 3.3.7; Cartledge 1979, 90, 181).

The evidence

The common tradition

There exists a remarkably consistent picture of Spartan iron money despite selectivity of detail. Plutarch provides the most important *testimonia*, to which the remaining evidence may be appended. Most substantial is *Lycurgus* 9.1–5, where iron money belongs to an array of institutions initiated by this fundamental lawgiver. This treatment can be used heuristically by us as a template, being supplemented by two other programmatic passages, a similar version of Lycurgan legislation from the *Apophthegmata Laconica* (*Mor.* 226B–D) and a short description in the *Comparatio Aristidis et Catonis* 3.1. Plutarch also briefly describes Spartan money in recounting the controversy about Spartan public finances in *Lysander* 17.1–5.

(1) According to Plutarch, iron money was not a forerunner of coinage in gold or silver. Rather it superseded such money, and, instead of expediting transactions, acted to impede them. Note *Lyc.* 9.1: πρῶτον μὲν γὰρ ἀκυρώσας πᾶν νόμισμα χρυσοῦν καὶ ἀργυροῦν, μόνῳ χρῆσθαι τῷ σιδηρῷ προσέταξε, 'accordingly, after first invalidating all gold and silver money, he enjoined the usage of iron money alone' (cf. *Mor.* 226C).[8] The terms 'counter-money' and 'anti-money' may be used to convey these ideas. The *Apophthegmata* treats its inauguration as a straightforward demonetization, speaking of a limited period for an exchange (*amoibē*) of superseded coins. Note a similar hint in Xenophon: coinage in precious metals was confiscated in an expropriation (*RL* 7.6: χρυσίον γε μὴν καὶ ἀργύριον ἐρευνᾶται, καὶ ἄν τί που φανῇ, ὁ ἔχων ζημιοῦται, 'most assuredly indeed is gold and silver sought out, and, if any would come to light anywhere, its possessor was punished'). Without a money economy, crimes of a monetary nature were supposedly absent, as both *Lycurgus* and *Apophthegmata* assert (9.2; *Mor.* 226D). Again, that motif is already implied in Xenophon, who speaks of Lycurgus suppressing *khrēmatismos* (money making) (*RL* 7.5–6).

(a) To deprive the iron money of convenience as a transactional medium, treatment with vinegar made subsequent utilization of the metal difficult, at least without reprocessing: *Lyc.* 9.2: ὄξει γάρ, ὡς λέγεται, διαπύρου σιδήρου τὸ στόμωμα κατασβέσας ἀφείλετο τὴν εἰς τἆλλα χρείαν καὶ δύναμιν, ἀδρανοῦς καὶ δυσέργου γενομένου, 'that was because, as is reported, quenching in vinegar the ingot of red-hot iron, he took away its utility and capacity for other purposes, as it became brittle and difficult to work'. This unusual practice is prominent in Plutarch, appearing in the *Comparatio* and *Lysander* too (17.2), and is highlighted elsewhere.[9] It constituted a deliberate disruption of normal metallurgical techniques (see the Appendix for discussion).

(b) The cumbersome character of Spartan money was a *topos* inaugurated by Xenophon (*RL* 7.5–6: Picard 1980; Luppino Manes 1988, 69–77). Both Xenophon and Plutarch use the example of ten *mnai* and the need for a wagon as conveyance, indicating that Xenophon was (at least) an indirect source for Plutarch (*RL* 7.5; *Lyc.* 9.1; cf. *Lys.* 17.2). Another short description in the pseudo-Platonic *Eryxias* also derives from the fourth century (400A–B; cf. 400D: Giacchero 1973). The treatment of the forged iron with vinegar and its great weight with low value also intrigued this author.

(c) Thus, the iron money was a curious token currency. Unlike base metal coins, its intrinsic metallic value was not enhanced by governmental authority. The *pelanors* were treated to lower their metallic value. Only then was a low artificial value affixed. The *Eryxias* nicely reflects this fiduciary quality, its dependence on political legitimization: καὶ ὁ πολὺν σταθμὸν σιδήρου τοῦ τοιούτου κεκτημένος πλούσιος δοκεῖ εἶναι, ἑτέρωθι δ' οὐδενὸς ἄξιον τὸ κτῆμα, 'and the person seems to be wealthy who possesses a great weight of iron, a possession worth nothing anywhere else'. The *Apophthegmata* specifies that iron weighing an Aiginetic *mna* (614–30 g.) had the value of four *khalkhoi* (*Mor.* 226E). *Khalkoi* were bronze fractions of which twelve constituted an Aiginetic obol. Thus, each *pelanor* was worth one-third of a silver obol, presumably on the Aiginetic standard, or *c.* 0.3 grams of silver. This is confirmed by a gloss in Hesychius (s.v. πέλανορ, π 1286 Latte): τὸ τετράχαλκον. Λάκωνες.[10] Hence, Xenophon's example of a monetary value of ten *mnai* envisages the astonishing mass of *c.* 11,000 kg. of iron (*RL* 7.5–6). Ever since the earliest commentary, this value ratio of the two metals (1:1800) seemed to value iron too cheaply (Müller 1839.15). This value ratio is discrepant with ancient comparative evidence.[11] Consequently, I emphasize that the value of the *pelanor* was determined by ideological concerns, and not by a market value for iron ingot.

(d) The interlocking motifs of superseding coinage in precious metal, demonetization, coercive exchange, and confiscation preclude Plutarch's developing a correlation between iron money and barter. That barter could, however, be integrated into an account of Spartan money is seen from Justin, *Epitome* 3.2.11–12: *emi singula non pecunia, sed conpensatione mercium* (Lycurgus) *iussit. Auri argentique usum velut omnium scelerum materiam sustulit*, '[Lycurgus] ordered that individual items be purchased not by money, but by the payment of goods. He abolished the usage of gold and silver as though the substance of all crimes'. Thus, the features of exclusion of conventional money and pre-emption of criminal incentives also appear in Justin. Moreover, Polybius could juxtapose iron money and 'exchange' of harvests (6.49.8–10).

(2) According to the ancient sources, the intention behind iron money was to isolate the Spartan economy. Neither goods nor service providers were attracted to Lakōnikē. The *Apophthegmata* notes that iron money replaced money that was *eukhrēstos* (easily-used) (*Mor.* 226D). The term *agōgimos*, used in the *Lycurgus* (9.3), may be glossed as 'transferable', and highlights the opposite character of the *pelanors,* their non-portability, inconvertibility, and general unattractiveness. For the *Apophthegmata*, importing and exporting became risky for the Spartiate because of iron money. Here Plutarch echoes the thematic linkages of Xenophon *RL* 7.1–4. Xenophon prefaces his treatment of Spartan money by describing Lycurgus prohibiting acquisition (*khrēmatismos*) in favor of inculcating 'whatever furnishes cities with freedom' (ὅσα δὲ ἐλευθερίαν ταῖς πόλεσι παρασκευάζει).

(a) A connection is made with *xenēlasia*, a practice in which the Spartans periodically expelled aliens.[12] In 431 Perikles proposed a partial termination of *xenēlasiai* as reciprocation for Athenian concessions just before the war (Thuc. 1.144.2). Plutarch's source envisages the Lycurgan monetary reform accompanied by a *xenēlasia*, apparently a first, paradigmatic recourse to the procedure (*Lyc.* 9.3; *Mor.* 226D).[13] A similar conjunction is made in *Agis* 10.3–5 in Agis' riposte to his adversary Leonidas (who had just mentioned Lycurgan *xenēlasiai*) that Lycurgus expelled indebtedness along with money (*nomisma*). Plutarch also plays on *xenēlasia* in *Comparatio* 3.2, using the participle ἐξοικίσας to describe the removal of precious metals. In his account of the confrontation over Spartan finances *c.* 400 (derived from Ephorus or Theopompus), Plutarch quotes the proposal of the anti-Lysandrians 'to banish ritually all gold and silver [money] as though imported curses' (ἀποδιοπομπεῖσθαι πᾶν τὸ ἀργύριον καὶ τὸ χρυσίον ὥσπερ κῆρας ἐπαγωγίμους). This rhetoric implies a religious purification, with the infinitive ἀποδιοπομπεῖσθαι 'to banish ritually' and the phrase κῆρας ἐπαγωγίμους 'imported curses' connoting scapegoat ritual (Lys. 6.53; Dio Cass. 37.46.1; Plut. *Mor.* 73D, 860E). This striking formulation was derived from the terminology of *xenēlasiai* (Arist. *Birds* 1010–20; *Suda* s.v. Διειρωνόξενοι, δ 997 Adler; cf. Plut. *Cleom.* 10.4; Figueira forthcoming).

(b) Notwithstanding any first *xenēlasia*, Spartan crafts were to be restricted by monetary reform. Not only is that directly stated in the *Lycurgus*, but the following text elaborates (*Lyc.* 9.4–5), observing that crafts were limited to *prokheira* (handy) and *anankaia* (necessary) objects. For the prime example, a military cup called the *kōthōn*, Plutarch cites

Critias from his *Constitution of the Lacedaimonians*. Critias' treatment is also known from Athenaeus (11.66.18, 483B), which reveals that the *kōthōn* exemplified for him Spartan practical craftsmanship (Critias DK fr. 34; cf. Poll. 6.97).

(3) In Plutarch, the purpose of the monetary reform was to suppress public manifestations of inequality among the citizens (*Lyc.* 9.1; *Mor.* 226C: τὸ ἄνισον καὶ ἀνώμαλον, 'the unequal and non-uniform'). In the *Lycurgus*, Plutarch groups the reform in a second phase of lawgiving with the *klēroi* (*Lyc.* 8.1). It has the goal of suppressing economic disparities (8.2: καὶ ζῆν μετ' ἀλλήλων ἅπαντας ὁμαλεῖς καὶ ἰσοκλήρους τοῖς βίοις γενομένους, 'and all to live with each other on a uniform basis and being equally endowed with the means of subsistence'). In *Comparatio* 3.2, the accent is on the danger of an impoverished underclass. Thus, the monetary reform was sumptuary legislation (cf. Barello 1993), the supposed outcome of which was attenuation of *truphē* (luxury). Without the mechanism of coinage, there could be no public differentiation of the wealthy – those with *euporia* (wealth). This idea was already present in Xenophon's *Respublica* (7.6). As an ideological signifier, iron money provided reassurance that Sparta had succeeded in suppressing characteristic transgressive behaviors associated with archaic aristocrats (*hybris* [arrogance], *pleonexia* [greediness], and *truphē* [luxury]). The usage of iron money sustained an agrarian/hoplite communalism, embodying *sōphrosynē* (moderation) and *dikē* (justice).

The sources of the 'Lycurgan' monetary tradition

The source(s) for Plutarch's treatments of Spartan money exhibit(s) an interest in institutional history. The two main descriptions in the *Lycurgus* and *Apophthegmata* are similar, but differences in details indicate that they utilized a common source rather than either of the two Plutarchean texts directly borrowing from the other. This authority distilled earlier material. The *Constitution of the Lacedaemonians* of Critias was explicitly used, and Plutarch was also indebted to the *Respublica* of Xenophon. Other lost polemical discussions of Spartan institutions from the late fifth and fourth centuries were probably also contributory. An important clue is the citation of Theophrastos in *Lycurgus* 10.2 on Lycurgan curbing of greed through the *syssitia* (fr. 512A Fortenbaugh: τὸ τὸν πλοῦτον ἄζηλον...καὶ ἄπλουτον ἀπεργάσασθαι, 'to engineer wealth as an object of no zeal...and to engineer unwealth'). Possible sources are the Theophrastean *Politika* (*Politika Ēthē*), *Nomothetai*, or *Nomoi* (589.1–3, 16–17). The concept of *zēlos* (zeal) for wealth is significant in Plutarch's main source tradition: its absence typifies Lycurgan norms (*Lyc.* 9.2, 10.1, 24.2; *Mor.* 226D, 226E, 227C, 239D); its presence their breakdown (*Lyc.* 30.1; *Lys.* 17.5, 6). The citation of Theophrastus in *Lycurgus* 10.2 has a parenthetical feel to it – and none of the parallel passages cite him – so that one ought not assume that he was Plutarch's main source on Spartan money. Yet, the affinities of the Theophrastean perspective with that principal source or sources are patent (note Hodkinson 1994, 210; 2000, 37).

Accordingly, a Peripatetic constitutional treatise, such as the Aristotelian *politeia* or the constitutional work of Dicaearchus, is also a likely candidate.[14] The Aristotelian work is cited a number of times in the *Lycurgus* (1.1, 5.9, 6.4, 28 [*bis*], 31.3). Plutarch includes figures for mess dues (*Lyc.* 12.3) congruent with those of Dicaearchus (*FHG* 2.242, fr. 23 = fr. 72 Wehrli). Thus, the amounts derive either from Dicaearchus or from another Peripatetic constitutional authority drawing on the same data about the messes.[15]

Such a provenance certainly fits the appearance of similar material in Olympiodorus (*In Plato Gorg.* 44.2 Westerink; cf. *In Plat. Alcib.* 1.18.164). If we ignore his apparent mistake about 'bronze' money, he parallels Plutarch on dissuasion of differentiation by wealth, exclusion of gold and silver money, bathing money in vinegar, alien expulsions, and discouragement of craftsmen by the disutility of the legitimate money.

Xenophon establishes the currency of the common tradition on Spartan money at the beginning of the fourth century, and the *Eryxias* confirms that currency for 335–290. Moreover, Plutarch's *Lysander* demonstrates the relevance of the tradition in actual politics *c.* 400. His broad context is the influx of precious metals after Aigospotamoi. The specific frame is the downfall of Gylippos, caught diverting booty Lysander dispatched home (Bommelaer 1981, 155–6).[16] Some leading Spartans linked his corruption to public possession of a treasury.[17] Their prospects for taking pre-emptive action depended on the credibility of that linkage. The debate that ensued cannot be placed precisely, as *gerousia* and assembly are both possible venues.

It seemed necessary to specify the traditional order under challenge, so Plutarch appends an account of Spartan money to the proposal of the anti-Lysandrians (ἀλλὰ χρῆσθαι τῷ πατρίῳ, 'but to use the traditional [money]'). Mindful of the link between the traditional money and prohibition of the open ownership of gold and silver, Plutarch recalls that Spartiates caught possessing money were liable to capital punishment. By implication that was also Lycurgan (note also Isidor. Pel. *Epist.* 2.146.192, *MPG* 78.593–4), for Plutarch goes on to criticize the decision in favor of a treasury on the basis of the spirit of Lycurgan lawgiving, because it promoted a defection from traditional mores and emergence of self-aggrandizement (Plut. *Lys.* 17.5–6). His employment of the term *philarguria* invokes a tradition that 'money-lust' would destroy Sparta (*Lys.* 17.4). This liability for the death penalty was reaffirmed, and not merely symbolically, for it soon claimed a prominent victim, Thorax, a Lysandrian partisan (*Lys.* 19.4).

Plutarch cites Ephorus and Theopompus for variant identifications of the anti-Lysandrian leader, Skiraphidas or Phlogidas (*FGH* 70 F 205; 115 F 332).[18] Therefore, fourth-century historiography had already highlighted this debate within reflections on Sparta's decline. That either historian digressed in order to explain traditional Spartan money is unlikely. Contemporary sources do not ever attest anyone utilizing iron money in any transaction, and their monetary citations concerning Spartans reflect use of, and the conceptual apparatus associated with, silver coinage. Instead, Ephorus and/or Theopompus seem merely to have noted that the anti-Lysandrians represented their alternative as a reversion to the traditional dispensation, for that is the connotation of the phrase τῷ πατρίῳ. Just as proposed for his other treatments, Plutarch probably took his sketch on iron money in the *Lysander* from a Peripatetic source.[19] The Plutarchean reflection of the 'constitutional' tradition leaves the same impression as Xenophon, who formulates his commentary on iron money in potential or hypothetical terms: '...a sum of only ten *mnai* would never escape the notice...' (*RL* 7.5). Contemporary non-Spartans knew about iron money solely as an item in an ideological construct. They lacked direct experience of the actual usage of *pelanors*, so any anti-Lysandrian alternative was unfathomable to them in its pragmatic application.

Nevertheless, late fifth-century anti-Lysandrians consciously pitched their opposition to retention of a monetary reserve in terms of Lycurgan precedent along the very lines outlined by Xenophon and Plutarch's Peripatetic authorities (cf. Hodkinson 2000, 160–1). Thus they were already tapping the authority of an imagined past whose contours were incised by the ideological imperatives of the 'Lycurgan' system. The forcefulness of this move argues that they could trust Spartan voters to share some of the same respect toward an inherited monetary order. Otherwise, they risked their counter-proposal unnecessarily to raise a provision in favor of iron money and a prohibition of coinage that lay almost unimaginably outside current Greek practice. Rather, they intended to offer a real alternative (in their own terms) to the proposal to maintain a reserve fund. Nor would the Lysandrians have jeopardized the authorization of a treasury by gratuitously acceding to a compromise that added onerous restrictions on private Spartiate behavior unless those rules were already standing in principle. Finally, if one assumes that this compromise (public usage of coinage/private prohibition) was imposed by those Spartiates who were not wholeheartedly committed either to the Lysandrians or to the anti-Lysandrians, then one should still conclude that they too would have been acting in the 'conservative' spirit of a Sparta, not only where local coins were not minted, but also where some inhibition surrounded the open use of foreign coins by individual citizens. Hence we should conclude that the legal status of the *pelanors* could not merely be a construct of *c.* 400.[20]

Appraisals of the tradition

Naturally, our evidence on Spartan use of money transcends this traditional portrait, with its roots in Spartan self-image, its reflection in fourth-century historiography, and its distillation in the testimony from Plutarch and other late sources. Ancient commentators critically engaged its ideological claims. Starting with a contemporary, Xenophon, they cast the history of late fifth- and early fourth-century Sparta in terms of increasing infidelity to inherited values. Chapter 14.2 of Xenophon's *Respublica*, dealing specifically with a supposed contemporary, degenerate interest in acquiring gold, set the tone. Similarly, Diodorus preserves Ephorus on a Delphic hexametric response supposedly given to Lycurgus that *philarguria* or *philokhrēmatia,* 'money-lust', would destroy Sparta (DS 7.12.5). The Aristotelian *Politeia* preserved the same tradition (fr. 550 Gigon). This oracle became proverbial,[21] being widely cited in retrospection on Sparta's decline.[22] It was current in the late fifth century, since our citation of Aristotle appears in the scholia to the *Andromache* of Euripides (445 Schwartz; cf. Philochorus *FGH* 328 F 124). There it comments on a denunciation of the Spartans in which a key term is *aiskhrokerdeis* (greedy), a charge whose tenor pervaded Athenian wartime polemics (*Andr.* 450–2).[23] Whether the oracle can be given an even earlier pedigree is uncertain. Noting the Doricism of the hexameter, van Wees suggests derivation from an early kitharodic poet (like Terpander) in allusion to the seventh-century Spartan social crisis (1999, 3–4). The shadowy Spendon, who may be early sixth-century and so commenting more prescriptively, might be another possibility (cf. Plut. *Lyc.* 28.5).

The mythographer Pherecydes of Syros (*fl.* 544/1) supposedly warned the Spartan kings not to honor gold and silver, being supported in his advice by a dream visitation to the kings by the hero Herakles (A 1 D/K *apud* DL 1.117; Olympiodorus *In Plat. Alcib.* 1.18.164). Naturally, this intervention is later fabrication, as the vacillation in attribution between Pherecydes and Pythagoras also indicates (DL 1.117). Other suspect stories linked Pherecydes with Sparta (Plut. *Agis* 10.6; *Pelop.* 21.2: Schibli 1990, 9–12). The main period for the accretion of his pseudo-biography lay within the fifth century (note Ion of Chios fr. 30 W). Significantly, his admonishment was mentioned by Theopompos in his *Thaumasia* (*FGH*

115 F 71). Thus fourth-century historiography (exemplified by Ephorus and Theopompus) treated contemporary Spartan greed as a flaring-out of an inherent vulnerability (cf. Hodkinson 2000, 165–7). Moreover, Plutarch in the *Lysander* was not alone in finding the root of later Spartan ills specifically in the Lysandrian influx (cf. Athen. 6.24, 233E–F; Posidonius *FGH* 87 F 48; Ael. *VH* 14.29).

The debate over a public reserve was paralleled externally in criticisms of the inadequacies of Spartan financial administration. Thucydides has both Arkhidamos and Perikles mention this area of weakness (1.80.4, 121.3–5, 141.3–7). Aristotle evaluated the absence of conventional finances as a major design flaw (Aris. *Pol.* 1271b10–18). His quip that the lawgiver made the city 'resourceless' (ἀχρήματον) but private individuals 'money-loving' (φιλοχρημάτους) demonstrates his intention to add a power-political dimension to contemporary moralizing on Sparta's decline. Polybius amplified with specific reference to the inadequacies of Spartan iron money (6.49.8–10). Hegemony required overseas campaigns and extra-Peloponnesian land expeditions, requiring 'money of general currency' (κοινοῦ νομίσματος), and an overseas logistical capacity. Both 'iron money' (τὸ νόμισμα τὸ σιδηροῦν) and 'exchange' (ἀλλαγὴ) of annual production failed hegemonic requirements. With a glance toward the 'constitutional' tradition, Polybius praises Lycurgus' achievement of unity by eradicating 'self-aggrandizement' (πλεονεξία: 6.46.6–7), but for hegemonic needs a policy 'in accordance with the lawgiving of Lycurgus' became unfeasible (6.49.9).

Furthermore, Spartan claims to aloofness from money and to egalitarianism were contested in the Academy. The *First Alcibiades*, a work of doubtful Platonic authorship, speaks of a mass of gold and silver, including money, entering Spartiate hands, with no discernible outflow (*Alcib.* 1.122D–123B). And this situation had supposedly prevailed for generations. In another suspect Platonic work, the *Hippias Maior*, Socrates quips to Hippias that lack of money forces the Spartans to shun his company, but Hippias answers that they have sufficient holdings of *khrēmata* (*Hippias Maior* 283D). Such explicit criticism drew on Platonic discourse on oligarchy in the *Republic* (Adam 1965, 2.211–20; Bertinelli 1997, 259). For Plato, a community devoted to military activities will conceal a savage greed and covert extravagance, intensified by its members' inability to indulge in open acquisition (*Republic* 548A–B). Their hidden store of precious metals is a powerful subversive force (550D; with reference to the lawlessness of citizens' wives striking a particularly 'peripatetic' note: cf. Aris. *Pol.* 1269b22). Plato proceeds to observe that *khrēmatistikē* (acquisitiveness) subverts respect for *aretē* (excellence) (*Republic* 550E).

Another way to appreciate Spartan monetary ideology is by exposing its mirror image in contemporary historiography on the non-Spartan 'money economy' of the Peloponnesus. Argos was the chief internal rival to the Peloponnesian hegemony of the Spartans. The Argive king and tyrant Pheidon was considered to have been the most successful champion of Argive aspirations. Even if one discounts as too poorly attested events like Pheidon's victory over the Spartans at Hysiai or the early archaic interventions of the Argives on behalf of the Messenians, Pheidon's involvement at Olympia and his dominance over the Peloponnesus must be interpreted as, at the least, a historiographical alternative to the later, historical Spartan hegemony (Figueira 1993, 19–23, 28–33). This tradition is attested as early as Herodotus (6.127.3). Here it is not historicity, but received tradition that most engages us.

Hence, it cannot be accidental that the alternative to the 'Lycurgan' monetary order was an economic system pioneered by Pheidon (Figueira 1981, 65–80). Pheidon was one claimant to having been the *prōtos heuretēs* (first discoverer) of coinage, having minted the first silver coins on Aigina.[24] Thus, Pheidon is said to have legitimized money in precious metal, while Lycurgus authorized only iron money. And Pheidon supposedly created the specific monetary medium, Aiginetan 'turtles', whose employment challenged Sparta's barter economy and use of the *pelanors*. While Lycurgus demonetized gold and silver coins, Pheidon demonetized and dedicated base metal *obeliskoi* at the Argive Heraion.[25] A related tradition credits him with establishing a metrological system for the Peloponnesus (Hdt. 6.127.3; cf. Aris. fr. 484 Gigon with Pollux 10.179). Consequently, in contrast to Lycurgus, who legislated an austere lifestyle restricted to the Spartans, in tradition Pheidon implemented an early version of the economy later conventional among neighboring states that shared regional coinages, standards, and metrological systems.

To be sure, this tradition commands little credence. If Pheidon had anything to do with Pheidonian *metra*, he merely codified pre-existing measures for wider, authoritative employment within his sphere of influence. Indeed, there is even some doubt whether the Aiginetic standard in later use was equivalent to the *metra* he standardized (Figueira 1993, 69, citing Theophrast. *Char.* 30.11; Tod, *GHI* #140.80–8). Even on the most recent chronology, Pheidon was too early for the inauguration of Aiginetan coining (Figueira 1993, 28–32). His disestablishment of a system based on *obeliskoi* is then improbable, even if one could acquiesce in the modernizing spirit of the tradition. While Aigina was dominated by Argos during the early and mid-seventh century, the island was independent by the period of its commercial vitality and minting activity.

These objections contribute toward a significant conclusion: the more unhistorical Pheidon's monetary legislation becomes, the more suitably it serves as counterpoint to the equally anachronistic monetary enactments of the even less historical Lycurgus.[26] Thus, the identities of the earliest authorities for Pheidon as monetary statesman are revealing: Ephorus, Heraclides Ponticus, and finally the Aristotelian *Constitution of the Sicyonians*. In comparison, Ephorus treated the Lysandrian influx of wealth as a crucial threshold for Sparta, while Peripatetic constitutional compilations are probable mediate sources for our portrait of Spartan money. Notably, for Ephorus, the lineaments of some other overarching themes can be made out. He may have incorporated the Pheidonian monetary system into a portrayal of early Argos beset by oscillations between royal or tyrannical authority and the autonomous urges of its *dēmos*.[27] The 'Lycurgan' system held the upper hand until it first proved ill-suited for war with Athens; it then accepted a weakening of monetary and sumptuary restrictions; and finally it collapsed through the demoralization of greed (DS 7.12.8).

Ideology and economy

The dossier of evidence on iron money presents a unitary portrait of one facet of a consolidated 'Lycurgan' program, which commentators praised, criticized, or contrasted with actual conditions. These positions should be assessed evidentially and subjected to a judgement on their probabilities. Before proceeding, however, it is necessary to acknowledge that the term 'ideology' deserves an exegesis. Let us define 'ideology' as pervasive systematization of cultural values that achieves a high degree of articulation. This articulation is both structural in that social processes and patterns of behavior are comparably more complex and expressive in that justifications for norms, behaviors, and procedures are relatively intricate and involuted. Expressive articulation and structural articulation develop in conjunction. Under this perspective, not every normative order qualifies as 'ideology'. 'Ideology' offers a characteristic formulation of group existential meaning that is essentially ahistorical. Not only is this meaning signified without recourse to historical methodology, particularly regarding causation, but it is also characterized by a sensibility in which present and past co-evolve. Because of their ahistoricism, ideological systems tend toward overdeterminism in accounting for historical conditions. Moreover, in their impetus to justify every social manifestation in terms of ideological leitmotifs, they often problematize the boundary between overt performance of normative mandates and opportunistic behavior grounded in appraisals of personal interest. A conjoined faith in their system both as behavioral praxis and as social analysis elevates the threshold of personal adherence for individuals and amplifies the gravity of any deviation. Commonly in early literate societies, invocation of an indigenous ideological system is more likely to happen where it is contended that deviation has occurred. In an environment of strong social conditioning, the main challenge to the prevailing system emerges out of incremental drift from behavioral conventions under the influence of optimizing personal choices. Unsurprisingly, to invoke Spartan money was to comment about degrees of adherence to economic norms of the 'Lycurgan' system.

The *pelanors* as monetary medium

One way to envisage Spartan *pelanors* is as a relict of a common early economic pattern that persisted in conservative Laconian society. They might be equated with other quasi-monetary transactional media, such as spits, tripods, and cauldrons, which are sometimes seen as stages in an evolution toward coined money (cf., e.g., Guarducci 1946). This approach takes its cue from Plutarch in *Lysander* 17.3, where he pierces the ideological barrier projected by the conventional portrayal to suggest that all early money approximated Spartan iron currency, with iron or bronze *obeliskoi* in use elsewhere (cf. *EM* s.v. δραχμή, δ 287; ὀβέλισκος, ο 612). He corroborates with the astute observation that obols comprise small change, of which six constitute a drachma (handful). By implication, the *pelanors* were not peculiarly Spartan or Lycurgan, merely preserving primitive practice, and could hardly have replaced gold or silver coins. This style of etymological anthropology descended from fourth-century commentary (note Aristotle, *Constitution of the Sicyonians* and Heraclides Ponticus).

In the early archaic period, Laconians possibly shared the culture-wide tendency to focus on certain craft products as repositories of value, such as *obeloi* (spits) or *lebētes* (cauldrons). These relatively standard items became signifiers of material value in donations and gifts, and evolved into units for primitive calculations of prices. The *pelanors*, however, differed in essential features from other quasi-monetary media. They were merely masses of iron, not utensils with recognizable function. Efforts to argue for monetary iron *pelanors* outside Laconia are unconvincing.[28] Nor were tripods or spits ever treated to deprive them of utility. That would have been counter-productive in assisting transactions. The acid bath of the *pelanors* was a prelude to assigning an artificial value that looks lower than market value, being intended to necessitate unwieldy transactions with huge amounts. Their artificially low official value offered a standing temptation to demonetize them by private initiative and reap the benefits of using their iron for barter. Yet, if quenching with vinegar created an etched, brittle surface, such demonetization was inhibited.[29] Requiring a blacksmith, reforging was probably beyond the competence of an *oikos*. Thus, paradoxically, the *pelanors* were both hard for Spartans to use monetarily and hard to demonetize, i.e., to stop using monetarily.

A system of ingot money was not inherently impractical or irreconcilable with silver money (Babelon 1912–17). But the iron tokens must be permitted to set prices autonomously or to reach an exchange rate with coins through market forces. In fifth-century Cretan laws, fines were reckoned in cauldrons and tripods (*IC* 4.1.1–8, 10, 11, 14, 21: Guarducci 1946). The circulation of Aiginetan coins and eventually local issues dominated the money supply there. Using quasi-monetary media alongside coins was a remedy for local economies starved for coined money, a phenomenon otherwise discernible through frequent recourse by Cretan cities to overstriking (Figueira 1981, 133–6; 1998, 122–3). The bulkiness/low value of the *pelanors* and the prohibition against silver coinage excluded this monetary model for Sparta. In Crete, quasi-monetary media supplemented coins in a nascent monetary economy. In Laconia, the 'anti-money' of *pelanors* presented an unpalatable alternative to non-monetary interchanges.

A conventional mint cannot have managed a *pelanor* currency. Mints struck coins from bullion, booty, dedicated or confiscated objects, foreign coins, and worn or obsolete local money. Income was generated by charging fees and by the premium accorded official tender over other silver. In contrast, a minter of *pelanors* subtracted value because his ingots were less valuable than untreated iron. He could not easily put *pelanors* into circulation, as Sparta lacked ordinary channels of dissemination, like paying wages. Moreover, if someone approached our hypothetical mint, he could provide raw iron, only to see its value drastically reduced after an acid bath (even if the same amount was returned, allowing for wastage). If he brought some natural product, the imbalance of the transaction shifted toward him, because the *pelanors* returned could be reforged (albeit with some difficulty) into usable iron ingots.

Pelanors were legitimized by shape, by the putative horse or horse head stamp, and by acid treatment, all easily duplicated. Rather than officially issued, *pelanors* could probably be procured from any perioecic blacksmith working in the *sidēros*, the Spartan iron market (Xen. *HG* 3.3.7). 'Minting' was nothing more complicated than depriving iron of other use than short-term circulation at a sanctioned value. As there were weak incentives for the use of *pelanors* by private agents, they were not much utilized, and especially not in the ways (such as hoarding, burial, or dedication) that gave them a good chance of survival and discovery. Not surprisingly, 630 g. iron cakes identifiable by a horse or horse head mark and by a distinct patina and brittle surface are absent from the archaeological record.

The employment of *pelanors* was possibly limited to where governmental mandate prevailed and could not be thwarted by collusion among private factors, namely in punitive exactions. If an affected party was forced to incur added cost, that stipulation only enhanced punishment. It is fascinating to contemplate the spectacle afforded by paying a large fine in *pelanors* (especially if they were seldom otherwise used in bulk). A fine of 100,000 Aiginetic drachmas (an attested amount) would entail amassing 1,800,000 *pelanors* or *c.* 11,000 metric tonnes of iron. Such sentences were tantamount to exile, as they could not be practically paid, at least in the short term or without mitigation.[30] The precedent that fines were dischargeable only in *pelanors* would account for the attitude of the anti-Lysandrians *c.* 400. For all their everyday impracticalities, the *pelanors* retained a powerful, if only potential, function in contemporary Laconia.

Our sources do not then describe mere survival of earlier archaic usage of quasi-monetary media. They suggest instead a remolding of economic behavior. Intractable, but not impossible to use, and rather inconvenient to demonetize, iron money may have inhibited an employment of coinage somewhat better than an absolute ban on any money at all (including the *pelanors* and other quasi-monetary media). Buttressed by the legal status of the *pelanors*, a fossilized barter economy was prolonged.

The inception of Spartan iron money

In grappling with the issue of how this reshaping occurred, we must analyze 'Lycurgan' economic ideology, abandoning its timeless paradigm and seeking to uncover a historical progression by exploiting incongruities and unearthing fault lines between ideological tenets and actual behavior. We begin by questioning the linkage between three features of the conventional portrait: prohibition of possession of precious metals,[31] barring use of coinage, and inception of iron money.

Each can be approximately dated. The Spartans would have forbidden using coinage only when coins were sufficiently prevalent to compel that decision. The earliest regional mint, Aigina, started 580–540 (Figueira 1981, 80–8; 1993, 62–4). Most Peloponnesian mints were strongly affected by the Aiginetan example, adopting its standard. Aiginetan 'turtle' staters achieved proverbial status as 'coins of the Peloponnesus',[32] but were not prevalent until the last few decades of the sixth century (Figueira 1981, 88–107; 1993, 62–4). Then or a little thereafter, Aiginetan fractional coinage became more common, allowing a wider range of monetary transactions. Peloponnesian hoards reveal the predominant role of Aiginetan money, but none were deposited before the 480s (Figueira 1981, 125–36; 1998, 36–8, 116–18). The presence, however, of older coins in these hoards establishes the origins of the Peloponnesian monetization well before 500. Given regional monetary circulation, a Spartan ban on silver coins was primarily a prohibition against Aiginetan/Aiginetic coinage.[33] Therefore, using coins in conducting transactions at Sparta was probably not forbidden before the last quarter of the sixth century or the reign of Kleomenes I (cf. Ehling 1997, 19 for 550–520).

The *pelanors* were distinctive by their acid treatment and artificial value. It is unlikely that a fiduciary value was affixed to iron tokens until the practice of authorities' enhancing the value of coins over bullion was firmly established. An equation of the *pelanor* with four bronze *khalkoi* certainly awaited the later emergence of base-metal coinage. Even if its value was originally a third-obol, however, that awaited the prevalence of fractional coinage (510–500). Indeed, the very idea of the *pelanors* as 'anti-money' bespeaks a setting where coins already predominated in regional commerce, as Plutarch and his sources appreciated. Their mistake was to connect them with Lycurgus anachronistically, assuming that coinage had theretofore been common at Sparta. The exclusive legitimacy of iron money was promulgated not earlier than 510–490. The reign of Kleomenes I provides several instances of apparent use of coinage in warfare and politics,[34] so that it is even conceivable that the status of the *pelanors* was codified in response.

Obvious reasons such as availability, weight, and low value affected the choice of iron ingots for this role. They may well have served previously as a quasi-monetary medium at Sparta, but not as the only such.[35] That iron monetary ingots were called *pelanors* was initially owed to wordplay about their shape.[36] Yet both fines and *pelanoi* were dedicated in sacred contexts, which might influence assigning a value to the *pelanor*. Perhaps the Spartans were aware how other Greeks commuted offerings of *pelanoi* to payments in silver coins, and chose a characteristic amount for such a commutation (one third-obol) as an arbitrary value for a *pelanor*. That *jeu d'esprit* would emphasize the role of *pelanors* as 'counter-money'.

The traditions concerning a wise Spartiate, Aristodemos, help us understand how Sparta came to be excluded from an emergent Peloponnesian monetary economy. Aristodemos was a candidate for inclusion among the Seven Sages, who supposedly competed for a prize as wisest Greek (DL 1.26–33). Andron of Ephesos in his *Tripod* had the Argives offer Aristodemos the prize that he presented to his countryman Kheilon (*FGH* 1005 F 2a at DL 1.30–1). The roster of these sages was controversial (DL 1.40–2). Dicaearchus put Aristodemos among six, from whom three supplemented a consensus contingent of four (fr. 32 Wehrli at DL 1.41). Hermippos in *Peri tōn sophōn* offered seventeen claimants, including Aristodemos (*FGH* 1026 F 10 = fr. 6 Wehrli at DL 1.42).[37]

Aristodemos' status was justified by a single, memorable gnomic pronouncement, attributed to him by Alcaeus (fr. 360 L/P):

> ὢς γὰρ δήποτ' Ἀριστόδαμον φαῖσ' οὐκ ἀπάλαμνον ἐν
> Σπάρται λόγον εἴπην· χρήματ' ἄνηρ, πένιχρος δ' οὐδ' εἶς
> πέλετ' ἔσλος οὐδὲ τίμιος.

> For they say once Aristodamos spoke a non-useless saying at Sparta: Money is the man, and there is not one pauper who is good (*eslos*) or honored.

While *khrēmata* could connote 'property', most commentators have opted for 'money,' following the lead of our sources that speak of *ploutos*. The term *es(th)los* has a strong status connotation, connoting 'of civic rank' or 'elite'. As well as being quoted in the *Suda* (χ 477 Adler), this citation is offered in a scholion to Pindar *Isthmian* 2.9–12 (Σ*Isth.* 2.17). Rather than being uttered by the recipient of an Argive prize, Pindar attributes the *dictum* to an Argive. The scholia provide more material (Σ*Isth.* 2.15b–c, 17). Not entirely convincingly, they explain the epithet 'Argive' as a Homeric touch, comparable to 'Argive' Helen. In addition to citing Andron, scholia establish the proverbial character of the gnome, citing *On Proverbs* of Chrysippos (45, fr. 2 von Arnim). This status is also corroborated by a number of citations from the collections of proverbs.[38]

There is no reason to deny Aristodemos' historicity, any more than that of the other Sages. If the Aeolic verses are genuinely Alcaeic, Aristodemos' *terminus ante quem* might be 610–590, or his *floruit* might be somewhat later, if synchronism with Kheilon is credited. He might have been a contemporary of both men. His passionate outburst makes best sense when awareness of money first permeated the Peloponnesus, but before monetization had advanced far in Laconia. While specific policy positions lie beyond recovery, the context for the saying was a panhellenic reaction to the introduction of coinage that adopted his maxim in protest against social mobility. Practical response, however, differed. Most elite Greeks bemoaned this 'new economy,' while embracing its affluence. The Spartans rejected it by eventually banning usage of silver coins.

Restricting the possession of precious metals appears considerably older than a ban on coinage (525–500) and exclusive status for iron money (510–490). It is a stringent form of sumptuary legislation, akin to restrictions on social presentation like dress or funerals that strove for status differentiation for aristocrats. Such legislation is commonly associated with lawgivers like Periander and Solon, analogies pointing toward *c.* 600. The deep integration of such inhibitions within Sparta's social matrix confirms this. Manifestations of elite material culture in seventh-/sixth-century Laconia, reflected archaeologically (including Laconian pottery) and in Alcman's *Partheneia*, were counterbalanced by impulses to suppress conspicuous display in the spirit of Aristodemos. That suppression of overt gesture (involving precious metals or dress – Thuc. 1.6.4; Aristotle at Heraclides 143.1.13 Gigon) is strongly correlated with the 'homogeneity nexus', including elongated *agōgē*, highly organized messes, and thorough politicization of *klēroi* and dependent labor.[39] Most historians would place the consolidation of this social order prior to 600.

The monetization of the Laconian economy

Whether iron money is viewed as a component within an ideological program, or its role as bulwark against a monetary economy is noted, the prescriptive monetary system of Sparta stood in dynamic tension with economic conditions prevailing elsewhere. The history of that tension is not the record of an archaic victory over coined money and a fourth-century surrender, but of a series of adaptations, adjustments, and concessions. During 500–300, Lakōnikē possessed by a huge margin the largest economy among states never minting gold or silver (or even among late minters, i.e., after 450–400).[40] The confrontation of the Spartans with monetization preceded codification of the function of iron money, emerging in the late seventh century with sumptuary restrictions amid consolidation of the 'Lycurgan' order.

Another important demarcation existed between rejection of internal use of coinage or precious metals and licit usage abroad. Posidonius gives the deeper background of the Lysandrian influx of precious metals by describing how the Spartans maintained deposits in Arcadia to thwart the prohibition against acquiring gold and silver (Posidonius *FGH* 87 F 48 = fr. 240a E/K at Athenaeus 6.24, 233E–F). These trustees were presumably Arcadian *xenoi* of prominent Spartiates engaged in a practice converse to the Spartiate Glaukos' service to a Milesian *xenos* (Hdt. 6.86α–86δ).[41] An inscribed bronze plaque of 450–400 from Tegea in Arcadian script may illustrate this phenomenon.[42] The dialect of the inscription is not Arcadian and, despite some peculiarities, can been identified as Laconian.[43] Terms are specified about redemption of two deposits of 200 and 400 *mnai* (presumably in Aiginetic silver), perhaps made at the treasury of Athena Alea, for Xouthias, son of Philakhaios. The text of side A (200 *mnai*) has been marred, suggesting recovery or revocation. A deposit of this magnitude – 6T, 4000 dr. (if side B supersedes A) or 10T (if taken cumulatively) – cannot have been an ordinary occurrence. Possibly, these sums were too great to be entrusted even to several aristocratic *xenoi*. If Xouthias and Philakhaios were indeed Spartiates, their names have an ideological resonance suggestive of affiliations with Sparta's non-Dorian neighbors and allies. That might explain the willingness of powerful Tegeans to oblige Xouthias. Despite the view of Posidonius, such a deposit outside Lakōnikē was probably not illegal. Presumably, the deposit that the Delphian historian Anaxandridas stated Lysander made at Delphi was also of this nature (*FGH* 404 F 3; Plut. *Lys.* 18.2). Undeniable traces of Spartan agonistic activity abroad had their material basis in such deposits at foreign religious centers (Holladay 1977, 118–19; Hodkinson 2000, 271–333).

The experience of another early-sixth-century Spartiate, Glaukos, also illustrates Spartan sensitivity toward the enticements of an early monetary economy. According to Herodotus, King Leotychidas used Glaukos as a monitory exemplum (at Athens in the 480s) against usurpation of a deposit (6.86α–86δ). An elite Spartiate reputed for his justice, Glaukos received half the wealth of a Milesian *xenos* in deposit as safeguard against unsettled conditions in Ionia. The tenor of the anecdote indicates that Glaukos' reception of the money did not violate a prohibition against holding coins. As yet, no such ban existed. Though one might doubt that an Ionian really did convert half his property into money at so early a date, Herodotus' Spartan informants did not find this arrangement inconceivable. Such deposits were subsumed within ancient *xenia,* and so kept separate from the taint of *khrēmatismos.* Nor was this a *public* holding of precious metals. Without any stigma of ostentation, such holdings nonetheless inaugurated an image of Sparta as a storehouse of hidden treasure.

However, such a large deposit of coins was perceived by the Spartans to have profoundly subversive implications. Even a Glaukos could be tempted not to return the deposit to the Milesian's heirs until he got a Delphic response directing him to do so. His hesitation, however, still condemned his lineage to extinction, in what, to Herodotus' informants, appeared exemplary punishment. The Spartans preserved the oracle, supposedly embodying the link between perjury and familial destruction, which is here the ultimate human chastisement. The Pythia also rejected Glaukos' plea for pardon for his *rhēthenta* (things said): consulting the god and acting were equivalent. That assertion collapses the distinction between an inner world of mere thoughts and words and the outer realm of public comportment in a manner illustrative of the pervasiveness of Spartan economic ideology.

Sparta maintained a barter economy that was characterized by the erection during the sixth century of 'firewalls' that isolated wealth in precious metals, secreted in elite *oikoi* and segregated abroad, from areas of civic interaction. These boundaries distinguished Sparta from other Peloponnesian states. During the seventh century, Arcadia had been penetrated by Aiginetan merchants, who brought by pack-mule *Aiginaia* (consumer goods) (Paus. 8.5.8–10). Since these expeditions were mounted from Elean Kyllene, perhaps they drew on contacts made at Olympia during Argive interventions there. This luxury commerce, seen earlier in the Saronic Gulf and Argolid, reached the borders and coasts of Laconia. But Arcadia and Laconia diverged in their response to monetization of Peloponnesian trade. Other Peloponnesians conducted private and eventually public business increasingly in coins. In time they started their own minting on the Aiginetic standard. Local monetary circulation fed reserves in Aiginetic coin for aristocratic *oikoi*, in and out of which money circulated to and from the public sphere. In contrast, the Spartans validated the *pelanors* as exclusive tender. Any Spartiate reserves were maintained 'offshore', as for a Xouthias, or in sequestration in Lakōnikē, as for a Glaukos or later for the *keimēlia* (treasures) of King Ariston and his *hetairos* Agetes (Hdt. 6.62.2; cf. 3.41.1). Consequently, they were supplied through obscure channels.

Although the legal standing of the *pelanors* buttressed a barter economy, there occurred striking infiltration of monetary consciousness into nearly every aspect of Spartan life, working gradually inward. Diplomacy conducted with non-Spartans and military activities early show the impact of money. Expenses for embassies were handled in money (e.g., Demaratos: Hdt. 6.70.1). Goals of public policy were pursued through monetary inducements.[44] As early as *c.* 525, the Spartans besieging Polykrates at Samos may have received payment for expenses, arguably their earliest mass exposure to coinage.[45] Possible ransoming of prisoners for cash is first attested at Sepeia in 494 (Hdt. 6.79.1). Booty sales are attested after Plataia, if only from unsanctioned sellers (Hdt. 9.80.3). Aiginetan buyers tricked unsophisticated Helots into accepting bronze prices for gold loot, a ploy both dependent on their ignorance of precious metals and expressive of their emergent monetary consciousness.[46] Thus, private treasuries at Sparta (*keimēlia* as in Hdt. 6.62.2) were not only well hidden in 479, but perhaps also restricted to a few aristocratic families. The mediation of money was also probably necessary for the dedication of spoils from Plataia.[47] Later there were the tithes from Dekeleia and from Aigospotamoi.[48]

Conversely, merchants expected to make money supplying Spartan forces, with a first instance again the Sepeia campaign (Hdt. 6.92.1–2). From the Peloponnesian War, booty was used to subsidize ongoing operations.[49] Experiments in military finances were undertaken during the Archidamian War.[50] During the Ionian War, Sparta duplicated the Attic naval establishment and exploited Persian subsidies.[51] Regionally dominant Aiginetan money played an important role in military finances, eventually codified in allied contributions in 382 (Xen. *HG* 5.2.21). It is likely that mercenary pay was calculated in Aiginetan money (cf. *IG* I³ 83.22–4; Thuc. 5.47.6–7). In naval warfare, a more complex pattern emerges. Athenian coins and their copies dominated calculations of pay and disbursements (Figueira 1998, 529–35), but Chian and Aiginetan coins were also important, so that defectors from Athens restructured minting on the Aiginetic or Chian/Rhodian standard.[52] After the war, a system of *phoros* (tribute) was emplaced, if only briefly, and Spartan allies minted coins compatible with both standards in order to provide contributions.[53] These coins with Herakles strangling a snake indicate that the Spartans were even aware how numismatic iconography might function as propaganda. The discontinuity between this sensitivity and the determination not to coin themselves points up the tenacity of the 'Lycurgan' monetary tradition.[54] At the end of the fifth century the debate between the Lysandrians and their opponents over establishing a treasury involved whether to make permanent and legitimize the wartime pattern of administration. At its heart stood the question whether the older system of recycling funds during hostilities and dedicating any surplus afterward was rendered nonviable by the broad hegemony won by victory over Athens.

The interior of Lakōnikē exhibited a slower assimilation of monetary behavior. Instances of bribery demonstrate dissonance between individual aspirations and communal expectations, although there is a risk of overplaying this point. Misuse of money at Sparta was almost as old as the regular circulation of money (and as any monopoly for the *pelanors*), as anecdotes involving bribery concerning Kleomenes imply.[55] Nonetheless, this clustering around the vilified Kleomenes indicates that Herodotus' mid-century informants still viewed covetousness centering on coined money as the hallmark of social deviancy. Later, subornation was alleged at crucial junctures regarding the Persians.[56] Another notorious case involved Periklean bribery of Kleandridas and Pleistoanax to thwart an invasion of Attica in 446.[57] Perikles' accounting for these bribes under the rubric εἰς τὸ δέον (for needful purposes) became proverbial. Theophrastus implies that he resorted to massive annual bribery (fr. 615 F *apud* Plut. *Per.* 23.1–2).[58]

These infiltrations of money were admittedly transgressive. More intriguing is the use of monetary amounts in calculating fines. The first attested case is the fining of Pleistoanax 15T for his aforesaid retreat from Attica.[59] In 418, after his abortive invasion of the Argolid, Agis was threatened with a similar punishment, 100,000 drachmas (Thuc. 5.63.2–4). Lest one suppose the kings were exempt from monetary prohibitions (*HCT* 4, 89–90), non-royal Spartiates were similarly punished in the fourth century.[60] One of these fines was actually discharged in some fashion, since Phoibidas continued his career under Agesilaos' patronage.[61] I have suggested above that the fines were to be paid in *pelanors.* Their calculation in coins (presumably Aiginetan) bears witness to the growing dominance of monetary consciousness. Moreover, such representation of penalties was the only means to signify their gravity to non-Spartans, who were in no small part the intended recipients in each case of messages about Spartan policy and ideology.

The last, most dramatic phase of monetary penetration involved basic social responsibilities. When Peripatetic *politeiai* were recounting the 'Lycurgan' order, Spartiate monthly mess dues involved a monetary calculation. Dicaearchus in his *Tripoliticus* reports that each messmate contributed *opsōnian* (payment for side dishes) worth ten Aiginetan obols.[62] Plutarch *Lycurgus* 12.3 taps a parallel tradition speaking of a small amount of money. So pervasive had monetary thinking become for the Spartiates that no other means existed to convey succinctly a traditional responsibility other than conversion into currency. This practice probably represented the domestication of the rules used for messes on campaign, where actual purchases in coins had long occurred. By the 340s, the use of a *xenēlasia* (expulsion of aliens) to combat a dearth (Theopompus *FGH* 115 F 178) implies the existence of a single market in grain conducted in money (Figueira, forthcoming). The attempt to lessen the number of the foreigners arises from their competition with other Laconians to acquire grain. The final citadel of the traditional economy was under assault in the hellenistic period, when the Helots began to accumulate assets from monetary income that were used under Kleomenes III to purchase release from Helotage.[63]

Money and social structure

During the seventh century, Sparta exploited the opportunities afforded by the *polis* structure and hoplite tactics to maximize the size of its phalanx, making its hoplite class co-terminal with the citizen body. The result was appreciable military power when coupled with comparatively stable politics and risk-averse decision-making. This hoplite polity was buttressed by curtailing elite aggrandizement. Not only was this restructuring a divergence of Laconian society away from paths of evolution elsewhere, but it may also have departed from the institutional pattern of early archaic Sparta, during Laconian consolidation and early expansion into Messenia. In that pattern, the upper class consolidated its internal dominance by bringing weaker community members into dependency through coercive patronage, by utilizing privileged access to resources, and by leveraging status networks into exploitation of external opportunities (e.g., for colonization). The outreach of elite assertion was absorption of a disproportionate share of the spoils of warfare through its base of capital assets, capacity for mobilizing manpower, and mastery of aristocratic warfare. In the southern Peloponnesus, ecological, geographical, and demographic conditions probably inhibited full emergence of these potentialities. Still, early archaic Sparta approximated contemporary Argos in structure more than it resembled 'Lycurgan' Sparta. The reaction to early archaic aristocratic dominance – although not peculiarly Spartan – was unusually forceful.

Early archaic Spartans achieved remarkable success in establishing hegemony over considerable territory, which the 'Lycurgan' order exploited (cf. Barello 1993). I cannot argue here the controversial features of my reconstruction, but intend rather a sketch of this economy.[64] At the point of reconfiguration, the Spartans conducted a redistribution of the land outside the *polis* core territory and its attached servile laborers. Available for allotment was fertile land cultivated by dependent laborers whose density fell below the threshold at which their settlements would qualify as *kōmai*. Perioecic villages, originally encompassing more marginal land, occupied the remaining territory, absorbing all non-agricultural assets. Recipients of restructured *klēroi* comprised the entire civic class, though right to possess a *klēros* was perhaps redeemed over time (the late seventh century). The *klēroi* were initially not exclusively transmitted through partible inheritance. Redistribution created the *Homoioi*, mitigating but not obliterating wealth disparities inherited from the typical early archaic property distribution within the core territory. Aristocratic status was retained; for one thing it imparted eligibility for the *gerousia*. Frozen in their elite status, aristocrats retained the assets for indulging in conspicuous consumption, but prevailing modes of exhibitionism were inhibited, except for certain restricted zones such as ritual activity and athletic competition (note Hodkinson 2000, 209–333).[65]

The elaboration over time of restrictions concerning monetary usage precluded any licit accumulation of assets by opportunistic economic behavior and inhibited much consequent differentiation in status. When viewed diachronically, the 'Lycurgan' monetary order was a precarious equilibrium in which principles of homogeneity, austerity, and blindness to economic opportunity were ostensibly defended against ordinary Greek practices. For the elite, the consolidation of the *Homoioi* delineated the boundary between the private and public spheres more sharply than for other Greeks. According to later critics, the inmost recesses of elite *oikoi* resembled their peers abroad.[66] The stigmatization of the outwardly visible possession of precious metals intensified the private/public delineation. This problematic boundary persisted as a central social 'fact'. Some gross effects were not unlike those generated by the Marxist-Leninist ideology of the 'peoples' democracies' or by Islamic fundamentalism in Iran, where stark incongruities could exist between outward conformity and covert indulgence in Euro-American consumerism in a pattern that might be called 'inconspicuous consumption'.

Sparta thrived on the reduction of social interrelations to highly articulated and simplified formulations, on the retardation in the evolution of group and individual identity, on a reduction of anxieties over social mobility, and on the predominance of formulae in mediating material circulation. The rigidity of this social structure promoted political stability, produced motivated and superb soldiers, and, ultimately, created a disproportionately powerful state for a *polis*. Naturally, social evolution was made difficult. Sparta had to a large degree forfeited its ability to exploit autonomous incremental adjustment emerging from the constituent institutions of society. Elsewhere, in contrast, some behavioral adjustments, indigenous innovations, and imitation of general Greek trends could be assimilated marginally without (at least, initially) requiring overt political sanction and reconciliation with a reticulated ideological system. The controversy over the creation of a public treasury (and its historiographical echoes) points up the dilemma of any Spartan reform initiative, i.e., its predication on large, pervasive corrections.

Laconian material culture remained comparable in regional terms, with crafts flourishing down to 550 or 525 (Huxley 1962, 62–5; Cartledge 1979, 155–7; Förtsch 1998). Almost everywhere in the Peloponnesus, circulation of goods was conducted through barter that sometimes utilized quasi-monetary standards. Perhaps an early version of the *pelanors* was one standard of evaluation within Lakōnikē. A lowered appetite for consumption of status-establishing goods dampened the inflow of other products. Yet consolidation of the 'Lycurgan' order offered economic advantages. An agrarian economy grew through an increasing labor supply and internal colonization. Perioecic craftsmen enjoyed settled conditions to serve that growing agricultural sector. The extractive portions of the economy presumably also prospered in perioecic hands. Nevertheless, the disadvantages of a barter economy and of (eventually) an intractable monetary medium grew as commerce conducted with coinage predominated nearby. The disadvantages of barter and ingot money transcend the drawbacks created by sacrificing coins' portability, divisibility, commonality, and acceptance. A natural economy forfeited the benefits accorded by prices in silver coins as quanta of information about the status of markets. Instead of an evolution toward a unified economy, a barter economy in a *polis* setting constituted an archipelago of economic sectors and separate markets. Much expertise, energy, and physical resources were probably used inefficiently in maneuvering among the compartments of this economy.

This lack of integration is mirrored on the behavioral level. By the late fifth and fourth centuries, Spartan economic life was characterized by cognitive dissonance,[67] despite the Spartiate reputation for a high degree of social cohesion and adherence to societal norms. The circulation of goods was ostensibly typified by sanctioned, stereotypical transfers between politically defined groups supplemented by barter and recourse to iron currency. In reality, Spartans reached valuations of material goods mainly in terms of silver coins. Over the horizon of conceptualization, conventional monetary behavior, both 'offshore' and away from public inspection, was enacted analogously to the operation of a modern 'black economy' involving actions shielded from governmental scrutiny. No *polis* possessed a sufficient apparatus for suppression of economic transgressions performed by complicit individuals outside the boundaries of the official marketplace.[68] Officials could occasionally resort to exemplary punishment of an isolated individual, one deviating too conspicuously. Accordingly, this monetary order was correlated with *xenēlasiai*, for the indiscriminate strategy of uprooting foreign 'carriers' of proscribed behaviors themselves was attractive.

The earthquake of 465 provided a first substantial shock to this system (Figueira 1986, 210). Thereafter, innovations in assignment of *klēroi* and transmission of property, however prudent-seeming, had a negative impact on social equilibrium because concomitant adjustments could not be carried through the whole societal structure. Consequently, efforts to achieve familial advancement appear to have intensified, as some *oikoi* benefited differentially from the aftermath of the earthquake. During the Peloponnesian War, Athenian raids and Helot flight constituted a second shock to the system. Spartan social entropy took the particular form of *oliganthropy*, an incapacity in sustaining the Spartiate class demographically. Against a social background egalitarian and nominally free of coinage, Spartan self-aggrandizement appeared outrageous to other Greeks (cf. Cawkwell 1983, 395–6). Coined money had become a means to remedy problems with the traditional, non-monetary circulation of goods. Spartans probably needed money to compensate for insufficient rents from the *klēroi*, to supply dues to the messes, and even to reward those persons serving them. And most destructively for the reputation of Sparta, the best means for procurement of money was foreign military and political activity.

Appendix

Acetic acid was the only strong acid available to the Greeks and Romans (Forbes 1955, 78–9; Healy 1999, 130–5). It is unknown whether it was ever concentrated in antiquity through distillation. Acetic acid, however, was used to weaken (limestone) rock in excavation (Livy 21.37.2, cf. Juv. *Sat.* 10.153; Pliny *NH* 23.57, 33.71; Vitruv. *De arch.* 8.3.1; Dio Cass. 36.18.2). The iron of the *pelanors* was treated with acetic acid during quenching, a process that regularly occurred in water or oil for iron forging (NB, not during smelting). For ancient procedures, see Blümner 1887, 340–8; Forbes 1964, 195–6; Healy 1978, 232–3; Healy 1999, 333–4. Quenching is a method for manipulating how heated metal cools (in general, see Johnson and Weeks 1977, 172–81; American Society of Metals 1964, 1–28). Even today quenching can occur in vegetable oils. Very rapid quenching techniques are an area for current scientific investigation. Thus, the emphasis in accounts of the *pelanors* on the quickness of application of the acid bath to red-hot iron may be seen as significant to ancient informants with experience of contemporary procedures. It is highly probable that ancient smiths experimented with various substances for quenching, including wine and vinegar. As a mixture of brine, alum, and vinegar was used to quench copper before gilding (Pliny *NH* 33.64), using vinegar is not far-fetched, even in a destructive process.

Quenching was a delicate process, so that the acid bath might possibly have been only a contributing factor to the brittleness of the *pelanors*. Pliny notes the difficulties of the process (Pliny *NH* 34.146). Sophocles has Kreon imagine Antigone will be brittle after quenching in *Antigone* 473–6. Accordingly, it is unclear whether the brittleness of the resultant ingot was owed primarily to its quenching in vinegar or whether the failure to quench conventionally perhaps had a damaging effect in itself. The other possible effect of quenching in acetic acid was an etching effect associated with a brittle surface layer. That result may have been useful in monetizing the *pelanors* by distinguishing them from ordinary iron (in various stages of oxidation?). The intersection of human and metallic orders at Sparta awaits semiotic analysis: Spartiate infants were bathed in wine not water (Plut. *Lyc.* 16.2), with the women assisting in birthing making a touchstone test (βάσανος) of their temperament (κρᾶσις).

I should like to thank Professor Victor A. Greenhut of the Department of Ceramics and Material Engineering, Rutgers University, for discussing this topic with me.

Acknowledgements

I should like to thank Professors Paul Cartledge of Cambridge University, Jack Kroll of the University of Texas at Austin, Nicolas Richer of the University of Strasbourg, and Stefan Rebenich of the University of Mannheim for their comments and suggestions, which improved this contribution greatly. I was also greatly assisted by the comments of the session participants for the panel 'Sparta' at the Celtic Conference in Classics at Maynooth. Subvention for my attending the conference was provided by the Faculty of Arts and Sciences of Rutgers University, New Brunswick. I should like to convey special thanks to Professor Barry Qualls, Dean of Humanities.

Notes

[1] Conventional treatments: Busolt-Swoboda *GS* 596, 661; Huxley 1962, 63; Cozzoli 1979, 36–9; Nafissi 1991, 232–34. Most are indebted to Müller 1839, 214–19. Coining Attic tetradrachms began under Areus (267–5: Grunauer-von Hoerschelmann 1978, 1–4).

[2] Pollux 9.79: σιδαρῷ δὲ νομίσματι καὶ Λακεδαιμόνιοι χρῶνται, ἐκ πολλοῦ ὄγκου ὀλίγον δυναμένῳ· ὄξει δ' αὐτοῦ τὴν ἀκμὴν εἰς τὸ ἄτομον κατασβεννύουσιν.

[3] Xen. *RL* 5.6; cf. Plut. *Lyc.* 9.1, *Lys.* 17.2, *Mor.* 226D; [Plato] *Eryxias* 400A–B.

[4] Confirmation might be sought in Nic. *Alex.* 488c Geymonat; cf. 488d, but see below n. 7.

[5] Note, e.g., Apoll. Rhod. *Arg.* 1076–7; Harpocration s.v. πέλανος, π 243–4; Paus. 8.2.3; cf. Lyc. fr. 6.15; *Suda* s.v. πέλανος, πέλανοι, π 927–8 Adler. For their shape, see *Suda* s.v. ἀνάστατοι, α 2082 Adler; cf. Σελῆναι, σ 204; Eur. fr. 350 N. See Stengel 1894; Ziehen 1937, 246–50.

[6] Laum 1925 countered by Michell 1946–7; Blinkenberg 1925, 108. See also A.M. Woodward in Dawkins 1929, 312; H.J. Rose in Dawkins 1929, 406.

[7] The issue is confused by the tendency in ritual either to specify the cost of *pelanoi* or to commute *pelanoi* to monetary amounts. Note Phot. s.v. πέλανοι, π 407; cf. Herodas *Mimiambi* 4.90–1. For commutations of a *pelanos* into money: *FD* 3.4 369.1–2 = *LSS* 39 = *CID* 1:8 (Delphi: 450–400); *SEG* 11.333.12–13 = 17.146a (Argos: mid-4th century); *SIG*[3] 1046.10 (Amorgos: *c.* 250); *SIG*[3] 1047.13–14 = *LGS* #98, 1.276–81 = *LSCG* #103B (Samians on Amorgos: 1st century). See also *P. Petr.* III, #142. See Ziehen 1937, 250; Amandry 1950, 86–103.

[8] The related idea of Lycurgus excluding gold and silver is emphasized in the *Comparatio.* Cf. Xen. *RL* 7.5; Ael. *VH* 14.29; Athen. 6.24, 233A–B with Posidonius *FGH* 87 F 48; Nic. Dam. *FGH* 90 F 103z, 144.7–8. A collective exemption stood for ritual purposes: e.g., Apollo at Thornax (Hdt. 1.69.4; cf. 1.51.3–4 for appropriation of another offering); the dedications of Lysander (Plut. *Lys.* 18.1).

[9] Cf. Pollux 9.79; [Plato] *Eryxias* 400A–B; Olympiod. *In Plat. Alcib.* 1.18.164; *In Plato Gorg.* 44.2.

[10] The value of an obol in ΣNic. Alex. 488c may represent a distortion, if the mandated cost of a *pelanos* or commutation of a *pelanos* is not at issue. See n. 8.

[11] At 4th-century Delphi, simple iron goods reveal silver:iron price ratios between 1:133 and 1:480 (*CID* 49.II.11–20; 56.I.83–6; 59.I.13–23, II.69–73); at early 4th-century Epidauros, the ratio spanned 1:375–1:409 (*IG* IV^2.1 103B.65, 80, 83, 92, 98, 112, 114, cf. 131, 133, 136, 138); at 3rd-century Delos, 1:100–1:

250 (*IG* IX 158.79–81, cf. 142.48, *ID* 406A.80–1). More elaborate iron fabrications were much more expensive (*IG* II^2 1672.68–9; IV^2.1 110A.37–40). For the evidence from Roman Egypt: Johnson 1936, 471; Bagnall 1985, 63; Drexhage 1991, 396–401. Cf. Clark and Haswell 1970, 152–3; Figueira 1981, 153.

[12] See Thuc. 1.144.2, 2.39.1; Arist. *Birds* 1012–14 with scholia; Xen. *RL* 14.4; Plato *Protag.* 342C, cf. *Laws* 950B, 953E; Aris. *Pol.* 1272b17; Theopomp. *FGH* 115 F 178; Plut. *Lyc.* 9.3, cf. 27.3–4; *Agis* 10.3–4; *Mor.* 226D, 237A, 238D; ΣArist. *Peace* 623a–c; *Suda* s.v. διειρωνόξενοι, δ 997 Adler; s.v. ξενηλατεῖν, ξ 25. See Figueira, forthcoming.

[13] Lycurgan origin: Plut. *Agis* 10.3–4; cf. Aris. *Pol.* 1272b17; also Nic. Dam. *FGH* 90 F 103z, 144.5; Olympiod. *In Plat. Gorg.* 44.2; Philostrat. *Epis.* 1.28; Apsines *Ars Rhet.* 356 Stengel ; Theodoret *Cur.* 9.18, 10.34.

[14] Figueira 1984, 88–90; also Richer 1998, 457; Hodkinson 2000, 46. Cf. Picard 1980. The *Politeia* of Dicaearchus was read officially to Spartiate youths annually (*Suda* s.v. Δικαίαρχος, δ 1062 Adler).

[15] Notwithstanding the issue of intermediation, from the 3rd century, Πολιτεία Λακωνική, 'Laconian Constitution', encompassed a historical sub-genre: *FGH* 584–6, 589–90, 703, cf. 587. For *Lakōnika,* see *FGH* 588, 591; and note also the works of Sosibios *FGH* 595.

[16] See also Plut. *Per.* 22.2–3; *Nic.* 28.3–4 (both of which strikingly contain cross-references to the *Lysander*); [Plut.] *Mor.* 10B–C; Ephorus *FGH* 70 F 193 (ΣArist. *Nubes* 859); DS 13.106.10; Posidonius *FGH* 87 F 48 ; cf. Timaeus *FGH* 566 F 100a–c. See Alessandrì 1985.

[17] See also Athen. 6.24, 233F ~ Posidonius *FGH* 87 F 48. See David 1979/80; Hodkinson 2000, 166–7, 423–8.

[18] See Alessandrì 1985 for Ephorus as main source in the *Lysander*.

[19] That he supplemented Ephorus and Theopompus here is also indicated by the absence of allusion to iron money in the corresponding passage on the influx of precious metals offered in his *Instituta Laconica* (*Mor.* 239F), the very work cited just below in the *Lysander* (17.6).

[20] Cf. Michell 1946–7; Picard 1980. The opposite conclusion cannot be carried merely through citing impracticalities of iron money and signs of usage of coins. For initiation of a coinage ban *c.* 400: Rebenich 1998 ad loc.; Hodkinson 1999, 165–7. Cf. Ehling 1997.

[21] Zenob. 2.24 (*CPG* 1.39); Diogen. 2.36 (*CPG* 1.201); Plut. 1.43 (*CPG* 1.327); Macr. 2.68 (*CPG* 2.150); Apostol. 4.54b (*CPG* 2.320); Apostol. 8.77 (*CPG* 2.452).

[22] The oracle was, alternatively, given to kings Alkamenes and Theopompos (Plut. *Mor.* 239F). For further references: Plut. *Agis* 9.1, Cic. *Off.* 2.22.7; Olympiod. *In Plat. Alcib.* 1.18.164; *Suda* s.v. διειρωνόξενοι, δ 997 Adler; ΣArist. *Peace* 623a–c.

[23] Arist. *Peace* 623–4; cf. Isoc. 8.96; 11.20; 12.241. Compare Hodkinson 1994.

[24] Ephorus *FGH* 70 F 115 (Strabo 8.3.33 C358), F 176 (Strabo 8.6.16 C376); Aris. fr. 485.1 Gigon (Poll. 9.77); Heraclides Ponticus fr. 152 Wehrli; Orion *Etym.*

s.v. ὀβολός (Sturz col. 118); *EM* s.v. ὀβελίσκος, ο 612–13; *Marmor Parium* 46 (Jacoby); cf. Pollux 9.83; Aelian *VH* 12.10.

25 Aris. 485.1; Heraclides Ponticus fr. 152 Wehrli; Orion *Etym.* s.v. ὀβολός (Sturz col. 118); *EM* s.v. ὀβελίσκος, ο 612–13. Cf. Cook 1958, 257–9.

26 For similar distortion about Solon in Atthidography: Figueira 1993, 61–77.

27 Paus. 2.19.1–2 with Andrewes 1951, 41–2. Plato reflects a similar line of interpretation (*Epis.* 8.354B; *Laws* 683D–86B, 690D–92E).

28 The suspect equation of *pelanoi* and iron spits is influential in this regard. Note, e.g., Head *HN* 438; Cook 1958, 258–9; and the authorities summarized in Chantraine 1957, 70–6. The idea that iron *pelanoi* or *obeliskoi* were first substituted for edible offerings should also be rejected. Cf. Nenci 1974, 653–5. See also n. 7 above.

29 The adulteration with iron of Italic bronze currency bars of the *ramo secco* type might be a parallel check against demonetization (Burnett 1987, 3–4).

30 Possibly, this practice lies behind the bitter irony of Thektamenes who preferred a death sentence he could discharge himself to having to beg or borrow (Plut. *Mor.* 221F; Cic. *TD* 1.42 [100]).

31 A general prohibition of ownership of precious metals was practically a ban on conspicuous possession, as *poleis* lacked the administrative means to control the interior of (elite) households.

32 Pollux 9.74; Eupolis fr. 141K = fr. 150, *PCG* 5.378; Apostolius fr. 12.31b (= *CPG* 2.550); Hesych. s.v. χελώνη, χ 343 Latte; cf. καλλιχέλονος, κ 495.

33 Corinthian coinage had less regional impact, passing the significant thresholds later than Aiginetan (Kraay 1976, 78–82), but Spartans were exposed to Corinthian money on campaign with the Corinthians.

34 Hdt. 3.56.2; 6.79.1; 6.82.1; 6.92.1–2.

35 Nikolaos of Damascus notes Spartan leather money (*FGH* 90 F 103z (144) 7–8; cf. Sen. *De benef.* 5.14.5). On Peripatetic lineage of his *Ethōn Synagōgē*, see Jacoby *FGH* 2C, 255–9; Gigon F 25.5, 143.7–8. On a Carthaginian analogy: [Plato] *Eryxias* 400A–B; Ael. Arist. 46.145; Nenci 1974, 643–6.

36 Jack Kroll reminds me (pers. comm.) that round, cake ingots – silver examples are known from hoards (*IGCH* #1645; *CH* 8.35) – may have been called *pelanors*; a possibility albeit unattested in literary sources.

37 Hermippus may have provided all 17 biographies (*FGH* IVa 3.126).

38 *Suda* s.v. χρήματα, χρήματ' ἀνήρ, χ 477 Adler (Spartiate Aristodemos); Zenobius 6.43 (Spartiate Aristodemos) (*CPG* 1.173); Greg. Cypr. 3.98 (*CPG* 1.377); Greg. Cypr. (Mosq.) 5.15 (*CPG* 2.129); Macarius 8.85 (*CPG* 2.226); Apostolius 18.32 (*CPG* 2.725).

39 Further corroboration derives from the Herodotean account of the aftermath of the Battle of Champions (1.82.7–8). Until Thyrea could be recovered, the Argives ritually forbade their men the wearing of long hair and their women gold jewelry. The Spartans in response ordained long hair. In the archaic vocabulary of social gesture, the Spartans could be expected to have mandated the wearing of gold by their women, at least in some ritual setting (cf. Hdt. 5.87.2–88.3; Figueira 1993, 41–4). This elision of symbolic reciprocity defers to the tradition

of prohibition against precious metals, dating it to the era of Herodotus' Laconian informants (480–440), at the latest. Nor can it be excluded that this imperfect symbolic mirroring was genuinely attributed to the historical actors themselves, placing the prohibition prior to the mid-6th century.

[40] Figueira 1998, 481–2; compare pp. 61–2 for the case of Byzantion.

[41] Posidonius is not to be followed in believing Spartan enmity with the Arcadians originated from hiding such deposits; for one thing that views Spartan relations with Arcadia from a hellenistic (or post-Leuktran) perspective.

[42] *IG* V.2 159; *DGE* #57; *SIG*[3] 1213; *RIJ* #22B (pp. 69–72); *GD*[2] #70 (pp. 267–8); *Epigraphica* 3.29 (pp. 42–3); *LSAG*[2] #27 (p. 212). See Bergese 1986 (bibliography: n. 7, p. 604); Thür 1986; Thür and Taeuber 1994, 1–11; Caravalho Gomes 1995. On Posidonius and the inscription, compare Hodkinson 2000, 157, 167.

[43] Most have opted for Laconian as the dialect, with Achaean being another option. See Thumb-Kieckers 1932, 78; Bergese 1986, 606. That Xouthias was an 'Achaean' *perioecus* is unlikely. Compare Cozzoli 1979, 58.

[44] Attestations, not all credible: Teisamenos after 480 (Hdt. 9.33.3; Paus. 3.1.7); enemies of Themistokles (DS 11.54.4); Adeimantos in 405 (Lys. 14.38; Paus. 4.17.3, 10.9.11; cf. Xen. *HG* 2.1.32; Plut. *Alcib.* 37.2); Boiotarchs in 369 (Theopomp. *FGH* 115 F 323; cf. Plut. *Ages.* 32.8). See Noethlichs 1987, 131–6.

[45] Hdt. 3.56.2, who was dubious. See Barron 1966, 17–18.

[46] The main thrust of the anecdote is to highlight Aiginetan greed and trace their affluence to unsavory roots, which does not negate the verisimilitude of background details.

[47] Hdt. 9.81.1; DS 11.33.2; cf. Thuc. 1.132.1–2; Paus. 5.23.1–3, 10.13.9; Nepos *Paus.* 1.3–4; Aristod. *FGH* 104 F 4.1, 9; Dem. 59.96–8.

[48] Dem. 2.128–9; Xen. *HG* 3.5.5, cf. Just. 5.10.12–13; regarding Lysander: Plut. *Lys.* 18.1–2, cf. *FGH* 404 F 3.

[49] e.g., harmost at Dekeleia (*Hell. Oxy.* XVII[XII].4); Iasos (Thuc. 8.28.2–4); Spartan ships at Aigina, 391–86 (Xen. *HG* 5.1.13, 24); booty-sellers (Xen. *RL* 13.11; *HG* 4.1.26; *Ages.* 1.18).

[50] Note the 'Spartan War Fund' (*SGHI* #67+): Loomis 1992; Figueira 1993, 308–10. For mercenaries: Thuc. 3.109.3, 4.80.5.

[51] Thuc. 8.8.1, 28.4–5, 29.1–2, 39.1, 44.1, 4; Xen. *HG* 1.5.3–7, 6.9; Plut. *Alcib.* 35.4–5; *Lys.* 4.3–4; cf. *Mor.* 233C.

[52] Thuc. 8.101.1; Xen. *HG* 1.6.12: Figueira 1998, 158–61, 474.

[53] DS 14.10.2, cf. 13.106.8–9: Karweise 1980; Figueira 1998, 474–6.

[54] As Anton Powell notes (pers. comm. 4/23/01).

[55] Hdt. 3.148.1–2; 5.51.2–3; 6.50.2; 6.66.2–3, cf. Paus. 3.4.3–5; Hdt. 6.82.1; *Ath Pol.* 19.4. See Noethlichs 1987, 137–9, 155–6.

[56] Themistokles: Hdt. 8.5.1–2; cf. Plut. *Them.* 7.5–6, Phaenias fr. 24 W; Theopompus *FGH* 115 F 85 *apud* Plut. *Them.* 19.1; cf. Andoc. 3.37–8. Thessalian Medizers: Hdt. 6.72.1–2; Paus. 3.7.9–10. Pausanias: Thuc. 1.131.2; Nepos *Paus.* 3.5; cf. DS 11.44.4. Megabyxos: Thuc. 1.109.1–3; DS 11.74.5. See

Noethlichs 1987, 139–44, 156.

[57] Thuc. 2.21.1, 5.16.3, cf. 1.114.2; DS 13.106.10, cf. 12.6.1; Plut. *Per.* 22.2–23.2, cf. *Nic.* 28.4; Arist. *Clouds* 859 with scholia, cf. also Ephoros *FGH* 70 F 193; *Suda* s.v. δέον, δ 243 Adler; Timaeus *FGH* 566 F 100.

[58] Later instances: Plut. *Nic.* 10.1 ~ Theophrast. fr. 617 F; Thuc. 8.50.3, 83.3; DS 14.4.4; Xen. *HG* 5.4.20, Plut. *Pel.* 14.4; Paus. 3.10.3 ~ Theopomp. *FGH* 115 F 312. See Noethlichs 1987.147–52. Concerning Lysander: Plut. *Lys.* 25.3 with Ephoros *FGH* 70 F 206; DS 14.13.3–5; Nepos *Lys.* 3.2.

[59] ΣArist. *Clouds* 859 ~ Ephoros *FGH* 70 F 193; *Suda* δ 243; cf. Plut. *Per.* 22.2–23.2.

[60] Phoibidas, 100,000 dr. in 382 (Plut. *Pelop.* 6.1, cf. *Mor.* 576A; also DS 15.20.2; Xen. *HG* 5.2.32); his son Isadas, 1000 dr. in 362 (Plut. *Ages.* 34.7–8); Lysanoridas, an unknown large amount in 379 (Plut. *Pelop.* 13.2, cf. *Mor.* 598F).

[61] Xen. *HG* 5.4.41–6; Plut. *Ages.* 23.7, *Pelop.* 15.6; DS 15.33.5–6; cf. Polyaen. *Strat.* 2.3.1.

[62] *FHG* 2.242, fr. 23 = fr. 72 Wehrli cited by Athen. 4.19.141C; cf. ΣPlato *Laws* 633A.

[63] Note Plut. *Cleom.* 23.1; Macrob. *Sat.* 1.11.34.

[64] For other systematic treatments Cartledge 1979, 160–95; 1987, 160–79, 395–412; Ducat 1983; Hodkinson 2000, esp. 113–86.

[65] Visualizing contexts for aristocratic assertion as niches or islands cautions against our over-playing attested analogies with panhellenic aristocratic culture. Tyrtean poetry implies the existence of a symposial context for its performance. Spartan archaic symposia, however, gave way to the classical *syssitia,* with their restricted opportunities for elite differentiation. Does (for example) Laconian fine pottery bespeak the survival of symposial culture or does the pottery constitute the relict of that culture, in which possession of the pots themselves must do duty for the whole behavioral repertoire that existed elsewhere? Note Smith 1998.

[66] Wealthy *oikoi* were plundered in 370 (Xen. *HG* 6.5.27; DS 15.65.5).

[67] Cognitive dissonance is 'a state of tensions that occurs whenever an individual simultaneously holds two cognitions…that are psychologically inconsistent with each other' (Aronson 2000).

[68] Restrictions on *xenoi* entering Sparta: *Suda* s.v. Διειρωνόξενοι, δ 997 Adler; ΣArist. *Peace* 623a. The would-be revolutionary Kinadon noted the presence of the ephors and *gerontes* in the *agora* (Xen. *HG* 3.3.5).

Bibliography

Adam, J.

1965 *The Republic of Plato*², Cambridge.

Alessandrì, S.

1985 'Le civette di Gilippo (Plut. *Lys.* 16–17)', *ASNP*³ 15, 1081–93.

Amandry, P.

1950 *La mantique apollinienne à Delphes,* Paris.

American Society of Metals, Committees on Quenching and Hardening.
1964 *Quenching and Martempering*, Metals Park, Ohio.
Andrewes, A.
1951 'Ephorus Book I and The Kings of Argos', *CQ* 1, 39–45.
Aronson, E.
2000 'Cognitive Dissonance', in A.E. Kazdin (ed.) *Encyclopedia of Psychology*, Oxford, 2, 141–2.
Babelon, E.
1912–17 'Lateres', in C. Daremberg and E. Saglio (eds.) *Dictionnaire des antiquités grecques et romaines*, Paris, 2, 954–6.
Bagnall, R.S.
1985 *Currency and Inflation in Fourth Century Egypt*, Chico.
Barello, F.
1993 'Il rifiuto della moneta coniata nel mondo Greco. Da Sparta a Locri Epizefiri', *RIN* 15, 103–11.
Barron, J.P.
1966 *The Silver Coins of Samos*, London.
Bergese, L. Burelli
1986 'Sparta, il denaro e i depositi in Arcadia', *ASNP*[3] 16, 603–19.
Bertinelli, M.G.A., Manfredini, M., Piccirilli, L., and Pisani, G.
1997 *Le Vite di Lisandro e di Silla*, Milan.
Blinkenberg, C.
1926 Review of B. Laum, *Heiliges Geld*; *Das Eisengeld der Spartaner*, *Gnomon* 2, 102–9.
Blümner, H.
1897 *Technologie und Terminologie der Gewerbe und Künste bei Griechen und Römer*, 4, Leipzig.
Bommelaer, J.-F.
1981 *Lysandre de Sparte: Histoire et traditions*, Paris.
Burnett, A.
1987 *Coinage in the Roman World*, London.
Cartledge, P.
1979 *Sparta and Lakonia: A regional history 1300–362 BC*, London.
1987 *Agesilaos and the Crisis of Sparta*, London.
Cawkwell, G.L.
1983 'The Decline of Sparta', *CQ* 33, 385–400.
Chantraine, H.
1957 'Peloponnes', *JNG* 8, 61–120.
Clark, C. and Haswell, M.
1970 *The Economics of Subsistence Agriculture*[4], London.
Cook, R.M.
1958 'Speculations on the origins of coinage', *Historia* 7, 257–62.
Cozzoli, U.
1979 *Proprietà fondiaria ed esercito nello stato Spartano dell' età classica*, Rome.

David, E.
1979/80 'The influx of money into Sparta at the end of the fifth century BC', *SCI* 5, 30–45.
Dawkins, R.M. (ed.)
1929 *The Sanctuary of Artemis Orthia at Sparta*, London.
de Carvalho Gomes, C.H.
1995 'Xouthias son of Philakhaios: On *IG* V.2. 159 and its possible historical placement', *ZPE* 108, 103–6.
Drexhage, H.-J.
1991 *Preise, Mieten/Pachten, Kosten und Löhne im Römischen Ägypten bis zum Regierungsantritt Diokletians*, St Katharinen.
Ducat, P.
1983 'Le citoyen et le sol à Sparte à l'époque classique', in *Hommages à Maurice Bordes, Annales de la Faculté des Lettres et Sciences Humaines de Nice* 45, 143–66.
Ehling, K.
1997 'Zur Datierung des gold und Silbergeld ‚verbots' in Sparta', *JNG* 47, 13–20.
Figueira, T.J.
1981 *Aegina*, New York.
1984 'Mess contributions and subsistence at Sparta', *TAPA* 114, 84–109.
1986 'Population patterns in late archaic and classical Sparta', *TAPA* 116, 165–213.
1993 *Excursions in Epichoric History*, Lanham, Md.
1998 *The Power of Money: Coinage and politics in the Athenian empire*, Philadelphia.
Forthcoming 'Xenelasia and social control in classical Sparta', *CQ*.
Finley, M.I.
1982 'Sparta and Spartan Society', in B.D. Shaw and R.P. Saller (eds.) *Economy and Society in Ancient Greece*, New York, 1–40.
Forbes, R.J.
1955 *Studies in Ancient Technology*, 3, Leiden.
1964 *Studies in Ancient Technology*, 9, Leiden.
Förtsch, R.
1998 'Spartan art: its many different deaths', in W.G. Cavanaugh and S.E.C. Walker (eds.) *Sparta in Laconia*, London, 48–54.
Giacchero, M.
1973 'Raggionamenti socratici sulla richezza e sulla moneta nel dialogo pseudoplatonico Eryxias', *RIN* 21, 7–38.
Grunauer-von Hoerschelmann, S.
1978 *Die Münzprägung der Lakedaimonier*, Berlin.
Guarducci, M.
1946 'Tripodi, lebeti, oboli', *RFIC* 22–3, 171–80.
Healy, J.F.
1978 *Mining and Metallurgy in the Greek and Roman World*, London
1999 *Pliny the Elder on Science and Technology*, Oxford.

Hodkinson, S.
1994 '"Blind Ploutos"?: contemporary images of wealth in classical Sparta', in A. Powell and S. Hodkinson (eds.) *The Shadow of Sparta*, 183–222.
2000 *Property and Wealth in Classical Sparta*, London and Swansea.

Holladay, A.J.
1977 'Spartan Austerity', *CQ* 27, 111–26.

Huxley, G.L.
1962 *Early Sparta*, Cambridge, Mass.

Johnson, A.C.
1936 *An Economic History of the Roman Empire, Volume II, Roman Egypt to the Reign of Diocletian*, Baltimore.

Johnson, C.G. and Weeks, W.R.
1977 *Metallurgy*[5], Chicago.

Karweise, S.
1980 'Lysander as Herakleiskos Drakonopnigon ('Herakles the Snake-Strangler')', *NC* 140, 1–27.

Köhler, U.
1882 'Zur Geschichte des griechischen Münzwesens', *AM* 7, 1–7; 'Peloponnesisches Eisengeld', *AM* 7, 377–9.

Kraay, C.M.
1976 *Archaic and Classical Greek Coins*, Berkeley and Los Angeles.

Laum, B.
1925 *Das Eisengeld der Spartaner*, Braunsberg.

Luppino Manes, E.
1988 *Un progetto di riforma per Sparta: La 'Politeia' di Senofonte*, Milan.

Michell, H.
1946–7 'The iron money of Sparta', *Phoenix* 1, 42–4.

Müller, C.O.
1839 *The History and Antiquities of the Dorian Race*[2], London.

Nafissi, M.
1991 *La nascita del Kosmos: Studi sulla storia e la società di Sparta*, Naples.

Nenci, G.
1974 'Considerazioni sulle monete di cuoio e di ferro nel bacino del Mediterraneo e sulla convenzionalità del loro valore', *ASNP*[3] 4, 639–57.

Noethlichs, K.L.
1987 'Bestechung, Bestechlichkeit und die Rolle des Geldes in der Spartanischen Aussen- und Innenpolitik vom 7.–2. Jh. V. Chr', *Historia* 36, 129–70.

Picard, O.
1980 'Xénophon et la monnaie à Sparte (*Constitution des Lacédémoniens*, c. 7)', *REG* 103, xxv–xxvi.

Price, M.J.
1968 'Early Greek Bronze Coinage', in C.M. Kraay and G.K. Jenkins (eds.) *Essays in Greek Coinage presented to Stanley Robinson*, Oxford.

Rebenich, S.
1998 *Xenophon. Die Verfassung der Spartener*, Darmstadt.

Richer, N.
1998 *Les éphores: études sur l'histoire et sur l'image de Sparte*, Paris.

Schibli, H.S.
1990 *Pherecydes of Syros*, Oxford.

Smith, T.J.
1998 'Dances, drinks and dedications: the archaic komos in Laconia', in W.G. Cavanaugh and S.E.C. Walker (eds.) *Sparta in Laconia*, London, 75–81.

Stengel, P.
1894 'ΠΕΛΑΝΟΣ', *Hermes* 21, 281–9.

Thumb, A. and Kieckers, E.
1932 *Handbuch der Griechischen Dialekte*, Heidelberg.

Thür, G.
1986 'IG V/2, 159: Testament oder Orakel?', in G.Wesener, H. Stiegler, G. Klingenberg, and M. Rainer (eds.) *Festschrift für Arnold Kränzlein*, Graz, 123–35.

Thür, G. and Taeuber, H.
1994 *Prozessrechtliche Inschriften der Griechischen Poleis: Arkadien*, Vienna.

van Wees, H.
1999 'Tyrtaeus' *Eunomia*: nothing to do with the Great Rhetra', in S. Hodkinson and A. Powell (eds.) *Sparta: New perspectives*, London and Swansea, 1–41.

Ziehen, L.
1937 'Πελανός', *RE* 37, 246–50.

6

IRON MONEY IN SPARTA: MYTH AND HISTORY

Jacqueline Christien

Sparta issued coins very late. The first minting was that of Areus I (*Fig.* 1).[1] This minting, it appears, was not carried out by the Lacedaemonian state. It took place at the beginning of the Chremonidean war,[2] shortly before Areus' death, and on the king's sole initiative. It seems to have been implemented outside of Lacedaemon (in Corinth?) and can be explained by the war which was commencing, the mercenaries who had to be paid, the support of Athens and Ptolemy II, and the personal role that Areus coveted of military leader of the land army. The tetradrachmas minted are simple reused coins in the style of Alexander and, when they bear an inscription, show Areus' name without indication of the other king of Sparta, or even of the state of the Lacedaemonians. However, the obols which are said to be part of the same experiment bear, on the obverse, the head of Herakles and, on the reverse, the mace of Herakles between the stars of the Dioscouroi, a monetary style subsequently adopted by Sparta.

In any event, the experiment was short-lived since, instead of the anticipated glorious outcome, Areus, and shortly afterwards his son Akrotatos, were to die.

Fig. 1. Tetradrachm of King Areus, 265 BC.

It is not the phenomenon of an unmonetarised city as such which is unusual. Other cities only stamped money late or irregularly. What is unusual is that Sparta was one of the most important Greek states, continuously implicated in general political life, and, after 404,[3] was even, admittedly for a short time, the most important state in the Greek world. At that moment the question became critical.

This is clearly set out by Polybios when, comparing different constitutions, he wrote:[4]

> For as long as they aspired to rule over their neighbours or over the Peloponnesians alone, they found adequate the supplies and resources furnished by Laconia itself as they had all they required ready to hand, and quickly returned home whether by land or by sea. But once they began to undertake naval expeditions and to make military campaigns outside the Peloponnese, it was evident that neither their iron currency nor the exchange of their crops for commodities which they lacked, as permitted by the legislation of Lycurgus, would suffice for their needs, since these enterprises demanded a currency in universal circulation and supplies drawn from abroad…

Now Polybios has just praised the Lacedaemonians for having laws which, contrary to those of the Cretans, protected them from immorality. Then, he continues, the laws of the Romans are better because they made available the resources necessary to achieve their aims. His logic seems difficult to understand; in fact Polybios is a prisoner of the mind-set of the fourth-century Greeks who compared aristocratic and democratic regimes, a process which is unhelpful for the historical undertaking that he intended. At this point, unfortunately for us, he rapidly abandons his analysis of the Lacedaemonians. His brief statement raises many questions, but they were not relevant to his purpose. Nevertheless he said something strange:[5]

> To pass to the constitution of Crete… How was it that the most learned of the ancient writers – Ephorus, Xenophon, Callisthenes, and Plato – state in the first place that it is one and the same as that of Lacedaemon… ?[6]

He says that he fails to understand his predecessors' opinions. But Polybios throws doubt on the description of the Cretan constitution. I propose rather to challenge that of the Lacedaemonians.

I. The context: ancient views on precious metal in Sparta.

One of the strangest aspects of the Spartan system and undoubtedly the one most praised by the moralists[7] concerns currency. The constitution of Sparta, attributed to Lycurgus, included a prohibition of gold and silver coins and prescribed the use of iron currency[8] (thus protecting its citizens from greed and corruption) and Xenophon says that gold and silver were forbidden.[9] Apart from the historical aberration of attributing to Lycurgus, who is supposed to have lived before the conquest of Messenia, the idea of using currency which did not exist at the time, this proposition contains a highly ideological flavouring. Indeed it has already been contested by a number of scholars.[10] This paper proposes to re-examine the issues on the basis of personal experience of Laconia.

Before 404

In a poem by Alcman, a girl, Hagesichora, wears purple clothes, a Lydian *mitra* and a golden bracelet.[11] Neither Herodotus, who appreciated such detail, nor Thucydides appears to be aware of a prohibition of precious metals in general or coins in particular. In various passages where they had an opportunity to refer to it, the opposite is suggested; for instance when Herodotus recounts a story of a Milesian who made a deposit in Sparta with Glaukos, the son of Epikydes, or tells of the corruption of Eurybiades by Themistocles.[12] Or when Thucydides describes how King Pleistoanax was bribed by Pericles, in discreet terms,[13] (but the episode is treated explicitly by other writers).[14] The final example of this kind is the history of Gylippos at the end of the Peloponnesian War, which will be discussed later.

The beginning of the fourth century

We can add to these texts Plato's first dialogues. Unfortunately this author had, according to P. Vidal-Naquet, a corrupt relationship with history. Also some of these texts are perhaps not from Plato;[15] but in any case the author enters into the world of Plato's society, the second part of the fifth century.[16] Therefore, these works have considerable interest.

In the *First Alcibiades* Socrates says to Alcibiades:

> If again you consider wealth…you have only to look at the wealth of the Spartans, and you will perceive that our riches here are far inferior to theirs. Think of all the lands that they have…and slaves…and horses…and herds. However, I pass over all these things; but there is more gold and silver privately held in Lacedaemon than in the whole of Greece (ἀλλὰ ταῦτα μὲν πάντα ἐῶ χαίρειν, χρυσίον δὲ καὶ ἀργυρίον οὐκ ἔστιν ἐν πᾶσιν Ἕλλησιν ὅσον ἐν Λακεδαίμονι ἰδίᾳ). For during many generations treasure has been passing in to them from every part of Greece, and often from the barbarians also, but not passing out to anyone; …the traces of money going into Lacedaemon are clear enough (τοῦ εἰς Λακεδαίμονα νομίσματος εἰσιόντος…).[17]

To the above we can add passages from *Hippias Major*. At the beginning of this dialogue, we learn that Hippias has made several recent visits to

Lacedaemon. Socrates therefore asks him, 'At which of the cities that you go to did you make the most money (ἀργύριον)? Surely it is Lacedaemon. Hippias replies in the negative and Socrates then says:

> Then it was for lack of money (χρήματων ἐνδείᾳ) that they avoided intercourse with you?
> Hippias: Not at all, since they have plenty of money.
> Socrates: What, then, could be the reason, that when they desired it and had money (χρήματα), they did not send you away loaded with money (ἀργυρίου)?[18]

The reply is that the Lacedaemonians are forbidden by law to bring up their sons outside the tradition.

These dialogues, if they are by Plato, are among his first, and if they are not by Plato, they refer clearly to a society before the *Lakedaimonion Politeia* of Xenophon.[19] In any event it is clear that the author has not incorporated here any prohibition of gold and silver in Sparta. The Sparta he is talking about is the Sparta that the Athenian oligarchs dreamt about at the end of the Peloponnesian War, where the rich were truly rich, with large expanses of land, pastures for horses, quantities of slaves and both gold and silver. It is undoubtedly a non-monetary economy, but one in which there is no prohibition on possessing precious metal. This emerges time and again in *Hippias Major.* The prohibition in question relates to the education to be given to the Spartan children, which is strictly organized by the state, and does not depend on owning gold or silver.

In the *Republic,* which is a much later text, Plato introduces the notion of a proscription. It is true that he does not clearly state on this occasion that the Lacedaemonians are involved, but scholars have generally understood him in this way:

> Such men will be avid for wealth, like those in an oligarchy, and will cherish a fierce secret lust for gold and silver…and will they not be stingy about money, since they prize it and do not possess it openly…[20]

Because there is a tendency to consider Sparta's laws as archaic, this quotation is very well known whereas the others do not appear to have generally attracted attention. However, we are lucky enough to have available historical texts for this period which allow us to understand how Plato's thinking developed, and the influences on him. The texts are those of Diodorus and Plutarch (*Life of Lysander*).

II. The situation around 404–403 BC: the events

The despatch of money to Sparta

According to Plutarch, at the end of the Peloponnesian War, after the fall of Athens,

> Lysandros…sailed to Thrace and sent to Lacedaemon through Gylippos who was *stratēgos* in Sicily, all the money remaining, and all the gifts, even the crowns received by himself… But Gylippos unsewed the bottom of the sacks and after taking a large amount of silver from each, sewed them up again, not knowing that there was a writing in each, indicating the sum it held. And when he came to Sparta, he hid what he had stolen under the tiles of his house…[21]

He was exposed by a servant.

Shortly afterwards, Plutarch gives his sources. He claims to follow the accounts of Ephoros and Theopompos. Diodoros, who – it is generally agreed – follows Ephoros' account, provides a slightly different version; after Lysandros' victories in Chersonesos

> He sailed at once to Samos with his troops and himself began the siege of the city, but Gylippos, who with a flotilla had fought in aid of the Syracusans in Sicily, he dispatched to Sparta to take the booty and with it fifteen hundred talents of silver. The money was in small bags, each of which contained a *scytalē* which carried the notation of the amount of the money. Gylippos, not knowing of the *scytalē*, secretly undid the bags and took out three hundred talents, and when, by means of the notation, Gylippos was detected by the ephors, he fled the country and was condemned to death…[22]

Diodorus' text seems both more sober and more precise. Plutarch allows himself to add moralizing touches. But some questions arise.

First, the date: Plutarch places the episode at the end of the war, Diodorus in 405. But we know from Xenophon that Lysander took control of the Hellespont and Thrace after Aigospotamoi[23] and returned to take Samos after the defeat of Athens. So it can be assumed that first Gylippos came back to Sparta with booty at the end of 405. The remainder of the booty went to Sparta at the end of the war, with Lysander, at the end of summer 404.[24]

Second: how could it be that Gylippos, who like Lysander has acted as a military leader with a mission abroad, did not know that any important communication was conveyed by a *scytalē* between the ephors and the chief of the expedition?

Finally: how can we believe the size of the amount stolen (300 times 1500 tetradrachms if we follow Diodorus and 30 times 1500 tetradrachms if we take the more reasonable assertion of Plutarch![25]), an amount allegedly warehoused in Sparta and not left in a temple elsewhere?

Unfortunately Diodoros' account of the episode stops here; no doubt because he was interested in the end of the Gylippos' career and not in the vicissitudes of Spartan internal history. For the sequel we have to turn to Plutarch. Plutarch explains:

> The wisest of the Spartans, being led by this instance in particular to fear the power of money, which they said was corrupting influential as well as ordinary citizens, reproached Lysander, and fervently besought the ephors to purify the city of all the silver and gold, as imported curses.[26]

Lysander's policy

We can now see how the system worked. At the end of the war, stripping systematically the former Athenian Empire, Lysander took care that the booty (and also precious gifts) be sent to Sparta. Athens surrendered at the end of March 404.[27] Samos, where a part of the Peloponnesian fleet had maintained the siege, surrendered in the summer of 404. Lysander then went back to Lacedaemon,[28] in the autumn of 404, but before him, Gylippos returned with the first part of the booty. The terms used by Plutarch make it clear that everything went to Sparta and that was obviously with the consent of the ephors.

It is also clear that a faction in Sparta was both irritated and troubled by Gylippos' and Lysander's glory. Lysander had carefully prepared the fall of the Athenian Empire and a new order. But the ruling classes in Sparta (those whose seniors constituted the Gerousia) and the kings, overshadowed by Lysander's glory, were not ready to make the necessary changes. Lysander had put in place everywhere governments which were faithful to him. Covered with honours, sometimes extravagant, by the cities of Asia Minor,[29] Lysander had not the slightest intention of abandoning them to the Great King. But, even if he had an agreement with Cyrus, their defence required a fleet and money. Until the fall of Athens, Cyrus had provided as much. But now this task had to be taken up. Sparta could not claim to assimilate its type of economy with trading economies which were fully monetarized,[30] and Sparta had no currency of its own. The booty sent by Lysander was a good opportunity for beginning to mint coins.

It seems that Lysander had already tested a method for the supply of currency for the symmachic system, one which would avoid dependence on Sparta (which, unlike Athens, could not supply the market with metal). An article by S. Karwiese[31] suggests how Lysander had tested his system. Coins depicting Herakles strangling two snakes, minted curiously in Asia Minor at this period, could in fact have been minted under Lysander's inspiration. He could be behind the ΣΥΝ coinage of Byzantion, Cyzicus, Lampsacos (*Fig.* 2), Ephesos, Samos (*Fig.* 3), Iasos, Cnidos (*Fig.* 4) and Rhodes (*Fig.* 5). These coins are generally tridrachms, with a drachma of particular weight: 3 g 84 (which became the Rhodian standard). This

Fig. 2. ΣΥΜ coinage, stater, Lampsacos, 8 g 41.

Fig. 3. ΣΥΜ coinage, Samos, tridrachm, 11 g 20.

Fig. 4. ΣΥΜ coinage, Cnidos, 10 g 82.

Fig. 5. ΣΥΜ coinage, Rhodes, tridrachm, 11 g 35.

type appeared in Ephesos, Lysander's headquarters, around 407. Karwiese provides a satisfactory meaning to a series that was previously difficult to place and throws a light on Plutarch's text. We can deduce from this that Lysander had established, in cities that were already monetarized (and provided with precious metal), a monetary system with its own characteristics and weight, specific to the new formation born from Spartan victory. These coins would have been symmachic coins.[32] He now waited for Sparta to stamp money and apparently the ephors of 405/404 were not opposed. Prudently, Lysander had also gained the support of Gylippos, the other hero of the Peloponnesian War.

The decisions of the assembly

Things went wrong in Sparta where persons not involved in external affairs (but who nevertheless had most of the power, and whose clients were apparently obedient) decided that it was time to set limits to the powers of the military commanders and to demonstrate that politics was not their domain; and to show above all that they should stay in line and that their victory did not allow them to rise above their families' situation in Sparta. An influential party, which was not in favour of Lysander's imperialism, provoked a debate at a well-chosen moment, in which conservative policy was victorious.

The chronology is very difficult[33] because Plutarch is a biographer, not an historian. We can see the problem clearly with Samos. Athens falls in March 404. During the summer Samos (according to the chronology of Xenophon)[34] falls and Thorax becomes harmost of the island. And here we meet the problem. Plutarch says that Thorax, harmost of Samos, went back to Sparta, and was condemned before Lysander's return.[35] This is impossible; because in that case we could not understand the return of Lysander with all the money and crowns and other precious things. If we think that the chronology of Plutarch is incredible, we must reckon that the rhetra forbidding coinage was made after Lysander's return, and even after the elections of the ephors.

When Lysander goes back to Sparta he thanks the gods. He asks to go to Libya because his family and he himself had a special concern with Ammon.[36] Lysander returns from Libya hurriedly because of troubles in Athens; we can see him asking to go to help the Athenian tyranny. The home authorities agreed to all that Lysander asked. Lysander was to be harmost, his brother navarch, and there were even to be 100 talents to pay mercenaries.[37]

Subsequently King Pausanias arrives with the regular army and with an ephor opposed to Lysander. We have have one mention of Lysander and then he disappears. The king seems to be alone near Athens. Lysander has lost the game.

We know from Xenophon that the ephor Naukleidas was not a friend of Lysander. The latter, it appears, later sought to vent his anger on both Naukleidas and Skiraphidas.[38] I believe that they were elected in the autumn of 404,[39] just after Lysander had gone to Athens.

The new ephors, it seems, summoned the assembly and the latter decided to vote against the introduction of a monetary system which risked overthrowing the whole social system, by dispossessing the landowners of their exclusive political power. Plutarch gives the text of the rhetra:

> The ephors deliberated on the matter. And it was Skiraphidas, according to Theopompus, or Phlogidas, according to Ephorus, who declared that they ought not to receive (προσδέχεσθαι) gold and silver coinage into the city but to use that of the country.[40]

In fact the word προσδέχεσθαι, a technical term which means to give the legal rate, seems to mean that the debate summarized by Plutarch related to the possibility of minting money from precious metal.[41]

Great efforts were expended to obtain this result. Lysander, though a Heracleid, was not of royal family, but his victory had made him more or less untouchable. His friends, however, were attacked. And Thorax, the harmost of Samos was killed.[42] All these events must be placed at the beginning of 403.[43]

Reasons for the failure

In summary, therefore, the idea of giving Sparta a currency was defeated at an assembly held in the absence of Lysander and managed by hostile ephors who, like many of the rich Spartans[44] (τοῖς πρώτοις καί ἰσοστίμοις) could give free rein to their jealousy now that the war was finished. This faction was also supported by King Pausanias. (Agis does not appear in the story.)[45]

The revival of a class of landowners, seeking to protect their traditional hierarchy and whose mediocre members were fiercely jealous of military glory, is not the whole explanation. As already noted, Sparta had no silver mines. The well-worked lead mines did not contain silver. Attempts a century earlier to set up a venture with Carthaginians had failed.[46] A family venture as in Thrace (on Athenian lines; compare the families and properties of Alcibiades or Thucydides) was excluded by the Spartan system. And the Spartan system was too self-sufficient to imagine setting up exchanges for supplying the treasury with metals. Lysander's idea of creating a symmachic coinage meant that the system would have been supplied by cities which were used to acquiring precious metals. But the Spartan authorities no doubt distrusted an external element that they did not control.

Lacedaemon had won the war, and that justified perpetuating the traditional system, and in particular Sparta's politico-religious structure. The army had to be led by one of the kings, who had magical qualities. As descendants of Zeus, they alone could lead the armies, with the gods' assistance. (Lysander learnt this lesson and subsequently tried to get the support of a king for the expedition in Asia that he wanted to initiate after the death of Cyrus.)

And, finally, in a society where old people and women were influential, peace was doubtless an objective. Lysander's policy involved foreign adventures, imperial wars and fleets in danger. But people lived well enough on the resources of Lacedaemon (with Messenia) which provided almost everything (apart from gold and silver): cereals, oil, grapes, figs and honey. There were large and small livestock, purple dye for cloth and even ordinary metals, some copper and above all plenty of iron.[47]

Thus the possible explanations of the refusal. But the assembly did not merely turn down Lysander's proposals. It also took some complementary decisions.

III. The implications of the decision

The Lacedaemonian treasury

The decision not to mint money was accompanied by other decisions. Not all Lysander's proposals were refused. The state was allowed to accumulate treasure in Lacedaemon:

> Since Lysander's friends opposed this measure, and insisted that the money remain in the city, it was resolved that money of this sort could be introduced for public use, but if any private person should be found in possession of it, he should be punished with death.[48]

We have a few indications concerning the Spartan treasure. There is a fragment of text by Strabon which locates[49] the Spartan treasury at Pharis and a very interesting inscription (*IG* V.1.1), recently completed by discovery of a new fragment.[50] The inscription was copied by Fourmont who found it in the church of Haghios Vassilios in the south of the plain of Sparta. The new fragment comes from a monastery in the south-west of the plain. This inscription describes the contribution of Spartan allies during the Peloponnesian War, probably when Sparta decided to built a fleet after 413. And effectively Pausanias locates Pharis[51] to the south of Amyklai, in that part of the plain. So it seems that there was something called the treasury of the Lacedaemonians.[52]

Why was the treasury not in Sparta or in the *naos* of Amyklai? First, Amyklai was not a temple. Second, because the state economy was not based on a currency, the treasury received an impressive miscellany that had to be stored in attics or even in compounds (for instance the royal tribute consisted of a small pig from each litter). The taxes due to the state and the contribution to *syssitia* had to be paid in kind and stored wherever space was available. The state's cellars were a superior version of those belonging to private individuals. At the end of the Peloponnesian War it seems that the looted silver and gold may also have been stored there, because the inscription *IG* V.I.1 (the two pieces) comes from that area. So the treasury was not completely a new thing.

The prohibition applying to private individuals

We have seen that Thorax, a friend of Lysander, and a well-known soldier, was condemned for possession of money.[53] By putting him to death, Lysander's enemies signalled their determination that the victors would not profit from their victories and that everyone had to respect the law.

Up to then, Sparta had been simply a non-monetarized economy,[54] though occasional finds of Aeginetic coins show that they were used in Lacedaemon.[55] From the end of the fifth century onward, there appear some coins of Tegea.[56] But in 403 the rhetra (of Skiraphidas or Phlogidas) prohibited coins of precious metals. And since in Sparta there was no written code, the new rules were immediately incorporated in the Lycurgan *politeia.*

Now we must see what happens after 403.

The iron nomisma

The rhetra has another adjoining clause: *use the money of the country. Now this was of iron…* Plutarch then gives us an extravagant description of this 'money',[57] and just afterwards speaks of *obeliskoi,* as if he has combined two different sources providing different explanations.

One of these explanations develops the myth born of the ambiguous text from Xenophon[58] who does not describe the currency, but emphasizes its unsuitability; the other is linked to an historical fact. We know the *obeliskoi* referred to by Plutarch. Examples have been found in various places in archaic Greece[59] and in Sparta itself, perhaps even up to the end of the fourth century.[60] In addition (and Plutarch knows this well since he provides the information himself), we are told that Epaminondas had brought one of these objects back from Laconia.[61]

Nevertheless, these are not coins. Before 404, when Aristophanes wants to make fun of iron coinage, he refers to Byzantion.[62] In fact perspectives have been distorted. *Obeloi* may have appeared as a form of coinage at a time when at least some people (and now a part of the Spartans were living abroad) had become used to living in a monetary universe.[63] In any event, it is interesting to note that the idea of iron coins had some success in the Peloponnese; the use of genuine iron coins at the beginning of the fourth century in Argos (*Fig.* 6), Phleious, Tegea and Heraia[64] has been demonstrated. Clearly this minting enjoyed no lasting success, since iron rusts. Its existence is nevertheless striking.

The emphasis on iron reflects one of the economic realities of the Lacedaemonian world. The Athenian miracle is due in large part to its silver-bearing lead mines. For its part, Sparta had only its iron mines. Cape Malea was an important mining area.[65] To the north and the south of present-day Neapolis there are workable lodes of iron (*Fig.* 7) and tons of slag at Boiai/Neapolis,[66] where there remain traces of furnaces. In antiquity, Lacedaemonian iron had a considerable reputation.[67] This allows us to make an interesting comparison. In Athens, they had money, a flourishing mercantilism, imperialism and defeat; in Sparta iron, a traditional life-style, a refusal of imperialism, and victory. But Sparta henceforward cut itself off from the right to mint silver coins. This refusal to adopt Lysander's imaginative policy weighed heavily on the city's future.

So we can see that Plutarch, in spite of his deficiencies, reveals (based in part on reliable sources, Ephorus and Theopompus) the origins of one of the most famous myths of the Lycourgan *politeia,* that of iron money. It appears in 403, when the traditional ruling class of Sparta rejects Lysander's measures for a monetarized system. They wanted above all to prevent people who had established links with the societies in Sicily and Asia Minor from becoming richer and more important than other Spartans. This explains the prohibition on individuals owning precious metal. The traditional social balance was to be maintained. And soon the myth of iron money started to influence the course of history.

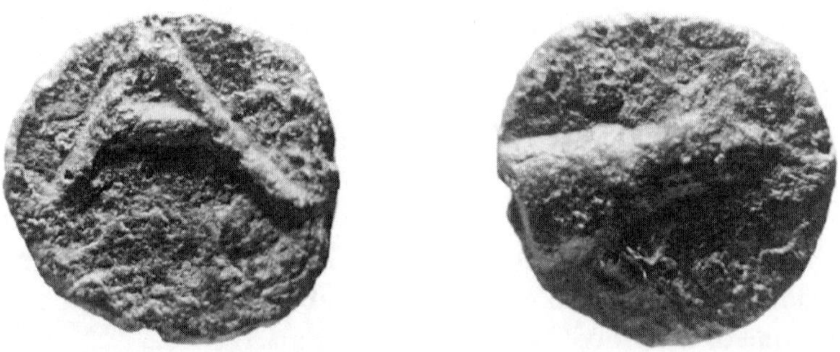

Fig. 6. Iron coin of Argos, *c.* 400.

Constantly involved in intrigues, Lysander managed to promote his friend Agesilaos, who was in favour of an expedition in Asia, to the throne of Sparta. The noble anti-imperialist policy adopted after the war was reversed. From then onwards the ambitious competed to be harmosts abroad. However, in 394 Aegean Asia was lost, and Conon defied the Spartans by retaking Kythera. Arguably these developments occurred because Sparta had let go the opportunity to mint money and, worse, had forbidden it. The prohibition had become constitutional. It was impossible for Sparta to acquire sea-power.

Fig. 7. Traces of iron in the rocks about 10 km NW of Neapolis.

The rest of the story

While it is easy to show that Sparta for a long time did not mint its own coins, the question remains open as to whether the prohibition on individuals' holding money remained in place.

No treasure has been found in Laconia in relation to the fourth century. Areus, at the summit of his glory, minted coins but only for the war of Chremonides and evidently to pay his Cretan allies and mercenaries. His intentions are difficult to fathom in view of his rapid death. His coinage (*Fig.* 1) was a personal one and not a coinage of the Lacedaemonian state, as he had profited from treasure found in Corinth in order to substitute his name on the Macedonian coinage. However the symbols on the obols – the Head of Herakles and, on the reverse, the club between the stars of the Dioscuri – were subsequently used on the civic coinage and give reason to think that Areus intended a Lacedaemonian currency.

Did people start to use money in Laconia? According to Dicearchus,[68] at the end of the fourth century, in addition to the basic products to be supplied for *syssitia*, there were various items to the value of ten Aeginetic obols. But it is impossible to know whether these were an equivalent or whether bronze coins had ultimately been exempted from the prohibition.

Few coins at all dating between 400 and the second quarter of the third century have been found in Laconia. Of 200 coins identified in the course of a year of excavation in Sparta,[69] the classical and hellenistic coins were extremely rare. Very few coins were found from pre-Roman times. The few hoards discovered in Laconia (including one recently in Geraki)[70] are mixed hoards which seemed to have been buried during the second half of the third century.

On consideration, the real revolutionary king was Leonidas II. He was the only king who, brought up outside of Sparta before becoming king, lived so far from Greece that he founded a family in Seleucid territory. When Akrotatos, Areus' son and successor, died early (263/2) Leonidas returned to become regent and afterwards king of Sparta. Agis IV, who sought to mitigate a profound social discontent, reacted against Leonidas II and his foreign-inspired habits. It was Leonidas who effectively created a monarchy by having the other king, Agis, killed (this was unheard of, being sacrilege) and virtually abolishing his descendance since the widowed queen was married to his son who thus became (at fifteen years) the guardian of Agis' sons. The brother of Agis had to flee from Sparta.[71]

I believe that all this was linked to a transformation of the socio-economic structures and in turn to the monetarization of the economy, even if Leonidas II himself decided not, or found it impossible, to mint money.

S. Grunauer places the first truly Spartan coins at the time of Cleomenes, son of Leonidas.[72] In fact it is more likely that the tetradrachms bearing on the reverse the Laconian Apollo[73] were issued during the reign of his successors.[74] As presented by Plutarch/Phylarchus, Cleomenes followed Agis' policy in the socio-economic area.[75] He set out to rebuild an effective Spartan army based on the attribution of *klēroi* and on a *paideia* reorganized by Sphairos who provided the young with military training from 14 years old. This Lycurgan policy would appear to exclude the coining of money. His successor Lycurgus, who did not come from a royal family but had bribed the ephors to make him king,[76] is a more likely candidate for issuing coin. He certainly gained some military success as he left straight away, in 219, to reconquer areas that had been seized by the Argives and the Messenians allied to Antigonos Doson in 221.

He had perhaps been in the East, since it appears that the head of the young king on the obverse of the coinage resembles Seleucos II. However he did not mark his name, but coins bear the city mark Λ A.

Sparta minted also bronze coins identical to a Ptolemaic original with an eagle on the obverse and thunderbolt on the reverse. But the exact attribution of these early Spartan coins is obscure. Perhaps we shall discover more when the coins excavated in Ithome have been published.

One of the most striking things about the four hoards found in Laconia (Sparta,[77] Gythion,[78] Talanta,[79] and now Geraki[80]) is that they include no coins struck in the surrounding cities, Megalopolis, Messenia, or Argos. We often have coins of the type of Philip or Alexander, and Seleucid and sometimes Ptolemaic issues, coins from cities of Athens, Aegina or Thebes often ancient enough, and, for the third century, from Sicyon. Because of the coin of Ptolemaios III found in Geraki, J.P.A. Van Der Vin tries to date the burial of these hoards at the time of the invasion of Laconia after Sellasia. I prefer a wider period starting in 243 (Agis IV's reforms) and ending in 218/217 (the invasion of Laconia by Philip V),[81] including 240/239 (invasion and sack by the Aetolians) and autumn 227 (Cleomenes' reforms). In any event, Laconia provides evidence of the use of coins from this period onward.

Conclusion

Overall, we have a few examples of silver coins dating from before 404 BC, but virtually nothing for the fourth century (in the present state of my knowledge). In the third century, particularly the second half, we start to find coins again. Sparta appears therefore to have retained a barter economy with also no doubt scriptural money; and the system would seem to have worked well enough since after the death of Nabis, coins are rare until the time of Julius Caesar. The reigns of the king who coined money, Lycourgos(?) and of Nabis, were too short to change things. After them, the decision of Philopoimen to destroy the Lycurgan *politeia* seems, by reaction, to give a new life to the prohibition of money.

Notes

[1] The photographs of coins were taken by D. Gérin, *conservateur* of the Cabinet des médailles in Paris.

[2] S. Grunauer-von Hoerschelmann, 1978. For the date of Areus' death cf. J. Christien 1987, 111–24.

[3] The situation was the same from 550 to 480, but the relationship between the authorities and currency did not exist.

[4] *Pol.* 6.49.7–9. Unless otherwise stated, the translation is that of the Loeb Classical Library.

[5] *Pol.* 6.45.1.

[6] We know from Strabon 10.476 ff. that Ephorus had indeed studied the Cretans. On the other hand there is nothing on that subject in the writings of Xenophon, strangely – given that Herodotus (1.65) raises the problem when writing of Lycurgus. We can imagine that the text of Plato in question is *Laws* 1.625 ff. It is surprising to find the name of Callisthenes when one might have expected that of Aristotle. D. Roussel 1970, 1309 n. 2, writes: 'On s'étonne qu'un esprit

ordinairement aussi méthodique ait pu s'égarer dans une telle confusion…'

[7] This is the view of Polybios.

[8] Plut. *Lyc.* 9.

[9] Xen. *Lac. Pol.* 7.6 'Χρυσίον γε μὴν καὶ ἀργύριον ἐρευνᾶται…ὁ ἔχων ζημιοῦται.'

[10] Fustel de Coulanges 1891, 90. H. Michell 1953, 228, 'Les Spartiates utilisaient les pièces d'or et d'argent aussi librement que toute nation.' More recently O. Picard, historian and numismatist, in a lecture given for the society of French Hellenic studies, expressed a similar opinion; cf. *REG* 90,1980, XXV–XXVI.

[11] Alcman, Frag. I, v. 64, 65. Clearly, we have no indication regarding a prohibition on precious metals; on the other hand adolescents were apparently not entitled to wear this clothing. Only a young woman who has finished her education has this right (unless the reference to her clothing means simply that she belongs to a richer family than her companions).

[12] Herod. 6.86; 8.5.

[13] Thuc. 1.114; 2.21.1.

[14] Plut. *Per.* 22.3.

[15] Cf. Guthrie 1976, 286 n. 3.

[16] P. Vidal-Naquet: 'Quiconque veut traiter aujourd'hui en historien de Platon doit tenir compte, non seulement de la date de rédaction des dialogues, mais de leur date dramatique, le plus souvent oubliée des commentateurs' ('La société platonicienne des Dialogues', in *La Grèce vue d'ailleurs*, 1990, 95–119).

[17] Plato, *Alc.* 1.122D–123A.

[18] Plato, *Greater Hippias*, 283B and D.

[19] And they are supposed to take place some years before, during the life of Socrates.

[20] Plato, *Republic* 548A and B.

[21] Plut. *Lys.* 16.1–2: Ὁ δὲ Λύσανδρος…ἐπὶ Θρᾴκης ἐξέπλευσε, τῶν δὲ χρημάτων τὰ περιόντα καὶ ὅσας δωρεὰς αὐτὸς ἢ στεφάνους ἐδέξατο, …ἀπέστειλεν εἰς Λακεδαίμονα διὰ Γυλίππου τοῦ στρατηγήσαντος περὶ Σικελίαν. ὁ δέ, ὡς λέγεται, τὰς ῥαφὰς τῶν ἀγγείων κάτωθεν ἀναλύσας καὶ ἀφελὼν συχνὸν ἀργύριον ἐξ ἑκάστου πάλιν συνέρραψεν, ἀγνοήσας ὅτι γραμματίδιον ἐνῆν ἑκάστῳ τὸν ἀριθμὸν σημαῖνον. ἐλθὼν δὲ εἰς Σπάρτην, ἃ μὲν ὑφῄρητο κατέκρυψεν ὑπὸ τὸν κέραμον τῆς οἰκίας…

[22] Diod. 13.106.8–9: εὐθὺς δὲ τῇ δυνάμει πλεύσας ἐπὶ Σάμον αὐτὸς μὲν ταύτην ἐπολιόρκει, Γύλιππον δὲ τὸν εἰς Σικελίαν τοῖς Συρακοσίοις τῷ ναυτικῷ συμπολεμήσαντα ἀπέστειλεν εἰς Σπάρτην τά τε λάφυρα κομίζοντα καὶ μετὰ τούτων ἀργυρίου τάλαντα χίλια καὶ πεντακόσια. ὄντος δὲ τοῦ χρήματος ἐν σακίοις, καὶ ταῦτ' ἔχοντος ἑκάστου σκυτάλην ἔχουσαν τὴν ἐπιγραφὴν τὸ πλῆθος τοῦ χρήματος δηλοῦσαν, ταύτην ἀγνοήσας ὁ Γύλιππος τὰ μὲν σακία παρέλυσεν, ἐξελόμενος δὲ τάλαντα τριακόσια, καὶ διὰ τῆς ἐπιγραφῆς γνωσθεὶς ὑπὸ τῶν ἐφόρων, ἔφυγε καὶ κατεδικάσθη θανάτῳ.

[23] Xen. *Hell.* 2.2.6.

[24] Xen. *Hell.* 2.2.10.

[25] Plut. *Nic.* 28.4 around 30 times 25 kg.

[26] Plut. *Lys.* 17.1.

[27] Bommelaer 1981, 171.

[28] With gold crowns and 490 silver talents, and many other things... Xen. *Hell.* 11.3. The issue of the amounts involved has been studied by E. David 1979; cf. idem 1981, ch. 1.

[29] Bommelaer 1981.

[30] The model of thalassocracy was Athens.

[31] Karwiese 1980, 1–27.

[32] The great political Spartan invention was symmachy. They led the Peloponnese for 150 years. And symmachy was the model adopted by Philip II. Even in the third century Areus tried to re-establish a symmachy.

[33] Bommelaer 1981, 134–171.

[34] Also Diod. 14.3.4.

[35] Plut. *Lys.* 19.7.

[36] Plut. *Lys.* 20.

[37] Xen. *Hell.* 2.4.28.

[38] N. Richer 1998, 463–4. I consider that they were colleagues in 404/403 contrary to op. cit. p. 528, which places them in successive years.

[39] N. Richer 1998, 301–4 (date of elections).

[40] Plut. *Lys.* 17.2.

[41] Cf. Bommelaer 1981, 155 n. 230.

[42] Plut. *Lys.* 19.7. Clearchos, who was harmost of Byzantion, was banished from Sparta (Diod. 14.12.2–7). Perhaps the story of Pharnabazos' claim involves a confusion, in Plutarch, between Lysander and Clearchos. In that part of Lysander's life he seems to follow Douris of Samos (18.1) and not Ephorus. In any case, Plutarch's chronology is not clear.

[43] And in the years after, 402 or 401, I place the rhetra of Epitadeus, which is a consequence of the decision above. J. Christien 1974,197–221.

[44] Plut. *Lys.* 19.1.

[45] But Plutarch speaks of the kings: *Lys.* 21.4.

[46] Herod. 5.42, cf. Malkin 1994, 192–218.

[47] Cartledge 1979, 13–22, 179–184.

[48] Plut. *Lys.* 17.4.

[49] Strab. 18.5.4. Unfortunately, the text is partly a conjecture.

[50] The second part of the inscription, discovered by G. Pikoulas, has been published by A. Matthaiou and G. Pikoulas in *Horos*, 1989, 7, 77–124 ; and also by Loomis 1992. Redated correctly by M. Pierart 1995, 253–82, to the years 411–410. See also J. Christien in Amouretti, Christien, Ruzé, Sineux, *Le regard des grecs sur la guerre*, Paris, 2000,154.

[51] Paus. 3.20.3.

[52] Waterhouse and Hope Simpson 1960, 78–81.

[53] Perhaps it was at that time that Lysander left what remained with him as a deposit with the Acanthians (Plut. *Lys.* 18.2–3). It was very little compared to all he had received. (But perhaps he made also another deposit in the temple of Ammon? cf. Plut. *Lys.* 25.3.)

[54] For the way in which an economy of this kind worked cf. Cardascia 1952. The book is enlightening. Also Aristotle, *Econ.* 1344b, emphasizes that the

Lacedaemonian system is close to the Persian and the opposite of the Athenian; see also Will 1960, 251–75.

[55] According to the latest information on these discoveries: at Ithome, the excavations directed by P. Themelis have provided two Eginetic drachmas (silver) and two demidrachmas (silver) with sea-turtle. And I am told by an epimelete of Sparta that a decade ago, a hoard of seventeen Eginetic drachmas (silver) was found in Sparta (but I have not been able to examine them). Cf. for general count Hodkinson 2000, 173.

[56] Abadie 1985, 404–5. Trihemiobol, fig. 40–1.

[57] Plut. *Lys.* 17.2: 'this was of iron, and was dipped in vinegar as soon as it came from the fire…', and 17.4–5.

[58] Xen. *Lac. Pol.* 7.5–6.

[59] Courbin 1953, 203–33.

[60] Hodkinson 2000, 162–3.

[61] Plut. *Fabius*, 27.

[62] Aristoph. *Clouds*, 249.

[63] We have examples of this phenomenon in the works of the ethnologists. Thus Bohannan, 1955. The author gives the example of societies who used iron bars on occasion in the course of trade. The Tivs' economy was in three trading areas and iron bars were used ritually on certain occasions. The early Europeans in contact with the Tivs interpreted iron bars as being their currency.

[64] Babelon 1914. Tegea, p. 655, n. 981, pl. 227, fig. 20; Argos, p 466, nn. 633 and 633a, pl. 215, fig. 28; Phleious, p. 514, n. 729a; Herala, p. 679, n. 1024, pl. 228, fig. 25.

[65] Christien 1989, 75–105, pp. 89–91.

[66] On the hill Psaphaki. Near the ancient wall the slag is mixed with Greek sherds. Nearer the mines existed remains of iron work slightly to the south at Palaiokastro (destroyed now for the new harbour) and to the north, near a site which was perhaps Aphrodisias.

[67] Steph. Byz. (Daimachos), Λακεδαίμων.

[68] Athen. 4.141.

[69] Th. Spyropoulos, archeologist of Laconia, provided me in 1982 with the list of excavated coins that had just been analysed. Dating from the end of the fifth century there was one silver coin of Tegea and one of Phleious. For the fourth and third centuries BC two silver coins and two bronze of Sicyon: later, two bronze of Nabis, and one triobol of Sicyon. Coinage began to be more common from 48 BC onwards. The great majority of coins dated from the lower Empire and pre-Christian times.

[70] Van Der Vin 1998, 71–92.

[71] Plut. *Agis* and *Cleom.*

[72] Grunauer 1978, 7–27 and pls. 1–4. Accepted by Cartledge and Spawforth 1989, 55.

[73] I cannot accept the interpretation of S. Grunauer that this is Artemis Orthia. On the other hand, as she says, it is not Amyklaean Apollo (because of the accompanying animal) but probably Apollo Karneios, the most important in Sparta.

[74] Van Der Vin 1998, 76.

[75] Even though, hidden away behind the propaganda, there are signs of hellenistic monarchy.

[76] *Pol.* 4.36. Lycourgos is accused of having given a talent to each ephor to accept him as Heracleid.

[77] *Inventory of Greek Coin Hoards* (*IGCH*) 2, New York 1973, n. 181. This is the only hoard where Spartan tetradrachms were found (a single one was found elsewhere, in a large hoard near Epidaurus) and yields a date between 220 and 210 BC.

[78] *IGCH* 2, n. 170:1 drachma of Aegina, 31 triobols of Sicyon, and 1 tetradrachm of Antiochos I. The hoard has been dated to 250–240 BC.

[79] Discovered in 1948(?) at Talanta (south-east of the temple of Apollon Hyperteleatas, between the perioecic towns of Cotyrta and Epidauros Limera). At first only six coins – *IGCH* 2, n. 132; the rest, to my knowledge, reappeared later, *IGCH* 3 n. 31. We therefore have 30 out of 31 coins: 4 dr of Alexander the Great, and 1 dr of Lysimachus, 1 of Philip III, 2 dr of Boeotia, 14 dr of Aegina, 6dr of Sicyon, 1 tetradr of Athens, and a triobol of Sicyon. The hoard has been dated 280–270 BC, but could be later.

[80] Van Der Vin 1998: 3 dr of Boeotia, 5 tetradr of Athens, 1 stater and 7 dr of Aegina, 2 tetradr and 22 dr of Alexander the Great, 1 tetradr of Lysimachos, 1 dr and 11 triobols of Sicyon… and 1 bronze of Ptolemaios III.

[81] This event could have given rise to the burial of the hoard in Sparta.

Bibliography

Abadie, C. and Spyropoulos, Th.
1985 'Fouilles à Helléniko', *BCH*, 385–466.

Amouretti, M.C., Christien, J., Ruzé, F. and Sineux, P.
2000 *Le regard des grecs sur la guerre,* Paris.

Babelon, E.
1914 *Traité des monnaies grecques et romaines*, II, Paris.

Bohannan, P.
1955 'Some principles of exchange and investment among the Tivs', *American Anthropology* 57.

Bommelaer, J.F.
1981 *Lysandre de Sparte. Histoire et tradition*, Paris.

Cardascia, E.
1952 *Les archives des Murashu, 450–403 BC*, Paris.

Cartledge, P.
1979 *Sparta and Laconia*, London.

Cartledge, P. and Spawforth, A.
1989 *Hellenistic and Roman Sparta*. London.

Courbin, P.
1953 'Le monnayage de la Grèce archaïque, valeur comparée du fer et de l'argent', *Annales ESC*, 203–33.

Christien, J.
1974 'La Loi d' Epitadeus: un aspect de l'histoire économique et sociale à Sparte', *RHD* 52, 197–221.
1987 'Les forteresses de la côte orientale de la Laconie et la guerre de Chrémonides', *Ktema*, 111–24.
1989 'Promenades en Laconie', *DHA*, 75–105.

David, E.
1979 'The influx of money into Sparta at the end of the fifth century BC', *SCI* 5, 30–45.
1981 *Sparta between Empire and Revolution; 404–243 BC*, New York.

Fustel de Coulanges, N.D.
1891 'Etude sur la propriété à Sparte', in C. Jullian (ed.) *Nouvelles recherches sur quelques problèmes d'histoire,* Paris, 52–118.

Grunauer-von Hoerschelmann, S.
1978 *Die Münzprägung der Lakedaimonier*, Berlin.

Guthrie, W.K.C.
1976 *Les Sophistes,* Paris.

Hodkinson, S.
2000 *Property and Wealth in Classical Sparta*, London and Swansea.

Karwiese, S.
1980 'Lysander as Herakliskos Drakonopnigon', *NC* 20, 1–27.

Loomis, W.T.
1992 *The Spartan War Fund, IG V 1, 1 and a New Fragment,* Stuttgart.

Malkin, I.
1994 *Myth and Territory in the Spartan Mediterranean*, Cambridge.

Matthaiou, A. and Pikoulas, G.
1989 ''Έδον τοῖς Λακεδαιμονίοις ποττὸν πόλεμον', *Horos* 7, 77–124.

Michell, H.
1953 *Sparte et les Spartiates*, Paris.

Pierart, M.
1995 'Chios entre Athènes et Sparte', *BCH* 119, 253–82.

Richer, N.
1998 *Les éphores; étude sur l'histoire et l'image de Sparte*, Paris.

Roussel, D.
1970 *Polybe*, Paris.

Thompson, M., Morkholm, O. and Kraay, C.
1973 *Inventory of Greek Coin Hoards* (*IGCH*) II, New York.

Van Der Vin, J.P.A.
1998 'A coin hoard from Geraki in Laconia', *Pharos* 6, 71–92.

Vidal-Naquet, P.
1990 *La Grèce vue d'ailleurs*, Paris.

Waterhouse, W. and Hope Simpson, R.
1960 'Prehistoric Laconia', *BSA*, 1960.

Will, E.
1960 'Chabrias et les finances de Tachos', *REA*, 251–75.

7

THE INVENTION OF TRADITION IN CLASSICAL AND HELLENISTIC SPARTA

Michael A. Flower

In 1983 a collection of essays was published called *The Invention of Tradition*, edited by Eric Hobsbawm and Terence Ranger. Although that collection broke new ground for the study of modern history, it seems to have had insufficient impact on the study of ancient history.[1] In Greek history the best known 'invented tradition' is the annual public burial of the war dead in a common grave at Athens, an 'ancestral custom' which Thucydides (2.34) wrongly believed to have existed at the time of the Persian wars, but which in all probability had been introduced after the battle of Drabescus in 464. Yet many scholars cannot accept that Thucydides could have been so greatly in error about so relatively recent a development.[2] Historians of modern history, by contrast, are acutely aware that many traditions are commonly believed, even by highly educated people, to be much older than they really are.

The purpose of this essay is to apply the methodology of the 'invention of tradition' to the study of classical and hellenistic Sparta. It has, of course, already been applied to Roman Sparta generally by Antony Spawforth, and to the Spartan upbringing, or system of education, by Nigel Kennell.[3] Furthermore, Lukas Thommen has recently argued that much of the Spartan *politeia* actually developed during the fifth century.[4] Thus some of my conclusions will not be new to scholars who are sympathetic to such treatments. Despite these advances, however, old habits of scholarship about Sparta show no signs of disappearing. Thus part of what I am attempting here is to give greater plausibility to recent trends by placing them within an overarching explanatory framework. Perhaps this essay will be useful also to the non-specialist who may be unaware of the historiographical pitfalls particular to the study of ancient Sparta.

What, then, is the precise meaning of the term 'invention of tradition', and how does it differ from the Spartan 'mirage'? The mirage was first explicitly studied by François Ollier as long ago as 1933 in his justly famous book *Le mirage spartiate*. More recently Paul Cartledge has succinctly defined it as 'the partly distorted, partly invented image created by and for non-Spartans (with not a little help from their Spartan friends) of what Sparta ideally represented'.[5] By the invention of tradition I mean the image of Sparta that the Spartans created primarily for themselves, but also, to a lesser extent, for outsiders. I have borrowed the phrase and the methodology from *The Invention of Tradition*. In his introduction to the volume, Hobsbawm provides the following definition: 'The term "invented tradition" is used in a broad, but not imprecise sense. It includes both "traditions" actually invented, constructed and formally instituted and those emerging in a less easily traceable manner within a brief and dateable period – a matter of a few years perhaps – and establishing themselves with great rapidity.' Perhaps the most famous article in that collection is Hugh Trevor-Roper's demonstration that the Scottish kilt woven in a design whose colour and pattern indicate its clan, was an invention of the first half of the nineteenth century. For my purposes, however, David Cannadine's article provides the closest parallel. As he demonstrates, the pageantry that surrounds the British monarchy in its public ceremonial manifestations, despite its seeming antiquity, is in its modern form the product of the late nineteenth and twentieth centuries.

In the present study, I am interested in only one variety of such inventions: traditions invented, constructed and formally instituted at a specific point in time and for a specific purpose. Of course, it has long been recognized that every time the Spartans changed something in their society, they attributed the change to Lycurgus. Such an attribution constitutes the invention of tradition. But I am going to argue that they did this so systematically and so pervasively that any synthetic history of Spartan institutions is impossible.

A traditional approach to the study of Sparta is to attempt to give a comprehensive description of Spartan political, social, and educational institutions during the fifth century BC, by combining evidence from every period and from diverse authors, all of it taken more or less at face value.[6] Alcman, Tyrtaeus, Herodotus, Xenophon, Polybius, and Plutarch are all treated as if they were contemporaries and their statements are accepted fairly uncritically and given equal weight. But all ancient evidence should not become primary evidence about classical Sparta, regardless of when and under what circumstances it was written. It is dangerous to assume that Spartan institutions were relatively static, coming into being at a certain point of time and then changing only slightly, if at all. That point is usually assumed to have been between 650 and 550 BC. But is it in fact possible to write a comprehensive, composite, and synthetic account of Spartan institutions for the period 550–350 BC? Can one legitimately include in a book on Spartan society, chapters on marriage, education, and land tenure, combining evidence from Xenophon, Plutarch, and other sources?

The impossibility of writing Spartan history according to that traditional method can be illustrated by a clear-cut example of the invention of tradition. According to Plutarch, in his *Life of Lysander*, there was a debate in Sparta in 404 BC about the importation of gold and silver money. Plutarch says (17): 'The ephors debated the matter. And it was Sciraphidas, according to Theopompus, or Phlogidas, according to Ephorus, who was of the opinion that they ought not to receive gold and silver coinage into the city, but to use their ancestral currency (which was of iron).' The compromise was reached that imported money could be used for public use, while private ownership of foreign currency was unlawful.

Interpretation is made difficult because the name of Lycurgus does not appear in the citation of Ephorus and Theopompus, but we may fairly assume that Lysander's opponents invoked his name.[7] Indeed, to call the iron currency 'ancestral' (πάτριος) was tantamount to calling it 'Lycurgan', for these terms became virtually synonymous.[8] And Xenophon, who actually wrote earlier than either Theopompus or Ephorus, implicitly attributes the ban on gold to Lycurgus himself (*Lac. Pol.* 14.3).[9] Now no one will doubt that Lycurgus, whoever he was and whenever he lived, could not have been responsible for a ban on coined money, as Plutarch elsewhere claims that he was (*Lyc.* 9.1).[10] Even the latest possible date for him antedates the striking of coins by Greek cities. It should also be clear that before 404 BC it was permissible for individual Spartans to possess gold and silver objects, and probably coinage too.[11] What happened in 404 was this: a group at Sparta, hostile to Lysander and represented by one or more of the ephors for that year, invented the tradition that Lycurgus had introduced iron currency and had banned the public and private ownership of gold and silver coinage (and surely of bullion as well).[12] This ban, they claimed, had subsequently lapsed. Their fear about contemporary conditions at Sparta was retrojected into the past. Indeed, it is a characteristic of invented traditions that they are responses to novel situations that take the form of references to old situations.

The ban on the ownership of precious metals is a patent invention. And it is possible to go even further. No undisputed example of Sparta's ancestral iron currency has ever been discovered,[13] and the earliest literary reference dates to the early fourth century (Xen. *Lac. Pol.* 7.5–6, although the metal is not specified). Could it be that the ancestral iron currency was also invented by Lysander's opponents at this moment, perhaps being a reinvention of something which either had existed or was thought to have existed in the distant past? Perhaps the Spartans, like Aristotle (*Pol.* 1257a28–41; frag. 481 Rose) and Plutarch (*Lys.* 17.1–5, probably drawing on Theopompus or Ephorus), believed that iron had once widely served as currency and thus recreated an iron currency in the tense atmosphere of 404.[14]

However that may be, this is an excellent example of the way invented traditions are built on cultural proclivities. Before 404 there had not been much coinage in Sparta, even though possession of it was not illegal, and the Spartans themselves did not begin to coin until the reign of Areus (309–265 BC). Their general unfamiliarity with coined money, which provided the basis for the claim that coinage had officially been banned, is well encapsulated by a story which Herodotus reports (3.56) – though he considered it silly – about the circumstances behind the Spartan withdrawal from their siege of Samos in 525/3: Polycrates bribed the Spartans to withdraw by giving them lead coins plated with gold. Herodotus' scepticism may have been unwarranted, given that some of these lead coins have actually survived; but that is not the issue here.[15] The logic of this story assumes that Spartans were so unused to coinage, and indeed to gold bullion, that they did not realize that the coins which Polycrates gave to them were too heavy to be gold. Given this general unfamiliarity with coined money, it was easy enough in 404 to invent the tradition that it had been illegal to possess it in the past.

Rather than proceed chronologically through the fifth century, it is more profitable, and more illuminating, to turn to an example which really constitutes a package of invented traditions that were fabricated and disseminated at the same time. This package was successful in a twofold sense. In the short term, it led to immediate political, social and economic reforms which served the purposes of the inventors. In the long term, it has profoundly distorted the way subsequent generations have reconstructed the archaic and classical history of Sparta. I am referring to the reforms of Agis and Cleomenes, who were responsible for what moderns have aptly dubbed 'the third-century revolution'.[16]

As my preceding remarks indicate, I take an extreme view of the amount of invention that their reforms entailed. Indeed, the invention of tradition is most clearly revealed when a 'tradition' is deliberately invented and constructed by a single initiator. There is, however, a historiographical problem concerning these reforms that must be faced at the outset. Our main source for the activities of Agis and Cleomenes is Plutarch, and Plutarch's main source was Cleomenes' possible friend and certain admirer, the historian Phylarchus.[17] Phylarchus was not an impartial source; he narrated the lives and deaths of Agis and Cleomenes in tragic style and he depicted them as heroes.[18] The relationship between literary representation and historical reality is always complex and allusive, and in this case it is especially so since what Agis and Cleomenes actually said and did is mediated through the double lens of Phylarchus and of Plutarch. Plutarch, moreover, has given a far briefer account than Phylarchus, and thus much important detail has been lost to us. This does not mean, however, that it is impossible to recover the political discourse of third-century Sparta from Plutarch's Lives of Agis and Cleomenes. It is here assumed that, even if certain episodes in these lives (such as death scenes) have been highly dramatized, Plutarch accurately represents the essential nature both of the reforms themselves and of the political discourse that was used to justify them.[19] For, although Plutarch is not giving us a mere transcript of Phylarchus, he has not invented new details out of whole cloth. [20] Nor was Phylarchus necessarily an inaccurate historian for being prone to sensationalism, any more than Simon Schama's *Citizens* is a less trustworthy work of history simply because of its strikingly vivid vignettes.[21]

By 244 BC, the year in which Agis became king, wealth in Sparta was concentrated in a very few hands. Plutarch states (*Agis* 5.4) that 'not more than 700 Spartiates were left, and of these there were perhaps 100 who possessed land and allotment'. Precisely what this means is uncertain,[22] but it may indicate that 700 was the total number of those who could exercise Spartan citizenship, while most land was controlled by a plutocratic elite. Moreover, the system of common messes, as well as the system of state education, called the *agōgē* in hellenistic times,[23] had long since lapsed. Although one cannot be certain of the exact date, I believe that the *agōgē* had been discontinued not too long after the devastating defeat of Agis III at Megalopolis in 330 BC, a disaster which was compounded by the surrender of fifty Spartiate hostages to Antipater.[24] By then losses in manpower would have been severe enough to render the old communal institutions obsolete. Furthermore, in a verbatim fragment, Phylarchus (*FGrHist* 81, F 44 = Athen. 141f–142c) implies that by the early third century BC, attendance at the public messes was no longer a regular part of Spartan life. He says that the Spartans did not go into the common messes according to their ancestral custom; whenever they did go, they feasted in luxury; and that these luxurious practices were begun by the Kings Areus and Acrotatus. I take Phylarchus to mean that the Spartans had desisted from attending the common messes sometime before Areus and Acrotatus introduced soft pillows and rich foods, which probably was between 272 and 268 BC. Incidentally, Pyrrhus' claim in 274 that he wanted his sons to be brought up in Laconian customs (τοῖς Λακωνικοῖς ἔθεσιν) does not necessarily demonstrate that even he believed that the old *agōgē* was still in full force (Plut. *Pyr.* 26.10). It may simply mean that life at Sparta was still considered rustic as compared to that in other cities, or that Pyrrhus was trying to flatter the Spartans with a now meaningless compliment.

The problems that faced Agis in 244 and Cleomenes in 235 were how to increase the number of hoplites, to convince the landholders to surrender their estates, to cancel debts, and to restore institutions such as the *agōgē* and the messes. It must be emphasized that by 244 there may have been no one left alive who had personal experience of those institutions, and the only written records to describe them in any detail were the works of non-Spartans. The Spartans' answer to these challenges was the invention of tradition. Agis wished to divide all of the land in Laconia into equal and inalienable lots: 4,500 for citizens and 15,000 for *perioikoi* (*Agis* 8). This was eventually carried out by Cleomenes (*Cl.* 11), who created a citizen body of 4,000 men. It is hardly coincidental that in Plutarch's life of Lycurgus (8, 16) we find the statement that Lycurgus himself had made a similar distribution, even if the original number of lots was a matter of dispute. Surely Agis, and later Cleomenes, claimed that they were merely reintroducing the original distribution of Lycurgus. But if Lycurgus had distributed the entire territory of Laconia in equal, inalienable, and indivisible lots, either to be passed down from father to son or to be redistributed by the state upon the father's death, whence arose the concentration of land in a few hands?

The answer can be found in another invention. This arrangement of Lycurgus had remained unchanged until the rhetra of Epitadeus in the early fourth century allowed a man to give or bequeath his estate to anyone he liked. It is striking that the only mention of the rhetra of Epitadeus appears in Plutarch's Life of Agis (5).[25] And surely it was either Agis or Cleomenes who was also responsible for the late tradition that Lycurgus had prohibited the giving of dowries, since large dowries had also contributed to the unequal redistribution of land.[26]

In sum, the whole concept of inalienable and indivisible lots of equal size was an invention of King Agis with no basis in historical fact.[27] There may have been an eighth- or seventh-century division of Messenian and/or Laconian land among the Spartan citizen body, but such allotments, even if made by someone called Lycurgus, were neither inalienable nor indivisible. Nor were they necessarily equal. And even if they were equal, the equality could not have lasted long. There is sufficient evidence in Alcman, Herodotus, and Xenophon that rich and poor Spartans coexisted at all periods.[28]

Agis did not stop with the rhetra of Epitadeus and inalienable lots. He also produced an oracle from the temple of Pasiphaë to this effect (*Agis* 9.3): Agis' supporters 'said the oracles from this goddess were enjoining the Spartans all to become equal according to the original law made by

Lycurgus'. The word for equal is ἴσοι. The Spartans traditionally called themselves the ὁμοῖοι (*homoioi*), which means not 'the equal ones', but 'the similar ones'.[29] What we have here is a development from similar to equal. Individuals who are similar dress alike, act alike, eat alike, but are not necessarily equal in terms of possessions and status. Individuals who are equal not only have the same habits, but the same possessions as well. This new concept of 'equality' served as the ideological basis for Agis' reforms,[30] and as such it needed to be justified in terms of what Lycurgus had originally ordained. But we should realize that this concept would have been alien to the way Spartans thought about themselves in the archaic and classical periods. In fact, the Spartan citizens had never been equal in any respect.

As opposition to his reforms mounted, Agis justified himself by attributing ever more to Lycurgus and to ancient tradition (*Agis* 10–12), such as the abolition of debts. The more his opponents impeded him, the more he and his supporters invented. In order to get rid of King Leonidas, who was against the reforms, the ephor Lysander set out to prosecute him according to 'a certain ancient law which forbids any of the descendants of Heracles to have children by a foreign woman and orders that any man who has left Sparta to live permanently among other people should die'. Far from being a law distinct from the law that forbade Spartans to travel abroad (which is more fully discussed below), this is manifestly an *ad hoc* invention that is based upon the earlier prohibition.[31] The general ban on foreign travel is mentioned by several fourth-century sources (Xenophon, Isocrates, Plato, and Aristotle), but these more specific restrictions are elsewhere unattested. That fact is enough to justify the suspicion that this 'ancient law' was actually no older than Lysander's citation of it. Lysander then reinforced this invention with another even more outrageous one. He and his fellow ephors proceeded 'to watch for the sign'. Plutarch (*Agis* 11.3) describes this procedure as follows:

> Every nine years the ephors pick a clear and moonless night, and sit in silence looking towards the sky. If a star shoots from one sector to another sector, they conclude that the kings have committed some fault relating to religion, and they suspend them from their office until an oracle comes from Delphi or Olympia to support the kings who have been convicted.

The sign was duly seen and King Leonidas was convicted of having had two children by an Asian woman. Not a few scholars have accepted the star-gazing as an ancient ritual.[32] Some have even speculated that it was used in the deposition of King Demaratus in 491 BC and that the more famous Lysander intended to employ it in his alleged plot to make himself king in the early fourth century.[33] I maintain, however, that it is invention. It may well appear to be a brazen invention, but even in societies with extensive written records such inventions are not unknown. In Sparta, where written laws could not easily be consulted, one group's collective memory could be opposed to another's. Agis and his supporters could claim that a hundred or more years earlier such a ritual had been observed, and none of their opponents had the historical knowledge required to refute them. Indeed, the new board of ephors attempted to prosecute the outgoing ephors Lysander and Mandrocleidas not for inventing spurious laws, but for illegally voting to abolish debts and redistribute land. Lysander and Mandrocleidas then played their final card, which was the unprecedented claim that the power of the kings was indissoluble when they were in agreement and that it was unlawful for the ephors to oppose them in such a circumstance; acting on that principle the kings then deposed the new board of ephors (*Agis* 12). All of this bears witness to the temporal and cultural gap that separated classical from hellenistic Sparta.

Cleomenes contributed as much, and perhaps even more, to the invention of the Lycurgan constitution as did Agis. In 227 BC, after canceling debts and dividing the land into 4,000 lots for citizens, he took a step whose relevance for the invention of classical Sparta has usually been underestimated. According to Plutarch (*Cleom.* 11.2): 'Next he turned to the training of the young men and to the so-called *agōgē*, most of the details of which Sphaerus, who was present, helped him in arranging. As they quickly took up again the proper order of both the physical training and the public messes, a few participated under compulsion, but the majority voluntarily subjected themselves to that frugal Laconian way of life'.

Plutarch here includes under the term '*agōgē*' both the public education, with its division into age classes and age grades, and the public messes.[34] The point that deserves emphasis is that Sphaerus arranged most of the details.[35] This Sphaerus was a philosopher of the Stoic school, reputedly a pupil first of Zeno and then of Cleanthes; he had also taught philosophy to Cleomenes when the Spartan was a youth (*Cleom.* 2.2). Why did Cleomenes need or want his former teacher's help? It was not, as an older generation of scholars once claimed, because Cleomenes was a Stoic philosopher in arms who wanted to liberate the starving masses throughout the Peloponnese. It was because at least fifty, and perhaps as many as a hundred, years had passed since the *agōgē* had been abandoned. Who would have remembered the details? The first Spartan to write about Sparta, Sosibius the grammarian, was probably active in the following century. Thus Cleomenes needed the help of Sphaerus. This point must be emphasized. In his book *Literacy in Ancient Sparta*, Terrence Boring says the following about Sphaerus (69):

> Once again, a foreigner dramatized the striking character of the Spartans – so rich in traditions (including written records) but unable to make effective use

> of them. And yet their failure does not seem to have been because of illiteracy. For how could Cleomenes have been so ignorant of the oral traditions of his own city?

That statement not only grossly overestimates the types of written records that existed at Sparta,[36] but also overestimates the ability of oral tradition to survive in a sterile environment. A community remembers something when it has a reason for doing so.[37] The plutocratic society of third-century Sparta would have had neither need nor reason to remember the precise details of arcane institutions that were fundamentally incompatible with their current affluent lifestyle. The degree of Spartan ignorance about their own past is underscored by the Suda's entry for Dicaearchus, the pupil of Aristotle: 'This Dicaearchus wrote the *Constitution of the Spartiates*, and a law was enacted in Lacedaemon requiring this work to be read annually at the meeting place of the ephors, while the youth of the city who were just coming of age, were required to listen. This custom was observed for a long time.' If this report is true, the most fitting historical context would be after 146 BC.[38] Yet, even if this is an invented biographical detail, it illustrates the general truth that Spartans of the post-classical period had to rely on outsiders for knowledge of their own past.[39]

There is, however, a more important consideration. Cleomenes is unlikely to have been concerned with reconstructing the past precisely as it had been; for his intent cannot have been to reproduce the inherent weaknesses and flaws which had contributed to Sparta's decline in the first place. His aim was to create a new Sparta which, although justified as a return to the ancestral polity, was in fact a radically new construction. If he had wished to construct a faithful model, he could have had recourse to the Spartan constitutions of Critias, Xenophon, Aristotle, and Dicaearchus. But the whole point was to construct a *politeia* that would serve and promote present needs and circumstances. Indeed, it was perhaps at this time that the tradition was invented that Lycurgus had not put his laws into writing and even had produced a rhetra prohibiting the use of written laws (Plut. *Lyc.* 13.1–3; cf. *Mor.* 227b). Despite some modern attempts to defend it, such a ban is extremely unlikely: Plutarch is the first writer to mention it and classical sources are wholly ignorant of it.[40] The Lycurgan rhetra that no laws should be written provided a useful template for recreating those very laws: it both explained why a particular law of Lycurgus had been forgotten and justified its reintroduction.

As friend and advisor to king Cleomenes, what role did Sphaerus play in reinventing the *agōgē*? Should we imagine that he had a passion for historical accuracy and antiquarian research? In addition to lending practical assistance, Sphaerus wrote two works. One was called *On the Laconian*

Constitution and consisted of at least three books; the other had the title *On Lycurgus and Socrates* and had a total of three books. Unfortunately, only two fragments survive, both from the former. On the surface, two considerations suggest that his emphasis was philosophical, and not antiquarian. First of all, we know the titles of 31 of his works, and with the exception of *On the Laconian Constitution*, all are philosophical (Diog. Laert. 177–8). And secondly, the mere fact that he wrote a comparison of Socrates and Lycurgus suggests a philosophical, rather than a historical interest. But when one looks at the fragments themselves, this expectation is not quite fulfilled. The first is Plutarch's statement (*Lyc.* 5.8) that he put the original number of elders at twenty-eight, because that was the original number of those who shared the confidence of Lycurgus. Here Sphaerus was disagreeing with Aristotle, who had written that two of the original thirty had abandoned the project. Perhaps Sphaerus' motive was to minimize the opposition to Lycurgus. The second fragment is a verbatim quotation by Athenaeus and comes as a surprise (Athen. 141c–d):

> And Sphaerus, in the third book of his *Laconian Constitution* writes: 'The members of the mess also contribute *epaikla* (extra dishes) to them. Sometimes the common people bring whatever is caught in the chase; but the rich contribute wheat bread and anything from the fields which is in season, as much as is needed for that one meeting, because they believe that to provide more than is sufficient is extravagant, if the food is not going to be eaten.'

Although no one has commented on this before, the distinction between 'the common people' (οἱ πολλοί) and the rich (οἱ πλούσιοι) is not what we would have expected. But the context is unclear. Sphaerus uses the present tense, and one might think that he is referring to the time of Cleomenes. But Cleomenes had supposedly redistributed all of the land into equal lots. He did not, however, confiscate moveable wealth, just as we are told Lycurgus had not. So perhaps the wealthier citizens could afford to plant wheat, whereas the poorer ones grew the traditional barley. Interpretation is made more difficult as soon as one realizes that this may be an example of research on Sphaerus' part. Xenophon (*Lac. Pol.* 5.3) also says that the rich contribute wheat bread to the messes. Be that as it may, if we had the whole work before us, I suspect that we would find that Sphaerus' version of the Spartan constitution both reflected Stoic ethical ideas and served the practical needs of Cleomenes.[41]

If my analysis of the purpose and nature of Sphaerus' writings is correct, it raises an important question. How much of Plutarch's account of the *agōgē*, of the public messes, and of Spartan institutions in general, is derived from the writings of Sphaerus and Phylarchus, and thus tells us nothing directly about the nature of those institutions in the classical period? This is not an easy question to answer, since Plutarch consulted a great many sources. But many of those sources were hellenistic (including the biographer Hermippus of Smyrna), and as a consequence Plutarch's conception of the substance and purpose of Lycurgus' reforms has been deeply influenced by the third-century revolution.[42] Matters are further complicated by the post-146 BC 'restoration', or rather 'reinvention', of Lycurgan customs; this occurred when Rome allowed the Spartans to revive their 'ancestral constitution' which had been dissolved by the Achaean general Philopoemen in 188 BC.[43] And there were further episodes of reinvention which took place as late as the Flavians. But to attribute long stretches of the *Lycurgus* to a single source, whether Sphaerus or Phylarchus, as some scholars have done, is too extreme and represents an outdated view of how Plutarch constructed his *Lives*. The work of Christopher Pelling has shown that even where Plutarch primarily follows a single source, he often interjects material from other sources,[44] and Plutarch did consult the now lost Spartan constitutions by Critias (late fifth century) and Aristotle (late fourth century). Nevertheless, I would assert that details about Spartan institutions found in Plutarch's *Lycurgus* and in his *Agis and Cleomenes*, as well as in the related parts of the *Moralia*, can be safely used as evidence for archaic and classical Sparta *only* if those details are confirmed by sources predating the third-century revolution.

Two examples can illustrate the general point. Plutarch records that Agis (*Agis* 8) proposed to divide the citizens into fifteen public messes, each containing either 200 or 400 men, which some scholars have argued was the correct number for the classical period as well. In his *Lycurgus* (12.2), however, Plutarch says that the messes had only about fifteen members each. Perhaps this discrepancy can be explained as follows: Agis was acting out of convenience, while Cleomenes, who had more time and a research assistant, divided the new citizens into smaller groups. In any case, we learn nothing about the number of messes in the classical period.[45] Secondly, a strong case has been made that the endurance test of whipping boys who knelt at the altar of Artemis Orthia was invented in the hellenistic period, perhaps by Sphaerus himself. In other words, the cheese-stealing ritual described by Xenophon (*Lac. Pol.* 2.9) was consciously reinvented as the brutal contest in endurance witnessed by Plutarch (*Lyc.* 18.1).[46]

One last point deserves attention here. The attribution by Agis and Cleomenes to Lycurgus of what was essentially their own constitution follows a pattern that was to be repeated throughout history. Again to quote Hobsbawm (7):

> It is clear that plenty of political institutions, ideological movements and groups – not least of all in nationalism – were so unprecedented that even historical continuity had to be invented, for example by creating an ancient

> past beyond effective historical continuity, either by semi-fiction (Boadicea, Vercingetorix, Arminius the Cheruscan) or by forgery (Ossian, the Czech medieval manuscripts).

If Agis and Cleomenes wanted their reforms to be acceptable and effective, they had to be attributed to Lycurgus. Their system of land tenure was so unprecedented that even historical continuity had to be invented.

After one has grasped the full range of traditions which were invented during the hellenistic period, it is easier to accept the idea that traditions may also have been invented during the fifth century. Whether they fully realized it or not, Agis and Cleomenes had good precedent for their penchant to innovate. Can we be sure that such typically Spartan customs as the expulsion of foreigners, the bans on manual crafts and foreign travel, wife-sharing, the civil disabilities for not marrying, the annual declaration of war against the helots and the *krypteia*, really predate the fifth century?

The invention of tradition often takes place at times of crisis and is a means of dealing with a crisis when older traditions are in themselves insufficient or outmoded. It is usually argued that most of Sparta's peculiar institutions were created in reaction to crises which had occurred before the fifth century. In particular, the revolt of Messenia around 650 BC and the struggle with Tegea in about 550 BC are thought to have shaped both the Spartans' mentality and their domestic institutions. What is not often recognized is that inducements to change and innovation were just as prevalent in the fifth century.[47]

First, let us start with another clear-cut case. A cavalry force was first introduced at Sparta in 424 BC, as is attested by Thucydides (4.55.2). Yet Xenophon can say that Lycurgus divided the Spartans into six *morai* (regimental units) of cavalry (*Lac. Pol.* 11.4), and Plutarch (*Lyc.* 23) cites Philostephanus (third century BC) for the view that Lycurgus distributed the cavalry into units called *oulamoi*. It seems that when this cavalry force was created – which was quite exceptional for men who had always trained to fight as heavy infantry (Thucydides calls it 'contrary to custom') – this development was attributed to Lycurgus. Indeed, such an attribution was the only way to make socially palatable so radical an innovation, born as it was of military necessity. There is, however, a further oddity in all of this. The number, and probably also the structure, of this force had changed between its initial creation in 424 and the time of Xenophon: there were only 400 cavalry in 424, as opposed to some 720 horsemen in the early fourth century (Xen. *Hell.* 4.2.16), and it is a reasonable inference that the division into *morai* took place when the number was increased.[48] So what was ascribed to Lycurgus by Xenophon at *Lac. Pol.* 11.4 was in reality not even the original creation but a later modification.

It is well known that, to a greater degree than other Greek cities, Sparta put restrictions on the personal freedom of her citizens. How ancient were these restrictions? We are told by Plutarch at *Lyc.* 27.3 that 'Lycurgus did not permit the Spartans to travel abroad and to wander about, acquiring foreign habits and imitating lifestyles that lacked education as well as different types of constitution'. The earliest reference to this prohibition on foreign travel dates to the early fourth century (Xen. *Lac. Pol.* 14.4), and the justification is consistent in a variety of authors from that time on (Isoc. 11.18; Plato, *Protagoras* 342c–d; Aristotle frag. 543 Rose; Plut. *Inst. Lac.* 19; Plut. *Agis* 11.2). But as far as our evidence goes, the first time that Spartans became concerned that other Spartans might be corrupted by foreign ways was in the 470s BC. Thucydides claims that the regent Pausanias, while serving as supreme allied commander in the Aegean (1.130), 'became so conceited that he was no longer able to live in the established manner, but took to wearing Median clothing when he ventured from Byzantium, was attended by a bodyguard of Medes and Egyptians as he traveled through Thrace, and had a Persian table set for himself.' It was also claimed that Pausanias was scheming, with Persian support, to make himself the 'ruler' (Thuc. 1.138.3) or 'tyrant' (Hdt. 5.32) of Greece. After his first recall to Sparta, when new commanders were rejected by the allies, we are told (1.95.7): 'And the Lacedaemonians sent out no other commanders thereafter, fearing that those who went out would be corrupted, as they saw had happened in the case of Pausanias.'

Although the Pausanias saga was surely more complex than Thucydides indicates, and the Spartans had various reasons for abandoning their leadership of the Hellenic League,[49] Pausanias' outward behaviour, whatever his motives, must have been a cause for alarm. Of equal if not greater concern, however, were Pausanias' actions subsequent to his recall and acquittal. He sailed to the Hellespont on his own initiative, residing first at Byzantium and then at Colonae, and some years later returned to Sparta only when the ephors threatened to have him declared a public enemy (1.128.3, 131). Even if the accusations of medism (which Thucydides himself believed to be true) were unfounded, it was still the case that Pausanias was engaging in diplomatic activities abroad without the official sanction of the Spartan state. That simply could not be tolerated. Thus the fall of Pausanias provides an appropriate context for the introduction of a ban on foreign travel without official authorization. The purpose was to keep other elite Spartiates from becoming like Pausanias, who not only adopted foreign habits, but apparently was pursuing his own foreign policy. Nor was Pausanias' disgrace an isolated incident. Between his first recall in 478 and his eventual death at Sparta in *c.* 466, came the prosecution of King

Leutychidas, who was convicted in *c.* 476 or 469 of accepting a huge bribe from the Thessalians and went into exile (Hdt. 6.72).[50]

According to Plutarch (*Lyc.* 24.2), 'Lycurgus absolutely prohibited the Spartans from practicing a manual craft.' Yet it is striking that Herodotus (who had probably finished his *Histories* by 425) knows of no such prohibition *per se*; he writes at 2.167 that the bias against citizens who practice a craft prevails throughout the whole of Greece, particularly among the Lacedaemonians, but least of all among the Corinthians. Here the Spartans are merely depicted as being at the extreme end of a widespread cultural norm (with the Corinthians being at the other end). By the time we get to Xenophon in the early fourth century, the Spartans are depicted as the opposite of other Greeks in this regard (*Lac. Pol.* 7.2–3):

> In the other cities everyone makes as much money as they are able: one man is a farmer, another is a ship-owner, another a trader, while crafts support others. But at Sparta Lycurgus forbade free men to engage in any activity concerned with moneymaking, and prescribed that their sole concern should be with the things that make cities free.

As with coinage, a cultural proclivity has been transformed into a strict prohibition.[51]

One can only guess why and when this transformation occurred. One possibility, which has been suggested recently, is that those Spartiates whose landholdings could no longer sustain their citizen status turned to banausic activities as a means of supplementary support; this situation prompted a formalized prohibition which was intended to define citizenship requirements more sharply and to draw a boundary between citizens and Inferiors (i.e. Spartiates who had lost their citizen status).[52] But a more general explanation may be sufficient. The Spartans, as a result of the stress which the Peloponnesian War placed upon their society and its institutions, came increasingly to represent themselves, and indeed to see themselves, as fundamentally different from their antagonists. They undertook the war against Athens in 431, believing – as did most Greeks (Thuc. 7.28.3) – that the Athenians could only hold out for two or three years at most. King Archidamus was apparently one of very few Spartans who did not share this widespread opinion. As it turned out, the fighting of a protracted war by land and sea over almost three decades put a tremendous strain on every aspect of Spartan society. Thus Xenophon is reflecting how the Spartans wished themselves to be viewed, as much as or even more than he is constructing his own personal image of them.

The alleged systematic expulsion of foreigners from Sparta (*xenēlasia*) is an elusive topic.[53] Yet one thing should be clear: in this case too, Herodotus does not refer to any such practice. He tells two stories of foreigners being told to leave Sparta, but those are the *ad hoc* expulsions of particular individuals and only one of them was by order of the ephors. Their significance lies not as purported evidence for this supposed Spartan institution, but in what they tell us about Spartan attitudes towards external influences; for both stories concern King Cleomenes' fear lest his fellow Spartans be corrupted by outsiders, to wit, by Maeandrius of Samos (3.148) and Aristagoras of Miletus (5.50–1). The Aristagoras story is highly complex and multi-layered;[54] he tries to bribe Cleomenes, but only after he had been told to leave. Cleomenes, however, requested that the ephors banish Maeandrius precisely because he feared his use of bribery. How are we to interpret these stories? As Robin Osborne has recently emphasized, an oral tradition reflects the concerns of the last person to tell it.[55] Thus these episodes show that in Herodotus' own time, as *perhaps* also in the late sixth century, there were serious misgivings about the influence of foreigners at Sparta. But these episodes do not indicate that there were any systematic deportations in the late sixth century; and if such wholesale deportations existed when Herodotus wrote Books 3 and 5 of his *Histories*, he chose not to allude to them.

The earliest references to systematic expulsions date to the period of the Peloponnesian war (Thuc. 1.144 and 2.39).[56] In the Funeral Oration, Thucydides has Pericles explain *xenēlasiai* in terms of keeping an enemy from learning or seeing anything that might profit him (2.39.1). Plutarch, disagreeing with Thucydides in this passage, claims (*Lyc.* 27.3) that Lycurgus drove away foreigners who gathered in Sparta, 'not, as Thucydides says, fearing lest they should become imitators of the constitution and should learn something useful for attaining virtue, but rather that they should not become teachers of some evil'. Plutarch is at best only partly correct; for Xenophon (*Lac. Pol.* 14.4) offers some confirmation when he says that the purpose behind *xenēlasiai*, which he couples with the ban on foreign travel, was to keep the Spartans from being infected with 'laziness' (ῥᾳδιουργία) caught from foreigners. Nonetheless, the idea expressed here by Plutarch (*Lyc.* 27.3–4 and especially in *Agis* 10) is that Lycurgus did not fear foreigners in themselves (οὐ τοῖς σώμασι πολεμῶν), but rather the harmful practices and alien ideas that they might introduce into Sparta (which is rather different from the fear of bribery found in Herodotus). It is possible that Plutarch's elaboration of the fear of foreign habits, which is so vaguely referred to by Xenophon, reflects the rhetoric of the third-century revolution and is connected with Agis' proposal to admit foreigners of the right sort (individuals who had been brought up as free men and were in excellent physical condition) to Spartan citizenship (*Agis* 8.2). That is to say, Agis faced opposition to his proposal on the grounds that Lycurgus, so far from admitting foreigners to citizenship, actually devised expulsions of them; accordingly, he needed to explain just what it was that Lycurgus was afraid of and why Lycurgus would not have objected to his plans. And it is Agis' explanation, as mediated through Plutarch's third-century sources, that dominates Plutarch's conception of *xenēlasiai*.

Thucydides' explanation of *xenēlasiai*, moreover, better fits the period of the Peloponnesian War, a time when the Spartans came to be obsessed with secrecy.[57] Indeed, Thucydides later remarks (5.68.2) that because of the secrecy of the Spartan state it was difficult to obtain information about the size of the Spartan army that fought at Mantinea in 418. It is a fair inference from Pericles' words at Thuc. 1.144.2 that all Athenians and all citizens of cities allied to Athens were expelled from Sparta during the months preceding the outbreak of the Peloponnesian War.[58] These expulsions are likely to have commenced with the declaration of war in 432 (Thuc. 1.125) and to have continued until the final defeat of Athens in 404. This situation was categorically different from the *ad hoc* banishments of specific individuals which we find in Herodotus, and as a new development needed to be justified as a Lycurgan institution (the attribution to Lycurgus is first found, even if implicitly, at Xen. *Lac. Pol.* 14.4). Once the war with Athens was over, restrictions on foreigners must have been eased or even lifted, since Xenophon (*Lac. Pol.* 14.4) implies that such expulsions were a thing of the past. Although Plato refers in general terms to *xenēlasiai* in his *Protagoras* and *Laws*, there is no specific evidence that any expulsions actually took place in the fourth century.

It is also probable that some of the institutions that were aimed at intimidating the helot population also date to the fifth century. There were, of course, two periods of extreme crisis in controlling the helots, roughly two hundred years apart: that is, during the revolt of Messenia in the mid-seventh century, and again during the revolt which followed the earthquake of 465 BC. The Spartans felt the need to institutionalize methods of control that would ensure that such revolts did not occur in the future. One means was to provide religious sanction for the killing of helots by annually declaring war upon them (Plut. *Lyc.* 28.4). The *krypteia* was another means. Select young men were sent out into the countryside, armed with only a dagger; they hid by day, and by night killed as many helots as they could find out of doors (Plato, *Laws* 633b; Plut. *Lyc.* 28.1–3). Plutarch tells us that Aristotle assigned the creation of the *krypteia* to Lycurgus, and it is usually assumed that these measures were instituted after the revolt of Messenia during the mid-seventh century. Yet it is certainly possible that both were created, or at least institutionalized, in the middle of the fifth century.[59]

The earthquake of 465 was devastating for Sparta, both physically and psychologically. Even allowing for considerable exaggeration in our sources, destruction was widespread and fatalities were high (Plut. *Cimon* 16.4; Diod. 11.63).[60] This precipitated a helot revolt that reputedly lasted for ten years and only ended when the remaining rebels were allowed to emigrate (Thuc. 1.103.1–3). It would not be at all surprising if this situation led to far-reaching changes in the treatment of helots.[61] Plutarch himself (*Lyc.* 28.5–6), because of his high esteem for Lycurgus' gentleness and justice, cannot accept the notion that he was responsible for the *krypteia* and other measures aimed at humiliating the helots, and he dates these measures to the period after the great earthquake. Unfortunately, he can cite no evidence for what must be only his personal view; and though his conclusion may be valid, his grounds for inference are obviously different from those expressed here. The authority of Aristotle in assigning to Lycurgus the *krypteia*, and presumably the annual declaration of war, was difficult to gainsay; nor would the Spartans themselves necessarily have wished to disagree with Aristotle's attribution. Even Sphaerus, who did disagree with Aristotle about the number of elders, may not have been minded to challenge the traditional ascription of these arrangements to Lycurgus.

By the end of the century the Spartans faced a crisis of their own making. Again, in contrast to other Greek cities, various forms of wife-sharing were permitted in Sparta (Xen. *Lac. Pol.* 1.7–9; Plut. *Lyc.* 15.6–10; Poly. 12.6b.8). Furthermore, there were civil disabilities for not marrying (Plut. *Lyc.* 15.2) and rewards for producing three or more sons (Arist. *Pol.* 1270b1–4). It would not be surprising if all of these provisions were introduced in the late fifth or early fourth century;[62] in any case, a date earlier than the beginning of the fifth century is extremely unlikely.[63] They were a reaction to the shortage of Spartan manpower, which had become critical by the early fourth century.[64] These new provisions were, of course, attributed to Lycurgus.

It is interesting, however, that there was at least one category of innovation intended to compensate for the decline in citizen numbers that the Spartans did not assign to Lycurgus. This category pertains to the use of hoplites who were not of Spartiate status in the Lacedaemonian army. Especially radical was the creation, *c.* 424–21, of the new military force of *neodamōdeis,* who were freed helots equipped as hoplites. Similarly, the brigading of *perioikoi* in Spartiate regiments, which was in effect by 425 BC, is nowhere attributed to Lycurgus. By contrast, the reorganization of the Lacedaemonian army from regiments called *lochoi* into ones called *morai,* which was probably the occasion for the integration of *perioikoi,* needed to be validated by reference to tradition.[65] Thus Xenophon in his *Constitution of the Lacedaemonians* says that Lycurgus created the *morai* (*Lac. Pol.* 11.4), but avoids stating explicitly that Spartiates and *perioikoi* were brigaded together. Although there are gaps in our evidence, a pattern does seem to emerge. It is a reasonable assumption that the Spartans did not wish to draw attention to their increasing reliance upon non-Spartiate hoplites, and so they did not invoke the name of Lycurgus in order to justify novel uses of such troops. At the same time, the presence of *perioikoi* and freed helots in the army did not directly alter the lifestyle and prerogatives of the Spartan citizen, and so did not absolutely require justification.

In conclusion, one last example of the invention of tradition can be cited, one that can be more confidently dated. Plutarch says in his *Lycurgus* (13.5–6):

> They mention a third rhetra of Lycurgus, which prevents making frequent expeditions against the same enemies, in order that these should not grow used to defending themselves and thus become skilled in warfare. And this was the accusation that was most of all brought against King Agesilaus in later times, namely, that by his continual and frequent invasions and expeditions into Boeotia he made the Thebans a match for the Lacedaemonians.

Plutarch then goes on to say that Antalcidas censured Agesilaus for teaching the Thebans how to fight. In light of the previous discussion it should be fairly obvious when and under what circumstances this third rhetra arose. It must have been the opponents of Agesilaus' foreign policy who invented this rhetra. Agesilaus had more prestige and influence than any single living Spartan. But he could be trumped by appealing to the authority of Lycurgus. And at the risk of making a circular argument, I would suggest that the invention of this rhetra can also be used as evidence for the degree of opposition to Agesilaus' Theban policy.

My purpose in exploring particular instances of the invention of tradition has been to suggest that the history of Sparta cannot be written as many modern scholars have tried to write it. This is not just a matter of deciding how much to attribute to a historical Lycurgus or, more generally, to the establishment of the 'Lycurgan' system in the seventh and sixth centuries. If the Spartans engaged in the invention of tradition as often and as profoundly as I have suggested, then it is impossible for us to write a history of Spartan institutions that combines evidence from authors who lived in different centuries. Nor can we say that in its 'fully developed form' the Spartan system of education, or position of women, or treatment of helots, or system of land-tenure was such and such. In other words, it is impossible for us to give a total description of Spartan society in its myriad aspects at any particular point in time which utilizes all of the available evidence. This is because Spartan society was continually in a state of flux and was continually being reinvented; for although the invention of tradition takes place in all societies, both past and present, it seems to have been exceptionally pervasive in Sparta, a society whose present realitites were always defined in terms of its semi-mythical and semi-legendary past. The only kind of Spartan history that one can write is one which traces the stages of development of specific aspects of Spartan society, such as Nigel Kennel's study of the *agōgē* and Stephen Hodkinson's article on the institutional structures of archaic Sparta as well as his various studies relating to Spartan property and wealth.[66] In a sense this kind of history is less satisfactory, because it does not allow us to imagine fully what it would have been like to live as a Spartan at a given time, say on the eve of the Peloponnesian War, since some of our evidence will not be valid for that particular period. It is also a type of history which is much more difficult for the non-specialist to appreciate. But it is preferable to face up to the limitations which our evidence imposes upon us, than merely to add another chapter to the Spartan mirage.

Acknowledgements
This essay has had a long genesis. It was first delivered at the University of Liverpool in 1994 and most recently at Harvard University in 2000. It here appears in a substantially revised form, and I am especially grateful to Judith Chien, Harriet Flower, Nino Luraghi, Ellen Millender, Graham Shipley, and Lukas Thommen, as well to as the editors of this volume, for their help and encouragement.

Notes

1 Notable exceptions are Finley 1971 and Kennell 1995. For an example in Roman history, see H.I. Flower 2000.

2 For bibliography and discussion, see Hornblower 1991 on Thuc. 2.34.1, and Flower and Marincola 2002, on Hdt. 9.85.2.

3 1989 and 1995 respectively.

4 1996.

5 1987, 118.

6 Recent examples are MacDowell 1986; Richer 1998; Ducat 1999. Pomeroy (1997, 48 n.71 and 51 n.9) cites three seminal articles by Stephen Hodkinson questioning the veracity of key sources, only to ignore them in her lengthy discussion of the Spartan family and system of land tenure (39–66; cf. the much more sophisticated treatment of Patterson 1998, 73–9). An otherwise interesting article on Spartan women (Kunstler 1987) states as a working hypothesis that Sparta's political and social institutions were fully developed by 600 BC. Many works

acknowledge the existence of the Spartan mirage, but ignore its consequences: especially egregious in this respect is Rahe 1992, 122–71.

[7] Hodkinson (2000, 166; cf. 1997, 84–5), however, argues that the accounts of Theopompus and Ephorus did not attribute the ban on foreign currency to Lycurgus and that this attribution was a later development. It is true that the name of Lycurgus does not appear in the single sentence in which Plutarch specifically cites those historians. Yet Plutarch's comment on the compromise ('as if Lycurgus had feared coinage and not the greed produced by coinage') implies that Lycurgus had been mentioned in their accounts of this debate; and we must keep in mind, judging from what we know of their historical method, that their accounts would have been fairly elaborate. Moreover, it is a fair inference from two passages in Diodorus (7.12.5 and 7.12.8) that Ephorus (who was Diodorus' source for Sparta) attributed the ban on coinage to Lycurgus.

[8] This was demonstrably the case by the third century: see Kennell 1995, 114.

[9] 'Should someone ask me whether I think that even now the laws of Lycurgus still remain unaltered (ἀκίνητοι), by Zeus I could no longer say so with confidence… I know that formerly they were afraid to appear to be in possession of gold, but now there are those who even take pride in possessing it.' This statement has force only if Xenophon believed that Lycurgus had banned the possession of gold.

[10] Cf. Christien and Figueira in this volume.

[11] See M.A. Flower 1991, 88–94 and Hodkinson 2000, 151–86.

[12] M.A. Flower 1991, 92 and Hodkinson 2000, 165.

[13] Iron spits have been found in the sanctuary of Artemis Orthia at Sparta, but it is doubtful if spits ever functioned as a form of currency in Greece (see von Reden 1997, 159–60). One might infer from Hesychius' use of the term *pelanor*, that the currency resembled round flat cakes, but no example has yet been found. For discussion and bibliography, see Hodkinson 2000, 160–5 and Figueira's article in this volume.

[14] I realize that other contributors to this book take a different view.

[15] See Barron (1966, 17–18), who thinks that the coins confirm the tale. Kraay (1976, 29–30), however, speculates that the existence of such coins gave rise to the story of the bribery.

[16] See Fuks 1962a and c; and Hodkinson 2000, 43–5, who gives an interpretation of their reforms that is similar to the one given here.

[17] Note in particular Bux 1925; Gabba 1957; Jacoby *FGrHist* 81, comm. 134; Africa 1961, 3; Schütrumpf 1987, 441 n. 2; Pédech 1989, 403; and Powell 1999, 401–13. It is also very likely that Phylarchus made some use of the writings of Sphaerus of Borysthenes (on whom see below): see Ollier 1943, 106 and Schütrumpf 1987, 475. It is sometimes claimed (e.g. Tigerstedt 1974, 53; Jacoby *FGrHist* 81, comm. 133) that Phylarchus was a personal friend or close associate of Cleomenes, but this is merely an inference.

[18] Phylarchus wrote a history of Greece from 272–219 BC in 28 books. Although it is no longer extant, the surviving fragments and citations in later authors are

sufficient to show that the tendency of his history was anti-Macedonian and pro-Spartan. See Africa 1961; Tigerstedt 1974, 54–5; Powell 1999, 401–13.

[19] The main points of Agis' programme of reform can be verified by sources which are independent of the Phylarchean tradition, as is demonstrated by Fuks 1962b. This is rejected by Erskine (1990, 126–31), whose overriding desire to prove the influence of Sphaerus on Cleomenes leads him to dismiss the evidence for Agis' plans.

[20] See Pelling 1990 and Powell 1999, 397–401.

[21] Cf. Africa 1961, 65–6.

[22] See Fuks 1962a, and Cartledge and Spawforth 1989, 42–3.

[23] As is well argued by Kennell 1995, 113–14; contra Ducat 1999, 63 n. 3.

[24] Kennell (1995, 13) gives 255 BC as the earliest possible date for the lapse of the *agōgē*, basing his argument on the fact that a certain Xanthippus, a Spartan mercenary who was hired by the Carthaginians in 255, is said by Polybius (1.32.1) to 'have taken part in the *agōgē* and to have commensurate practise in military affairs'. But we are not told how old he was in 255; he is most unlikely to have been a recent 'graduate' (especially in view of his military experience) and he may well have been an old man, given that Agesilaus undertook mercenary service in Egypt in his 80s.

[25] Although some have accepted it as fact, Epitadeus' rhetra has no historical basis: see Schütrumpf 1987 and Hodkinson 2000, 90–4.

[26] See Hodkinson 2000, 98.

[27] The definitive treatment of Spartan land tenure is Hodkinson (2000, 65–112), who, expanding on his earlier work, decisively refutes the modern notion that there were two categories of Spartiate land: state-controlled equal allotments and private estates. Yet old myths die hard (cf. Rahe and Pomeroy cited in n. 6 above).

[28] See n. 11 above.

[29] This point is well made by Murray 1993, 175. See also Cartledge 2001, 73–4.

[30] For what their notion of social and political equality entailed in practical terms, see Fuks 1962c. Erskine (1990, 141–9) argues that the Stoic emphasis on equality permeated the revolution and its ideology. It should be noted that the stress laid on equality by Agis and Cleomenes, while reflecting contemporary Stoic ideas, need not be entirely due to the influence of Sphaerus.

[31] MacDowell (1986, 115–16) infers from this passage that there were two separate laws, one dealing with travel abroad and the other with residence abroad.

[32] So den Boer 1954, 210–11, and, at great length, Richer 1998, 155–98. *Contra*, Powell 2000, 505–6.

[33] So Parke 1945, 108.

[34] Kennell (1995, 98–114) argues that the age grade structure of the *agōgē*, according to which there were precisely named age grades for boys 14 to 20, was invented by Sphaerus. Ducat (1999, 50) rejects this, but only on general grounds: 'I do not see how the classical *agōgē* could have functioned otherwise than by annual "promotions"'. But that is a rather subjective judgment (Ducat

cites Plato, *Laws* 666e, in support of his position, but the word *agōgē* does not appear in that passage).

[35] On Sphaerus' contribution, see Kennell (1995, 98–114), who follows Ollier (1936) and Erskine (1990, 123–49) in stressing his fundamental importance. Tigerstedt (1974, 69–70) and Schofield (1991, 42) are skeptical about the extent of Sphaerus' influence.

[36] The evidence, such as it is, suggests that there were archives of oracles (Hdt. 6.57.2–4) and perhaps of treaties (Plut. *Lys.* 30.3; and see Millender 2001, 129–30), but not of the type of documents that pertained to the structure and organization of cultural institutions. Cf. n. 40 below.

[37] See the seminal works of Vansina (1965 and 1985) on the nature of oral traditions.

[38] This is well argued by Kennell 1995, 19.

[39] For a different view, see Thommen 2000.

[40] Millender (2001, 132–7) persuasively argues that some written laws must have existed in archaic and classical Sparta. As she points out, the Athenian orator Lycurgus had a Spartan law on desertion read out loud to a jury (*Against Leoc.* 129) and Aristotle knew the text of the Great Rhetra (Plut. *Lyc.* 6). But such written laws would never have been numerous and I am not convinced that the Great Rhetra consisted of much more than what is quoted by Plutarch. Indeed, the very scarcity of written laws made it possible to invent the tradition that they had been prohibited.

[41] Kennell (1995, 102–7; cf. 20–3) argues that the first 17 apophthegms of the Plutarchan *Instituta Laconica* derive from Sphaerus' work on the Spartan constitution. Hodkinson (2000, 48–9) is cautious about this attribution; Cartledge (1997) calls it wishful thinking.

[42] See especially Tigerstedt 1974, 81–5, 238 (who summarizes earlier, mostly German, scholarship, in his extensive notes). There are many striking similarities between Plutarch's account of the reforms of Lycurgus and his account of the reforms of Agis and Cleomenes. There is no scholarly consensus on how to account for this, but two popular explanations have been that Plutarch used Phylarchus in both works or that Phylarchus and Plutarch each made extensive use of Sphaerus. Kessler (1910), for example, argued that *Lyc.* 12–27 derives from Sphaerus.

[43] Plut. *Philop.* 16.6 and Paus. 8.51.3. See further Kennell 1995, 8–11.

[44] Pelling 1980 and 1988, 31–6. Note also Tigerstedt 1974, 231–3.

[45] *Pace* Singor (1999, 77), who accepts that there were about 15 in each *syssition* on the basis of Plut. *Lyc.* 12.2.

[46] See Cartledge and Spawforth 1989, 207. Kennell (1995, 111) assigns the transformation to the hellenistic phase of the *agōgē* and attributes it to the work of Sphaerus because of the mention of the endurance contest in *Instituta Laconica* 40 (= 239d), which he considers to be a work of the mid-second century BC.

[47] But see Thommen 1996, 115–46, on the fifth-century transformation of Spartan society.

[48] See Lazenby 1985, 11–12 and Hodkinson 2000, 311–12. Xenophon records that 600 Lacedaemonian cavalry participated in the battle of the Nemea river in

394: if only five of the six cavalry *morai* were present (as seems probable), the total strength of all six *morai* would have been 720.

[49] See Cawkwell 1970; Rhodes 1970; and Badian 1993, 130–3.

[50] For the dates of Leutychidas' exile, see *CAH*^{5}, 97–8.

[51] Cartledge (1976 and 1979, 183–4) has demonstrated that Spartan citizens could not have been legally banned from practicing manual crafts before the fifth century. See also Thommen 1996, 71–4.

[52] This is the suggestion of Hodkinson 2000, 177–8.

[53] See Thommen 1996, 145–6 and especially Rebenich 1998, both of whom deny the existence of regular and systematic expulsions.

[54] See M. A. Flower 2000, 70–3.

[55] 1996, 7.

[56] Cf. Aristop. *Birds* 1012–14, Xen. *Lac. Pol.* 14.4; Plato *Protagoras* 342c and *Laws* 950b. The reference in the *Lac. Pol.* is enough to demonstrate (pace Thommen 1996, 145–6) that *xenēlasiai* were not a myth created by Athenian propaganda.

[57] Although the context is ironic, at *Protagoras* 342c Plato also sees the desire to maintain secrecy as the reason for expulsions.

[58] I here follow Chrimes, 1949, 310–11.

[59] Thommen (1996, 128–9) argues that the killing of helots was an innovation of the mid-fifth century. But elsewhere I have suggested (1998, 373) that the three hundred Spartans at Thermopylae may have been able to undertake a night attack on the camp of Xerxes, as Ephorus claimed that they did, because some of them had participated in the *krypteia*. Perhaps the transformation of the *krypteia* from adolescent rite of passage to instrument of terror (on which see Murray 1993, 178–9) took place in the 450s; that would still enable us to explain how the Spartans were competent to attack the Persian camp at night.

[60] See Hodkinson 200, 417–18.

[61] It is noteworthy that in 479 the 5,000 Spartan hoplites who marched out to fight at Plataea trusted the helots enough to take 35,000 lightly armed helots with them, and that these helots actually participated in the fighting. It seems that so large a number of helots was never again used in warfare and it is tempting to find the explanation in the revolt of 465. For discussion and bibliography, see Flower and Marincola 2002, on Hdt. 9.10.1; 28.2; 29.1–2.

[62] See Mossé 1991, 143.

[63] Cartledge (1979, 309–10, following Daube 1977) dates these measures to around 500 BC (with a preference for 490); Hodkinson (1989, 109–10; 2000, 422–3) places them in the mid-fifth century. MacDowell (1986, 76), while not necessarily believing in a historical Lycurgus, nevertheless asserts that the attribution to Lycurgus precludes a date as late as 500. Sallares (1991, 160–92) dates the origin of wife-sharing and the penalties against bachelorhood to the archaic age, but he is refuted by Hodkinson 1997, 89–92.

[64] Hodkinson (1989, 90–3, 105–6; 2000, 406–7), however, argues that wife-sharing was (or rather became: 1989, 110) a private response to the Spartan inheritance system and served to retain land within the kin group. But this explanation

for its purpose depends on the claim of Philo (*On Special Laws* 3.4.22) that the Spartiates permitted marriage between uterine half-siblings, something which is otherwise unattested.

[65] On the reorganization of the army, see Cartledge 1979, 255–7 and Lazenby 1985, 48–52.

[66] As Hodkinson (1997) demonstrates, the essential structures of the Spartan system had surely been formed during the archaic period, whereas the particular institutions and practices through which that system was articulated continued to develop in subsequent centuries. Yet even so we can say very little about archaic Sparta, and even Hodkinson uses some later evidence of questionable relevance to archaic times (e.g. on p. 93, citing Plut., *Lyc.* 22.4 and *Quaest. Conv.* 2.639e for Olympic victors fighting in the kings' bodyguard).

Bibliography

Africa, T.W.
1961 *Phylarchus and the Spartan Revolution*, Berkeley.
Badian, E.
1993 'Thucydides and the outbreak of the Peloponnesian War', in *From Plataea to Potidaea. Studies in the history and historiography of the Pentekontaetia*, Baltimore, 125–62.
Barron, J.P.
1966 *The Silver Coinage of Samos*, London.
Boring, T.A.
1979 *Literacy in Ancient Sparta*, Leiden.
Bux, E.
1925 'Zwei sozialistische Novellen bei Plutarch', *Klio* 19, 413–31.
Cartledge, P.A.
1976 'Did Spartan citizens ever practise a manual *tekhne*?' *LCM* 1, 115–19.
1979 *Sparta and Lakonia: A regional history, 1300–362 BC*, London.
1987 *Agesilaos and the Crisis of Sparta*, London.
1997 Review of Kennell 1995, *CR* 47, 98–100.
2001 *Spartan Reflections*, London.
Cartledge, P.A. and Spawforth, A.
1989 *Hellenistic and Roman Sparta: A tale of two cities*, London.
Cawkwell, G.L.
1970 'The Fall of Themistocles', in *Auckland Classical Essays Presented to E.M. Blaiklock*, Auckland and London, 39–58.
Chrimes, K.M.T.
1949 *Ancient Sparta: A re-examination of the evidence*, Manchester.
Daube, D.
1977 'The duty of procreation', *Proceedings of the Classical Association* 74, 10–25.
den Boer, W.
1954 *Laconian Studies*, Amsterdam.

Ducat, J.
1999 'Perspectives on Spartan education in the classical period', in S. Hodkinson and A. Powell (eds.) *Sparta: New perspectives*, London, 43–66.
Erskine, A.
1990 *The Hellenistic Stoa: Political thought and action*, London.
Finley, M.I.
1971 *The Ancestral Constitution: An inaugural lecture*, Cambridge.
Flower, H.I.
2000 'The Tradition of the *Spolia Opima*: Marcus Claudius Marcellus and Augustus', *Classical Antiquity* 19.1, 34–64.
Flower, M.A.
1991 'Revolutionary agitation and social change in classical Sparta', in M.A. Flower and M. Toher (eds.) *Georgica: Greek studies in honour of George Cawkwell,* Institute of Classical Studies, University of London, Bulletin Supp. 58, 78–97.
1998 'Simonides, Ephorus, and Herodotus on the Battle of Thermopylae', *CQ* 48, 365–79.
2000 'From Simonides to Isocrates: the fifth-century origins of fourth-century panhellenism', *Classical Antiquity* 19.1, 65–101.
Flower, M.A. and Marincola, J.
2002 *Herodotus, Histories, Book IX,* Cambridge.
Fuks, A.
1962a 'The Spartan citizen-body in the mid-third century and its enlargement proposed by Agis IV', *Athenaeum* 40, 244–63.
1962b 'Non-Phylarchean tradition of the programme of Agis IV', *CQ* 12, 118–21.
1962c 'Agis, Cleomenes, and equality', *CP* 57, 161–6.
Gabba, E.
1957 'Studi su Filarco. Le biographie plutarchee di Agide e di Cleomene', *Athenaeum* 35, 3–55, 193–239.
Hobsbawn, E. and Ranger, T.
1983 *The Invention of Tradition*, Cambridge.
Hodkinson, S.
1989 'Marriage, inheritance and demography: perspectives upon the success and decline of classical Sparta', in A. Powell (ed.) *Classical Sparta: Techniques behind her success*, London and Norman, Okla., 79–122.
1997 'The development of Spartan society and institutions in the archaic period', in L.G. Mitchell and P.J. Rhodes (eds.) *The Development of the Polis in Archaic Greece*, London and New York, 83–102.
2000 *Property and Wealth in Classical Sparta*, London.
Hornblower, S.
1983 *The Greek World 479–323 BC*, London.
1991 *A Commentary on Thucydides, I: Books I–III*, Oxford.
Kennell, N.
1995 *The Gymnasium of Virtue: Education and culture in ancient Sparta*, Chapel Hill and London.

Kessler, E.

1910 *Plutarchs Leben des Lykurgos*, Berlin.

Kraay, C.M.

1976 *Archaic and Classical Greek Coins*, London.

Kunstler, B.L.

1987 'Female dynamics and female power in ancient Sparta', in M. Skinner (ed.) *Rescuing Creusa: New methodological approaches to women in antiquity*, Lubbock, Tex., 31–48.

Lazenby, J.F.

1985 *The Spartan Army*, Warminster.

MacDowell, D.M.

1986 *Spartan Law*, Edinburgh.

Millender, E.G.

2001 'Spartan literacy revisited', *Classical Antiquity* 20.1, 121–64.

Mossé, C,

1991 'Women in the Spartan revolutions of the third century BC', in S.B. Pomeroy (ed.) *Women's History and Ancient History*, Chapel Hill and London, 138–53.

Murray, O.

1993 *Early Greece*, 2nd edn, London.

Ollier, F.

1933–43 *Le mirage spartiate: Étude sur l'idéalisation de Sparte dans l'antiquité grecque*, 2 vols., Paris.

1936 'Le philosophe stoïcien Sphairos et l'oeuvre réformatrice des rois de Sparte Agis IV et Cléomène III', *REG* 49, 536–70.

Osborne, R.

1996 *Greece in the Making, 1200– 479 BC*, London.

Parke, H.W.

1945 'The deposing of Spartan Kings, *CQ* 39, 106–12.

Patterson, C. B.

1998 *The Family in Greek History*, Cambridge, Mass., and London.

Pédech, P.

1989 *Trois historiens méconnus: Théopompe, Duris, Phylarque*, Paris.

Pelling, C.B.R.

1980 'Plutarch's adaptation of his source material', *JHS* 100, 127–40.

1988 *Plutarch, Life of Antony*, Cambridge.

1990 'Truth and fiction in Plutarch's Lives', in D.A. Russell (ed.) *Antonine Literature*, Oxford, 19–52.

Pomeroy, S.B.

1997 *Families in Classical and Hellenistic Greece*, Oxford.

Powell, A.

1999 'Spartan women assertive in politics?: Plutarch's Lives of Agis and Kleomenes', in S. Hodkinson and A. Powell (eds.) *Sparta: New perspectives*, London, 393–419.

2000 Review of Richer 1998, *CR* 50, 504–7.

Rahe, P.A.
1992 *Republics Ancient and Modern*, Chapel Hill and London.
Rebenich, S.
1998 'Fremdenfeindlichkeit in Sparta? Überlegungen zur Tradition der spartanischen Xenelasie', *Klio* 80, 336–59.
Rhodes, P.J.
1970 'Thucydides on Pausanias and Themistocles', *Historia* 19, 387–400.
Richer, N.
1998 *Les éphores*, Paris.
Sallares, J.R.
1991 *The Ecology of the Ancient Greek World*, London.
Schofield, M.
1991 *The Stoic Idea of the City*, Cambridge.
Schütrumpf, E.
1987 'The *rhetra* of Epitadeus: a Platonist's fiction', *GRBS* 28, 441–57.
Singor, H.W.
1999 'Admission to the *syssitia* in fifth-century Sparta', in S. Hodkinson and A. Powell (eds.) *Sparta: New perspectives*, London, 67–89.
Thommen, L
1996 *Lakedaimonion Politeia: Die Entstehung der spartanischen Verfassung*, Historia Einzelschriften 103, Stuttgart.
2000 'Spartas fehlende Lokalgeschichte', *Gymnasium* 107, 399–408.
Tigerstedt, E.N.
1974 *The Legend of Sparta in Classical Antiquity*, vol. 2., Stockholm.
Vansina, J.
1965 *Oral Tradition*, Chicago.
1985 *Oral Tradition as History*, Madison.
von Reden, S.
1997 'Money, law and exchange: coinage in the Greek polis', *JHS* 117, 154–76.

8

NOTES ON THE INFLUENCE OF THE SPARTAN GREAT RHETRA ON TYRTAEUS, HERODOTUS AND XENOPHON

Michael Lipka

There is a huge bibliography on the so-called Spartan Great Rhetra, the earliest and virtually only more-or-less directly transmitted legal text on inner Spartan affairs of the classical period or earlier. In writing about the Rhetra, scholars normally focus on such controversial issues as meaning and (inextricably connected with it) historical setting and dating.[1] By contrast, my contribution will *not* deal with these issues. Rather, my topic will be the influence of the Great Rhetra on three texts, to which we owe much if not all of what we know or think we know about early Spartan institutions – Tyrtaeus' *Eunomia*, chapters 56–58 of Herodotus' Book 6 and chapters 13 and 15 of Xenophon's *Spartan Constitution*. I will take for granted the little which (almost) all scholars would accept anyway – that the Rhetra predates Herodotus and Xenophon, and that the source of Plutarch's quotation is Aristotle's largely lost *Spartan Constitution*, in other words, a source that is generally considered to be reliable.

The text of the Rhetra is transmitted in Plutarch's *Life of Lycurgus*. I quote the relevant passage (*Lyc.* 6.1–4):

> Οὕτω δὲ περὶ ταύτην ἐσπούδασε τὴν ἀρχὴν ὁ Λυκοῦργος ὥστε μαντείαν ἐκ Δελφῶν κομίσαι περὶ αὐτῆς, ἣν ῥήτραν καλοῦσιν. ἔχει δὲ οὕτως· Διὸς Συλλανίου καὶ Ἀθανᾶς Συλλανίας ἱερὸν ἱδρυσάμενον, φυλὰς φυλάξαντα καὶ ὠβὰς ὠβάξαντα, τριάκοντα γερουσίαν σὺν ἀρχαγέταις καταστήσαντα, ὥρας ἐξ ὥρας ἀπελλάζειν μεταξὺ Βαβύκας τε καὶ Κνακιῶνος, οὕτως εἰσφέρειν τε καὶ ἀφίστασθαι· δάμῳ δὲ τὰν κυρίαν ἦμεν (text: γαμωδανγοριανημην) καὶ κράτος.[2]

I. Xenophon

To begin with the connection between the Rhetra and chapters 13 and 15 of Xenophon's *Spartan Constitution*. My discussion focuses on three aspects:(a) the general resemblance of the king–*damos* relationship as depicted by Xenophon and the Rhetra; (b) the use of the word συνθῆκαι at the beginning of chapter 15 in Xenophon; (c) the joint worship of Zeus and Athena in both the Rhetra and chapter 13 of Xenophon's *Spartan Constitution*.

(a) Since Xenophon's chapter 15 and the Rhetra, as transmitted by Aristotle, both refer to the king–*damos* relationship, as it presented itself at more or less the same historical period,[3] one would expect Plutarch to note differences (as he does elsewhere),[4] if Aristotle and Xenophon had contradicted each other or differed from one another fundamentally. The fact that Plutarch does not record any such contradictions or differences suggests that the political situation as indicated by Aristotle coincides (in Plutarch's mind, at least) with the situation as indicated by Xenophon. Now, if Xenophon and Aristotle depicted the same or a similar state of affairs, Xenophon is likely to have taken into account the Rhetra or – at least – the political reality based on the regulations of which the transmitted Rhetra text formed a part.

(b) The topic of chapter 15 is, as Xenophon himself stresses at 15.1, how Lycurgus defined the relation between the king and the city (ἃς βασιλεῖ πρὸς τὴν πόλιν συνθήκας ὁ Λυκοῦργος ἐποίησε). In this context the term συνθῆκαι is noteworthy: the word, which occurs only here in Xenophon's *Spartan Constitution*, normally denotes a paragraphed, written 'compact' between two parties.[5] In the context of chapter 15 these parties can hardly be any other than the Spartan king and the Spartan *damos*. Hence, it is plausible to postulate a 'compact' between the king and the *damos* which lies behind some or all pieces of information of chapter 15 in Xenophon's *Spartan Constitution*.

What did this hypothetical 'compact' referred to by συνθῆκαι look like? The text of a treaty between the Lakedaimonians and the Aitolians may give an idea of such early Laconian συνθῆκαι. I quote the beginning:[6]

> [συνθε̂κ]αι Αἰτολοῖς κ̣[αττάδε]
> [φιλία]ν καὶ hιράναν ἐ̂[μεν ποτ]
> [Αἰτο]λ̣ος καὶ συνμα[χίαν … 3–4 …]
> (a number of infinitive constructions follows)

The dating of the treaty is much debated, but most scholars believe that it belongs to the fifth century.[7] The quoted passage makes it clear that such treaties could be called συνθῆκαι.[8] Furthermore, it shows the grammatical structure of such treaties: the introductory section is followed by a series of infinitive constructions by which the individual 'paragraphs' of the treaty are listed.[9]

Some similarities between the Rhetra and the aforementioned treaties are interesting. The Rhetra is a Laconian *prose text*, with infinitives so characteristic of treaties (ἀπελλάζειν, εἰσφέρειν, ἀφίστασθαι, ἦμεν). In addition, the regulations of the internal organization of the Spartan state are simply *listed.* Thus in quoting the Rhetra Aristotle probably drew on a text that was very similar to the aforementioned συνθῆκαι between Lakedaimonians and Aitolians (and quite different from, say, an ordinary oracle, which would conventionally have been written in hexameters).[10] It is at least conceivable that the Rhetra was only a part of a longer document, i.e. the συνθῆκαι between king and *damos* as mentioned by Xenophon in chap. 15.

(c) According to 13.2 of Xenophon's *Spartan Constitution*, the Spartan king crosses the border after sacrificing to Zeus and Athena (θύεται Διὶ καὶ Ἀθηνᾷ). In other words, Zeus and Athena are regarded here as boundary deities. Likewise, the Rhetra mentions the ritual community of Zeus and Athena.[11] The epithet συλλάνιος applied to both deities in the Rhetra is unexplained and the specific function of both deities unknown. But if we assume that they were the boundary deities to which Xenophon refers at 13.2, the immediately following instruction of the Rhetra, according to which the Spartan territory should be divided into *phylai* and *obai*, would make perfect sense.

II. Herodotus

Another major classical source on Spartan kingship is Herodotus' famous section on the Spartan kingship at 6.56–8.[12] There is a direct structural parallel between this section and the Rhetra: like the Rhetra Herodotus gives an *enumeration* of a number of royal privileges. In doing so, he avails himself of infinitive constructions, found also in the Rhetra and Laconian συνθῆκαι in general, as shown above. Far from being a means of stylistic variation, this infinitive construction appears 22 times (sic!) in the two Herodotean paragraphs (6.56f.).

There are also marked resemblances between Herodotus 6.56–8 and chapter 15 of Xenophon's *Spartan Constitution*. Both Xenophon and Herodotus mention the right of the king to the hides and chines of the sacrificed animal (Hdt. 6.56, 6.57.1 / Xen. *Lac.* 15.3), the double ration (διμοιρία) at the common meal (Hdt. 6.57.1, 3 / Xen. *Lac.* 15.4), the Pythioi as royal messmates (Hdt. 6.57.2, 4 / Xen. *Lac.* 15.5) and the splendid funeral of the Spartan king (6.58 / Xen. *Lac.* 15.8f.). Most striking is fact that these details occur in both authors in exactly the same order:

	Hdt.	Xen. *Lac.*
1. Right of the king to the hides and chines of the sacrificed animal	6.56, 6.57.1	15.3
2. The double ration (διμοιρία) at the common meal	6.57.1, 3	15.4

3. Pythioi as royal messmates	6.57.2, 4	15.5
4. Royal funerals	6.58	15.8 f.

Since Xenophon has pieces of information that are not found in Herodotus,[13] Herodotus cannot be the source of Xenophon here (unless we assume that Xenophon draws on one or more different sources apart from Herodotus). Anyway, on general grounds Herodotus is unlikely to have been Xenophon's source, given the latter's first-hand knowledge of Sparta and his access – via his friend, the Spartan king Agesilaus – to all sorts of otherwise rather inaccessible information about Sparta. Therefore one may suspect that the source of the similarities between Herodotus and Xenophon is the συνθῆκαι mentioned by Xenophon at 15.1 of his *Spartan Constitution* and represented by the Rhetra of Plutarch / Aristotle.[14]

III. Tyrtaeus' *Eunomia*

One may speculate a bit further. Spartan political institutions are closely connected with the Tyrtaean poem called *Eunomia.*[15] It is tempting to ask whether the poem has anything to do with the postulated συνθῆκαι. Due to the absence of any reference to popular sovereignty in the *Eunomia*, van Wees has recently argued that the Great Rhetra post-dates the *Eunomia.*[16] However, the concept of a linear decline of royal power and simultaneous increase of the people's vote from Homeric times onwards, as implied by van Wees, cannot be verified in the case of Sparta. Tyrtaeus' presentation may be influenced by Homeric concepts here, as it certainly is by Homeric language. Furthermore, the linkage of Spartan legislation with the oracle at Delphi, found in the *Eunomia*, was probably a secondary phenomenon.[17] It is notable that the crucial fr. 4 [W.] of *Eunomia* offers the same chain of infinitive constructions (five infinitives) as the above-mentioned συνθῆκαι. It seems a reasonable guess that *Eunomia* is based – at least partly – on the συνθῆκαι that also influenced Herodotus and Xenophon.

To conclude, I suggest that the Tyrtaean *Eunomia*, Herodotus at 6.56–8 and Xenophon in chapters 13 and 15 of his *Spartan Constitution* were all influenced – directly or indirectly – by a 'compact' (συνθῆκαι) between the Spartan king and the *damos*, part of which is preserved literally via Aristotle / Plutarch in the form of the so-called Great Rhetra. Like other treaties this 'compact' consisted of an enumeration of a number of legal issues, expressed in a series of infinitive constructions, which are documented in fr. 4 [W.] of the Tyrtaean *Eunomia*, the relevant Herodotean passage and the Aristotelian quotation of the Great Rhetra. From the content of the later passages we can deduce that the complete version of the 'compact' between the king and the *damos*, the original 'Great Rhetra', covered a much wider range of subjects than is represented in the surviving Aristotelian / Plutarchan excerpt: including regulations about the borders of the Spartan territory, the constitutional relationship between the king, the *damos* and the Elders,[18] the role of the kings at sacrificial meals, the communication of the community with Delphi, and Spartan royal funerals. In an influential article published over 30 years ago Chester Starr called the Great Rhetra an 'undoubtedly genuine constitutional document *in prose* before 600 BC' and highlighted the amazing fact that 'we have no other precise statement of governmental organization this early'.[19] The conclusions of this study enable us to perceive more clearly the magnitude and scope of this early Spartan political achievement.

Acknowledgements
I want to express my gratitude to Stephen Hodkinson and Anton Powell for helpful suggestions.

Notes

1 For recent discussions cf. e.g. Thommen 1999, 186–207; van Wees 1999.

2 'When thou hast built a temple to Zeus Syllanius and Athena Syllania, divided the people into *phylai* and into *obai*, and established a senate of thirty members, including the *archagetai*, then from time to time *appellazein* between Babyca and Cnacion, and there introduce and rescind measures; but the people must have the deciding voice and the power' (Perrin's Loeb translation).

3 This is especially true if we read δάμῳ δὲ τὰν κυρίαν ἦμεν for the corrupt γαμωδανγοριανημην, as proposed by Sintenis and Müller.

4 Cf. Plu. *Lyc.* 1.5.

5 e.g. Xen. *HG* 1.5.5, 2.2.11, 4.8.15.

6 M/L p. 312.

7 Cf. Thommen 1996, 59 n. 28. Besides, the treaty between Sparta and Tegea (cf. Arist. frg. 592 [Rose]), for which the latest dating is the first half of the 5th century (Cawkwell 1993, 368–70), clearly indicates that written treaties are quite conceivable in 5th century Sparta.

8 The reading [συνθῆκ]αι is generally accepted by all editors, though mainly supplied (the reading of the rest of the text is, of course, highly controversial). συνθῆκαι as a technical term occurs in Attic inscriptions from early on (e.g. *IG*[3] I.1 42.8; 76.21 f., 26 f.), cf. also Th. 5.18.9 (the oath annually taken by both the Athenians and the Spartans according to the Nicias Peace): ἐμμενῶ ταῖς ξυνθήκαις καὶ ταῖς σπονδαῖς ταῖσδε δικαίως καὶ αδόλως.

9 Cf., e.g., the beginning of the treaty between Athens and Sparta as concluded in 421 (Th. 5.18.1 f.): σπονδὰς ἐποιήσαντο Ἀθηναῖοι καὶ Λακεδαιμόνιοι καὶ οἱ ξύμμαχοι κατὰ τάδε, καὶ ὤμοσαν κατὰ πόλεις. περὶ μὲν τῶν ἱερῶν τῶν κοινῶν,

θύειν καὶ ἰέναι καὶ μαντεύεσθαι καὶ θεωρεῖν κατὰ τὰ πάτρια τὸν βουλόμενον καὶ κατὰ γῆν καὶ κατὰ θάλασσαν ἀδεῶς.

[10] For prose oracles cf. van Wees 1999, 34 n. 63.

[11] Cf., in general, Thommen 1996, 41.

[12] For the following cf. Carlier 1984, 251.

[13] e.g. the right to take a porker of every litter of pigs (15.5), water supply near the royal residence (15.6), exchange of oaths between king and ephors (15.7).

[14] The plural of ῥήτρα at Tyrt. fr. 4.6 [W.] (εὐθείαις ῥήτραις ἀνταμειβομένους) may indicate that the singular originally denoted only a single paragraph, though poetic licence may help to explain the plural here; on the meaning of ῥῆτραι in general cf. Huxley 1962, 120 f. n. 283; van Wees 1999, 22 f. It remains conceivable that Xenophon deliberately – but inaccurately – adopted the word συνθῆκαι from the Athenian / Laconian texts of treaties at 15.1, whether because he did not know the source underlying chapter 15 as ῥῆτραι, or because he considered the term ῥήτρα as unsuitable for the ears of his Athenian public.

[15] Tyrt. fr. 1–4 [W.].

[16] van Wees 1999, 23–5.

[17] Herodotus stated that while some (οἱ μὲν δή τινες) supported the connection of the Lycurgan legislation with Delphi, the Spartans themselves believed that Lycurgus had adapted his laws from Crete (Hdt. 1.65.3 f., cf. Plu. *Lyc.* 4.1 (Crete) but also 5.4, 6.1 (Delphi). Xenophon derives the Spartan laws from Delphi only, cf. Xen. *Lac. Pol.* 8.5.). It was natural that the supporters of a Delphic connection produced oracles given to Lycurgus by the Delphic god. Herodotus already mentions Lycurgus as the addressee of an oracle (Hdt. 1.65.3; generally for oracles connected with Lycurgus, Ephor. *FGrH* 70 F 118; Paus. *FGrH* 582 T 3 with van Wees 1999, 14). The συνθῆκαι (like the Great Rhetra), however, as reconstructed above, are very unlikely ever to have existed in the form of an oracle, given the fact that the Great Rhetra is a prose text and, besides, straightforward in terms of contents (in contrast to the riddling style of oracles, cf. van Wees 1999, 22). The most likely scenario is that according to the oldest (Spartan) version Lycurgus brought a legal prose text (the συνθῆκαι) from Crete to Sparta. It was only later that the Lycurgan legislation became connected with Delphi (possibly for political reasons [divine legitimation of Spartan kingship?]) and thus with various oracles in dactylic shape.

[18] Hdt. 6.57.5 points out that the Spartan senate numbered 28 members plus the two kings. It is very noteworthy that the Great Rhetra too refers to the exact number of members in the senate.

The expression τριάκοντα γερουσίαν σὺν ἀρχαγέταις καταστήσαντα could be interpreted as 'established a senate of 30 members *plus* the two kings' or as 'established a senate of 30 members, *including* the two kings'. On the basis of Herodotus and Plu. *Lyc.* 5.12–14 (immediately preceding the quotation of the 'Great Rhetra') most scholars normally follow the latter interpretation, but the Plutarchan passage shows that the origin of the number was debatable and discussed already by Aristotle and Sphaerus.

[19] Starr 1965, 267. Although we cannot absolutely prove that the συνθῆκαι were

written down by the Spartans, the nature of such legal texts requires accuracy, homogeneity and verifiability to an extent that practically excludes a long-term oral tradition. Such an assumption is strengthened by the existence of the so-called 'Rider' to the Great Rhetra (Plu. *Lyc.* 6.8). The Rider shows that the συνθῆκαι were open to amendments, but that these amendments were apparently handed down separately from the main text, although in the same grammatical form (i.e. with infinitives). The fact that the Spartans added a new regulation which modified an earlier one, rather than reformulating the original text, suggests that the original text was considered as fixed and unalterable, and hence was in written form.

Bibliography

Carlier, P.

1984 *La royauté en Grèce avant Alexandre*, Strasbourg.

Starr, C.G.

1965 'The credibility of early Spartan history', *Historia* 14, 257–72. Reprinted in A. Ferrill and T. Kelly (eds.) *Essays in Ancient History*, Leiden, 1979, 145–59; and in M. Whitby (ed.) *Sparta*, Edinburgh, 2002, 26–42.

Thommen, L.

1996 *Lakedaimonion Politeia. Die Entstehung der Spartanischen Verfassung*, Stuttgart.

van Wees, H.

1999 'Tyrtaeus' *Eunomia*. Nothing to do with the Great Rhetra', in: S. Hodkinson and A. Powell (eds.) *Sparta. New Perspectives*, London, 1–41.

9

HELOTIC SLAVERY RECONSIDERED

Nino Luraghi

> Nicht die in völliges Dunkel gehüllte dorische Wanderung, sondern die Bildung der Gemeinde Sparta und ihrer Verfassung ist der Ursprung der Helotie wie der Periökie.
>
> Benedictus Niese, 1906

It is probably fair to say that in current research on Sparta a consensus dominates as far as the origins of helotry are concerned. With varying degrees of confidence, the helots are considered to have been the descendants of pre-existing free populations, pre-Dorians in Laconia and a mix of pre-Dorians and Dorians in Messenia, who had been subdued by the Spartiates when the latter conquered their land, at the time of the Dorian migration in Laconia and after the first or second Messenian war respectively. From that point on, the helots tilled the land of the Spartiates, that is, what had formerly been their own land, and fed their masters with its products. In other words, the helots are usually seen as the sum of two homogeneous ethnic groups subdued in their own territory by invaders.

The goal of the present contribution is to show that there are good reasons to question this consensus and to suspect that helotry may not have been a direct result of Spartan conquest in Laconia or Messenia, and therefore that the helots may not have been the descendants of aboriginal populations of those regions, enslaved *en masse* by incoming conquerors. A careful scrutiny of the ancient sources, which has been undertaken elsewhere (Luraghi, forthcoming), shows that the *communis opinio* has much less direct support in the evidence than usually assumed. On a more general level, it is at least doubtful that the origins of helotry can be reconstructed based on the ancient literary sources in the same way in which scholars reconstruct, for instance, a campaign of the Peloponnesian War. The evidence on the origins and early history of helotry is much too scanty and late, and leaves central points completely in the dark.[1] As is generally the case with archaic Spartan history, the only reasonable way to proceed is to produce models, by making explicit use of comparative evidence, from other Greek cities in the first place, but also from other areas and periods.[2] The merit of such models will be inversely proportional to the number of undocumented facts that they have to postulate, and directly proportional to their ability to make sense of the sources in their respective historical contexts. An important aspect of this process is the attempt to delimit the range of possible solutions. Excluding avenues of interpretation narrows down the field in which to look for the most satisfactory one.

1. The status of the helots

Any discussion of the origins of helotry involves necessarily a brief review of the evidence on the peculiarities of their status and of the interpretations of such evidence in the research. It is generally assumed that the key difference in status between helots – or helot-type dependants – and chattel slaves in the Greek world consisted in the fact that the former enjoyed some limited amount of personal rights, of which the latter were almost completely deprived. In the case of the helots scholars refer to customary rights over their persons and over property, recognition by their masters of their family ties, and to the existence of some form of religious community (Cartledge 1988, 38). In this perspective, the difference between helots and chattel slaves seems best characterized in terms of the opposition between slavery and serfdom.[3] While earlier research saw analogies between helotry and dependent peasantry in the Middle Ages, more recent advocates of the interpretation of helotry as a form of serfdom have looked for a more general model and found it in the definition of serfdom provided by the 1956 Convention of the United Nations, according to which serfdom is 'the tenure of land whereby the tenant is by law, custom or agreement bound to live and labour on land belonging to another person and render some determinate services to such other persons, whether for reward or not, and is not free to change his status'.

The idea that the helots were bound to the land they tilled and could not be removed from it represents the very core of the interpretation of helotry as a form of serfdom,[4] and therefore deserves close scrutiny. The only directly relevant piece of evidence is a famous quotation from Ephorus in Strabo's *Geography* (*FGrHist* 70 F 117 = Strab. 8.5.4).[5] After describing the Dorian conquest and colonization of Laconia, Ephorus narrated how king Agis, the son of Eurysthenes, had deprived the peripheral settlements of their equality of rights with Sparta, where the Dorians had settled, and imposed a tribute upon them. The inhabitants of Helos refused and were therefore besieged and enslaved by the Spartans on particular conditions: it was forbidden for the Spartiate master to manumit his helots or to sell them abroad, πωλεῖν ἔξω τῶν ὅρων ('outside the borders'). Only preconceived ideas about helotry can explain how some scholars have been able to interpret this clause as if it meant that it was forbidden to sell helots altogether.[6] A quick look at the text shows that, in order to convey that meaning, it would have been enough to conclude the sentence with πωλεῖν, without mentioning the borders. Ephorus is describing the conditions that made the status of the helots different from that of all other slaves: normal slaves could be sold within the boundaries of their master's city or abroad, the second possibility was excluded in the case of the helots. If it had been forbidden to sell helots altogether, and Ephorus had known that, the sentence would make no sense. In other words, this passage constitutes positive evidence that it was allowed to sell helots inside *Lakōnikē* – or at least, that Ephorus thought so.

Although they might seem contradictory, at a closer look the two rules mentioned by Ephorus are perfectly consistent with one another and can be seen both as acting in the masters' interest. In fact, these two rules made sure that the biological reproduction of the helots also guaranteed their reproduction as a social group. Comparative evidence from other slave systems shows that the true reason why some societies that made use of slave labour were constantly dependent on slave trade was not that slave populations normally do not reproduce biologically, as has sometimes been maintained, but rather that there is a strong and universal trend towards manumitting second- or third-generation slaves, curtailing the reproduction of the slaves as a social group (Patterson 1982, 132–3). Seen from this viewpoint, the Spartan regulations would make perfect sense. Helotry would have worked in a way not unlike another slave system characterized by an extremely low manumission rate and little input of new slaves from outside, that is, the South of the United States after the Atlantic slave trade ceased in the early nineteenth century (Patterson 1982, 161–2 and 245; Cartledge 1985, 27). Besides keeping the manumission rate low, state monopoly on manumission also made sure, in a very Spartan way, that only merits towards the community could bring freedom to a helot.[7]

Evidence for further rights of the helots is equally elusive. For example, there is no hint in the sources to the effect that the Spartiates recognized family ties among helots any more than other Greek slave owners recognized those among their slaves. The fact that in the mid-fifth century, when, after ten years of war, the rebels entrenched on Mount Ithome were finally allowed to leave their redoubt, they went away 'with their wives and children', as Thucydides says (1.103.3), cannot be seriously treated as evidence that in everyday life the Spartiates recognized marriages among helots.[8] The only piece of evidence that could justify speaking positively of rights of the helots over the produce of the land they worked is a passage in Plutarch's *Customs of the Spartans* (239d–e), according to which it was forbidden under curse to the Spartiates to exact from the helots more than the amount of a fixed rent in kind. However, this passage, like two more from the *Life of Lycurgus* (8.3–8; 24.2) mentioning the fixed rents imposed by the Spartiates on the helots, should not be separated from its context, that is, Plutarch's highly idealized description of Lycurgus' reform of landed property at Sparta, with the introduction of equal lots for all citizens. Such a description has long since been recognized by scholars for what it is – a retrojection of the programme of Cleomenes' reforms in the last quarter of the third century (Ducat 1990, 56–8; Hodkinson 2000, 126 with further references). As for the fact that the extraction of produce from the helots in classical Sparta was somehow regulated, in the form of a fixed amount or a fixed proportion of the produce (Myron *FGrHist* 106 F 2), this would be a reasonable assumption in itself and would find parallels in practices associated with slavery in ancient Greece and in other times and places.

Apart from the prohibition on selling them outside the Spartan territory and on manumitting them, all we really know is that the helots worked the fields of their masters and lived off the product of those fields, after having given either a fixed proportion or a fixed amount of that product to the masters. The question is, how really untypical their plight was when compared to Greek slavery in general. Surely all the helots, male and female, who were serving in the households of their masters, would live like other household slaves across Greece, and obviously no quota of product was expected from them.[9] To assess the conditions of helots working the land of their masters' estates, it will be useful to leave Sparta for a moment, and look at the situation of a well-to-do Athenian, someone like the Hermokopids or the characters of Xenophon's *Oeconomicus* – someone who would own portions of land in different locations across Attica, some of them with a farmstead.[10] Like any free adult male Greek who could afford it, he would live in the city, because that is where politics was going on, for him the only conceivable occupation. His fields would be worked mostly by slaves. He would visit them every so often, particularly at the time of the harvest, to collect his share of the products. Obviously, since his slaves had to survive the winter, he would leave a part of the product to them, but they would not receive their sustenance from their master on a daily basis. What precisely would differentiate their situation from that of farming helots? Admittedly, the function of the absentee master in the Attic farmstead would often be played by an overseer, himself a slave (e.g. Xen. *Oec.* 13.9 ff.). However, it stands to reason that the Spartiates' estates would also be led by overseers, of helotic status, to be sure.[11] Again, the true difference between Sparta and the rest of Greece consists in the fact that the *homoioi* formed a homogeneous group of absentee landlords.

In this connection, there is a further factor that has to be addressed, since it may seem to speak against an interpretation of helotry as a form of slavery and in favour of seeing it as serfdom or dependent peasantry. This factor is the geographical structure of the Spartan state. Although the Spartiates owned land lots not only in Laconia, but also in Messenia, probably in the northern plain and in the Soulima Valley, perhaps elsewhere in the region as well (Luraghi 2002, n. 73 with further references), their community life required their presence at Sparta even more than would have been the case for normal Greek oligarchies. Except perhaps as *kruptoi*, Spartiates must have been rarely present on their Messenian land.

The notion that slaves could be located in a position on which their masters could exercise such a precarious control may seem implausible, the more so if Susan Alcock (2002, 190–8) is right in maintaining, based on the results of the Pylos Regional Archaeological Project, that helots lived in small villages, not in isolated farms separated from each other at night by the terror of the *krupteia*. However, there is evidence suggesting that keeping their territory and their helots under control was a problem to which the Spartiates devoted a lot of energy,[12] and besides, in Messenia as in Laconia the helots were surrounded by a belt of perioikic settlements: as long as the latter were loyal, the former had much less freedom of action (Lotze 1993/94, 51). Unsurprisingly, in the case of the only helot revolt on which we have good evidence, the one that followed the earthquake at Sparta in the sixties of the fifth century, we happen to know that at least two perioikic settlements took part in the revolt as well, and one of them was one of the most important perioikic settlements of Messenia (Luraghi 2001, 297–9). Furthermore, the evidence from the Pylos area may be only one part of the story. Even if it were certain that this area was inhabited by helots, the settlement pattern observed in it should not necessarily be extended to the whole of the Spartiate land in Messenia. After all, bits of evidence from the Soulima Valley, where the probability of being on Spartiate land is higher, seem to show a different pattern. In the modern village of Kopanaki, a large building has been excavated, so massive that it was at first mistaken for a Roman villa. It turned out to be a residential building of the late archaic period, whose size and structure suggest its identification as the main building of a large estate.[13] Near Vasiliko, not far from Kopanaki, a strikingly similar building had been excavated earlier in the twentieth century.[14] Although it was interpreted originally as a small fortress, its position in the middle of a gentle slope overlooking the valley of the Pamisos, distant from any possible natural defence, shows that this interpretation is untenable,[15] and the similarities with the Kopanaki building, in terms of shape and size, chronology, and pottery types, strongly encourage us to see them both as instances of the same kind. In neither case is there evidence of other buildings nearby, and at least at Vasiliko the location of the building speaks clearly against seeing it as a part of a larger settlement. Rather, the structure and location of these two buildings suggest a plantation-like sort of settlement, with big and isolated buildings forming the centre of large landholdings.

On the comparative side, evidence on slavery in pre-colonial Africa shows that nucleated settlement is not incompatible with slavery, and more generally, that the settlement pattern of unfree peasants is not necessarily connected with the way in which they or their ancestors lost their freedom. Nucleated settlement is attested in various regions of nineteenth-century West Africa, where unfree peasants could be settled in semi-autonomous villages from which an agricultural surplus was extracted by the masters in the form of a fixed amount of produce. In spite of their wide-ranging organizational autonomy, such settlements were populated by individuals who had been violently captured in some other place, normally far away, and then sold, or by their offspring – slaves, by any other name. They were controlled by overseers, themselves mostly slaves.[16] Different patterns of exploitation are attested, ranging from the one just sketched to more intrusive ones, as it were, in which the masters would exact labour not produce.[17] Normally, under this latter pattern the slaves would have a proportion of time to work for themselves, to which some portion of land would correspond, while giving up a half or more of their working capacity to their masters. This system could generate productive units that have been compared to the slave plantations of the New World (Lovejoy 1979, esp. 1271–2). Interestingly, this seems to have been the result of a general development of regional economic structures towards mass production of specialized crops for a growing export trade; in a word, a modernization process supported by a more market-oriented mentality among the masters (Lovejoy 1979, 1286–7). On the other hand, a system of exploitation based on the alienation of produce not labour allowed the master to have as little as possible to do with the productive process, an attractive goal for members of ruling groups in which economic activities were seen as inferior and contrary to the set of shared values that constituted the group's moral code. Judging from the few available figures, at least in the late period the percentage of slaves that had to be imported from outside was relatively low, while many were sold from one master to another (Hogendorn 1977, 373). If we keep in mind that their manumission rate was not reduced by a ban on private liberation as at Sparta, they provide an interesting *comparandum* for helotry, all the more so, since even here some scholars have been seduced into applying definitions like serfdom or peasantry to what was clearly a form of slavery.[18]

It is time to sum up this first part of the argument. Ancient evidence about helotry satisfies or does not contradict Orlando Patterson's definition of slavery (1982, 13): 'the permanent, violent domination of natally alienated and generally dishonored persons'. Violence and dishonour were a central aspect of the relationship between Spartiates and helots, as Jean Ducat has brilliantly shown (Ducat 1974; see also 1990, 105–27). Natal alienation requires some qualification. Patterson understands it not only as the alienation of the free person reduced to slavery, but also as the lack of recognized family ties for a second-generation slave (1982, 5–9). Taken in this sense, there is no ancient evidence preventing the applicability of it to helots. This conclusion is to some extent paradoxical. If we think of the helots as a self-reproducing slave population, in practice, whatever their origin, after some generations their condition would have acquired more and more the characteristics associated with serfdom: although it was not forbidden to sell helots to other Spartiates, there would be no general reason to do this particularly often, so that *de facto* helots, like African slaves in the Old South, would experience some family continuity. Alienation would occur mostly in the mediated sense defined by Patterson; it would always be possible, but there is no way to imagine how often helots would really be sold far away from their family group. Nevertheless, the absence of positive evidence for the rights associated with serfdom, together with the violence that characterized the relations between helots and their masters, and finally also the fact that all ancient authors, including Plato and Aristotle, considered helotry a kind of *douleia*, encourage us to consider helotry as a form of slavery. The little we know about the status of the helots explains their persistence as a group, but not their origin.

2. Helotry and the *kosmos*

One crucial point distinguishes modern reconstructions from ancient perceptions of the origins of the Spartan *kosmos*. The ancient sources, starting with Herodotus (1.65) and Thucydides (1.18.1), usually depict it as the result of a single reform, brought about by the legendary lawgiver Lycurgus very early in what is for us the archaic age. Some authors, like Plato (*Leg.* 3.691d–2a), admit that the *kosmos* had received some adjustments at a later stage, but apparently no ancient author thought that anything important had happened after the late eighth century (Paradiso 1995, with further references). Modern scholars, instead, are convinced that Spartan political institutions were the result of a piecemeal process, which reached completion at some point during the sixth century.[19] Hans van Wees' recent work on the Great Rhetra (van Wees 1999) has made a very strong case for the view that the origin of the Spartiates, as a group of full-time warriors characterized by conspicuous equality and contempt of economic activities and of luxury in general, was a product of a development that took place between the age of Tyrtaeus and the sixth century. Even among more conservative scholars, probably no-one would today locate the emergence of the Spartiate *homoioi* earlier than the seventh century. Strangely enough, this rearrangement of the chronology of Spartan history has left a central aspect untouched, namely the helots. The ancient evidence on the origins of helotry has received a distinctively different treatment from any other piece of ancient evidence on archaic Sparta. In the face of their ideas on the origins of the Spartan *kosmos*, modern scholars' readiness to accept the ancient chronology of the emergence of helotry or even to push it further back in time is somewhat puzzling,[20] all the more so since helotry was obviously functional to the Spartan *kosmos* in a very specific way, as a closer look at it easily shows.

As noted above, the law or custom[21] inhibiting the sale of helots abroad and their manumission made of them a self-reproducing slave population, which in its turn allowed the Spartiates to be self-sufficient in terms of labour-force and freed them from the necessity to acquire slaves regularly by trade or war. In other words, relying upon the helots, the Spartiates could reduce their involvement with the productive process, keep away from economic activities like slave trade, and minimize their contacts with the outer world, three obviously attractive goals for late archaic and early classical Sparta. Furthermore, if helotry can be seen as a way of regulating a private institution such as slavery (and dependent labour, see below), refunctionalizing it in order to transform it into a cornerstone of the Spartan *kosmos*, its introduction would strongly recall a pattern that seems typical of late archaic Sparta and can be observed for instance in the transformation of the archaic aristocratic *sumposion* into the Spartan *sussition*.[22] Referring to the fundamental aspects of the structure of the Spartan state as it emerged during the archaic age, Stephen Hodkinson wrote (1997b, 88): 'These different elements may have had different origins and timetables of development, but they shared some essential common features. Each was created through the transformation of existing institutions. Warrior groups, male commensality and the exploitation of helot labour[23] all predated their extension to the whole community… Each element moreover was the product of a conscious design.'

The way that helotry specifically fits the Spartan *kosmos* prompts a reflection: in many ways, the differences between helots and chattel slaves of other Greek cities seem to mirror the differences between the Spartan *homoioi* and the citizen bodies of other Greek cities. This is particularly clear if we observe the interference of the community in the relationship between Spartiates and their helots. On an ideological level, the close connection between helots and *homoioi* is emphasized in the field of social interaction by a set of practices of ritualized contempt by which the Spartiates produced a despicable collective identity for the helots, which was a mirror image of the Spartiates' image of themselves (Ducat 1990, 179). But then, one starts wondering if the process that produced helotic slavery, at least in the form in which we know it from classical Sparta, could not have been connected with the very emergence of the *homoioi*. This is perhaps not a direct argument against the traditional view of the origin of helotry and of its chronology, but it casts more than a shade of doubt on it.

Against this proposal to down-date the emergence of helotry and make it a part of the Spartan revolution, it should not be objected that helotry is in fact attested already for the mid-seventh century by Tyrtaeus' famous verses (fragments 6–7 West^2, trans. Gerber):

> Like asses worn out by heavy burdens,
> bringing to their masters out of grievous necessity
> half of all the produce that the land brings forth.

And again:

> Wailing for their masters, they and their wives alike,
> whenever the baneful lot of death came upon any.

It should not be overlooked that according to Pausanias (4.14.5), who is the only direct testimony for these verses, they describe the condition of the Messenians after the first Messenian war. This condition for Pausanias was not helotry: for him, it was only after the second Messenian war that the Messenians had been reduced to the condition of helots (4.23.1 and 24.5). After the first war, they had only been compelled to swear allegiance to the Spartans, to pay half of their products and to take part in the funerals of Spartan kings and magistrates (Paus. 4.14.4). Incidentally, the fact that Tyrtaeus' 'masters' are transformed into 'kings and magistrates' in Pausanias' paraphrase is probably to be explained as a reminiscence of the famous description of the funerals of the Spartan kings in Herodotus' *Histories* (6.58). Herodotus says explicitly that a certain number of *perioikoi* was compelled (ἀναγκαστούς: 6.58.2) to come to the funeral, and this probably induced Pausanias – or perhaps his source?[24] – to conflate Tyrtaeus and Herodotus: Pausanias must have imagined the plight of the defeated Messenians as in some ways similar to that of the *perioikoi*.

Parallel to Pausanias, Aelian, in a passage that obviously draws directly or indirectly on the same verses of Tyrtaeus, describes the condition of the Messenians after the first war as follows (*VH* 6.1, trans. Wilson):

> When the Spartans conquered the Messenians they took possession of half of all property found in Messenia, and they compelled the freeborn women to attend funerals to mourn over the corpses of men who had no connection or relation with them. Some men were left to farm the land, some were sold into slavery, and others killed.

Just like Pausanias, Aelianus clearly assumes that the Messenians had not been reduced to the status of helots, since he speaks of free women (τὰς γυναῖκας τὰς ἐλευθέρας). It is likely that this theory had been developed in the fourth or third century by Messenian propaganda, attempting to down-date the enslavement of the Messenians as far as possible (Oliva 1971, 110–12), but this would be immaterial in the present perspective. Pausanias may have misunderstood or misconstrued Tyrtaeus, but it must be emphasized that here he is using Tyrtaeus as evidence of the fact that the Messenians had not been transformed into helots after the first war. If what Tyrtaeus describes were helotry, Pausanias would be even more stupid than any modern scholar has ever thought, and his argument mere nonsense.[25] The point becomes even stronger if Pausanias had not been the first to use Tyrtaeus' verses as evidence for the conditions imposed on the Messenians after the first Messenian war, as the passage from Aelian makes virtually certain. Had these verses described the condition of the helots, for someone writing at a time when helotry was still in existence, as would be the case with authors echoing fourth- or third-century Messenian propaganda, it would have been self-defeating to use them as evidence of the non-helotic status of the Messenians after the first Messenian war.[26]

Two conclusions are inescapable: first, in the remaining part of this elegy Tyrtaeus did not call helots the people whose plight he described (Ducat 1990, 61 n. 21), and second, in Pausanias' times, and most probably already in the fourth or third century, nobody would have recognized in these verses of Tyrtaeus helotry as it was commonly known. In other words, Tyrtaeus was not speaking of helotry, at least not in the form in which it existed from the fifth-fourth centuries onwards.

3. The mirage of mass enslavement

The main reason for being sceptical of the modern *vulgata* on the origins of helotry concerns its inherent implausibility, in a purely Greek perspective as well as in the light of comparative evidence. It has often been emphasized in recent research that, whether or not the division between Spartiates and helots was based on an original conquest by the former of the latter's territories, the Spartiates treated the helots as a conquered people.[27] However, such a view seems to take little account of how the Greeks really dealt with conquered peoples, Greek or not. Pierre Ducrey's study of the treatment of war captives in Greece illustrates the basic options available when Greeks conquered in war the population of a city or region: they could kill all adult males and sell all women and children as slaves, or sell the whole population, or, more often, ransom at least a part of the captives (Ducrey 1968, 107–47); in the latter case, some sort of subordinate status would often be imposed on the conquered polity. Obviously, the option chosen depended also on whether the conquerors were going to appropriate directly the conquered land or not: if they were, they would try to get rid of the local population. Correspondingly, when sale into slavery was the choice, the sources make it absolutely clear that the defeated were sold abroad, away from their land. In Greek history, there is not a single case of a city being conquered and its citizens being kept there as slaves of the conquerors. This is not at all surprising. Orlando Patterson's comparative study of slavery (Patterson 1982, 110) brought out 'a strong tendency on the part of a conquering group not to enslave a conquered population *en masse* and *in situ*. This, however,' Patterson continues, 'is no more than a strong tendency, to which there have been many exceptions. The exceptions bring us to a second generalization: attempts by a conquering group to enslave a conquered population *en masse* and *in situ* were almost always disastrous failures.' Patterson goes on to explain why this is so. It was the solidarity among the enslaved population, the fact that they were on their own ground, whereas the enslavers were the outsiders in the conquered land, that doomed any attempt of this sort to failure (Patterson 1982, 111–13). A formerly independent group, with a full social structure and its own ruling elites, cannot be reduced to slavery without huge bloodshed. Moreover, comparative evidence shows that ethnic solidarity among large numbers of slaves, particularly if they had been enslaved recently, has always been strongly conducive to revolts even if the slaves had been removed from their original environment (Patterson 1970, 320), and therefore, when mass enslavement did take place, a tendency to scatter the slaves can be observed.[28] The Greeks themselves, who had a lot of experience in the field, knew this all too well, as is shown by concrete examples of the scattering of homogeneous bodies of enslaved people[29] and by theoretical remarks of Plato (*Leg.* 6.777c–d) and Aristotle (*Pol.* 7.9.1330a25–8; see also *Oec.* 1.5.1344b18) on the drawbacks of ethnic homogeneity among slaves.

Patterson himself (1982, 112) records the case of the helots as an exception to his rule – apparently, the only exception known to him, or at least, the only one he mentions. He explains it by following Moses Finley[30] and observing that 'the helots remained non-slaves in the collective nature of their bondage and in the fact that they were a subject community'. Patterson adds that apparently the helots had custodial claims on their parents and children, which conflicts with his analysis of the constitutive elements of slavery and induces him to follow Finley in insisting on the distinction between helots and chattel slaves. However, as mentioned before, there is not a single source that says that family ties among the helots were acknowledged by the Spartans. As for the definition of the helots as a subject community, all that can be said is that the sources show clearly that each helot belonged to a single Spartiate master (Ducat 1990, 19–29; Hodkinson 2000, 114–15). To be sure, the use of helots, as Ducat and Hodkinson emphasize,[31] reflected the strong sense of community that characterized most Spartan institutions.[32] For instance, according to Xenophon's *Constitution of the Spartans* (6.3), each Spartiate was allowed to borrow another Spartiate's helots in case of need. But it would be rash to conclude that the helots were communal property among the Spartiates: after all, Xenophon also says that Spartiates were allowed to make use of each other's wives to produce offspring, although wives were obviously not held in common.

Now, if each helot belonged individually to a single Spartiate and – as has been argued above – the condition of the helots was basically a form of slavery, then, if we want to keep to the traditional view of helotry, we have to accept the paradox of a native population enslaved *en masse* and *in situ*, in Patterson's words. As was the case with the argument about the functionality of helotry for the Spartan *kosmos*, this is perhaps not a fatal blow against the view that the helots were the descendants of aboriginal populations enslaved as a group, but it should suffice to justify a strong scepticism.

4. Helotic ethnicity

Apparently, the strongest argument in favour of the origin of at least part of the helots from a homogeneous ethnic group is the history of Messenia in the fifth and fourth centuries. It is obviously tempting to see the revolt in Messenia in the sixties of the fifth century and finally the foundation of Messene by Epameinondas in 369 as the culmination of centuries of resistance and the triumph of Messenian ethnic consciousness, all the more so since Plato (*Leg.* 6.777c) singles out the helots of Messenia as an example of the rule according to which ethnic homogeneity among slaves produces revolts. But at a closer look, the whole history of Spartan domination and revolts in Messenia does not necessarily confirm the view that Messenian helots had been a homogeneous ethnic group from the outset. If the Spartans had subdued the original population of Messene and transformed it into helots, we would expect a cluster of revolts in the first period of Spartan domination, and then, had such revolts been unsuccessful, fewer and fewer signs of resistance as time passed. What we have is the shadowy second Messenian war, sometime in the mid-seventh century,[33] and then nothing at all until the even more shadowy revolt in the year of Marathon,[34] and finally the one triggered by the earthquake in Sparta.[35] During the whole sixth century there are no traces of revolts in the sources. On the other hand, in the late fifth century unrest among the helots was clearly a central concern for the Spartans. In other words, though ethnicity obviously played a role in the revolt after the earthquake, the general chronological pattern of revolts in Messenia suggests that ethnic solidarity among the helots in Messenia was more likely to be a result of their shared condition under their Spartiate masters.[36]

The rise of a secondary ethnic consciousness among a group of slaves descending from people of mixed origin would not be unparalleled in the annals of slavery (e.g. Caron 1997; Chambers 1997), and the very conditions in which the helots were held formed the ideal substratum for such a process.[37] If, as has been suggested above, helotry was formalized at some point in the first half of the sixth century, by the mid-fifth century the helots, having been *de facto* a self-reproducing group over generations, probably without inputs from outside, were bound to start perceiving themselves as a group, regardless of their ethnic origin. Furthermore, the Spartiates themselves imposed a collective identity on the helots by way of practices such as ritualized contempt or the annual declaration of war by the ephors. This was of course a purely negative and despicable identity, functional to Spartan domination, but as a matter of fact it emphasized the perception of the helots as a group and probably gave them more cohesion than other slaves had in the Greek world. As soon as the helots started perceiving themselves as a group, the normal Greek way of understanding group identities, whereby only an ethnic group can have legitimate aspirations to a homeland, was bound to produce ethnic consciousness among them (Luraghi 2001, 293–4). At the same time, this same mechanism ensured that other Greeks, except of course the Spartiates, would be ready to accept this identity. The *mythomoteur* of Messenian identity was highly plausible from a Greek perspective. As for the fact that ethnicity among the helots was stronger in Messenia, the geography of the Spartan state and perhaps to some extent the settlement pattern in Messenia is a sufficient explanation.[38] Moreover, Thomas Figueira's brilliant study of Messenian identity has shown that during the Peloponnesian war every helot who successfully escaped the control of the Spartans became a Messenian, regardless of whether he came from Messenia or Laconia; in his words (1999, 224), 'instead of reflecting genealogy, feeling "Messenian" or identifying oneself as "Messenian" appears to be inversely correlated with the degree of compliance with the Spartan government and with the Spartiates as a social class'. In conclusion, ethnic consciousness among the helots in fifth century Messenia is not a direct clue as to their origin, and the chronological pattern of revolts in Messenia fits better the assumption that helots in Messenia did not form a homogeneous ethnic group from the beginning.

5. Towards an alternative view of the origins of helotry

If the common view of the origins of helotry is rejected, or at least questioned, it is necessary to look for alternatives, at least in a preliminary way. A first step should be to reformulate the question, and consider the problem of the origins of helotry as a sub-unit of a wider problem, that is, how wealthy and powerful individuals in seventh and early sixth century Greece were able to secure a workforce to till their lands. The answer to this second question would bring us much closer to the answer to the first. Unsurprisingly, this means that it is necessary to turn to Athens, the only Greek polis for which we have evidence about the conditions of poor peasants in the relevant period. Ulrich Kahrstedt once wrote that, in terms of dependent labour, Sparta was what Athens would have become without Solon,[39] and much as one feels uncomfortable in expressing agreement with Ulrich Kahrstedt, there may be something to this view.

Although the details are extremely controversial, there can be no doubt that in Solon's age poor Athenians were experiencing much pressure from their more wealthy and powerful fellow-citizens. Probably this pressure took at least in part the form of pushing them into a situation in which inability to repay loans would endanger their personal freedom.[40] At any rate, arbitrary enslavement and sale abroad of freeborn citizens, and a sort of dependence that also approached slavery, if it was not outright slavery, but did not involve removal from Attica, are envisaged in a famous poem of Solon's (36.13–5 West^2, trans. Gerber):

> And I brought back to Athens, to their homeland founded by the gods, many who had been sold, one legally, another not, and those who had fled under necessity's constraint, no longer speaking the Attic tongue, as wanderers far and wide are inclined to do. And those who suffered shameful slavery right here, trembling before the whims of their masters, I set free.

These verses shed a sudden light on what is otherwise a rather murky landscape. In some ways, they bear an uncanny resemblance to Tyrtaeus' verses discussed above. However, the context remains obscure. At least, they seem to imply that powerful Athenians contemplated enslaving their fellow-citizens to secure additional labour for their lands, since one cannot see any other reason for the enslavement. In the long run, the answer to the need for a workforce in most of Greece would be an increase in the use of chattel slaves acquired from abroad, unsurprisingly in view of the unease always associated with internal enslavement (Patterson 1982, 178–9). But Solon's verses show that imported chattel-slaves, who were certainly there already, did not represent the only form of unfree labour in early sixth-century Athens. By the fifth century they did, just as the helots represented the only form of unfree labour in Sparta.

Let us postulate for a moment that in seventh-century Sparta, just as in Athens or anywhere else in Greece, chattel slaves were used as agricultural workforce, alongside poor free peasants and dependants of other kinds, such as the (enslaved?) sharecroppers Tyrtaeus mentions or perhaps also debt slaves. Although the proportions cannot be defined, one could then suggest that helotry originated by regulating and making permanent the condition of these different kinds of unfree or free and impoverished labourers. After all, the idea of the free citizen was just developing in archaic Greece, and comparative evidence invites us not to underestimate the ability of wealthy landowners to push even free peasants into conditions approaching or equalling slavery. The unification of this multiplicity of statuses in the state-regulated form of helotic slavery would have a distinctively Spartan flavour. Besides, if the original helots were in part not outsiders at all, but rather former impoverished members of the community, the attempt on the part of the Spartiates to emphasize their otherness by way of social rituals makes even better sense. In this perspective, the fact that by the late sixth century many helots were working fields in some parts of Messenia would not be a consequence of the fact that those areas had formerly belonged to them as free Messenians, but rather, of the fact that the Spartiates, the ruling elite of the Lakedaimonian state, had appropriated the best agricultural areas of Messenia – and of Laconia, for that matter.

The views of origin and status of the helots advanced here are admittedly tentative and sketchy, but they might open some interesting perspectives. A late emergence of helotry – and probably of other forms of unfree labour resembling helotry, on Crete and in Thessaly for instance – would make a number of facts easier to understand – for instance the absence of anything approaching helotry in the world of Homer and Hesiod – and would allow one to reconstruct in a more consistent way the development of the use of dependent workforce in archaic Greece. However, the arguments against the *communis opinio* on the origins of helotry are self-sufficient and should be assessed as such: the destructive side of the argument developed here does not depend on the constructive side. If the former is considered convincing, this contribution will have reached its goal.

Acknowledgements

This is a revised version of the paper presented at the Sparta panel of the first Celtic Conference in Classics at Maynooth in September, 2000. I am very grateful to Steve Hodkinson and Anton Powell for inviting me to take part in the conference, and to the other participants of the Sparta panel. Subsequently, the paper has been submitted for discussion in March 2001 at Harvard, in the workshop 'Helots and their masters in Laconia and Messenia', organized by Sue Alcock and myself, and in April of the same year at Utrecht, in the first meeting of the European Network for the Study of Greek History. In both cases I have received precious and stimulating feedback. I am very grateful to Paul Lovejoy (York University), Massimo Nafissi (Perugia University) and Eric Robinson (Harvard), who have read this contribution in its final form. In the following, references will be kept to a minimum. The proceedings of the Harvard workshop will soon provide a fuller body of scholarship on the topic. Since in most of the paper I shall be criticizing previous research on helotry, it is appropriate for me at this point to stress the superb quality of scholarship on this topic. For a general orientation, Lotze 1959, 26–47 and 60–78 and Ducat 1990 are the best starting points. The influence of the latter, not only of his book but also of his many articles, will be easily recognizable in my pages. Cartledge 1985 provides a model of how to apply fruitfully a comparative approach to the study of ancient slavery in general and of helotry in particular. Hodkinson 2000, esp. 65–149, offers a very detailed and insightful discussion of the social and economic side of the phenomenon. The fact that I often find myself disagreeing with his views does not detract in the least from my great admiration for his outstanding contribution to the economic and social history of Sparta.

Notes

[1] In this case as in general, Starr's (1965) *caveat* against reconstructing the archaic history of Sparta based on sources from the second century AD is still very relevant.

[2] '...sticking firmly to the principle that comparison cannot supply the primary evidence we lack but rather can only serve to provoke hypotheses to explain the evidence we have' (Cartledge 1985, 21).

[3] The characterization of helotry as a form of serfdom has been recently advocated by de Ste Croix 1983, 135–6 and 149–50; see also Cartledge 1988. For a recent discussion of the opposition slavery/serfdom see Engerman 1996, esp. 19–26.

[4] The fact that serfs could not be sold apart from the land they tilled is the first difference between serfdom and slavery in Engerman's checklist (1996, 21), although, as he notices, this does not apply to Russian serfs from the seventeenth century onwards (see Kolchin 1987, 41–2) who could be sold.

[5] The extension of the quotation is well marked by Jacoby in his edition; see the important observations of Hodkinson 2000, 117–18.

[6] MacDowell's suggestion (1986, 35) that the borders meant here are the borders of each single estate seems a particularly telling example.

[7] State manumission does not imply state ownership; the manumission of slaves who have acquired merits in the eyes of the community of the free, in particular fighting for it, is not rare in general (Patterson 1982, 287–93), and is attested for Greece, e.g., by the case of Athenian slaves freed after taking part in the battle of Arginusae (Ducat 1990, 26).

[8] *Pace* Lombardo 1999, 133–6, in part based on an untenable interpretation of Paus. 4.14.5. Note that some of the rebels were *perioikoi* not helots, and also that the revolt had lasted for ten years. Furthermore, in cases where relevant evidence exists it is clear that, even though the masters did not recognize family ties among slaves, the slaves themselves had a strong attachment to what they regarded as their family (e.g. Patterson 1982, 6). The permission to leave with their families was part of an agreement in which the Spartans were certainly making concessions to the rebels.

[9] On helots serving in Spartiate households see Hodkinson 1997a, 46–53 and Paradiso 1997, 73–7.

[10] On agriculture and labour in Attica, see Jameson 1992, 142–6 with further references.

[11] See Cartledge 1985, 41. One could also suspect that one or more of the shadowy categories discussed by Ducat 1990, 166–8, such as *mothakes* or *mothōnes*, could have served in this function.

[12] Whether or not this was one function of the *krupteia*. Cf. the famous passage in Thucydides (4.80.3–4), whatever the exact translation of the sentence in 4.80.3. As for the Spartiate control over the territory, consider, e.g., the Aulon affair embedded in the Cinadon story in Xen. *Hell.* 3.3.8–9.

[13] The building has been published by Kaltsas 1983. It was in use between the mid-sixth and the first quarter of the fifth century, when it was destroyed, perhaps in connection with the uprising in Messenia (Kaltsas, 220–21); see also Kiderlen 1994, 26–7 and 108–13 on the general typology.

[14] For the original publication, see Valmin 1941 (interpretation as a fortress: 72–3); see also Pikoulas 1984.

[15] I am very grateful to Yanis Pikoulas (Athens/Volos) for discussing with me the interpretation of this building.

[16] On slave villages, see Cooper 1979, esp. 115 with further references; Lovejoy 1979; Hogendorn, 1977; and the general overview by Lovejoy 2000.

[17] For a typology of systems of exploitation of slaves in pre-colonial Africa see Meillassoux 1991, 116–18.

[18] Against this confusion see Lovejoy 1979, 1273–4.

[19] See the careful and detailed discussion by Nafissi 1991, 31–150, with full references to previous scholarship.

[20] As Ducat 1990, 69 rightly stresses, no ancient source connected helotry immediately with the Dorian conquest of Laconia, as many modern – particularly German – scholars do (e.g. Lotze 1959, 71; Clauss 1983, 110).

[21] Ephorus (*FGrHist* 70 F 117, discussed above) explicitly describes the conditions imposed on the people of Helos when they surrendered to the Spartans, which makes it impossible to decide whether he is generalizing based on common

practice observed in Sparta in his times or more specifically retrojecting the laws that regulated the status of the helots.

[22] On which see Nafissi's comprehensive analysis (1991, 173–226).

[23] For 'helot labour' I would of course substitute 'unfree labour'.

[24] Pausanias (4.14.4) also says that the Messenians had to wear a black cloth at the funerals; this detail, which appears neither in Tyrtaeus nor in Herodotus, might possibly come from an intermediary source.

[25] This point has been made forcefully by Kiechle 1959, 61. Incidentally, since Pausanias is able to use Tyrtaeus' verses in this way in spite of their twice referring to masters (which Pausanias took metaphorically, one supposes), it must be the sharecropping arrangement that made this condition unmistakably different from helotry.

[26] It should be noted that one of the strongest candidates to be identified as a source of Pausanias on the first Messenian war, the mid-third century historian Myron of Priene, seems to have been particularly interested in helotry; see *FGrHist* 106 F1–2.

[27] See, e.g., Singor 1993, 31: 'Whether or not the division between Spartans and helots was based on an original conquest of Laconia – as it certainly was in Messenia since its annexation by the Spartans – it was as a conquered people that the helots were treated.'

[28] This tendency surfaces in the most different times and places; for a late antique example see Heather 1998, 103–4.

[29] e.g., the demos of Megara Hyblaea enslaved by Gelon (Hdt. 7.156.2), or the Rhegians enslaved by Dionysius I (Diod. 14.111.4).

[30] Patterson refers to Finley 1980, 72 (= Finley 1998, 140). For Finley's interpretation of helotry, see also Finley 1981, 109 and 116–49, esp. 119 and 123–4.

[31] Ducat 1990, 29 and Hodkinson 2000, 115–16, and 199–201 on communal use of private property at Sparta. Not very dissimilar is Lotze's view, 1959, 40–2 and 47.

[32] This might be the reason why Strabo (8.5.4) calls the helots 'in a sense public slaves' but see Kennell, forthcoming, for a different – and to my mind more convincing – explanation.

[33] Pre-fourth-century sources on this war are almost non-existent, and the fact that fifth-century authors such as Herodotus and Antiochus of Syracuse seem to know of only one war does not encourage us to believe in its historicity (Luraghi 2002, n. 3). However, for argument's sake I assume here the historicity of this war. Although attempts at down-dating the Messenian wars leave me somewhat sceptical, what is relevant for my argument is not the date of the second Messenian war but the distance between it and the first, which is established as not shorter than two generations by Tyrtaeus fr. 5 West^2.

[34] The historicity of this revolt has been and will probably endlessly be disputed, since in the end it depends on accepting Plat. *Leg.* 3.692d and 698e as historical evidence. See the discussion in Ducat 1990, 142. Among the most recent scholarship, note Dusanic 1997, arguing that the Messenian aggression against Sparta at the very moment when the barbarian was invading Greece was a politically

biased invention of the early fourth century, and Hunt 1998, 28–31, in favour of its historicity and imputing Herodotus' silence on this episode to his general bias against the military capacity of slaves.

[35] Sources and development are discussed in Luraghi 2001, 280–90.

[36] Admittedly, since sources on Sparta before the reign of Ariston and Anaxandridas are desperately scarce and late, one could also speculate that the helots in Messenia had been fighting through the first half of the sixth century. Even in that case, though, the chronological pattern of helotic unrest would not fit well the assumption that ethnic homogeneity was there from the beginning.

[37] See esp. Ducat 1990, 181–2, developing Vidal-Naquet's observations on the collective identity of the helots (1981, 211–22).

[38] For an illuminating analysis of the conditions that made possible revolts among the helots, see Cartledge 1985, 40–6. Referring to Cartledge's checklist, factors 3, 4 and 8 (and 7, perhaps underestimated by Cartledge; cf. Ducat 1990, 163–4) seem to suffice to explain helotic revolts (to these factors I would add the role of *perioikoi* living in Messenia; see Luraghi 2001, 297–301, and 2002).

[39] Kahrstedt 1919, 292. This article represents the first sustained attempt at arguing that helotry was not a direct consequence of conquest, a thesis that Eduard Meyer and Niese had advanced in passing, without arguing it in full. Oliva's criticism of Kahrstedt's views (1961, 9–12) is not completely justified: in the 1919 article the parallels with medieval and modern serfdom had a purely typological function, without the implications that they would acquire thirty years later in Kahrstedt's theory of historical cycles. Certainly Kahrstedt's proud mention of his service in the police and in the Volkssturm (Oliva 1961, 11) has not predisposed later scholars to sympathy for any of his ideas; on Kahrstedt's political side see Wegeler 1996.

[40] Finley 1981, 155–6: 'debt was a deliberate device on the part of the creditor to obtain more dependent labour rather than a device for enrichment through interest'.

Bibliography

Alcock, S.E.

2002 'A simple case of exploitation?', in P. Cartledge, L. Foxhall and E. Cohen (eds.) *Money, Labour and Land: Approaches to the economies of Ancient Greece*, London, 185–99.

Caron, P.

1997 '"Of a nation that the others do not understand": Bambara slaves and African ethnicity in colonial Louisiana, 1718–60', *Slavery and Abolition* 18, 98–121.

Cartledge, P.

1985 'Rebels and Sambos in classical Greece: a comparative view', in P. Cartledge and F.D. Harvey (eds.) *Crux: Essays in Greek history presented to G.E.M. de Ste Croix on his 75th birthday*, London, 16–46.

1988 'Serfdom in classical Greece', in L.J. Archer (ed.) *Slavery and Other Forms*

of Unfree Labour, London and New York, 33–41.
Chambers, D.B.
1997 '"My own nation": Igbo exiles in the diaspora', *Slavery and Abolition* 18, 72–97.
Clauss, M.
1983 *Sparta. Eine Einführung in seine Geschichte und Zivilisation*, Munich.
Cooper, F.
1979 'The problem of slavery in African Studies', *Journal of African History* 20, 103–25.
de Ste Croix, G.E.M.
1983 *The Class Struggle in the Ancient Greek World: From the archaic age to the Arab conquests*, 2nd edn, London.
Ducat, J.
1974 'Le mépris des Hilotes', *Annales (ESC)* 30, 1451–64.
1990 *Les Hilotes, Bulletin de correspondance hellénique, Suppl.* XX, Athens and Paris.
Ducrey, P.
1968 *Le traitement des prisonniers de guerre dans la Grèce antique, des origines à la conquête romaine*, Paris.
Dusanic, S.
1997 'Platon, la question messénienne et les guerres contre les Barbares', in P. Brulé and J. Oulhen (eds.) *Esclavage, Guerre, Économie en Grèce Ancienne: Hommage à Yvon Garlan*, Rennes, 75–86.
Engerman, S.L.
1996 'Slavery, serfdom and other forms of coerced labour: similarities and differences', in M.L. Bush, *Serfdom and Slavery: Studies in legal bondage*, London, 18–41.
Figueira, T.
1999 'The evolution of the Messenian identity', in S. Hodkinson and A. Powell (eds.) *Sparta: New perspectives*, London, 211–44.
Finley, M.I.
1980 *Ancient Slavery and Modern Ideology*, London.
1981 *Economy and Society in Ancient Greece*, ed. by B.D. Shaw and R.P. Saller, London.
1998 *Ancient Slavery and Modern Ideology*. Expanded edition ed. by B.D. Shaw, Princeton.
Heather, P.
1998 'Disappearing and reappearing tribes', in W. Pohl and H. Reimitz (eds.) *Strategies of Distinction*, Leiden, 95–111.
Hodkinson, S.
1997a 'Servile and free dependants of the classical Spartan "oikos"', in M. Moggi and G. Cordiano (eds.) *Schiavi e dipendenti nell'ambito dell'"oikos" e della "familia"*, Pisa, 45–71.
1997b 'The development of Spartan society and institutions in the archaic period', in L. Mitchell and P.J. Rhodes (eds.) *The Development of the Polis in Archaic Greece*, London and New York, 83–102.

2000 *Property and Wealth in Classical Sparta*, London and Swansea.

Hogendorn, J.

1977 'The economics of slave use on two "plantations" in the Zaria Emirate of the Sokoto Caliphate', *International Journal of African Historical Studies* 10, 369–83.

Hunt, P.

1998 *Slaves, Warfare, and Ideology in the Greek Historians*, Cambridge.

Jameson, M.H.

1992 'Agricultural labor in ancient Greece', in B. Wells (ed.) *Agriculture in Ancient Greece*, Stockholm, 135–46

Kahrstedt, U.

1919 'Die spartanische Agrarwirtschaft', *Hermes* 54, 279–94.

Kaltsas, N.

1983 ' Ἡ ἀρχαϊκὴ οἰκία στὸ Κοπανάκι τῆς Μεσσηνίας', *AE*, 207–37.

Kennell, N.

Forthcoming '*Agreste genus*: helots in hellenistic Laconia', in S. Alcock and N. Luraghi (eds.) *Helots and their Masters in Laconia and Messenia: The history and sociology of a system of exploitation.*

Kiderlen, M.

1994 *Megale oikia. Untersuchungen zur Entwicklung aufwendiger griechischer Stadthausarchitektur von der Früharchaik bis ins 3. Jh. v. Chr.*, Hürth.

Kiechle, F.

1959 *Messenische Studien*, Kallmünz.

Kolchin, P.

1987 *Unfree Labor: American slavery and Russian serfdom*, Cambridge, Mass.

Lombardo, M.

1999 'Le donne degli Iloti', in F. Reduzzi Merola and A. Storchi Marino (eds.) *Femmes-esclaves. Modèles d'interprétation anthropologique, économique, juridique*, Naples, 129–43.

Lotze, D.

1959 *Μεταξὺ ἐλευθέρων καὶ δούλων. Studien zur Rechtsstellung unfreier Landbevölkerungen in Griechenland bis zum 4. Jahrhundert v.Chr.*, Berlin.

1993/94 'Bürger zweiter Klasse: Spartas Perioken. Ihre Stellung und Funktion im Staat der Lakedaimonier', *Sitzungsberichte der Akademie der Wissenschaften zu Erfurt, Geisteswissenschaftliche Klasse* 2, 37–51.

Lovejoy, P.E.

1979 'The characteristics of plantations in the nineteenth-century Sokoto Caliphate (Islamic West Africa)', *AHR* 84, 1267–92.

2000 *Transformations in Slavery: A history of slavery in Africa*, 2nd edn, Cambridge.

Luraghi, N.

2001 'Der Erdbebenaufstand und die Entstehung der messenischen Identität', in D. Papenfuß and V.-M. Strocka (eds.) *Gab es das griechische Wunder? Griechenland zwischen dem Ende des 6. und der Mitte des 5. Jahrhunderts v. Chr.*, Mainz, 279–301.

2002 'Becoming Messenian', *JHS* 122.

Forthcoming 'The imaginary conquest of the helots', in S. Alcock and N. Luraghi (eds.) *Helots and their Masters in Laconia and Messenia: The history and sociology of a system of exploitation.*

MacDowell, D.M.

1986 *Spartan Law*, Edinburgh.

Meillassoux, C.

1991 *The Anthropology of Slavery: The womb of iron and gold*, London.

Niese, B.

1906 'Die lakedämonischen Periöken', *Nachrichten von der Königl. Gesellschaft der Wissenschaften in Göttingen, philologisches-historische Klasse*, 101–42.

Oliva, P.

1961 'On the problem of the helots: critical study', *Historica* 3, 5–34.

1971 *Sparta and her Social Problems*, Prague.

Paradiso, A.

1995 'Tempo della tradizione, tempo dello storico', *Storia della Storiografia* 28, 35–45.

1997 'Gli iloti e l'"oikos"', in M. Moggi and G. Cordiano (eds.) *Schiavi e dipendenti nell'ambito dell'"oikos" e della "familia"*, Pisa, 73–90.

Patterson, O.

1970 'Slavery and slave revolts: a socio-historical study of the First Maroon War, 1655–1740', *Social and Economic Studies* 19, 289–325.

1982 *Slavery and Social Death: A comparative study*, Cambridge, Mass.

Pikoulas, Y.A.

1984 'Τὸ φυλακεῖον στὸ Βασιλικὸ καὶ ἡ σημασία του γιὰ τὴν ἱστορικὴ τοπογραφία τῆς περιοκῆς', in Πρακτικὰ τοῦ Β' τοπικοῦ συνεδρίου Μεσσηνιακῶν σπουδῶν, Athens, 177–84.

Singor, H.W.

1993 'Spartan land lots and helot rents', in H. Sancisi-Weerdenburg, R.J. Van der Spek, H.C. Teitler and H.T. Wallinga (eds.) *De agricultura. In memoriam Pieter Willem de Neeve*, Amsterdam, 31–60.

Starr, C.G.

1965 'The credibility of early Spartan history', *Historia* 14, 257–72.

Valmin, N.

1941 'Ein messenisches Kastell und die arkadische Grenzfrage', *Opuscula archaeologica* 2, 59–76.

van Wees, H.

1999 'Tyrtaeus' Eunomia. Nothing to do with the Great Rhetra', in S. Hodkinson and A. Powell, (eds.) *Sparta: New perspectives*, London, 1–41.

Vidal-Naquet, P.

1981 *Le chasseur noir. Formes de pensée et formes de société dans le monde grec*, Paris.

Wegeler, C.

1952 *'Wir sagen ab der internationalen Gelehrtenrepublik.' Altertums-wissenschaft und Nationalsozialismus: das Göttinger Institut fur Altertumskunde 1921–1962*, Vienna.

10

HELOTAGE AND SPARTAN SOCIAL ORGANIZATION

Nikos Birgalias

The helots are commonly thought to have been a servile peasant population which posed a permanent threat to the Spartiates. The conventional view is that their enmity and hatred for the Spartiates, their constant uprisings, the fear which they instilled in the Spartiates and Sparta's need to keep them under its control,[1] determined the city's internal politics and dictated its political and social reforms. In other words, the system of helotage[2] is considered as perhaps the most important factor which influenced the history of Sparta and its political and social make-up.

This view is based upon four different and inter-related points: (a) the appearance of the Dorians, (b) the military orientation and nature of the Spartan *politeia*, (c) the helot rebellions and the behaviour of the *homoioi* towards them, and (d) the social status of the helots. In this article, I will re-examine these four points as well as the general theories which associate helotage with Spartan social organization.

The purpose of this article is, once having explored the above four points, to integrate them into the course of Spartan history from the late seventh to the fourth century BC. This will call into question certain stereotypes and demonstrate that the system of helotage was a product of the attempt to find a resolution to the agricultural question which affected not only Sparta but the whole of the Greek world from the mid-seventh and throughout the whole of the sixth century. I will attempt to show that it was in this way that the helots influenced the organization of Spartan society, and not as a population group that created a sense of fear and insecurity in the citizen body, which consequently resulted in political and social choices or extreme actions.

The Dorians

The belief in the arrival of the Dorians in Lakonia through a large-scale invasion, from which the institution of helotage as well as the structure and form of Spartan society originated, is today doubted. Of the social and political consequences of the Dorian presence in the area, we know almost nothing. Equally doubtful is the origin of the term helot.[3] Indeed, there was confusion even in antiquity as to the exact origin of the helots.

We can be more certain, however, that the social position of one section of the population, in this case the helots, was not necessarily due to its descent, its phyletic origin or a foreign occupation, but was the result of a series of social and political changes. Indeed, the dependence of a section of the rural population on a ruling class of citizens is known elsewhere in Greece and is not an exclusively Spartan phenomenon. Moreover, the references to an antithesis between Dorians and Ionians[4] in terms of customs and political structure, date to a much later period – from the fifth century onwards – and were written within the context of the antagonism between Athens and Sparta, acting more as a reflection of Athenian ideology. The antithesis between the two cities was often reduced to, and interpreted in terms of, political differences as well as descent and origin.

Hoplites and helots

One of the stereotypes of the myth of Sparta which continues from antiquity until today is a belief in the military character of society and, for some scholars, of the political system. The justification given for this belief is the prominent position of the helots in Spartan society. I will attempt to outline the factors that are thought to constitute the military character of Spartan society and will discuss the political choices upon which this city was based and evolved in antiquity. This will enable us to see that Sparta's choices were not dictated by any danger posed by the helots.

If a society was truly exclusive and oriented only towards war, either because it feared the uprisings of its servile peasant population or because it had constantly to watch over it, then it would reinforce its military capabilities. It would not reduce them to the point where it would have to rely for its military campaigns, or for the defence of the *polis* itself, on the servile population that it supposedly had to control. Spartan society's obsession with war was not only a Platonic construct,[5] but was the only acceptable interpretation that democratic Athens, loser of the Peloponnesian War, could give.[6] It is, of course, true that, faced with the Persian threat at the dawn of the fifth century, Sparta was considered the most militarily experienced *polis* of Greece[7] and the *polis* most likely to guarantee the freedom of the Greeks.

From the mid-fifth century onwards, the rest of the Greek world was becoming increasingly distanced from the model of citizen-hoplite.[8] In the eyes of the other Greeks, especially the Athenians, Spartan insistence on this model in the classical period, if only theoretical, was seen as an anachronism and a reflection of militaristic zeal.

Yet helotage was not the factor most responsible for Spartan political and social development. Sparta began to take on the appearance of a fully developed city-state on every level of public and private life in the mid-seventh century and after its victory in the Second Messenian War (640–620),[9] by which it conclusively resolved the agricultural problem that was to burden other Greek *poleis* for over a century. I believe that this success was due in great measure to the adoption of the hoplite phalanx and the social and political repercussions of this.[10] As a consequence of this long war, Spartan society was radically transformed from a society of *aristoi* to a society of *hoplites*.

In the decades that followed, Sparta, in order to deal successfully with the political and social problems which had arisen, redefined its criteria for political participation and gave political rights to the peasant-hoplites, who, along with the aristocracy, now formed a new body of citizens, the *homoioi*.[11] On an economic and political level, the *homoioi* were all equal.[12] At the same time the Great Rhetra,[13] a new legislative and constitutional framework (one of the first in the ancient Greek world) was created, on the basis of which the relationship of the *damos* with the various political bodies (the *ekklēsia*, kings and *gerousia*) was reformed and redefined, and new organs created (the *ephorate*). Social issues were resolved through a redistribution of the land, in keeping with the constitutional and political changes which took place, and the population was divided into three large social groups or categories (*homoioi*, *perioikoi*, helots), each with distinct roles.

The income from the ownership of land, upon which, theoretically at least, the political equality of the *homoioi* was based, did not simply permit a *homoios* to maintain himself and his family and satisfy the obligations which the status of citizen entailed. The goal, again theoretically, was to relieve the *homoios* from the need to engage in any gainful work or employment which would have led to the acquisition of wealth, so that he could devote himself exclusively to his political and especially military duties. Unfortunately, we know very little as to how the absence of 'crude' work from the life of the Spartiates operated in practice. There was no legal decree which prohibited any kind of gainful employment. On the contrary, the acquisition of wealth through the exploitation of land or through other means was one of the most important economic and political objectives of a Spartiate, as it secured his membership and that of his family in the body of the *homoioi*.

These reforms secured Spartan political and social stability. They gave the city a new and original constitution, as well as a significant political, social and military advantage over other *poleis*. By satisfying the social and political demands of the peasants, the Spartan aristocracy managed far earlier than any other aristocracy both not to endanger its own position and not to have its character radically altered. By instituting a social system and a political legislation of its own liking, and by broadening its membership, it secured an important and powerful position for itself within this new political body.[14] The basic traditional criteria of aristocratic society for the acquisition of political rights and the exercise of power (descent, ownership of land, right to partake in battle, education, adherence to a particular code of social conduct) were not relinquished, but were supplemented with the criteria of wealth. A stable oligarchy was thus created.

In contrast with the rest of the Greek world, sixth-century Sparta was not plagued by political and social upheavals, nor by tyranny.[15] By the end of this century, Sparta had contracted a series of alliances with other Peloponnesian cities and created what modern historians call the Peloponnesian League. This was a primarily political, as well as military, alliance which secured Sparta's sphere of influence,[16] shifting the city's area of interest from Lakonia to the wider region of the Peloponnese.

The fifth century BC, however, was a period of change for Sparta, during which the city's political and social balance was gradually undermined. The end of the Persian Wars marked a new era in which Athens emerged as a competitor *polis*, not only on a military and economic level, but on a primarily political one. Athens and Sparta[17] competed for hegemony of the Greek world, leading to the catastrophic Peloponnesian War (431–404), which was to change the political and social make-up of both *poleis*. The war overturned the traditional structure of Spartan society, and had a massive impact on the behaviour of the citizens and the operation of its institutions. Thousands of helots now participated as hoplites in the army with the promise that their social status would change.[18] The creation of new military positions with broad powers (such as that of admiral),[19] mercenary soldiers, gold from Persia, the increase in corruption and the availability of education to children whose parents were not *homoioi* are just some aspects of this transformation.[20]

If, on a political level, the institutions appear unchanged, the social foundation on which they were based, that is the class of *homoioi*, was shrinking, with the result that the social conflicts and political differentiations were intensified. The balance between the various forms of power was also under threat. The *dēmos*, in an attempt to have a greater role over a political situation which it was increasingly unable to control,[21] reinforced the role of the ephors, thus increasing their antagonism with the kings. The presence of the ephors became increasingly stifling and it almost controlled the political life of the city, attempting to curb the personal power of the kings whilst also satisfying the conservative policies of the overwhelming majority of *homoioi*.[22]

The social and economic distinctions within the citizen body were intensified, and this undermined the political balance among the *homoioi*, as well as increasing the conflicts between them. The citizen-hoplite of the sixth century was gradually transformed, at the expense of his fellow citizens, into a large landowner, whilst a large number of citizens was also removed from the body of the *homoioi*, primarily for economic reasons. The ever-decreasing membership of the citizen body created the problem of *oliganthrōpia*, which became even more pronounced after the catastrophic earthquake of 464. This resulted in political and judicial power resting in the hands of fewer and fewer citizens, giving the political system an even more pronouncedly oligarchical character. At the same time, the antagonism, and subsequently the war, with Athens, as well as the exercise of hegemony over the Greek world, increased the *polis*' military needs, to which the small number of *homoioi* was no longer in a position to respond. The participation of helots and mercenaries in the hoplite body, the creation of a navy, the long and distant military campaigns, the cavalry, and the need to besiege fortified places were factors which not only exceeded the capabilities of the city; they also gradually transformed the social composition of the Spartan army and began to distance Spartan society from its traditional models.

The great economic and, by extension, social and political inequalities, as well as the concentration of wealth in the hands of a few families in classical Sparta resulted from the system of land ownership[23] upon which the Spartiate's political participation in the body of *homoioi* depended. This suggests that the Spartiates and, in this particular case, the state were not particularly concerned with maintaining a stable number of landholdings, nor with the distribution and transmission of land within the family.[24] And this despite the fact that in order to remain within the body of *homoioi* it was essential to own sufficient land to secure a reasonable level of income.[25]

Oliganthrōpia, however, resulted in (especially from the mid-fifth century) the creation of new social classes[26] (*hypomeiones*, *tresantes*, *mothakes*, *trophimoi*, *neodamōdeis*) which had not existed in the previous centuries, at least not with the characteristics which now distinguished them. The number of the members within these groups is remarkable, as are their different social origins. We can presume that they included those Spartiates who, either for economic reasons or because of their behaviour in battle, had fallen from the body of the *homoioi*; the offspring of *homoioi* and non-*homoioi*; those who in youth had participated in the education system although they were not the children of *homoioi*; unrecognised children of *homoioi*; helots who had participated in battle and had thus gained some kind of status, etc. The above factors do not simply demonstrate the lack of homogeneity within these groups or the different reasons for their creation, but also the different relations, ties or interests which each group may have had with the *homoioi* as well as with the helots and the *perioikoi.*

Under the existing social stratification, these new groups included within them *homoioi*,[27] *perioikoi* and former helots, thus creating informal binding ties with the class of *homoioi*, but also profound dividing lines. The new social classes may, then, have participated in a united effort of the city (such as a war), but they also undermined the balance between the political body (the *homoioi*) and the peasant population (the helots). The creation of these new classes altered the social structure of the population and led to demands for their political recognition. In addition, the fact that they were called upon to resolve the city's military weaknesses undermined the exclusive military prerogative of the *homoioi.* The only movement that we know of that sought political recognition was that of Kinadon (Xenophon, *Hellenika* 3.3), which highlights for us not only an attempt to forward an alternative political proposal, but also the way in which the institutions at Sparta operated, during this period at least. Even so, it is reasonable for us to presume that this movement was not created overnight, but had been preceded by a sufficient period of agitation for the consciousness of the common position shared by the members of these groups to form. Moreover, the granting of freedom and land, before Kinadon's movement, to non-*homoioi* who had participated in wars from 430 BC, cannot be explained simply on the grounds that the Spartiates were fulfilling a promise that they had given, but primarily by the fact that they were attempting to satisfy certain demands that had been expressed.

Spartan hegemony after the Peloponnesian War did not last for long. The defeat at the hands of the Thebans at Leuctra in 371 and the defeat at Mantineia in 362, marked the complete loss of Messenia, and Sparta was now a *polis* of no special importance.[28] On a political and social level, the inequalities which had been created during the previous century had become entrenched. A minority of large land-owners, who continued to be called *homoioi* and who used their traditional political ties to impose their will, dominated the *dēmos.* In addition, various kings (Agesilaos,[29] Archidamos III, Leonidas II) led mercenary armies. Sparta became, then, an aristocratic society with pronounced plutocratic features. Whilst the criteria for political rights which had been established centuries before continued to exist in theory, in practice only a few families – rich ones of noble descent – were able to fulfil these criteria.

The *homoios* of the fifth and fourth centuries had other priorities and other problems to resolve from those of his sixth-century namesake. He was less warlike, richer, one of a smaller group and, particularly from the late fifth century, conducted his wars using mercenaries or other categories of the population, and attempted ever more zealously to maintain the status quo and the privileges which it offered him.

Helot rebellion?

The attempted helot uprisings are considered as not only both the cause and the result of the bad treatment which helots received at the hands of the *homoioi*, but also as proof of the anxiety and fear which the *homoioi* felt towards them, and of the tense relationship between the two groups.

Plato (*Laws* 776c and 777cd) notes that the issue of the helots was something which divided the Greeks. Some writers argued that helotage was a good institution and that the Spartans behaved well towards the helots, whilst others maintained the exact opposite. Aristotle (*Pol.* 1272b and 1269a) claimed that the helots were in a constant state of revolt. This observation not only reflects the confusion and differences in views among Athenian circles on this particular issue, but also their ignorance as to precisely how the helots were treated.

It is noteworthy that from the end of the Second Messenian War[30] – from around 620 until the beginning of the fifth century – absolutely no reference is made to a helot uprising.[31] Essentially, the whole debate focuses on the years 490–425, when we have references to four attempted revolutions. The first was that of Kleomenes I in 490. This particular case indirectly involved Kleomenes, who appears to have exhorted the helots to rebel. Even so, this is not evidence for an actual helot revolution.

The next attempted revolution was that of Pausanias. Even if Thucydides' (1.132 and 4.80) criticisms are true, we can see that Pausanias himself urged the helots on, aiming to create a movement, when the helots during that period did not pose any danger or threat for the *homoioi* at all.

The revolt under Archidamus in 464 was the first serious expression of discontent against Sparta, albeit limited.[32] Sparta here had to face a double problem. The first was to find ways of integrating the helots better and of quelling their anxieties. The second was to suppress the uprising and resolve the issue of Messenian independence. I believe that, with the gradual incorporation of the helots into the army as well as the promise to grant freedom or political rights, Sparta managed to resolve the first problem and at the same time guarantee a good ally in order for the second problem never to arise again.

The final tension was that under Agis II in 425. Again, our main source is Thucydides (4.14, 54–55, 4.41, 7.26). This case did not involve an uprising of the helots but concerns instead the anxieties of the *homoioi* as regards the

Messenians, who had reappeared and settled at Pylos during the Peloponnesian War. Indeed, the *homoioi* continued to use the helots in the army.

Of these four purported crises during the fifth century, we can only retain that of 464, a rebellion that was isolated, limited and which did not spread. Moreover, after 464, the helots did not even attempt to rebel, despite having many opportunities to do so.

There are three important elements relating to the conduct of the Spartans towards the helots:[33] Thucydides' reference (4.80, 3) to the mass murder of 2000 helots, Plutarch's reference to the annual proclamation of war, and the *krypteia*.

Thucydides notes that (in 424?) the Spartiates killed 2000 of the more vigorous helots who had offered their services to Sparta. This single and unclear piece of evidence raises many questions.[34] The figure of 2000 seems to me especially large. Moreover, how are we to interpret the lack of protest on the part of the helots? And what of the *krypteia*, for all those who consider it to be the 'murder' of helots? Plutarch (*Lyc.* 28.6) did not believe that such a thing happened. Bearing in mind the willingness of helots to fight alongside the Spartiates a little later, such as the 700 of Brasidas in Thrace and, in the same period, the *neodamōdeis* at Lepreon, it is possible that Thucydides has been misinterpreted. The annual proclamation of war, to which only Plutarch (*Lyc.* 28.7) refers – as something that Aristotle believed took place – is peculiar and otherwise unknown. If we are, however, to accept its veracity, then we should date its origins to the period after the defeat at Leuctra and the loss of Messenia, which coincided with the period in which Aristotle was active. That is, the Spartans symbolically proclaimed war on the Messenians (and not necessarily the helots), sending thus a message in two directions. To the Spartans themselves, to remind them that they must not give up their efforts to regain Messenia, which belongs to them by right, and also to the Messenians, proclaiming opposition to the new status quo in Messenia.

As for the *krypteia*,[35] this should not be thought of as the murder of helots either. Indeed, how one views the *krypteia* depends on how one interprets the system of helotage.

In no circumstance should we suppose that the *homoioi* systematically annihilated the peasant population which cared for their land and secured their political position. This would have been catastrophic for the *homoioi* and would also have caused continual strife and conflict, something which the *homoioi* were always careful to avoid. Moreover, they would not have used the helots in the army at a time when they themselves numbered less than a few hundred, nor would the helots have willingly participated in the army. Finally, the fact that the helots had a peculiar legal status, somewhere between free and slave,[36] reflects a peculiar conception of their position and consequently a different form of behaviour towards them from that directed at slaves.

Helot social status

The social status of the helot is, as Polydeuces correctly observed (*Onomastikon* 3.83), somewhere between free and slave. This implies that the fortune of the helots differed significantly from those of the slaves of Athens.[37]

The helots were a homogeneous peasant population who, although they did not belong to the citizen community, were not foreigners brought to Sparta from other parts of Greece. They spoke the same language, reproduced themselves as a class, and were primarily farmers. A helot would farm the land of a *homoios* with the obligation of giving him a portion of the yield or income, but also with the right to retain a share of it for himself.[38] This demonstrates the existence of some kind of settlement between *homoioi* and helots, as well as a direct and common economic interest. For the helots, it was a question of survival, since this settlement allowed them to be self-sufficient and not dependent upon their *homoioi*-masters. It also allowed them to enrich themselves,[39] as is suggested by the existence of rich helots who were in a position to buy their freedom[40] and fight as hoplites. As for the *homoioi*, it was a question of political existence, since their position within the political community depended on the cultivation of the land by the helots.

When we say, therefore, that the helots were public slaves we mean that they did not belong individually to each *homoios*. The *homoios* did not have any property rights over the helot who cultivated his land. He did not have the right to free the helot nor to sell him as a commodity (Ephorus at Strabo, 8.5,4), nor to kill him or to transfer him elsewhere without the permission of the authorities.[41] The helots, therefore, were a dependent peasant population, a dependency which was basically determined by the fact that they were not the owners of the land which they cultivated and that they were not members of the citizen body, so as to be able to take decisions for themselves.[42]

Conclusions

To clarify my position, I do not believe in a difference between the helots of Lakonia and the helots of Messenia,[43] a difference which supposedly justifies a distinction between their respective positions in relation to the Spartiates, and which presents the helots of Messenia as a separate nation, with its own culture and history,[44] relegating the system of helotage to two different sets of historical conditions. One wonders what exactly was this

Messenian civilization, what was the history of Messenia, and what was the political identity of the Messenians before the First Messenian War. Political activity in Messenia during this period mainly centred around an attempt by the aristocracy to maintain its privileged position. It then attempted to cultivate the concept of an independent 'country', with the support of those who would benefit from the removal of Messenia from Sparta's sphere of influence.

The idea that the *homoioi* feared the helots (especially those of Messenia) and that the helots hated their masters and were constantly rebelling against them, resulting in the idiosyncratic structure of Spartan society, is a great exaggeration. It is more a product of the ideological conflict which began in fifth-century Athens and of later cultural constructs of the Messenians themselves.[45]

We do not know much about the exact status of the helots after the First Messenian War. Even so, it is commonly acknowledged that, whilst the rest of the Greek world adopted the practice of sending out colonies in order to resolve the demographic problem, Sparta at the end of the eighth century began to occupy the fertile valley of Pamisos.

Thus, with the First Messenian War (735–715), the Spartiates divided the land of the Messenian nobles, who lost the exclusive right to exploit this land along with their political privileges. As for the poor or landless peasants of Messenia, they must have either maintained the same status they had before annexation by Sparta or gained some benefit from the new system of land ownership. According to Pausanias (*Messen.* 9.1), many of them went over to the Spartan side during the war.

Seventy years later, the ring-leaders of the Messenian uprising against the Spartans, who rebelled with the help of nobles from other Greek *poleis*, were in fact descendants of the Messenian nobles[46] who had lost their privileges, not the poor peasants of Messenia.

If we agree that the predominant problem of Greek society at the end of the seventh century BC and throughout the sixth was the agrarian question and the granting of political rights to the peasant-hoplites, then the case of Sparta becomes more comprehensible and less paradoxical. Both during the Second Messenian War and after it, Sparta, as we have mentioned, created the new citizen body of the *homoioi*. At the same time, through the land redistribution, it institutionalized the status of the peasants who were poor, indebted, landless or had been ruined by the war. These peasants had contributed to the Spartan victory, yet they had not been able to participate as hoplites and thus be included in the new citizen body.

I am not claiming that the system of helotage appeared at this point, but that the relationship between *homoioi* and helots was reoriented and reformed in order to achieve a workable compromise. Given the historical context, and in comparison with what was going on in the rest of the Greek world, the social security provided for the poor peasant, even if it was a form of dependency, was revolutionary and pioneering, guaranteeing them a better, safer and institutionally more secure life.

The social status of helotage, then, was the result of a series of social changes which took place over many decades. If we examine helotage within the historical context of the archaic period, then we can see it as an economic and social development analogous to that which took place in Attica in the seventh century BC, leading to the creation of the class of *hektēmoroi*. Whilst Solon abolished this class without securing a better future for the indebted peasants, in Sparta the problem was resolved much earlier and in a far more radical way. The Spartan reforms secured significant privileges for this category of peasants and a more stable, secure and better status than that of the 'free' *hektēmoroi*.

Of course, the position of the helots at the end of the seventh and throughout the sixth centuries appears to be an anachronism when compared to that of the free peasants of Athens in the fifth century. Yet, these were two different chronological moments and two different political systems.

What the helots initially gained, then, in this reform between helots (i.e. indebted or landless farmers) and *homoioi* (i.e. wealthy farmers) during a period of land redistribution, was the securing of their freedom as well as an institutionally-safeguarded status. In exchange they gave up any demand for, or right to, a new redistribution of land or aspirations to own land, or to gain political rights – problems which plagued other *poleis* at the time and which the tyrants exploited. With this agreement, Sparta managed to resolve a serious problem, that of the peasant population, which Athens, for example, needed over a century, as well as many reforms, a tyrannical regime, and the invention of a new political system, that of democracy, in order to resolve.

Of course, the helot did not evolve into a free peasant, and the *homoioi*, by weakening the possibilities for the establishment of a tyrannical regime, could maintain their aristocratic character.

The political and social stability and consensus which Sparta maintained for so many years, and which was especially tested from the mid-fifth century onwards, was truly impressive. It would not otherwise be possible to understand how, with the dangers which Sparta incurred from war and the continuing decline in the number of *homoioi*, the helots, who participated in and contributed to the war efforts, lacked any sustained or widespread inclination to overthrow the regime. This arrangement is one of the factors which allowed Sparta to face successfully the challenge of the Persian Wars, the conflict with Athens, the Peloponnesian War and, subsequently, the exercise of Greek hegemony.

From the mid-fifth century, as the number of *homoioi* began to decline and the peasant population began increasingly to bear the burden of war, this arrangement no longer truly existed in practice. This does not mean that all helots participated in war, nor that they all demanded their political recognition – only those who had the financial ability to fight as hoplites, given that hoplite armour was expensive and was not provided by the city. This situation created tension and rupture in their relationship with the *homoioi* and undermined the existing balance. We must also bear in mind the possibility that many Spartiates who had been excluded from the body of *homoioi* quite likely felt more solidarity with the helots than with the *homoioi* (see the discussion on the movement of Kinadon above). During 430–360, then, Sparta attempted to resolve or to alleviate this problem in a manner similar to that which had successfully been implemented at the end of the Second Messenian War. This effort was part of a wider reform of the political body, incorporating other social groups aside from wealthy helots, such as, for example, the new and very large category of *neodamōdeis*. This attempt at reform was never completed, as the needs which created it disappeared along with the loss of Messenia and the hegemony of the Greek world.

Acknowledgements

I would like to thank Anton Powell and Stephen Hodkinson for their comments on an earlier draft of this article.

Notes

[1] For the use of such fear as a pretext, see Osborne 1996, 177 and Devereux 1965, 18–44.

[2] For the system of helotage and its problems, see Ducat 1978, 5–46 and 1990.

[3] See Ducat 1990, 7–12.

[4] Roussel 1976.

[5] Plato, *Laws* 666e.

[6] There is a remarkable increase in the number of references to the military character of the Spartans from 430 BC on: see Birgalias 1999, 29 ff. and 369 ff. Despite the fact that the writers of the classical period avoided direct discussion of Sparta's military achievements during the Peloponnesian War, referring instead to those of the 6th century or the Persian War, it is clear that Sparta's great victory

against Athens was lurking at the back of their minds. See, e.g., Euripides *Andromache*, 742–726; Thucydides, 1.10 and 1.84; Xenophon, *Lak. Pol.* 13.5; Aristotle *Politics*, 1271b, 1333b, 1334a; Isocrates, *Panathenaicus*, 45–8 and 253–6 and *On the Peace*, 97; Lysias *Olympiakos*, 7 and *Epitaphios*, 31–2; Lycurgus *Against Leocrates*, 129–30; Aeschines *Against Timarchus*, 181.

[7] For the Spartan army, see Lazenby 1985.

[8] For the importance of this as the political model *par excellence* in Sparta, see Birgalias 1999, 321–83.

[9] Finley 1981; 1965, 110–22; Mossé 1973, 7–20; Hodkinson 1997a, 83–102.

[10] See Snodgrass 1965, 110–22; Detienne 1985, 119–42; Cartledge 1976, 115–19 and 1977, 11–27.

[11] This is according to the tradition cultivated from the 5th century onwards, and which has been accepted by some contemporary scholars.

[12] For the rumoured equality between the *homoioi* as well as an undermining of this view, see the exceptional study by Hodkinson 2000, esp. 19–64.

[13] Many views have been given as to the chronology of the Great Rhetra. I believe that its creation coincides with the Second Messenian War and is related to the hoplite phalanx. See the prologue in van Wees 1999.

[14] See Birgalias 1997, 35–52.

[15] It has often been commented that there were important changes in Sparta around the mid-6th century, changes which had either political or economic causes. From Ehrenberg 1929, 1373–1453, where Chilon is characterized as the Lycurgus of the 6th century BC, to Powell 1998, 119–46, many thoughts have been expressed on the content of the 'revolution' which took place around 550. It is not impossible that during this period there really was internal tension, as reflected especially in the rivalry between the ephor Chilon and the King Alexandrides. Independent of the content that we could ascribe to these changes, I do not believe that they transformed the deeper internal political and social structures of the city.

[16] See Cawkwell 1993, 364–76.

[17] See Powell 1988, esp. 96–135 on Sparta's internal problems during the period 478–431. On the Peloponnesian War, see de Ste Croix 1972.

[18] The participation of helots in battle dates already from the Second Messenian War (Paus. 4.16, 6). 35,000 lightly-armed helots took part in the battle of Plataia, whom Herodotus (9.28–29) describes as 'combatants' and who buried their dead in a special tumulus. The helots later took part in the navy as rowers and in the army as light-armed troops (Herod. 7.229, 9.10; Thuc. 7.19.3; Xen. *Hell.* 7.1.12). From at least the mid-5th century, the helots were used as hoplites. During the Peloponnesian War in particular, the promise that they would be freed if they took part in the war as hoplites became common (Thuc. 4.80.2–5 and 7.19.3; Theopompus in Athenaeus 271cd, Diod. Sic. 15.65.6). Helots made up a section of the army on all the long and great Spartan military campaigns (Xen. *Hell.* 3.1.4; 5.2.24; 6.5.28–9). In 421 they were indeed freed and settled at Lepreon, along with the *neodamōdeis* (Thuc. 5.34.1). The Spartan army directed against Argos

in 418 was made up of Lacedaimonians and many helots (Thuc. 5.57.1). Helots and *neodamōdeis* were sent to Sicily in 413 (Thuc. 8.19.3 and 8.58.3). Finally, we should recall Xenophon's comment that 6000 helots joined the Spartan army after the defeat at Leuctra (Xen. *Ages*. 2.24, *Hell.* 7.2.2 and 6.5.28). 1000 of these were granted their freedom by way of compensation (Plut. *Ages*. 32.12). See also Cozzoli 1978, 213–32, and Hunt 1998.

[19] For the role of Lysander, see Bommelaer 1981, and Hodkinson 1993, 146–76.

[20] Birgalias 1999, 291–7.

[21] For the level of participation of the *dēmos*, see Ruzé 1997, 173–240.

[22] Aristotle's description (*Politics* 1270b–1271a) of these two institutions is of exceptional interest. For the policies of the kings, see Cloché 1949, 113–38 and 343–81, Carlier 1984, 24–324, Thomas 1974, 257–70. For the relationship between the ephors and the kings, as well as a general discussion of the whole issue, see Richer 1988, 389–430.

[23] For the system of land ownership, see Hodkinson 1986, 378–406 and 2000; Ducat 1983a, 194–225 and 1983b, 143–66; Cozzoli 1979.

[24] This situation was especially aggravated by the law of Epitadeus. For the significance of this law, see Christien 1974, 196–221, but also Hodkinson 2000, 90–6.

[25] Birgalias 1998, 207–34, and esp. Schutrumpf and Hodkinson 2000, 76.

[26] Christien 1993, 33–40; Ruzé 1993, 297–310; Carlier 1994, 25–41; Alfieri-Tonini 1975, 305–16; Lotze 1962, 427–35.

[27] See Hodkinson 1997b, 45–71.

[28] For Spartan society after the 4th century BC, see Cartledge and Spawforth 2001.

[29] For the political and social situation during this period, see Cartledge 1987 and Hodkinson 1996.

[30] If, as Osborne 1996, 177–8 argues, the history of the Second Messenian War, as presented by Pausanias, was a construct of the Messenians after their liberation from Sparta in the 4th century, then this reduces even more the number of supposed Messenian rebellions.

[31] On the helot rebellions, see the interesting article by Roobaert 1977, 141–55, and Ducat 1990, 129–44.

[32] See Diod. Sic. 11.63.7, Plut. *Lyc*. 28.12 and Thuc. 4.41.2–3, 5.14.3 and 5.23.3.

[33] Whitby 1994, 87–126.

[34] See Powell, 1998, 250–1 and re-edition 2001, 269; and Talbert 1989, 22–40; Cartledge 1991, 379–81; Richer 1998, 383–7.

[35] See Birgalias 1999, 97–126; Ducat 1997, 9–38.

[36] See Lotze 1959.

[37] See Kyrtatas 1987, 94–5, and N. Luraghi, 'Helotic slavery reconsidered', in this volume.

[38] Hodkinson 1992, 123–34.

[39] We do not know the exact proportion of the agricultural produce which they

gave to the *homoioi*. A difference of opinion over this issue can be observed among the ancients. For Strabo (8.5.4) and Myron of Priene (Athenaeus 657d), the helots gave a proportion of the produce and kept the rest themselves. In contrast, Ailianos (*Poikile Istoria*, 6.1) and Pausanias (*Messen.* 14.4) argued that the helots handed over half their produce. Plutarch's view (*Lyc.* 24.2 and *Lac. Apophth.* 239 E, 41), whereby the helots paid a pre-arranged sum from the income from the produce, is of interest. A pre-arranged sum, retaining thus a surplus, would provide a motive for increasing agricultural output. Despite the fact that Plutarch considered that any *homoios* who attempted to gain more – and, by extension, the profit-earning helot who would thus have been working quite willingly – was cursed, there was no doubt that such 'exchanges' constituted a mutual interest between helot and *homoios*: for the former, so that he would not depend upon the owner of the land-holding for his livelihood, and for the latter so that he would remain a citizen.

[40] The figure of 6000 helots who had access to the 5 minas required under Kleomenes III (Plu. *Kleom.* 23.1) to purchase their freedom is remarkable.

[41] However much we might believe that the state held responsibility, there is no doubt that the personal relationships between a *homoios* and a helot were more important than the sources allow us to believe. See Herod. 7.229.

[42] The debate as to whether the helots were public or private property is still open. Cf. Ducat 1990, 19–29 and Hodkinson 2000, 113–49.

[43] Not all Messenians were helots and, as such, we should not identify Messenian expressions of discontent with the system of helotage.

[44] As Talbert 1989, 22–40, esp. 28–30, quite correctly argues, the Messenians did not have a 'political' consciousness as their region had been conquered before the city had fully developed.

[45] See the interesting article by Figuera 1999, 211–44.

[46] On the image of Aristomenes and his companions as constructed in Messenia after 370 BC, see Themelis 2000.

Bibliography

Alfieri-Tonini, T.

1975 'Il problema dei Neodamodeis nell'ambito della societa spartana', *RIL*, 109, 305–16.

Birgalias, N.

1997 'Ερις περί αρετής', *Ελληνικά*, τ. 47, 35–52.

1998 'Ο Μύθος του Καιάδα', *Αρχαιογνωσία*, 207–34.

1999 *L'odyssée de l'éducation spartiate*, Βασιλόπουλος, Athens.

Bommelaer, J.F.

1981 *Lysandre de Sparte. Histoire et traditions*, Paris.

Carlier, P.

1984 *La royauté en Grèce avant Alexandre*, Strasbourg, 240–324.

1994 'Les inférieurs et la politique extérieure de Sparte', *Mélanges Pierre Lévêque*, vol. 8, Besançon, 25–41.

Carlier P. (ed)
1996 'Spartan society in the fourth century: crisis and continuity', in *Le IVe siècle av. J- C.: Approches historiographiques*, Nancy.
Cartledge, P.
1976 'Did Spartan citizens ever practice a manual *techne*?', *LCM* 1, 115–19.
1977 'Hoplites and heroes: Sparta's contribution to the technique of ancient warfare', *JHS* 97, 11–27.
1979 *Sparta and Lakonia*, London.
1987 *Agesilaos and the Crisis of Sparta*, London.
1991 'Richard Talbert's revision of the Spartan-helot struggle: a reply', *Historia* 40, 379–81.
2001 *Spartan Reflections*, London
Cartledge, P. and Spawforth A.
2001 *Hellenistic and Roman Sparta. A tale of two cities*, 2nd edn, London and New York.
Cawkwell, G.L.
1993 'Sparta and her allies in the sixth century BC', *CQ*, 43, 364–76.
Christien, J.
1974 'La loi d'Epitadeus: un aspect de l'histoire économique et sociale à Sparte', *RD* 2, 196–221.
1993 'Les bâtards spartiates', *Mélanges Pierre Lévêque,* vol. 7, Besançon, 33–40.
Cloché, P.
1949 'Sur le rôle des rois de Sparte', *LEC* 17, 113–38 and 343–81.
Cozzoli, U.
1978 'Sparta e l'affrancamento degli iloti nel 5 e 4 sec.', *Studi pubblicati dall' Instituto Italiano per la Storia Antica* 27, 213–32.
1979 *Proprietà fondiaria ed esercito nello stato spartano dell'età classica*, Rome.
de Ste Croix, G.E.M.
1972 *The Origins of the Peloponnesian War*, London.
Detienne, M.
1985 'La Phalange: problèmes et controverses', in J.-P. Vernant (ed.) *Problèmes de la guerre en Grèce ancienne*, Paris, 119–142.
Devereux, G.
1965 'La psychanalyse et l'histoire. Une application à l'histoire de Sparte', *Annales (ESC)*, 18–44.
Ducat, J.
1978 'Aspects de l'hilotisme', *Ancient Society* 9, 5–46.
1983a 'Sparte archaïque et classique. Structures économiques, sociales, politiques, *REG* 96, 194–225.
1983b 'Le citoyen et le sol à Sparte à l'époque classique', in *Hommage à Maurice Bordès, Annales de la Faculté des Lettres et Sciences Humaines de Nice* 45, 143–166.
1990 *Les Hilotes*, *BCH* Supplément XX, Paris.
1997 'Crypties', *Cahiers du Centre Gustave Clotz* 8, 9–38.

Ehrenberg, V.
1929 'Sparta (Geschichte)', *RE* III, A.2, 1373–1453.
Figueira, T.
1999 'The evolution of the Messenian identity', in S. Hodkinson and A. Powell (eds) *Sparta: New perspectives*, London, 211–44.
Finley, M.I.
1981 'Sparta and Spartan society', in *Economy and Society in Ancient Greece*, London, 24–40.
Forrest, W.G.
1968 *A History of Sparta 950–192*, London.
Hodkinson, S.
1986 'Land tenure and inheritance in classical Sparta', *CQ* 36, 378–406.
1992 'Sharecropping and Sparta's economic exploitation of the helots', in Sanders (ed.) ΦΙΛΟΛΑΚΟΝ, 123–34.
1993 'Warfare, wealth and the crisis of Spartiate society', in J. Rich and G. Shipley (eds.) *War and Society*, London, 146–76.
1996 'Spartan society in the fourth century: crisis and continuity', in P. Carlier (ed.) *Le IVe Siècle av. J- C.: approches historiographiques*, Nancy.
1997a 'The development of Spartan society in the archaic period', in L.G. Michell and P.J. Rhodes (eds.) *The Development of the Polis in Archaic Greece*, London and New York, 83–102.
1997b 'Servile and free dependants of the Spartan *oikos*', in M. Moggi and G. Cordiano (eds.) *Schiavi e Dipendenti nell'Ambito dell'Oikos e della Familia*, XXII Colloquio GIREA, Pisa, 45–71
2000 *Property and Wealth in Classical Sparta*, London.
Hodkinson, S. and Powell, A. (eds.)
1999 *Sparta: New perspectives*, London.
Hooker, J.T.
1980 *The Ancient Spartans*, London.
Hunt, P.
1998 *Slaves, Warfare and Ideology in the Greek Historians*, Cambridge.
Huxley, G.L.
1962 *Early Sparta*, London.
Jones, A.H.M.
1967 *Sparta*, Cambridge.
Κυρτάτας, Δ.
1987 *Δούλοι, Δουλεία και δουλοκτητικός τρόπος παραγωγής*, Athens.
Lazenby, J.F.
1985 *The Spartan Army*, Warminster.
Lotze, D.
1959 *ΜΕΤΑΞΥ ΕΛΕΥΘΕΡΩΝ ΚΑΙ ΔΟΥΛΩΝ*, Berlin.
1962 'ΜΟΘΑΚΕΣ', *Historia* 11, 427–35.
MacDowell, D.M.
1986 *Spartan Law*, Edinburgh.
Michell, H.
1952 *Sparta*, Cambridge.

Mossé, Cl.
1973 'Sparte archaique', *PP* 28 , 7–20.
Oliva, P.
1971 *Sparta and her Social Problems*, Prague.
Osborne, R.
1996 *Greece in the Making 1200–479 BC*, London and New York.
Powell, A.
1988 *Athens and Sparta. Constructing Greek political and social history from 478 BC*, London.
1998 'Sixth-century Laconian vase-painting: continuities and discontinuities with the "Lykourgan" ethos', in Fisher and van Wees (eds.) *Archaic Greece*, 119–46.
Powell, A. (ed.)
1989 *Classical Sparta: Techniques behind her success*, London.
Powell, A. and Hodkinson, S. (eds.)
1994 *The Shadow of Sparta*, London and New York.
Richer, N.
1998 *Les Éphores. Études sur l'histoire et l'image de Sparte (VIIIe–IIIe siècles av. J.-C.)*, Paris.
Roobaert, A.
1977 'Le danger hilote?', *Ktèma* 2, 141–55.
Roussel, D.
1976 *Tribu et Cité*, Paris.
Roussel, P.
1961 *Sparte*, Paris.
Ruzé, F.
1994 'Les inferieurs libres à Sparte: exclusion ou integration', *Mélanges P. Lévêque*, vol. 7, 297–310.
1997 *Délibération et pouvoir dans la cité grecque de Nestor à Socrate*, Paris.
Snodgrass, A.M.
1965 'The hoplite reform and history', *JHS* 85, 110–22.
Talbert, R.J.A.
1989 'The role of the helots in the class struggle at Sparta', *Historia* 38, 22–40.
Themelis, P.
2000 *Ηρωες και Ηρώα στη Μεσσήνη*, Βιβλιοθήκη της εν Αθήναις Αρχαιολογικής Εταιρείας 210, Athens.
Thomas, C.G.
1974 'On the role of the Spartan kings', *Historia* 23, 257–70.
van Wees, H.
1999 'Tyrtaeus' *Eunomia*: nothing to do with the Great Rhetra', in S. Hodkinson and A. Powell (eds) *Sparta: New perspectives*, London, 1–41.
Whitby M.
1994 'Two *Shadows*: images of Spartans and helots', in A. Powell and S. Hodkinson (eds.) *The Shadow of Sparta*, London and New York, 87–126.

11

SETTLEMENTS OF SPARTAN *PERIOIKOI*: *POLEIS OR KŌMAI*?

Andrey Eremin

Scholars who study the history of ancient Sparta have always considered the *perioikoi* an enigmatic part of Spartan society.[1] Evidently, such an opinion is connected, in the first instance, with the condition of the literary sources we have at our disposal. The material contained in them is so fragmentary that we are able to give a definitive answer to practically no question concerning the place of the *perioikoi* in Spartan society.

Against this background one of our main issues is the question of whether Spartan *perioikoi* of the classical period were citizens of the Spartan *polis*. The controversy on this point has continued for several decades, without general agreement among scholars having been reached.[2] Indeed, in our opinion it is simply not possible to solve this problem merely on the basis of the sources dated to the classical period (that is, fifth/fourth centuries BC), or retrospectively relating to it.[3] A related issue is the question of the typological affiliation of the perioikic settlements of Laconia and Messenia, or, to be more exact, to which of the two general categories of settlements most widely attested in ancient Greece – *poleis* or *kōmai* – we should attribute the many perioikic settlements. Although this question has been raised comparatively recently,[4] it is not so narrow and particular as it might seem at first sight. Below I will try to demonstrate that these two issues are interconnected, and that they cannot be solved independently of each other.

I would argue that the character of Spartan *perioikia* can be understood only in historical perspective, that is, not unless it has been considered in its historical development from its origin up to the ultimate fate of this specific form of intercommunity dependency. In pursuing this approach, the so-called retrospective method, or the method of reverse temporal conclusions, seems to be the most suitable in our case. As is well known, Kathleen Chrimes, who was one of the first to study Sparta of the Roman period, was also the first to apply this method to Spartan history of the archaic and classical periods, in her 1949 book.[5] Nevertheless, an additional approach may be offered, one which, I suggest, will help us clarify some problems connected with the Spartan *perioikoi*. One important aim is to identify any changes in settlement practice affecting both contemporary and former Spartan *perioikoi* in the hellenistic and Roman periods.

However, before proceeding to an analysis of the sources, we must define the terms *polis* and *kōmē*.[6] Clearly, we are not in a position to give here a thorough analysis of sources and historiography on this issue. This is a subject for its own inquiry, but, for the present, the reader can be referred to the papers published under the aegis of the Copenhagen Polis Centre.[7] Briefly speaking, it should be noted that our sources are quite inconclusive, since they denote the same settlement both as *polis* and as *kōmē*, even when referring to the same period. This phenomenon is especially well attested for classical authors, including those on whose evidence writers of later periods relied.[8] Nor have modern historians yet worked out a unified approach to these concepts. Most often quantitative approaches to the problem have been used, which do not allow us to draw a sociological distinction between, let us say, a small *polis* and a large *kōmē*.[9] Historians are nowadays, however, increasingly critical of the once orthodox idea of the Greek *polis* as city-state, elaborated in the nineteenth century.[10] Accordingly, more attention is being given to the conceptualization of the *polis* reached by the Greeks themselves. As a result, it has been noted that ancient sources refer not so much to cities as such, but to their inhabitants, the citizens of these cities, that is, to the Athenians, the Spartans, the Corinthians, with the implication that a *polis* could be 'movable' and have, at least temporarily, no territory.[11] This idea is most manifest in a formulation which Thucydides (7.77.7) puts into Nikias' mouth in his speech delivered before the Athenian retreat from Syracuse in 413 BC: 'for *polis* is men not walls and vessels without men' (ἄνδρες γὰρ πόλις, καὶ οὐ τείχη οὐδὲ νῆες ἀνδρῶν κεναί).

However, we must assume that a *polis* is not just its people but a definite structured organization of people, whose character manifests itself through specific social relations between particular social groups. From this point of view, the largest social groups were the *phylai* (which typically bore different specific names in different *poleis*). Viewed anthropologically, *phylai* were associations of fictive kinship that had emerged long before the *polis* formation.[12] It is because of their quasi-kinship nature that in the process of *polis* formation the social relations between *phylai* became essentially citizenship relations. According to this formal criterion, a citizen of a classical *polis* had first of all to be a member of a *phylē*, that is, a *phyletēs*.[13]

Probably, the same could be assumed regarding the *kōmē*. In this case, however, the main social groups constituting the *kōmē* were most probably *phratriai*, which represented, as is well known, associations of *genē* or clans.[14] The relationship between the *phratriai* within the *kōmē* apparently could be either of fictive or of actual kinship through intermarriages (*epigamiai*) of their particular *oikoi* members.[15] From this perspective, the process of *kōmai* merging into the *polis* (or, to be more correct, of *oikoi* merging and through their fusion joining *phratriai* and *genē*) can be viewed as the process of synoikism.[16] This is the idea that Aristotle had of *polis* formation – namely, through the merging of *kōmai* which for him were not spatial or territorial units any more than was the *polis* itself.[17] In other words, what present-day research sometimes tends to visualise as geographical and political synoikisms,[18] were in reality secondary manifestations of an inner synoikism, a synoikism occurring at the level of smaller kinship groups.

Now that we have broached the issue of synoikism in our argument, we have grounds to ask whether there is any evidence to indicate that the process of synoikism had any effect on perioikic settlements. On the basis of our previous discussion, we should make no distinction between whether over the course of their history the settlements remained *perioikoi* as such (remaining dependent vis-à-vis Sparta) or became independent or autonomous, or even dependent on some other *polis*. Indeed we are going to analyse them from the point of view of internal organization, irrespective of any external influence. If we succeed in revealing the traces of participation of perioikic settlements (or, as it would be more correct to say, communities) in synoikism, we shall clearly be justified in considering them not as *poleis* but as *kōmai* on a path toward evolving into *poleis*, in the context of the classical period.

Given the above, it is important to trace the participation of perioikic communities in the process of synoikism not only in the classical period, but also in the hellenistic and Roman epochs, especially since the process could be quite lengthy. To trace such long-term processes, it is necessary to turn to the archaeological data which have been schematised in the maps compiled by the participants in the recent archaeological project 'The Laconia Survey'.[19] Also essential are the detailed catalogues compiled by Graham Shipley, without which any work with the cartographic material is impossible.[20] For our purpose we need only three maps, reflecting settlement practice in the classical, hellenistic and Roman periods (*Figs.* 1–3).[21]

Even at first sight the following two developments seem evident: first, the nucleation of settlements in different regions; and, second, a decline in number of settlements themselves. Thus, in particular, according to my calculations, the map of archaeological sites in Laconia shows the following number of settlements with definite dating: 136 settlements in the classical period, 112 settlements in the hellenistic period, and 107 settlements in the Roman period. So we can see a more than 21 per cent, or one-fifth, decline in the number of settlements in the Roman period in comparison with the classical period.

If we analyse in the same way the data from individual Laconian sub-regions, the picture becomes much more diverse. In some sub-regions we discover a drastic decline in the number of archaeological sites (regions CC of the Laconia Survey – North-Western Borderlands; DD – Karyes and Surrounding Area; EE – Kelephina Valley; KK – Helos plain; NN – Malea Peninsula), while in other regions we can even see some growth in their number (regions AA LS – Thyreatis; LL – Mani).[22] However, we should take into consideration the fact that in the Roman period there appeared an absolutely new type of settlement – the so-called country villa (*villa rustica*). The most famous example of such a villa is that of Herodes Atticus just inside the Thyreatis, probably on the site of, or near, perioikic Eua (region AA 5 or AA13).[23] It is quite evident that this type of settlement is not a result of the historical development of settlement practices in the classical period, and consequently we should exclude its instances from our calculations. As a result, we shall have roughly the same picture qualitatively in these sub-regions as well.

It is evident that these figures are approximate, but the general tendency seems to be quite clear. At first sight these data confirm the evidence of later authors, in particular Strabo and Pausanias, about the devastation and depopulation of Greece in the Roman period.[24] The evidence of later authors in this regard has in fact generated a deep-rooted judgement in our historiography about the decline and depopulation of Greece in the Roman period, an opinion that has become a truism in almost every ancient history textbook. However, in 1993, Susan Alcock brilliantly argued against this conclusion. Basing herself on the results of the available archaeological surveys in various regions of Greece, she concluded that the process of depopulation of rural regions, beginning in the hellenistic period and continuing in the Roman period, was accompanied by a process of nucleation and growth of urban settlements.[25] In other words, the processes that we have identified for Laconia and Messenia in the hellenistic and Roman periods were occurring in other regions of Greece as well.

It is patent that these two processes should be viewed together, as parallel and interconnected evolutions, and, indeed, as one single process. According to this interpretation, one ought not to speak about a decline, devastation or depopulation of Greece, at least as far as the whole hellenistic and Roman periods are concerned. Moreover, Alcock particularly notes that the advance of nucleation and urbanization was a direct continuation of tendencies in settlement practices which originated not later than the

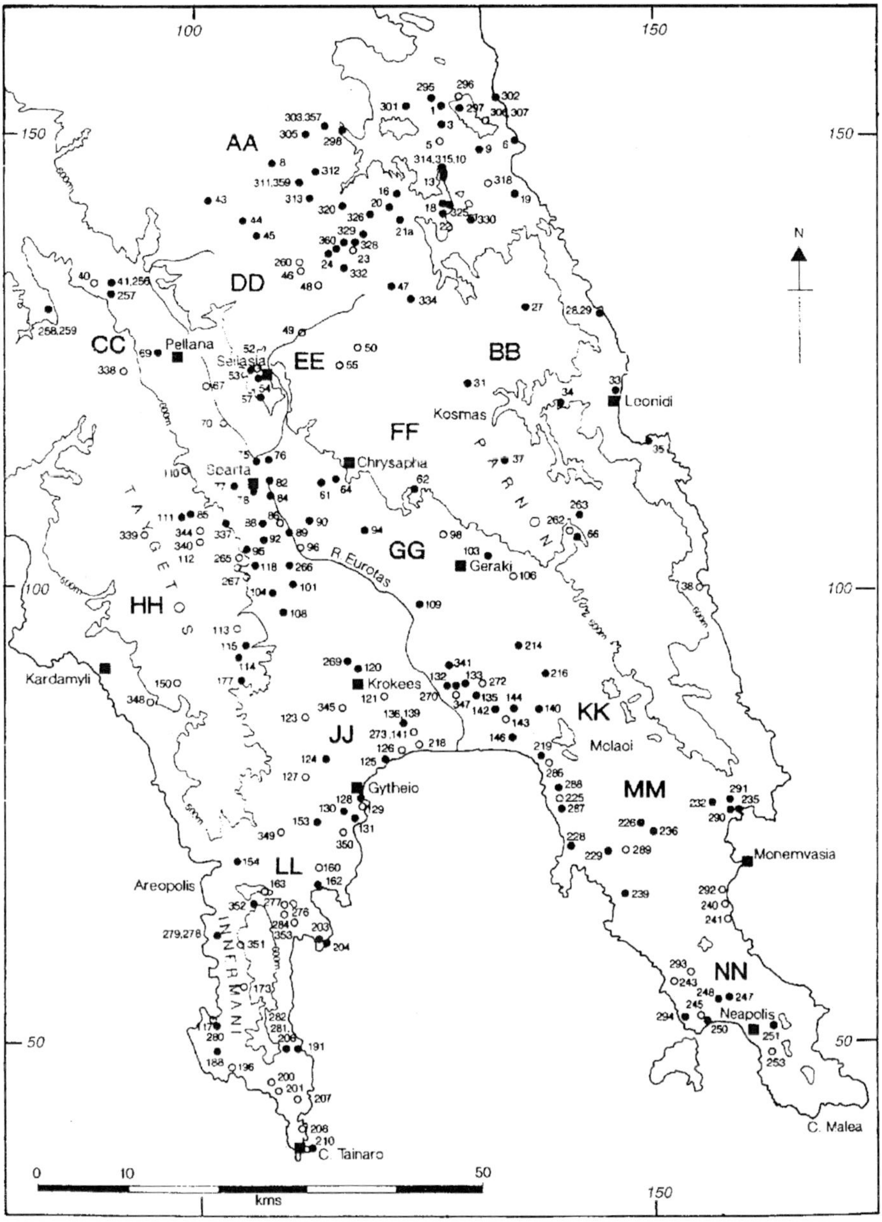

Fig. 1. Classical sites in Laconia.

classical period. The main outcome of these tendencies was the formation of new and larger settlements and communities, that is, new *poleis*.[26] In addition, such synoikism may be viewed as the most widely spread and peaceful mode of *polis* formation. Here it is unimportant exactly which

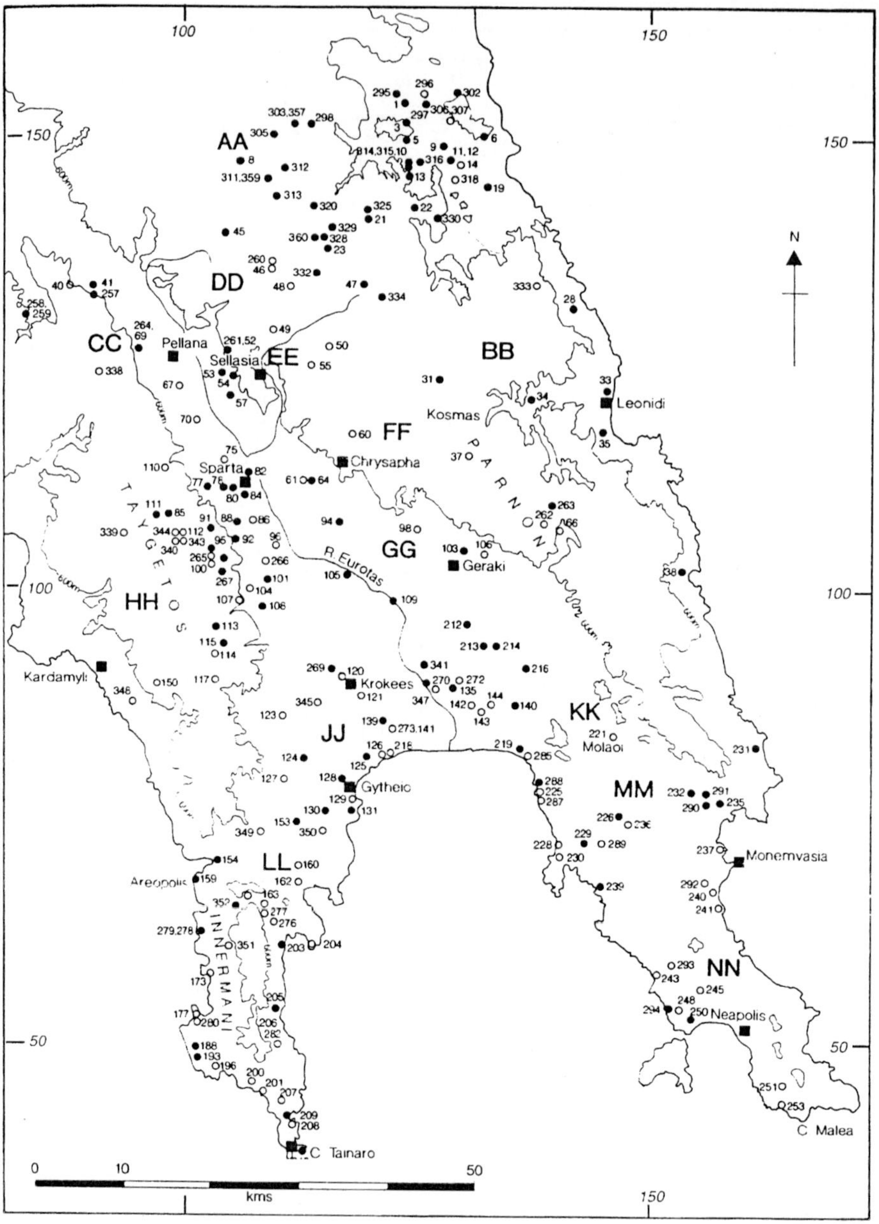

Fig. 2. Hellenistic sites in Laconia.

form one or another *polis* took as a result of a synoikism, whether a *polis* with one urban and civil centre, or a *polis* κατὰ κώμας οἰκουμένη. The important thing is that rural settlements, *kōmai*, primarily understood as related or quasi-related associations consisting of *phratriai*, *genē* and big

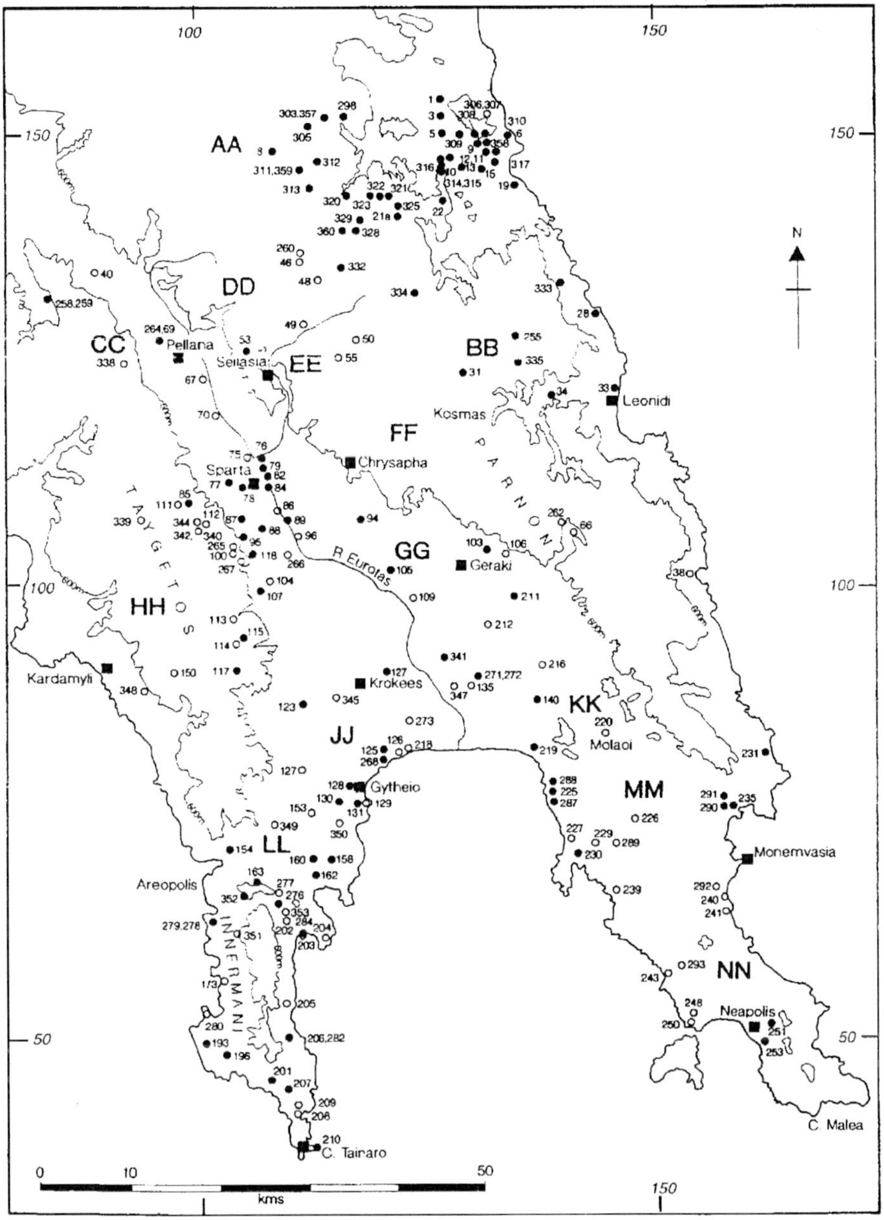

Fig. 3. Roman sites in Laconia.

families (*oikoi*), were merging into a single autonomous community, which was gradually acquiring all the structures characteristic of a *polis*.

Evidently, the process of the formation of these structures, i.e., the process of synoikism, could take quite a long period of time, depending on the general geographic or regional ecological conditions, or even on external factors. That is why ancient authors were not always able to trace such long-term processes which often took more than one generation. Hence in the sources, especially the later ones, we often read such phrases as 'the ruins of the former *polis*', 'a *polis* abandoned by its citizens', or 'a *polis* before, but now *kōmē, chōrion, polisma, polichnē*' and so on, which creates an impression that Greece was really depopulated and deserted.

Nevertheless, there is some evidence that shows how it all really happened, and it should be especially noted that perioikic settlements participated in this process. For example, let us consider the synoikism of Megalopolis,[27] which can be recognized as the earliest and best documented example of the participation by Spartan *perioikoi* in synoikism. Megalopolis was founded in the period between the battle of Leuktra (371 BC) and the battle at Mantinea (362 BC). Our main sources are Diodorus (15.72.4) and Pausanias (8.27.3–4). Diodorus' account is disappointingly brief: in particular, when speaking about the participants, he mentions twenty κῶμαι (sic) of Maenalian and Parrhasian Arcadians. Pausanias is more detailed. He gives us a list of forty-one πόλεις, which participated in the foundation of Megalopolis. In this list there are at least four names of settlements which were either explicitly or arguably perioikic. These are Aigys, Kromoi, Blenina and Leuktron. These settlements Pausanias describes as παρὰ δὲ Αἰγυτῶν, that is, as settlements of the Aigytians.

The Aigytians who lived in these settlements, took part in the foundation of Megalopolis alongside the Maenalians, Eutresians, Parrhasians, Cynurians and the citizens of several settlements belonging to Orchomenos (Paus. 8.27.3–4). It is interesting to note that in an inscription from Megalopolis itself,[28] dated to the first half of the second century, we find the names of five phylai, φυλὴ Μαιναλίων and φυλὴ Παρρασίων among them. Several conclusions can be drawn from this circumstance. First, *phylai* in Megalopolis were formed, at least partially, on a tribal basis. This is confirmed by the name of at least one other *phylē* – φυλὴ Ἀπολλωνιατῶν, which existed in Tegea as well,[29] and, as is known from Pausanias, two *oikistai* from this city took part in the foundation of Megalopolis. We may suggest that both of them belonged to the *phylē Apollōniatōn.*

Secondly, the Aigytians probably could not form even a separate *phylē* at Megalopolis out of all their supposed *poleis*, and had to enter one of the other newly formed *phylai* as one part of it. This demonstrates how small, to say the least, these former perioikic settlements could be. The fact that both the Parrhasians, by their eight settlements, and Maenalians, by their nine settlements, each formed a *phylē*, surely proves that neither their settlements, nor certainly Kromai, Blenina, Leuktron and Aigys can be considered *poleis*. In other words, they all took part in synoikism, or, to be more correct, in its initial stage, being *kōmai*, in accordance with widespread Greek practice.

As for further examples of synoikism with participation by perioikic or ex-perioikic settlements, written sources are less concrete. Nevertheless, Ulrich Kahrstedt in his *Das wirtschaftliche Gesicht Griechenlands in der Kaiserzeit* was able to trace at least four cases of late synoikism with a participation by perioikic communities. He dates one of them, Boiai, to the hellenistic period, and three others to the imperial period (Kainepolis and Las – region LL Mani, and Asopos – region MM Apidea and Molaoi Plains).[30]

According to Pausanias' evidence (3.22.11), Boiai emerged as far back as the legendary times of the Heraclids by means of a synoikism of three *poleis* – Etis, Aphrodisia(s) and Side.[31] Of these three settlements, Thucydides mentions Aphrodisia (4.56.1) and Pseudo-Scylax mentions Side (46.10) as still being in existence in their respective periods. Pausanias also speaks about the ruins of Etis within seven stadia of Boiai (3.22.13). Apparently, we should date the end of the process of synoikism to the hellenistic period, as Kahrstedt does.[32] In the Roman period, Boiai was quite a large and flourishing city.

The other three cases of synoikism and the relevant sources were analysed in detail by Kahrstedt, so we need only allude to the respective pages of his work. However, these three instances show us different modes of synoikism. In the case of Kainepolis the inhabitants of the two nearby communities – Psamathus and Hippola – joined a third community, Tainaron, and created a 'New' *polis*.[33] In the case of Las, the inhabitants of two neighbouring communities – Las and Asina – merged, moving to a new place and founding a new city, which Kahrstedt named 'New Las'.[34] Approximately the same sequence happened in the case of Asopos, where the members of this community joined the people of neighbouring Kyparissia. However, the newly-founded city remained in the old place of Asopos, and perhaps even absorbed the population of nearby Kotyrta.[35]

We should assume, therefore, that there were multiple paths toward synoikism, which could hardly be reflected precisely in the written sources. There was the mode in which a larger perioikic (or ex-perioikic) settlement was gradually joined by smaller settlements situated nearby within one geographical micro-zone. This type of synoikism, I believe, may be better documented if more detailed archaeological surveys are carried out in such zones as, for example, small shore plains or the small valleys of the western Taygetos foothills. Judging by the descriptions of Philippson and Bölte[36] and the maps of the valleys where such settlements as Prasiai,[37] Zarax[38] or

Marios[39] were situated, there could be additional smaller perioikic settlements relevant to this mode. Thus, I believe we can hope that further archaeological surveys will give us additional arguments to support the point of view expressed above.

Let me sum up the foregoing discussion, stressing its most salient conclusion. We cannot use the term *polis* when speaking about perioikic settlements of the classical period, or at least about most of them, even though this term is sometimes used by ancient authors. Most probably, these settlements can be attributed to a type of settlement (and, I emphasize, of community), which the Greeks themselves called *kōmai* or villages. Under certain conditions, perioikic *kōmai* could develop into *poleis* by way of synoikism, and this is what we observe in the hellenistic and Roman periods.[40]

In addition, we can identify their dependence on Sparta, the economic resources of the micro-zones where they initially emerged, and the various historical vicissitudes of their existence, as factors that all hindered the process of evolution from *kōmai* into *poleis*, beginning in the archaic period. And it may indeed be true that the initially unfavourable influences of geographic, environmental and, conjoined to them, demographic and socio-economic factors, strongly conditioned that these settlements turned out to be dependent on Sparta.

One further conclusion inevitably follows. As *perioikoi* of the classical period lived κατὰ κώμας and unlike, say, the Amyclaians,[41] were not included in the phyletic organization of the Spartiates, we cannot consider them citizens of the Spartan polis in the narrow, technical sense of the concept, denoting the citizenship community, where the membership of the citizen body was realized through membership of the *phylē*. It would also be incorrect to speak about a 'Lacedaemonian *polis*' where *perioikoi* could belong as citizens, even though not possessing full citizen rights.[42] Membership in the *polis*-citizenship, at least in the classical period, depended not on having certain political rights or honoured responsibilities, but rather on belonging to a kinship, or rather to quasi-kinship groups, the best known of which were *phylai*.[43] Moreover, we should assume that the perioikic communities of the classical period, which from the demographic point of view were small villages – *kōmai*, and from the social point of view were phratrial associations, could not have the idea of citizenship which was a characteristic feature of the classical Greek *poleis*.

Acknowledgements

I would like to express my sincerest and deepest gratitude to Prof. Thomas Figueira whose permanent and invaluable support I have felt for several years beginning from 1997. As it stands, this article could not have appeared without his generous help and support. I am also grateful to Dr Stephen Hodkinson and Dr Anton Powell for their invitation to take part in the Celtic Conference at Maynooth which stimulated writing this article. Dr Graham Shipley kindly agreed to read the initial version of the paper and his critical notes gave me the opportunity to define more precisely many of my theses and conclusions. I am thankful to all of them for having supplied the materials which were inaccessible to me in Russia, as well as for their commentaries and proof-reading of the English text.

My special thanks are to the Council of the British Archaeological School at Athens and to the editors of the Laconia Survey volumes (William Cavanagh, Joost Crouwel, R.W.V. Catling and Graham Shipley) for their kind permission to reproduce the maps drawn by Debora Miles on the basis of the site catalogue composed by Graham Shipley.

Notes

[1] See, e.g., Ridley 1974, 281–92; Mossé 1977, 121–4.

[2] Here it will suffice to list only major works on Spartan *perioikoi*: Niese 1906, 101–42; Hampl 1937, 1–49; Larsen 1937, 816–33; Zaikov 1988, 19–29; Shipley 1992, 211–26; Shipley 1997, 189–281; Hall 2000, 73–89; Mertens 2002.

[3] The main reason for this seems to be the inability or unwillingness of ancient authors, in the conditions of a predominantly rural mode of life, to draw in each particular case a strict sociological distinction between city (πόλις, ἄστυ) and village (κώμη, δῆμος). This distinction was only formed gradually, and both these concepts were continuously evolving under the influence of various socio-economic factors, such as, for example, the development of crafts and trade, *synoikism*, *dioikism*, the formation of different forms of dependence between communities, etc. Cf. Lévy 1986, 117–27.

[4] Cavanagh 1991, 112–13; Shipley 1992, 222.

[5] Chrimes 1949, V–VI. Naturally, I do not endorse all of her conclusions.

[6] I shall speak only of the 'classical Greek *polis*', the basic structure of which had formed by the end of the 6th/beginning of the 5th centuries BC, but not of the so-called 'Homeric' and 'Hesiodic' as being essentially different from it as well as from each other. Cf. Andreev 1976, referring to the so-called 'Homeric Polis'; Yailenko 1990, who defines Hesiodic Thespiai as an 'archaic *polis*' or a 'proto-*polis*'.

[7] Of the studies published recently in the collections of the *Centre*, an article by M.H. Hansen (1995) is of most interest for our purposes.

[8] See, e.g., the discussion on Stephanus Byzantius and Pausanias in Whitehead 1994, 99–124 and in Rubinstein 1995, 211–19.

[9] See especially Hansen 1995, 80–1. Cf. Swoboda 1924, 950–61. In this respect V. Yailenko's position (1990, 9–17) seems to me especially well grounded and considered, especially with reference to the interrelation of gentile and territorial communities, characteristic of archaic Greek society. In particular, he draws the

following scheme of this interrelation (13):

GENTILE UNITS			TERRITORIAL UNITS
ethnos (nation)	*phylai* (its subdivisions)	—	*gē, chōra* (territory, occupied by nation)
|			|
phratria (association of clans)	*genos* (clan)	—	*dēmos, kōmē* (village with its territory)

We may assume this scheme to be in general true for the classical period as well, taking into consideration, however, the fact of the emergence of the classical *polis*. As a result this scheme may probably be modified in the context of the classical period as follows:

polis (citizen community)	*phylai* (its subdivisions)	—	*politikē chōra* (territory, occupied by citizen allotments)
|			|
phratria (association of clans)	*genos* (clan)	—	*dēmos, kōmē* (village as territorial subdivision of a polis)

[10] Cf. the historiographical outline of the concept of *polis* development from classical antiquity to the present in Frolov 1988, 5–54.

[11] See especially Hampl 1939, 1–60. Cf. Gschnitzer 1958, 159–72; Utchenko 1977, 18–41; Koshelenko 1983, 9–36; Frolov 1988, 5 ff.; Demand 1990, 7–8; Raaflaub 1991, 566.

[12] This formulation follows a traditional interpretative line, according to which the original *phylai*, unlike later artificial ones, were gentile rather than territorial communities. See, e.g., Latte 1941, 994–1010; Yailenko 1989, 9–12. Cf., however, Roussel 1976, 311. For the difference between social relations within Spartan *phylai* and *syssitia*, see the brief but important note by Singor 1999, 72–3.

[13] See, e.g., Lambert 1993, 25–56 (with relevant literature in notes); Yailenko 1989, 13 with n. 25.

[14] See, e.g., Latte 1941, 746–56.

[15] With reference to the interrelation between phratries and *dēmoi/kōmai* on the one hand, and, on the other the necessary connection between membership in them and the right to belong to the citizens' community in Athens, see especially Lambert 1993, 25–57. Thus we may assume that such interrelations also existed in other Greek *poleis*.

[16] Apart from the obvious etymology of the word *synoikism* itself, I would cite a passage from Xenophon (*Hell.*, 5, 2, 12–19), which seems quite significant in this connection. In 382 BC Kleigenes, an Akanthian ambassador, draws the Spartans' attention to Chalcidian communities uniting around Olynthos and emphatically advises them to interfere immediately in this process, as later 'this union will be hard to break…if they, in accordance with the decision already adopted <by the assembly> (ἅς ἐψηφισμένοι εἰσὶ), will merge into a single unity by means of

intermarriages and acquiring property from each other (συγκλεισθήσονται ταῖς τε ἐπιγαμίαις καὶ ἐγκτήσεσι παρ' ἀλλήλοις). Kleigenes (or Xenophon) describes here the actual mechanism of synoikism and polis formation through the merging of separate families or *oikoi*. Cf. Arist., *Pol.*, 1280b30–1281a5.

[17] Arist., *Pol.*, 1252a25–1253b1. A brilliant and delicate analysis of Aristotle's *Politics* from the point of view of his methods and approaches as well as his usage of the concepts *polis*, village-*kōmē* and family-*oikos* can be found in Vilatte 1995, 27–81. See also Dovatur 1965, 7–8.

[18] See, e.g., Hansen 1995, 52–61 passim.

[19] Cavanagh W. et al. 1996.

[20] Shipley G., 'Archaeological sites in Laconia and the Thyreatis', in Cavanagh W. et al. 1996, 263–313; Shipley G. 1996, 223–281 (Part III: Catalogue: *Poleis* and Other Ancient Sites in Laconia and Messenia).

[21] Cavanagh W. et al. 1996, Ill. 23.5 (Classical Sites in Laconia); Ill. 23.6 (Hellenistic Sites in Laconia); Ill. 23.7 (Roman Sites in Laconia).

[22] The indications of regions are given in accordance with the above mentioned Laconia Survey maps and catalogues. See n. 20.

[23] Cavanagh W. et al. 1996, 277.

[24] See, e.g., Polyb., 36.17.5; Strabo, 8, C362 (with reference to Messenia and Laconia); 8, C388 (with reference to Arcadia). Pausanias constantly reports depopulated and deserted cities. See Rubinstein 1995, 211–19.

[25] Alcock 1993, 33–128 passim.

[26] Alcock 1993, 95–6.

[27] Hiller v. Gaertringen, 1931, 127–140; Moggi 1974, 71–107.

[28] *IG* V, 2, 452. Cf. Jones 1987, 136.

[29] Cf. Jones 1987, Chapter III, §6 Tegea, 130–42.

[30] Kahrstedt 1954, 192–220 (Lakonien).

[31] Philippson 1907, 718; Hirschfeld 1894, 2725; Geyer 1923, 2208.

[32] Kahrstedt 1954, 212–13. Cf. Oberhummer 1897, 627–8.

[33] Kahrstedt 1954, 207–8. Cf. Shipley 2000, 384 with nn. 151–3.

[34] Kahrstedt 1954, 209–10. Cf. Shipley 2000, 384 with n. 148.

[35] Kahrstedt 1954, 210–11. Cf. Wace and Hasluck 1907–1908, 163–5 (Asopus and Kyparissia).

[36] Philippson 1959, 412–508; Bölte 1929, 1294–1349.

[37] Wace and Hasluck 1908–1909, 174–5.

[38] Bölte 1967, 2319–21; Wace and Hasluck 1907–8, 167–73.

[39] Bölte 1930, 1804; Wace and Hasluck 1907–1908, 166–7.

[40] This tendency in the development of perioikic settlements was intuitively expressed by N. Kennell (1999, 189–210) in the title of his article 'From *Perioikoi* to *Poleis*', which is, however, to a greater extent devoted to the so-called 'League of Free Laconians'. Cf. Gitti 1939, 189–203.

[41] Pausanias calls Amyklai κώμη (3.19.6), though it is generally accepted that the Amyklaeans were a part of the Spartan citizen community, and Amyklai was one of the five Spartan ὠβαί.

[42] Cf., e.g., Hampl 1937,1 ff.; Zaikov 1988, C.20 ff.; Shipley 1996, 201 ff.; Hall 2000, 73 ff.

[43] It is from this point of view that phyletic and citizen relations were absolutely the same. Lambert is quite right when noting, regarding Athens, that the main condition of citizenship was not the place of birth or residence, but descent from parents who were Athenian citizens. This main condition in its turn involved automatic inclusion into a certain *phratria* and at the same time into a *phylē* (Lambert 1993, 27 ff.). We can assume that in Sparta this is also proved by the famous custom of bringing a new-born Spartiate to the oldest of the *phyletai* (τῶν φυλετῶν οἱ πρεσβύτατοι), which meant, among other things, an 'official' inclusion into the *phylē* and at the same time into the citizen body (Plut., *Lyc.* 16.1).

Bibliography

Alcock, S.E.

1993 *Graecia Capta. The Landscapes of Roman Greece*, Cambridge.

Andreev, Y.V.

1976 *Ranne-grecheskii polis: gomerovskii period* (Early Greek Polis: Homeric period), in Russian, Leningrad.

Bölte, F.

1929 'Sparta (Geographie)', *RE*[2] III, cols. 1294–1349.

1930 'Marios', *RE*[2] XXVIII, col. 1804.

1967 'Zarax', *RE*[2] IX A 2, cols. 2319–21.

Cavanagh, W., Crouwel, J., Catling, R.W.V., Shipley, G.

1996 *Continuity and Change in a Greek Rural Landscape: The Laconia Survey* 2, London.

Cavanagh, W.G.

1991 'Surveys, cities and synoecism', in J. Rich and A. Wallace-Hadrill (eds.) *City and Country in the Ancient World*, London and New York, 112–13.

Chrimes, K.M.T.

1949 *Ancient Sparta. A re-examination of the evidence*, Manchester.

Demand, N.H.

1990 *Urban Relocation in Archaic and Classical Greece: Flight and consolidation*, Norman.

Dovatur, A.I.

1965 *Politika i Politii Aristotelya* (Aristotle's Politics and Polities), in Russian, Moscow and Leningrad.

Frolov, E.D.

1988 Rozhdeniye grecheskogo polisa (The Birth of the Greek Polis), in Russian, Leningrad.

Geyer, F.

1923 'Side', *RE*[2] IV, col. 2208.

Gitti, A.

1939 'I perieci di Sparta e le origini del KOINON TON LAKEDAIMONION', *RAL* 15, 189–203.

Gschnitzer, F.
1958 *Abhängige Orte im griechischen Altertum*, Munich.
Hall, J.M.
2000 'Sparta, Lakedaimon and the nature of perioikic dependency', in Pernille Flensted-Jensen (ed.) *Further Studies in the Ancient Greek Polis*. Papers from the Copenhagen Polis Centre 5, Stuttgart, 73–89.
Hampl, F.
1937 'Die Lakedämonischen Periöken', *Hermes* 72, 1–49.
1939 'Poleis ohne Territorium', *Klio* 32, 1–60.
Hansen, M.H.
1995 '*Kōmē*. A study in how the Greeks designated and classified settlements which were not *Poleis*', in M.H. Hansen and K. Raaflaub (eds.) *Studies in the Ancient Greek Polis*, Papers from the Copenhagen Polis Centre 2, Stuttgart, 45–81.
Hiller v. Gaertringen, F.
1931 'Megala Polis', *RE* XXIX, cols. 127–140.
Hirschfeld, G.
1894 'Ἀφροδισία', *RE*, Halbbd. II, cols. 2725.
Jones, N.F.
1987 *Public Organization in Ancient Greece: A documentary study*, Philadelphia.
Kahrstedt, U.
1954 *Die wirtschaftliche Gesicht Griechenlands in der Keizerzeit. Kleinstadt, Villa und Domäne*, Bern.
Kennell, N.M.
1999 'From *Perioikoi* to *Poleis*. The Laconian cities in the late hellenistic period', in S. Hodkinson and A. Powell (eds.) *Sparta: New perspectives*, London, 189–210.
Koshelenko, G.A.
1983 'Drevnegrecheskii polis (Greek Polis)', *Antichnaya Greciya* (Ancient Greece) 1, in Russian, Moscow, 9–36.
Lambert, S.D.
1993 *The Phratries of Attica*, Ann Arbor.
Larsen, J.A.O.
1937 'Perioikoi', *RE* XIX, cols. 816–33.
Latte, K.
1940 'Phyle', *RE*. Halbbd. XXXIX, cols. 994–1010.
1941 'Phratrie', *RE*. Bd. XX, 1, cols. 746–56.
Lévy, E.
1986 'Apparition en Grèce de l'idée de village', *Ktema* 11, 117–27.
Mertens, N.
2002 'οὐκ ὁμοῖοι, ἀγαθοὶ δέ. The *perioikoi* in the classical Lakedaimonian *polis*', this volume.
Moggi, M.
1974 'Il sinecismo di Megalopoli', *ASNP* 4, 71–107.

Mossé, Cl.
1977 'Les perièques lacédémoniens. A propos d'Isocrate, *Panathénaique*, 177 sqq.', *Ktema* 2, 121–4.
Niese, B.
1906 'Neue Beiträge zur Geschichte und Landeskunde Lakedämons. Die Lakedämonischen Periöken', *Göttingische gelehrte Nachrichten*, 101–42.
Oberhummer, E.
1897 'Boiai', *RE*, Halbbd. V, cols. 627–8.
Philippson, A.
1907 'Etis', *RE*, Halbbd. XI, col. 718.
1959 *Die Griechischen Landschaften*, 3, 2, Frankfurt an Main.
Raaflaub, K.A.
1991 'City-state, territory, and empire in classical antiquity', in A.Molho et al. (eds.) *City States in Classical Antiquity and Medieval Italy*, Stuttgart.
Ridley, R.T.
1974 'The economic activities of the perioikoi', *Mnemosyne* 27, 281–92.
Roussel, D.
1976 *Tribu et cité*, Paris.
Rubinstein, L.
1995 'Pausanias as a source for the classical Greek *polis*' in M.H. Hansen and K. Raaflaub (eds.) *Studies in the Ancient Greek Polis*, Papers from the Copenhagen Polis Centre 2, Stuttgart, 211–19.
Shipley, G.
1992 '*Perioikos*: the discovery of classical Lakonia', in Jan Motyka Sanders (ed.) *ΦΙΛΟΛΑΚΩΝ*, *Lakonian Studies in Honour of Hector Catling*, London, 211–26.
1996 '"The other Lakedaimonians": the dependent perioikic poleis of Laconia and Messenia', in M.H. Hansen (ed.) *The Polis as an Urban Centre and as a Political Community*, Acts of the Copenhagen Polis Centre 4, Copenhagen, 189–281.
1997 'Archaeological sites in Laconia and the Thyreatis', in W. Cavanagh J. Crouwel, R.W.V. Catling, G. Shipley (eds.) *Continuity and Change in a Greek Rural Landscape: The Laconia Survey* 2, London, 263–313.
2000 'The extent of Spartan territory in the late classical and hellenistic periods', *BSA* 95, 367–90.
Singor, H.W.
1998 'Admission to the syssitia in fifth-century Sparta', in S. Hodkinson and A. Powell (eds.) *Sparta: New perspectives*, London, 67–89.
Swoboda, H.
1924 'Κώμη', *RE*. Supplbd. IV, cols. 950–61.
Utchenko, S.L.
1978 *Politicheskiye ucheniya drevnego Rima* (Political Doctrines of Ancient Rome, III–I centuries BC), in Russian, Moscow.
Vilatte, S.
1995 *Espace et temps. La cité aristotélicienne de la* Politique, Paris.

Wace, A.J.B. and Hasluck, F.W.
1907–1908 'Laconia, II. Topography. East-Central Laconia', *BSA* 14, 163–5 (Asopus and Kyparissia).
1908–1909 'Laconia, II. Topography. East-Central Laconia', *BSA* 15, 174–5.
Whitehead, D.
1993 'Site-classification and reliability in Stephanus of Byzantium', in D. Whitehead (ed.) *From Political Architecture to Stephanus Byzantius*, Papers from the Copenhagen Polis Centre 1, Stuttgart, 99–124.
Yailenko, V.P.
1989 *Archaicheskaya Gretsiya i Blizhny Vostok* (Archaic Greece and the Near East), in Russian, Moscow.
Zaikov, A.V.
1988 'Perieki v strukture spartanskogo polisa (*Perioikoi* in the structure of the Spartan Polis)', *Antichnaya drevnost' i sredniye veka* (Classical Antiquity and the Middle Ages), in Russian, Sverdlovsk, 19–29.

12

οὐκ ὁμοῖοι, ἀγαθοὶ δέ. THE *PERIOIKOI* IN THE CLASSICAL LAKEDAIMONIAN *POLIS*

Norbert Mertens

After the victory at Thermopylae in 480 BC, the Persian king Xerxes questioned Demaratus, the exiled Spartan king, about the remaining Lakedaimonians. According to Herodotus (7.234.2), Demaratus characterized them thus:

> King, the mass of all the Lakedaimonians is great and the *polies* are numerous. What you wish to learn, I shall tell you. In *Lakedaimōn* is the *polis* Sparta with about eight thousand men. All those are the same as the ones who fought here. Well, the other Lakedaimonians are not the same as those, but they are good men.[1]

Herodotus' detailed knowledge of a private conversation between Xerxes and Demaratus may be questionable.[2] Nevertheless, the passage at least provides us with a concise summary of his own perception of *Lakedaimōn* and the Lakedaimonians in the mid-fifth century BC. Since there can be hardly any doubt that the last sentence refers to the *perioikoi*, and that the term *polies* in the first sentence comprises the town Sparta as well as the perioikic settlements, two pivotal questions arise from the statement: what conclusions can be drawn, first, from the designation of the *perioikoi* as Lakedaimonians, and second, from the use of the term *polis* with reference to the perioikic settlements by Herodotus – and many other classical authors? In the present study, I want to address both these questions.

The first part deals with the status of the *perioikoi*. I shall endorse the view that they were citizens of the Lakedaimonian *polis* even though they lacked the rights of political participation enjoyed by the Spartiates. In the second and third part, I shall then turn to the status of the perioikic communities. The Copenhagen Polis Centre (CPC) has exerted a strong influence on the study of the archaic and classical Greek *polis* in recent years; under its auspices, Shipley (1997) and Hall (2000) have dealt with the perioikic communities. Based on the main assumptions advocated by the CPC, they regard them as 'city-states' in their own right which were 'dependent' on

Sparta. In this article, I shall argue for an alternative view, beginning with a critical review of the CPC's central propositions in the second part. Unlike the CPC, I think that neither the designation of the perioikic communities as *poleis*, nor the occurrence of ethnics sufficiently proves that they were 'city-states'. In the third part of this article, I shall then take a closer look at the ancient evidence concerning the perioikic communities. Apparently, they lacked some of the central features which may be associated with a *polis* according to Hansen (1997b, 31). This suggests to me that they were integrated components of the Lakedaimonian *polis* rather than 'city-states' of their own. Moreover, it sheds some doubt on the feasibility of general categorizations such as those put forward by the CPC.

It needs to be stressed that this study is restricted to the period between the Persian wars and the battle of Leuctra in 371 BC. The first individual *perioikoi* to be mentioned explicitly in the extant sources fought at Plataea (479 BC); the Boeotian confederacy's invasion of *Lakedaimōn* following the crushing defeat at Leuctra had a deep impact on Spartan history in general and – at least in a number of cases – on the relations between Spartiates and *perioikoi*.[3]

The status of the *perioikoi*

It is well known though often blurred by modern terminology that the classical sources usually refer to the Spartan state, the inhabitants of Sparta and to the Spartan army as οἱ Λακεδαιμόνιοι ('the Lakedaimonians'). In a number of cases, we can deduce from further information that *perioikoi* were included in this designation. For example, according to Herodotus' account (9.81) of the battle of Plataea, the Lakedaimonians commemorated on the Serpent Column at Delphi (*ML* 27) must have included perioikic hoplites. Thucydides (4.53.2) is even more straightforward when he refers to the inhabitants of Kythera as Λακεδαιμόνιοι...τῶν περιοίκων ('Lakedaimonians from among the *perioikoi*') in a brief general description of the island.[4] This characterization, although part of his account of an Athenian invasion, shows that the denomination of the *perioikoi* as Lakedaimonians was not restricted to military contexts.[5] The same applies to Demaratus' statement quoted above; its immediate context is the battle of Thermopylae but in itself it represents a brief description of Lakedaimonian society. First, Herodotus provides some basic information about the Lakedaimonians as a whole (they are numerous and dwell in many different settlements). After that, he distinguishes between the eight thousand Spartiates living in the *polis* Sparta and 'the other Lakedaimonians', i.e. the *perioikoi*.

Furthermore, classical authors regarded the territory roughly equivalent to modern Lakonia and Messenia as a single unit and usually termed it ἡ Λακωνική ('the *Lakōnikē*') or ἡ γῆ / ἡ χῶρα ἡ Λακεδαιμονίων ('the land / the territory of the Lakedaimonians').[6] Thus, when Thucydides (1.10.2) states that the Lakedaimonians inhabit two of the five 'parts' of the Peloponnese, he obviously has both Lakonia and Messenia in mind.[7] For him and for his contemporaries the perioikic settlements were located inside the *Lakōnikē*;[8] and this itself was not only a geographical region but identical with the territory of the Lakedaimonian *polis*.[9] Consequently, the Argives, Arkadians and others are described as 'bordering on'[10] or as direct 'neighbours'[11] of the Lakedaimonians. Xenophon (*HG* 4.7.2), for instance, explains the Spartan reluctance to send out an army against Athens or Boeotia in 388 BC with their fear of leaving 'in their rear a hostile *polis* bordering upon *Lakedaimōn* and one so large as that of the Argives'.[12] The *diabatēria*, or 'border-sacrifices', are a further case in point: the commanding king performed these before leaving *Lakedaimōn* with his army. Agis II, for example, twice unsuccessfully tried to receive good omens before entering Arkadia in 419 BC.[13] Finally, the initial reception of foreign embassies not at Sparta itself but at perioikic towns nearer the borders, such as Sellasia, and the use of a single calendar throughout *Lakedaimōn* apparently based on the name of the eponymous Spartan ephor, point towards a politically unified Lakedaimonian *polis*.[14]

These observations have led a number of scholars to the conclusion that the *perioikoi* were citizens of the Lakedaimonian *polis* who lacked the rights of political participation enjoyed by the Spartiates, particularly the right to partake in the Spartan assembly.[15] Since I am in agreement with this view, it may suffice here to refer to the detailed discussion by Hampl (1937) which was subsequently refined and in some respects expanded by Gschnitzer (1958), Shipley (1997) and Hall (2000). It needs emphasis, however, that the *perioikoi* were not 'full-citizens' as defined by Aristotle in the third book of his *Politics*. He took active participation in the process of political decision-making, and the right to hold an office, as pre-requisites of full citizenship. Aristotle was, however, well aware of the fact that his definition applied to democracies only and was not universally shared by his contemporaries.[16] As Hall (2000, 80) has put it, the *perioikoi* 'were *politai* of the Lakedaimonian state insofar as they were the freeborn male children of *Lakedaimonioi*, even if they were not fully enfranchised'.[17] Apart from descent, one may refer to the following points:

1. Kingship: the sources usually refer to a Spartan king as Λακεδαιμονίων βασιλεύς ('king of the Lakedaimonians'), i.e. king of both the Spartiates and the *perioikoi*. The kings possessed landholdings in perioikic regions which were located inside the territory of the Lakedaimonian *polis*. Furthermore, their death was announced in the whole *Lakōnikē* and a certain number of *perioikoi* took part in a royal funeral.[18]

2. Army: the *perioikoi* contributed a permanent, increasingly important and by 425 BC fully integrated part of the Lakedaimonian army. They could rise to high positions and even if an author fails to mention them explicitly, we may assume that they usually participated in a campaign, especially when the so-called *politikon strateuma* ('citizen-army') was involved.[19]
3. Cult-practice: apart from the fact that the *perioikoi* were normally present at the *diabatēria* mentioned above, they also participated in important festivals of the *polis*, such as the Promakheia and, probably, the Hyakinthia.[20] Most notably, however, the so-called Damonon stēlē (*IG* v.1.213) provides evidence for the participation of Spartiates at a range of festivals in the perioikic regions of Lakonia.[21] Among those mentioned in the inscription are the Parparonia: the festival took place at Thyrea near the Argive border and on its occasion the Lakedaimonians commemorated their victory over Argos in *c.* 546 BC and the subsequent incorporation of the Thyreatis into the territory of the *polis*.[22]
4. 'Public limitations': as is well known, many facets of Spartiate life were subject to public regulation and limitation, for instance: among males 'the right to a commemorative inscription was reserved to those who died in battle'.[23] The archaeological evidence strongly suggests that the *perioikoi* also complied with this rule because six of the nineteen ΕΝ ΠΟΛΕΜΟΙ *stēlai* we know come from the perioikic regions of Lakonia.[24]

In sum, I agree with those scholars who regard the *perioikoi* as a distinct status-group within the Lakedaimonian citizen-body. Despite their minor political status, they were born as Lakedaimonians, 'subjects' of the Spartan kings and integrated into the military and religious structure of the *polis*. Furthermore, the memorials suggest that some 'public limitations' applied to all Lakedaimonians.

Since the *perioikoi* lacked the right of political participation, the Spartiates determined the state's policy on behalf of all Lakedaimonians. Consequently, treaties concluded by the *polis* of the Lakedaimonians automatically applied to the *perioikoi*. Considered from this angle, I think it is tenable to regard the Spartiates as a governing minority.[25] Thucydides (5.31.6) seems to support this view when he explains why the Megarians and Boeotians declined to join the alliance of Argos, Corinth and Elis in 421 BC: they regarded 'the Argive democracy [as] not so advantageous for them, with their oligarchical form of government, as the Lakedaimonian constitution'.[26]

Perioikic 'city-states'?

I turn now to the status of the perioikic communities. The fundamental question is whether these communities constituted political entities of their own which could and still can be appropriately regarded as *poleis* in the sense of 'states'. Two well known facts are central to the argument: first, various classical authors recorded the perioikic settlements as *poleis* both collectively and individually and, second, ethnics are attested for some of them, such as οἱ Κυθήριοι ('the Kytherians') for the inhabitants of Kythera.[27]

According to the CPC, this is sufficient proof that the perioikic communities were *poleis* in the sense of 'town' and 'state'. Shipley (1997) described them as 'dependent *poleis*' of Sparta.[28] Subsequently, Hall (2000) has reinforced this analysis. He has also pointed out a further implication of this view, namely that the *perioikoi* enjoyed a form of 'dual membership': in their capacity as Lakedaimonians they were – together with the Spartiates – citizens of the Lakedaimonian *polis*; at the same time, they were citizens of their own 'city-states'. Hall (*op. cit.,* 81) differentiates two 'superimposed systems which structure political, civic and territorial space in Lakedaimon'. On the one hand a 'polycentric' or 'horizontal' system of numerous neighbouring *poleis* featuring their own institutions, urban centres and territories and, on the other, a 'monocentric' or 'vertical' system of one Lakedaimonian *polis* with the urban centre Sparta which comprised the whole *Lakōnikē.*

Unlike Shipley and Hall, I do not regard the perioikic communities as dependent 'states'. In this article, I shall try to argue for an alternative view. As a first step, we need a brief discussion of the assumptions and principles underlying Shipley's and Hall's as well as most other publications of the CPC.

1. One of the CPC's principles has been invested with the quality of a scientific law. According to Hansen's *Lex Hafniensis de civitate*, the archaic and classical sources applied the term *polis* in the sense of 'town' only to an urban settlement which was simultaneously considered a *polis* in the sense of 'city-state':[29] that is to say, in the sense of 'a small self-governing community of citizens living in an urban centre and its hinterland' (Hansen 1997a, 13). Hence, the undisputed designation of perioikic communities as *poleis* has been interpreted as sufficient proof that they were 'city-states'.

In contrast, Rhodes (1997, 238) has criticized the idea of a systematic and consistent use of the word *polis* by archaic and classical authors. It is not only hard to imagine their contemplating the 'appropriateness' of the term at every instance; more fundamentally, it appears questionable whether 'the Greeks' did in fact share a consistent 'ancient concept' of the *polis* at all.[30] The term was applied to all sorts of political systems and localities: to the '2,000 *poleis* in Egypt' as well as to the whole Persian empire.[31] Even though the CPC has limited the validity of the *lex Hafniensis* to Greek *poleis* for this particular reason,[32] varying usages still occur. For example, while Pindar (*O.* 7.18) called Rhodes ἡ τρίπολις νᾶσος ('the three-city island'), Herodotus (2.178.2–3) simply referred to it as one *polis* decades before the synoecism of 408/7 BC. Apparently, contemporary Greeks could use the term differently and according to diverse 'standards'. This is the implication of Isocrates' (12.179) criticism when he says that the *perioikoi* were 'in name...spoken of as dwelling in *poleis* though they had less power than our [Athenian] demes'.[33] I would, therefore, maintain that an ancient author may equally well have applied the term *polis* to a Greek settlement in the urban sense only.[34]

Consequently, when we study the use of complex concepts such as *polis*, the immediate context, the motivation of the author etc. have to be taken into consideration at every instance. I doubt that an empirically-derived 'principle' can release us from this necessity. The mere designation of a settlement, sometimes in a single source, does not constitute a sufficient basis for far-reaching conclusions about its political status.

2. According to the CPC, an ethnic which derived from a toponym designating an urban centre – as opposed to a 'civic subdivision' or a region – is a very strong indicator of the place's *polis*-status.[35]

Among others, van Wees (1997, 230) has disagreed and argued that the mere existence of an ethnic does not permit conclusions about the status of a settlement.[36] The perioikic community Oion may serve as an illustration. Xenophon (*HG* 6.5.26) called its inhabitants Οἰᾶται ('Oiatians'). According to CPC orthodoxy, he should have thus regarded Oion as a *polis*, i.e. a 'town' and a 'state'. A few lines earlier, however, he calls it a *kōmē* ('village'; *op. cit.* 6.5.24). Now, Hansen (1996) has conceded a number of what he regards as 'exemptions' from the 'rule' in the very article in which he developed it. He exempts, for instance, the use of an ethnic in a 'remote region' such as the Pontos. In these cases he claims, as opposed to Hellas 'proper', city-ethnics could be used 'to denote the place of habitation or origin only'[37] – and not necessarily citizenship. It seems to me, however, that the cumulative force of the 'exemptions' invalidates the principle altogether. A similar use of ethnics derived from other Greek toponyms cannot simply be ruled out.

3. The classification of the perioikic communities as 'dependent *poleis*' is based on the CPC's objective to dissociate the concepts of *polis* and αὐτονομία ('*autonomia*'). According to Hansen (1995), unlike the English term 'autonomy' the Greek '*autonomia*' denoted complete and unrestricted independence. Thus, since many Greek *poleis* were clearly subordinate to others, he has dismissed '*autonomia*' as one of its defining characteristics and introduced the category 'dependent' *polis*. It comprises all sorts of

communities lacking, in most cases, full independence of action in external relations – among them the perioikic *poleis* of *Lakedaimōn*.

This approach has also met with criticism.[38] While it is true that if we accept Hansen's definition of '*autonomia*', it cannot be maintained as a necessary characteristic of the *polis*, parallel to what has been said above about the term *polis*, it is again problematic simply to define the concept in the first place and regard it as invariable.[39] Again, we should allow for a wider range of meanings of '*autonomia*' and especially for subjective uses depending on the immediate context. For instance, in 386 BC the Thebans claimed that Boeotian federalism was compatible with the provisions of the King's Peace concerning '*autonomia*'. Quite understandably, Sparta disagreed and insisted on the opposite. Eventually, her greater military power at the time secured her privilege to define the concept.[40]

To sum up this discussion, I would endorse the view that neither the collective nor the individual designation of perioikic communities as *poleis* nor the occurrence of an ethnic which derived from the name of a perioikic settlement sufficiently proves them to have been 'city-states' in their own right.

The status of the perioikic communities

Explicit statements about the status of the *perioikoi* or their settlements in the Lakedaimonian *polis* are very rare in the extant ancient literature. A passage from Isocrates' *Panathēnaikos* (12.177–81) comes closest to a detailed account in both respects. He described the *perioikoi* as the *dēmos* ('people') and the *plēthos* ('mass') of the Lakedaimonians which was excluded from political participation by the Spartiates in the course of inner struggles, divided up into small groups and settled in numerous small places which, although called *poleis*, possessed less power than the Athenian demes.

Scholars disagree about Isocrates' reliability. While Mossé (1977) argues that his account is, to a certain extent, trustworthy, Shipley (1997, 202) regards it as unreliable because of Isocrates' age and, more importantly, his political bias. I agree that we should not uncritically accept his statements at face value, in particular his alleged knowledge of the origins and early development of the perioikic status. Nevertheless, we should not reject all aspects of his account outright. In fact, his comparison between the perioikic communities and the Athenian demes is not as far-fetched as might initially be suspected.

I turn now to other sources which might help to clarify the status of the perioikic communities. Hansen's (1997b, 31) distinction between a *polis* and a 'civic subdivision' (e.g. an Athenian deme or a *kōmē* of Argos) serves as a central thread for my discussion.[41] He lists a number of features which can be found not only in *poleis* but also in 'civic subdivisions': a variety of local institutions, among them assemblies in which magistrates could be elected, trials held, or honours conferred; local cults and festivals; a variety of urban features such as a defensive wall, an acropolis, temples or a theatre. At the same time, according to Hansen a 'civic subdivision' lacks a number of characteristics which apply exclusively to a *polis*:

> in contradistinction to a *polis*...a civic subdivision had [1] no prytaneion, no bouleuterion and no boule; [2] its members were citizens of the *polis* of which the subdivision was a part, and were not citizens of the civic subdivision as such; [3] a local assembly had no right to pass citizenship decrees and proxeny decrees; and [4] a local court could impose fines but was not empowered to pass a sentence of death or exile. [5] A civic subdivision did not have its own coins, and it had no right to enter into relations with foreign states. [6] The members of a civic subdivision could form a unit of the army of the *polis*, but would not operate as a separate army.

1. Concerning the first of Hansen's six features, there is no positive evidence for the existence of a *prytaneion*, a *bouleutērion* or a *boulē* in a perioikic community during the classical period. This is, of course, an argument *e silentio*, especially considering the scarcity of classical inscriptions from *Lakedaimōn* and the need for more intensive archaeological exploration of this area.[42] However, it would be hard altogether to deny the existence of local institutions and the buildings associated with them in perioikic communities. Every aspect of daily life in the vast territory of *Lakedaimōn* simply cannot have been administered by central *polis*-institutions located in Sparta.[43] I would nevertheless suggest that the designation of a perioikic town as a *polis* by a classical author does not suffice to place assumed local magistrates and institutions on a level with *prytaneis* or *boulai*. Rather, as far as we can tell from the extant sources, the competences of administrative bodies in perioikic towns did not exceed those of the institutions in 'civic subdivisions' of other *poleis*.

The existence of local administrative bodies or magistrates may also form the background to the rare allusions to some sort of communal deliberation or action in our sources.[44] For example, Thucydides (5.54.1) tells us that the Lakedaimonian army marched out in 419 BC 'and no one knew whither they were marching, not even the *poleis* from which they were sent'.[45] The *poleis* in question were those of the *perioikoi*.[46] Shipley (1997, 208) has interpreted Thucydides' statement as an indication of the perioikic communities' capacity 'to resolve to send out troops.' However, this was not for the *perioikoi* to decide. According to the *communis opinio* they were fully integrated into the structure of the Spartan army by 425 BC at the latest.[47] The ephors in Sparta mobilized the whole army and determined its overall strength. Messengers would, I suppose, transmit the number of the required age groups to the local magistrates or directly to the local assemblies of the *perioikoi* and those concerned would then march to the meeting place.[48] We may conclude from the passage quoted above that the messengers would normally also state the destination of the campaign since the *poleis*' ignorance in 419 BC appears to have been extraordinary. This case might serve as an illustration of Thucydides' (5.68.2) often-cited complaint about the Lakedaimonian state's secrecy.

2. The issue of citizenship has already been dealt with above: the *perioikoi* were citizens of the Lakedaimonian *polis*. The further assumption that they were also citizens of their own *poleis* is based entirely on the CPC's principles. There is no attestation of a *perioikos* being called a '*politēs*' of his *polis*. Special significance has been attributed to the ethnics attested for a number of perioikic communities because they are interpreted as 'city-ethnics' as opposed to 'sub-ethnics' deriving from 'civic subdivisions'. The main reason for this interpretation is Xenophon's frequent mention of Neon ὁ Ἀσιναῖος ('the Asinaian', from the perioikic town of Asine) among the Ten Thousand in Asia.[49] This is considered to be good evidence because, according to Hansen (1996, 172–3), 'sub-ethnics' are 'commonly' replaced by 'city-ethnics' abroad. Even if the objections towards the use of ethnics as evidence for the status of a settlement pointed out earlier are rejected, the qualifying expression 'commonly' should induce us to take this rule with a grain of salt. Certain Athenians operating abroad are described by their 'sub-ethnics' rather than their 'city-ethnics'. Herodotus (6.92.3), for instance, tells us that Sophanes ὁ Δεκελεύς ('the Dekeleian') killed Eurybates from Argos during a fight on the island of Aigina in 488/7 BC; and Xenophon (*HG* 5.1.26) states that Thrasyboulos ὁ Κολλυτεύς ('the Kollytean') was commander of an Athenian fleet in Thrace during the 380s BC.[50]

3. Regarding the assembly's right to grant citizenship and proxeny we can again only note our sources' silence.[51] But in the light of what has been said so far, I would not attribute this gap to the fragmentary state of our evidence.

4. A court in a civic subdivision 'could impose fines but was not empowered to pass a sentence of death or exile'.

Again, we lack explicit information about local courts in perioikic communities but I would still endorse the view that they probably existed.[52] On the other hand, there is some evidence for judicial procedure involving central *polis*-institutions: first, in the case of the island Kythera, the Spartiates each year send a *Kythērodikēs* with a company of hoplites.[53] The name of the official points towards a judicial function which apparently exceeded the authority of local institutions or magistrates.

Second, in Xenophon's (*HG* 3.3.4–11) account of the abortive conspiracy of Kinadon, the ephors send Kinadon on an ostensibly official mission to perioikic Aulon with orders to arrest a number of helots and locals. As Xenophon points out, Kinadon does not become suspicious because he had carried out similar missions before. It is difficult to assess the authenticity of the whole story but I would agree with Lazenby (1997, 442), who has argued that, even if some details about Kinadon himself and his conspiracy appear exaggerated, Xenophon's depiction of its setting is to a great extent reliable.[54] Therefore, under specific circumstances *perioikoi* stood under the direct jurisdiction of central authorities. It appears to have been quite normal for the ephors to send out somebody (who was not himself a Spartiate) to a perioikic town with a warrant of arrest and to deal with these persons in Sparta. On Kythera the situation was different; the practice of sending out an official with (among others?) judicial powers who stayed there for one year may, I suppose, not only be due to the great vulnerability and strategic importance of the island but also to its remoteness which rendered the alternative procedure impracticable.

Irrespective of this, the question remains how the ephors would deal with an arrested *perioikos*. In this connection we may recall Isocrates' (12.181) assertion that 'the ephors have the power to put to death without trial as many [*perioikoi*] as they please'.[55] This has been rejected as an exaggeration.[56] However, Xenophon's account of the regime of the so-called Thirty Tyrants in Athens in 404/3 BC includes an interesting parallel: Whitehead (1982/83) and Krentz (1982, 64–8 and 82) saw the Thirty's main objective as emulating the example of the idealized Spartan *politeia* by deliberately remodelling the Athenian constitution and society.[57] Individual members of the group (most notably Kritias)[58] have been identified as sympathisers of *Lakedaimōn* and strong 'Spartan overtones' have been attributed to certain measures and institutions.[59] For instance, the institution of the Thirty itself – which is said to have been modelled on the *gerousia* – the five ephors who preceded them and the 300 lash-bearers.[60] Furthermore, the Thirty compiled a catalogue of three thousand Athenians who supposedly had a share in the status of full-citizens and were thus turned effectively into Athenian *homoioi*.[61] Their number has been explained as an estimate of the total number of Spartiates at the time.[62] In contrast to them, the Athenians 'outside the catalogue' not only lacked the right of political participation but were also expelled from the *asty* ('inner city').[63]

Of particular interest is the diverging judicial treatment of the two groups. Xenophon (*HG* 2.3.51) has Kritias mention 'new laws' which gave the *boulē* the final say whenever a capital punishment was imposed on one of the Three Thousand. In contrast to that, the Thirty could simply decide to put to death an Athenian 'outside the catalogue'. If interpreted as a part of the imitation of Sparta,[64] these 'new laws' might offer a feasible background for Isocrates' description of the *perioikoi*'s judicial treatment by the ephors. In both cases, leading *polis*-institutions would have been able to sentence to death citizens who were not fully enfranchised, without a 'proper' trial. However, the ephors' use of their legal power was not necessarily as cruel and repressive as Isocrates wants us to believe, since they had no reason for killing *perioikoi* at random. On balance, Hansen's dictum that courts in 'civic subdivisions' could not pass death sentences seems to hold true for the putative local courts in perioikic communities as well.

5. First, it is well known that no coins were minted in *Lakedaimōn* before *c.* 260/50 BC; instead, those of other *poleis* were used.[65] Second, there is widespread agreement that perioikic communities had no foreign relations of their own.[66]

6. I have pointed out above that the perioikic hoplites were integrated into the smallest units of the Lakedaimonian army together with the Spartiates – with the sole exception of the *Skiritai*.[67] Even the *Skiritai*, however, constituted 'a unit of the army of the *polis*, but would not operate as a separate army'.[68]

In sum, there is no evidence in perioikic communities for the existence of institutions and competences associated with a 'state'. Rather than citizens of their own communities, the *perioikoi* were Lakedaimonians. The perioikic communities did not grant citizenship or proxeny. The power over life and death, as well as foreign relations, was restricted to central *polis*-institutions. The *perioikoi* were an integral part of the Lakedaimonian army.

The perioikic communities appear to fit Hansen's category of 'civic subdivision' more closely than the category of 'dependent *polis*'. However, they were clearly not incorporated into the political mechanism of the Lakedaimonian *polis* in a way comparable to the incorporation of Attic demes in the Athenian *polis* – which is, in my opinion, what Isocrates (12.179) was getting at in his comparison of the perioikic communities and the Attic demes: even though they are sometimes called *poleis*, they are relatively 'powerless'. Consequently, since the perioikic communities do not exactly fit into either category, the present example suggests that the stark choice between the two is a simplification. Alternatively, we should reckon with a more varied spectrum of 'levels of integration' in classical Greece. Within such a spectrum, the perioikic communities represent a lower level of integration into the overall structure of the *polis* than the Attic demes. Nevertheless, on a sliding scale they are nearer to the highly integrated demes than they are to Hansen's ideal type of a 'dependent *polis*'. At the same time, some Greek communities may have been even less integrated than the perioikic ones and others even more so than the Attic demes. In each individual case, the exact 'level of integration' can only be determined by a close study of the extant sources.

Conclusion

The evidence suggests that the Lakedaimonian *polis* of the fifth and early fourth centuries BC was a politically unified entity. The *perioikoi* were Lakedaimonian citizens who lacked the right of political participation, most notably in the assembly. The facts that the perioikic communities were on some occasions called *poleis* and could generate an ethnic do not automatically make them distinct political entities in the sense of 'dependent states'. Instead, they were 'components' of *Lakedaimōn*, i.e. integrated into the political structure of the Lakedaimonian *polis* – although on a relatively low level when compared with the Attic demes.

This view is compatible with the probable existence of local administration and institutions. It does not contradict the existence of a feeling of local identity and of belonging to a small community. This sort of local identity is independent of the political status and may be considerable even in highly integrated 'civic subdivisions': according to Thucydides (2.16.2), the Athenians who had to leave the countryside and move into the area enclosed by the Long Walls because of Perikles' strategy felt 'as if each of them had to leave his own *polis*'.[69]

Thus, I would agree in principle with Hall's (2000, 81) analysis of the two systems 'which structure political, civic and territorial space in Lakedaimon'. There was a 'polycentric' one of numerous local communities scattered all over the *Lakōnikē* and a 'monocentric' one of a single Lakedaimonian *polis*. However, in contrast to Hall, I would not place the two systems on the same political level. As Demaratus points out to Xerxes in the passage quoted at the start of this article: the *perioikoi* were Lakedaimonians and good men – but they were not *homoioi*.

Acknowledgements

I would like to thank the editors for their comments on the original version of this paper. Special thanks are due to Stephen Hodkinson for his longstanding and tireless support of my work. I am also grateful to the audience at Maynooth for helpful advice and citicism, especially Graham Shipley, Stefan Rebenich, Thomas Figueira, and Nino Luraghi, and to Hans van Wees and Peter Spahn who have read and commented on earlier drafts of this paper.

Notes

[1] Ὦ βασιλεῦ, πλῆθος μὲν πολλὸν πάντων τῶν Λακεδαιμονίων καὶ πόλιες πολλαί· τὸ δὲ θέλεις ἐκμαθεῖν, εἰδήσεις. ἔστι ἐν τῇ Λακεδαίμονι Σπάρτη πόλις ἀνδρῶν ὀκτακισχιλίων μάλιστα. [και] οὗτοι πάντες εἰσὶ ὁμοῖοι τοῖσι ἐνθάδε μαχεσαμένοισι· οἵ γε μὲν ἄλλοι Λακεδαιμόνιοι τούτοισι μὲν οὐκ ὁμοῖοι, ἀγαθοὶ δέ.

[2] Cf. Fehling 1989, 205: 'How anyone can see anything more than absolutely free creations by the author in Xerxes' conversations with Demaratus in 7.101–4 and 7.234–7 ...is incomprehensible to me, and I see no need to put forward any special arguments on these.' *Pace*, among others, Hornblower 1987, 25 who thinks that Herodotus may have met Demaratus in the Troad in Asia Minor where he settled on land given to him by the Persian king.

[3] *Perioikoi* at Plataea: Hdt. 9.11.3; for Leuctra and its consequences see Cartledge and Spawforth 1989, 3–15.

[4] Cf. also Thuc. 4.54.3. For 'Lakedaimonians of the ὅμοιοι' (i.e. Spartiates) see Xen. *An.* 4.6.14: ὑμᾶς γὰρ ἔγωγε, ὦ Χειρίσοφε, ἀκούω τοὺς Λακεδαιμονίους ὅσοι ἐστὲ τῶν ὁμοίων εὐθὺς καὶ ἐκ παίδων κλέπτειν μελετᾶν...

[5] *Pace* Cartledge 1979, 178; 2001, 23.

[6] Cf. Shipley 1997, 272–3.

[7] The five μοίραι were Lakonia, Messenia, Achaia, Argolis and Arkadia/Elis; cf. Hornblower 1992, 34.

[8] Cf., e.g., Hdt. 7.168.2, 8.73.2 (Pylos, Tainaron and Kardamyle); Thuc. 2.25.1 (Methone) and Xen. *HG* 7.1.25 (Asine).

[9] Cf., e.g., Thuc. 8.2.3, 8.5.3; Xen. *HG* 2.1.14. Isocrates (6.28) provides further illustration of this point from a Spartan perspective when his 'Archidamus' laments the loss of Messenia: μὴ τοῦτ' εἶναι χαλεπώτατον, εἰ τῆς χώρας στερησόμεθα παρὰ τὸ δίκαιον, ἀλλ' εἰ τοὺς δούλους τοὺς ἡμετέρους ἐποψόμεθα κυρίους αὐτῆς ὄντας.

[10] Lys. 34.7: τοὺς [Ἀργείους] μὲν ὁμόρους ὄντας Λακεδαιμονίοις...

[11] Aristotle (*Pol.* 1269b3–4) refers to the Argives, Arkadians and Messenians (after their liberation) as 'neighbours' (γειτνιῶντες) of Sparta.

[12] ὄπισθεν καταλιπόντας ὅμορον τῇ Λακεδαίμονι πολεμίαν καὶ οὕτω μεγάλην τὴν τῶν Ἀργείων πόλιν...

[13] Thuc. 5.54.2 and 5.55.3.

[14] Cf. Xen. *HG* 2.2.13–19; Hodkinson 2000, 148 n. 41 (foreign embassies) and Xen. *HG* 2.3.10; *IG* v.1.1228–32 (calendar).

[15] For a different view cf. Eryomin (this volume).

[16] Arist. *Pol.* 1275a22–3 and 1275b5–6. Cf. Schütrumpf 1991, 388: 'D.h. der Bürger bei Ar[istoteles] ist der Aktiv- oder Vollbürger.' Schütrumpf (ibid.) interprets Aristotle's definition as a polemic against Plato (e.g. *Plt.* 414e5, 416d1 and 463a4): 'Hiermit unterscheidet Ar[istoteles] sich von der Bürgerbestimmung des platon[ischen] Staates, wo Krieger, Handwerker und Bauern, die *keine* politischen Rechte haben, doch Bürger genannt waren...'.

In an inscription from Cyrene (*SEG* 9.1) – dated to 321 BC (Bertrand 1992, 145) – the right of political participation is restricted to 10,000 men who constitute the *politeuma*, i.e. the politically effective citizen-body. Nevertheless, men not belonging to this group are also termed *politēs*. According to Taeger (1929, 439–41), this inscription finally falsified the dominant Aristotelian view of Greek citizenship. Similarly, Gschnitzer 1958, 154 n. 2: 'Unter 'Bürgerrecht' verstehe ich...die Staatsangehörigkeit, die Mitgliedschaft im Staatsverband, die in der Führung des Ethnikons zum Ausdruck kommt. Ich kann diesen Begriff nicht auf den (in aristokratischen Staaten viel engeren) Kreis jener einschränken, die zur Teilnahme an der Regierung berechtigt sind...'. See also Busolt 1920, 220; Hampl 1937, 3 n. 3; Lauffer 1981, 377–8; Spahn 1988, 415–16; Whitehead 1991, 135–41.

[17] Accordingly, liberated helots were – as *neodamōdeis* – promoted to the same Lakedaimonian *dēmos*; cf. Shipley 1997, 203.

[18] Cf. Xen. *Lac.* 15.3 (landholdings); Hdt. 6.58.1 (royal funeral).

[19] Individual *perioikoi* in the army: Thuc. 8.6.4–5, 8.22.1; πολιτικὸν στράτευμα: Xen. *HG* 4.4.19, 5.3.25, 5.4.41, 7.4.20–7. A detailed reconstruction is hardly possible; however, most scholars agree that Spartiates and *perioikoi* jointly formed the smallest units of the army, the *enōmotiai*, following a military reform before 425 BC; cf. Toynbee 1969, 366; Cartledge 1979, 256–7.

[20] Cf. Sosibius *FGrH* 595 F 4 (Promakheia); Polycrates *FGrH* 588 F 1 (Hyakinthia). *Pace* Cartledge (2001, 20), who claims that 'the only non-Spartans [i.e. non-Spartiates] present at the Hyakinthia...were Helots'. However, in my opinion the *politai* mentioned by Polycrates may have included *perioikoi*; furthermore, according to Thucydides (5.23.4) even foreign guests could be present at the Hyakinthia.

[21] For the *stēlē*: Hodkinson 2000, 303–7.

[22] Cf. Ziehen 1929, 1510.

[23] Hodkinson 2000, 251; cf. his detailed discussion of the 'restrictions on the deployment of wealth', ibid. 209–70.

[24] *IG* v.1.918, 921, 1124, 1125, 1320, 1591; cf. Hodkinson 2000, 267 n. 42.

[25] Cf., e.g., Welwei 1998, 12–13; Walter 1993, 174–5.

[26] νομίζοντες σφίσι τὴν Ἀργείων | δημοκρατίαν, αὐτοῖς ὀλιγαρχουμένοις, ἧσσον ξύμφορον εἶναι τῆς Λακεδαιμονίων πολιτείας.

[27] Thuc. 7.57.6; cf. Shipley 1997, 207–9 and 226–36.

[28] Op. cit. 206–12.

[29] Hansen 1997, 19.

[30] Cf. also van Wees 1996, 236; Burckhardt 1998, 513. Hornblower (1987, 97) points out Thucydides' imprecise usage of 'crucial words' such as αὐτονομία.

[31] Cf. Hdt. 2.97.1, 2.177.1 (Egypt); A. *Pers.* 213 (Persia).

[32] Hansen 1997, 19.

[33] ὀνόμασι μὲν προσαγορευομένους ὡς πόλεις οἰκοῦντας, τὴν δὲ δύναμιν ἔχοντας ἐλάττω τῶν δήμων τῶν παρ' ἡμῖν.

[34] Cf. e.g. Hampl 1937, 48–9.

[35] Hansen 1996, *passim*.

[36] Cf. also Bowden 1996, 30: The ethnic Ναυκρατίτης on a late-fifth-century tombstone from Athens 'is not proof that Naukratis had formal citizenship.'

Furthermore, even though the κληροῦχοι on Imbros and Lemnos were Athenian citizens (cf. *IG* i³.1164 and 1165), Thucydides (3.5.1; 4.28.4) calls them Ἴμβριοι and Λήμνιοι; cf. Welwei 1999a, *passim*.

37 Hansen 1996, 185.

38 Cf. Mitchell 1999, 150; van Wees 1997, 230; Rhodes 1997, 238 and Welwei 1999, 506.

39 Cf. Spahn 1999, 720: 'Es ist evident, daß man einen so komplexen historischen Grundbegriff wie "Polis" weder einfach definieren noch allein am griechischen Wort und seinem Auftauchen in den Quellen festmachen kann. Das gleiche muß aber auch für solche eng mit der Polis zusammenhängende Kategorien wie *autonomia* gelten.'

40 Cf. Xen. *HG* 5.1.31–4.

41 In general, Hansen's description follows the findings of Jones (1987), who has used the alternative designation as 'public units'.

42 However, even extensive archaeological exploration would not solve the difficulties of identification due to the general modesty of classical buildings of the specified type; cf. Hansen and Fischer-Hansen 1994, *passim*.

43 Cf. Shipley 1997, 210.

44 Cf. the sources collected by Shipley (op. cit. 207–9).

45 ᾔδει δὲ οὐδεὶς ὅποι στρατεύουσιν, οὐδ' αἱ πόλεις ἐξ ὧν ἐπέμφθησαν.

46 Cf. de Ste Croix 1972, 345–6.

47 Cf. above n. 19.

48 Cf. Thuc. 4.8.1; Xen. *HG* 3.5.7, 5.1.33.

49 Xen. *An.* 5.3.4, 5.6.36 etc.

50 Dekeleia was a mesogeia-*dēmos* north-east of Athens and Kollytos an asty-*dēmos* in the centre of Athens (south-west of the acropolis); cf. Traill 1975, map 2.

The ancient authors' usage of 'ethnics' probably should not be given too much weight: Neon, although normally called Ἀσιναῖος, can also be termed Λακωνικός (Xen. *An.* 7.2.29). Dexippos ὁ Λάκων περίοικος (Xen. *An.* 5.1.15) is probably identical with Dexippos ὁ Λακεδαιμόνιος who, according to Diodorus (13.85.3, 87.5, 88.7, 93.1) citing Timaios of Tauromenion (*c.* 350–260 BC), enjoyed high regard in Sicily in 406 BC διὰ τὴν πατρίδα. Although this source does not disprove it, it might shed some doubt on Hansen's (1996, 185) argument *e silentio* that 'there is no attestation [in an archaic or classical source] of Λακεδαιμόνιος being used individually as the surname of one of the perioikoi'.

51 One may point towards the proxeny decree from Argos (*SEG* 13.239; cf. Jeffery 1990, 169 No. 22; *c.* 475 BC) and the proxeny-list from Keos (*IG* xii.5.1.542; *c.* 360 BC). However, according to the former, the Argives made Gnosstas of Oinous (Γνόσσταν τὸν Ϝοινόντιον) their proxenos; we do not hear of a similar measure by a local assembly in Oinous. The same applies *mutatis mutandis* to the inscription from Keos. Furthermore, as Cartledge (1979, 216) points out, the Argives' decision 'has rightly been interpreted as a deliberate affront to Sparta [and] could represent a deliberate attempt to create or exploit sympathy for Argos at least among the Perioikoi of northern Lakonia…' .

52 Cf. Larsen 1937, 821.

[53] Thuc. 4.53.2.

[54] Xenophon had no reason to insert wrong details in these relatively minor points which would have put the credibility of the whole narrative at risk.

[55] ἔξεστι τοῖς ἐφόροις ἀκρίτους ἀποκτεῖναι τοσούτους ὁπόσους ἂν βουληθῶσιν.

[56] Cf., e.g., Cartledge 1979, 179.

[57] Cf. also Lehmann (1997, 51) who regards the 'Faszinationskraft eines Programmes der konsequenten inneren Umgestaltung Athens nach dem Staatsmodell der seit 405/4 so triumphal dominierenden Siegermacht Sparta' as one of the main reasons for the oligarchs' political unity during the revolution.

[58] Whitehead (1982/83, 114) dubbed him the 'philolakon-in-chief'. Cf. op. cit. 111–17 for other individuals.

[59] Brock 1989, 163 with n. 31.

[60] Cf. Lys. 12.43–4; Xen. *HG* 2.3.21–2. Whitehead 1982/83, 123: 'in constituting themselves as a body of thirty (having previously operated through a five-man ephorate), Kritas and his associates were perceiving themselves as a gerousia in the Spartan mould'. Besides, the brutal attacks on rich metics smack of Spartan ξενηλασία; cf. Arist. *Ath.* 31.1; Xen. *Lac.* 4.3, *HG* 3.3.9.

[61] Xen. *HG* 2.3.18: ἐκ τούτου μέντοι Κριτίας καὶ οἱ ἄλλοι τριάκοντα…καταλέγουσι τρισχιλίους τοὺς μεθέξοντας δὴ τῶν πραγμάτων. Cf. op. cit. 2.3.19, Arist. *Ath.* 36.2.

[62] Cf., e.g., Brock 1989, 163.

[63] Cf. Xen. *HG* 2.3.20; 2.4.1; Lys. 25.22: τοὺς δὲ ἄλλους πολίτας ἐκ τοῦ ἄστεως ἐκκεκηρυγμένους. Lysias here calls the Athenians 'outside the catalogue' πολίται even though they were not fully enfranchised. According to Krentz 1982, 66, the oligarchs and the Three Thousand dominated the city while the other Athenians were reduced to the status of Athenian *perioikoi*. In addition, it is noteworthy that Xenophon's (*Mem.* 2.7.2) Aristarchos complains about the ὀλιγανθρωπία…ἐν τῷ ἄστει during that time.

[64] As done by Lehmann (1997, 51 n. 60): 'Als imitative "Anleihe" bei der Staatsordnung des spartanischen "Kosmos" dürfen die von Kritias im Theramenes-Prozeß angesprochenen "neuen Gesetze" des Regimes gelten…, die ausdrücklich alle Athener, die nicht zum Bürgerverband der "Dreitausend" zählten, ohne Anspruch auf rechtliches Verfahren mit Leib und Gut den Willkürentscheidungen und Maßnahmen des Regierungsgremiums der "Dreißig" unterwarfen und sie damit dem Status der deklassierten Perioiken Lakedaimons oder gar der Heloten-Existenz annäherten…'.

[65] Cf. Hodkinson 2000, 154–82 and Christien and Figueira (this volume).

[66] Cf., e.g., Cartledge 1979, 178.

[67] Σκιρῖται: Xen. *Lac.* 12.3, 13.6; Thuc. 5.67.1; Diod. 15.32.1; army-organization cf. above n. 19.

[68] Hansen 1997b, 31.

[69] ἢ πόλιν τὴν αὐτοῦ ἀπολείπων ἕκαστος.

Bibliography

Bertrand, J.-M.

1992 *Inscriptions historiques grecques*, Paris.

Bowden, H.

1996 'The Greek settlement and sanctuaries at Naucratis: Herodotus and archaeology', in Hansen and Raaflaub (eds.) *More Studies in the Ancient Greek Polis*, 17–37.

Brock, R.

1989 'Athenian oligarchs. The numbers game', *JHS* 109, 160–4.

Burckhardt, L.

1998 Review of Hansen (ed.) 1995, *Klio* 80, 513–14.

Busolt, G.

1920 *Griechische Staatskunde. Erste Hälfte: Allgemeine Darstellung des griechischen Staates*, Munich.

Cartledge, P.

1979 *Sparta and Lakonia. A regional history, 1300–362 BC*, London.

1987 *Agesilaos and the Crisis of Sparta*, London.

2001 *Spartan Reflections*, London.

Cartledge, P. and Spawforth, A.

1989 *Hellenistic and Roman Sparta. A tale of two cities*, London and New York.

de Ste Croix, G.E.M.

1972 *The Origins of the Peloponnesian War*, London.

Fehling, D.

1989 *Herodotus and his 'Sources': Citation, invention and narrative art*, trans, J.G. Howie, Leeds.

Gschnitzer, F.

1958 *Abhängige Orte im Griechischen Altertum*, Munich.

Hall, J.

2000 'Sparta, Lakedaimon and the nature of perioikic dependency', in P. Flensted-Jensen (ed.) *Further Studies in the Ancient Greek Polis*, Stuttgart, 73–89.

Hampl, F.

1937 'Die Lakedaemonischen Perioeken', *Hermes* 72, 1–49.

Hansen, M.H.

1995 'The 'autonomous city-state'. Ancient fact or modern fiction?', in Hansen and Raaflaub (eds.) *Studies in the Ancient Greek Polis*, 21–43.

1996 'City-ethnics as evidence for polis identity', in Hansen and Raaflaub (eds.) *More Studies in the Ancient Greek Polis*, 169–96.

1997 'The Copenhagen inventory of the poleis and the *Lex Hafniensis de Civitate*', in L.G. Mitchell and P.J. Rhodes (eds.) *The Development of the Polis in Archaic Greece*, London, 9–23.

1997a 'Πόλις as a generic term for state', in Nielsen (ed.) *Yet More Studies in the Ancient Greek Polis*, 9–15.

1997b 'A typology of dependent poleis', in Nielsen (ed.) *Yet More Studies in the Ancient Greek Polis*, 29–37.

Hansen, M.H. (ed.)

1995 *Sources for the Ancient Greek City-State, Symposium August, 24–27 1994*, Copenhagen.

1996 *Introduction to an Inventory of Poleis. Symposium August, 23–26 1995*, Copenhagen.

Hansen, M.H. and Fischer-Hansen, T.

1994 'Monumental political architecture in archaic and classical Greek *poleis*. Evidence and historical significance', in D. Whitehead (ed.) *From Political Architecture to Stephanus Byzantius. Sources for the ancient Greek polis*, Stuttgart, 23–90.

Hansen, M.H. and Raaflaub, K.A. (eds.)

1995 *Studies in the Ancient Greek Polis*, Stuttgart.

1996 *More Studies in the Ancient Greek Polis*, Stuttgart.

Hodkinson, S.

2000 *Property and Wealth in Classical Sparta*, London.

Hornblower, S.

1987 *Thucydides*, London.

1992 *A Commentary on Thucydides, Vol. I, Books I–III*, Oxford.

Jeffery, L.H.

1990 *The Local Scripts of Archaic Greece*. Revised edn of the original 1961 edn, with a supplement by A.W. Johnston, Oxford.

Jones, N.F.

1987 *Public Organization in Ancient Greece: A documentary study*, Philadelphia.

Krentz, P.

1982 *The Thirty at Athens*, Ithaca.

Larsen, J.A.O.

1937 'Περίοικοι', *RE* XIX,1, cols. 816–33.

Lauffer, S.

1981 'Πολίτης', in E.C. Welskopf (ed.) *Soziale Typenbegriffe im alten Griechenland und ihr Fortleben in den Sprachen der Welt. Band 3: Untersuchungen ausgewählter altgriechischer sozialer Typenbegriffe*, Berlin, 376–84.

Lazenby, J.F.

1997 'The conspiracy of Kinadon reconsidered', *Athenaeum* 85, 437–47.

Lehmann, G.A.

1997 *Oligarchische Herrschaft im klassischen Athen: zu den Krisen und Katastrophen der attischen Demokratie im 5. und 4. Jahrhundert v. Chr.*, Opladen

Meiggs, R. and Lewis, D.M. (eds.)

1988 *A Selection of Greek Historical Inscriptions to the end of the 5th Century* BC, rev. edn, Oxford.

Mitchell, L.G.

1999 Review of Hansen and Raaflaub (eds.) 1996, *CR* 49, 149–51.

Mossé, C.

1977 'Les périèques lacédémoniens. A prospos d'Isocrate, *Panathénaïque*, 177 sqq.', *Ktema* 2, 121–4.

Nielsen, T.H. (ed.)

1997 *Yet More Studies in the Ancient Greek Polis*, Stuttgart.

Rhodes, J.P.

1997 Review of Hansen (ed.) 1996 and Hansen and Raaflaub (eds.) 1996, *JHS* 117, 236–8.

Ridley, R.T.

1974 'The economic activities of the Perioikoi', *Mnemosyne* 27, 281–92.

Schütrumpf, E.

1991 *Aristoteles. Politik, Buch II–III*, Darmstadt.

Shipley, G.

1997 '"The other Lakedaimonians": The dependent perioikic poleis of Laconia and Messenia', in M.H. Hansen (ed.) *The Polis as an Urban Centre and as a Political Community. Symposium August, 29–31 1996*, Copenhagen, 189–281.

Spahn, P.

1988 'Aristoteles', in I. Fetscher and H. Münkler (eds.) *Pipers Handbuch der Politischen Ideen, Band 1*, Munich, 397–437.

1999 Review of Hansen and Raaflaub (eds.) 1996, *HZ* 268, 720–1.

Taeger, F.

1929 'Zum Verfassungsdiagramm von Kyrene', *Hermes* 64, 432–57.

Toynbee, A.

1969 *Some Problems of Greek History*, Oxford.

Traill, J.S.

1975 *The Political Organization of Attica. A study of the demes, trittys, and phylai, and their representation in the Athenian council*, Princeton.

van Wees, H.

1996 Review of Hansen (ed.) 1995 and Hansen and Raaflaub (eds.) 1995, *G&R* 43, 236–7.

1997 Review of Hansen (ed.) 1996 and Hansen and Raaflaub (eds.) 1996, *G&R* 44, 229–31.

Walter, U.

1993 *An der Polis teilhaben: Bürgerstaat und Zugehörigkeit im archaischen Griechenland*, Stuttgart.

Welwei, K.-W.

1998 *Die griechische Polis. Verfassung und Gesellschaft in archaischer und klassischer Zeit*, rev. edn, Stuttgart.

1999 Review of Hansen and Raaflaub (eds.) 1996, *Klio* 81, 505–6.

1999a 'Kleruchoi', *DNP* 6, cols. 598–9.

Whitehead, D.

1982/3 'Sparta and the Thirty Tyrants', *AncSoc* 13/14, 105–30.

1991 'Norms of citizenship in ancient Greece', in A. Molho, K.A. Raaflaub and J. Emlen (eds.) *City States in Classical Antiquity and Medieval Italy*, Stuttgart, 135–54.

Ziehen, L.

1929 'Sparta (Kulte)', in *RE* IIIA2, 1453–1525.

13

SPARTA COMPARED: ETHNOGRAPHIC PERSPECTIVES IN SPARTAN STUDIES

Marcello Lupi

> Among the Maasai, as in Sparta, young men are expected to live and eat together as a way of inculcating them with the virtues of self-denial and respect for authority. Maasai warriors, like Spartans, also disclaim possession, and those who have married can only steal furtive visits to their wives. Both societies have been admired by their more progressive neighbours for the vitality of their austere conservatism and self-regard. (Spencer 1988, 275)

Some years ago Pietro Janni observed that if Sparta's peculiar fate is that of having represented an ideal model of political and social order, then it comes as no surprise that Sparta is thought to have been re-discovered in all the four corners of the world. The article in which Janni made this observation was meant to contribute to the familiar theme of the Spartan mirage, and showed, on his sifting through Greek travel literature, that the ancient authors frequently came across customs and institutions of an apparently 'Spartan' character among barbarian peoples. Starting out with a few familiar passages of the classical period, the Italian scholar went on to review a multitude of ancient sources up to the authors of the first century AD, revealing the constant presence of a 'Spartan model' in ancient ethnography. He noted, incidentally, that when comparing Spartan institutions with those of barbarian peoples, the ancient authors 'crudely anticipated without any real methodical basis what was later to become an important trend in modern research into Sparta and Spartan society'.[1]

On the other hand, the presence of a Spartan model even in the embryonic stage of modern ethnography has been pointed out by Elizabeth Rawson, who gave a chapter of her book on the Spartan tradition the title 'In Utopia and among the Savages'. She thereby acknowledged the presence of continuity between sixteenth-century utopian literary production and the works of missionaries and travellers who, during that same period, discovered certain 'Spartan' customs among the peoples of the New World. The classical culture, on which the authors of both these productions were nurtured, clearly explains why the idealization to which Sparta had been subjected in the age of antiquity continued to influence western culture as soon as Europe undertook its colonial expansion.[2] In referring to the pages of Rawson, Janni concluded his reflection on the Spartan ethnographic model with the following words: 'Spartans are discovered just as good savages are discovered' (Janni 1984, 58).

Thus, in a sense, the history of recourse to ethnological comparison in the studies on Sparta represents yet another chapter of the Spartan mirage; not because comparison necessarily produces a distorted image of Spartan society, but because the frequency with which modern historiography has tried to interpret certain Spartan customs on the basis of ethnographic parallels – in the same way as the ancient authors tried to interpret certain barbarian customs on the basis of the Spartan model – reflects the awareness of a Spartan otherness which renders it particularly apt for comparison with societies of ethnological interest. This otherness makes it very difficult to resist the temptation of comparing Sparta to societies which belong to very different cultures. Recently, in introducing his account of the similarities between Spartan pederasty and that of the Sambias, a New Guinea people, Daniel Ogden has confessed that as a structuralist he is wary of comparisons between different societies, for he believes that every institution of a given society may be better understood in terms of its relationship with other institutions of the same society rather than with presumed similar institutions from different societies and cultures; he has also added, however, that 'the ostensible similarities between Sambian and Spartan initiation rites are so striking that they beg to be aired, if only for curiosity's sake' (Ogden 1996, 140). Although curiosity does not in itself represent a research method, Ogden's confession reveals the impossibility of avoiding comparison. It is my impression that curiosity which has driven many scholars to collate similarities between Spartan customs and those of societies distant both in time and space, has produced studies which, although not always convincing, have nevertheless acted as a driving force for the elaboration of new research perspectives. What I propose to do here is not so much to provide an exhaustive picture of these studies, but rather to dwell on certain major episodes of such recourse to ethnological comparison over the last century, and examine past and present perspectives of this method of interpretation.

There is no doubt that recourse to the comparative method gives rise to perplexity; the possibility of arriving at really productive comparisons and, through them, at a more correct interpretation of Spartan society is far from being acknowledged among classicists, many of whom tend to be conservative. To the more conservative one may reply that the whole of history is comparative, and that, as has already been observed, 'when historians avoid comparative studies they fall most easily into the trap of assimilating the society they study to the only other society they know – that in which they live' (Humphreys 1978, 19).[3] Yet, while comparison between Sparta and other Greek societies is relatively unproblematic in that they are societies which share a common historical and cultural background, the principle behind detection of analogies among societies which are not historically connected is more difficult to justify.[4] Consequently, although recourse to anthropological perspectives is nowadays widespread in classical studies, the use of ethnographic data for comparative purposes often meets with scepticism.[5]

1. The search for ethnographic parallels: approval and disapproval

It was especially in the first two decades of the twentieth century, at a time of close collaboration between anthropology and classical studies and of an evolutionist research perspective, that certain comparative works enriched the bibliography on Sparta. The comparative approach introduced by evolutionist anthropology in the second half of the nineteenth century was based on the assumption that humanity had passed through a series of stages along a similar journey of evolution starting from a greater simplicity and moving towards a greater complexity. Thus, primitive societies were at a stage of evolution which the western world had already passed through; by transforming cultural differences in space into cultural differences in time, the task of the evolutionists consisted mainly in fixing a given custom in a certain time. In this perspective the notion of fossil played a central role, wherewith were indicated those cultural or social elements considered historical hangovers from an earlier stage of evolution.

In the comparative study which in 1902 the German ethnologist Heinrich Schurtz dedicated to age-classes and male associations the notion of fossil is explicitly referred to, and Sparta is defined as 'an authentic museum of ancient customs elsewhere generally made to disappear from civilization' (Schurtz 1902, 98). When a decade later Martin Nilsson wrote his seminal article on the foundations of Spartan life, he used Schurtz's work and drew various anthropological parallels from it.[6] Other parallels appear in the famous study which Eric Bethe (1907) devoted to Spartan – or, as he calls it, Doric – pederasty, and abound in the study of Henri Jeanmaire (1913) on the *krypteia*. However, when in 1918 W.S. Ferguson produced a comparative study in which he collated similarities between Zulu and Spartan military systems, this intensive period of interdisciplinary collaboration was coming to an end.

Since Jeanmaire's work has enjoyed considerable influence, especially on the Parisian School,[7] it is useful to consider it in greater detail. It is an article which almost a century later leaves one somewhat perplexed at how little discussion there is of the ancient evidence, and how much space the author in contrast devotes to the ethnographic material. After rapidly naming the main ancient sources in his opening lines, Jeanmaire states that the *krypteia* is nothing but 'a variety of a type of widespread phenomena': namely, a sort of secret society which one enters through initiation. Starting from this assumption he considers a series of ethnographic data of most disparate provenance, relating to the Arunta (or Aranda) of Australia, to populations of sub-Saharan Africa (above all Maasai and Zulus) and of North America. For example, after quoting Plato's scholion in which it is argued that the *krypteia* brought about the estrangement of some young men from the city and their wanderings through the mountains living on whatever they managed to find (Schol. Plat., *Leg.* 633a), he concludes that 'every comment would be superfluous. There are no details of this text…whose reference to the previous ethnographic facts does not provide us with the explanation.' Finally, mindful of the fact that the Spartan *kryptoi* were able to kill the helots they met with impunity, Jeanmaire engages in further comparison with the custom of head-hunting widespread in areas of Melanesia and Malaya.[8]

When, a quarter of a century later, he referred in his major work – *Couroi et Courètes* – 'to the rather inordinate and indiscreet way in which, more especially at the beginning of this century, reference was sometimes made to the data taken from the most varied fields of descriptive ethnography' (Jeanmaire 1939, 156), it cannot be ruled out that he was also referring to his own article on the *krypteia*. Conversely, in *Couroi et Courètes* the use of the comparative method is much less hazardous: comparison is limited, yet within a section of some eighty pages, to the African area which offered numerous and homogeneous material regarding initiation rites and age classes.[9] Furthermore, Jeanmaire (id., 157–8) is aware of the criticisms levelled against those who cause 'savages' or 'primitives' to intervene in order to focus on certain aspects of the mentality and society of the Greeks, but argues that such criticisms are the outcome of an erroneous premise in that comparative ethnography is not a question of 'primitive' societies but of complexes of civilizations; more especially, he stresses that the designation of archaic cultures is more fitting to African societies, and justifies the comparison between Sparta and African cultures on this basis.

However, when Jeanmaire published his book, collaboration between classical studies and anthropology had undergone a setback. Within classical studies the discredit which had surrounded the Cambridge ritualist school led to suspicion of comparison between the Greeks and presumed primitive societies. Within anthropology the inter-war period saw the functionalist paradigm gaining the upper hand: Malinowski and Radcliffe-Brown published their celebrated monographs in which they recognized the need for field research involving immersion, through the technique of participant observation, into the daily life of the community examined.[10] This brought about the multiplication of monographic studies on single communities and a lesser interest in a comparative perspective. Although Radcliffe-Brown himself had maintained that 'without systematic comparative studies anthropology will become only historiography and ethnography',[11] the functionalists in fact applied the comparative method with caution, and preferably among societies belonging to the same geographical area. Moreover, since the functionalist paradigm rejected the existence of cultural fossils by considering that each element of a society must be interpreted in the light of the functions it performs within the social structure of which it forms part, the theoretical basis on which the crosscultural comparison was founded was missing.

It is in this context that the severe criticism is to be read which Moses Finley, in his influential article 'Anthropology and the Classics', levelled against recourse to ethnographic comparison in studies on Sparta:

> For more than a century scholars have drawn upon anthropological parallels for an explanation of Sparta: comparative materials on primitive age-classes, polyandry, blood-letting as an initiation rite, marriage by capture, even the Zulu barracks appear and re-appear in modern books about Sparta. What has been largely overlooked is that all the anthropological models are inadequate for classical Sparta...; inadequate because those 'peculiar' features in Spartan life that appear to be illuminated by anthropology were, by the classical period, fossilized rites which had lost their original function (and which the Spartan themselves no longer understood) and had acquired new functions within a complex society of a kind that eludes meaningful comparison with non-literate, primitive groups. What anthropology illuminates about Sparta, paradoxically, are certain aspects of her lost early history rather than the Sparta from which the fossilized evidence comes.[12]

Finley does not adopt a negative position with regard to comparative method, the more so since he himself, in his celebrated book *The World of Odysseus*, had interpreted the ritualized exchanges of gifts in the Homeric world in the light of the data gathered by Marcel Mauss in his *Essai sur le don*.[13] However, he explains that, unlike in the case of the Homeric world, the use of anthropological material is not of much value for archaic and classical Greece, the period which saw the birth of the city-state and the first appearance of democracy. Thus, having identified the approximate date beyond which recourse to ethnographic materials was of limited value as being towards the middle of the eighth century BC, Finley assumes that the data deriving from societies of ethnographic interest are comparable only with those of primitive Sparta.

What is most striking in Finley's writing is the synthesis of two different paradigms, the one evolutionist, the other functionalist. In holding that the majority of anthropological parallels generally referred to in Spartan studies represent solely fossils of a more ancient age, Finley appears to be referring explicitly to an evolutionist paradigm. Yet, in sharply contrasting primitive cultures with classical Greece, he does not seem to take account of Jeanmaire's approach, which through the notion of archaism had set the bases, as has been seen, for a comparison between the societies studied by ethnologists and classical Sparta.

Yet it would be short-sighted to interpret Finley's words only from an evolutionist viewpoint; in a sense his recourse to an evolutionist paradigm is itself a sort of fossil preserved within a mainly functionalist approach. Finley's functionalism, however, could not be that of the anthropologists. Since the societies which the anthropologists examined were considered societies 'without history' – not so much because they had remained unchanged, but because it was deemed impossible to reconstruct history in the absence of written sources – functionalist theorists tended, at any rate until the 1950s, to avoid tackling the question of change in history, being convinced that knowledge of history was not essential for understanding the present functioning of a society.[14] As a historian Finley was unable fully to accept this view.[15] Consequently, he decides to take a different route: on the one hand he considers that each element of archaic and classical Sparta is to be interpreted on the basis of the function that it performs within that society, and on the other hand he reappropriates a historical perspective by formulating the thesis he developed in his leading article on Sparta (Finley 1968) of 'reinstitutionalization' to which many of the more ancient Spartan customs would have been subject in the course of the 'sixth-century revolution' from which the classical city would have sprung. Thus, for example, Finley argues that the archaic division between old and young is something completely different from the complex age class system of the classical age utilized within the so-called *agōgē*; the age-class system and the *agōgē* would thus be a substantially original creation of the sixth-century revolution, which had been made possible through the refunctionalization of a primitive division of society between young and old.

Nevertheless, in regaining a *spatium historicum*, Finley is only able to exploit it through an evolutionary paradigm which had for some time been abandoned by the social sciences. Nigel Kennell has recently observed that the persistence of such a paradigm – so much the more lasting if one considers that Finley's authority has been such that his point of view has been accepted favourably even in several more recent studies[16] – is indeed surprising. Since it has been demonstrated that even assumed primitive cultures undergo change, and that certain rites believed to be traditional ones often represented innovations which were not at all primitive, Kennell argues that the claim of being able to pin down to a prehistoric date those Spartan institutions for which it is possible to single out anthropological parallels is clearly untenable. Yet, Kennell goes much further: 'ancient historians have no warrant for reconstructing early Greek initiation rites from African "parallels" that grew out of historical situation utterly dissimilar to those of prehistoric Greece'.[17]

In my view, there exists an alternative to the historical particularism to which Kennell condemns us, that consists not in *reconstructing from* but in *rethinking through* ethnographic parallels.

2. Updating the ethnographic dossier

The preliminary condition for new recourse to comparison is the updating of the ethnographic dossier. The need for such updating has been recently stressed by Pauline Schmitt Pantel who has shown with regard to Spartan and Cretan *syssitia* – another institution for which reference was normally made to an ethnographic notion: the 'house of men' – that even more recent works often continue to rely upon the comparative studies of the early decades of the twentieth century (Schmitt Pantel 1992, 67–8). The fact that such studies drew upon ethnographic works published in the second half of the nineteenth century, or, at the latest, in the opening years of the twentieth century is one reason why they are of very little use nowadays, the more so since the ethnographic material was mostly made up of reports compiled by colonial officials, missionaries and travellers.

However, the outdatedness of the bibliography varies according to what Spartan customs are under discussion. In this regard it may be useful to examine studies of collective education and the age-class system on the one hand, and Spartan pederasty on the other. Generally, age-class studies have looked, with Jeanmaire, towards Africa. Doubts have been expressed regarding this tendency and it has recently been written that 'if we really wish to look for some terms of comparison, we will find fewer in an African tribe than in the British colleges of Rudyard Kipling, which trained the future officers of the armies in India' (Lévy 1997, 160). Although a similar comparison may be useful for understanding certain logics of the Spartan educational system, the fact remains that the initiation rites and Spartan education are encapsulated within an age-class structure, and the rich supply of ethnological material on age-class systems which the African continent provides is such that comparison tends preferably to be directed towards Africa.[18] This is the reason why the Zulus and the Maasai are so often quoted in Spartan studies.[19] However, since the publication of Jeanmaire's book there has been no systematic confrontation of the new data provided by ethnographic research, a remarkable fact considering the flood of ethnological monographs on Africa since the 1940s, which have given a new impulse to our knowledge of African cultures and their age-class systems.[20] The publication in 1969 of *Paides e Parthenoi* – in which Angelo Brelich proposed the thesis that Spartan initiations were not hangovers of a primitive initiatory cycle but rather constituted a perfectly-functioning system of age-class and initiations – represents a partial exception.[21] But not even Brelich had at his disposal at that time the two anthropological syntheses on the age-class systems of Frank Stewart (1977) and Bernardo Bernardi (1984), which brought order to the new ethnographic material which had mounted up and were the first to underline the demographic consequences of such systems, by opening up a perspective which Robert Sallares (1991) has applied in a recent monograph to the analysis of Spartan and Cretan age-class systems.

In contrast, in the studies of pederasty the ethnological parallels more frequently drawn refer to cultures of New Guinea, or at any rate to those situated in the area of the South-West Pacific.[22] It is towards this area that Bethe (1907, 463–4) had already turned when formulating his celebrated thesis whereby during the performance of the act of pederasty the lover transmitted to the beloved boy his own personal qualities of physical and military excellence through his semen. Yet, since systematic interest in homosexuality in the ancient world has largely developed only since the work of Kenneth Dover (1978), and since in the intervening period our knowledge of the cultures of New Guinea had expanded enormously, all comparative studies of Spartan pederasty have perforce undergone bibliographic updating. Paul Cartledge's 1981 article on Spartan pederasty refers to three societies none of which was known to Bethe.[23] The same year saw the publication of Herdt's celebrated monograph on the Sambias of New Guinea, which opened up new routes into the symbolic analysis of homosexual initiation rituals (Herdt 1981). Cartledge had time to mention Herdt's book only in a note, and recently Daniel Ogden has been able to make a systematic comparison between Spartan and Sambian homosexual rituals.[24]

3. Towards an interpretative approach: 'Spartan marriage' as a case study

One may wonder whether it is worth bothering to update the ethnographic dossier in a context of anthropological studies which today do not particularly favour comparison. The contemporary anthropological panorama is undoubtedly marked by the considerable reduction in the amount of comparative research. Generally speaking, this reduction is to be associated with the crisis of the positivist idea that anthropology can succeed in singling out cross-culturally valid laws, and that comparison is anthropology's equivalent of experiment in the natural sciences.[25] Nevertheless, the prevalence of interpretative paradigms in contemporary anthropology has not caused comparison to disappear, but has led to the development of 'forms of comparison founded on processes of translation' (Fabietti 1999, 218). In the perspective of interpretative anthropology, the researcher's main task consists of continuous negotiation among the significances of his own – generally western – culture and those of the culture which he, as anthropologist, intends to describe. The search for a translation which may prove adequate for rendering the significances of the culture investigated requires continuous comparison between these two cultures. In a certain sense, 'all our analysis is ultimately comparative in that we have to translate to be able to describe' (Holy 1987, 15).

What particularly characterizes comparison in interpretative trends is the fact that it is no longer directed towards generalization, but towards facilitating the description of a particular ethnographical reality. In other words, one no longer tries, on the basis of assumed cross-cultural similarities, to single out a generalizing category into which to fit the ethnographic datum that is object of the comparison, but rather one attempts to examine whether the comparative category being utilized is really adaptable to the meanings of the culture analysed (Holy 1987, 9–12). The analysis of the usefulness of the idea of marriage may serve to clarify this point. The idea of marriage especially lends itself to this purpose both because the attempt to provide a definition of marriage which has cross-cultural value has long tormented those anthropologists who have tried to construct a form of anthropology as a comparative science, and also because Spartan marriage is another of those customs whose apparent difference from Greek practice has encouraged the use of ethnographic parallels.

First of all let us see how anthropological reflection has attempted to arrive at a definition of marriage. In the final edition of *Notes and Queries in Anthropology* (1951) marriage was defined as 'a union between a man and a woman such that the children given birth to by the woman are recognized as the legitimate offspring of both parents';[26] that is to say marriage was defined by identifying its presumed universal functions. Subsequent studies were also directed towards the search for such an assumed function, by identifying it as the sanction of the legitimacy of the children that are born therefrom 'under circumstances not prohibited by the rules of the relationship' (Gough 1959, 32), or as the recognition of a 'continuing claim to the right of sexual access to a woman' (Goodenough 1970, 12–13). The limitations of these various definitions of marriage led Edmund Leach, in a pioneering study, to argue that not only are the various rights associated with marriage never present together in every society, but also that it is impossible to identify one of them which is constantly present and which may serve as a basis for a definition of marriage; hence the uselessness of all the universal definitions of marriage (Leach 1961, 105). It is not by chance that Leach has also been the one to uphold the idea that cross-cultural comparison is a process analogous to that of collecting butterflies, which believes it can catalogue every social custom and institution on the basis of types and sub-types. By rejecting the validity of such approaches, he was among the first to decree the crisis of the old positivist paradigms. Later Rodney Needham, further developing Leach's arguments, has said that the word 'marriage' is 'an odd-job word: very handy in all sorts of descriptive sentences, but worse than misleading in comparison and of no real use at all in analysis' (Needham 1971, 7–8).

It is thus natural that no anthropologist working in the field of a given society may expect to find a custom that corresponds perfectly with a given definition of marriage. Yet, although aware that any translation is imperfect, it is likely that our anthropologist, after reviewing the various forms of relationships among the sexes which he comes to know through his native informants, will single out one of them to which to attribute the name of marriage at least for descriptive purposes.

We may attempt to tackle the question as it relates to Sparta: a hypothetical anthropologist of ancient Sparta would examine the functions of the various relationships between the sexes described in the ancient texts in order to identify the one to which to attribute the label of 'Spartan marriage'.[27] The question is apparently simple: a long-established tradition of classical studies assures us that the Greek term for marriage is *gamos*; thus, although the Greek term at times appears to be used also for sexual relationships which do not involve any social tie, our anthropologist would look for the term *gamos*, and would find it in the well-known passage by Plutarch (*Lyc.* 15.4–10), in which the biographer describes a wedding ceremony with very special characteristics which on the one hand sanctioned the legality of sexual relationships between the wedded couple, but on the other required that these took place secretly for a period which might be considerable. The originality of this marriage phase characterized by secret meetings has certainly not passed unobserved by scholars of Spartan history, but even those who considered Plutarch's testimony trustworthy have limited themselves to considering it an ethnographic curiosity, and have tried to explain this custom by recourse to a comparative category, namely the 'trial marriage'.[28] Although this is a rather dated notion, it is nevertheless clear: the expression 'trial marriage' refers to the usage encountered in certain traditional societies of not officializing the marriage until the wife had given proof, through the birth of the first child, of being able to perpetuate her husband's lineage. It is easy to understand how this comparison leads to a very significant outcome in the interpretation of the first phase of Spartan marriage, as it suggests that the secret meetings were aimed at procreation.

Since I have already elaborated my own radically different interpretation in a recently published monograph (Lupi 2000), I will now stick to the main issues.

1. According to Plutarch the bride, before associating with her groom, was entrusted to a woman who 'shaved her head to the scalp, then dressed her in a man's cloak and sandals, and laid her down alone on a mattress (*stibas*) in the dark' to wait for her bridegroom (*Lyc.* 15.5). Thus, the wedding involved a disguise by which the bride became similar to a male. Note that Plutarch also states, while speaking of the boys' upbringing, that it was customary to shave their heads to the scalp and dress them in a cloak; moreover, when the boys reached age 12, they slept together on mattresses (*stibades*) and had pederastic relationships with young men (*Lyc.* 16.11–17.1). We infer therefrom that during these secret meetings Spartan young men associated with girls dressed up not as adult males but as teenage boys who were undergoing their communal education.

2. In a short passage Athenaeus, quoting the Academic Hagnon of Tarsus, writes that 'for the Spartans it is customary before marriage to associate with maidens as with *paidika*' (Athen. 13.602d–e). In other words, it was normal for Spartan young men not yet married to have heterosexual intercourse with girls which were modelled on the homosexual relations they used to have with boys. This means that Hagnon is referring to anal or intercrural – and therefore infecund – coitus.[29]

3. The simplest hypothesis is that the two texts refer to the same social practice. If so, Plutarch's secret meetings, which lasted until the bridegroom reached the age of 30,[30] were sterile. While the theory of the trial marriage suggested that the Spartans tended to have children at a relatively early age, my view implies that Spartan males abstained from legitimate procreation until the age of 30.

4. Consequently, the scarcely-known Hagnon and Plutarch have attached two different categories to the same custom, since for Hagnon sexual intercourse takes place before marriage, whereas Plutarch sets it during a first phase of marriage. If Plutarch considers the secret meetings as matrimonial

it is because in his work a philo-Spartan tradition is reflected which aimed at justifying the supposed immodesty of Spartan girls by including the secret meetings within the category of marriage; hence we can infer that in Hagnon the presence of the anti-Spartan tradition is felt.

What is of interest here, however, is that neither author was a participant observer of Sparta, nor does either reflect what we might call the native's point of view, since neither of them was Spartan. It is also highly unlikely that their sources were Spartan. Their position is analogous to that of travellers or colonial officials, who lacked conceptual tools for a correct understanding of the customs they described and of which they often had second-hand information. Nevertheless, the convergence between the two passages not only makes Hagnon's isolated evidence reliable,[31] but also shows that the marriage is not a phenomenon to be described, but rather a construction of meaning, which can be manipulated. Note that this new interpretation has been facilitated by insights gained from comparative studies of the problematic nature of a cross-cultural notion of matrimony. By problematizing the notion of marriage and by analysing two testimonies which apparently refer to different customs, we can arrive at a closer understanding of the specific Spartan reality.

It is now possible to formulate a new interpretation of the Spartan age-class system, by having further recourse to cross-cultural comparison. The increase in our knowledge of the functioning of the age-class systems of Eastern Africa, which recent research has made possible, sheds light on the presence among some of them of a generational structure. The main example of such a generational model occurs among the Borana, a people dwelling in Southern Ethiopia and Northern Kenya. The rule governing the recruitment of members to the age-class system among the Borana defines the structural distance between a father's position in the scale of grades and the position of his sons; this rule dictates that a son be placed at a distance of five grades or forty years (a grade covering a period of eight years) from the grade occupied by the father. The peculiar consequence of this generational rule is that the members of an identical age-class may be of considerably different ages. In order to avoid this, the generational systems try to limit the period of time during which a man may generate legitimate children.[32]

I do not intend to claim that the Spartan age-class system was closely similar to those of the Borana, indeed it certainly did not present the rule which prescribes the distance between a father's age-class and that of his children (Lupi 2000, 113–14). Yet I believe that comparison with an ethnographic reality which presents a great multitude of age-class systems, and which hence represents a sort of experimental laboratory for the elaboration of theoretical models with which to interpret age-organization systems, provides us with categories which deserve to be put to the test in the analysis of the Spartan social system. So, the thesis which I have developed is that the prohibition on procreating legitimate children before the age of 30, together with the punishment of both bachelors and those who married late (Plut. *Lyc.* 15.1–3; *Lys.* 30.7), served to keep the generation gaps constant and conferred on Spartan society a generational aspect.

To conclude, the comparison cannot be resolved through singling out ethnographical parallels. The fact that a Spartan rite is similar to an African initiation, or that it is possible to trace convergences between Spartan and Sambian pederasty, does not represent in itself a considerable gain in our knowledge. These parallels, if used prudently, may provide us with some useful ideas for directing research, but in my view the real usefulness of cross-cultural comparison lies elsewhere: comparison with data from other cultures must represent the means for discussing the categories which we use in interpreting Spartan society. Marriage, age-classes, pederasty are not empirical realities, but constructions of meaning. Comparison may then constitute the way for coming close, through a continuous negotiation of significances, to the meaning that these customs assume in Spartan culture.

Notes

[1] Janni 1984 (the quotation is taken from p. 56); the title of this contribution of mine refers to that of Janni's, to which it may be considered a sort of sequel.

[2] Listed among the works quoted by Rawson 1969 is to be found the *Historia de las Indias* by the Dominican Bartolomé de Las Casas (p. 178), as well as the well-known *Moeurs des sauvages Amériquains comparées aux moeurs des premiers temps*, with which at the turn of the eighteenth century the Jesuit father Joseph Lafitau laid the foundations of the comparative approach (p. 222). For a discussion of Lafitau and of the early ethnographic approaches to ancient Greece, including Sparta, cf. Vidal-Naquet 1975.

[3] On the difficulty of communication between anthropology and classical studies see also Redfield 1991.

[4] Unless one wants to claim the right to compare the incomparable, as Detienne 2000 did somewhat provocatively in a recent pamphlet.

[5] Some reflections on the use of the comparative method in anthropology, and on the problems which it raises, are developed in Holy 1987, Remotti 1991, Fabietti 1999, 189–226.

[6] Nilsson 1912, 319–25; note, in particular, the recourse to ethnographic data relating to the Maasai.

[7] See Vidal-Naquet 1968.

[8] Jeanmaire 1913 (the two quotations are taken from p. 122 and p. 140, respectively).

[9] Jeanmaire 1939 devotes the entire third chapter – from the title *Rites d'éphébie et classe d'âge dans l'Afrique contemporaine* – to the analysis of the ethnographic material.

[10] Malinowski 1922; Radcliffe-Brown 1922.

[11] Radcliffe-Brown 1951, 16.

[12] Finley 1975, 116–17. The paper was originally delivered in Cambridge in 1972.

[13] Finley 1954; cf. Morris 1998, 24.

[14] Cf. Viazzo 2000, 30–41.

[15] *Anthropology and the Classics* is in fact a criticism levelled against the functionalist's claim to reject history, but, at the same time, an attempt to re-open the dialogue between anthropological and historical studies.

[16] Cf. Cartledge 1981, 24; 1987, 24–5; Nafissi 1991, 196–7; Ducat 1999, 59–62. Particularly significant are the words with which Cartledge takes up and comments on Finley's observations: 'we cannot therefore treat Sparta and the communities studied by modern ethnographers as strictly analogous entities. If the evidence from the latter can shed light on the former, what will be illuminated are the origins or prehistory of certain customs or customary complexes. Comparative ethnography, in other words, may only be used as a kind of geological tool to lay bare the strata of cultural deposit below those exposed for us by the surviving literary sources' (1981, 24).

[17] Kennell 1995, 143–6 (the quotation is taken from p. 145).

[18] The choice of the society to be compared obviously depends on the type of questions one wishes to answer; Golden (1992, 324) has recently emphasized that 'we should accept no comparison as given or inevitable; on the contrary, each will implicate some theory, some hypotheses about why things are one way or another'.

[19] The converse is also true: I have had occasion to verify that Sparta is often quoted in studies regarding the African age-class systems; see, for instance, the passage of Spencer 1988 quoted as epigraph to this article, and Peatrik 1995, 20.

[20] Especially thanks to the initiative of the Institute of African Culture; on the role held by this Institute in the development of studies on the African world cf. Bernardi 1998, 34–5.

[21] Brelich 1969 makes reference to a large number of ethnographic parallels in the notes to the introduction (pp. 52–112), but only incidentally so in the chapter dedicated to Spartan initiations (for example at p. 127 n. 35: comparison with Zulus).

[22] For a global view of the diffusion in this area of homosexual initiation customs see Herdt 1984.

[23] Cartledge 1981, 24–5 (where reference is made to the Aranda of Central Australia, the Keraki of Papua and the Marind Anim of New Guinea). On the use of anthropological data in reference to Greek homosexuality see also Dover 1988, 120–2; he too is very critical of the persistence of evolutionist interpretations:

'the equation of contemporary primitive with prehistoric universal may be rather misleading' (p. 122).

[24] Cartledge 1981, 34 n. 49; Ogden 1996, 139–44. Cf. also Gilmore 1990, who refers fleetingly to convergences between Sambian and Greek (particularly Spartan) homosexuality.

[25] Cf. Borutti 1999, 151–4. The assimilation of the comparison to an experiment reflected the aspiration of the anthropologists to provide their own discipline with a strong scientific status (cf. Evans-Pritchard 1951, 89–90).

[26] It is useful to bear in mind that *Notes and Queries* was especially meant for colonial officials and administrators and was thus not concerned with purely theoretical questions.

[27] The bibliography on Spartan marriage is vast: I limit myself to Paradiso 1986 on the initiatory aspects of the wedding ceremony, and Hodkinson 1989 on its patrimonial aspects.

[28] For references to this notion in the studies on Spartan marriage see Lupi 2000, 97–8.

[29] On the reading of Hagnon's passage there is now general consensus: cf. Lupi 2000, 65–71; on his reliability, however, doubts have arisen (Brelich 1969, 158 n. 138; Cartledge 1981, 35 n. 69), which I hope my interpretation may expel.

[30] On the basis of Plut. *Lyc.* 15.8 it is generally considered that the secret meetings lasted for the whole period in which the bridegroom was obliged to take part in collective education with his fellows, that is until the age of 30 (see for example Hodkinson 1989, 109).

[31] With regard to Plutarch's reliability, I do not think there are any reasons for doubting it, the more so since the attestation of secret meetings between bride and groom is already in the sources of the classical age (Xen. *Lac. Pol.* 1.5).

[32] On the generational systems of Eastern Africa cf. Bernardi 1984, 137–72, and the recent synthesis of Peatrik 1995; on the Borana in particular see Baxter 1978.

Bibliography

Baxter, P.T.W.

1978 'Boran age-sets and generation-sets: *Gada*, a puzzle or a maze?', in P.T.W. Baxter and U. Almagor (eds.) *Age, Generation and Time: Some features of East African age organization*, London, 151–82.

Bernardi, B.

1984 *I sistemi delle classi d'età. Ordinamenti sociali e politici fondati sull'età*, Turin.

1998 *Africa. Tradizione e modernità*, Rome.

Bethe, E.

1907 'Die dorische Knabenliebe. Ihre Ethik und ihre Idee', *RhM* 62, 438–75.

Borutti, S.

1999 *Filosofia delle scienze umane. Le categorie dell'Antropologia e della Sociologia*, Milan.

Brelich, A.
1969 *Paides e Parthenoi*, Rome.

Cartledge, P.
1981 'The politics of Spartan pederasty', *PCPhS* 207, 17–36.
1987 *Agesilaos and the Crisis of Sparta*, London and Baltimore.

Detienne, M.
2000 *Comparer l'incomparable*, Paris.

Dover, K.J.
1978 *Greek Homosexuality*, London.
1988 'Greek homosexuality and initiation', in K.J. Dover, *The Greeks and Their Legacy. Collected Papers* II, Oxford, 115–34.

Ducat, J.
1999 'Perspectives on Spartan education in the classical period', in S. Hodkinson and A. Powell (eds.) *Sparta: New perspectives*, London, 43–66.

Evans-Pritchard, E.E.
1951 *Social Anthropology*, London.

Fabietti, U.
1999 *Antropologia culturale. L'esperienza e l'interpretazione*, Rome and Bari.

Ferguson, W.S.
1918 'The Zulus and the Spartans: a comparison of their military systems', *Harvard African Studies* 2, 197–234.

Finley, M.I.
1954 *The World of Odysseus*, New York.
1968 'Sparta', in J.-P. Vernant (ed.) *Problèmes de la guerre en Grèce ancienne*, Paris and The Hague, 143–60.
1975 *The Use and Abuse of History*, London.

Gilmore, D.D.
1990 *Manhood in the Making: Cultural Concepts of Masculinity*, New Haven and London.

Golden, M.
1992 'The uses of cross-cultural comparison in ancient social history', *Échos du Monde Classique* 11, 309–31.

Goodenough, W.
1970 *Description and Comparison in Cultural Anthropology*, Chicago.

Gough, K.
1959 'The Nayars and the definition of marriage', *Journal of the Royal Anthropological Institute* 89, 23–34.

Herdt, G.
1981 *Guardians of the Flutes. Idioms of Masculinity*, Chicago.

Herdt, G. (ed.)
1984 *Ritualized Homosexuality in Melanesia*, Berkeley and Los Angeles.

Hodkinson, S.
1989 'Inheritance, marriage and demography: perspectives upon the success and decline of classical Sparta', in A. Powell (ed.) *Classical Sparta: Techniques behind her success*, London, 79–121.

Holy, L.
1987 'Description, generalization and comparison: two paradigms', in L. Holy (ed.) *Comparative Anthropology*, Oxford, 1–21.
Humphreys, S.
1978 *Anthropology and the Greeks*, London.
Janni, P.
1984 'Sparta ritrovata. Il modello spartano nell'etnografia antica', in E. Lanzillotta (ed.) *Problemi di storia e cultura spartana*, Rome, 29–58.
Jeanmaire, H.
1913 'La cryptie lacédémonienne', *REG* 26, 121–50.
1939 *Couroi et courètes. Essai sur l'éducation spartiate et sur les rites d'adolescence dans l'antiquité hellénique*, Lille.
Kennell, N.M.
1995 *The Gymnasium of Virtue. Education and Culture in Ancient Sparta*, Chapel Hill and London.
Leach, E.R.
1961 *Rethinking Anthropology*, London.
Lévy, E.
1997 'Remarques préliminaires sur l'éducation spartiate', *Ktema* 22, 151–60.
Lupi, M.
2000 *L'ordine delle generazioni. Classi di età e costumi matrimoniali nell'antica Sparta*, Bari.
Malinowski, B.
1922 *The Argonauts of the Western Pacific*, London.
Morris, I.
1998 'Poetics of power: the interpretation of ritual action in archaic Greece', in C. Dougherty and L. Kurke (eds.) *Cultural Poetics in Archaic Greece: Cult, performance, politics*, New York and Oxford, 15–45.
Nafissi, M.
1991 *La nascita del* kosmos. *Studi sulla storia e la società di Sparta*, Naples.
Needham, R.
1971 'Remarks on the analysis of kinship and marriage', in R. Needham (ed.) *Rethinking Kinship and Marriage*, London, 1–34.
Nilsson, M.P.
1912 'Die Grundlagen des spartanischen Lebens', *Klio* 12, 308–40.
Notes and Queries
1951 *Notes and Queries in Anthropology*, 6th edn, London.
Ogden, D.
1996 'Homosexuality and warfare in ancient Greece', A.B. Lloyd (ed.) *Battle in Antiquity*, London, 107–68.
Paradiso, A.
1986 'Osservazioni sulla cerimonia nuziale spartana', *Quaderni di Storia* 24, 137–53.
Peatrik, A.-M.
1995 'La règle et le nombre: les systèmes d'âge et de génération d'Afrique orientale', *L'Homme* 134, 13–49.

Radcliffe-Brown, A.R.
1922 *The Andaman Islanders*, Cambridge.
1951 'The comparative method in social anthropology', *Journal of the Royal Anthropological Institute* 81, 15–22.
Rawson, E.
1969 *The Spartan Tradition in European Thought*, Oxford.
Redfield, J.
1991 'Classics and Anthropology', *Arion* 1.2, 5–23.
Remotti, F.
1991 'La comparazione inter-culturale: problemi di identità antropologica', *Rassegna Italiana di Sociologia* 32, 25–46.
Sallares, R.
1991 *The Ecology of the Ancient Greek World*, London.
Schmitt Pantel, P.
1992 *La cité au banquet. Histoire des repas publics dans les cités grecques*, Rome.
Schurtz, H.
1902 *Alterklassen und Männerbünde*, Berlin.
Spencer, P.
1988 *The Maasai of Matapato. A Study of Rituals of Rebellion*, Manchester.
Stewart, F.H.
1977 *Fundamentals of Age-Group Systems*, New York.
Viazzo, P.P.
2000 *Introduzione all'antropologia storica*, Rome and Bari.
Vidal-Naquet, P.
1968 'Le chasseur noir et l'origine de l'éphébie athénienne', *Annales ESC* 23, 947–64.
1974 'Le cru, l'enfant grec et le cuit', in J. Le Goff and P. Nora (eds.) *Faire de l'histoire*, vol. III, Paris, 137–68.

14

FROM THERMOPYLAE TO STALINGRAD: THE MYTH OF LEONIDAS IN GERMAN HISTORIOGRAPHY

Stefan Rebenich

ὦ ξεῖν', ἀγγέλλειν Λακεδαιμονίοις, ὅτι τῇδε
κείμεθα τοῖς κείνων ῥήμασι πειθόμενοι.

Foreigner, go tell the Lacedaemonians
that we lie here obedient to their commands.

We all, of course, know this famous epitaph which has been attributed to the poet Simonides and which glorifies the futile battle at Thermopylae fought in 480 BC by Leonidas and his brave comrades against the Persian host.[1]

The historical setting of the notorious episode is easy to outline. In order to punish the city-states of the Greek mainland which had assisted the Ionian Revolt, the king of Persia ventured upon two expeditions. The first attack was shipwrecked in the storm-swept Aegean Sea; the second reached Marathon in 490 where the Athenian hoplites and their allies from Plataea, fighting with the courage of despair, decisively defeated the invasion-force although it was superior in number. Ten years later, another attempt was made to discipline the insubordinate *poleis* on the edge of the world. Now nothing was left to chance. In spring 480 the time had come. The Persians approached Greece by land and sea. There the issue was raised where the invader should be met. Three natural positions of defence were considered. First the Tempe defile in north-eastern Thessaly, then the Thermopylae pass separating northern and central Greece, and finally the Isthmus joining central Greece and the Peloponnese. The first line was abandoned without a fight; in consequence the Thessalian aristocracy who had supported the defensive strategy changed sides. It was then decided to send a Peloponnesian force under the command of the Spartan king Leonidas to Thermopylae to defend the pass against the Persian ground troops; at the same time the fleet moved into position at the promontory of Artemisium. After two days of fighting Thermopylae was turned through the treachery of a local Greek. When Leonidas learnt of the Persian approach he told the allies to go. The king and his 300 Spartans, with some hundred Thespians and Thebans, decided to stay and fought to the last.

It is not my intention here to discuss the reasons why the Spartan king decided to stand on the hillock, and to die. They are still subject to scholarly dispute.[2] Rather, I want to present 'one of the most famous days in the history of warfare'[3] as a paradigm of the 'Spartan tradition' in German historiography.[4] Leonidas' obedience to the decrees has again and again been celebrated as duty of the highest order,[5] from Cicero, who gives a Latin translation of the epigram in *Tusculan Disputations,*[6] to R. Glover in the eighteenth century,[7] who, like so many others, let the king die for the salvation of his native land; from Origen, who believed that the devotion of Leonidas helps Christians to understand that of Jesus,[8] to the *citoyens* of the French town Saint-Marcellin, who abandoned their Christian faith in 1793, and adopted the name 'Thermopyles' for their community.[9]

In the following pages, I shall concentrate on certain aspects of the Leonidas-myth in German historiography. After a short introduction on the perception of Sparta in the second half of the eighteenth and the first half of the nineteenth centuries (i), I shall analyse the accounts of the battle of Thermopylae in German scholarship first from about 1850 to 1918 (ii) and then in the period up to 1945 (iii). The popular glorification and political manipulation of the 'three hundred' in the educational system of Nazi Germany will then be examined (iv). In this context, it seems necessary to compare contemporary German studies with interpretations of Leonidas' last stand in other European countries (v). I shall end with a glance at the presentation of Leonidas' death in German historiography after the Second World War (vi). Since some Austrian and Swiss scholars are cited, it should also be said that I do not maintain a national concept of German historiography, either *großdeutsch* or *kleindeutsch,* but have scrutinized their respective works since their authors considered themselves as belonging to a culturally or politically defined German nation.

(i) 1750 to 1850

In the second half of the eighteenth century, idealization of the hellenic world brought with it the gradual emergence of a positive picture of Sparta. Johann Gottfried Herder and Friedrich Schiller, though criticizing the Lycurgan constitution as objectionable and praising the enlightened citizenship of Athens, nevertheless admired the 'principle of Thermopylae', i.e., the political virtue and patriotism of the Spartans.[10] To Schiller we owe the well-known German translation of Simonides' epitaph quoted above:

> *Wanderer, kommst du nach Sparta, verkündige dorten, du habest*
> *Uns hier liegen gesehn, wie das Gesetz es befahl.*[11]

In Herder's view, Athens and Sparta represented the two eternal poles of human development, i.e. enlightenment and patriotism. This polarized classification also characterizes Georg Wilhelm Friedrich Hegel's approach, according to whom Athens is far superior to Sparta. In Athens – at least in the fifth century BC – democracy, expressing an objective will, guaranteed individual freedom, strong community feeling and the active pursuit of beauty and truth, or in Hegel's words: *freie Individualität* and *Sittlichkeit.* In Sparta, a forced equality destroyed liberty, while an over-powerful state suffocated civil responsibility and intellectual life. So it is not surprising that Hegel dedicates only a marginal note to Leonidas and Thermopylae when describing the Persian War as a battle of Asiatic despotism versus Greek culture and individuality.[12]

Hegel's dialectic rendering of the two Greek *poleis* is also to be read as a reaction to a new understanding of the Spartans proposed by Friedrich Schlegel and, above all, by Karl Otfried Müller. This tradition, which later became most influential in German political theory and classical scholarship, perceived the Dorian tribe as the most authentic of all the Greeks. Sparta was the model for reconstructing the institutions and customs of the older and purer hellenic past. Hence the Spartans were converted into the Dorians *par excellence.* In Leonidas' sacrifice Schlegel recognizes not a patriotic deed, but a symbol of the Dorian obedience to law. 'Their holy death was the pinnacle of all joy', he exults.[13] Müller, on the other hand, mentions the battle of Thermopylae only *en passant,* but he defines Dorian Sparta as a Greek model state, praises the subjection of the individual to the community, and emphasizes the conservative orientation of Sparta's institutions. His romantic idealization was successful in the first place because he integrated some of the new political feelings of his age into his work, and also because he combined mythology and religion, archaeology and geography, philosophy and philology, political and institutional history.[14]

Although the Spartans, especially through Müller's *Dorier*, won some popularity, we should not forget that, as Elizabeth Rawson has observed, in Germany 'even in philhellenic literature, of which there was a flood, Leonidas is a great deal harder to find than he was in France and England'.[15] In the first modern, one may say 'critical', history of Sparta by J.C.F. Manso, a Prussian schoolteacher and patriot, the battle of Thermopylae is described without solemn overtones.[16] Leonidas' great time was yet to come.

(ii) 1850 to 1918

Leonidas was a new discovery in the period of historicism and nationalism. Classical scholarship received an unparalleled impetus in the nineteenth century. The first systematic archaeological campaigns and an intensified

Quellenforschung gradually transformed the picture of Sparta. A long series of 'Histories of Greece' tried to put back together again the fragments generated by ever more specialized academic research. The historical interpretation of the battle of Thermopylae was based upon the most detailed source criticism, topographical reconstruction, military exegesis and discussion of the different reasons why Leonidas fought to the last. In those days, scholars asked the same questions that we still do.[17] Why did Sparta send fewer of its citizens against the Persian invaders than did Corinth? Is Herodotus' account convincing that Sparta planned to send a full contingent when the Karneia festival was over? Was Sparta pursuing a narrow, Peloponnesian policy in sending an inadequate force to Thermopylae? Why did Leonidas and his 300 Spartans take their stand on the hillock? Did they simply refuse to contemplate retreat? Or was there a strategic advantage? Was there really a prophecy that either Sparta would be destroyed or would lose a king? Were the 300 Thebans kept back as hostages? Did the 700 Thespians volunteer to stay? Can Herodotus' account be reconciled with that of Diodorus?

There were, of course, different shades and emphases. Military historians, for instance, like Hermann Köchly and Friedrich Rüstow, discussed possible tactical reasons why the king stayed. They thought that he wanted to protect the retreat of the remaining army.[18] According to Hans Delbrück, the defence of Thermopylae was, in military terms, '*ein Fehler, eine Halbheit*' ('a mistake, a half measure') since the king's position could be outflanked by the enemy;[19] nevertheless, Leonidas' heroic death remained 'a moral postulate' and was of immense value, since 'the babarians were not allowed to enter real Hellas without a fight'.[20] Often the Spartan's civil duty and obedience to law was underlined.[21] Leopold von Ranke, for example, adopted this view in his *Weltgeschichte.*[22] Robert von Pöhlmann, the author of the 'Greek History' for the *Handbuch der klassischen Altertumswissenschaft,* said that Leonidas had to stand, otherwise he would have violated Spartan martial law: 'The splendid heroic death of the fighters at Thermopylae strengthened rather than weakened the confidence of the Greeks and was thus not futile for the national cause.'[23] Other scholars complained about the missing support of the Spartan authorities and their narrow-minded policy; among these are to be found Ernst Curtius,[24] Adolf Holm[25] and Georg Busolt.[26]

Not only the tactical, but also the moral importance of the battle was stressed. Thermopylae was now understood in the context of the national movement. Already in 1812, the poet Theodor Körner praised the 'bloody valley of Thermopylae' (*das blut'ge Tal der Thermopylen*) to encourage his compatriots in their fight against Napoleon.[27] In scholarship too the dead were transformed into the embodiment of self-sacrificing courage, their tomb was, according to Ernst Curtius, 'an everlasting monument of heroic civic virtue' (*ein unvergängliches Denkmal heldenmüthiger Bürgertugend*).[28]

Certainly, there were also critical voices. Jakob Burckhardt, in his *Griechische Kulturgeschichte,* accused the Spartans of blind egoism in the Persian War: they had deliberately sacrified Leonidas so that Sparta could retain her honour and protect the main force of her army from being defeated.[29] In accordance with Plato's political philosophy, Sparta appeared to Burckhardt as the perfect Greek *polis* and he deeply admired the ephorate. On the other hand, he did not ignore the oppressive nature of Spartan institutions, the exploitation of the helots and was full of distaste for the educational system.

Others showed no sympathy whatever with the action of the 'Kamikaze squadron'[30] led by Leonidas. Barthold Georg Niebuhr, in his 'Lectures on Ancient History', vigorously defended a pro-Athenian perspective. Hostile to the *polis* of the Eurotas, he argued that later generations have honoured Leonidas and his Spartans but ignored the helots and the 700 Thespians, who were also killed in the battle.[31] According to Nikolaus Wecklein, it was 'a fruitless bloodshed';[32] and Franz Rühl, a leftist, complained that Leonidas gave his life for an obsolete sense of martial honour deriving from his boyhood education.[33] Some years earlier he had simply called the disaster 'quixotic'.[34] The most prominent of all critics was Karl Julius Beloch, an ardent nonconformist and *bête noire* of the academic establishment,[35] who made a clean sweep of the legend. His de-mystification resulted in the conclusion: 'The catastrophe at Thermopylae had only one advantage for the Greek case: it liberated the federal army from an incompetent commander.'[36]

That hurt. Most of Beloch's colleagues were indignant. Eduard Meyer, for example, who since 1902 had held the Chair of Ancient History at Berlin,[37] refused any serious discussion of Beloch's position. Instead, he celebrated *ex cathedra* Leonidas' heroic death, which was 'a shining example showing the nation the way it had to go; this example made men realize more deeply and more vividly than any words that the only choice was to gain victory or to die with honour'.[38] That the battle of Thermopylae was of tactical as well as moral significance was also argued by Max Duncker. He rejected modern critics of Leonidas' death in battle, on the grounds that such statements showed only that their authors had no idea of the moral powers which also rule war.[39] These quotations are typical of the interpretations proposed during this period. Only a minority of outsiders criticized Leonidas' action; the overwhelming majority of professional historians celebrated the Spartan king as a shining example of patriotism and heroism. Leonidas had become a paragon of nationalism.

(iii) 1918 to 1945

The military break-down of the German *Kaiserreich* and the democratic revolution in November 1918 had deep consequences for the subsequent political, social and intellectual development of Germany. The old system had collapsed, a new one was to be built up. In this time of crisis, historians and classicists categorically demanded a prominent position for their subjects as leading disciplines (*Leitdisziplinen*) to give guidance and orientation to the masses. It is well-known that the majority of university teachers did not identify with the Republic of Weimar but advocated an anti-parliamentary, autocratic system and glorified the good old days of the Empire. Specialized positivist research, though struck by the severe economic problems at the beginning of the twenties, was carried on; but at the same time a historical and classical education was presented as the ideal means of mastering the present and the future.[40] In this context, Sparta became one of the most popular patterns of classical antiquity, and not only among professional historians. Expressionist German authors often referred to Sparta as an example of Doric manhood and homosexual, antifeminist elitism. I mention only Theodor Däubler's essay on Sparta, written in 1923, which praises the homoerotic couples killed at Thermopylae for the sake of their country,[41] and Gottfried Benn's article on the 'Doric World' of 1934. According to the latter, the Dorian's 'dream is reproduction and ever-lasting youth, equality with the gods, great will, strongest aristocratic belief in the race, care for the entire tribe', and 'Doric is pederasty…Doric is love of fighting, such couples stood like a wall and fell'.[42]

But not only poets adored the *Soldatenstaat* and the *Männerlager* on the Eurotas. Sparta seems to have been a model for a whole generation of academics who were shaped by the terrible experience of the trenches in the First World War and could not accept the military defeat of Germany. They propagated instead the myth of the 'stab in the back'. At Langemarck in Flanders, where in the autumn of 1914 thousands of badly-trained and poorly-equipped young German soldiers were sent to their slaughter, the perished regiments were celebrated with the following inscription:

> *Wanderer kommst Du nach Deutschland, verkündige dorten Du habest*
> *Uns hier liegen gesehen, wie das Gesetz es befahl.*[43]
>
> Tell them in Germany, passer-by:
> Obedient to the orders, here we lie.

In scholarship, however, the discussions of the preceding decades continued, though it is striking that criticism of Leonidas' action slowly but steadily subsided. Carl Friedrich Lehmann-Haupt[44] and Thomas Lenschau, the author of the article 'Leonidas' in Pauly-Wissowa's *Realencyclopädie der classischen Altertumswissenschaft*,[45] defended the king's glory considering him to have remained on the hillock to act as a rearguard for the Greek allies. Whereas Johannes Kromayer and Georg Veith presented an exhaustive analysis of the topography of Thermopylae and the battle, and interpreted the sacrifice as successful cover for the retreat of the Greek army,[46] Ulrich Wilcken emphasized in his popular 'Greek History', first published in 1924 and often reprinted, that Leonidas, as soldier and general, carried out duty of the highest order and defined the slaughter as a moral victory. He concluded: 'Leonidas and his followers shall forever remain an example and an object of adoration for our youth.'[47] This passage is also to be found in the revised editions of 1951, 1957, 1962 and 1973 and disturbed some students of Greek history, at least at Leiden University in the late fifties and early sixties. They wanted the book removed from their reading list.[48] Franz Miltner at Innsbruck considered a defence of Leonidas necessary in 1935 and tried to prove that the Spartan king had won not only a moral, but also a strategic victory which saved the Greek fleet at Artemisium from destruction.[49]

Yet the scholarly and public discourse about Sparta in the twenties and thirties was mainly influenced by the accounts of two ancient historians, namely Victor Ehrenberg and Helmut Berve. Ehrenberg, a liberal Jew, who in 1939 had to emigrate to England, was attracted by the manly community of the Spartiates. In his *PW*-article on Sparta he wrote:

> The one-sidedness of this race indicates its greatness. Never again has the ideal of disciplined manhood been set down in such purity. But the greatest achievement is that this masculine and soldierly society devotes itself to unrestricted service of the Nomos, which as incarnation of their state, their religious belief, their customs and tradition is their only sovereign. Only thus was this society able to sacrifice almost entirely its individual existence to the state.[50]

One can hardly imagine a better place for such a statement than Pauly-Wissowa's *Realencyclopädie.* It may be added that only five years later Ehrenberg sang the palinode of his colourful picture of a 'totalitarian' state in antiquity.[51]

Ehrenberg's famous theory of a single Spartan legislator, who in the sixth century BC refounded the *polis* and attributed his reforms to the mythical statesman Lycurgus,[52] met the immediate disapproval of Helmut Berve: 'The strange *kosmos* and the Spartan spirit...were not made, but grew from the ultimate, timeless depths of a collective soul (*Volksseele*)...'[53] Berve formulated his concept of Sparta already in the twenties[54] and popularized it in his *Greek History*, the first volume of which appeared in 1931. There one could read that

> the Spartans sacrificed themselves deliberately, not only out of strategic necessity but for the law of Doric manhood. With good reason they are

> considered as the true fighters at Thermopylae. They were the ones in whom autonomous Greek man consciously opposed fate, they were prepared to be defeated but were not prepared to submit themselves to their fate.[55]

Berve's view of Sparta depended on the idealizing tradition which derived from Schlegel and Müller and thus advocated a strict dichotomy between Dorians and Ionians.[56]

Although some Nazis may have had personal reservations about Berve's political loyalty, he identified himself entirely with the 'national revolution' of 1933 and strongly influenced the academic development and profile of his discipline in the Third Reich.[57] He became *rector magnificus* at the university of Leipzig and *Kriegsbeauftragter der deutschen Altertumswissenschaft* ('war representative of German classics').[58] It is therefore not surprising that Richard Walther Darré's blood-and-soil mysticism and his confusing interpretation of Sparta as an ideal peasant society (*Bauernstaat*)[59] did not meet the taste and ideology of an academically trained public, but Helmut Berve's concept of the Lacedaemonian *polis* did.[60] Berve, who had warmly welcomed the Nationalsocialist re-evaluation of history, did not hesitate to criticize[61] the eccentric theories of Darré's epigoni and other ignorant zealots.[62] At the same time he, like Fritz Schachermeyr, Hans Oppermann, Joseph Vogt and others, adopted racist categories, developed, for example, by Hans F.K. Günther,[63] to interpret ancient history.[64] The Greek city states were integrated into the concept of Nordic world history (*Nordische Weltgeschichte*) and a pseudo-scientific biologistic approach propagated close racial relations between *Deutschtum und Hellentum*.[65]

In his little book on Sparta, which was aimed at a general audience and published in 1937, with reprints in 1944 and in 1966,[66] Berve depicted Sparta as an ideal historical model for Nationalsocialist government. He conjured up the Nordic spirit embodied in the aristocracy of Sparta and idealized the institutions and customs of the Doric polis, above all the racial laws which were consequently applied, and the elitist clanship which efficiently suppressed every individualistic notion. Consequently, he reduced the soldiers killed at Thermopylae to the 300 aristocratic Spartiates and deliberately ignored the Lacedaemonian *perioikoi*, the Thespians and the reluctant Thebans. The heroism of the 300 Spartiates was based upon the fact, 'that they, far away from their home, at a place where the command had put them, took their stand for no other reason but the command'. And Berve continued:

> How could a Lacedaemonian king, how could troops of Spartiates have left their post to save a life whose highest fulfilment was to stand in battle regardless whether they won or died! Unthinkable the return of such a company! Certainly, the sacrifice was of no avail for central Greece and the

> Lacedaemonians themselves, whose aristocratic troops lost one twentieth of their numbers; but he who, in this case, asks for such a shallow benefit or even bases his judgement upon it, misunderstands Spartan warfare and fails to appreciate the strength which finally enabled Hellas to gain the victory over the Persian. The greatness as well as the impact of the deed lay in its futility.[67]

Indeed, this lesson was about to be learned by soldiers of the *Wehrmacht*. The Nazi elite did not hesitate to refer to the supposed Spartan 'virtues' to drive army corps to their doom. In the last days of the battle of Stalingrad, the *Reichsmarschall* Hermann Göring reminded the troops of the hopeless fight of Leonidas and his 300 comrades, pointed to this heroic example of 'highest soldiership' and predicted a new reading of the famous epitaph:

> *Kommst Du nach Deutschland, so berichte, du habest uns in Stalingrad kämpfen sehen, wie das Gesetz der Ehre und Kriegführung es für Deutschland befohlen hat.*[68]

> If you come to Germany, tell them you have seen us fighting in Stalingrad, obedient to the law of honour and warfare.

(iv) Leonidas in Nationalsocialist Education

Berve, like other prominent German ancient historians, was not only a collaborator, but a 'willing executioner' of Nazi ideology, to use a phrase that has recently won some popularity. He was prepared to offer an *interpretatio fascistica* of Spartan history which corroborated the 'Aryan' or 'Nordic' view of the past and was easily adopted by schoolteachers and classicists who hastily embraced the Nationalsocialist *Weltanschauung*, ardently advocated racist theories and opportunistically emphasized the central importance of antiquity for the proper education of German '*Volksgenossen*' (fellow countrymen).[69] In those days pupils had to write essays on 'Xenophon in the *Anabasis* and Adolf Hitler in his struggle for and in power' or 'The heroism in the *Odyssey* and today, especially as embodied in the *Führer* of ancient and modern times'.[70] Contemporary curricula reflected the relevance of Sparta to Nazi Germany. The tough military aristocracy commanded respect. Sexual asceticism and the bringing up of children were praised, the laws concerning marriage were approved as an outstanding means of eugenics. Scholars pointed to the freshness and youth of an uncivilized 'barbarian' community, but homoerotic and pederastic relations were only briefly mentioned or absurdly explained and Sparta's fall was reduced to the process of denordicization (*Entnordung*).[71]

Already in 1934, Berve had postulated that a classical education must produce a man like Leonidas.[72] In the same year, a teacher at a *Humanistisches Gymnasium* interpreted Greek history as the grand fight of the Nordic race against the aliens from Asia and Africa and praised the spirit of Leonidas and his followers:

> spirit of the spirit of our youth who, at Langemarck, died for *Volk und Reich,* spirit of the spirit of the heroic souls who, in the last fifteen years, have sacrificed blood and life to the revival of the German nature.[73]

One year later, 1935, in an official journal, it was suggested that of all political organizations in Greece Sparta, under the aspect of racial history, must be most carefully scrutinized.[74]

The case of Sparta and, above all, of the fighters at Thermopylae clearly proves the influence of a Nazified classical scholarship on school teaching in the Third Reich. Berve also provided the ideological legitimation for teaching pupils the new image of ancient Sparta, since as he wrote in the preface of his little book on Sparta:

> The education of youth, the spirit of community, a soldierly way of living, integration and heroic testing of the individual, tasks and values indeed which have again arisen for ourselves, seem to have been coined here in such a lucidity, to have been put into existence with such an implicitness that frankly demands us to go deeply into this unique constitutional creation.[75]

Hence W. Schröter, *Studienrat* at the *Altes Gymnasium* in Bremen, collected, in 1937, the most important sources for the battle of Thermopylae; the booklet, entitled 'Leonidas', was published as volume iii in the series *Führergestalten des Altertums.*[76] Finally in 1940 Otto Wilhelm von Vacano edited the pamphlet *Sparta: Der Lebenskampf einer nordischen Herrenschicht* ('Sparta: The struggle for life of a Nordic master race'),[77] which was meant to be a textbook for the Adolf-Hitler-schools and gave Leonidas' final struggle a most prominent place. His example was exploited to justify heroic self-sacrifice and to encourage last-ditch resistance. Among the contributors were Richard Harder, Franz Miltner and Helmut Berve. The latter was to deliver his last lecture on Sparta on May 2nd, 1945.[78]

(v) The European perspective

The peculiarities of the German Sparta-reception since 1918 become more evident if one views contemporary historiographical discussions about Sparta in a broader European context. First, it should be noted that the battle at Thermopylae has always been glorified and the 'equal heroism' of Leonidas and his comrades, to quote George Grote,[79] has been mystified right across all borders and ideologies. Leonidas has for many generations been a popular example in a political culture based upon the classical tradition and national patriotism.[80] So it is not surprising that the Thermopylae story was used in the American civil war to encourage bloodletting.[81] The Swedish poet Hjalmar Gullberg, in his verse 'Död amazon', composed in April 1941, pointed to the courage of the small troop who recklessly fought against the far superior enemy. At the same time the *Wehrmacht* was advancing through central Greece on the ancient route and met the hopeless opposition of the inferior Greek units at Thermopylae. There is certainly no typical German approach to Sparta, and even over a racist interpretation of Greek history German scholarship cannot claim exclusive rights. I only mention Professor Wade-Gery who, in the first edition of the *Cambridge Ancient History*, insisted on the notion of Doric race and the racial division of the Greek tribes into Ionians and Dorians.[82]

This is not the place to examine in detail the numerous contributions to Greek, especially Spartan, history written in the twenties and thirties outside Germany. I will concentrate on two examples, one from England, the other from France. In the *Cambridge Ancient History* J.A.R. Munro described Xerxes' invasion of Greece and gave a straightforward account of the battle of Thermopylae, explicitly 'putting aside the retrospective interpretations imported by subsequent controversies, and endeavouring to envisage the situation as it may have presented itself to Leonidas at his last council of war'. The Rector of Lincoln College, Oxford, argued that the Spartan king believed that with 2000 men he could keep the pass for one more day,

> and to his eternal honour he made the gallant attempt. But at the moment it was no forlorn hope, no desperate sacrifice, but a well-calculated scheme which offered fair promise of success. The descent of Hydarnes by the Anopaea was a complete surprise.[83]

The French historian Pierre Roussel published a book on Sparta in 1939 in which he dealt with the history and the social and political institutions of the *polis.* On Leonidas he wrote:

> Leonidas, without any doubt, was neither a blind man nor a mystic... He died with his people; a Spartan king could not act differently... He left his name and the memory of a deed that made him incarnate the ideal of a Spartiate.[84]

Comparing these English and French descriptions with Berve's account, the differences in style, vocabulary and argument are obvious. Roussel moreover had written his monograph also as a response to the contemporary re-enactments of the supposed 'Doric city' and thus to Berve's *Sparta,* as he stated in his last chapter on 'L'idéalisation de Sparte'. He did not criticize Berve explicitly, but he questioned the aristocratic character of the Spartiates and denied the idea of Doric race as 'singulièrement arbitraire'[85] and concluded: 'Et Sparte, mystérieuse et secrète, après avoir alimenté la pensée de Platon et de Rousseau, enfante une nouvelle mystique.'[86] Berve answered in *Gnomon*: Roussel had failed to write a convincing study on Sparta, since he lacked *die tiefere innere Anteilnahme an Lakedämon, seiner Art und seinem Geschick* ('the deeper inner sympathy for Lacedaemon, its nature and its fate').[87]

What do we learn? The glorification of the 300 Spartans killed at Thermopylae, when they defended their country, was a common feature of the academic *oikoumenē* of ancient historians. The halo of a patriotic fighter, or even of a Doric fighter, does certainly not constitute a German *Sonderweg*. But German historiography, after the hiatus of the First World War, exclusively transformed the *polis* on the Eurotas into a positively connotated historical model of a better state and Leonidas, the Spartan king, into the ideal representative of a *Führerstaat*. After 1933 scholars who identified themselves with the new regime defined Sparta as a quasi-Nationalsocialist institution. The former pluralism of approaches and judgements was liquidated, academic discourse was allowed only within the ideological lines of the system. Sparta and Leonidas barely mattered as historical figures, but were integrated by intellectuals into a religious system, as Arnaldo Momigliano once put it, 'che ebbe i suoi maggiori santuari a Dachau e Auschwitz (which had its major sanctuaries at Dachau and Auschwitz).'[88]

(vi) 1945 to the present

In 1950, Heinrich Böll published a short story entitled *Wanderer kommst du nach Spa* in which the narrator sees not a bronze inscription eternalizing the heroic deed but a man with torn-off limbs, a bleeding body above whom the renowned words could be read, only a bit garbled and repeated seven times on the dirty blackboard of the 'good old Humanist gymnasium.'[89] This comfortless fragment crystallizes the rejection of classical education by German intellectuals and authors who after thirteen years of Nazi barbarism and the holocaust could no longer believe in the force of the traditional school training.

In German scholarship Sparta was not very popular after 1945. New themes and methods, new perceptions and ideas were now introduced to the international discourse mainly by French and English scholars. It was not until 1983 that a professional historian wrote a concise 'History of Sparta' in German.[90] In the years between, some older contributions[91] were reprinted, even translated into other European languages, and were not warmly welcomed everywhere. Momigliano for instance harshly attacked Berve in his review of the Italian version of the latter's *Greek History*.[92] The criticism was right, but we may ask today whether Momigliano was the right person to criticize.[93] At Erlangen, where Berve taught Ancient History in the fifties and early sixties, a younger generation of academics wrote some important studies on Sparta.[94] The Nationalsocialist manipulation of history led scholars back to specialized research – *Quellenkritik* and political abstinence instead of ideology and political commitment were now demanded. Leonidas and the battle of Thermopylae became less attractive objects of research. There is an article by Hans Schaefer, written immediately after the end of World War II, in which the author tries to show that Leonidas in following his mission to the bitter end and refusing to retreat sanctioned the ephorate's claim for supremacy.[95] Twenty years later, a classicist discussed recent interpretations of the epitaph attributed to Simonides.[96] In addition, the battle of Thermopylae is mentioned in the handbooks and general accounts of Greek history. A wide range of opinion underlines the restoration of academic pluralism in West Germany. Some authors just mention the battle without any assessment,[97] some leave the question of Leonidas' motives open,[98] and some discuss various hypotheses to make the Greek strategy plausible.[99] Alfred Heuß harshly criticized the Spartan king who had underestimated the danger of being outflanked and spoke of a military and strategic disaster.[100] Fritz Schachermeyr, in his erratic 'Greek History', interpreted the action as a 'voluntary self-sacrifice' (*freiwillige Selbstaufopferung*).[101] The most old-fashioned description is to be found in Hermann Bengtson's 'Greek History' in the *Handbuch der Altertumswissenschaft*: 'The sacrifice was not in vain, Leonidas' deed gave a shining example of duty to the Greeks fighting for liberty.'[102] At least in this respect Professor Nicholas Hammond might have agreed with his German colleague: 'In the pass of Thermopylae the Spartans had shown the iron will and the undaunted courage which inspired others to follow their example.'[103] It goes without saying that modern Greek authors have also been ready to immortalize the glory of their illustrious ancestor.[104]

Even in the former German Democratic Republic, which was normally more interested in the slave-system than the military history of Greece and Rome, Leonidas was not entirely forgotten.[105] In the *Lexikon der Antike,* published by Johannes Irmscher, the heroic death of the Spartans is apostrophized,[106] on the very page where Lenin's merits for the understanding of classical antiquity are praised.

(vii) Conclusion

After this *tour d'horizon* one may feel compelled to agree with Hignett's deep scepticism over the grounds of Leonidas' death in the battle of Thermopylai: 'In face of the breakdown of all modern explanations, the "final problem" of Thermopylai is best left as an unsolved riddle; agnosticism is preferable to a pretence of knowledge.'[107] Such a conclusion seems the more attractive the closer one looks at the scattered evidence provided by the sources and the political exploitation of the myth of Leonidas in Nationalsocialist Germany.

Following the end of the First World War, in German historiography the pluralist interpretation of this famous day, which had characterized earlier research, was abandoned. Certainly, a patriotic and militarist reading had also been predominant in former days. But the Sparta-maniacs were now fascinated by the idea that the people on the Rhine and on the Eurotas were racially closely connected and had a common Nordic background. The ancient Spartans liked a strong state and took care of the *Volk* as the modern Germans did. However, the new image of the battle of Thermopylae, which was popularized through a flood of racist and *völkisch* publications, was not the result of the 'national revolution' of 1933, but emerged from a complex amalgam of ideas and ideologies which were virulent long before the Nazis came into power. The image of Sparta, propagated in the Third Reich, was essentially influenced by the adaptation of obscure racial categories, the revival of the Romantic dichotomy between Dorians and Ionians, the idealization of military duty and sacrifice after the military disaster of the First World War, the yearning for a strong *Führer* instead of a 'democratic' government and the glorification of the *Volk*. Professional historians and classicists painted the new picture of Sparta as a proto-Nationalsocialist state. Thus Leonidas became the most purely Nordic leader of all Greeks.

Thermopylae, Langemarck, Stalingrad. But this story ends in Berlin. There, on April 20th, 1945, the cream of the collapsing Nazi regime met for the last time to commemorate the *Führer*'s birthday. It was a sad celebration in the air-raid shelter underneath the *Reichskanzlei,* since the Red Army had crossed the Oder and nobody could stop its march on the capital. Hitler was contemplating retreat to the Alps, but then decided to stay in Berlin. 'A desperate fight will always be remembered as a worthy example', he said to Martin Bormann. 'Just think of Leonidas and his 300 Spartans.'[108]

Acknowledgements

An earlier version of this paper was read at the Craven Seminar in Cambridge in May 1999, 'Greek Historiography in National Context', organized by Paul Cartledge. I am grateful to William M. Calder III, Peter Heather and Keith Hopkins who commented on earlier drafts and improved my English. Many thanks too to Anuschka Albertz, Katja Bär, Thomas J. Figueira and Tomas Hägg for pertinent observations and suggestions. All renderings of German texts are my own.

Notes

[1] Cf. Hdt. 7.228.

[2] Cf. Dascalakis 1962; Hignett 1963, 105 ff. 371 ff.; Hooker 1989; Lazenby 1993, 117 ff.; Green 1996; Hammond 1996; Flower 1998. For a new, though controversial, account of the topography of the battlefield see Szemler et al. 1996 and Szemler and Cherf 1999. For a related discussion, Clarke (this volume).

[3] Lazenby 1993, 142.

[4] Of fundamental importance for the subject are Christ 1986 and Rawson 1969; cf. also Christ 1999; Losemann 1977; Marchand 1996; MacGregor Morris 2000; Näf 1986; Nickel 1995 and Watt 1985.

[5] Cf. Ollier 1933–4 and Tigerstedt 1965–78.

[6] Cic. *Tusc.* 1.42.101: *Dic, hospes, Spartae nos te hic vidisse iacentes, | dum sanctis patriae legibus obsequimur.*

[7] R. Glover, *Leonidas. A Poem,* London, 2nd edn, 1738, 1, 1–11: 'Rehearse, O Muse, the deeds and glorious death / Of that fam'd Spartan, who withstood the pow'r / Of Xerxes near Thermopylae, and fell / To save his country. When from Asia's coast / With half the nations of the peopled globe / The Persian king the Hellespont had pass'd, / And now in Thrace his boundless camp was spread / Soon to the Isthmus, where th'assembled chiefs / Of Greece in anxious council long had sat / How best their menac'd liberties to guard, / The dreadful tidings reached...' Cf. MacGregor Morris 2000, 211 ff.

[8] Orig. *Contra Celsum* 2.17.404; 8.6.747; 8.35.768.

[9] Cf. Christ 1986, 8.

[10] J.G. Herder, *Ideen zur Philosophie der Geschichte der Menschheit* [1784–91], Darmstadt 1966; F. Schiller, 'Die Gesetzgebung des Lykurgus und Solon' [1790], in Christ 1986, 73–86; cf. Rawson 1969, 310 ff.

[11] F. Schiller, 'Der Spaziergang' [1795], ll. 97–8. Cf. Baumbach 2000 and Gelzer 1997.

[12] G.W.F. Hegel, 'Vorlesungen über die Philosophie der Geschichte', in *Sämtliche Werke*, vol. xi, Stuttgart 1928, 335 f.

[13] F. Schlegel, 'Studien des Klassischen Altertums', in *Kritische Friedrich-Schlegel-Ausgabe,* vol. i, Paderborn, München and Wien 1979, 42: 'Ihr heiliger Tod war der Gipfel aller Freude.'

[14] Müller 1844, vol. ii, 78 n. 1, 391 n. 4. Cf. Calder and Schlesier 1998 and Christ 1999, 18 f.

[15] Rawson 1969, 320. But cf. Löbker 1998, 111 ff.

[16] Manso 1800–5, vol. i, 319 ff.

[17] Cf., e.g., Cartledge 1979, 204 f. and Lazenby 1993, 144.

[18] Köchly and Rüstow 1852, 61.

[19] Delbrück 1887, 89 f.

[20] Delbrück 1920, 79: 'In sich selber hatte die Verteidigung von Thermopylä so gut wie keine Aussichten; sie war, isoliert betrachtet, ein heroischer Versuch, ohne daß man gleich das Ganze aufs Spiel setzen wollte. Formal, man könnte auch sagen, materialistisch-militärisch war es ein Fehler, aber es war ein moralisches Postulat und in seiner Erfüllung von unermeßlichem Wert, daß den Barbaren

der Eintritt in das eigentliche Hellas nicht kampflos preisgegeben wurde.' Cf. ibid. 81.

[21] Cf., e.g., Curtius 1878–80, vol. ii, 70 f. and Busolt 1893–1904, vol. ii, 686 n. 1.

[22] Ranke 1883, 230 f.

[23] Pöhlmann 1914, 127: '...dieser glänzende Heldentod der Thermopylenkämpfer [hat] das Vertrauen der Hellenen eher gesteigert, als geschwächt und [war] insoferne für die nationale Sache kein vergeblicher.'

[24] Curtius 1878–80, vol. ii, 828 n. 34.

[25] Holm 1886–94, vol. ii, 57 f.

[26] Busolt 1893–1904, vol. ii, 677.

[27] Th. Körner, Auf dem Schlachtfelde von Aspern [1812], ll. 54–6: 'Wandrer! sag's den kinderlosen Eltern, / daß für's Vaterland auf diesen Feldern / Spartas kühne Heldenjugend sank!'

[28] Curtius 1878–80, vol. ii, 70 f.

[29] Burckhardt 1956–57, vol. i, 114. Cf. Christ 2000 with further reading.

[30] Cartledge 1979, 204.

[31] Niebuhr 1847, 406.

[32] Wecklein 1876, 40.

[33] F. Rühl in *Jahrbücher für Klassische Philologie* 128 (1883) 746 ff.

[34] F. Rühl in *Literarisches Zentralblatt* 33 (1877) No. 33, 1095.

[35] On Karl Julius Beloch, see Christ 1972, 248–85; Christ 1999, 81 ff. and Polverini 1990.

[36] Beloch 1912–27 (1893–1904), vol. ii, 91–105 ('Die Legende von Leonidas'), esp. 104 f.: '...Nur *einen* Vorteil hat die Katastrophe an den Thermopylen der griechischen Sache gebracht; sie hat das Bundesheer von einem unfähigen Oberfeldherrn befreit...'

[37] For Meyer cf. Christ 1972, 286–333 and id. 1999, 99–124 with further reading.

[38] Meyer 1939 (1901), vol. iv.1, 361: 'Der Heldentod des Leonidas und seiner Schar aber hatte vollends das Vertrauen eher gestärkt als gebrochen; in glänzendem Vorbild zeigte er der Nation den Weg, den sie zu gehen hatte, und brachte ihr, tiefer und lebendiger als alle Worte es vermocht hätten, zum Bewußtsein, daß es für sie keine Wahl gebe, als zu siegen oder in Ehren unterzugehen'. Meyer adds in n. 3: 'Auf die wirklich ganz ernsthaft geführte Diskussion einzugehen, ob Leonidas, statt den Tod zu suchen, richtiger abgezogen wäre, wird man mir hoffentlich erlassen.'

[39] Duncker 1882, 256.

[40] Cf., e.g., Flashar 1995.

[41] Th. Däubler, 'Sparta. Ein Versuch' [1923], in id., *Dichtungen und Schriften,* München 1956, 331–46, esp. 338: 'Bei den Thermopylen fielen bloß Freundespaare, überhaupt kämpften meistens dorische Lakedämonier nur in Liebesgemeinschaft: sie schien ihnen nämlich alles, der Tod fürs Vaterland, mit dem Geliebten, heilig, ja willkommen.'

[42] G. Benn, 'Dorische Welt' [1934], in id., *Das Hauptwerk,* vol. ii: *Essays, Reden,*

Vorträge, Wiesbaden and Munich 1980, 139–71, esp. 151: 'Ihr [sc. der Dorier] Traum ist Züchtung und ewige Jugend, Göttergleichheit, großer Wille, stärkster aristokratischer Rassenglaube, Sorge über sich hinaus für das ganze Geschlecht' and 153: 'Dorisch ist jede Art von Antifeminismus. ...Dorisch ist die Knabenliebe... die Liebe der Kriegszüge, solche Paare standen wie ein Wall und fielen.'

[43] Lüdemann 1939, 143. For the battle of Langemarck cf. Unruh 1986.

[44] Lehmann-Haupt 1923, 32.

[45] Lenschau 1925, 2017 f.

[46] Kromayer and Veith 1924–31, 21–63, esp. 61.

[47] Wilcken 1943, 116: 'Mögen unserer Jugend Leonidas und seine Getreuen immer ein Vorbild und ein Gegenstand der Verehrung bleiben!' On Wilcken's 'Greek History' cf. Christ 1999, 176 ff.

[48] Wes 1997, 219.

[49] Miltner 1935, 236 and 240 f.

[50] Ehrenberg 1929, 1383: 'Aber die Einseitigkeit dieses Menschentums ist seine Größe. Niemals wieder ist das Ideal disziplinierter Männlichkeit in solcher Reinheit aufgestellt worden. Das größte aber ist, daß diese männliche und soldatische Gesellschaft im uneingeschränkten Dienste des Nomos steht, der als Verkörperung ihres Staates, ihres religiösen Glaubens, ihrer Sitte und Tradition ihr einziger Herr ist. Nur dadurch ist es möglich gewesen, daß diese Gesellschaft ihr Eigenleben fast völlig dem Staate geopfert hat.' Ehrenberg also rejects the theory that Leonidas failed to gain stronger support of the ephorate, cf. ibid. 1386. On Ehrenberg cf. Christ 1999, 195 ff., 271 ff.

[51] Ehrenberg, 'A Totalitarian State' in id. 1946, 94–104.

[52] Ehrenberg 1925.

[53] H. Berve in *Gnomon* 1 (1925) 311.

[54] Berve 1931.

[55] Berve 1931–3, vol. i, 248 f.: '...die Spartaner...opferten sich bewußt, nicht nur einer strategischen Notwendigkeit, sondern dem Gesetz dorischer Mannheit. Mit Recht gelten sie als die Thermopylenkämpfer schlechthin. Sie waren es, in denen der autonome griechische Mensch bewußt sich dem Schicksal entgegenstemmte, bereit, ihm zu unterliegen, aber nicht sich freiwillig ihm zu beugen.'

[56] Nippel 1993, 282; cf. Will 1956 and Losemann 1998.

[57] For Berve cf. Canfora 1995, 126–78; Christ 1990, 125–87; Christ 1999, 202 ff., 246 ff.; Losemann 1977, *passim*; Momigliano 1966, 699–708; Näf 1986, 146 ff.; Ulf 2001; Näf 2001, esp. 315 ff., 357 ff., 383 ff., 397 ff. and Rebenich 2001.

[58] Cf. Hausmann 2002, 143 ff.

[59] Darré 1929, esp. 157 ff. For Darré cf. Corni 1994; Corni and Gies 1994; D'Onofrio 1997 with further reading.

[60] Cf. Christ 1986, 50 ff.; Losemann 1980, esp. 63 ff.; D'Onofrio 1996.

[61] Cf. Berve in *Vergangenheit und Gegenwart* 30 (1940) 138 and *Gnomon* 17 (1941) 1–11.

[62] Cf., e.g., Bullemer 1938; Lüdemann 1939; Meier 1939.

[63] Cf. Günther 1929, esp. 37 ff. and id. 1935.

[64] Berve 1934; cf. Rebenich 2001, 471 ff.

[65] Cf., e.g., Schachermeyr 1933.

[66] Berve 1966, 58–207. The collection of essays was published by Berve's pupils Edmund Buchner and Peter Robert Franke on the occasion of his 70th birthday.

[67] Berve 1937, 78 f.: 'Denn nicht darin, daß sie gleich den Thespiern den väterlichen Boden verteidigend fielen oder in Verzweiflung über das sichere Schicksal der Heimat lieber den Tod suchten als Versklavung und Zerstörung schauten, lag ihr Heldentum, sondern darin, daß sie fern von der Heimat, an einer Stelle, wohin der Befehl sie gestellt hatte, aushielten aus keinem anderen Grunde, als weil es so Befehl war. ...Wie hätte überhaupt ein lakedämonischer König, wie hätte eine Spartiatenmannschaft ihren Posten verlassen können, ein Leben zu retten, dessen höchste Erfüllung die Bewährung im Kampfe war, gleich, ob er Sieg oder Tod brachte! Undenkbar die Rückkehr einer solchen Schar! Genützt war freilich mit dem Opfer weder Mittelgriechenland noch den Lakedämoniern selbst, deren Adelstruppe fast ein Zwanzigstel ihres Bestandes verlor, aber der mißversteht spartanische Kriegführung und verkennt die Kräfte, welche letzten Endes Hellas über den Perser haben siegen lassen, der hier nach äußerem Nutzen fragen oder gar nach ihm werten wollte. Wie die Größe, so lag auch die Wirkung der Tat gerade in ihrer Nutzlosigkeit.'

[68] Watt 1985, 874 and Fest 1973, 909. A slightly different version is to be found in Wieder 1962, 327 f. (cited in Christ 1986, 52 n. 190): 'Kommst Du nach Deutschland, so berichte, du habest uns in Stalingrad kämpfen sehen, wie das Gesetz, das Gesetz für die Sicherheit unseres Volkes es befohlen hat.' – For the Nazi corruption and exploitation of Leonidas and his Spartans cf. also Watt 1985, 873–7; for Berve's political manipulation of Leonidas in a paper given in 1941 cf. Hausmann 2002, 150.

[69] Cf. *inter alia* Apel and Bittner 1994, esp. 221 ff.; Bittner 1989; Dithmar 1989; Horn 1996; Irmscher 1966; Keim 1995–7; Nickel 1970; id. 1972.

[70] Schlossarek 1934, 148 f. ('Xenophon in der Anabasis und Hitler in seinem Kampfe um die und in der Macht'; 'Der Heroismus in der Odyssee und in unserer Zeit, besonders verkörpert an dem antiken und dem neuzeitlichen Führer').

[71] Cf., e.g., Lüdemann 1939, 103 ff.

[72] Berve 1934, 270.

[73] Holtorf 1934, 270: 'Die griechische Geschichte werten wir als einen "grandiosen Kampf" der nordischen Rasse gegen die artfremden Völker Asiens und Afrikas. So verstehen wir die heldenmütigen Kämpfe gegen die Perser als einen Kampf der Rassen, als einen Kampf des Lichtes gegen die Unterwelt. In völkischer Verbundenheit vermochte Hellas den Ansturm der Asiaten aufzuhalten. Der Geist des Leonidas und seiner Getreuen gab die Kraft dazu, Geist vom Geiste unserer Jugend, die bei Langemarck in den Tod für Volk und Reich ging, Geist vom Geiste der Heldenseelen, die in den letzten fünfzehn Jahren Blut und Leben opferte für die Erneuerung der deutschen Art'.

[74] Cf. *Deutsche Wissenschaft, Erziehung und Volksbildung. Amtsblatt des Reichsministeriums für Wissenschaft, Erziehung und Volksbildung und der Unter-*

richtsverwaltung der Länder 1 (1935) 28: 'Von den staatlichen Gebilden der Griechen verdient Sparta unter dem Gesichtspunkt der Rassengeschichte die eingehendste Betrachtung.'

[75] Berve 1937, 7: 'Jugenderziehung, Gemeinschaftsgeist, soldatische Lebensform, Einordnung und heldische Bewährung des einzelnen, Aufgaben und Werte also, die uns selbst neu erstanden sind, scheinen hier mit einer Klarheit gestaltet, mit einer Unbedingtheit verwirklicht, die geradezu aufruft, sich in diese einzigartige Staatsschöpfung zu vertiefen.' This preface was not reprinted in the 1966 edition (cf. above n. 66).

[76] Schröter 1937.

[77] Vacano 1940. Cf. Losemann 1998, 344 ff.

[78] Losemann 1977, 231 n. 173.

[79] Grote 1869–70, vol. iv, 440.

[80] Cf., e.g., Glotz and Cohen 1931, 69: 'En ce jour, les Spartiates avaient, jusqu'au sacrifice suprème, obéi 'aux lois' qui étaient pour eux les lois de l'honneur militaire.'

[81] Cf. Clingman 1878, 112; *Southern Historical Papers* 24 (1896) 308; Hughes 1996, 222; Jeffrey 1998, 182 with n. 69. I owe the references to the courtesy of Thomas J. Figueira.

[82] *CAH* vol. ii (1926), 525; *CAH* vol. iii (1929), 566. Jardé 1923, however, denied any racial implications in Greek history; cf. Corbetta 1979.

[83] *CAH* vol. iv (1926), 299; cf. Hdt. 7.215 ff.

[84] Roussel 1939, 123 f.: 'Léonidas ne fut sans doute ni un aveugle ni un mystique. ...Il périt avec les siens: un roi de Sparte ne pouvait agir autrement. ...Il a laissé son nom et le souvenir d'une action qui lui valut d'incarner le Spartiate idéal.'

[85] ibid. 25.

[86] ibid. 216.

[87] *Gnomon* 17 (1941) 11.

[88] Cf. Momigliano 1966, 707 f.

[89] H. Böll, 'Wanderer kommst du nach Spa', Opladen 1950. On the Thermopylae tradition in post-war German writing cf. Watt 1985, 877 ff.

[90] Clauss 1983; cf. Christ 1999, 408 f.

[91] Berve's *Griechische Geschichte* [Berve 1931–33] was reprinted in 1951–52, his essay on *Sparta* [Berve 1937] is to be found in Berve 1966, 58–207. For minor changes in the revised editions cf. Momigliano 1966, 699 ff.; Näf 1986, 163 and Ulf 2001, 380 and n. 9.

[92] Cf. Momigliano 1966, 699–708 (= *Rivista Storica Italiana* 71 [1959] 665–72) and id. 1980, 837–40 (= *Athenaeum* 43 [1965] 441–3).

[93] Documents published by Riccardo Di Donato in 1995 show that Momigliano was a member of a Fascist organization when he was a student, and later of the Fascist party itself. On the discussions about 'The politics of Arnaldo Momigliano' in Fascist Italy cf. e.g. Di Donato 1995; Fabre 1995; id. 2001 and in *TLS*, May-June 1996.

[94] Cf. Christ 1986, 63 and n. 222 f.; id. 1999, 301 and 408.

[95] Schäfer 1948, 504–17 (= id. 1963, 153–66).

[96] Philipp 1968.
[97] Weiler 1988, 233.
[98] Bayer 1987, 161.
[99] Baltrusch 1998, 50; id. 1999, 313 f.
[100] Heuß 1962, 230.
[101] Schachermeyr 1960, 147.
[102] Bengtson 1977, 173: 'Das Opfer war nicht vergeblich, die Tat des Leonidas hat den Hellenen in ihrem Freiheitskampf ein leuchtendes Beispiel erfüllter Pflicht gegeben'; cf. id. 1983, 58: 'Der Widerstand der Spartaner unter dem König Leonidas und sein Untergang an den Thermopylen sind als leuchtendes Beispiel treuester Pflichterfüllung in die Annalen der Geschichte eingegangen. Wäre Leonidas nicht gewesen, so wären auch die Flotte und der ganze Krieg verloren gewesen.'
[103] *CAH* vol. iv (1988), 558.
[104] Cf. esp. Dascalakis 1962, 171 ff., esp. 184. For the use of Thermopylae to encourage support for Greek liberation at the end of the 18th and the beginning of the 19th century cf. MacGregor Morris 2000, 222 ff.
[105] Kreissig 1978 (1991), 140 f.
[106] Irmscher 1974, 316 s.v. Leonidas (H. Schulz-Falkenthal); cf. ibid. 553 s.v. Thermopylen (H. Schulz-Falkenthal).
[107] Hignett 1963, 378.
[108] Bormann 1981, 51: 'Ein verzweifelter Kampf behält seinen ewigen Wert als Beispiel. Man denke an Leonidas und seine dreihundert Spartaner.' And Hitler continued: 'Es paßt auf jeden Fall nicht zu unserem Stil, uns wie Schafe schlachten zu lassen. Man mag uns vielleicht ausrotten, aber man wird uns nicht zur Schlachtbank führen können.' Cf. Fest 1973, 989; Christ 1999, 244; and Demandt 2002.

Bibliography

Apel, H.J. and Bittner, St.
1994 *Humanistische Schulbildung 1890–1945. Anspruch und Wirklichkeit der altertumskundlichen Unterrichtsfächer*, Cologne etc.

Baltrusch, E.
1998 *Sparta. Geschichte, Gesellschaft, Kultur,* Munich.
1999 'Leonidas und Pausanias', in K. Brodersen (ed.) *Große Gestalten der griechischen Antike: 58 historische Portraits von Homer bis Kleopatra,* Munich, 310–8.

Baumbach, M.
2000 '"Wanderer, kommst Du nach Sparta...". Zur Rezeption eines Simonides-Epigramms', *Poetica* 32, 1–22.

Bayer, E.
1987 *Griechische Geschichte*, 3rd edn, Stuttgart.

Beloch, K.J.
1912–27 *Griechische Geschichte*, 2nd edn, 8 vols., Berlin and Leipzig.

Bengtson, H.
1977 *Griechische Geschichte*, 5th edn, Munich.
1983 *Griechische Staatsmänner des 5. und 4. Jahrhunderts v.Chr.*, Munich.
Berve, H.
1931 'Sparta', *Historische Vierteljahresschrift* 25, 1–22.
1931–3 *Griechische Geschichte*, 2 vols., Freiburg.
1934 'Antike und nationalsozialistischer Staat', *Vergangenheit und Gegenwart* 24, 257–72.
1937 *Sparta*, Leipzig.
1966 *Gestaltende Kräfte der Antike. Aufsätze und Vorträge zur griechischen und römischen Geschichte*, 2nd edn, Munich.
Bittner, St.
1989 'Rassentheoretische Vorstellungen und ihre Bedeutung für den humanistischen Unterricht (1925–1936)', *Comenius* 36, 424–39.
Bormann, M.
1981 *Hitlers politisches Testament. Die Bormann-Diktate vom Februar und April 1945*, Hamburg.
Bullemer, K.
1938 'Die Frage der Erbhöfe im Kriegerstaate Sparta', *Vergangenheit und Gegenwart* 28, 264–81.
Burckhardt, J.
1956–57 *Griechische Kulturgeschichte*, 4 vols., Basel.
Busolt, G.
1893–1904 *Griechische Geschichte bis zur Schlacht bei Chaeroneia*, 2nd edn, 3 vols., Gotha.
Calder III, W.M. and Schlesier, R. (eds.)
1998 *Zwischen Rationalismus und Romantik. Karl Otfried Müller und die antike Kultur*, Hildesheim.
Canfora, L.
1995 *Politische Philologie. Altertumswissenschaften und moderne Staatsideologien*, Stuttgart.
Cartledge, P.
1979 *Sparta and Lakonia. A Regional History 1300–362 BC*, London.
Christ, K.
1972 *Von Gibbon zu Rostovtzeff. Leben und Werk führender Althistoriker der Neuzeit*, Darmstadt.
1986 'Spartaforschung und Spartabild. Eine Einleitung', in id. (ed.) *Sparta*, Darmstadt, 1–72 (= id. 1996, 9–57; 'Nachträge' 219–21).
1990 *Neue Profile der Alten Geschichte*, Darmstadt.
1996 *Griechische Geschichte und Wissenschaftsgeschichte*, Stuttgart.
1999 *Hellas. Griechische Geschichte und deutsche Geschichtswissenschaft*, Munich.
2000 'Jacob Burckhardts Weg zur "Griechischen Kulturgeschichte"', *Historia* 49, 101–25.
Clauss, M.
1983 *Sparta*, Munich.

Clingman, T.L.
1878 *Selections from the Speeches and Writings*, 2nd edn, Raleigh.
Corbetta, C.
1979 'Un mito etnico della storiografia moderna: Dori, Spartani e la "purezza della razza"', in M. Sordi (ed.) *Conoscenze etniche e rapporti di convivenza nell'antichità*, Milan, 79–89.
Corni, C.
1994 'Richard Walther Darré – Der "Blut-und-Boden"- Ideologe', in R. Smelser and R. Zitelmann (eds.) *Die braune Elite*, 3rd edn, vol. i, Darmstadt, 15–27.
Corni, C. and Gies, H.
1994 *Blut und Boden: Rassenideologie und Agrarpolitik im Staat Hitlers*, Idstein.
Curtius, E.
1878–80 *Griechische Geschichte*, 5th edn, 3 vols., Berlin.
Darré, R.W.
1929 *Das Bauerntum als Lebensquell der Nordischen Rasse,* Munich.
Dascalakis, A.
1962 *Problèmes historiques autour de la bataille des Thermopyles*, Paris.
Delbrück, H.
1887 *Die Perserkriege und die Burgunderkriege*, Berlin.
1920 *Geschichte der Kriegskunst, vol. i: Das Altertum*, 3rd edn, Berlin.
Demandt, A.
2002 'Klassik als Klischee: Hitler und die Antike', *Historische Zeitschrift* 274, 281–313.
Di Donato, R.
1995 'Materiali per una biografia intellettuale di Arnaldo Momigliano', *Athenaeum* n.s. 83, 213–44.
Dithmar, R. (ed.)
1989 *Schule und Unterricht im Dritten Reich,* Neuwied.
D'Onofrio, A.
1996 'Antichità classica e la nuova visione storica nella Germania nazista', in C. Montepaone (ed.) *L'incidenza dell'antico. Studi in memoria di Ettore Lepore*, vol. iii, Napoli, 233–62.
1997 *Ruralismo e storia nel Terzo Reich. Il caso 'Odal',* Napoli.
Duncker, M.
1882 *Geschichte des Altertums*, 5th edn, vol. vii, Leipzig.
Ehrenberg, V.
1925 *Neugründer des Staates,* Munich.
1929 'Sparta (Geschichte)', in *PW* iiiA.1, 1373–1453.
1946 *Aspects of the Ancient World,* Oxford.
Fabre, G.
1995 Arnaldo Momigliano: autobiografia scientifica, *Quaderni di storia* 41, 85–96.
2001 Arnaldo Momigliano: materiali biografici, *Quaderni di storia* 53, 309–320.

Fest, J.
1973 *Hitler. Eine Biographie,* Frankfurt a.M., Berlin and Vienna.
Flashar, H. (ed.)
1995 *Altertumswissenschaft in den 20er Jahren. Neue Fragen und Impulse,* Stuttgart.
Flower, M.A.
1998 'Simonides, Ephorus and Diodorus on the Battle of Thermopylae', *CQ* 48, 365–79.
Gelzer, T.
1997 'Woher kommt Schillers Wanderer nach Sparta? Etappen der Geschichte eines berühmten Epigramms' in D. Knoepfler (ed.) *Nomen Latinum. Mélanges de langue, de littérature et de civilisations latines offerts au professeur André Schneider*, Neuchâtel and Geneva, 409–28.
Glotz, G. and Cohen, R.
1931 *Histoire Ancienne,* vol. ii 2*: Histoire Grecque: La Grèce au V*[e] *siècle,* Paris.
Green, P.
1996 *The Graeco-Persian Wars* (= rev. ed.: *The Year of Salamis*), Berkeley.
Grote, G.
1869–70 *History of Greece,* 12 vols., London.
Günther, H.K.F.
1929 *Rassengeschichte des hellenischen und des römischen Volkes*, Munich.
1935 'Der Einschlag nordischer Rasse im hellenischen Volke', *Vergangenheit und Gegenwart* 25, 529–47.
Hammond, N.G.L.
1996 'Sparta at Thermopylae', *Historia* 45, 1–20.
Hausmann, F.-R.
2002 *"Deutsche Geisteswissenschaft" im Zweiten Weltkrieg. Die "Aktion Ritterbusch"*, 2nd edn, Dresden and Munich.
Heuß, A.
1962 'Hellas' in id. et al. (eds.) *Propyläen Weltgeschichte*, vol. iii, Berlin and Frankfurt a. M., 69–400.
Hignett, C.
1963 *Xerxes' Invasion of Greece,* Oxford.
Holm, A.
1886–94 *Griechische Geschichte*, 4 vols., Berlin.
Holtorf, H.
1934 'Platon im Kampf gegen die Entartung der nordischen Rasse', *Deutsches Philologenblatt* 42, 269–72.
Hooker, J.T.
1989 'Spartan Propaganda' in A. Powell (ed.) *Classical Sparta: Techniques behind her success*, London, 122–41.
Horn, K.-P.
1996 *Pädagogische Zeitschriften im Nationalsozialismus: Selbstbehauptung, Anpassung, Funktionalisierung,* Weinheim.

Hughes, N.Ch.
1996 *Bentonville: The final battle of Sherman and Johnston*, Chapel Hill and London.

Irmscher, J. (ed.)
1966 'Altsprachlicher Unterricht im faschistischen Deutschland', *Jahrbuch für Erziehungs- und Schulgeschichte* 5/6, 225–71.
1974 *Das große Lexikon der Antike,* Leipzig.

Jardé, A.
1923 *La formation du peuple grec,* Paris.

Jeffrey, Th.E.
1998 *Thomas Lanier Clingman: Fire eater from the Carolina mountains*, Athens and London.

Keim, W.
1995–97 *Erziehung unter der Nazi-Diktatur,* 2 vols., Darmstadt.

Köchly, H. and Rüstow, F.
1852 *Geschichte des griechischen Kriegswesens von der ältesten Zeit bis auf Pyrrhos*, Aarau.

Kreissig, H. (ed.)
1978 *Griechische Geschichte bis 146 v.u.Z.,* [2nd edn 1991], Berlin.

Kromayer, J. and Veith, G.
1924–31 *Antike Schlachtfelder*, vol. iv, Berlin.

Lazenby, J.F.
1993 *The Defence of Greece 490–479 BC*, Warminster.

Lehmann-Haupt, C.F.
1923 'Griechische Geschichte bis zur Schlacht bei Chaironeia', in: A. Gercke, Ed. Norden (eds.) *Einleitung in die Altertumswissenschaft*, 2nd edn, vol. iii, Leipzig and Berlin, 3–125.

Lenschau, Th.
1925 'Leonidas I.', in *PW* xii 2, 2015–34.

Löbker, F.
1998 *Antike Topoi und Reminiszenzen in der deutschen Philhellenliteratur zur Zeit des griechischen Unabhängigkeitskrieges (1821–1829). Untersuchungen zur Antikerezeption*, Ph.D. Münster (= id. *Antike Topoi in der deutschen Philhellenliteratur. Untersuchungen zur Antikezeption in der Zeit des griechischen Unabhängigkeitskrieges*, Munich 2000).

Losemann, V.
1977 *Nationalsozialismus und Antike. Studien zur Entwicklung des Faches Alte Geschichte 1933–1945*, Hamburg.
1980 'Programme deutscher Althistoriker in der Machtergreifungsphase', *Quaderni di storia* 11, 35–105.
1998 'Die Dorier im Deutschland der dreißiger und vierziger Jahre', in Calder and Schlesier1998, 313–48.

Lüdemann, H.
1939 *Sparta. Lebensordnung und Schicksal,* Leipzig and Berlin.

MacGregor Morris, I.
2000 '*To Make a New Thermopylae*: hellenism, Greek liberation, and the Battle

of Thermopylae', *Greece & Rome* 47, 211–30.

Manso, J.F.C.
1800–5 *Sparta. Ein Versuch zur Aufklärung der Geschichte und Verfassung dieses Staates*, 3 vols., Leipzig.

Marchand, S.L.
1996 *Down from Olympus. Archaeology and Philhellenism in Germany, 1750–1970*, Princeton.

Meier, Th.
1939 *Das Wesen der spartanischen Staatsordnung, nach ihren lebensgesetzlichen und bodenrechtlichen Voraussetzungen,* Leipzig.

Meyer, Ed.
1939 *Geschichte des Altertums*, 3rd edn, 5 vols., Stuttgart.

Miltner, F.
1935 'Pro Leonida', *Klio* 28, 228–41.

Momigliano, A.
1966 *Terzo contributo alla storia degli studi classici e del mondo antico,* Rome.
1980 *Sesto contributo alla storia degli studi classici e del mondo antico*, Rome.

Müller, K.O.
1844 *Die Dorier*, 2nd edn, 2 vols., Breslau.

Näf, B.
1986 *Von Perikles zu Hitler? Die athenische Demokratie und die deutsche Althistorie bis 1945*, Bern and Frankfurt a.M.

Näf, B. (ed.)
2001 *Antike und Altertumswissenschaft in der Zeit von Faschismus und Nationalsozialismus*, Mandelbachtal and Cambridge.

Nickel, R.
1970 'Der Mythos vom Dritten Reich und seinem Führer in der Ideologie des Humanistischen Gymnasiums vor 1945', *Paedagogica Historica* 10, 111–28;
1972 'Humanistisches Gymnasium und Nationalsozialismus. Erziehung zum Rassenbewußtsein im altsprachlichen Unterricht vor 1945', *Paedagogica Historica* 12, 485–503.
1995 'Der Leonidas-Komplex. Das Thermopylen-Epigramm als ideologischer Text', *Der altsprachliche Unterricht* 38, 15–26.

Niebuhr, B.G.
1847 *Vorträge über alte Geschichte*, vol. i, Berlin.

Nippel, W.
1993 *Über das Studium der Alten Geschichte,* Munich.

Ollier, F.
1933–4 *Le mirage spartiate. Etude sur l'idéalisation de Sparte dans l'antiquité grecque.* I. *De l'origine jusqu'aux cyniques.* II. *Du début de l'école cynique jusqu'à la fin de la cité*, Paris.

Philipp, G.B.
1968 'Wie das Gesetz es befahl? Bemerkungen zu einer neuen Leonidaslegende', *Gymnasium* 75, 1–45.

Pöhlmann, R. von
1914 'Griechische Geschichte mit Quellenkunde', 5th edn, *HAW* iii 4, Munich.
Polverini, L. (ed.)
1990 *Aspetti della storiografia di Giulio Beloch*, Perugia.
Ranke, L. von
1883 *Weltgeschichte*, vol. i, Leipzig.
Rawson, E.
1969 *The Spartan Tradition in European Thought*, Oxford.
Rebenich, S.
2001 'Alte Geschichte zwischen Demokratie und Diktatur. Der Fall Helmut Berve', *Chiron* 31, 457–96.
Roussel, P.
1939 *Sparte,* Paris.
Schachermeyr, F.
1933 'Die Aufgaben der Alten Geschichte im Rahmen der nordischen Weltgeschichte', *Vergangenheit und Gegenwart* 23, 589–600.
1960 *Griechische Geschichte. Mit besonderer Berücksichtigung der geistesgeschichtlichen und kulturmorphologischen Zusammenhänge,* Stuttgart etc.
Schäfer, H.
1948 'Die Schlacht in den Thermopylen', *Die Wandlung* 3, 504–17 (= id., 1963,153–66.)
1963 *Probleme der Alten Geschichte,* Göttingen.
Schlossarek, M.
1934 'Humanismus und alte Sprachen auf nationalsozialistischer Grundlage und der Mader-Breywischianismus', *Deutsches Philologenblatt* 42, 148–9.
Schröter, W.
1937 *Leonidas, Führergestalten des Altertums* vol. iii, Bielefeld and Leipzig.
Szemler, G.J, Cherf, W.J. and Kraft, J.C.
1996 *Thermopylai. Myth and Reality in 480 BC,* Chicago.
Szemler, G.J. and Cherf, W.J.
1999 '"Nochmals" Thermopylai, 480 BC and AD 1941: Some Parallels', in R. Mellor, L. Tritle (eds.) *Text and Tradition. Studies in Greek History and Historiography in Honour of Mortimer Chambers,* Claremont, 345–66.
Tigerstedt, E.N,
1965–78 *The Legend of Sparta in Classical Antiquity*, 2 vols., Stockholm.
Ulf, Ch.
2001 'Die Vorstellung des Staates bei Helmut Berve und seinen Habilitanden in Leipzig: Hans Schaefer, Alfred Heuß, Wilhelm Hoffmann, Franz Hampl, Hans Rudolph', in Peter W. Haider and Robert Rollinger (eds.) *Althistorische Studien im Spannungsfeld zwischen Universal- und Wissenschaftsgeschichte. Festschrift für Franz Hampl,* Stuttgart, 378–454.
Unruh, K.
1986 *Langemarck. Legende und Wirklichkeit,* Koblenz.

Vacano, O.W. von
1940 *Sparta. Der Lebenskampf einer nordischen Herrenschicht*, Kempten.
Watt, R.H.
1985 '"Wanderer, kommst du nach Sparta". History through propaganda into literary commonplace', *The Modern Language Review* 80, 871–83.
Wecklein, N.
1876 *Über die Tradition der Perserkriege*, Munich.
Weiler, I.
1988 *Griechische Geschichte. Einführung, Quellenkunde, Bibliographie*, 2nd edn, Darmstadt.
Wes, M.A.
1997 'Ulrich Wilcken, de Mittwochs-Gesellschaft, en de "Atem der Geschichte"', *Lampas* 30, 213–44.
Wieder, J.
1962 *Stalingrad und die Verantwortung des Soldaten*, Munich.
Wilcken, U.
1943 *Griechische Geschichte im Rahmen der Altertumsgeschichte*, 5th edn, Munich and Berlin.
Will, Ed.
1956 *Doriens et Ioniens. Essai sur la valeur du critère ethnique appliqué à l'étude de l'histoire et de la civilisation grecques,* Paris.

INDEX

Greek names have been hellenized wherever possible: thus, 'Damaratos', 'Lykourgos' but 'Thucydides'.

Acheron 118
Achilles 66–7, 72
Aeschines 88–9
Africa 232–3, 308, 311–12, 316–17
Agamemnon 67
Agesilaos 94–5, 183, 208, 254
Agis I 228
Agis II 156, 287
Agis III 195
Agis IV 93, 95, 184, 194–8, 201, 205–6
Aigina 12, 146, 149–51, 155–7, 181
Aigitians 274
Aineias 66–7
Aitolians 220
Ajax 73
Akrotatos 171
Aktaion 114–15
Amyklai 181
Anaxandridas 13, 16
Antalkidas 208
Aphrodisia 275
Apollo 184
Arcadia, Arcadians 153–5, 274
Archidamos III 254
Archilochus 123
Areopagus 88–9
Areus I 171, 183, 194–5
Argeia 14
Argilios, Argilos 119–25
Argos 12, 18–19, 32 n. 7, 146–7, 182
Aristagoras 29, 205
Aristodamos (noted for dictum on wealth) 151–2
Aristodamos (survivor of Thermopylai) 75–6
Ariston 13, 17, 155
Aristophanes 101 n. 26
Aristotle 90
Constitution of the Spartans 219–21
Arkhonides 127
Artaÿktes 17
Asopos 275
Athena 112–3, 221
Athena Chalkioikos, temple of 111–12, 117, 120, 126
Athens 2, 8–9, 21–4, 26–30, 73, 88, 156, 182, 240, 250, 257–9, 294–5
Atossa 14

Beloch, K.J. 327
Benn, G. 328
Berve, H. 329–34
Boiai 275
Böll, H. 334
Borana (E. Africa) 316
Boulis 27–8
Burckhardt, J. 327
Byzantion 116–17, 137, 176, 181

Caligula 116
Cambyses 9, 17, 20–1
Carians 9
Chios 156
coinage of gold and silver, forbidden chs. 6–7 *passim*, 193
coinage, iron ch. 6 *passim*
Crete 149, 224 n. 17, 241
Croesus 51 n. 148
Cyrene 114
Cyrus 20
Cyrus (prince) 176

Damaratos 2, 11–15, 17, 28–30, 285–6
Danae 4
Darius 14
Däubler, T. 328
Davis, Thomas 64
Delbrück, H. 326
Delphi 18–19, 69–70, 111–15, 144, 154, 222
Dikaiarkhos 199
Dioskouroi 12, 112, 171, 183
Dorians 227–8, 249–50, 333
  in German thought 325, 328, 330, 336
Dorieus 2, 13
Duncker, M. 327

earthquake (465 BC) 207
Egypt 4–6
Ehrenberg, V. 329
Epameinondas 181, 238
Ephesos 176, 178
Ephoros 228–9
Epidotes 112, 114
Epitadeus, 'rhetra of' 196
ethnography 3, 4, ch. 13 *passim*
Etis 275
Euripides 8, 24, 69–70, 75–6, 101 n. 26
Eurybiadas 173

Germany, and myth of Leonidas ch. 14 *passim*
Glaukos 154, 173
Goering, H. 331
Gullberg, H. 333
Gylippos 142, 175–6, 178

Hagesichora 173
Haghios Vassilios 180
Halicarnassus 22
Hegel, G.W.F. 324
Hektor 73
Hellanikos 70
Helos 228
helots 155, 157, 206–7, chs. 9–10 *passim*
  helot revolts 238–9, 255–7
Heraia 182
Herakles 12, 171, 183
Herder, J.G. 324–5
Herodotus ch. 1 *passim*, 65–6, 69, 71, 75, 85, 285
  and 'Great Rhetra' 221–2
Hikesios 114
Hitler, A. 336
Homer 65, 72
hoplites 250–1, 253
Hyakinthia 288

Iasos 176
Iran 158–9
Ireland 63–6
iron mines 182
iron money chs. 5–6 *passim*, 194
Isokrates 87–9

Justin 113

Kaiadas 111, 115
Kainepolis 275
Kandaules 16–17
Kinadon 254, 294
Kleandridas 156
Kleomenes I 2, 11–21, 25–6, 29, 127, 156, 205, 255
Kleomenes III 93, 95, 184, 194–6, 198–201, 230
Kleonike 116–19, 121–3, 127
Knidos 176–7
Kodros 70
Konon 183
Kopanaki 231–2
Körner, T. 326
Krateia 119
Kritias 87, 294
  as character in Platonic dialogue 90–1
Kroton 113
Kyllene 155
Kypselos 15
Kythera 183, 289, 293–4
Kyzikos 176

Lakonia 257, 269–70, 286–7
Lampsakos 176–7
Langemarck (Flanders) 328
Las 275
Leonidas I 21, chs. 2, 14 *passim*
Leonidas II 184, 197, 254
Leotychidas 204
Leuktra 254
Lykourgos (king) 184
Lykourgos (mythical lawgiver) 93, 95–6, 138–40, 147, 172–3, ch. 7 *passim*, 230, 233
Lysandros (admiral) 94–5, 142–3, 154, 175–6, 178–80, 183, 193, 196
Lysandros (ephor) 197–8

Maasai 305, 308, 312
Maenalians 274
Malea, Cape 182
Mandrokleidas 198
Manso, J.C.F. 325
Mantineia (Battle of) 254
Megabyzos 24
Megalopolis 195, 274
Melissa 118
mercenaries 254–5
Messene 238
Messenia, Messenians 227, 235–6, 238–41, 255–8, 287
Metaponton 113
Meyer, E. 327
Midea 113
Miltner, F. 329, 332
Momigliano, A.D. 334
  as fascist 335, 341 n. 93
Müller K.O. 325, 330
Munro, J.A.R. 333

Nasamones 7
National Socialism (German) 330–2, 334–6
Naukleidas 179
Neapolis 182
neodamōdeis 207
Neon of Asine 293
Nepos, Cornelius 120, 124–5
Niebuhr, B.G. 327

obeliskoi, *obeloi* 181–2
Orchomenos 114–15
Origen 324
Otanes 1, 16–17, 24

Pamisos, valley of 258
Pantites 75
Parparonia 288
Parrhasians 274
Pausanias (king) 178–9
Pausanias (periegete) 114
Pausanias (regent) 17, ch. 4 *passim*, 203, 255
pederasty 312, 315, 328, 331
Peisistratids 26
Peisistratos 1, 15
pelanor, *pelanos* 137, 139, 148–51, 155, 159, 161
Periandros 16, 118–19
Perikles 156
perioikoi 158–9, 207–8, 231, 235, 243 n. 8, 251, 254, chs. 11–12 *passim*
Perseus 4
Persia, Persians 6–8, 14, 24
Pharis 180
Pheidon 146–7
Pheretime 20, 38
Phleious 182
Phlogidas 179, 181, 193
Phoibidas 156
Phylarchos 95, 194–5
Plato 90–2, 96–7, 145, 173–4
Pleistoanax 156, 173
Plutarch 92–8, 138, 140–3, 194–5 200–1
Polybius 97, 172
Polykrates 194
Promakheia 288
Pylos 231
Pyrrhos 195–6

Rhadine 118
'Rhetra, Great' ch. 8 *passim* 234, 251
Rhodes 156, 176–7
Roussel, P. 333–4
Rühl, F. 327

St Marcellin (France) 324
Sambia (New Guinea) 306, 312, 317
Samos 176–8, 194
Schiller, F. 324
Schlegel,F. 324–5, 330
Selinous 114
Sepeia 19
Side 275
Simonides 64–5, 76–7
Siris 113
Skiraphidas 179, 181, 193
Skiritai 295
slavery, slaves 228–35, 237–41, 257
Sokles 1, 25–26
Solon 9, 240–1, 259
sōphrosynē ch. 3 *passim*
Sosibios 198
Soulima Valley, Messenia 231
Sparta
  agōgē 195–6, 198, 310
  cavalry 202
  damos 219–20
  despotism ch. 1 *passim*
  ekklēsia 3, 251
  ephors 3, 11, 111, 124, 251–2, 293–5
  funerals 5–13, 71, 223, 235
  and German scholarship ch. 14 *passim*
  gerousia 3, 11, 88–9, 95, 158, 251
  homoioi 158, 197, 231, 234–5, 251–4, 257, 259–60
  hypomeiones 253
  kings ch. 1 *passim*, 198, 220–3, 251–2
  krypteia 206–7, 231, 256, 308
  marriage 313–15, 317
  messes 195, 200
  mothakes 253
  neodamōdeis 253, 256
  religion 18, ch. 4 *passim*, 180, 196–7, 287–8
  tresantes 253
  trophimoi 253
  whip 19, 30, 201
  women 14–15, 93, 95, 103 n. 58, 106 n. 93, 186 n. 11, 207, 238
  xenēlasia 140, 157, 160, 204–6
Sperthias 27
Sphairos 105 n. 82, 184, 198–201, 207
Stalingrad 331
synoikism 269, 271–6

Tainaron 119–20, 122–3, 125–6
Taras (Tarentum) 33 n. 7
Tegea 181–2
Thebes 291
Theopompus 91, 95
Thera 114
Thermopylai chs. 2, 14 *passim*
Thessaly 241
'Thirty Tyrants' 294–5
Thorax 178–9, 181
Thucydides 86–7, 111, 113–15, 119–22, 124–6
Tivs 188 n. 63
Tomyris 20
tradition, invention of ch. 7 *passim*
Tyrtaios 65, 74–5, 101 n. 31, 235–6, 241
  and 'Great Rhetra' 222

United Nations, Convention of, on serfdom 228
USA 229, 233, 332

Vasiliko 231–2
von Pöhlmann, R. 326

Wade-Gery, H.T. 333
Wilcken, U. 329
women 15 236.
  See also 'Sparta, women'

Xenophon 89–90
  and 'Great Rhetra' 219–22
Xerxes 9, 14, 16–17
Xouthias 153–4

Zeus 114, 221
Zopyros 9
Zulus 308, 312